Outdoor Recreation in American Life:

A National Assessment of Demand and Supply Trends

H. Ken Cordell
Principal Investigator
and
Carter J. Betz
J.M. Bowker
Donald B.K. English
Shela H. Mou
USDA Forest Service
Southern Research Station
Athens, GA

—

John C. Bergstrom
R. Jeff Teasley
Michael A. Tarrant
The University of Georgia
Department of Agricultural and Applied Economics
and
Department of Recreation and Leisure Sciences
Athens, GA

—

John Loomis
Colorado State University
Department of Agricultural and Resource Economics

Sagamore Publishing
www.sagamorepub.com

Production Coordinator: Anne E. Hall
Cover Design: Joe Buck and Terry Hayden
Editor: Susan M. McKinney

ISBN: 1-57167-246x
Library of Congress Catalog Card Number: 98-83130

Printed in the United States.

We would like to dedicate this book to the memory of Dr. Marion Clawson, whose work in outdoor recreation at Resources for the Future over many years established the conceptual foundations for much of the research we report here. We also dedicate this book to the thousands of professional and lay people who work in federal, state, local, or private organizations to provide quality outdoor opportunities and services for the American public.

CONTENTS

ACKNOWLEDGMENTS

Sincere appreciation is extended to the many dedicated scientists, authors, students, and advisors who contributed to this work. Those not elsewhere acknowledged as authors or other contributors to the following 10 chapters include:

Linda Langner and David Darr, USDA Forest Service, Washington, DC, for their support and financial assistance.

Marilyn Howard, Project Secretary, USDA Forest Service, Athens, GA, for administrative assistance and reassuring smiles.

Joanne Norris, The University of Georgia, Athens, GA, for text and graphics production on Chapter IV.

And for reviews of chapter drafts as follows:

Chapter III:	Dean F. Tucker, National Park Service, Ft. Collins, CO; and Robert D. Bixler, Cleveland Metroparks, Cleveland, OH.
Chapter IV:	Brett Wright, George Mason University, Fairfax, VA; and Bryan Hubbell, The University of Georgia, Griffin, GA.
Chapter V:	George Seihl, Gaithersburg, MD; and Patricia Winter, USDA Forest Service, Riverside, CA.
Chapter VI:	David H. Newman and Christopher McIntosh, The University of Georgia, Athens, GA.
Chapter VII:	Thomas H. Stevens, University of Massachusetts, Amherst, MA; and Armando Gonzalez-Caban, USDA Forest Service, Riverside, CA.
Chapter IX:	Michael Patterson, University of Montana, Missoula, MT; Myron Floyd, Texas A&M University, College Station, TX; and Michael Schuett, Southwest Texas State University, San Marcos, TX.

Special thanks is also extended to a special friend and colleague, Bob Biesterfeldt, for editing the entire manuscript.

FOREWORD

H. Ken Cordell

For most of the first two centuries of its existence, the United States was primarily an agrarian society and most of its population made a living from the land. Resources were seemingly limitless, space infinite, and opportunities for economic expansion unbounded. The last few decades, however, have seen this country making a drastic departure from its rural beginnings as the population has continued to move farther and farther away from its close attachment to and direct dependence on making a living from the land. With this transition away from rural lifestyles and livelihoods, have come changes in American society and its culture. Along with cultural changes, have come much heavier demands on the rich natural resource base of the United States—demands of a magnitude much greater than ever before been seen in this country.

Outdoor recreation is one of these growing demands. Because of high interest across almost the entire population, it is closely entwined with the sweeping social, economic, cultural and resource evolution occurring in the United States. As a key component of our "modern" lifestyles, outdoor recreation is both affected by and directly contributes to shaping the transition in the way American people live and think. The technology and consumption-driven urban society of today demands in many ways a very different mix of recreational pursuits, settings and services than was in demand by our more rural and land-based society of past times. Yet, in some ways, the mix of contemporary recreational demands resembles those of the past.

This book is the United States' only ongoing, comprehensive assessment of the trends, current situation, and likely futures of outdoor recreation demand and supply. New and different aspects of national demand, as well as resemblances to the past are examined.

As the character of the demand for outdoor recreation settings and services change, so too will this Country's infrastructure which provides those settings and services. Government at all levels has always been a very significant part of the outdoor recreation supply infrastructure in the U. S. To be responsive and efficient in its provider role, the public sector must have up-to-date information detailing demand trends. Unlike the private sector, most of the opportunities provided by the public sector are available free to whoever wishes to take advantage of them. Thus the price, revenue and profit signals, which for the most part guide the private sector, are absent in the public sector. To help in monitoring trends in public demands for outdoor recreation in the United States, this national assessment is conducted every 10 years to identify significant shifts that may signal a need for policy, budget, management, and/or infrastructure adjustments.

In this book, we overview national demand and supply trends, the current situation and likely futures of outdoor recreation and Wilderness, as these trends and futures are driven by ever more rapid social, technological and economic change. The main text of this book begins with an overview of the benefits and histories of outdoor recreation and wilderness to set the tone and context for the chapters that follow. Then, a description of the framework that guides the assessment of trends and market shifts is provided in Chapter II. Following Chapter II, in-depth descriptions of the recreation resources of the country, with emphasis on private land access, are presented. In Chapter V, outdoor recreation participation trends are examined, with specific coverage of social group differences, regional differences, international tourism, federal and state system visitation trends, and consumer spending for outdoor recreation. In Chapter VI, models and projections of recreation participation (numbers of persons, total days of participation and trips taken away from home) are described. The status and trends in the National Wilderness Preservation System are analyzed in Chapters VII and VIII, covering demand and supply aspects as well as the makeup of users, uses and values about Wilderness. In Chapter IX, preferences, perceptions and attitudes of public land recreation users are reviewed. Chapter X highlights key findings of this Assessment and discusses their implications for the future of outdoor recreation.

Publication of this Assessment responds to the Congressionally mandated Renewable Resources Assessment as specified in the Forest and Rangeland Renewable Resources Planning Act of 1974 (RPA), P.L. 93-378, 88 Stat. 475. In addition to outdoor recreation and wilderness, national assessments of timber, wildlife and fish, minerals, range, water, and global change are also developed by specialists in the USDA Forest Service.

PROLOGUE

PERPETUAL MOTION, UNICORNS, AND MARKETING IN OUTDOOR RECREATION

Francis Pandolfi
United States Forest Service
Washington, D.C.

THE RISING IMPORTANCE OF OUTDOOR RECREATION

Outdoor recreation is but one of the many multiple uses we have for our lands, public and private. Yet, its importance in Americans' lives and the benefits it provides seem to be increasing faster than many other uses of our precious land. The rise in importance of outdoor recreation in Americans' lives is one of the dramatic changes, as well as challenges, now occurring in the United States.

Greater demand for outdoor recreation opportunities across an increasingly diverse spectrum of social groups and interests creates greater responsibility to consider carefully the way we as providers of those opportunities do business. As some of the methods and ideas that worked well in the past become less effective or practical, there will be a mandate to become more innovative and creative. Some of the issues associated with steadily rising demand will be difficult to address. For example, as people travel more seeking the beauty of our public lands and recreation areas, how can crowding at some of the better known locations be avoided and some of the impact of increased use be shifted to lesser known areas of equal or nearly equal quality? Will new forms of access be required as the number seeking recreational experiences increases to levels that recreation managers have never before experienced?

Realization of the rapid rise in the importance of outdoor recreation and of the challenges this increased importance brings is relatively recent among public land management interests. Growing importance and growing numbers of visitors will surely require greater investments in maintenance and improvements as wear and tear take their toll. But what will be the sources of the capital that will be needed to finance maintenance and improvements? Finding financing and other such issues, while extremely important today, are likely to become even more critical in the future as demand growth and other changes continue into the 21st century.

There are numerous important reasons for accelerating development and planning strategies to provide high quality outdoor recreation opportunities more effectively and responsively. Some of the more prominent of these reasons were highlighted in a recent national study conducted by Roper Starch Worldwide for The Recreation Roundtable. (The Recreation Roundtable represents many of the largest recreation-oriented companies in our country. *Outdoor Recreation in America* has been published annually since 1994 for the Recreation Roundtable by Roper Starch Worldwide).

While there is abundant information on what people do to recreate in America, there is usually much less research-based information describing why Americans do what they do, how satisfied they are with the opportunities available to them, what barriers restrain them from additional recreation participation, and how they learn about recreation choices. The Recreation Roundtable study helps address these questions.

Consistent with other outdoor recreation research, the Roundtable study points out that in this society marked by rapidly advancing technology, growing stress and time constraints, Americans clearly value having time away from it all. Americans are placing an increasing emphasis on the leisure portions of their lives and on outdoor recreation as an important leisure outlet. Whether or not they choose to participate frequently in outdoor recreation, the activities they chose lead to positive individual and social benefits. Valuing health, fun, family togetherness and environmental education benefits, people understand the importance of outdoor recreation for individuals, families, and society as a whole.

The Benefits of Outdoor Recreation

A sound environment.
Healthy rural economies.
Strengthened families.
Better personal health.
Quality of life and perceived success in life.

Outdoor recreation clearly has a positive image, and providing high quality opportunities contributes importantly to society's goals. Among the key findings of the Roper-Starch report is that outdoor recreationists are more satisfied with the quality of their lives than are others among the public at large who do not participate. The same is also true of people for whom outdoor recreation was important when they were growing up. The evidence strongly suggests that participation in outdoor recreation at any time of life, but particularly as a child, leads people to have more satisfying and fulfilling lives. This concept of "quality of life" was measured including such factors as satisfaction with friends, career, health, fitness, and leisure time. But while quality of life is an interesting concept, it usually is viewed as too intangible to be useful in guiding planning efforts.

It is also productive to look at the top motivations for outdoor recreation, shown below:

Why We Spend Our Leisure Time Outdoors

Fun (rated important by 76%)
Relaxation (71%)
Health and exercise (70%)
Family togetherness (68%)
Stress reduction (66%)
Teach kids values (64%)
To experience nature (64%)

Source: *Outdoor Recreation in America*, Roper Starch Worldwide, 1996.

Finally, outdoor recreation can increase appreciation for and understanding of our environment and provide opportunities for children to learn.

MARKETING OUTDOOR RECREATION

Perpetual motion, unicorns, and marketing outdoor recreation all have one thing in common—many people believe them to be fiction. Yet, the strong trends driving the increases in demand for outdoor recreation and its growing importance and value to our nation offer us an opportunity to consider seldom-used techniques for better delivering recreational services. We have: (a) solid research documenting market needs, (b) outstanding product, and (c) growing consumer demand. These factors all but require that we move toward managing for strong outdoor recreation "products" or "brands" to provide to committed consumers. For example, a product or brand could be defined as "Hiking," "Fishing," "Camping," "Skiing," and other activities. Thinking of outdoor recreation activities as products or brands, of course, suggests applying the principles of sound, private-sector marketing as an approach for meeting recreation demands and providing satisfying outdoor recreation products and services.

Let us consider a number of quotes from a prominent organization to understand better how a change in the approach to outdoor recreation policy and management might be viewed:

"We will need to strengthen our ability to deliver breakthrough product innovation."

"The strongest brands of the 21st century will respond to consumers' increasing demands for good value. In fact, the best of these brands will push consumers' value expectations even higher by continually resetting the standard for delivering the highest possible quality."

"We're working hard to ensure that our brands are among those that set the standard for good value."

"Great brands are built by the best employees serving loyal customers with good value of superior products."

"Great brands always stand for something—something that consumers care about, something the brand delivers better than any other competitor, something that can last and is consistent over time. This 'something' is what we think of as a brand's 'equity.' It is the fundamental reason that consumers purchase any given brand on a sustained basis."

"Great brands earn customers' trust by meeting their needs—better than anyone else—with truly superior products."

...and finally....

"Loyal customers rely on their favorite products week in and week out. They don't have to worry whether they're getting the best deal because they know the brands they love deliver the best products at a good value every day."

These comments came from the 1996 annual report of the Procter & Gamble Company, provider of some of the most successful consumer products in the world. P&G's leading brands include Tide, Ivory, Mr. Clean, Pampers, Charmin, Cover Girl, Crest, Scope, Duncan Hines, and Pringles. They offer enlightened ideas and guidance for examining new ways of looking at public sector outdoor recreation management.

Have we fully explored our gold mine of recreation opportunities in this country and managed it as if it were consumer product brands? How could it be done? As federal agencies and others transition from providing outdoor recreation at no cost to the consumer to charging for access and services, we can expect to see many changes in the way we operate. Selling a product, even to an eager customer, is very different from giving it away. In an increasing-demand environment, additional funding or investment will be required for both the public and private sectors if we are to improve the quality and amount of opportunities in the years ahead.

As the level to slow-paced growth of public funding for outdoor recreation continues from year to year, management may need to reorient to a product's mind-set where opportunities are priced, as opposed to free, if supply is to keep pace with demand. To make this transition from free to priced recreational opportunities and services, a number of considerations will be increasingly important:

- A well-articulated strategy based on a thoughtful analysis of information about demand and supply trends, such as are reported in this book.
- Up-to-date, credible data for evaluating decisions, alternatives, and their potential consequences.
- A focus of energy and resources on investing in those options where the returns will be greatest. Which opportunities are most valued by our customers relative to their costs?
- A careful transition from a mostly extractive resource emphasis on much of our public lands to a more balanced emphasis between commodities, recreation, and ecosystem health.
- Adequate staffing by employees with appropriate skills and an improved organizational structure for effectively providing high-quality recreation opportunities. For example, moving toward pricing and products will require people with marketing skills, grown or acquired. Appropriately building the right mix of skills will be particularly important in government where marketing and customer service have not historically been widely practiced.

- Continue to conduct (and even accelerate) research to define clearly what people want in their outdoor recreation experience and how satisfied they are with what they experience. This practice is fundamental in the commercial world of building brand loyalty.
- Improve information and educational materials (printed literature, on-site signage, etc.) for delivering quality customer service and for improving product development as technology yields new recreation equipment.
- Most importantly, establish partnerships with others with knowledge and expertise in areas we in government do not have.

PARTNERSHIPS

The public and private sectors and non-government organizations (NGOs) can be effective partners in meeting the nation's recreation needs. Such partnerships, together with a branding/marketing approach and full sharing of knowledge, technology, and financing, can provide stronger underpinnings for successful market expansion. To the extent the public sector can improve the opportunities for recreation, private sector partners will benefit as well. And the members of NGOs, customers to us all, benefit as well with superior experiences.

Partners can include a number of different interests:

- Recreation equipment manufacturers.
- Mail-order retailers of outdoor recreation products.
- Relevant industry associations.
- Travel and tourism providers.
- The media, both general and outdoor-oriented.
- Recreation and environmental NGOs (these groups often overlap).
- All levels of government.

WHERE WE GO FROM HERE

To evaluate any new plan, we must be able to measure its results. Proper monitoring of opportunity accessibility and visitor satisfaction will be essential to managing our brands effectively and putting our investments in the most appropriate areas. As we near the 21st century and a new way of providing outdoor opportunities, there will be a need for awareness of a number of emerging concerns.

Federal funding of recreation opportunities will increasingly be supplemented by user fees and partnership dollars to maintain existing infrastructure and improve customer experiences. As additional sources are developed, however, appropriations will have to be maintained and not offset by the newly acquired financing.

There is an opportunity to build environmental education into outdoor recreation experiences. The growing market of users can be given the opportunity to learn more about our natural resources and the challenge of keeping them healthy. Research by Forest Service outdoor recreation scientists has continued to show that recreationists not only seek the fun and relaxation outdoor settings offer, they also want to learn. Based on the 1994-95 National Survey on Recreation and the Environment, it was found that viewing- and learning-oriented activities, such as visiting historic sites, viewing wildlife, and sightseeing, are among the most popular of recreational pursuits (see Chapter V of this book).

Volunteerism is increasingly an opportunity for improving outdoor recreation opportunities. Volunteerism directed toward maintaining and improving recreation areas can be viewed as an additional resource to accomplish the goals mentioned above, even though it is actually in-kind services.

Monitoring the level of visitation at the more popular locations will help by alerting managers of potential overloads that can lessen outdoor experiences.

Affordable and accessible opportunities for urban and underprivileged youth will be important in the future for improving the quality of their lives.

There is no single constituency for the outdoor recreation experience since activities vary so greatly and the agendas of the various user groups range across a broad spectrum of interests. But we do know that outdoor recreation provides unique social and economic benefits. If it is well marketed and managed for the benefit of current and future generations, it will create an *annuity and legacy* of great value to the American people for as far into the future as we can see.

CHAPTER I

OUTDOOR RECREATION AND WILDERNESS IN AMERICA: BENEFITS AND HISTORY

. . . .

B. L. Driver, USDA Forest Service (Retired)
Robert W. Douglass, Ohio State University
John B. Loomis, Colorado State University

Invited Papers:

B. L. Driver, USDA Forest Service (Retired)

The text that follows was provided by three prominent scientists who are highly respected colleagues. They each have worked in the areas of outdoor recreation and wilderness for many years. Their coverages of the benefits from and histories of outdoor recreation and wilderness are meant to provide the broad context within which we subsequently examine, in depth, trends and futures in demand and supply.

If no one believed outdoor recreation and wilderness provided benefits, then obviously public funding and private investments would not occur on the vast scale they now occur. In fact, no one believes such benefits do not exist. Some of these benefits are pretty obvious and immediate. Recreation is fun and enjoyed instantly; it can fill voids people perceive in their lives. Other benefits are less obvious; they often accrue steadily over time and are more indirect. Building valued memories and better health are among these less obvious and less immediate benefits. Dr. Bev Driver has devoted many years of study to the topic of benefits. The following article he has provided is based on his and others' work to better understand the benefits of outdoor recreation and how improved understanding of them can help aid in building better management strategies.

The histories which follow Dr. Driver's paper are contributed by two very knowledgeable scientists and highly valued colleagues. Dr. Bob Douglas writes of the rich history of outdoor recreation in the United States and traces how Americans' view of it has changed from the formative years to now. In a very real sense, the overall national assessment this book represents is the latest chronicle of the continuing story of outdoor recreation. Sometime in the future, this work, too, will be read for its historical value.

Dr. John Loomis provides a brief tracing of wilderness in the United States. There was a time when EuroAmerican eyes viewed the whole continent of North America as wilderness. Now, wilderness is remnant patches of public land mostly in remote places.

With Drs. Driver's, Douglas', and Loomis' contributions thus acknowledged, we launch this fourth national *Assessment of Outdoor Recreation and Wilderness*.

—Ken Cordell, Principal Investigator for *Outdoor Recreation in American Life*

MANAGEMENT OF PUBLIC OUTDOOR RECREATION AND RELATED AMENITY RESOURCES FOR THE BENEFITS THEY PROVIDE

B. L. Driver, U.S. Forest Service

Introduction and Purposes

Historically, every nation has used its natural resources to meet multiple social needs. In the United States, such an orientation to that country's renewable natural resources (also referred to here as the hinterland, wildlands, or just the land including water) is called multiple-use management, which represents how that nation's hinterlands are generally managed by both private enterprises and public agencies to accommodate a wide range of human needs and values. In fact, few, if any, wildlands are managed for a single use, even though some private firms and some public agencies emphasize a narrower set of uses and values than others, even though some land areas are managed for highly restricted uses (e.g., designated wilderness areas and a mineral deposit that will be exploited for its valuable ores and then restored). But beyond these restrictive uses, those areas provide multiple benefits to society because they also serve as habitats for wildlife, provide opportunities for some types of outdoor recreation, and protect watersheds.

Hikers trek the Appalachian Trail through the north Georgia mountains, circa 1936. Photo courtesy of the Hargrett Rare Book and Manuscript Library, University of Georgia.

While our nation's privately and publicly managed renewable resources have always provided outdoor recreation and related nature-based amenity services under multiple-use management, the prominence of these uses has been gradually increasing since the end of World War II. However, only recently have these uses been recognized as the dominant ones of many public lands and as a very important use of many private wildlands.

For example, the USDA Forest Service now acknowledges recreation as a dominant use of the National Forests. The reported number of recreation visits to the National Forests has increased from 560 million in 1980 to about 860 million in 1996 (Dombeck, 1997a). Because that agency is the single biggest provider of outdoor recreation opportunities in the nation, it is reorienting its management to better accommodate these amenity uses. Mike Dombeck, Chief of the U.S. Forest Service, recently explained the need for this reorientation by saying "Today, society's priorities are shifting. Our management priorities must keep pace with . . . society's values" (1997b). This changing orientation applies both to private and public wildland management.

This chapter plays on the theme that management of wildlands must accommodate the shifting social values and priorities referred to by Dombeck. The focus is on those changing social values that have impacted management of wildlands and what those impacts have been. The chapter contains four sections after this introductory one.

- The first section proposes that the clear trend in society of people trying to increase the quality of their lives has significantly impacted management of all recreation resources, including wildland recreation resources for four reasons:

  (1) More people sense that recreation services contribute strongly to the quality of their lives.
  (2) This awareness has caused dramatic increases in demands for recreation services, including those provided on wildlands.

(3) This awareness has helped cause significantly increased public understanding of the wide scope, great magnitude, and pervasiveness of the benefits that accrue from the provision and use of recreation services.
(4) The public now expects managers of recreation resources to provide not only recreation activity opportunities, but also to provide "benefit opportunities." A discussion of the nature, scope, and magnitudes of these benefits of leisure services leads to two bold propositions:
  (1) Leisure services provide more total benefits to society than any other social service.
  (2) The "leisure services sector" is the largest sector of the U.S. economy.

- The second section narrows the focus to the benefits of wildland recreation. It considers whether any of the benefits of recreation described in the previous sections can be attributed uniquely to our nation's renewable natural resources and must be provided on those resources.
- The third section of the chapter describes how the growing recreation use of wildland and other recent changes in society have impacted the management of wildlands. It describes these other social changes and the consequent slow, but perceptible, changes they are causing in private and public wildland management. One such change is the recent implementation of science-based amenity resource management systems designed to accommodate changing social values. A system, called Benefits-Based Management (BBM), is described because it helps to optimize realization of the benefits of recreation.
- The chapter ends with a brief consideration of future directions and issues related to capturing the benefits of outdoor recreation and related nature-based amenities.

In this discussion of wildland recreation services, no distinction is made between public and private land or between different jurisdictions of public land.

Because many of the amenities provided on wildlands cannot strictly be defined as recreation (e.g., nature-based renewal of the human spirit or psychological attachment to a special place), the words *outdoor recreation and related nature-based amenities*, or just *amenity services* will be used to more accurately represent the services being considered. For a detailed discussion of these amenity values, see Driver, Dustin, Baltic, Elsner, and Peterson (1996).

Growing Recognition of the Social Significance of Leisure

Shifting Social Priorities

Several significant social priorities have shifted in the past decade:

- Political authority and action have shifted from the federal government to state and local governments.
- Stakeholders are demanding to be involved in environmental decision-making, and voters expect all units of government to be more efficient, cost-effective, responsive, and accountable.
- People are increasingly concerned about the quality of their lives and committing increasing amounts of personal resources to improve that quality. Together, these factors have caused people to demand and exercise more control over their lives to enhance its quality.

Shifting of authority and power to state and local governments has not yet significantly affected the provision of leisure services. Demands for increased public involvement in park and recreation decisions have led to collaborative partnerships with stakeholders. For example, the U.S. Forest Service now uses the term *collaborative stewardship* to capture its current management philosophy. This public involvement has provided better opportunities for the public to express to the land managers the types of goods and services they prefer, including opportunities to realize specific types of benefits.

People also have become more introspective, now consciously evaluating positive and negative impacts of alternative choices and behaviors. Most people now consider the following contributors to the quality of their lives: good nutrition, physical exercise, avoiding substance abuse (including alcohol and tobacco), managing stress, networking that provides social support and cohesion (including trying to retain a perceived loss of sense of community), seeking and using "alternative" medical practices (e.g., acupuncture, use of proven herbal remedies, massage, etc.), and exploring alternative means of finding and expanding the spiritual meanings of their lives (including the growing use of natural areas for spiritual renewal) (Driver, et al., 1996).

Analysis of positive and negative consequences of alternative personal behaviors to the quality of one's life has pervaded leisure behavior in two significant ways. First, people are more serious about how they can balance their work with their leisure. Levels of economic security remain fairly high for most people and time available for leisure has tended to increase, but in smaller blocks of time (Robertson & Godbey, 1997). For example, a national household telephone survey conducted during January and February 1992 (Godbey, Graefe, & James, 1992, p. 25) found that only 35 percent of the respondents said that their work was more important to them than their leisure. Thirty-eight percent said work and leisure were equally important, and 26 percent said leisure was most important. In a 1989 national survey (Roper, 1990), 41 percent responded that leisure was most important, 36 percent said work was most important, and 23 percent said both were of equal importance. Despite their slight discrepancies, these two surveys document that 64-73 percent of the U.S. population perceive leisure to be at least as important as their work. One can assume these data reflect a strong correlation between leisure and perceived quality of life. Such a relationship was documented by a recent survey by Roper Starch Worldwide, Inc. of 2,000 households conducted in April 1994. The report, *Outdoor Recreation In America: A 1994 Survey for the Recreation Roundtable* (The Recreation Roundtable, 1994, p. 61) states "Americans who recreate regularly are consistently more apt to be completely satisfied with virtually all aspects of their lives compared to people who recreate infrequently or not at all."

The second impact of people analyzing the consequences of their leisure behaviors is that many people now have a fairly clear understanding of the consequences of alternative leisure options; they understand the benefits and costs (see Chapter V) (Godbey, et al., 1992; Driver, Tinsley, & Manfredo, 1991). This increased awareness of the benefits has contributed to growing levels of recreational use, to more clearly articulated demands by the public for specific types of benefits, and, slowly but surely, to managers of park and recreation resources adopting management systems, such as Benefits-Based Management (BBM), that accommodate these demands.

Scope and Magnitude of the Benefits of Leisure in General

This section examines the nature and scope of the benefits of leisure. While it would be desirable to focus only on the benefits of outdoor recreation, that is impossible. Such an attempt would be subjective, speculative, and overly qualitative because there are few benefits of leisure that, when taken singly, can be attributed to a particular recreational setting. Put differently, each identified benefit of leisure can be realized in indoor as well as outdoor settings. For that reason, this discussion will first consider the benefits of all types of leisure activities and then attempt to relate those benefits to outdoor recreation. Prior to that, some basic concepts and definitions must be established.

There has been considerable confusion about what is meant by a benefit of leisure. To help prevent that confusion, the developers of the BBM system defined the three types of leisure benefits.

- A change in the condition of individuals, groups of individuals (a family, a community, society at large, or the natural environment) that is viewed as more desirable than the previously existing condition. Examples include improved health, a more economically stable local community, and improved habitat for a species of wildlife.
- The maintenance of a desired condition and therefore the prevention of an unwanted condition. Examples include maintenance of health, pride in local community, and an erosion-free trail.
- The realization of a satisfying psychological recreation experience, such as mental relaxation, closer family bonds, learning of many types, tranquility, enjoying natural scenery, and testing, applying, and/or developing one's skills. See Driver and Bruns (in press) for an elaboration of these three benefits of leisure.

These definitions are meant to include all benefits realized both on and off the recreation sites. They include effects on stakeholders, such as local business enterprises and local communities, and on the biophysical environment. Benefits can be psychological, physiological, social, economic, or environmental. They may be immediate (learning new things about a particular culture or subculture at a particular heritage site) or delayed (greater pride in one's locale, region, or nation because of accumulated increased historical cultural understanding and personal reflection about that knowledge). And one type of benefit (relaxation from a demanding job) can lead to another benefit (increased quality or quantity of work performance), which in turn can lead to other benefits (increased job satisfaction and maybe increased income). See Driver, Tinsley, and Manfredo (1991) for a discussion of this "benefit chain of causality." Of course, managers must also consider negative outcomes of recreation experiences. In fact, they must try to optimize net benefits, or positive outcomes minus negative outcomes.

Until the early 1980s, research on the benefits of leisure focused on cardiovascular benefits of physical exercise, promotion of self–concept, promotion of positive character traits, economic benefits of tourism, and economic value of nonmarket services such as outdoor recreation. The motivations for recreation choices were studied.

Scientific concerns about the benefits of leisure have recently increased rapidly. Since 1992, two national household surveys have provided useful anecdotal and other documentation that the public values its leisure pursuits highly. Several reports have documented the state of knowledge about the benefits. The results of the national surveys and of systematic research that evaluates specific types of benefits will be reviewed separately.

Results of National Household Surveys on Benefits: Two national household surveys have considered the benefits of leisure: (1) the study by Godbey, Graefe, and James (1992) entitled *The Benefits of Local Recreation and Park Services: A Nationwide Study of The Perceptions of the American Public*; and (2) the survey by Roper Starch Worldwide, Inc. done for The Recreation Roundtable (1994). The second will be reviewed in the next section.

The Godbey et al. (1992) survey was done for the National Parks and Recreation Association. In January and February of 1992, telephone interviews were conducted with a nationally representative sample of 1,305 individuals aged 15 and over. Interviews were followed by a mailed questionnaire to obtain additional information. The questionnaire was sent to 882 of those telephoned. Some key findings are:

- 75 percent of the respondents reported that they used local recreation and park services. Fifty-one percent reported they used them occasionally and 24 percent said they used them frequently.
- Respondents were asked to report benefits they perceived to themselves individually, to their households, and to their local communities. By degree of benefit, the percentage responses were as follows.

Degree	Individual	Household	Community
No Benefit	16.3%	20.8%	5.6%
Some Benefit	47.0%	47.9%	33.1%
Great Benefit	36.7%	31.3%	61.3%

Thus, 83.7, 79.2, and 94.4 percent perceived some to great benefits for them individually, for their households, and for their local communities, respectively. Interestingly, 61.3 percent perceived great benefit to their local communities.

- Both users and nonusers were asked about the benefits they perceived, and surprisingly 71 percent of the nonusers reported perceived benefits to themselves, their households, or their local communities.
- Respondents who perceived benefits were asked to name the most important benefit they received and then to list the additional benefits they perceived for themselves, for their households, and for their local communities. Space limitations prevent a listing of these specific types of benefits. Suffice it to say now that results from Godbey et al. (1992) support the underlying contention of this chapter, which is that benefits of leisure are very broad and very large.

Results of Systematic Research on Specific Benefits

Since 1991, three publications have comprehensively documented results of systematic research on specific types of benefits. They are the *Benefits of Leisure* (Driver, Brown, & Peterson, 1991), *The Benefits of Parks and Recreation: A Catalogue* (Parks and Recreation Federation, Ontario, Canada, 1992), and the *Benefits of Recreation Research Update* (Sefton & Mummery, 1995). Other sources that also document the benefits of leisure include Kelly (1981), the section on recreation values and benefits in the *Literature Review* done by the President's Commission on Americans Outdoors (Driver & Peterson, 1986), *Outdoor Recreation in America* (The Recreation Roundtable, 1994), and research publications by Allen (1996), Bruns (1997), Driver (1994, 1996), Lee and Driver (1996), Tindall (1995), and Stein and Lee (1995). Also, very recent systematic inquiry has led to documentation of the very important social benefits of leisure programs in preventing and helping resolve problems of at-risk youth (Schultz, et al., 1995; Witt & Crompton, 1996). The fall 1996 issue of the *Journal of Park and Recreation Administration* is devoted to these benefits of leisure programming. The very recent dates of these publications indicate that much attention is now being devoted to the benefits of leisure. Research now in progress and future research will advance that state of knowledge even further.

Research has disclosed a vast number of general categories and specific types of benefits of leisure (Table I.1). Much better scientific documentation exists for some categories and types of benefits than for others. For example, more research has been done on health-related benefits of physical exercise and on the economic benefits of tourism to local communities than other types of benefits attributed to leisure. Little study has been done on the role of leisure in building social networks and support systems which are especially important for many elderly people. Too many of the benefits attributed to leisure in Table I.1 require greater confirmation. And lastly, in qualification, most of the research on the many psychological benefits of leisure has, by necessity, relied on perceived measures. While results are valid and useful, they are frequently viewed as less reliable than those based on "hard" measures.

Many park and recreation managers have observed the emergence of many of the benefits listed in Table I.1 during their professional careers, and there is wide consensus among those practitioners about the reality of these benefits. While these professional judgments are subjective, they should not be ignored, because they add credibility to the results of the research shown in Table I.1.

Table I.1: Specific Types and General Categories of Benefits that Have Been Attributed to Leisure by Research

- I. Personal Benefits
  - A. Psychological
    - 1. Better mental health and health maintenance
      - Holistic sense of wellness
      - Stress management (prevention, mediation, and restoration)
      - Catharsis
    - Prevention of and reduced depression/anxiety/anger
    - 2. Personal development and growth
      - Self-confidence
      - Self-reliance
      - Self-competence
      - Self-assurance
      - Value clarification
      - Improved academic/cognitive performance
      - Independence/autonomy
      - Sense of control over one's life
      - Humility
      - Leadership
      - Aesthetic enhancement
      - Creativity enhancement
      - Spiritual growth
      - Adaptability
      - Cognitive efficiency
      - Problem solving
      - Nature learning
      - Cultural/historic awareness/learning/appreciation
      - Environmental awareness/understanding
      - Tolerance
      - Balanced competitiveness
      - Balanced living
      - Prevention of problems to at-risk youth
      - Acceptance of one's responsibility
    - 3. Personal appreciation/satisfaction
      - Sense of freedom
      - Self-actualization
      - Flow/absorption
      - Exhilaration
      - Stimulation
      - Sense of adventure
      - Challenge
      - Nostalgia
      - Quality of life/life satisfaction
      - Creative expression
      - Aesthetic appreciation
      - Nature appreciation
      - Spirituality
      - Positive change in mood/emotion

Table I.1 Cont.

B. Psycho-physiological
- Cardiovascular benefits, including prevention of strokes
- Reduced or prevented hypertension
- Reduced serum cholesterol and triglycerides
- Improved control and prevention f diabetes
- Prevention of colon cancer
- Reduced spinal problems
- Decreased body fat/obesity/weight control
- Improved neuropsychological functioning
- Increased bone mass and strength in children
- Increased muscle strength and better connective tissue
- Respiratory benefits (increased lung capacity, benefits to people with asthma)
- Reduced incidence of disease
- Improved bladder control of the elderly
- Increased life expectancy
- Management of menstrual cycles
- Management of arthritis
- Improved functioning of the immune system
- Reduced consumption of alcohol and use of tobacco

II. Social/Cultural Benefits
- Community satisfaction
- Pride in community/nation (pride in place/patriotism)
- Cultural/historical awareness and appreciation
- Reduced social alienation
- Community/political involvement
- Ethnic identity
- Social bonding/cohesion/cooperation
- Conflict resolution/harmony
- Greater community involvement in environmental decision making
- Social support
- Support democratic ideal of freedom
- Family bonding
- Reciprocity/sharing
- Social mobility
- Community integration
- Nurturance of others
- Understanding and tolerance of others
- Environmental awareness, sensitivity
- Enhanced world view
- Socialization/acculturation
- Cultural identity
- Cultural continuity
- Prevention of social problems by at-risk youth
- Developmental benefits of children

III. Economic Benefits
- Reduced health costs
- Increased productivity
- Less work absenteeism
- Reduced on-the-job accidents
- Decreased job turn-over
- International balance of payments (from tourism)
- Local and regional economic growth
- Contributions to net national economic development

IV. Environmental Benefits
- Maintenance of physical facilities
- Stewardship/preservation of options
- Husbandry/improved relationships with natural world
- Understanding of human dependency on the natural world

Table I.1 Cont.

Environmental protection
Ecosystem sustainability
Species diversity
Maintenance of natural scientific laboratories
Preservation of particular natural sites and areas
Preservation of cultural/heritage/historic sites and areas

Source: Driver, B.L. (1990a) as updated and not published elsewhere since.

Table I.1 is of central importance to this chapter because it clearly shows that the benefits of leisure are broader and larger than one would first envision. Those benefits pervade practically all aspects of human behavior and performance: mental and physical health; family and community relations, self-concept, personal value clarification, perceived personal freedom, sense of fitting in, pride in one's community and nation, performance in college and at work, ethnic identity, formation of social networks and systems of social support, spiritual renewal, involvement in community affairs, environmental stewardship, and economic development, growth, and stability.

Consider the scope of the benefits listed in Table I.1. Reflect on the large number of people who perceive these benefits. Ponder their pervasiveness and likely total magnitude, and reflect further on the associated benefits they nurture, create, and promote. For example, satisfactory leisure activities can reduce health-care costs, reduce crime and prevent the high costs of incarceration, increase economic value of work performance, and increase pride in community and nation. It is easy to reach the conclusion that leisure services provide more total benefits to society than any other social service, including health and education.

This strong conjecture is supported by two other types of data. First, statistics show that large percentages of the U.S. population engage in various recreation activities each year. For example, Godbey et al. (1992) report that 75 percent of the respondents said they used local recreation and park services either occasionally or frequently. In addition, very recent data from the 1994-95 National Survey on Recreation and the Environment (see Chapter V) showed that 95 percent of the population of the United States 16 years of age and older participated in at least one of the following selected recreation activity groups between January 1994 and April 1995: fitness activities (68.3 percent), outdoor team sport activities (26.4 percent), outdoor spectator activities (58.7 percent), camping (26.3 percent), swimming (54.2 percent), and picnicking (49.1 percent).

Another contention of this chapter is that the leisure services sector is the largest economic sector in the United States. That proposition rests on the tenet that consumers gain utility (i.e., benefit) commensurate with their expenditures. To explore this proposition, we first need to evaluate the size of this leisure economic sector.

It has been factually established, but not widely recognized, that the leisure services sector is very big business in the United States and other countries (Stynes, 1993). For example, in most U.S. states, recreation and tourism rank in the top three economic sectors as generators of income and employment. It has also been established that expenditures on tourism-related international travel generate greater flows of funds between nations than any other economic transaction, including sales of grain, automobiles, or electronic parts and equipment, each of which is a big ticket item.

In the United States, the following statistics on the economic impacts of domestic and international travel document the size of the "leisure industry":

- In 1995, international travelers spent $79.7 billion in the U.S., and American travelers spent $60.2 billion outside the U. S., creating a trade balance surplus of $19.5 billion. The size of the surplus rose 4 percent over 1994. The surplus from travel grew for the seventh straight year. Travel is one of the few economic sectors that generates a positive trade balance.
- During 1995, domestic and international travelers together spent $421.5 billion in the U.S., which is a 5.8 percent increase over 1994. When induced and indirect effects are added to those expenditures, the estimated total expenditures for 1995 were about $1,017 billion. That total translates into about 16.5 million jobs, travel-related payrolls of about $116 billion, and $64 billion in federal, state, and local tax revenues for that year.
- Pleasure-related travel accounted for 69 percent of all U.S. domestic/resident travel in 1995. Seventeen percent of domestic business trips in 1995 combined business with pleasure, which represents a 4 percent increase over 1994. No statistics could be found for the percentage of international travel that

is estimated to be pleasure-related, but it is logical to assume it is as high or higher than that for resident travelers.

- In 1995, travel and the related tourism it stimulated was the third largest retail industry in the U. S., after automotive dealers and food stores. The projections for the foreseeable future are for expenditures in that sector to continue to increase as a percent of total expenditures of the retail sale industries of the U.S. (The Tourism Works for America 1996, U.S. Travel Data Center, 1994).

While these statistics document that recreation and tourism are very large, they are just portions of the leisure services sector.Current systems of accounting exclude many components that should be included. A few examples of components that should be included are:

- all entertainment expenditures, such as cassette tapes and CDs, operas, symphonies, rock groups, all professional sports, the winter and summer Olympics, and all nonbusiness uses of TV and radio—including the costs of production, distribution, salaries, travel, capital investments in buildings and other infrastructure—and costs of viewing equipment, gate fees, and travel paid by the spectators/patrons/viewers,
- the costs of acquiring, maintaining, and using summer homes, boats/yachts, airplanes, guns, fishing rods, cameras, and clothes for leisure,
- the costs of acquiring, maintaining, and using personal vehicles (e.g., sports utility vehicles, vans, pick-ups) and personal computers that should be allocated to leisure,
- the costs of entertaining guests both inside and outside one's home,
- and a leisure-related share of the total costs of public libraries and continuing education courses.

It seems likely that a leisure services sector that includes all its parts would be the biggest economic sector of the U.S. economy in terms of salaries paid, employment generated, and expenditures made by consumers. If reasonably sovereign consumers willingly allocate so much of their resources to support that leisure services sector, the benefits they receive must be reasonably commensurate with the expenditures. Thus, leisure services must be extremely valuable.

In fairness, it should be mentioned that many expenditures on leisure services also lead to disbenefits, such as recreation injuries, human damage to resources, and other costs, such as those related to abuse of alcohol, but negative impacts accompany all consumer purchases. The purpose here, however, is to estimate the contributions of the leisure services sector to the U.S. economy.

The Benefits of Outdoor Recreation

While outdoor recreation can occur in one's own back yard or on small green spaces in municipalities, the discussion here will focus on outdoor recreation opportunities provided by federal, state, and large regional public agencies, and by private land management firms.

This section describes public perceptions about the benefits of outdoor recreation found by the 1994 Roper Starch survey (The Recreation Roundtable, 1994). It then considers whether policies pertaining to the provision of outdoor recreation opportunities on wildlands can be based on the argument that the benefits of outdoor recreation, when taken individually or separately, are uniquely dependent upon the hinterland-renewable natural resources of the United States.

The Roper Starch Survey

The household survey was conducted in April of 1994 among a representative sample of 1,993 men and women 18 years of age and older. Some relevant findings are:

- Two-thirds of Americans participate in outdoor recreation every year, half do so at least once a month, and one-third take an outdoor vacation.
- Respondents were asked to rate 12 reasons for participating in outdoor recreation in a response format that offered five alternatives ranging from "not at all important" to "very important." For each motivation, the percentages that responded "important" or "very important" were:

To have fun	76%
For relaxation	71%
For health and exercise	70%

For the family to be together	69%
To reduce stress	66%
To teach good values to children	64%
To experience nature	64%
To be with friends	60%
For excitement	53%
To learn new skills	48%
To be alone	39%
For competition	24%

Responses to two other questions showed that 90% and 87%, respectively, agreed strongly or mostly agreed (in contrast to disagreeing) with the statements that "Outdoor recreation is a good way to increase people's appreciation for nature and the environment" and "Outdoor recreation is an excellent way for parents to teach good values to their children." In addition, Francis Pandolfi, then vice president of the Recreation Roundtable, stated "The data clearly demonstrate that providing appropriate opportunities for outdoor recreation contributes to other societal goals, including a sound environment, healthy rural economies, strengthened families, and better personal health."

- Participation in outdoor recreation at any time in life, but particularly as a child, leads to a more satisfying and fulfilling life. The survey disclosed that the proportion of those completely satisfied with the quality of their lives is significantly higher among those who recreate outdoors several times a week (38 percent) than those who do so monthly (32 percent), less often (24 percent), or never (also 24 percent). While other factors, such as income, could explain these relationships, the report stated that the respondents' perceived satisfaction with "the amount of money you have to live on" was the least correlated with recreation participation and that the statistical relationship between recreation and satisfaction persists even when socio-economic status is held constant. Thus, active outdoor recreators are more completely satisfied with the quality of their lives than is the general public.

These findings document that the American public perceives sizable benefits of many different types from their outdoor recreation pursuits.

Unique Dependency of Specific Benefits on Outdoor Settings

The 1994 Roper Starch survey and many other studies show that the public assigns great value and personal and social benefit to outdoor recreation. Are any of those benefits uniquely dependent on outdoor settings?

Intuitively, one would think that many specific benefits of leisure can only be realized in particular settings. However, careful reflection about each of the benefits listed in Table I.1 reveals that each of those benefits individually can be realized in many different environments or settings. I might prefer to enjoy a sense of solitude and tranquility in Central Park of New York City, while you might prefer the Maroon-Bells Wilderness in Colorado. You might prefer to demonstrate, apply, and develop your technical climbing skills on a wall in an exercise center, while another person might prefer Mt. Everest. Recreation experiences and benefits commonly attributed to wildland recreation can also be realized from smaller natural areas in cities. Nature learning and appreciation can also result from nature-oriented programs on television, from magazine articles and books, from environmental education courses, from gardening, and from walks in natural areas in cities. Thus, while each of the benefits listed in Table I.1 can be realized from outdoor recreation, none of them is uniquely dependent on a particular recreation setting or facility. It is therefore misleading to argue here that particular benefits should be provided on the public land administered by federal, state, and large regional agencies because they cannot be realized elsewhere.

But the issue of setting- or facility-dependency of a particular type of benefit is not the important managerial or public allocation issue. The real issue is customer preference. Individual recreationists prefer specific recreation settings just as they prefer specific types of wine, beer, soda pop, cars, homes, music, and most other goods and services. Strong preferences in the minds of the customers represent needs for specific attributes of the desired recreation setting. In this sense, there is resource dependency.

Research has shown that recreationists prefer specific recreation settings to realize a specific benefit or set of benefits for many reasons, including personal taste, effects of past experience, social and cultural conditioning, cost, time available, skill level, and information available on alternative options. A particularly important consideration is the "recreation experience and benefit gestalt," which relates to the qualitative dimensions of leisure preference. To illustrate, I can attain a sense of solitude and tranquility in Central Park, but you prefer to realize those experiences in the Maroon-Bells Wilderness because you get a sense of self-sufficiency, independence, and nature-based spiritual renewal there. And those recreation experience and benefit gestalts definitely depend on specific recreation settings. This is the factor that differentiates demand for outdoor recreation from demands for other types of recreation. It is also here that the supply and the demand sides of outdoor recreation management come together. Managers must mesh their professional skills in managing recreation settings with appraisals of customer needs and preferences to determine which packages of benefit opportunities to provide in which settings.

Management for outdoor recreation and related amenities creates tremendous benefits to individuals, to society and to the natural environment. These benefits have been clearly documented in the following ways:

- Each of the benefits in Table I.1 can result from managing and using wildlands for recreation and related amenity services.
- The several national surveys reviewed in this chapter have established that large percentages of the population of the United States engage in outdoor recreation. One can assume they do this because of the benefits they receive. The 1994 Roper Starch survey found that two-thirds of Americans participate in some form of outdoor recreation each year. The 1994-95 National Survey on Recreation and the Environment also documented that 95 percent of the population over age 15 participated at least once in outdoor recreation. For example, 46.4 percent visited a nature center, 31.3 percent viewed wildlife, 20.7 percent camped in developed sites, 24.4 percent did freshwater fishing, 23.5 percent motorboated, and 23.8 hiked in natural areas. These percentages represent big numbers and logically connote benefits of tremendous magnitude.
- Another indication of the magnitude of the social benefits of outdoor recreation is that outdoor recreationists would not spend so much of their personal time and income on recreation if the rewards were not reasonably commensurate with those expenditures. It is known that a significant part of domestic and international tourism travel is directed toward wildland recreation and related amenity services. The expenditures for this travel and for related tourism are tremendous. In addition, preliminary results of the recent survey the U.S. Bureau of the Census conducted for the U.S. Fish and Wildlife Service showed that in 1966, hunters, anglers, and wildlife watchers spent $97 billion, which now represents 1.3 percent of gross domestic spending. It should be pointed out that while hunters and anglers together spent $68 billion of the $97 billion, they represent only 14 million and 35.5 million people in the United States. Similarly, it should be emphasized that these expenditures pertain only to hunting, angling, and viewing wildlife and thus say nothing about the expenditures for other types of outdoor recreation. The point is that these large expenditures must connote large personal benefits.
- A related indication of the benefits of outdoor recreation is its contribution to the value of domestically produced goods and services, or Gross Domestic Product (GDP). For example, the Draft 1995 RPA Program (USDA Forest Service 1995) states "Forest Service programs in 1993 are estimated to have generated about $123.8 billion toward the GDP: a little less than 2 percent of the national total. By the year 2000, Forest Service programs, as outlined in this strategic plan, would contribute $130.7 billion to GDP, of which $97.8 billion (75 percent) would be generated by recreation, $12.9 billion by wildlife and fish, $10.1 billion by minerals, and $3.5 billion by timber." These high estimates for recreation have been contested and the economic impact analyses made for this draft RPA program statement, scheduled for release in 1995, are being revised and updated for the Recommended RPA Program. While it is expected that the magnitude of the economic effects from individual resources will change, the majority of the economic activity associated with Forest Service programs will continue to be stimulated through the recreation, fish, and wildlife resource areas (Personal conversation with Forest Service RPA staff analysts). Thus, recreation and related amenity resources make large contributions to GDP. Put simply, the pursuit of wildland recreation generates big bucks.

Managing Wildland Recreation Resources for the Benefits They Provide

This section describes some of the ways managers of wildlands are responding to demands for recreation and related amenities. Management priorities are being reoriented to accommodate shifting social priorities as advocated by Forest Service Chief Dombeck (1997b) earlier in this chapter.

Shifting Social Priorities Affecting Management of Wildlands

People are attempting to have more control over their lives by deliberating more carefully about the consequences of specific behavioral alternatives to the quality of their lives. Self-examination has led to increased awareness and appreciation of the benefits of leisure. Perceived benefits have increased recreation participation and demands by the public that managers of recreation resources provide specific benefits opportunities. Accompanying this shifting social priority toward individuals making choices to enhance the quality of their lives have been pressures to increase amenity services from public wildlands. Three of the most significant social changes reflecting increased pressures for changes in management of public wildlands are:

- Public involvement: Since the National Environmental Policy Act was passed in 1969, other legislation and agency directives have required that public agencies systematically involve the public in environmental decision-making.
- Fiscal stringency and accountability: All agencies that manage public land operate under increasing fiscal stringency and increasing demands for accountability.
- Public concerns about the biophysical environment: Since the early 1970s, public opinion polls have shown that the American people remain highly concerned about the state and quality of the biophysical environment.

Although these three social changes, along with people's growing awareness of and demands for the benefits of recreation, have been occurring for a decade or two, their cumulative and interactive effects on management of outdoor recreation resources have been most visible only in the past five to 10 years. During that short period, these changes have been truly revolutionary in some agencies and considerable in others. The nature and impacts of these changes on management of outdoor recreation resources are discussed in detail elsewhere (Driver & Bruns, in press).

- The focus of multiple-use management of public land has shifted away from commodity and toward recreation and related amenity uses. This reorientation has required the agencies to develop and apply sophisticated and science-based amenity resource management systems; acquire more personnel with training in the social sciences to complement existing personnel trained in timber, range, fishery, and wildlife management; and modify their budgeting processes to justify additional appropriations for recreation and related uses.
- Recreation and related amenity resource agencies have moved considerably away from activity-oriented management, which focuses on supply considerations, toward outcomes- or benefits-oriented management. In the new focus, the major goal of management is to add value to the lives of the customers served while protecting and improving the basic biophysical resources being managed.
- There has been wide adoption of total quality management (TQM), with solicitation of information on customer preferences for specific recreation activities, experiences, and other benefits. TQM has stimulated monitoring of customer satisfaction.
- Many park and recreation agencies have substituted the concept of *customer* for the words *user* and *visitor*, and they are involving all stakeholders in planning and plan implementation.
- There has been greater recognition that several to many collaborators, both public and private, affect the type, quality, and amount of recreation benefits that are realized.
- Public involvement has gone far beyond soliciting input from the public at a few selected steps in the land–planning process. Involvement now includes development and maintenance of collaborative partnerships. This approach promotes an atmosphere of trust and respect within which the customers feel they are an active part of the decision processes. Especially significant here has been movement away from the philosophy that the professional managers are technical experts who can determine the one right decision. Managers now recognize that there are several right decisions that differ in terms of which values and interests are accommodated and compromised.
- There has been a distinct trend toward more efficient, cost-effective, and accountable management by public agencies. As a result, higher administrative levels and stakeholders are able to review the performance of field-level personnel more objectively. While public agencies do not operate as profit-making firms, there has been wide adoption of business principles to help assure more efficient operations.
- There has been widespread adoption by private and public wildland managers of a holistic sustainable ecosystem philosophy. Management plans, therefore, often cross administrative boundaries because ecological processes cross these boundaries.

Adoption of Better Management Systems

To keep pace with these changes, most agencies that provide outdoor recreation opportunities have reevaluated and changed many of their goals as well as their managerial philosophies and practices. To meet those new goals and directions, many of those agencies have recently begun to refine older recreation and related amenity resources management systems. They are developing and applying newer science-based systems that are consistent with modern theories of leisure behavior. To meet growing social demands, these systems are being developed to promote TQM, a customer orientation, collaborative partnerships with both on- and off-site customers, sustainable ecosystem management, and responsive, cost-effective, and accountable managerial actions.

The U.S. Forest Service, for example, has adopted four amenity resource management systems: (1) the Meaningful Measures for Quality Recreation Management System (Jaten & Driver, in preparation), (2) the Scenery Management System (USDA Forest Service, 1995), (3) the Recreation Opportunity Spectrum System (USDA Forest Service, 1982; Driver, Brown, Gregoire, & Stankey, 1987; Driver, 1990); and (4) Benefits-Based Management (Allen, 1996; Driver, 1996; Driver & Bruns, in press). The fourth, which is the most recent, comprehensive, and integrative, was developed to better accommodate social changes and especially to provide guidance on how to practice outcomes-oriented management. Under that approach, customers can determine which types of recreation opportunities will best enhance the quality of their lives, and management agencies can improve their promotion of rural economic stability and growth. Because this chapter focuses on the benefits of outdoor recreation and how to manage wildlands to optimize realization of those benefits, Benefits-Based Management (or BBM for short) will be elaborated on briefly. For more information, see Driver and Bruns (in press).

Benefits-Based Management

Historically, recreation has been defined as the human behavior of participating in a designated activity at particular sites and locations. Examples are camping at a particular site and driving on a specific scenic highway. Thus, recreation was considered a human behavior in the same sense as spelling, studying, and sleeping. Little managerial attention was directed to why such a behavior was chosen or how it positively and negatively impacted the recreationist. Recently, this orientation has changed. Most public parks and recreation agencies have adopted, or are adopting, an "outcomes orientation." In the new orientation, participation in a recreation activity is viewed as a means for optimizing personal beneficial outcomes (Driver, 1994). By identifying desired outcomes, parks and recreation managers have found a much broader array of benefits that they must accommodate more fully than in the past. For outdoor recreation, this broader array of beneficial outcomes includes:

- nature-based spiritual renewal (Rolston, 1996) and wellness (Montes, 1996),
- psychological attachment to special places (Roberts, 1996; Greene, 1996),
- appreciation of early American landscapes (Bruns & Stokowski, 1996),
- use of heritage and historic resources not only for better understanding of the evolution of a culture or subculture, but also for maintenance of particular ethnic identities (Lee & Tainter, 1996),
- strategically programming leisure services as a social intervention to prevent or help ameliorate particular social problems or to capture a targeted type of benefit; e.g., help at-risk youth, promote physical health, promote environmental awareness, including that of natural ecological processes, and through tourism help stabilize the economy of a local community (Witt & Crompton, 1996).

BBM was developed and is being used and refined by leisure researchers, educators, policymakers, and managers to integrate and direct thinking about the management of recreation service delivery systems. It is not only a philosophy about the roles of leisure in society, but also a system for directing leisure research, instruction, policy development, and management (Allen, 1996; Driver & Bruns, in press).

The fundamental question raised by BBM is "why should a particular leisure service be provided?" The answer is formulated in terms of clearly defined positive and negative consequences of delivering that service. The objective is to optimize net benefits—to add as much positive value as possible. To succeed, leisure policy analysts and managers must: (1) understand what benefits are associated with each leisure service that is provided; (2) decide what benefits opportunities will be provided; (3) articulate to higher level administrators, to the customers, and to the general public why particular benefits opportunities were chosen; and (4) understand how to manage different recreation settings to deliver those opportunities. BBM is science-based and requires the leisure policymaker and manager to keep abreast of improving knowledge about the benefits of leisure.

BBM is a major shift in the way we conceive of and manage recreation resources and programs. It is more than a management system because it influences how we think about leisure. BBM is an expanded conceptual framework that uses concepts from general systems theory to integrate the inputs and the physical structure of the leisure/recreation service delivery systems with the outputs of those systems. Under conventional approaches, attention focuses primarily on the inputs to the system and on management of the physical structure. Too often, these inputs are viewed as the ends of management with little attention given to why services are provided. In sharp contrast, the BBM views inputs and system as necessary means for capturing desired outcomes. It views the goal of management as optimizing net benefits that accrue to individuals. BBM requires the writing of clear management objectives for explicitly defined "benefit opportunities." It requires benefits-oriented management prescriptions, guidelines, and standards that help to assure provision of the types and amounts of the benefit opportunities targeted for delivery both on and off the physical site. By considering both on- and off-site impacts, the BBM requires a comprehensive appraisal of the impacts to on-site users, to local communities, to other stakeholders, and to the biophysical resources. It defines these impacts in terms of beneficial changes that occur, whether desired conditions are maintained, and whether or not on-site customers have opportunities to realize satisfying recreation experiences.

While the notion of managing recreation resources to realize benefits is not novel, a systematic, conceptually integrated, and operational means of promoting and applying that approach did not exist until BBM was conceptualized and articulated.

The benefits or outcomes perspective is the fastest growing trend in parks and recreation management, including management of outdoor recreation and related amenity resources. BBM is growing in acceptance at all levels of government. It has been endorsed by the National Parks and Recreation Association (NPRA) which has set up a Task Force to train parks and recreation professionals to implement BBM, and it is preparing training manuals and BBM implementation guidelines. More significantly to outdoor recreation, the National Society for Park Resources, which is the branch of NRPA most concerned with outdoor recreation, has endorsed and is promoting BBM.

Future Directions and Issues

Directions: The 1994 Roper Starch national household survey (The Recreation Roundtable, 1994) asked respondents to assess the importance of outdoor recreation to them as they were growing up. About 25 percent said it was very important, 37 percent said it was somewhat important, and 32 percent said it was not important. The remaining respondents did not know. Those respondents who engaged in outdoor recreation selected the *very important* response much more frequently than any other group. Conversely, those who said outdoor recreation was not important to them early in life were most apt to forego outdoor recreation now. It is disturbing that 32 percent in 1994 said outdoor recreation was not important to them when growing up, because only 16 percent said so in a survey done in 1986 for the President's Commission on Americans Outdoors. The percentage responding *very important* then was 32 percent, compared to the 25 percent in 1994. Some possible causes are decline in availability of extended blocks of leisure time (Robertson & Godbey, 1997), more single-parent families, and more households in which both parents work. It probably is not caused by greater urbanization, because the percentage of the U.S. population living in essentially urban areas did not change appreciably between 1986 and 1994. The Roper Starch report for the Recreation Roundtable (1994, p. 59) concluded, "given the significance of parents in forming our future recreation participation and values, this trend is disturbing."

The shifting social priorities and changes discussed earlier will continue to occur, but perhaps not at the same intensity as in the recent past. Nevertheless, they will continue to influence the goals and managerial directions of wildland management firms and agencies. Use of wildland for recreation and related amenity values and benefits will continue to grow. Public agencies will face increased public pressure to be customer-oriented, cost-effective, and accountable in their operations. And private firms and public agencies will be expected to continue to practice sustainable ecosystem management.

It is highly probable that the benefits and outcomes approach will be used much more widely to guide management of park and recreation resources. This approach also will guide development of leisure policies, including the justification of budget requests and allocations. And the benefits approach will continue to attract leisure scientists and educators.

Because of the continuation of the social changes and the needs for management systems such as BBM to accommodate them, parks and recreation policymakers, administrators, and managers probably will continue to sharpen their interests in the benefits of leisure.

Issues: While the 1994 Roper Starch survey indicates a trend toward a decreasing number of Americans saying that outdoor recreation was very important to them when they were growing up, it is unclear if and how this trend can be reversed. Doubt about how to address societal problems is pervasive in contemporary America, where polarization is increasing and aid-giving behaviors, charitable giving, voter turnout, and confidence in public governance are decreasing (Godbey, 1995). Parks and recreation services, including outdoor recreation, can help alleviate these problems, but that role will not be optimized until leisure has gained political parity with the other social services and until leisure professionals understand and articulate the social benefits of leisure more widely (Driver, 1995; Driver & Bruns, in press).

Considerably more training of parks and recreation professionals, at all levels of government, is needed to help them understand the philosophy and concepts of the benefits and outcomes approach. They should understand why it is needed, and how to implement it.

Leisure professionals need to better understand the scope, magnitude, and true social significance of leisure, including its great economic significance.

Leisure professionals must not only be able to articulate the benefits of leisure to their customers, other stakeholders, and the public at large; they also must clearly and accurately convey the important message that leisure adds much positive value to individuals and society at large. Leisure may well be the most important social service and the largest economic sector. Nevertheless, it does not now have parity with the other social services (education, health, social welfare/public assistance, justice, communication, transportation) with which it competes for public funds. It does not because park and recreation agencies have not positioned themselves in the eyes of the public as a social service that adds great value to society (Crompton, 1993).

Considerably more funding is needed for research on the benefits of leisure to advance that state of knowledge. The needed research is complex and multidisciplinary. It is costly because it covers many dimensions of human behavior (psychological, physiological, psychophysiological, social, economic), requires expensive longitudinal studies, and must consider the positive and adverse impacts of leisure on the biophysical environment. That funding should include studies to document much more accurately the economic magnitude of leisure in general, and outdoor recreation in particular, as a sector of the U.S. economy.

HISTORY OF OUTDOOR RECREATION AND NATURE-BASED TOURISM IN THE UNITED STATES

By Robert W. Douglass, Ohio State University

Introduction

Outdoor recreation pursued during leisure time and by free choice that provides its own satisfaction has continued to play an increasing role in people's lives through good times and bad. World wars, major economic troubles, record rises in the standard of living, and general increases in our overall quality of life all appear to have boosted outdoor recreation and tourism. Good and bad economic times seem to direct changes in style, but increases in involvement in outdoor recreation have accompanied both of them. There has been an increasing trend in outdoor recreation and nature-based tourism participation from the time that record-keeping began. Some activities have decreased in popularity, but new ones have come forward to continue the overall upward trend. That upward trend has continued through the mid-1990s, even while discretionary or free time appears to be getting harder to find.

The upward trends in outdoor recreation and nature-based tourism reflect the changes in our society. We are an urban society that still clings to the concepts of the great outdoors and self-reliance. We now share our landscapes with millions of foreign visitors, while we have become globe-hopping tourists ourselves. As a group, we are getting older, more affluent, busier, more culturally diverse, and maybe even more mellow in our outlook. Today, our recreation participation appears to be an accommodation of, or even a reaction to, the society we share.

New technologies are being adapted by the public as rapidly for recreation as for business activities. Exchanging faxes for road-race registrations has become the norm. Internet enquiries keep the skier informed on daily snow conditions. Hiking plans for a trip to a national forest 2,000 miles away can be planned on maps obtained from a net search. Airline tickets and ocean cruises are booked electronically, while all sorts of "chat" groups provide opportunities to exchange questions and answers about favorite activities. New toys and advanced equipment constantly appear, challenging us to try new activities.

It is useful to look back on our history for a feeling of how we have arrived where we are today. Outdoor recreation and nature-based tourism have been developing on the American landscape for more than 100 years. They have responded to the changes society has dealt. While developing in the United States, outdoor recreation and nature-based tourism moved through three overlapping phases. The formative years defined the roles of the public and private sectors and were rooted in the establishment and management of public land. Definition and expansion of the infrastructures to support nature-based recreation and tourism followed World War II. Societal integration and accommodation to science and the environment, which were always part of recreation and tourism, accelerated after the Cold War presented the world with a new set of problems. Where recreation- and nature-based tourism will be carried in the future is a subject for conjecture, but their place in the future appears assured.

The Formative Years

Recreation serves as America's direct contact with its natural resources. It is one of the nation's most influential attitude-builders on use of natural resources. Recreation has played direct and indirect roles in the evolving concept of how America's land should be cared for, used, and valued. Recreation areas and parks were established to supply recreation opportunities directly. Indirectly, the accommodation of outdoor recreation demands caused changes in the management of land meant primarily for other purposes. The formative stages of America's land-use policy include conquest, conservation and wise use, multiple use, sustained use, and stewardship.

Recreation and nature-based tourism have been around in this country since its beginnings. However, recreation was not formally recognized during the nation's formative years as a force that would eventually shape land management policies of the private and public sectors. During the late 19th and early 20th centuries, the romanticism and conservation movements were at their peaks. George Perkins Marsh had introduced the concept of land stewardship into the literature in 1864, but the country had something else on its mind at that time. With 90 percent of its population living in rural areas and served by slow and limited transportation, the country did not seem to care about a national recreation policy. People of the time were too busy carving a living from the landscape to revisit it in their scarce leisure time.

But as society changed, its view of wilderness and "untamed" land evolved. Eventually, wilderness was described in friendly terms as a thing of beauty and no longer as the enemy. Authors such as James Fenimore Cooper produced novels that presented a romantic view of the natural landscape. Using his European training, Albert Bierstadt produced magnificent paintings of the western mountains that influenced many people, including members of Congress, to preserve tracts of land for their unique beauty. People vigorously supported, or went along with, setting aside large areas of the country in the public interest. However, early in the 20th century, there was no perceived need for the government to have a cohesive policy for recreation and tourism. None was needed because outdoor experiences and exposure to nature were parts of the everyday life and outdoor spaces were plentiful. Americans exerted little or no pressure on federal and state governments to provide outdoor recreation opportunities.

At the turn of the 20th century, there were abundant recreation opportunities in this country. But they did not exist as a result of government policy or as a public good. Hunting, fishing, boating, and many other activities were common, but they were not within the realm of government and were not always considered to be outdoor recreation experiences. The playground movement gave rise to city-oriented recreation activities, and the American railroads were making excursions to their parks and associated resorts early in this century. Excursions to Mont Alto Park in Pennsylvania, to Riverview Beach and Cape May in New Jersey, and to several other places were responsible for establishing resorts that have survived in one form or another into the present time. But widespread consideration of recreation was yet to follow on the large federal estate that was being developed by the establishment of the national forests and national parks. Even Gifford Pinchot and John Muir were looking at the need to set aside lands in the public's interest without specifically recognizing tourism or recreation.

Local needs for recreation were addressed in some urban environments. New York's Central Park was designed in 1850 by Frederick L. Olmstead, who went on to champion core parks in major urban areas. These parks, along with village greens, commons, plazas, and other institutional open spaces, were used by city dwellers as *de facto* parks, even though the open spaces were not the result of recreation planning. Many forms of open space owe their existence to needs for survival and community defense. Many actions taken early in the American colonial period led to what later became outdoor recreation opportunities for their citizens. Legal actions of the early settlers led to establishment of laws guaranteeing access to natural resources for human survival. Those "fishing and fowling" laws became the forerunners for today's concepts of recreational hunting and fishing. As far back as 1641, the Massachusetts Bay Colony enacted the "Great Ponds Act" to open bodies of water for hunting, fishing, and ice gathering by the public. Those access acts established the tradition of public entry onto land. Today, outdoor recreation is often the purpose of such access.

Cities led the way in establishing areas that were to become parks or recreation areas even before the formal efforts of Olmstead and his associates took place. William Penn's plan for Philadelphia included five open squares. Penn also required farmers to keep one-fifth of their farms in woodlots. That tradition still marks the rural Pennsylvania landscape with forestland. Newington, New Hampshire, established the country's first city forest in 1710. The playground movement, which first was directed at providing wholesome activities in safe places for children, created pressures in the cities for parks and play areas (Van Doren & Hodges, 1975).

Playgrounds helped to improve the quality of city life for both children and adults in the prewar years. City of Atlanta park, circa 1930s. Photo courtesy of the Hargrett Rare Book and Manuscript Library, University of Georgia Libraries.

However, no popular, broad-based support existed for outdoor recreation areas at the national or state levels prior to the close of the 19th century. Yellowstone was established as a federal park in 1872 because some farsighted individuals held out for its public ownership at a time when the land appeared to be valueless and lost in distance from civilization. The Yosemite Grant to California and the reservation of Yellowstone Park were carved from public domain land when there was no opposition to the ideas (USDI, 1962). They were harbingers of things to come, but they did not reflect a national policy at that time.

Government actions for recreation were scattered, but they did begin to show a pattern early in the 20th century. The establishment of the forest reserves in 1891, the Forest Service in 1905, the Antiquities Act in 1906, the Agriculture Appropriations Act in 1915, and the National Park Service in 1916 placed the federal government in the recreation management business. Although recreation was not, in itself, the reason for the federal government to get into the land management business, recreation became a major component of the management strategy almost from the start. By creating the National Park System, Congress introduced a concept that would spread to almost every country in the world by the end of the 20th century. Congress also opened national parks for recreation by the charge that it gave to the National Park Service for managing its areas. When, in 1905, the Forest Service was established in the United States Department of Agriculture, then Secretary of Agriculture James Wilson (USDA, 1974) set the Forest Service on its way into recreation management when he directed the first chief of the Forest Service to consider the policy, " when conflicting interests must be reconciled, the question will always be decided from the standpoint of the greatest good of the greatest number in the long run."

The national forests contained the ingredients of attraction, space, opportunities for solitude, setting, and accessibility that make up the potential for recreation areas. That potential eventually made the Forest Service the nation's largest host to outdoor recreation. Americans quickly recognized the potential for outdoor recreation in national forests. In 1921, Chief William Greeley declared outdoor recreation to be a major use of the National Forest System.

Recreation was first mentioned in federal legislation as a legitimate use of public land in the 1902 Morris Act which reserved lands on the Chippewa Indian Reservation for recreation use and provided for protection of scenic values (Van Doren & Hodges, 1975). Impacted by the Agriculture Appropriations Act of 1915, the Forest Service responded to the requirement for establishing cabin lease sites on national forests. Formalization of the wilderness concept at the federal level was a product of that cabin-site leasing program. Protection of a unique area of wilderness where no development would take place was a concept advanced by some Forest Service employees who were sent into an area to suggest where cabin lease sites might be located. Arthur Carhart and other Forest Service employees in the Trapper Lake region of the Carson National Forest in 1924 suggested the concept of wilderness on federal land that has developed into the National Wilderness Preservation System. More than 20 percent of today's national forest area is managed as wilderness. The Forest Service was not the first government agency to act on wilderness preservation. Pennsylvania had already set the pattern. Under the leadership of its Commissioner of Forestry, Gifford Pinchot, Pennsylvania established a state wilderness system that preceded the action by the federal government (Frome, 1984).

The Department of the Interior's Bureau of Land Management is the nation's largest landholder. It manages the land left over from the public domain as well as the nearly 3 million acres that were returned to the Department of the Interior from the Oregon and California Railroad by the Reinvestment Act of 1916 (Forest Service, 1976). During the formative years, most of the land associated with recreation was managed by the National Park Service, the Bureau of Land Management, and the Forest Service. The roles of the other agencies increased later. Eastern national forests were established and added to the National Forest System through purchase of lands at the headwaters of navigable rivers as authorized by the Week's Law of 1911. Today, there are some 130 national forests and 19 national grasslands that cover more area than France, Belgium, and Switzerland combined. In all, the federal government manages 761 million acres of land. Of that land, 691 million acres are available for recreation and nature-based tourism. Seven federal land managing agencies care for approximately 34 percent of the nation's land and host more than 500 million visitor days of recreation use (National Park Service, 1989).

States have only six percent of the country's land, but offer impressive opportunities for outdoor recreation opportunities. Most of the state park land is in eastern states, where the federal estate is the smallest. When the national parks and national forests were getting their start on western public-domain land, the state forestry-conservation movement began in the eastern states, which had seen their land ravished by poor farming practices, careless logging, charcoaling, and other destructive activities. Several northeastern states organized state agencies to care for their land during the late 19th century. New York began the Adirondack and Catskill Preserves in 1885; Pennsylvania followed by creating state forests and wildlife and watershed protection areas in 1889. As with the federal government, preservation and conservation were the driving forces behind the state programs. However, the large tracts established for conservation purposes eventually became extensive recreation areas and, in some cases, parks. Yosemite Valley almost became the first state park in this country when it was granted to the state of California for public use and recreation for all time (Van Doren & Hodges, 1975). However, California not did meet its obligations for the park and eventually ceded it back to the federal government. Illinois acquired its first park in 1903 and established a park system in 1917.

State parks were given a big boost in 1921 when the National Park Service hosted the first National Conference on State Parks. That conference, presently entitled the National Society for Park Resources, has been meeting on a regular basis ever since and has been instrumental in defining and supporting the role of state parks (Van Doren & Hodges, 1975). Other federal actions gave land to the states for parks, and the Civilian Conservation Corps built the infrastructures of many of those parks. States realized early on that their role was to provide balanced outdoor recreation opportunities to their citizens. Therefore, they did not follow the preservationist model of the National Park Service for very long. Showing flexibility, the state parks attempted to respond more to the regional needs for developed facilities and active recreation.

The Years of Definition and Expansion

After the Great Depression and World War II, recreation became a major component of the American way of life. It demanded recognition and attention. That demand engendered a massive development period. As part of, or as a result of, that development, millions of people were brought into contact with nature and introduced to the need to protect natural environments. That awareness has manifested itself in the environmental concerns being voiced in many countries today. During that period, the world became more affluent and mobile. Jetliner travel became common, and the interstate highway system began connecting all parts of the nation. Large numbers of people began to travel for recreation. The tourist industry has been a major economic force around the world ever since.

After World War II, Americans took to the open road to see and experience the great outdoors. They did so in such numbers that they overwhelmed the existing recreation facilities. Many of those facilities had been built by the Civilian Conservation Corps and were completely outmoded in design and intent. Leisure activities that had been put off by World War II and the Korean Conflict were causing strain on the outdated recreation infrastructure. Recognizing a need to improve the situation caused by the increasing recreational demands, Congress passed legislation to study the outdoor recreation situation. The Outdoor Recreation Resources Review Commission (ORRRC) was established in 1958 (85th Congress, 1958) and charged with studying the present and future needs for outdoor recreation and with determining the available and future supply of outdoor recreation resources. *Outdoor Recreation for America,* commonly known as the ORRRC report, presented to Congress in early 1962, contained the findings and recommendations of the ORRRC. The ORRRC report was the beginning of a massive federal movement to create more recreation opportunities in the United States.

The ORRRC action was not the only congressional action on recreation at that time. Congress was aware of the unsatisfied demand for outdoor recreation and was moving to address the situation even before the Outdoor Recreation Resources Review Commission had completed its report. A major concept for public land management was articulated by Congress when it passed the Multiple-Use and Sustained Yield Act of 1960 to establish the policy for managing the national forests. This piece of legislation was intended to place recreation on the same level of importance as timber, water, wildlife, and range. The multiple-use mandate has the same ring as the doctrine Agriculture Secretary Wilson's direction that the national forests "should provide the greatest good to the greatest number in the long run." In the vast National Forest System, outdoor recreation opportunities would have the same footing as timber and other uses of the forest. Today, national forests provide more recreation opportunities than any other land management system.

The multiple-use concept was extended to the Bureau of Land Management's national resources land, which makes up the largest acreage under one jurisdiction. The Bureau of Land Management oversees approximately 175 million acres in 11 Western states and 165 million in Alaska. This is land that was not claimed from the public domain under the homestead acts and other land transfer programs. Historically, the great recreation potential of this land was slow to develop because the Bureau of Land Management had been dispersing and leasing land rather than providing outdoor recreation opportunities. Congress provided a new charter for the Bureau in the Federal Land Policy and Management Act of 1976. Also, much of the land it managed was inaccessible or not attractive for mass recreational activities until recently.

The release of the ORRRC report in 1962 set off a chain of related activities that defined the national and state policies on outdoor recreation, began a large transfer of land from the private sector to the public sector, and led to a two-tiered recreation management complex on federal land. As a direct result of that report, Congress passed a series of acts. That legislation, mostly crowded into the 1960s, included acts that established the National Wilderness Preservation System, the National Wild and Scenic Rivers System, the National Trails System, and national recreation areas. Legislation funded acquisition of recreation land under the Land and Water Conservation Fund Act of 1965 and provided for a method of directing state involvement in the push to meet the recommendations of the ORRRC report.

The Outdoor Recreation Act of 1963 declared the desirability of assuring adequate outdoor recreation resources and called for all levels of government and private interests to conserve, to develop, and to use those resources for the benefits and enjoyment of the American people. Statutory recognition for the newly established Bureau of Outdoor Recreation was intended by this act, even though the Bureau of Outdoor Recreation was never mentioned. Authorization was given to the secretary of the interior for performing several activities and functions. The president and the 88th Congress understood that the secretary of the interior, Morris Udall, would delegate the charges of this act to the Bureau of Outdoor Recreation for implementation (Fitch & Shanklin, 1970).

The Outdoor Recreation Act requires the preparation and maintenance of a continuous inventory and evaluation of the outdoor recreation needs and resources in the United States. It was from the authority of this act that the national policy for outdoor recreation was established in the form of a comprehensive outdoor recreation plan. That plan was eventually built upon the states' comprehensive outdoor recreation reports and plans and presented by the president to the American people on an approximate five-year cycle. State plans came about when they were required by the Bureau of Outdoor Recreation for individual states to receive the large sums of federal money that were to become available.

Three five-year comprehensive nationwide outdoor recreation plans were produced by the Department of the Interior. *The Recreation Imperative*, the first plan, was too controversial to release. The second national outdoor recreation plan, *Outdoor Recreation; A Legacy for America,* was presented by the Bureau of Outdoor Recreation in 1973. It provided guides for coordinating federal and nonfederal public agencies' recreation efforts. It also established roles for various levels of government and the private sector in meeting recreation needs in America. *The Third Nationwide Outdoor Recreation Plan,* presented in 1979, sought to establish continuous recreation planning and assessment rather than periodic efforts.

Assessment of outdoor recreation was continued by the Department of the Interior, even though the Bureau of Outdoor Recreation was being eclipsed by rival agencies.

By 1978, the Bureau of Outdoor Recreation had been renamed the Heritage, Conservation, and Recreation Service (HCRS). But this agency too was short-lived in part because of the constant opposition to it by the National Park Service (Fairfax, 1978). Also, many original objectives given to it by the Outdoor Recreation Act of 1963 and the ORRRC report had been accomplished. By 1981, the last independent remnants of HCRS were abolished, and any remaining duties were transferred to the National Park Service. With that action, the federal government eliminated one of the few agencies concerned specifically with outdoor recreation. With abandonment of national assessments and the Nationwide Outdoor Recreation Plan, assessment of outdoor recreation in America became the responsibility of the Forest Service. Authority for this assessment was through the Renewable Resources Planning Act of 1976 as described in Chapter 2 of this book.

A back-country preservation system that was begun by the Forest Service in 1924 with a half-million acres has blossomed into the National Wilderness Preservation System (NWPS) containing approximately 91 million acres. The wilderness concept—originated at the federal level by Arthur Carhart in 1924—has grown to become a major component of federal land administration. Public opinion has supported establishing, keeping, and enlarging the National Wilderness Preservation System.

More than 677,000 acres are designated as part of the National Wilderness Preservation System in Yosemite National Park. Photo courtesy of USDI National Park Service. Photo by Richard Frear.

Once the battle to pass the Wilderness Act was won, Congress moved rapidly to establish other recreation systems at the national level and to fund recreation land acquisition. Compromises needed to get the Wilderness Act through Congress served as models for the ensuing recreation legislation that faced the same sort of opposition. Prior activities that were exceptions to the intent of the legislation were permitted where they had been established. Private land rights were given some protection against eminent domain proceedings. And, mining interests were protected under an existing mining law until it expired in 1984. Having established the ground rules, Congress rolled on to pass the acts establishing the National Trails System and the Wild and Scenic Rivers System and creating several more national recreation areas.

The Land and Water Conservation Fund Act of 1965 (LWCFA) did more than any other piece of legislation to get federal agencies and states to develop outdoor recreation areas and facilities in response to the recommendations of the ORRRC report. LWCFA provides funds to state and local governments for the development of outdoor recreation on a planned, nationwide scale. Balancing the nation's supply of recreation opportunities with its needs is the expressed purpose of LWCFA. Substantial sums of money were made available to agencies and states that cooperated and complied with certain requirements. Some of that money was spent by the Forest Service, the National Park Service, and the Fish and Wildlife Service for land acquisition. Sixty percent of the LWCFA money was intended for the state governments on a 50-50 matching basis. Use of matching funds was intended to double the total monies spent under this act. It also signified a commitment by the receiving state. An investment in recreation resources of more than $2.5 billion has resulted from the Land and Water Conservation Act. More than one million acres have been added to federal recreation areas, and 27,000 state and local projects received matching funds. Many of the original goals set by the ORRRC report were accomplished through the LWCFA.

Federal and state responses to the ORRRC report brought about significant changes in outdoor recreation. In some ways, the success of that report also brought about its obsolescence. As time passed, people's outdoor recreation involvement changed to the point that by 1980, many national leaders were concerned about the overall recreation situation. Twenty years after the ORRRC report was published, Resources for the Future (Outdoor Recreation Policy Review Group, 1983) published a private assessment of the outdoor recreation situation entitled, *Outdoor Recreation for America—1983*. That report pushed the Congress and the president into ordering another serious study to update the 1958 ORRRC project. The President's Commission on Americans Outdoors (PCAO) was established by executive order in 1985 and produced its report, *Americans Outdoors: The Legacy, the Challenge*, in 1987. This new study produced a new approach by the government in its role of providing a national policy for recreation. Instead of concentrating upon supply and demand numbers, the new policy focused upon societal concepts. The needs for an outdoor recreation ethic, private property rights, landowner liability, cooperative partnerships, and environment quality were the topics forming the new federal policy for outdoor recreation.

Since the 1970s, state parks have rearranged their priorities so that outdoor recreation, rather than preservation, defines their mission. Increased demand for state park land between 1960 and 1990 fueled the development of facilities and recreation programs—often at the expense of passive use and preservation. Today, every state has a park system, and state parks host an estimated 700 million visitors a year on just over 11 million acres. Land acquisition for state parks rose rapidly through the 1970s, but has tapered off since then. That decreasing rate of expansion has paralleled the leveling off of attendance that occurred unevenly in state park systems. Apparently, the State Park System was again able to adjust to the situation. As the rate of increase in use slowed down, so did the expansion of parkland area. And, the State Park System became less dependent upon uncertain tax support—turning instead to more revenue generation—to support its operations.

State and federal land got the most attention during the development of the nation's outdoor recreation infrastructure. However, private land was also providing a major share of recreation opportunities. During the years of expansion and definition, private land continued to provide opportunities for outdoor recreation and tourism. Much of the private land that is available for recreation is in the East where it helps to balance the lack of sufficient public recreation land. In the past, one of the major reasons for closing private land to public recreation was the fear of liability. States wanting the private land to be open to public use in some form passed legislation to shield landowners from liability in certain situations. All 50 states passed recreation user statutes to limit liability of landowners for injuries occurring to recreational visitors while on their land (Voth & Wright, 1995). Although the states differ in how much immunity their statutes provide, they agree on the concept of shielding the landowner who does not charge entry fees (Van Der Smissen, 1987). Charging a fee usually negates the protective laws.

Recreation was considered to be a social need that should be provided to everyone as a public good. That notion was declared in the Outdoor Recreation Act of 1963—much as the Declaration of Independence referred to inalienable rights. The approach appears to minimize the role of private recreation opportunities and place the responsibility for providing all the recreation land and opportunities through public funding. As is typical of long-term government programs, the situation changed as recreation demand was being satisfied. The perceived role of recreation shifted. Society changed its mind. It no longer looked at recreation solely as a public good with common benefits paid for by public funds. Rather, people began to respond to the myriad of new recreation choices being offered by the private sector both on and off public land.

Long trips during extended vacations gave way to short, intensely active vacations that fit into the changing life styles in the developed nations. Both spouses worked and time was becoming the most valuable commodity when the national policy for recreation had run its course in the early 1990s. A sort of "pay-to-play" principle had replaced the public-good view of recreation. People who were paying to pursue recreation were becoming less likely to vote for higher taxes to support the public-good aspect of it. Rapid and relatively cheap transportation permitted fast travel to destination vacations anywhere in the world. Improved equipment allowed people to get involved in activities that would have been impossible for them a decade or two earlier.

Rapid transportation and high-quality equipment allowed many people to do more than just view the scenery. Close involvement with nature during outdoor recreation and tourism set the stage for learning more about the natural environment and for becoming more closely associated with its many facets. The physical fitness movement enabled a large segment of the population to safely enjoy some newly available high risk activities. Recreation activities of all sorts were moved into the natural setting. Running, bicycling, and other competitive activities have become common activities in parks and forests. Although they are not likely to displace conventional parkland activities, these recreational pursuits are here to stay and they are growing, changing, and getting more intrusive all of the time. Individual watercraft, mountain bikes, in-line skates, super sidecut skis, small snowshoes, new clothing materials, and hundreds of other items are changing the way the public is participating in the great outdoors.

Non-traditional activities such as snow volleyball are seen increasingly on recreation areas. Photo courtesy of National Ski Areas Association.

Only the private sector of the economy has the flexibility to adjust quickly and continuously to the desires of recreationists and tourists. Large companies recognized the potential for good investments in recreation and tourism and established facilities both independent of and dependent upon public attractions. Now, private capital and private management of facilities are common on public land. This concept was introduced by Stephen Mather when he was director of the National Park Service in 1916. Demands for more expensive and elaborate facilities and services got to the point where the public sector did not want to, or could not, provide them. Mather's earlier idea of introducing private capital and management onto public land to provide facilities and services was seen as the way to provide those specialized services. Hotels in national parks were part of Mather's earliest plan, but the idea did not spread very much until after the large LWCFA expansion of recreation land. Lodging, ski resorts, and similar developments were established as concessions on public land to provide opportunities that were too expensive or outside of the agency's responsibility. As available tax monies shrank, state and federal agencies turned more and more to partnership agreements in which private organizations met changing demands for recreation on public land. The partnerships are successful because recreators are willing to pay more of the cost for specialized, high-quality opportunities.

Integration and Accommodation of Science and the Environment

Outdoor recreation and nature-based tourism are adjusting to new realities. Technology innovations and economic and social structural changes are evident everywhere. Unprecedented affluence and economic advancement have followed the end of the Cold War in many parts of the world. The citizens of many nations are investing their time, energy, and money in recreation pursuits. Tourism is moving people to all corners of the earth—even to places where the attractions only recently have been defined. Recreation participation has been increasing in this country for over 100 years, and that trend is continuing. Recent work by the National Survey on Recreation and the Environment indicates that in 1995, approximately 95 percent of Americans participated in outdoor recreation and that the popularity and marketplace opportunities are still increasing faster than the general population (Cordell, Lewis, & McDonald, 1995).

For Americans, the length of a vacation averages 8.5 days. Less time and more money to invest have made some changes in the way that we now view the use of our leisure. There seems to be an interest in more economical use of leisure. People are doing those things that reflect a previous investment of time and money rather than just "hanging out" at the beach. Certainly, beach vacations are popular if one surveys the shorehouse rental success these days. However, many people look for more ingredients in the vacation package than they once did. Computer games and the Internet go with them. Individual watercraft, mountain bikes, portable CD players, and hundreds of new concepts enhance vacation activities. Where safe drinking water is scarce, tiny, portable water filtration systems now allow serious backpackers to stay out longer than they once could. Lightweight clothing and associated gear provide warmth, waterproofing, and safety.

Pursuit of an activity of choice appears to have replaced the vacation as the primary reason for outdoor recreation participation. Children's soccer leagues, adult golf outings and tournaments, triathlon camps, specialized theme cruises, and ecotourism are small parts of the new wave of outdoor recreation involvement. A "been there, done that" group of travelers is looking for new and ultimate adventures. These people now can begin their activities from such far away bases as Tahiti or Bora Bora. New concepts in marine cruises have been introduced. All three cruises of a new 420-passenger cruise liner operating on the Great Lakes were sold out to European tourists in 1997. The northern border of the United States appears to have an appeal to European travelers, who are stopping over at Toledo, Ohio, on their 10- and 11-day cruises between Montreal and Chicago.

In today's marketplace, "green" sells. Environmental interest is high, and it attracts paying visitors. Nature-based tourism implies travel to interact with a natural environment for education, observation, or recreation (Richards, 1996). Visiting an area to appreciate its natural attributes has been the rationale for nature-based tourism as we commonly accept the term. Now, a new term, "ecotourism" has been introduced. Ecotourism is defined by the Ecotourism Society as "socially and environmentally responsible travel to natural areas which conserve the environment and improves the welfare of the local people." Ecotourism has developed from the 1990s' nature-based tourism desires to benefit from unique environments while contributing to their protection and improvement.

There is a downside to worldwide nature-based tourism. Tourists are able to fly to many locations that may not be ready to offer them the best of hospitality. Tourists who are stretching their horizons to include more extreme cultural situations sometimes find themselves coping with more than the trip. The end of the struggle between the superpowers left many vacuums of undefined power that are bringing life to local, but violent conflicts. Completely innocent and impartial nature-based tourists are stepping into these settings. The nature-based tourist can be a pawn in forceful negotiations. Governments encourage tourism as an excellent industry for boosting local economies. Hard currency is brought from home and left in developing countries as tourists come to see cultural, scenic, and historical attractions. People seeking power occasionally resort to the ultimate weapon of the disenfranchised—terrorism. Disrupting tourism or holding tourists hostage is a rare, but real, situation. Violent attacks have occurred in Egypt, hostages have been taken in Nepal, and outright banditry has occurred in Belize and Guatemala. Tourists are vulnerable to violence. The threat of violence upon tourists for political purposes is not unique to modern tourism, but it is something to consider. Quick and visible impacts make tourism an attractive target for terrorists and bandits.

New equipment and the desire to learn something new drive much of today's outdoor recreation participation. A four-wheel driving school is available for people who purchased a sport–utility vehicle, but have neither a place to use its capabilities nor the knowledge to do so. Just $664 buys two hours of lessons in the school's Land Rovers and a night's hotel stay (Sloan, 1997). Bicycle tours of European countries attract Americans who want to pedal around while looking at wineries, art, castles, or some other theme. Many Asians come to this country to climb its mountains using the equipment that new technologies provide.

Hand-held global positioning satellite (GPS) receivers and cellular telephones have changed the way people interface with the wilderness experience. Today, it is possible to be in touch with the office while camping in the middle of a wilderness area. Some resistance is surfacing from organizations dedicated to more primitive experiences. Those groups believe that the new technologies are incongruous with wilderness experiences. However, the safety and convenience of GPS receivers and cellular or satellite telephones mean that they are in the back-country to stay. The same is true for satellite transmitters carried by ocean-going yachts and back-country skiers for location tracking in emergencies. While these devices are not for everyone, the ability to "be in touch" while isolated on a recreation trip into remote places makes sense for people concerned about their safety or needing to monitor business or family situations. Why not have your computer available, send faxes, or receive telephone messages in the wilderness?

New alliances are forming as conflicting views rise or decline in this new period of integration and accommodation of science into outdoor recreation. Personal computers, faxes, electronic mail, and the Internet have permitted new, small budget organizations to present their cases to the public and to lawmakers in ways that were not possible just a decade earlier. Highly funded preservation organizations no longer have the lobbying and public information fields to themselves. Recently founded organizations interested in using, rather than simply preserving, outdoor resources have learned how to use the modern technologies to effectively state their cases. A case in point is the successful campaign to keep the Reserve Status 2477 roads open for access on federal land in spite of strong attempts by preservation groups and government agencies to close them and thereby exclude mounted and mechanized recreationists.

Different technologies have created different situations—not all of them good or bad in the long run. These technologies will enable people to enjoy the out-of-doors in ways unknown to their parents. Anglers can use the GPS systems to determine their location, mark a fishing spot for a return visit, have an automatic course plotted for home or the next fishing site, and have a standby man-overboard locator. As the price per unit has dropped, GPS receivers have become a popular method of traveling in back-country areas because they give all the directions needed to get where one wants to go. However, they are best used when backed up with a compass and a map.

Internet users gather all sorts of information about their destinations before leaving home. Maps, trail conditions, camping availability, snow conditions, and costs of events are just a few items that are learned from the Internet. Reservations, tickets, and equipment use can be arranged electronically. Completing the recreation planning and obtaining all the required information in advance fits into the new style that demands time efficiency.

Even hunting is swept up in the new style of outdoor recreation. "Sporting-clays" shooting courses are substituting for live bird harvesting. They present compact, ready experiences to the person wanting to develop shooting skills or compete against others without spending long periods of time in the field looking for live targets to fly up. Managers are perplexed in eastern public forests as the white-tailed deer population climbs while hunting pressure declines. But hunting is more appealing on private domains where conditions can be controlled by the hunting organization or the property manager.

Some of the same camaraderie can be developed that is associated with the game of golf where people play in small groups on a known course. Golf is another growing outdoor pursuit that is succeeding predominantly in the private sector. Golf was here to stay before the present trends developed. However, it now has a new face with an appeal to Asian and Black Americans that it never had before. The young and minority group members see golf as an activity in which they can achieve greatness or just have fun now that Tiger Woods has arrived.

Conclusion

The changes in outdoor recreation taking place today may be more dependent on attitude than upon toys. People are willing to pay to recreate, but they want to spend their money on their terms. Public sector recreation helped to meet the country's recreational needs when opportunities were in short supply. Now that there are plentiful supplies of outdoor recreation opportunities and public money is getting scarce, people have begun to focus on more specialized and costly activities. Recreation opportunities still exist on the public estate. But many of the new activities are in the private sector or in cooperative partnerships between the public and private sectors. Partnerships in funding and in supplying outdoor recreation opportunities will continue to grow. Where outdoor recreation and nature-based tourism go in the future might be linked to the economy. If the past is a predictor of the future, however, outdoor recreation participation will go up regardless of where the economy goes.

EVOLUTION OF THE NATIONAL WILDERNESS PRESERVATION SYSTEM

John B. Loomis, Colorado State University

Origins of the Concept of Wilderness Preservation

The concept of wilderness has evolved in human perception over the past centuries. Wilderness as a primeval, natural environment was viewed as a forbidding place during most of human history. Wilderness was something to be conquered and a source of wood for heating, cooking, and buildings. Three factors led to the changing perception of wilderness as something desirable. First was the rise of incomes brought about by the success of the industrial revolution. A growing proportion of the American public was less concerned with survival needs such as food, clothing, and shelter. Their interests began to enlarge to outdoor recreation. Second, the industrial revolution and urbanization of America resulted in less direct contact with nature. The noise and crowding of factories and cities made the contrasting quiet and solitude offered by wilderness refreshing rather than forbidding. Finally, Nash (1973) pointed out that wilderness was becoming scarce relative to farmland, suburbs and cities. At the margin, another million-acre wilderness was now something of value, rather than something to be cleared for farms and houses.

Early Reservations

It was a sense of this rising scarcity of wilderness that led Arthur Carhart and Aldo Leopold to suggest to the U.S. Forest Service that some land be preserved in a roadless state. Their first reservation was the Gila Wilderness Reserve in 1924 in New Mexico. In 1929, the first official policy was established for protecting such roadless areas as primitive areas. Ten years later, the Forest Service issued "U" regulations that administratively established wilderness areas (Dana & Fairfax, 1980; Hendee, et al., 1990). These regulations provided that tracts larger than 100,000 acres could be protected from road building, logging, hotels, and motorized access. At that time about 14 million acres were classified as wilderness (Hendee, et al., 1978). The Forest Service retained authority to reclassify lands from wilderness to other uses, however.

Early Legislative Efforts

The ability to reclassify lands from wilderness to allow more developed uses led many groups to push for more permanent protection of wilderness through Congressional designation. From the original proposals in 1956 to the final Wilderness Bill in 1964, 65 different bills were introduced into Congress (Hendee, et al., 1990). During this time, 20 of these bills passed one house or the other, but not until 1964 was a bill finally passed by both Houses of Congress (Dana & Fairfax, 1980, 217)

Wilderness Act of 1964

In September of 1964 the Wilderness Act was passed. The act defined wilderness as:

> an area where the earth and its community of life are untrammeled by man, where man himself is a visitor who does not remain . . . an area of undeveloped Federal (sic) land retaining its primeval character and influence, without permanent improvements or human habitation, which is protected and managed so as to preserve its natural conditions and which (1) generally appears to have been affected primarily by the forces of nature, with the imprint of man's work substantially unnoticed; (2) outstanding opportunities for solitude or a primitive and unconfined type of recreation.

The act "hereby established the National Wilderness Preservation System . . . and shall be administered for the use and enjoyment of the American people in such a manner as will leave them unimpaired for future use and enjoyment as Wilderness (sic)."

The act formally designated all national forest land that had been classified under the U regulations as *wilderness* or *wild*. The act required the Forest Service to recommend whether areas classified as *primitive* should be recommended for *wilderness* designation. The act required the secretary of interior to review every roadless area of over 5,000 acres the National Park Service and National Wildlife Refuge System for potential as wilderness.

The act specified that "there shall be no temporary road, no use of motor vehicles, motorized equipment or motorboats, no landing of aircraft, no other form of mechanical transport..." This latter requirement has been interpreted to ban the use of mountain bikes in wilderness areas.

It is very important to note that wilderness is compatible with multiple-use management. Wilderness allows for continuation of livestock grazing in the same manner and degree as prior to designation. Many multiple uses are enhanced by wilderness protection, for example, water quality, wildlife, fisheries, and primitive recreation.

Eastern States Wilderness Act

Given the strict definition of wilderness in the act, the Forest Service felt that many of the previously "cut-over" but regrown forests in the eastern U.S. did not meet the definition of Wilderness (Hendee, et al., 1978). However, there was significant public support for protecting many of these less–than–pristine areas from future logging and development. From 1972 to 1974 several bills were introduced for an Eastern States Wilderness Act. In 1975, the act passed. The act designated 16 areas in 13 states as Wilderness and added them to the National Wilderness Preservation System (Hendee, et al., 1978, 77). The act identified 17 Wilderness Study Areas for review and recommendation as Wilderness. While this act provided less stringent admission criteria for eastern areas, it dictated that the areas would be managed in accordance with the principles in the 1964 Wilderness Act (Hendee, et al. 1978).

BLM Made Eligible for Wilderness

The Bureau of Land Management was not included among federal land agencies when the Wilderness Act of 1964 passed. However, the BLM is the largest public land manager in the 11 Western States. BLM did not receive authority to review its land for Wilderness until it received its "organic" act in the form of the Federal Land Policy and Management Act of 1976, nearly 12 years after the Wilderness Act first passed. Due to the tens of millions of roadless acres on BLM land, the agency's Wilderness review process was a major undertaking. Some offices of BLM approached the effort as part of its new planning process, while others tried to "fast track" the Wilderness review process to "release" as many roadless areas as possible to other multiple uses. While the BLM largely completed its review and recommendation of roadless areas as Wilderness by the mid 1980s, Congress has been very slow to act on these recommendations. With the exception of California and Arizona, most areas recommended for Wilderness are still labeled as Wilderness Study Areas (WSA's). Generally, WSA's are managed as Wilderness to protect their qualities until Congress makes final determinations on these areas.

Wilderness Management

While the concept of wilderness management might be thought of as a contradiction in terms, protection of the wilderness qualities of solitude and naturalness requires explicit user guidelines when visitation levels rise beyond the natural resiliency of the environment. Wilderness management has become a professional career path within many federal and state agencies. The joint publication in 1978 by the USDA and USDI of the landmark book *Wilderness Management* by USDA Forest Service scientists John Hendee, George Stankey, and Robert Lucas did much to upgrade the standards of wilderness management. The second edition of that book in 1990 continues to be a standard text for wilderness management courses throughout the world. Wilderness management has emphasized visitor use management, including carrying capacity, limits of acceptable change, and the merits of different ways to ration visitor use. However, wilderness management is much broader than visitor management and includes wildlife, fire, and air quality. For example, wilderness areas are provided special air quality protection as Class I areas under the Clean Air Act of 1977 and subsequent amendments.

Summary

As is shown in Chapter VII on wilderness, the National Wilderness Preservation System is a diverse collection of natural ecosystems. These ecosystems range from deserts to alpine areas. Wilderness areas range in size from a few hundred acres of wetland on national wildlife refuges in the lower 48 states to million-acre tracts in Alaska, Idaho, and Minnesota. There has been growing recognition that wilderness is for more than recreation use. Wilderness is now playing a major role in protecting critical habitat for endangered species such as the northern spotted owl and salmon.

REFERENCES

Allen, L. (1996, March). A primer: Benefits-based management of recreation services. *Parks And Recreation*, 64-76.

Bruns, D. (1997). Benefits-based management's role in shifting recreation-tourism management paradigms. In M. Johnson, D. Twynam, & W. Haider (Eds.), *Proceedings of shaping tomorrow's North: The role of tourism and recreation*. Thunderbay, Ontario, Canada: Lakehead Center for Northern Studies.

Bruns, D., & Stokowski, P. (1996). Sustaining opportunities to experience early American landscapes. In B. Driver, D. Dustin, T. Baltic, G. Elsner, & G. Peterson (Eds.), *Nature and the human spirit: Toward an expanded land management ethic* (pp. 321-330). State College, PA: Venture Publishing, Inc.

Congress of the United States, 85th. (1958). *The Outdoor Recreation Resource Review Act of 1958*. Washington, DC: U.S. Government Printing Office.

Cordell, H. K, Lewis B., & McDonald, B. L. (1995). Long-term outdoor recreation participation trends. In J. L. Thompson, D. W. Lime, B. Gartner, & W. M. Sames, (Comps.), *Proceedings of the Fourth International Outdoor Recreation & Tourism Trends Symposium* (pp. 35-38). St. Paul, MN: University of Minnesota.

Crompton, J. (1993). Repositioning recreation and park services: An overview. *Trends, 30*(4), 2-5.

Dana, S., & Fairfax, S. (1980). *Forest and range policy* (2nd ed.). New York: McGraw Hill.

Department of Agriculture. (1974). *The principal laws relating to forest service activities.* (Agriculture Handbook No. 453). Washington, DC: US Government Printing Office.

Department of the Interior. (1962). *Forest Conservation.* (Bulletin 42). Washington, DC: US Government Printing Office.

Dombeck, M. (1997a). Remarks at Public Lands Forum of Outdoor Writers' Association of American Public Lands Forum. June 24, 1997. Grenefee, Florida.

Dombeck, M. (1997b). Remarks to USDA Forest Service Regional Foresters and Directors. April 8, 1997.

Driver, B. (1990). Recreation opportunity spectrum: Basic concepts and use in land management planning. In R. Graham & R. Lawrence (Eds.). *Toward serving visitors and managing our resources*: Proceedings of a North American workshop on visitor management on parks and protected areas (pp. 159-183). Waterloo, Ontario, Canada: University of Waterloo, Tourism Research and Education Center.

Driver, B. (1994). The recreation production process: The benefits-based approach to amenity resource policy analysis and management. In Friluftsliv: Effekter og goder, Dn-notat, 1994-7, (pp. 12-30). [In Proceedings, Scandinavian Conference on Recreation: Benefits and Other Positive Effects. Norwegian Institute of Nature Studies]. Direktoratet for Naturforvaltning Tungasletta 2, 7005 Trondheim, Norway.

Driver, B. (1995). Reaction to Godbey: Change and leisure—and being civilized. In J. Thompson, D. Lime, B. Gartner, & W. Sames (Compilers), *Proceedings of the Fourth International Outdoor Recreation and Tourism Symposium and the 1995 National Recreation Resources Planning Conference* (pp. 14-16). St. Paul, MN: Minnesota Extension Service, University of Minnesota.

Driver, B. (1996). Benefits-driven management of natural areas. *Natural Area Journal, 16*(2), 94-99.

Driver, B., Brown, P., Gregoire, T., & Stankey, G. (1987). The ROS planning system: Evolution, basic concepts, and research needed. *Leisure Sciences, 9*(3), 203-214.

Driver, B., Brown, P., & Peterson, G. (Eds.). (1991). *The benefits of leisure*. State College, PA: Venture Publishing, Inc.

Driver, B., & Bruns, D. (In press). Concepts and uses of the benefits approach to leisure. In T. Burton, & E. Jackson, (Eds.), *Leisure studies at the millennium*. State College, PA: Venture Publishing, Inc.

Driver, B., Dustin, D., Baltic, T., Elsner, G., & Peterson, G. (Eds.). (1996). *Nature and the human spirit: Toward an expanded land management ethic*. State College, PA: Venture Publishing, Inc.

Driver, B., & Jaten, A. (In preparation). *Meaningful measures for quality recreation management: Managing the recreation program of work at the site or project level*. Available from B. L. Driver, USDA Forest Service, Fort Collins, CO.

Driver, B., & Peterson, G. (Compilers). (1986). Values section (comprised of 11 papers). In *A literature review: President's commission on Americans outdoors*. Washington, DC: U.S. Government Printing Office.

Driver, B., Tinsley, H., & Manfredo, M. (1991). The paragraphs about leisure and recreation experience scales: Results from two inventories designed to assess the breadth of the perceived benefits of leisure. In B. Driver, P. Brown, & G. Peterson (Eds.), *The benefits of leisure* (pp. 263-286). State College, PA: Venture Publishing, Inc.

Fairfax, S. (1978). A Disaster in the Environmental Movement. *Science,* 189 (February): 743-48.

Fitch, F. M., & Shanklin, J. F. (1970). *The bureau of outdoor recreation.* New York: Praeger.

Forest Service. (1976). *Highlights in the history of forest conservation.* (US Department of Agriculture A1B-83). Washington, DC: U.S. Government Printing Office.

Frome, M. (1984). *Twentieth anniversary of the Wilderness Act: Heroes who made it happen—heroes in the making.* Natural Resources Days Keynote Address. Ft. Collins, CO: Colorado State University.

Godbey, G. (1995). Things will never be the same: Prospects for outdoor recreation and tourism in an era of exponential change. In J. Thompson, D. Lime, B. Gartner, & W. Sames (Compilers), *Proceedings of The Fourth International Outdoor Recreation and Tourism Symposium and the 1995 National Recreation Resources Planning Conference* (pp. 3-13). St. Paul, MN: Minnesota Extension Service, University of Minnesota.

Godbey, G., Graefe, A., & James, S. (1992). *The benefits of local recreation and park services: A nationwide study of the perceptions of the American public.* State College, PA: The Pennsylvania State University.

Greene, T. (1996) . Cognition and the management of place. In B. Driver, D. Dustin, T. Baltic, G. Elsner, & G. Peterson (Eds.), *Nature and the human spirit: Toward an expanded land management ethic* (pp. 301-310). State College, PA: Venture Publishing, Inc.

Hendee, J., Stankey, G., & Lucas, R. (1978). *Wilderness management.* (Miscellaneous Publication No. 1365). Washington, DC: USDA Forest Service.

Hendee, J., Stankey, G., & Lucas, R. (1990). *Wilderness management* (2nd ed.). Golden, CO: North American Press.

Jaten, A., & Driver, B. (In preparation). *Meaningful measures for quality recreation management: Managing the recreation program of work at the site or project level.*

Journal of Park and Recreation Administration. (1996) . Vol. 14, No. 3.

Kelly, J. (1981). *Social benefits of outdoor recreation.* Urbana-Champaign, IL: University of Illinois.

Lee, M., & Driver, B. (1996). Benefits-based management: A new paradigm for managing amenity resources. In W. Burch, Jr., J. Aley, B. Conover, & D. Field (Eds.). *Survival of the organizationally fit: Ecosystem management as an adaptive strategy for natural resource organizations in the 21st century.* New York: Taylor & Francis Publishers.

Lee, M., & Tainter, J. (1996). Managing for diversity in heritage values. In R. Driver, D. Dustin, T. Baltic, G. Elsner, & G. Peterson (Eds.), *Nature and the human spirit: Toward an expanded land management ethic* (pp.339-349). State College, PA: Venture Publishing, Inc.

Montes, S. (1996). Uses of natural settings to promote, maintain, and restore human health. In R. Driver, D. Dustin, T. Baltic, G. Elsner, & G. Peterson (Eds.), *Nature and the human spirit: Toward an expanded land management ethic* (pp. 105-115). State College, PA: Venture Publishing, Inc.

Nash, R. (1973). *Wilderness and the American Mind.* New Haven, CT: Yale University Press.

National Park Service. (1989). *Statistical abstract—1988.* Denver, CO: U.S. Department of the Interior, Denver Service Center.

Outdoor Recreation Policy Review Group. (1983). *Outdoor recreation for America—1983.* Washington, DC: Resources for the Future, Inc.

Outdoor Recreation Resources Review Commission. (1962). *Outdoor recreation for America.* Washington, DC: U.S. Government Printing Office, Superintendent of Documents.

Parks and Recreation Federation of Ontario. (1992). *The benefits of parks and recreation: A catalogue.* Ottawa, Canada: Parks and Recreation Federation of Ontario.

The Recreation Roundtable. (1994). *Outdoor recreation in America: A 1994 survey for the Recreation Roundtable.* Orlando, FL: Roper Starch Worldwide, Inc.

Richards, S. (1996). *A strategic plan for sustainable rural system tourism development in the Toledo district of southern Belize.* Graduate thesis. Columbus, OH: The Ohio State University, School of Natural Resources.

Roberts, E. (1996). Place and spirit in public land management. In R. Driver, D. Dustin, T. Baltic, G. Elsner, & G. Peterson (Eds.), *Nature and the human spirit: Toward an expanded land management ethic* (pp.61-80). State College, PA: Venture Publishing, Inc.

Robertson, J., & Godbey, G. (1997). *Time For life.* State College, PA: Pennsylvania State University Press.

Rolston, H. III. (1996). Nature, spirit, and landscape management. In R. Driver, D. Dustin, T. Baltic, G. Elsner, & G. Peterson (Eds.), *Nature and the human spirit: Toward an expanded land management ethic* (pp.17-24). State College, PA: Venture Publishing, Inc.

Roper Poll. (1990, May/June). *The American enterprise, 1*(3),118-120.

Sefton, J., & Mummery, W. (1995). *Benefits of recreation research update.* State College, PA: Venture Publishing, Inc.

Schultz, L., Crompton, J., & Witt, P. (1995). A national profile of the status of public recreation services for at-risk children and youth. *Journal of Park and Recreation Administration, 13*(3), 1-25.

Sloan, G. (1997, April 18). 4X4 school teaches the rules of the road. *USA Today*, D9.

Stein, T., & Lee, M. (1995). Managing recreation resources for positive outcomes: An application of benefits-based management. *Journal of Park and Recreation Administration, 13*(3), 52-70.

Stynes, D. J. (1993). Leisure—the new center of the economy? *SPRE Newsletter,17*(3), 15-20.

The Tourism Works for America Council. (1996). *Tourism Works for America: 1996 report*. Washington, DC: The Tourism Works for America Council.

Tindall, B. (1995, March). Beyond fun and games. *Parks And Recreation*, 87-93.

USDA Forest Service. (1982). *ROS users' guide*. Washington, DC: USDA Forest Service.

USDA Forest Service. (1995). *Landscape aesthetics: A handbook for scenery management*. Agriculture Handbook 701 System. Washington, DC: USDA Forest Service.

U.S. Travel Data Center. (1994). *Impact of travel on state economies 1994*. Washington, DC: Travel Industry Association of America.

Van Der Smissen. (1987). *Recreational user statutes: A review of landowner hold-harmless laws in the United States*. Columbus, OH: American Motorcyclist Association.

Van Doren, C., & Hodges, L. (1975). *America's park and recreation heritage: A chronology*. Washington, DC: U.S. Department of the Interior, Bureau of Outdoor Recreation.

Voth, D., & Wright, B. (1995). Supply of private land and water access and use. In J. L. Thompson, D. W. Lime, B. Gartner, & W. M. Sames (Compilers), *Proceeding of the fourth International Outdoor Recreation and Tourism Trends Symposium* (pp 113-119). St. Paul, MN: University of Minnesota.

Witt, P., & Crompton, J. (Eds.). (1996). *Recreation programs that work for at-risk youth: The challenge of shaping the future*. State College, PA: Venture Publishing, Inc.

CHAPTER II

FRAMEWORK FOR THE ASSESSMENT

. . . .

H. Ken Cordell[1]

INTRODUCTION

In 1974 the United States Congress established a process for assessing the state of the forest and range resources in this country through passage of the Forest and Rangeland Renewable Resources Planning Act (RPA). The RPA directed the secretary of agriculture to assess the demand, supply and condition of all forest and range resources in the United States and to submit the first of these assessments by December 31, 1975. A five-year update to this first assessment was mandated for 1979. The act then directed the secretary to establish an ongoing process for updating the national RPA assessment every 10 years after reporting the findings from the 1979 assessment.

The intention of the RPA assessment was and is to describe recent trends, current condition and likely futures for timber, water, wildlife and fish, range, minerals, and outdoor recreation and wilderness in the United States. This book represents the fourth of the outdoor recreation and wilderness studies done to meet the mandates of the 1974 RPA. The other studies covering the other resource areas mentioned above are published elsewhere by the specialists covering each of those areas.

The scale of outdoor recreation and wilderness assessments prior to this one was primarily national. Secondarily, as was possible given data limitations, regional differences were described and interpreted. As the assessment process has evolved and capabilities have progressed from the first one in 1975, demands for regional information have grown. While the overall national picture is still very much of interest and is the major focus of this assessment, more emphasis has been placed on identifying regional differences and on examining geographic patterns of the primary study variables at the scale of individual counties. The makeup of the four assessment regions is shown in Figure II.1. More easily accessible data at county level and advances in GIS tools for microcomputers have now made county-scale examinations of geographic patterns of outdoor recreation and wilderness resources and uses feasible. This assessment of outdoor recreation and wilderness provides national, regional and county-scale results.

Past assessments also focused on comparing demand and supply trends through a constructed "gap" analysis. The gap of reference was the difference between demand for outdoor recreation and wilderness opportunities and the supply of these opportunities. Chapter IV of the 1989 assessment was devoted to such a gap analysis (Cordell, et al., 1990). This had been the traditional econometric approach to identifying imbalances between supply and demand where such differences could be viewed as problems, or opportunities, for setting policies and programs to better match demand and supply. While the RPA assessment has always been carefully designed to deal only with fact finding and non-prescriptive interpretation, findings indicating gaps between demand and supply were found useful in identifying areas where policy changes could be considered. Indeed, this is the reason for conducting such an assessment in the first place.

---

[1]H. Ken Cordell is a Research Forester and Project Leader, USDA Forest Service, Athens, GA.

Figure II.1: The four RPA Assessment Regions, 1997

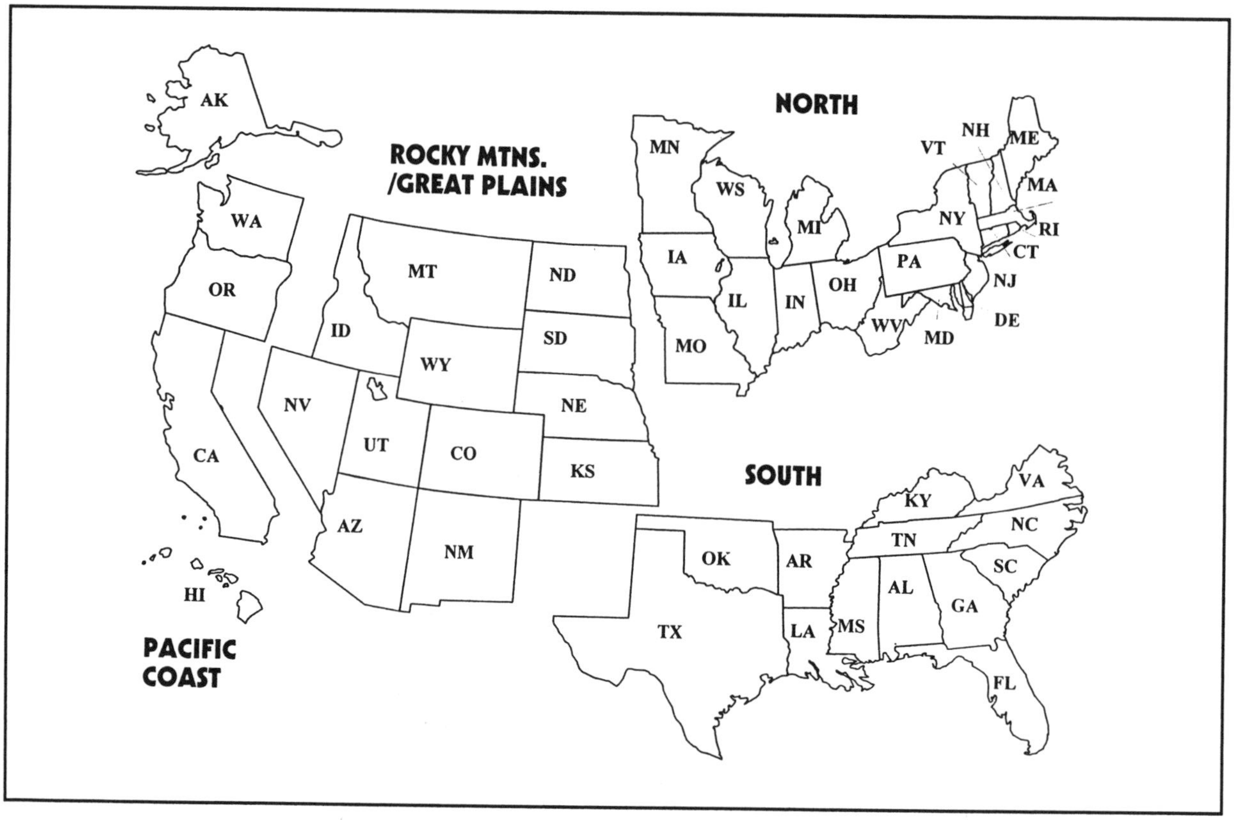

While comparisons between demand and supply in the form of a gap analysis were highly informative, the complexity and assumptions underlying such an analysis made communication of its findings difficult. For this assessment, a formal gap analysis is not attempted. Less of a statistical approach has been adopted. Primarily the approach in this assessment is to use the expert judgement of the assessment specialists to examine supply trends across the spectrum of opportunities the public and private sectors provide in light of demand trends and projections. From this less formal "gap analysis" and based on knowledge of issues in outdoor recreation and wilderness, we attempt to identify policy, management and research implications for the country. It is the authors' opinion that this form of qualitative comparison can provide valid insights just as the more quantitative econometric gap analysis does.

Thus, the *framework* for this national assessment of outdoor recreation and wilderness includes the following activities:

- Inventory and describe trends in the availability of the land and water *resources* of this country for outdoor recreation uses, both publicly and privately owned.
- Examine in depth the availability of *private rural lands* for outdoor recreation and the conditions under which access is permitted.
- Describe recent trends and current *participation* in outdoor recreation by region of the country and across social groups.
- Forecast *future participation* trends under widely accepted assumptions about future population growth, changes in population makeup and shifts in the availability of recreation opportunities.
- Describe recent trends, the current situation, and likely future *wilderness system* designations, uses, and values.
- Describe the public's *perceptions* and evaluations of recreation opportunities in the United States.
- Interpret the *implications* of resource availability, demand, and other trends for future resource management, policy, and research.

In the preceding chapter, introductory text was provided about the benefits and the histories of outdoor recreation and wilderness. Dr. Beverly Driver is internationally known for his work on the meaning of and management for benefits of outdoor recreation. He offered the first section of Chapter I on benefits as he was retiring from the U.S. Forest Service.

Following Dr. Driver's treatise on benefits, Dr. Robert Douglas provided a review of the history of outdoor recreation in the United States. Dr. Douglas has written his own books on the subject, has completed numerous studies of participants and management issues, and has taught for a number of years in one of the country's larger universities. This history helps set the context for the analysis and examination of issues that follow in later chapters. Following Dr. Douglas' history is Dr. John Loomis' history of wilderness in this country as it moved toward and ended up as the National Wilderness Preservation System in 1964. Dr. Loomis' history helps set the context within which we later examine in detail wilderness demand and supply trends in the U. S.

In the following sections, brief descriptions are provided of the thought, data, analyses, and approaches used to address each of the core elements of the earlier described assessment framework. Details of the data and analysis for any one of these elements are provided as technical appendices to each chapter as needed. The chapters themselves are devoted to describing the findings of the analyses.

RESOURCES AND OPPORTUNITIES–CHAPTER III

As with the other resource areas about which the overall RPA assessment is concerned (wildlife, etc.), this assessment covers all sources of outdoor recreation opportunities. These sources include federal agencies, states, local government, and•private lands and businesses. While our primary emphasis is natural-resource-based recreational opportunities, some attention also is given to facilities for outdoor sports and other activities that are usually found in urban settings. Private sources of opportunities are viewed as being as important as public-sector opportunities. For the most part, in fact, public and private opportunities complement one another.

To add depth to the assessment analyses, numerous agency, professional, and industry representatives were invited to contribute short papers for this chapter. These contributed pieces have added enormously to our understanding of the trends uncovered in the data. Outdoor recreation touches almost all the individuals and institutions in this country, and having the short papers from some of these individuals and institutions adds insight into the ways recreation opportunities are made available to Americans.

A key concept in our assessment of outdoor recreation resources is "availability." Not all land, water and snow/ice resources are available, and the nature of availability varies widely among individual outdoor recreational sites. For example, portions of most military bases are closed to the public for security reasons. Some private holdings are closed to the public to protect crops or because of potentially conflicting other uses. Our intention is to identify the land, water, snow/ice and developed resources which are available for outdoor recreation use and which thus represent opportunities for the public. We attempt to describe these opportunities as they currently exist and to identify and describe trends in the area, number, and location of these opportunities.

The content of our examination of outdoor recreational opportunities includes:

- Federal properties across the seven major land management agencies, plus coverage of military, Indian, and marine sanctuary properties.
- Specially designated federal systems including wilderness, national recreation areas, national trails, and national rivers.
- Campgrounds and other camping facilities, both public and private.
- Public/private partnership resources, specifically two umbrella programs that have grown substantially in the 1990s: Scenic Byways and Watchable Wildlife.
- State recreation lands including state parks, forests, wilderness, fish and game lands, state trails, and scenic rivers.
- Local government park and recreation agencies, local facilities and sites, park districts, outdoor recreation in urban areas, and greenways.
- Recreational access to private lands, industrial and nonindustrial; nature conservancy preserves; and private recreation businesses, both the providers of facilities and the providers of services.

The above categories of recreation resources and opportunities are covered in a data base referenced as NORSIS. NORSIS is the acronym for the 1997 National Outdoor Recreation Supply Information System. NORSIS contains over 400 separate measures of recreation opportunities from boat ramps, campgrounds, and downhill ski lift capacity, to area in national parks and national forests. Where extant at county scale, the supply measures were entered at that scale directly from the secondary sources. Where available at site scale, data were aggregated across sites and summed to totals for each county. For some measures of recreation resources and opportunities, data were available only at state, regional, or national scale. In presenting the findings from our analysis of the data in NORSIS, county-scale maps were produced for key measures to indicate the geographic pattern of availability. To see the overall pattern of availability across the many measures in NORSIS, indexes were estimated across related measures of opportunities, enabling display of a more limited number of measures to provide a more comprehensive look at the patterning of outdoor opportunities. Trends in these indices were also examined.

PRIVATE RURAL LANDS—CHAPTER IV

Private rural lands make up over 60 percent of the land base of the 48 contiguous states—approximately 1.28 billion acres. Especially in the East, private land is an extremely important potential resource for outdoor recreational use. Unlike public lands, there is very little information available from existing sources covering recreational opportunities on private lands. Because of the magnitude of the recreational opportunities these lands represent and because lack of data meant it was necessary to conduct a national survey of private land holders for this assessment, Chapter IV is devoted specifically to recreational access and ownership issues on rural private lands.

Continuing with application of the concept of availability, the approach for examining recreational opportunities on private lands was to survey land owners to obtain the data needed to estimate four types of availability:

(1) Portions of private holdings on which recreational use was restricted to family, friends, neighbors or employees only.
(2) Portions of holdings leased to individuals or groups for their exclusive use.
(3) Portions of holdings available to anyone for recreational use, including both those holdings requiring permission or a fee and those not requiring permission.
(4) Portions of holdings completely closed to anyone except the immediate household of the owner.

The survey was entitled the National Private Land Owners Survey (NPLOS). To enable tracing of trends in availability, this most recent NPLOS was designed so that the essential measures were consistent with those in previous surveys. The 1995 NPLOS is the third in a continuing series of NPLOS studies conducted at 10-year intervals. The first was in 1975.

The primary interest driving NPLOS is in estimating the area of private land, nationally and by region, that is available for public recreational use. The estimate of this area of available land derived from NPLOS data is the sum of above accessibility categories two and three.

A continuing concern within the overall RPA assessment process is avoiding inconsistencies in reporting area of land and water across assessments of the different resource areas. For example, area of forested land estimated one way for the outdoor recreation assessment could easily disagree with area of forest estimated another way for the timber assessment, unless common definitions and sources of data were used. To avoid such inconsistencies, statistical estimates of area from the NPLOS study focused only on proportions of private land among the above-listed access categories. The end step in estimating area was to use the NPLOS-derived estimates of proportions with widely accepted sources of areal data, including the National Resources Inventory, which is conducted every five years by the Natural Resources Conservation Service. Also used was total land area at county scale as maintained by the Bureau of the Census. Areal estimates for this assessment were generated at regional scale and disaggregated to county scale.

In addition to the primary emphasis on estimating area by type of accessibility, descriptions of private land and of the owners were developed from the NPLOS survey data. Land ownership objectives, land uses and vegetative cover types, problems encountered from others' use of private lands, and characteristics of owners were attributes analyzed to identify associations with different levels of availability for recreation.

PARTICIPATION—CHAPTER V

A central element of this assessment is the description of recent trends, current levels and likely future trends in participation in outdoor recreation activities by the American public. To enable fully covering participation trends and patterns across the country, an update of the ongoing series of National Recreation Surveys was planned and executed (Cordell, et al., 1996). This most recent of the National Recreation Surveys was entitled the *National Survey on Recreation and the Environment* (NSRE). The data from the NSRE provided the primary basis for estimating percentages of the population, numbers of participants, number of days during which people participated, and number of trips taken primarily for outdoor recreation. Where possible, current participation estimates were compared with estimates from previous National Recreation Surveys (1960, 1965, & 1982-83) to describe trends, both recent and long term. In keeping with the structure of the resources and opportunities analysis, participation was categorized as primarily land, water, or snow/ice based. In addition, estimates of participation for individual activities were generated.

Other sources of data were employed as needed to describe types of participation outside the scope of the NSRE. These sources included studies of mountain biking, information on bird watching participation, federal and state visitation data, industry and Department of Commerce data on sales and consumer spending, and data on international visitation to the U.S. for tourism.

The principal elements of the data and analysis for describing participation and trends from the NSRE and the other sources described above included:

- Current participation levels for land, water, and snow/ice recreational activities and types of participation (summaries across related activities, e.g., all types of hunting). Included also are participation in outdoor sports (not nature based), estimates of number of days and trips participants took during the year of the survey, and participation patterns by the most active of participants, the enthusiasts.
- Long-term (from 1960) and recent (from 1982-83) participation trends in comparable activities across the various National Recreation Surveys, including land, water, and snow/ice activities.
- Comparisons of participation across activities by various groups within American society, including racial, age, sex, and income groupings.
- Comparisons of participation across regions of the country, including the four assessment regions (North, South, Rocky Mountains and Great Plains, and Pacific Coast) and nine more disaggregated forest regions (Alaska, Pacific Northwest, Pacific Southwest, Intermountain, Northern Rockies, Rocky Mountain, Southwestern, North, and South).
- Estimates of visitation at developed sites and in dispersed areas managed by the federal land and water managing agencies and visitation at state park systems.
- Recent trends (since 1986) in consumers' spending on outdoor recreation equipment and services and industry sales and revenues associated with outdoor recreation purchases.
- Trends and current levels of international visitation to the United States with emphasis on visitation associated with nature-based tourism.

These elements of Chapter V covering outdoor recreation participation were examined closely to surface new trends, as well as to determine if trends of the past were continuing.

FUTURE PARTICIPATION—CHAPTER VI

This portion of the assessment provides a method for examining the effects that demographic, population, and resource availability factors may have on outdoor recreation participation in future years. The factors examined include age, income, sex, region of the country, nearby recreation opportunities, and population growth. From this analysis, projections of likely participation changes in the future for winter, water, wildlife, dispersed land, and developed land recreation activities have been developed.

As in the previous assessments of outdoor recreation, the approach is to estimate cross-sectional models by measuring the association between variation in observed recreation participation and variation in demographic makeup and recreation opportunities available to participants. With these associations estimated, future participation can be estimated using projections of change in the factors identified in the models as having significant cross-sectional associations with participation. The factor representing availability of recreational opportunities was measured using the resource measure in the NORSIS data set that best reflected the nature of the resources (sites, facilities, and services) important to each activity.

Two forms of models were estimated to support projections of future participation patterns. The first was a logistical regression model, which is the appropriate form for estimating association between incidence of participation/nonparticipation and the demographic and opportunities factors. The second was a count data model, which is appropriate for estimating the association between counts of numbers of days of participation and trips away from home for recreation. Both forms of models were estimated for 23 separate recreational activities for each of the four assessment regions. Projections of the factors in the models were obtained from the Bureau of Census and the USDA Economic Research Service.

Following is the structure used for reporting the results of the projections:

- Of the 23 separate activities, similar ones were grouped into winter, water, wildlife-related, dispersed-land and developed-land groups.
- Projected future participation was reported by activity and for activity groups at national and regional levels.
- All projections were developed for the year 2000 and then for each decade after that up to 2050.

In using and discussing these projections, the uncertainty of how recreation may trend in this country in the future and of the ability of statistically estimated cross-sectional models to predict this future was kept in mind. Our interpretation of the projections, therefore, is that they provide useful information about potential changes in outdoor recreation demand if the population and its characteristics trend as predicted.

NATIONAL WILDERNESS PRESERVATION SYSTEM—CHAPTERS VII AND VIII

Two chapters were devoted to the wilderness portion of this assessment. For the most part, this assessment includes federal lands identified by congressional designation in the National Wilderness Preservation System (NWPS) as the wilderness resource. A widely accepted convention, and one used here, is to identify designated Federal Wilderness by capitalizing the first letter of the term. This helps distinguish designated Wilderness from the many other conceptualizations of wilderness, many of which see it simply as remote areas seldom entered by humans.

The base analysis underlying the Wilderness assessment is presented in Chapter VII. This chapter begins with an examination of the long-term trends in the Federal Wilderness System since its beginnings in 1964. The emphasis is on Wilderness Areas within the National Forest and the National Park Systems. Examined also are qualified federal roadless areas and the representativeness within the current system of the different types of ecosystems across the United States.

In addition to the Federal Wilderness System, composition of the eight state wilderness systems is described, including their recreational uses. Impacts of use and threats to resource health of these state systems are covered.

Acknowledging the importance of Wilderness as a recreational opportunity, use trends on areas managed by the four administering agencies are traced. Lack of good data on recreational uses of Wilderness is a limitation of this section of the assessment. In addition to the "on-site" recreational benefits of Wilderness, "off-site" benefits are explained and research exploring these benefits is described. These benefits include option, existence, and bequest benefits. Another benefit of Wilderness is protection of remnant portions of natural ecosystems. GIS maps illustrate which ecosystems are protected under the National Wilderness Preservation System.

Parallel with the modeling completed for projecting future recreation participation, as presented in Chapter VI, models were estimated of trends in Wilderness visitation using a time-series, fixed-effects approach. Since reliable visitation trend data were available only for the Forest Service and the National Park Service Wilderness Areas, models were developed for these two portions of the NWPS only. Demographic, area designation, and regional effects on visitation trends were estimated. Future recreational use of Wilderness was estimated using the resulting models and forecasts of the values of the variables found important in the models for future years of interest. One effect of interest was changes in visitor use resulting from increased Wilderness designation.

In addition to assessment of the status and use of the National Wilderness Preservation System, coverage is included in Chapter VIII of Wilderness uses, users and values and of current challenges to managers of the Federal Wilderness System. The material covered in this chapter deepens the understanding of trends in Wilderness recreational uses and users and provides an update of Wilderness management policies and issues from the perspectives of the managing agencies.

Drs. Watson and Cole of the Leopold Wilderness Research Institute describe changes in demographics of users and in use patterns of Wilderness from their and others' research in recent years. Also examined are changes in attitudes toward wilderness management. Drs. Friese, Kinziger, and Hendee of the University of Idaho follow with an examination of a particular use of Wilderness, visiting areas for personal growth reasons. Mostly, this section of the chapter covers wilderness experience programs and the trends in popularity of these programs in recent years. Next, Drs. Watson and Landres of the Leopold Wilderness Research Institute trace values and the evolution of values toward Wilderness from the time of establishment of the Wilderness System. The effect on Wilderness values of the many and dramatic societal changes that have occurred since the 1960s is examined, as is the importance of understanding value shifts in Wilderness management.

Following the above described papers on use, users and values, three of the four federal agencies which manage portions of the National Wilderness Preservation System discuss management issues. Wilderness specialists in each of the four federal agencies were invited to develop papers describing recent trends, current conditions, and likely future challenges. Perspectives from the U.S. Forest Service (Geary and Stokes), the Bureau of Land Management (Jarvis), and the National Park Service (Henry) are included. The philosophies underlying Wilderness management and the issues and challenges facing federal agencies are obviously different from those of the 1960s and 1970s and are trending from where they were at the time of the last assessment in 1989. A major change has been the establishment of the Interagency Wilderness Management Strategy, which is described.

MOTIVATIONS, PREFERENCES, AND SATISFACTIONS—CHAPTER IX

To improve understanding of trends and likely futures of outdoor recreation and Wilderness supply and demand, a review of recreationists' preferences, perceptions, and expectations is provided in Chapter IX. The first section of this part of the assessment is an analysis of the CUSTOMER data covering the preferences and satisfactions of visitors to a sample of recreation sites across the country. CUSTOMER is an acronym for Customer and Use Survey Techniques for Operations, Management, Evaluation and Research. CUSTOMER was conceptualized and designed by Cordell and others at the Forest Service Outdoor Recreation and Wilderness Assessment Research Unit in Athens, Georgia. Interviews of over 11,000 visitors at 31 recreation areas across the country were conducted from 1991 to 1994, and participants were asked their preferences for and satisfactions with both general and setting-specific attributes of recreation sites. Preferences and satisfactions were analyzed using the importance-performance framework to identify the importance of various attributes (facilities, scenery, and services) and their satisfactions with these attributes during the visit on which they were interviewed. The importance-performance analysis was then used to identify attributes that may warrant greater management attention in the future.

The second section of this chapter examines findings from a review of published literature on preferences and expectations for outdoor recreation experiences. First examined are the motivations for participating in outdoor recreation among segments of the American public. Next, the review covers experience preferences among recreation participants and attitudes toward encountering other recreation participants while at an outdoor recreation site. This latter portion includes the perceptions and effects of user crowding at recreation areas and visitors' preferences for the optimum number of others they encounter while recreating. This literature review is intended to provide a better understanding of the implications of continued growth in the popularity of outdoor recreation in the United States as the limited number of recreation sites and opportunities seem likely to become more heavily used.

IMPLICATIONS—CHAPTER X

Chapters III through IX contain the key findings for this assessment of supply and demand. These key findings are the basis for describing the implications of trends in outdoor recreation and wilderness as we near the end of the 20th century and look beyond. It is acknowledged by the assessment team that the implications identified are those of the team. It is likely that a somewhat different set of implications could result from the interpretations of others. The reader of this book is encouraged to think of the implications of this assessment's findings as reading and studying proceed.

COMMENTS ABOUT THE CURRENT ASSESSMENT CAPABILITIES AND DATA

As with any undertaking that relies in part on secondary data, has a limited budget, and is staffed with a particular team of scientists and analysts, this assessment has strengths and weaknesses which need to be acknowledged. For this fourth national assessment of outdoor recreation and wilderness, strengths to be built upon and areas where improvements would be desirable are noted below.

Strengths

The assessment of trends in the availability of outdoor recreation opportunities is the most comprehensive compilation to date of supply indicators across both public and private sectors in this or any other country. The data were developed at county scale wherever possible; this relatively fine level of aggregation enabled much greater capabilities for modeling, indexing, and mapping.

Lacking up-to-date data on recreational access to private rural lands, examination of recreational opportunities across the vastness of the private lands of this country was undertaken by conducting an original survey of the owners of these lands.

Participation trends and current demand for outdoor recreation were, for the most part, supported by an original population survey designed specifically to meet the assessment requirements for descriptive and model-based results. The National Survey on Recreation and the Environment also tied back to the National Recreation Survey series originating in 1960.

Recent past and current trends provide only limited information about the future beyond the year 2000. Original research was conducted to estimate forecasting models of future demand as it might occur given changes in population, demographics, and availability of opportunities.

Coverage of the National Wilderness Preservation System and complementary state systems and candidate roadless areas has been improved over the work done for the 1989 assessment. Added were future demand models and reviews of changes in preferences, attitudes, and values people hold about Wilderness in this country.

Much more coverage was given in this assessment to recreation visitors' preferences, satisfactions, motivations, and expectations. This additional coverage provides much deeper understanding of the possible implications of growth in outdoor recreation participation in the United States, a growth that seems assured to continue into the future.

Numerous user and provider groups and special topic experts have added specific short papers to Chapters III, V, and VIII. These papers provide depth and diversity of information about specific interests and industries that would not otherwise be possible.

Weaknesses

While public participation in outdoor recreation has grown to unprecedented levels, public budgets and professional interest in maintaining up-to-date data about the status of outdoor recreation and Wilderness in the United States has waned. In some cases, data that existed in the past exist no more. In other cases, the indicators of supply changes used were indirect measures because directly applicable data were not available.

Reliable measures of the amount and kind of recreational activity at outdoor areas in general, and of Wilderness specifically, are practically nonexistent for the 1990s. Reported visitation statistics are usually not based on actual counts or statistical sampling designs.

In addition to the National Survey on Recreation and the Environment, other population surveys are conducted using different designs and sample sizes. It is difficult to use the results of other surveys, given their differences in design and in some cases differences in estimates of recreation participation.

Time series data on recreation participation are not adequate to support time series model estimation, which is viewed by many as superior to cross-sectional models to predict changes in demand across future times.

The analysis of demand and supply in this assessment stops at the U.S./Mexican and U.S./Canadian borders. Yet it is obvious that recreation trends and recreational travel do not stop at these borders. This situation has likely led to some bias in the estimates of trends reported in the chapters that follow.

REFERENCES

Cordell, H. K., Bergstrom, J. C., Hartmann, L. A., & English, D. B. K. (1990). *An analysis of the outdoor recreation and wilderness situation in the United States: 1989-2040*. Ft. Collins, CO: USDA Forest Service, Rocky Mountain Forest and Range Experiment Station, GTR RM-189.

Cordell, H. K., et al. (1996). United States of America. In G. Cushman, A. J. Veal, & J. Zazanek (Eds.), *World leisure participation: Free time in the global village*. Wallingford, England: CAB International.

CHAPTER III

OUTDOOR RECREATION RESOURCES

. . . .

Carter J. Betz[1]
Donald B. K. English
H. Ken Cordell

Invited Papers:

Kimberly H. Anderson, USDA Forest Service
Cheryl S. Beeler, Florida State University
V. Robert Leeworthy, National Oceanic and Atmospheric Administration
Douglas McEwen, Southern Illinois University
Daniel D. McLean, Indiana University
Hugh Morris, Rails-to-Trails Conservancy
Gary L. Rankel, USDI, Bureau of Indian Affairs
George H. Siehl, Congressional Research Service (Retired)
Joan W. Tannen, National Scenic Byways Clearinghouse
George L. Peterson and James M. Williams, USDA Forest Service
Donald W. Fisher and Lyle Laverty, USDA Forest Service
Rodger Schmitt, Michelle M. Dawson, Hal Hallett, and Cal McCluskey, Bureau of Land Management
Merle Van Horne, National Park Service
Terry Villanueva, U.S. Fish and Wildlife Service
Richard A. Crysdale, U.S. Bureau of Reclamation (Retired)
R. Scott Jackson, David J. Wahus,and H. Roger Hamilton, US Army Corps of Engineers
James DeLoney, Texas Parks and Wildlife Department
Roger L. Moore and Mark I. Ivy, North Carolina State University
Ney C. Landrum,National Association of State Park Directors
John F. Dwyer, USDA Forest Service
Robert D. Bixler, Cleveland Metroparks
Edward T. McMahon, The Conservation Fund
Wilfred E. Richard, Outdoor Ventures North, Inc., and Lloyd C. Irland,
The Irland Group Forestry Consultants
Connie Coutellier, American Camping Association
Stacy Gardner, National Ski Areas Association
Chris Frado, Cross Country Ski Areas Association
Gilbert M. Clark, International Inline Skating Association

Acknowledgments:
The authors appreciate the valuable suggestions of Dr. Dean F. Tucker and Dr. Robert D. Bixler and important contributions made by Chris Gray, John Hayes, Cassandra Johnson, and Virginia Lasly.

---

[1]Carter J. Betz is Outdoor Recreation Planner, Donald B. K. English is Research Social Scientist, and H. Ken Cordell is Research Forester and Project Leader, all with Outdoor Recreation and Wilderness Assessment Research, USDA Forest Service, Southern Research Station, Athens, Georgia.

INTRODUCTION

Outdoor recreation is as broad and diverse as America itself. It covers a wide spectrum of resources, from the most pristine wilderness setting to urban streets and playgrounds. At its broadest definition, outdoor recreation is any leisure activity that takes place out-of-doors, regardless of setting. Under this definition, most outdoor recreation in the United States probably occurs very close to where people live—in backyards, on streets and playgrounds, and in local neighborhoods. Much of this recreation can be characterized as unstructured "play" or relaxation. This chapter examines the outdoor recreation resources and settings that are provided and managed by both government and the private sector. Outdoor recreation on rural private land is covered more thoroughly in Chapter IV.

The traditional view of outdoor recreation focuses mostly on natural resources in rural settings such as parks, forests, lakes, and rivers. However, recreation resources also exist in urban environments where they are extremely important in meeting urban demand for recreation experiences. This chapter attempts to provide a broad-based overview of the current status of outdoor recreation resources in the United States. The focus is on the availability, distribution, and general description of the outdoor resources rather than on their quality or condition.

We examine recreation resources and opportunities by the four types of providers: federal, state, local governments, and the private sector.[2] We also discuss the trend of partnerships in the provision of outdoor recreation opportunities, especially two types that emerged in the 1990s: Scenic Byways and Watchable Wildlife opportunities. Where possible, we discuss changes and trends in recreation resources since the mid-1980s. Those trends, in turn, point to anticipated future trends.

Also included are brief articles from government agencies, environmental organizations, and recreation industry groups. The authors of these articles address issues and trends that have emerged over the past decade or so and offer their outlooks for the future. Near the end of this chapter, we offer summary indexes that describe categories of recreation resources and how they have changed over the past 10 years. These indexes provide a more general indication of how resources are distributed with respect to population, and how their availability has changed in recent years. The final section of this chapter presents observations about the outdoor recreation resource base in the United States by summarizing the current status, trends, and future outlook.

FEDERAL LAND AND WATER RESOURCES FOR OUTDOOR RECREATION

The Federal Estate

The most widely held images of outdoor recreation are probably those of adventurous backcountry visitors trying to "get away from it all" and of families camping and sightseeing. Much of the land and water where these activities occur are managed by the federal government. Despite the continually increasing demand for recreation opportunities close to home, the federal government manages thousands of special places throughout the country, many remote and distant, that are highly popular. Often, however, federal resources (especially water) are close to population centers. The popular perception of the "Great Outdoors" is that of national parks, national forests and other federal land. All estimates put the amount of federal land in the United States at around 650 million acres (Table III.1).[3] This acreage represents about 28 percent of the total land area in the United States of just under 2.3 billion acres. All Western states, except Hawaii, have more than 25 percent of their total area in federal ownership. Nevada, Alaska, Utah, and Idaho each is more than 60 percent of their area in federal ownership. Federal acres in the United States are roughly equal to an area the size of the seven largest contiguous states—Texas, California, Montana, New Mexico, Arizona, Nevada, and Colorado.

---

[2]The authors assembled a national, county-level database (called the "National Outdoor Recreation Supply Information System") covering the four types of recreation providers from a variety of source datasets.

[3]Because of the enormous size of the Federal estate and the dynamic nature of land sales and swaps, inholdings, etc., it is difficult to get an exact total of Federal land at any given time. In this chapter, "Federal land" refers to only the resources held by the seven principal land-managing agencies of the Federal government and does not include Department of Defense land, land managed by the General Services Administration and other miscellaneous agency resources. Defense Department land is covered elsewhere in this chapter but is not included in general references to "Federal land."

Table III.1: Land and Water Area[1] Administered by Federal Land-Managing Agencies by Agency and Region, 1995

	Region (1000 acres)				
Agency	**North**	**South**	**Rocky Mountains**	**Pacific Coast[2]**	**U.S. Total**
USDA Forest Service	11,957	12,900	100,093	66,665	191,615
National Park Service	1,882	5,412	10,830	65,072	83,196
Fish & Wildlife Service[3]	1,209	3,809	7,193	78,239	90,450
Bureau of Land Management	388	796	144,237	122,219	267,640
U.S. Army Corps of Engineers	2,907	5,634	2,475	540	11,556
Tennessee Valley Authority	0	1,032	0	0	1,032
Bureau of Reclamation	0	197	5,470	854	6,521
All Agencies	18,343	29,780	270,298	333,589	652,010

[1]Numbers may not sum exactly to totals because of rounding. Table does not include Department of Defense land or other miscellaneous Federal agencies with minor land holdings.

[2]Alaska accounts for 242.4 million of the Pacific Coast's 333.6 million acres. Agency breakdown is: FS, 22.0 million; NPS, 54.7 million; FWS, 76.8 million; BLM, 88.9 million. There is one COE project in Alaska with 19,709 acres.

[3]U.S. Fish and Wildlife Service acreage includes National Wildlife Refuges and Waterfowl Production Areas. About 23.6 million acres of the 90.5 million acres of FWS managed land are not open for recreational use.

Sources: Land Areas of the National Forest System, As of September 1995.
National Park Service, Master Deed Listing. State and County Report by State. As of October 31, 1995.
U.S. Army Corps of Engineers Natural Resource Management System (NRMS). 1994.
Bureau of Land Management. Public Land Statistics. 1993.
Annual Report of Lands Under Control of the U.S. Fish and Wildlife Service. As of September 30, 1995.
Bureau of Reclamation. Recreation Areas on Bureau Projects. 1992.
Development of TVA Recreation Facilities Cumulative Through September 30, 1992.
TVA Areas Above Full Pool Level, By County, September 30, 1987.

The West (Rocky Mountain and Pacific Coast regions), including Alaska, accounts for just under 93 percent of federal land or about 604 of the 652 million acres. Excluding Alaska, the West still accounts for over 88 percent of the federal land. By contrast, the East (North and South regions) has only about 7 percent, even though it contains over 75 percent of the U.S. population—199.6 of 262.8 million people based on a 1995 Census estimate. Despite the fact that the West has the fastest current and projected population growth rates, the great disparity between the location of federal land (a product of historical settlement patterns) and the population distribution of the United States is not likely to change significantly in the near future.

Generally, the least populous states—e.g., Alaska, Montana, Idaho, and Wyoming—have the greatest amounts of federal land. Many of the most heavily populated states—e.g., New York and New Jersey—have very little federal land. California is a notable exception. It is the largest state in population, yet has a considerable amount of federal land. Because of topography, geologic features, and historic land uses, many outdoor recreation experiences that depend on alpine elevations and vast stretches of unroaded land are available only in the West.

Alaska, of course, is a special case. While Alaska is second only to Nevada in percentage of land area owned by the federal government, it has over four times as much federal acreage. By itself, Alaska has over one-third of the country's 652 million federal acres. Excluding Alaska reduces the ratio of federal to nonfederal land from more than one in every four U.S. acres to about one in every five acres.

The large majority of federal land is available for recreation. However, accessibility varies widely depending on the presence of roads and location with respect to population. Furthermore, not all federal land is available for all recreation activities. Federal land in Alaska is not very accessible to most Americans. Unlike most federal land, many national wildlife refuges managed by the U.S. Fish and Wildlife Service are closed to public use. These properties cover 23.6 million acres, most of which are in Alaska.

There are also other instances of federal properties that are unavailable for recreation use. The federal water resource agencies—U.S. Army Corps of Engineers, Bureau of Reclamation, and Tennessee Valley Authority—have some dams and reservoir operations that are not open for recreation. However, such areas represent a very small percentage of their total property. Likewise, research natural areas, fish hatcheries, experimental areas, and similar properties generally are not open to public use. Some land, especially in national forests, is inaccessible because it is surrounded by private property or because private access roads have been closed. The amount of such land is becoming significant enough to be of concern to federal land managers, especially the Forest Service.

ACCESS TO NATIONAL FOREST LAND[4]

(By George L. Peterson, Project Leader, USDA Forest Service, Fort Collins, CO; and James M. Williams, Lands Specialist, USDA Forest Service, Washington, D.C.)

Background

As reported by the United States General Accounting Office (US GAO) (1992), limited access to the national forests and other public lands is a significant problem that prevents the American public from fully utilizing and enjoying these lands. During the early history of the USDA Forest Service, little thought was given to public right of access. With some exceptions, adjacent landowners did not object to people crossing their lands to use the national forests. Unfortunately, the willingness of private landowners to accommodate the public has diminished. Over the past few decades, the situation has changed dramatically with landowners increasingly closing historic routes of access. Existing roads and trails that have long provided public access across private lands are being closed by landowners at an increasing rate. Some of the reasons for this change in behavior include a fear of vandalism, growing concern over liability, concern for spread of exotic vegetation, and general incompatibility between the owner's use and public access.

Of the 465 million acres of public land managed by the Forest Service and the Bureau of Land Management, about 50.4 million acres (roughly 14 percent) lack adequate public access (US GAO, 1992). Overbay (1993) reports that as of November 1993, 17.3 million acres, or approximately 9 percent of the 191 million acres of National Forest System lands, did not have adequate access. Inadequate access, as defined by the General Accounting Office in its report, means "that the federal government does not have the permanent, legal right for the public to enter federal land at the point(s) needed to use the land as intended by the managing agency." According to Overbay (1993), approximately 28,000 easements involving an estimated 7,500 miles of rights-of-way were needed in 1993 to provide adequate access to the Forest Service lands. The majority of needed easements are located in the Western regions where most of the inaccessible land is located. Over 90 percent of inaccessible land is in the West, most of that (about 13.2 million acres) being in the Rocky Mountains region.

The most immediately identifiable effect of inadequate access is seen in the reduction of the general public's ability to recreate on public land, including national forests. For example, over 10 percent of managers surveyed for the GAO report (US GAO, 1992) stated that hunting and off-road vehicle use were greatly or extremely reduced due to the lack of adequate access. Other activities, such as hiking and viewing wildlife, have also been significantly affected. To a lesser extent, important management activities, such as habitat improvement in support of biological diversity (4.2 percent of managers cited great or extreme interference), have been hampered by inadequate access. Activities and the percent of Forest Service supervisors and land managers who said inadequate access greatly or extremely reduced recreation opportunities were as follows:

Activity	Percent
Hunting	12.7
Off-road vehicle use	10.2
Hiking	7.6
Viewing scenery and wildlife	5.9
Driving for pleasure	5.1

[4]This article is based in large part on Overbay (1993).

Camping	4.2
Horseback riding	4.2
Mountain biking	4.2
Fishing	3.4
Wilderness area uses	3.4
Rafting, canoeing, etc.	1.7
Cross country skiing and snowmobiling	1.7
Recreational mining	1.7
Developed recreation site use	0.8
Commercial uses (e.g., outfitters/guides)	0.8

The Existing Situation

With increased emphasis on recreation and wildlife resources and opportunities to promote rural economic development, many individuals and interest groups are demanding that the Forest Service improve accessibility to National Forest System lands (For example, see Times Mirror magazines, Inc.). Access needs are identified through the forest planning process mandated by the National Forest Management Act. This process allows for substantial public involvement and is an important tool in identifying those areas where the public feels a need for better access to the national forests. The Forest Service maintains an ongoing program to resolve access issues using a variety of authorities to accomplish program objectives. These include: (a) fee simple acquisition, the acquisition of all rights and interests associated with the land needed for access, and (b) perpetual access easements, which are irrevocable rights granted by private landowners for access across their property. Either type of access can be acquired through purchase, donation, exchange, or condemnation.

The GAO report shows that the Forest Service acquired public access to about 2.6 million acres during fiscal years 1989 through 1991. Of these acquisition actions, approximately half were through perpetual easements, a quarter through fee simple land acquisition, and another 17 percent through other methods such as cooperative agreements with other agencies or private entities. Only three percent were a result of condemnations, many of which were used to perfect title or to establish an equitable value for the property involved. The overwhelming majority of acquisitions were the result of an amicable transaction, beneficial to both parties.

The principal funding source for the access program has been construction dollars, both road and trail. Historically, the road rights-of-way acquisition activities have been largely associated with the timber sale program. The program, with funding of $4.5 to $6.0 million in annual appropriations, has been declining, however. At current funding levels, the Forest Service is able to acquire about 375 road and trail right-of-way easements and eliminate the need for about 275 more on an annual basis through land exchanges, acquisitions, and other means.

Acquisition of needed rights-of-way has also been hampered by changing public preferences. The increased number of closures of historic access facilities, a declining willingness of owners to sell their land or interest in land, escalating land values, and ownership fragmentation all serve to complicate acquisition efforts. At the current rate of acquisition, adequate access to all national forest systems lands will not be guaranteed in the next 40 years. According to Overbay (1993), however, the Forest Service does not need new authorities to carry out its program of access acquisition, but this does not mean that improved performance in this area is not needed.

One of the major obstacles in providing access to public lands is a growing reluctance on the part of county and state road agencies to defend the status of historic roads that are being gated and closed. Limited resources are the prime reason for this trend. On a case-by-case basis, the Forest Service enters into cooperative agreements with local governments that allow use of these important means of access to be maintained. However, this is not a comprehensive approach. In the future, there will be a need to work with national associations of state and local governments in developing incentives that will encourage them to maintain legal rights, services, and travel-way facilities to and on National Forest System lands. In addition to these actions, there is a need to review the adequacy of existing authority to defend, perfect, and maintain historic public rights-of-way that provide access to federal lands that might otherwise be abandoned.

As mentioned, liability considerations detract from the willingness of many private landowners to allow the public access across their property. The Forest Service is addressing this problem by working to develop cooperative agreements with private landowners, user groups, and state and local governments to meet the need for reduced tort liability and enhanced law enforcement. There is also a need for the Department of Justice and the USDA Office of General Counsel to continue to defend United States interests aggressively in protection of existing rights.

The Forest Service public access program also receives attention through internal activities such as Renewable Resources Planning Act updates, the annual budgeting process, and the annual report of the Forest Service. Resolution of identified access problems has also been included as a specific item in the Forest Service's annual management attainment report. For example, a 1988 memo from agency leaders to the regional foresters identified the problem of access to national forest lands as an emerging issue in much of the West. Although the driving force behind acquisition of access had been resource harvesting and management, continuing to operate on that basis would not be effective because of increased concern about lack of access for recreation and other purposes. Regional foresters were directed to "get out in front on this issue" and "develop a program to acquire rights needed to provide access to the large acreage of land that does not have adequate access."

This question of access to public land is part of the larger problem of travel management, including development, maintenance, and closure of access to and travel within national forest land. The more comprehensive problem was addressed in the National Access and Travel Management Conference held in Denver in August of 1991. The Forest Service National Access and Travel Management strategy team participated in that conference and followed up by preparing a report summarizing the issues and recommending a national strategy for travel management (National Access and Travel Management Strategy Team, 1992). Then Chief Dale Robertson accepted the goal and strategy recommendations and appointed the associate deputy chief for the National Forest System as national travel management coordinator. He also appointed a national travel management coordinating council comprised of national staff directors (Robertson, 1992).

Assessment of Recent Progress and Future Prospects

At the end of fiscal year (FY) 1996, the deputy chief for the National Forest System prepared a summary of recent accomplishments (Reynolds, 1996). In FY 1996, the Forest Service acquired a total of 569 road, trail, and other rights-of-way through their Rights-of-Way Acquisition Program. Furthermore, it secured 256 perpetual access easements nationwide. Approximately 75 percent of both the rights-of-way and easements were acquired in the western United States. Since FY 1992, the trend has been a decreasing number of both right-of-way and easement acquisitions. Rights-of-way peaked at 729 nationally in FY 1993, and easements were also greatest that year (387 easements in FY 1993) and the previous year (388 easements in FY 1992). From FY 1994 through FY 1996, easement acquisitions declined more than 25 percent from those peak years. Approximately 10 percent, or 17 million acres, of National Forest System lands lacked adequate access (Reynolds, 1996). Furthermore, there was a significant increase in the number of temporary rights-of-way. These temporary solutions appeared to be the dominant access effort in some forest service regions. Lands and engineering staffs in each region were directed to "jointly monitor this activity to insure that these temporary actions are consistent with Forest Service Policy" (Reynolds, 1996).

The 17 million acres, or 10 percent, of National Forest System lands lacking adequate access at the close of FY 1996 shows little change from the situation described in the 1992 GAO report. As stated in that report, Forest Service land managers told GAO that 17.3 million acres of Forest Service land lacked adequate access in 1991. We may assume, therefore, that the statistical summaries in the GAO report continue to be a reasonable assessment of the current situation.

Multiple-Use Agencies

The USDA Forest Service (FS) and Bureau of Land Management (BLM) manage the most land among federal agencies (Table III.1). Together, the FS and BLM manage almost three-quarters of all U.S. federal land that is open for outdoor recreation. These agencies have a multiple-use mandate in which outdoor recreation is one of several concurrent uses. As a result, a great deal of their acreage is undeveloped and suitable for dispersed activities such as hiking, backpacking, hunting, and off-road driving. Other uses, such as timber harvesting, grazing, mining, and watershed protection, may temporarily restrict outdoor recreation.

USDA Forest Service

The FS manages more than 191 million acres of national forests and national grasslands in 42 states. About 87 percent of FS acreage is in the two Western regions, including 52 percent in the Rocky Mountains. The large majority of FS acreage is in undeveloped areas that the agency refers to as "general forest areas."

The 1995 *Report of the Forest Service* lists a total of more than 125,000 trail miles in the National Forest System. About 53 percent of the miles are classified as "maintained." Almost two-thirds of the total trail mileage is located in six Western states—California, Colorado, Idaho, Montana, Oregon, and Washington.

The FS maintains developed recreation areas in the following categories: boating sites, swimming sites, camping sites, picnic grounds, ski areas, interpretive sites, and all other developed sites. In 1996, there were 12,730 of these developed sites throughout the National Forest System, seven percent more than in 1992 (Table III.2). This net increase was due to the addition of boating sites, picnic grounds, and other developed sites. Despite the overall net gain in recreation sites, numbers of swimming, camping, interpretive, and skiing sites all decreased between 1992 and 1996.

The two Western regions account for just under 75 percent of FS developed recreation sites, a somewhat smaller proportion than their shares of land. Eastern national forests have slightly more developed recreation sites per acre than those in the West. Recreation sites in the East grew at the rate of 13 percent between 1992 and 1996, while those in the West grew only 5.0 percent. The Pacific Coast was the only region with a decrease in the number of sites, due mostly to a significant drop in the number of camping sites (15 percent). Boating and swimming sites are the only types of recreation areas which are more plentiful in the eastern than in the western United States. The East had over half of the boating sites and two-thirds of the swimming sites in 1996.

Fees are charged at some FS recreation sites but not at others. Most sites are managed by the FS itself, but a substantial number are operated by concessionaires. About three-fourths of concessionaire-operated sites charge a fee. Concessionaires operated just under half of the nearly 4,000 fee sites in 1996, compared to only seven percent of nonfee sites. Despite the increased use of concessionaires to operate developed recreation sites, the number of these sites operated by the FS was almost four times greater than the number operated by concessionaires in 1996.

Table III.2: Number of U.S. Forest Service-Developed Recreation Sites by Type of Site and Region, 1992 and 1996[1]

Type of Developed Site	Year	Region: North	South	Rocky Mountains	Pacific Coast	U.S. Total
Boating sites	1992	448	227	323	218	1,216
	1996	474	262	385	226	1,347
Swimming sites	1992	121	106	61	35	323
	1996	107	99	66	36	308
Camping sites	1992	411	388	1,958	1,773	4,530
	1996	413	396	1,923	1,509	4,241
Picnic grounds	1992	265	260	596	343	1,464
	1996	273	312	710	369	1,664
Ski areas	1992	34	2	87	65	188
	1996	11	0	81	63	155
Interpretive sites	1992	23	10	195	117	345
	1996	34	17	211	67	329
All other developed sites	1992	428	351	1,516	1,521	3,816
	1996	604	481	2,003	1,598	4,686
All developed sites	1992	1,730	1,344	4,736	4,072	11,882
	1996	1,916	1,567	5,379	3,868	12,730

[1]Includes fee and nonfee sites. Each site is included in only one category.

Source: USDA Forest Service. Washington Office: Recreation, Heritage and Wilderness Resources Management.

Overall, more than 31 percent of the FS recreation sites charged a fee for public use in 1996. This percentage was up significantly from 1992, when about 26 percent of sites charged a fee. With the exception of ski areas, camping sites were the clear leader with almost two-thirds of the sites charging a fee. The North led all other regions in proportion of fee camping sites with 69 percent. No other type of FS recreation site had as many as 50 percent of sites charging a fee, the closest being swimming areas with 41 percent.

USDA Forest Service: Trends, Issues, and Futures in Outdoor Recreation

(By Donald W. Fisher, assistant director, Recreation, Heritage and Wilderness Resources, USDA Forest Service, Alaska Region, Juneau, AK; and Lyle Laverty, Regional Forester, Rocky Mountain Region, USDA Forest Service, Washington Office, Washington, D.C.)

Current Situation

The national forests play a significant role in the provision of outdoor recreation opportunities in the United States with over 191 million acres of public lands. As the largest public provider of outdoor recreation in the country, the national forests received over 850 million visits in 1996. International visitation currently exceeds 78 million annually, reflecting growth of over 66 percent since 1987. With over 4,200 campgrounds and 60 percent of the nation's alpine skier days, the national forests are increasingly the nation's outdoor playground.

Spending by recreationists visiting the national forests in 1996 contributed almost $100 billion to the nation's gross domestic product, and more than 2.5 million jobs were associated with these expenditures. Revenue to the U.S. Treasury from national forest recreation and special use fees exceeds $46 million annually.

The national forests serve an important niche in American society by providing programs and services that are open and accessible to a diversity of people, communities, families, and organizations. The USDA Forest Service is an agency of choice for a large, knowledgeable, and supportive group of customers and partners. The national forests provide value to people's lives by providing recreation opportunities for physical, emotional, and spiritual renewal, as well as healthy productive forests for a diversity of other benefits.

The national forests provide a wide spectrum of outdoor opportunities, from the more developed to the most primitive, primarily in a forest setting. Developed areas, such as resorts, ski areas, visitor centers, developed campgrounds, and boating facilities are highly valued by users. Natural settings offer opportunities for primitive activities such as backpacking, fishing, hiking, and wildlife viewing that attract many visitors. The Forest Service has developed and implemented a scenery management system to protect the inherent qualities of the forest landscape.

The National Forest System includes many unique and special areas for outdoor recreation. These include 18 national recreation areas, seven national scenic areas, four national monuments, 133 Scenic Byways, 96 wild and scenic rivers, and four national scenic or historic trails. To enhance visitor information and interpretive services, the Forest Service manages 55 major visitor centers, which host 10 million visitors a year. For those seeking very primitive recreation opportunities, the national forests contain approximately 35 million acres of wilderness. The national forests provide more than half the country's network of trails with over 125,000 miles for hiking, riding, snowmobiling, and cross-country skiing. The national forests will host all, or at least important components, of several upcoming events, such as the Lewis and Clark Bicentennial, the 1999 World Downhill Ski Championships, and the 2002 Winter Olympics.

Currently there are over 100,000 heritage sites inventoried on national forests, representing over 10,000 years of human history. These range from the renowned Anasazi cliff dwellings in the Southwest to more subtle indicators of our past, such as scatterings of obsidian chips from a maker of spear points. The Forest Service's "Windows on the Past" program enhances visitor use and enjoyment of heritage resources.

The Forest Service's state and private forestry program works in partnership with states to assist communities in promoting tourism, recreation, and preventing human-caused wildfires. Much of the tourism and recreation use in national forests is carried out by private recreation service providers through partnerships and special-use permits. There are approximately 23,000 recreation special-use permit holders providing a diversity of recreation experiences for visitors.

Recent Trends

A number of recent trends are having a significant effect on national forest recreation opportunities. Federal budgets are being reduced and are projected to continue declining. The same trend is projected for the size of the federal work force. Therefore, the number of Forest Service recreation professionals available to deliver good quality recreation products and services has fallen. The result is a loss of technical expertise when demand is dramatically increasing. Consequently, the Forest Service is finding it difficult to maintain the level of visitor services offered in the past, and the backlog in maintenance of recreation facilities has increased. These trends have created an emphasis on the use of the private sector as partners in providing recreational opportunities on public lands. This shift in delivery methods has resulted in new tasks and responsibilities for the federal work force.

Community economic vitality is also receiving strong emphasis nationally, with a priority being placed on enhancement and revitalization of jobs at the community level. These factors result in a renewed emphasis on collaborative stewardship to involve communities and the private sector more intimately in providing outdoor recreation opportunities on National Forest System lands. These activities highlight the tradeoffs communities face between economic growth and unencumbered rural lifestyles involving a more primitive environmental setting.

These trends are encouraging the Forest Service to initiate and emphasize different ways of providing outdoor recreation services for visitors and non-traditional customers. These include cost recovery through visitor fees, public/private ventures, expanded concession operations, and embracing partnerships and volunteerism as an integral way of doing business.

Additional trends impacting recreation opportunities on national forests involve ecotourism. The recent growth in ecotourism has increased the demand for educational and interpretive services and has created a tremendous growth opportunity for commercial outfitting and guiding services. It has also resulted in greater demand for a diversity of recreation experiences, such as hiking and backpacking, wildlife viewing, water-based activities, and camping. One of the fastest growing areas affecting use of the national forests is heritage tourism, which involves viewing and interpretation of historic and prehistoric sites. Much of national forest heritage tourism involves an additional component of existing opportunities, such as those provided by outfitters' and guides. The Forest Service's emphasis on ecosystem management is also affecting outdoor recreation management. Recreation activities and services are being managed to assure ecosystem sustainability while providing direct benefits to individuals, families, and communities.

Key Current Programs and Initiatives

There are a number of key programs and initiatives being implemented by the Forest Service to accommodate current trends affecting the way the agency has historically provided outdoor recreation services. Examples include a recreation fee demonstration, a tourism strategy, enhanced collaborative stewardship, an emphasis on public/private ventures, expanded opportunities for concession operations, expanded use of partnerships, volunteers, and cooperation with the National Forest Foundation.

A significant recent trend in recreation management affecting the national forests is a movement toward expanded visitor fees. This trend was emphasized by the recreation fee demonstration authorized project in Public Law 104-134, the Omnibus Consolidated Rescission and Appropriations Act of 1996. This act initially approved up to 50 fee demonstration projects on national forests. Authorization for 50 more projects and a one-year extension of the program through September 1999 were given under the Interior and Related Agencies Appropriation Act for fiscal year 1997. The purpose of the program is to test ways of providing improved customer service through many different methods of establishing, collecting, and reinvesting recreation use fees where they were collected. A critical component of the test is monitoring the public's acceptance of the increase in costs and the benefits they receive. The program is particularly important to the Forest Service at a time of existing and projected declining federal budgets and work force. The projected revenue to be generated through the recreation fee demonstration during the start-up of fiscal year 1997 was $7.6 million. Initial evaluations show that while fees may be a useful tool, new fees are not universally accepted by customers, and the program does have impacts on the work force for fee collection and security.

With travel and tourism being the world's largest industry, the Forest Service is planning an integrated strategy that will demonstrate commitment to community vitality and the tourism industry. The tourism strategy will be a benefits-based management approach emphasizing collaboration and enhancements to people and the environment. This approach will produce measurable benefits to visitors, local residents, private industry, communities, and the recreation resources. Positive outcomes anticipated through this strategy include enhanced physical, psychological, and spiritual health of people, rural economic development and diversification, historic preservation, increases to the national gross domestic product, natural resource enhancements, and an increase in partnership opportunities and volunteerism.

To provide enhanced public service, the Forest Service has embraced collaborative stewardship. Through collaborative stewardship, the agency is focusing on building sustained relationships with constituents, with an anticipated outcome of reduced adversity, appeals, and litigation. A cornerstone of collaborative stewardship is the creation and maintenance of partnerships. This rapidly expanding activity is creating tremendous opportunities for the agency to provide high quality recreation products and services, and to develop a knowledgeable and supportive constituency.

In order to stimulate private sector participation in outdoor recreation services, the Forest Service is emphasizing public/private ventures. Through joint private and public-sector investment in recreation facilities and/or services on national forests, viable business opportunities may be made available to private industry, resulting in high–quality recreation experiences for visitors.

Concessioning recreation facilities and services is another area which is receiving strong emphasis by the Forest Service. Through concession agreements the Forest Service, while working with the private sector, can continue to provide and enhance a diversity of recreation services and camping opportunities for the public.

The Forest Service has implemented an aggressive "Windows on the Past" program to provide visitors access to heritage sites and experiences. This includes Passport in Time, the Historic Structure Rental program, and Heritage Expeditions. The Passport in Time is a highly popular program that pairs volunteers with national forest archaeologists and historians to work on projects ranging from archaeological excavations to restorations of historic structures. The Historic Structure Rental program provides historic cabins and fire lookout towers for public rental, offering a unique way to learn history. The Heritage Expeditions program is a component of the recreation fee demonstration. Under this program, the Forest Service and the private sector co-host heritage resources expeditions, such as retracing historic explorers and visiting rock art sites with professional conservators and interpreters.

To help improve the quality of service to national forest visitors, the Forest Service has adopted "Meaningful Measures." Under this internal process, quality standards for work accomplishment are set, work is prioritized by visitor preferences, and work plans are developed consistent with program funding.

Future Trends, Issues, and Directions

In the foreseeable future, outdoor recreation participation will continue to increase, assuming continued economic stability and availability of fossil fuels. Increased use places greater demands on the natural settings available in national forests. Access to private lands for outdoor recreation will become increasingly constrained, as more lands are closed for public use. An increasingly urban population will seek out natural settings for recreation. This will result in greater demands and impacts on national forests, particularly those in close proximity to urban areas.

Other public providers of outdoor recreation will be reaching visitor carrying capacity and will implement limitations on visitation to avoid natural setting degradation. This is already happening in some national parks. As a result, some areas such as national forests, which have not reached carrying capacities, will see increased visitation. This increase will require development of management strategies and collaborative actions to meet the demand effectively while continuing to maintain ecosystem sustainability.

Users of national forests are changing. Demographic shifts that are taking place will present unique challenges in providing outdoor recreation opportunities on national forests. Programs and services will need to be structured to serve an increasingly diverse, older, and more international visitor, while continuing to accommodate the traditional forest recreationist.

New technology and equipment are constantly evolving or creating new recreation uses, such as improved 4-wheel-drive vehicles, snowboards, personal GPS units, cellular phones, and mountain bikes. Managers of the future will be challenged to maintain compatibility of new technology and equipment uses with national forest stewardship.

Research indicates that forest users are demanding increased access to accurate information they need to plan their recreation trips. Therefore, on-site, off-site, and computer technology accessible information will be more important than ever in providing for visitor needs and ensuring a positive visitor experience.

With anticipated increased visitation to national forests in the future, greater pressures will be made on special areas, such as components of the National Wilderness Preservation System and the National Wild and Scenic Rivers System. Preserving the inherent qualities of these special areas for future generations is and will remain a significant management challenge.

Heritage values are a growing interest to many Americans who enjoy tracing their cultural heritage and examining various types of heritage information. As interest in heritage tourism continues to grow, management strategies will need to be in place to protect heritage resources on national forests, as well as provide expanded opportunities for visiting historic and prehistoric sites.

The Forest Service is embarking on the creation of a national image marketing strategy. Although the program will ultimately embrace all program areas of the agency, it will initially focus on areas discussed in this section and fish and wildlife management. The goals of the effort are to:

1. Develop a large, supportive, and knowledgeable constituency now and into the 21st century.
2. Become a partner of choice for corporate America.
3. Develop a positive image as the premier land-managing agency in America.
4. Provide clarity in the public's eye regarding the agency's niche by both enhancing agency recognition and creating distinction from other agencies.
5. Rally the internal force and focus this tremendous energy to expand capability to provide high–quality products, services, and opportunities.
6. Develop champions and support in Congress.
7. Provide focus for agency activities with a consistent message to the public.
8. Do a better job of managing the nation's forests.

As a strategy for accommodating increasing outdoor recreation demands in the future, the Forest Service will be developing a wide range of management tools and techniques, such as improved permit systems, increased public/private sector investments, enhanced developed sites, improved and efficient fee systems, and increased emphasis on partnerships and volunteerism. In many instances, a balance will be needed between more intensive management, preservation of unique areas, and providing public access to an ever increasing range of outdoor recreation opportunities.

Bureau of Land Management

The BLM manages about 268 million acres, more than any other federal agency (Table III.1). BLM land is almost exclusively Western. Only about one million acres are located in the two Eastern regions. BLM land is nearly evenly split between the Rocky Mountain (54 percent) and Pacific Coast (46 percent) regions, but 89 out of 122 million acres of the Pacific Coast BLM land is in Alaska. BLM acreage is often called "the land nobody wanted" because most of it is the residual that was neither homesteaded nor transferred to other agencies. Most of the land is in dry and barren environments. For example, 69 percent of the total area of Nevada (the "Sagebrush State") is BLM land. A major and controversial development occurred on BLM land in September, 1996 when President Clinton created the 1.7-million-acre Grand Staircase-Escalante National Monument in southern Utah by executive fiat (Satchell, 1997a). This is the first national monument under jurisdiction of the BLM. Management of the area will be closely watched by many interests since it encompasses some of the nation's richest coal, oil, and natural gas reserves.

The BLM manages a variety of resources and facilities devoted to outdoor recreation. The publication of *Recreation 2000: A Strategic Plan* in 1989 articulated the agency's planning and policy direction for recreation management. BLM land is zoned into Recreation Management Areas (RMA), which are further classified as either Extensive or Special. Extensive RMAs are similar to the Forest Service general forest areas where development is minimal and the emphasis is on dispersed recreation. They may contain recreation sites, but typically, backcountry areas are not a part of Special RMAs. In Special RMAs, a specific commitment (i.e., investment) has been made to provide recreation services or facilities.

Special RMAs outnumber Extensive RMAs almost two to one, but the acreage in each is reversed. According to BLM's 1994 Recreation Management Information System (RMIS), there were 338 Special RMAs compared to 180 Extensive RMAs. The Special RMAs account for about 28.6 million acres, while Extensive RMAs account for about 193.5 million acres.[5] The BLM lists 2,213 designated recreation sites in the 1994 RMIS. These may occur in either type of RMA, but more than two-thirds (1,484) are in Special RMAs. The BLM manages 7.6 million acres developed specifically for recreation. In addition to dispersed use areas, the types of recreation sites listed in the RMIS indicate the variety of facilities provided by BLM: boat launches, cabins, campgrounds, caves, environmental education centers, picnic areas, resorts, swimming areas, trail heads, comfort stations, and visitor centers.

---

[5]About 45 million acres were not classified as either Special or Extensive RMAs.

Outdoor Recreation and the Bureau of Land Management

(By Rodger Schmitt, Recreation Group Manager, Bureau of Land Management, Washington, D.C.; Michelle M. Dawson, Partnership/Marketing Specialist, Bureau of Land Management, Washington, D.C.; Hal Hallett, Outdoor Recreation Planner, Bureau of Land Management, Washington, D.C.; and Cal McCluskey, Wildlife Biologist, Bureau of Land Management, Boise, ID)

Background

The BLM in the Department of the Interior administers one-eighth of the nation's original vast land holdings—the 1.8 billion acre public domain. In the nation's earliest years, the federal government and Congress became the legal guardians of the public lands, where policy generally provided for the disposal of the public lands. Millions of acres of public land were set aside to establish Indian reservations, national parks, forests, wildlife refuges, and military reservations. The land disposal policy built the country's economic foundation, opened the West to settlement, and united the vast expanses of land into one nation. In 1812, Congress established the General Land Office (GLO) to administer the public domain. The passage of the Taylor Grazing Act in 1934 established the U.S. Grazing Service to provide active range management on public domain land. In 1946, the GLO and the U.S. Grazing Service merged to create the BLM.

Originally viewed as the "Great American Desert," BLM land for years was regarded primarily as a source of livestock forage, timber, and energy and mineral resources. Since the 1980s, the BLM public land has become more valued for its environmental resources, significant cultural resources, recreation opportunities, and in an increasingly urban nation, its vast open spaces. The BLM's mandate under the Federal Land Policy and Management Act of 1976 requires the agency to manage the public land to accommodate many uses, while protecting the long-term health of the land.

Recreation Resources and Opportunities

The BLM public lands offer abundant opportunities for outdoor recreation notable for their undeveloped, wild nature. Dispersed recreation activities that occur on BLM lands include, but are not limited to, camping, hiking, fishing, hunting, whitewater rafting, hang gliding, horseback riding, wildlife viewing, and driving for pleasure. Examples of the diversity that recreationists enjoy include the solitude of Arizona's Aravaipa Canyon wilderness area, riding all-terrain vehicles in New Mexico's North Dunes, whitewater rafting on Utah's Green River, canoeing and island hopping in Minnesota, snowmobiling in Alaska, hunting for world-renowned big game in Colorado, fishing for steelhead trout in Idaho, retracing the Oregon Trail by horseback in Oregon, and caving in Wyoming.

Modern explorers can hike, horseback ride, mountain bike, motorcycle, four-wheel drive, and cross country ski across trails on BLM public lands. The diverse terrain ranges from 14,000 foot summits in Colorado to the depths of Paria Canyon in Utah, from the Alaska wilderness to the geysers and cypresses of California. The BLM public lands contain nine national historic trails, two national scenic trails, and 26 national recreation trails encompassing nearly 5,000 miles. Off-highway vehicle (OHV) hobbyists, motor bikers, and horseback riders enjoy over 141 million acres for OHV, over 6,200 miles for motorbikes, and 17 equestrian trails spanning almost 5,300 miles. An additional 4,500 miles of trail are open to all-terrain vehicle use.

Those seeking less crowded and pristine areas can escape to the 134 designated wilderness areas managed by the BLM covering 5.2 million acres. Additionally, the BLM is currently managing 622 wilderness study areas that encompass over 17 million acres awaiting Congressional action. Further, the BLM manages the 1.7 million acre Grand Staircase Escalante National Monument in Utah.[6] The BLM is also responsible for eight

[6]Presidential, Congressional, and Secretarial designations provide instant visibility to otherwise unknown areas. With visibility, visitation is not far behind. The Grand Staircase Escalante National Monument did not exist until the September 1996 monument proclamation by President Clinton. The new status has resulted in extensive media coverage heightening the public's curiosity for visiting this monument, which is a unique combination of archeological, historical, paleontological, geological, and biological resources.

national conservation areas in Alaska, Arizona, California, Nevada, and New Mexico. Other congressional designations managed by the BLM include the Santa Rosa Mountains National Scenic Area in California, the Yaquina Head National Outstanding Natural Area in Oregon, and the one-million-acre White Mountain National Recreation Area in Alaska.

Although not known as a water resource management agency, the BLM manages 174,000 miles of fishable streams, 2.6 million acres of lakes and reservoirs, more than 5,400 miles of floatable rivers and 127 boat ramps. Under special designation, the BLM manages parts of 34 rivers in five Western states as National Wild and Scenic Rivers. For wildlife enthusiasts, the BLM public lands provide habitat for more than 3,000 species of mammals, birds, reptiles, and fish. Hunters have access to big game animals, such as pronghorn, mountain sheep, caribou, deer, and moose, as well as numerous waterfowl and small game animals species.

National Trends in Recreation and Tourism on BLM Lands

The BLM, the American Recreation Coalition's Recreation Roundtable, Tennessee Valley Authority, USDA Forest Service, and the Federal Highway Administration sponsored the 1997 Roper Starch Worldwide National Survey on "Outdoor Recreation in America." Key findings from this research reaffirm trends BLM managers have been experiencing on the ground about the widespread popularity of outdoor recreation. Cultural tourism has surfaced as a key trend. Families are seeking unique experiences and educational information. Historic and prehistoric sites are increasingly popular. The BLM public lands hold a tremendously large and varied body of cultural resources. More than 180,000 prehistoric and historic sites have been found on BLM public lands. This legacy includes ancient stone tools and dwellings, dusty trails, crumbling and half-forgotten cabins, forts, and mines. Enthusiasts can pan for gold near old placer mines, trace an abandoned railroad line, or photograph petroglyphs that recall stories of ancient triumphs. Two outstanding attractions are the Garnet Ghost Town in Montana, which preserves 30 buildings much as they were in 1895; and the Anasazi Heritage Center and Museum in Dolores, Colorado, which features the ruins of two late Anasazi communities and interprets the culture of the people known as the "Ancient Ones."

Paleontological discoveries are another significant resource found on BLM public lands. For example, in Utah, the BLM's Cleveland-Lloyd Dinosaur Quarry has yielded nearly 10,000 bones representing at least 14 species of Jurassic animals. Material from the Cleveland-Lloyd Quarry has been the basis for more public exhibits than any other dinosaur quarry in the world, contributing specimens to 40 museums in 19 states and eight foreign countries. The challenge for the BLM is to channel the public's enthusiasm for archaeological, historical, and paleontological resources on the public lands to protect and preserve this fragile and irreplaceable legacy.

Scenic driving and sightseeing are among the most popular forms of outdoor recreation in the U.S. The BLM developed its Back Country Byway program to complement the National Scenic Byway program. The BLM manages 64 back country byways covering over 3,000 miles. An example is Colorado's Alpine Loop which links Lake City, Silverton, and Ouray following roads built by miners over 60 years ago. The byway passes through old mines, mining camp mill ruins, tram lines, and ghost towns. Another BLM program designed to help meet the demand for recreational touring, particularly among seniors, is the establishment of eight long-term visitor areas in Arizona and California. Designed primarily for winter travelers in recreational vehicles, visitors may stay for months at a time by purchasing a long-term visitor pass for a nominal fee. The permit covers the season from September 15 to April 15. BLM public lands are more accessible to automobile travelers than many people realize. Approximately 40 percent of BLM lands are located within a day's drive of 16 major urban areas in the West.

The BLM has 300 Watchable Wildlife areas offering adventure for recreationists to observe and learn about wildlife in their natural habitat. Enthusiasts may see a steelhead struggling upstream to spawn, a peregrine falcon wheeling high over a canyon, a killer whale breaching in the Pacific, pronghorn bounding across the plains, or the elusive Roosevelt elk hiding in the wooded forest of the Northwest. This program provides the public with meaningful opportunities to enjoy wildlife resources. Watchable Wildlife is a program signaling the BLM's efforts to balance recreation resources and wildlife habitat considerations.

Another interesting trend, dramatically impacting the BLM, is the emergence of Las Vegas, Nevada as one of America's most visited destinations. The BLM's Red Rock Canyon National Conservation Area (NCA), just 15 minutes by automobile from Las Vegas, offers much—especially scenic beauty and wildlife—to families seeking a natural experience away from the Las Vegas strip. Red Rock Canyon is also a world-class rock climbing area. In addition, the BLM public lands are experiencing increasing international visitation. International visitation to the United States is a growing market. International travelers are looking for a real "American" experience and have a keen interest in adventure travel in the American West. Another management challenge for the BLM is appropriate signage in several languages to ensure international visitors have a good quality recreation experience.

BLM Strategic Planning and Recreation 2000

Many popular forest areas and parks in the U.S. are overcrowded with decreasing visitor services and crumbling infrastructure. Visitation to the BLM public lands has increased from 51 million visits in 1994 to nearly 60 million visits in 1997, as more and more people pursue outdoor activities. The growth in recreational use has had various impacts and consequences. Some areas are deteriorating from overuse. The very resources that attract visitors may be in jeopardy. If these resources are impaired or damaged, they will lose their value and appeal. When visitor use exceeds capacity, it is often a difficult management task to protect resources from degradation, while at the same time ensuring visitor safety. The BLM is expanding its efforts to educate the public about protecting and conserving its public land heritage through interpretation, environmental education, permit stipulations, and environmental stewardship efforts. Visitors are asked to use and enjoy the public lands with minimal environmental impact by incorporating the Leave No Trace and Tread Lightly principles.

Leave No Trace principles are techniques that visitors can use to help reduce evidence of their presence on the public lands. By following the Leave No Trace land ethic, visitors can enjoy public lands, the back country, and wilderness areas, while preserving the beauty and solitude of this public land legacy. Tread Lightly is an educational program dedicated to increasing awareness about how to enjoy public and private lands while minimizing impacts. The emphasis is responsible use of off-highway vehicles and other forms of back country travel, and low–impact principles that are applicable to outdoor recreation activities. The Tread Lightly pledge involves traveling only where permitted; respecting the rights of others; educating oneself; avoiding streams, meadows, and wildlife; and driving and traveling responsibly. Well-informed, environmentally sensitive recreation users can play a key role in protecting cultural, natural, and scenic resources, as well as sustaining the health of the nation's public lands.

While the recreation public continues to increase, funding has not kept pace with the rising costs of managing recreation sites and providing services that the public expects and demands. Consequently, routine and corrective maintenance needs are not being met, BLM recreation employees are not sufficiently present on site, and critical visitor services are lacking. In 1989, the BLM developed the comprehensive document, *Recreation 2000: A Strategic Plan*, which outlines specific policy guidance for the BLM's recreation program. Through the strategic plan, the BLM's recreation program was recognized as a major component of the BLM's multiple use mandate. In 1994, the BLM updated its strategic plan and crafted the *Recreation 2000 Update*. These two documents establish a clear image of the BLM in providing quality recreation and tourism opportunities for the public while sustaining healthy land and water resources.

Well-designed, universally accessible facilities, combined with sound management techniques, can stabilize and restore natural values, increase safety, and improve the recreation experience. This sometimes poses a dilemma for management. Facilities require long-term maintenance and are an added expense. Facilities and costly visitor centers represent a break from the BLM's traditional recreation niche—providing a primitive and dispersed experience consistent with the wide-open landscapes the BLM manages. Furthermore, the BLM should complement, not compete, with other federal, state, tribal, regional, and local governments and private entities that also supply recreation opportunities.

The BLM attempts to customize the management of each local area according to its own unique attributes. The BLM focuses on resource-dependent opportunities, as well as responding to the demands for facility development where necessary. Most recreation-related development involves protecting resource values and serving as staging areas for resource-based use—not as visitor attractions in and of themselves. Through collaborative efforts, recreation providers must strive to provide a diversity of opportunities and make them available to the public. The BLM is developing a marketing strategy for the next five years on recreation, travel, and tourism to accompany and complement the *Recreation 2000 Update* strategic plan. Each BLM district office must identify its niche and concentrate on furnishing high–quality recreation opportunities in cooperation with other providers. For example, BLM's New Mexico's Roswell District contains many caves adjacent to Carlsbad Caverns National Park. In defining one of its primary recreation niches, the district decided to concentrate on providing "wild" cave opportunities. Visitors wishing a more structured cave visit are directed to Carlsbad Caverns National Park. Within this region, a broad spectrum of customers is served by both the BLM and the National Park Service, providing complementary—not competing—opportunities.

The tremendous growth in recreation visitation is having a significant impact on the economy of many Western communities. One of the challenges facing the BLM is to help local communities understand, anticipate, and plan for the economic and social impacts of travel and tourism from the outdoor recreation that occurs on BLM public lands. The BLM is now evaluating methods to improve its understanding of customer expectations, needs, and motivations. This deeper understanding will lead to the improved management of outdoor recreation, travel, and tourism opportunities.

The Bureau of Land Management's "Windy Arch" (top) and "Kink Area" (bottom) in Alaska offer opportunities for remote recreation experiences. Photos courtesy of the USDI Bureau of Land Management.

The BLM is currently working with the USDA Forest Service, Southern Research Station, and Old Dominion University to identify the economic impact of recreation accurately from public lands to neighboring communities. Preliminary studies indicate significant positive impacts. An example of this economic impact is the study results of recreationists visiting Yaquina Head, Oregon. In 1995, almost $21 million was spent locally by tourists visiting and recreating at Yaquina Head. The rugged beauty of this promontory is one of the most outstanding features of the Oregon coast. It includes a century-old lighthouse, marine gardens, viewing platform, paved parking areas, and stairway access to the beach and tide pools. The BLM public lands are not only valued for their revenue-raising potential and economic benefits to rural and local economies, but also for the exceptional and challenging recreation opportunities.

The BLM is working to develop innovative approaches for securing additional funding to satisfy the growing desire of the recreating public to use public lands. Using existing legal authorities, the BLM is methodically implementing a recreation fee program and building partnerships at local, county, regional, state, and national levels to leverage its fiscal resources. Partnerships increase the staffing, equipment, facilities, printing services, maintenance capabilities, and funding available to improve the quality of services and level of maintenance provided at many outdoor recreation sites.

The BLM is aggressively pursuing challenge cost-share partnerships, grants, and alternative funding sources to strengthen its relationship with local communities and to provide high-quality customer service to public land users. Selection of cost-share partners is focused on recreation site management that reduces risk to public health and safety, decreases environmental degradation, provides recreation facilities that meet use requirements, improves the quality and diversity of the resources, and provides customer service that is the "best in the business." Also important is the delivery of messages to the public on environmental stewardship ethics about conserving and protecting its treasured public lands legacy.

Public lands are administered by the BLM for the benefit and enjoyment of all Americans. The public lands were once considered the "lands nobody wanted." Today, they are recognized for their rich legacy—both a link with the past and a trail to the future.

Resource Protection and Public Use

The National Park Service (NPS) and the U.S. Fish and Wildlife Service (FWS) are agencies of the Department of the Interior that, by law, emphasize resource protection. Both have major land holdings throughout the United States, especially in Alaska. The NPS is much better known by the American public and has far more annual visitation. The NPS' higher profile may be because recreation or "public enjoyment" is an explicit part of the NPS mission. The NPS, however, seems to fight a continuing battle over the proper balance of preservation versus public use (Satchell, 1997b). The enormous popularity of the national parks results in ongoing problems of crowding and its associated impacts. Crowding is not a widespread problem on FWS resources, but the issue of "appropriate use" on national wildlife refuges has received a great deal of attention. The FWS recognizes recreation as a "legitimate use," allowable so long as it does not conflict with conservation objectives.

National Park Service

The NPS is arguably the best-known federal land-managing agency due to its famous "crown jewel" national parks such as Yellowstone, Yosemite, and the Grand Canyon. Almost two-thirds of NPS land is in Alaska. Including Alaska, the two Western regions account for 91 percent of NPS resources (Table III.1). Without Alaska, the Eastern portion of NPS land rises from nine to 26 percent. The other 49 states have about 28.5 million acres of NPS land, with approximately 7.3 million acres in the North and South regions combined. As important as the size of NPS resources is their variety. In 1996, there were 374 separate NPS units, including national parks, monuments, historic sites, battlefields, parkways, recreation areas, seashores, and others. Although the larger areas are mostly in the West, the diverse NPS units are well distributed throughout the contiguous states.

The NPS is also responsible for several "affiliated areas," which are not technically NPS units but are managed with NPS assistance. Chimney Rock National Historic Site in Nebraska and the Historic Camden District in South Carolina are two examples of NPS affiliated areas. The NPS has a presence in several of the nation's urban areas with National Historic Sites and National Recreation Areas (NRAs). Nearly all of the NRAs are primarily water-based resources; the Gateway NRA in New York, the Chattahoochee River NRA in Atlanta, and the Golden Gate NRA in San Francisco are three well-known and highly popular urban sites managed by the NPS.

In addition to the natural and cultural interpretation that visitors enjoy at NPS units, many of them, especially national parks, host a variety of traditional outdoor recreational uses. The NPS *Map and Guide* lists the following facilities, services, and activities at each of the units: visitor centers, guides for hire, campgrounds, boat ramps, cabin rentals, access for disabled persons, back country permits, and areas for mountain climbing, horseback riding, swimming, boating, fishing, hunting, bicycling, snowmobiling, and cross-country skiing.

Two recent laws passed by Congress had major implications for NPS resources. First and foremost, the California Desert Protection Act of 1994 (P. L. 103-433) protected more land in the lower 48 states than any other legislation with the exception of the 1964 Wilderness Act, most of it under NPS' jurisdiction (Zinser, 1995). Death Valley National Monument was upgraded to national park status after 1.3 million acres of BLM land were transferred to the NPS. More BLM land was transferred to the NPS near the Joshua Tree National Monument, which was also upgraded to a national park. Further, a new NPS unit, the Mohave National Preserve, was created from 1.4 million acres of the former BLM East Mohave Scenic Area. In addition to numerous minor provisions, the act also established a number of new wilderness areas and wilderness study areas in the NPS, BLM, FS, and FWS.

Another significant law passed by Congress was the Omnibus Parks and Public Lands Management Act of 1996 (H.R. 4236). It created five new NPS units: the Tallgrass Prairie National Preserve and Nicodemus National Historic Site (NHS) in Kansas, the Washita Battlefield NHS in Oklahoma, and the New Bedford Whaling National Historic Park and the Boston Harbor Islands NRA in Massachusetts. The Tallgrass Prairie National Preserve is the first of its kind in the United States. The act also defined a management structure for the Presidio, the former military installation on a spectacular setting in San Francisco, which was recently transferred to the NPS. Further, the Omnibus Act provided funding toward the protection of the highly regarded Sterling Forest natural area, located just 40 miles from New York City along the New Jersey border. And the act also created nine "heritage areas," a new NPS designation that is not technically an NPS unit, but that provides technical assistance to historic and cultural districts created through local initiatives.

The National Park Service and Outdoor Recreation in the United States

(By Merle Van Horne, National Park Service, Washington, D.C.)

The mission of the National Park Service, as stated in its 1997 strategic plan, is:

> The National Park Service preserves unimpaired the natural and cultural resources and values of the National Park System for the enjoyment, education, and inspiration of this and future generations. The Service cooperates with partners to extend the benefits of natural and cultural resource conservation and outdoor recreation throughout this country and the world.

The two elements of this mission statement—the park system and the cooperative outreach effort—while entirely complementary, are sufficiently different to warrant separate treatment here.

The National Park System

The National Park Service Organic Act of 1916 created a new federal bureau within the Department of the Interior to protect and manage the 40 national parks and monuments then in existence and those yet to be established (USDI-NPS, 1995, p.6). Since then, the system has grown to more than 370 such "units" designated Congress and in some cases (by the president) designates new areas. The service is responsible for the protection of resources as varied as the White House (18 acres) and the Wrangell-St. Elias National Park and Preserve (13 million acres), as well as more than 35 million museum objects and 22,000 linear feet of archives. Table III.3 summarizes the status of the National Park System as of December 31, 1996.

A number of trends are affecting the National Park System and will continue to do so. They all pose challenges to the adaptability of the service.

Congress continues to create new units for the National Park Service to manage, often with little or no increase in dollars or personnel to do the job. The growing gap between means and ends is leading to major adaptations, some tentative and experimental, in how the National Park Service does its work. Here are a few examples:

> Entrance and service fees are always controversial, but surveys have consistently shown that visitors would accept higher fees if they were sure the revenue would go for improved facilities and services at the site where the money was collected. Both Congress and past administrations have been most reluc-

tant to relinquish any of their control over where the money goes, but these kinds of fee "plowback" experiments are now being conducted with congressional approval.

- Partnering with both commercial and nonprofit organizations is seen as a path to more cost-effective management of the National Park System. This has always been so. More than 650 concessionaires provide lodging, transportation, food, shops, and recreational services to park visitors (USDI-NPS, 1997, p. xi). Numerous "cooperating associations" serve the visitor with literature and information. Consideration is being given to using partners in more—and more responsible—roles. A current study is exploring the possible role of bond issuance in funding major capital projects. Also, the National Park Service has traditionally benefitted from the services of many fine volunteers. They are even more avidly sought in the present climate of fiscal constraint.
- A worrisome trend in recent years is a rise in the number and severity of "external threats" to park resources from adverse changes in the use of nearby (and not so nearby) lands in other ownerships. This trend has led to much strife between parks and their neighbors, both public and private. Efforts are now underway to mitigate these conflicts and establish more cooperative relationships with park neighbors. Often, "ecosystem management" is seen as an appropriate framework for improved relationships of this type.

Table III.3: The National Park System[a] as of December 31, 1996

Type of Area	Number in System	Acreage
International Historic Site	1	35
National Battlefield	11	13,144
National Battlefield Park	3	8,776
National Battlefield Site	1	1
National Historic Site	74	23,913
National Historical Park	38	162,239
National Lakeshore	4	228,936
National Memorial	26	8,058
National Military Park	9	38,028
National Monument	73	2,066,178
National Park	54	51,700,937
National Parkway	4	170,765
National Preserve	16	23,616,704
National Recreation Area	19	3,703,211
National Reserve	2	33,407
National River[b]	6	424,786
National Scenic Trail	3	183,105
National Seashore	10	592,608
National Wild and Scenic River[c]	9	219,540
Other Areas[d]	11	38,947
System Totals	374	83,233,318

[a]Does not include National Park Service-affiliated areas nor national heritage areas and corridors, since those resources have not been designated as units of the National Park System.
[b]These six rivers are designated and managed as units of the National Park System, but they have *not* been designated as components of the National Wild and Scenic Rivers System.
[c]These nine rivers are designated and managed as units of the National Park System, *and in addition*, have been designated as components of the National Wild and Scenic Rivers System. Certain other rivers, which are components of the National Wild and Scenic Rivers System, are managed by the National Park Service but are not units of the National Park System. Those rivers are not included in this table, which is limited to National Park System units.
[d]Includes the White House, the National Mall, and various other sites.

The Visitors

There are many. Over the 10-year period of 1987-1996, recreation visits to the National Park System ranged between 246 million and 275 million, with a long-term increasing tendency. Over the same period, overnight stays held fairly steady between 16.6 million and 18.3 million, with tent and back country camping gaining and recreation vehicle camping declining (USDI-NPS, 1987-1996).

The National Park Service encourages "appreciative" recreation activities, such as hiking and wildlife observation, which have relatively little adverse impact on resources and generally do not impair the quality of other people's experiences. Some sensitive natural and cultural areas are restricted to such activities exclusively. The National Park System includes some urban parks and national recreation areas which permit a broader range of recreation pursuits. Even in such areas, however, the service has been relatively successful (with the support of the majority of visitors) in avoiding clearly inappropriate recreation activities.

In recent years, much of the media coverage of the national parks has consisted of horror stories of gross overcrowding. In actuality, such episodes are mostly limited to peak weekends at the most popular parks. The service takes the crowding problem seriously, however, since these crush-load instances may be harbingers of things to come. Various remedies are being tested and applied.

Reservations are required more often and at more places. Alternative transportation systems are replacing the space-consuming private automobile in the most crowded front country areas. New information technologies are being used to divert people from the most crowded sites and times to equally rewarding alternative destinations.

Off-season visitation is increasing, but the inflexibility of the school year continues to force most family recreation travel into major seasonal peaks.

Visitors to the National Park System as a whole are quite diverse. However, those who travel outside metropolitan regions to visit the more remote sites continue to be disproportionately white and of above average education and income. Tourists from other countries constitute a substantial and increasing share of national park visitors. This trend is a major plus. International travel is one of the few segments of our country's balance of payments that consistently shows a surplus. Market studies show that the national parks are one of America's best inducements for foreign travelers to visit our shores.

Partnerships—The Outreach Effort

Since the 1930s, the National Park Service has had broad authority to extend its expertise and support to communities throughout the nation, regardless of their proximity to units of the National Park System. The service experienced a major expansion of its outreach mandate in 1981, when it assumed most of the recreation and cultural resources assistance and monitoring responsibilities formerly exercised by the Heritage Conservation and Recreation Service and its predecessor, the Bureau of Outdoor Recreation pursuant to the Outdoor Recreation Act of 1963.

The service collaborates with other federal agencies, tribes, states, local, and county governments, nonprofit organizations and commercial enterprises in carrying out this work. Descriptions of some of the major outreach programs follow.

Through the national historic and natural landmarks programs, Historic Preservation Fund grants, the tribal historic preservation program, the archeology and ethnography program, and the historic American buildings survey/historic American engineering record, the National Park Service bolsters community preservation efforts nationwide. In partnership with the State Historic Preservation Officers, more than 67,000 resources have been listed on the national register of historic places. The preservation tax credit program alone has leveraged more than $17 billion in private investment, restoring over 26,000 historic buildings. Over the next five years, an increase of 15 to 20 percent in the number of resources protected by these partnership programs is envisaged.

Since 1964, the Land and Water Conservation Fund has provided more than $3.2 billion in 50 percent matching grants to states and territories for the acquisition and development of recreation and conservation sites. The 37,000 parks and recreation facilities assisted through this program and the 1,800 properties rehabilitated with grants from the Urban Park and Recreation Recovery program are largely administered by counties and municipalities. Most of them serve community recreation and open-space needs.

Similarly, the Federal Lands-to-Parks program has recycled over 1,200 "surplus" federal properties into locally managed parks, open space and recreational facilities. Over the past 10 years, the Rivers, Trails and Conservation Assistance program has responded to over 500 requests for help with locally developed conservation and recreation projects by providing technical assistance. Over the next five years, these two partnership programs plan to assist in the conservation of 1,100 additional miles of trail, 1,200 miles of protected river corridor, and 35,000 acres of new parks and open space—largely at the community level (USDI-NPS, 1997, p. 43).

Other recreation resources and opportunities are conserved through partnerships with states and other federal agencies. In cooperation with other land managing agencies, the National Park Service exercises the Secretary of the Interior's oversight responsibility for the National System of Trails and the National System of Wild and Scenic Rivers. More than 150 wild and scenic river segments conserve key free-flowing waterways. Twenty national scenic and historic trails and over 800 national recreation trails mark and commemorate many famous pathways and travel routes.

In the Urban Resources Partnership, the National Park Service cooperates with six other federal agencies to focus various assistance programs on the environmental problems of 13 American cities. The program responds to community-defined needs with projects ranging from erosion control, to community gardens, to anti-litter campaigns.

Recently, Congress has begun to designate national heritage areas—locally-driven partnerships that protect resources and provide educational and recreational opportunities. Fifteen such areas have been designated so far. Each national heritage area recognizes an exemplary local or regional effort to conserve and interpret a distinctive "cultural landscape" that has evolved over time through the interaction between the land and the human communities thereon. Management of these areas is entirely local, but the management entities are eligible for targeted technical assistance from applicable National Park Service programs.

America is changing rapidly. Each succeeding generation of National Park Service managers and employees faces new problems and opportunities arising from a changed environment and a different clientele. Constant and thoughtful adaptation is the key to success in accomplishing the service's dual mission of resource preservation and effective service to the American people.

U.S. Fish and Wildlife Service

The purpose of the FWS is to protect and enhance wildlife and fish habitats in the National Wildlife Refuge System. Most refuges were established for migratory bird conservation and endangered species protection. The National Wildlife Refuge Administration Act of 1966 established the refuge system with the standard that any public uses must be "compatible" with the management of the individual refuges. The 1966 law, however, did not define a unifying mission for the agency. The National Wildlife Refuge System Improvement Act, passed by the House of Representatives in 1997 but still awaiting Senate action, defined a mission for the Fish and Wildlife Service and established priority public uses. A key provision is the recognition of wildlife-dependent recreation as a "legitimate and appropriate" public use, so long as it is compatible with wildlife conservation.

As of September 1997, there were 512 refuges with approximately 90 million acres in the United States, not counting U.S. territories. In addition, the FWS manages about 2.5 million acres of waterfowl production areas. These areas consist of wetlands management districts (WMD) managed as part of the National Wildlife Refuge System. WMDs are located in the upper Great Plains and Great Lakes states (plus Iowa and Montana). Many provide recreation opportunities similar to those found on National Wildlife Refuges.

FWS's "Visitor's Guide" map and brochure describes recreation facilities and services available at all refuges and WMDs that allow public use. These facilities and services include: visitor centers, walk-in-only and day-use-only areas, hiking trails, wildlife viewing sites and best seasons for viewing wildlife, archaeological sites, wilderness areas, allowable use of nonmotorized and motorized boating, and the availability of hunting and fishing. More than one-third of the refuges (176), about 23.6 million acres, are not open for outdoor recreation. Most FWS land is in Alaska. Of the refuge acres closed to public use, almost 95 percent are in three refuges in Alaska. Excluding Alaska, the majority of FWS land in the contiguous states is in the Rocky Mountain region (53 percent), followed by the South with 28 percent (Table III.1).

Outdoor Recreation and the U.S. Fish and Wildlife Service

(By Terry Villanueva, Recreation Specialist, U.S. Fish and Wildlife Service, Arlington, VA)

The U.S. Fish and Wildlife Service (FWS) is the principal federal agency with responsibility for conserving, protecting, and enhancing fish and wildlife and their habitats for the continuing benefit of the American people. The FWS manages 512 National Wildlife Refuges covering about 90 million acres in all 50 states and U.S. territories, as well as 64 National Fish Hatcheries. The agency also enforces federal wildlife laws, manages migratory bird populations, stocks recreational fisheries, and conserves and restores wildlife habitat such as wetlands. In addition, it oversees the Federal Aid program that directs federal excise taxes on angling and hunting equipment to state wildlife agencies. This program is a cornerstone of the nation's wildlife management efforts, funding fish and wildlife restoration, boating access, hunter education, shooting ranges, and related projects across the U.S.

In great American tradition, the hunting and angling community likewise has become a cornerstone of conservation. Whether in the form of a local Izaak Walton League or Bass Angler Sportsman Society Chapter, fighting to preserve water quality in local lakes and rivers or an effort to conserve wetlands sponsored by a Ducks Unlimited Chapter, these small partnerships have become hugely important parts of national conservation efforts. Keeping hunting and fishing as healthy, vibrant recreational activities is, therefore, important to the future of wildlife conservation. And newer forms of wildlife recreation, like photography, observation and conservation education are presenting new ways for Americans to get involved in conservation.

Recreation in the National Wildlife Refuge System

The debate over how National Wildlife Refuge lands, managed by the U.S. Fish and Wildlife Service, ought to be managed and used by the public has intensified and become more visible over the last two decades as the system expanded and visitation grew to nearly 30 million people per year. The first national wildlife refuge was established in 1903, when President Teddy Roosevelt set aside a tiny Florida island as a protected area for birds being indiscriminately harvested for their plumage to meet the fashion demands of the day. Today, the National Wildlife Refuge System forms a network of diverse landscapes wildlife call home, providing habitats where migratory birds thrive and endangered species mark their recovery.

To help balance the refuge system's central wildlife conservation mission with legitimate public recreation interests, on March 25, 1996, President Clinton issued Executive Order 12996, Management and General Public Use of the National Wildlife Refuge System, the first major presidential action to clearly define the mission, purpose and priority public uses of the system. The Executive Order defined the mission of the system as preserving "a national network of lands and waters for the conservation and management of the fish, wildlife, and plants of the United States for the benefit of present and future generations." The Administration opposed subsequent attempts by Congress to elevate recreational use to a "purpose" of the refuge system. In a display of bipartisan cooperation, Secretary of the Interior Bruce Babbitt joined Congressmen Don Young (R-AK), John Dingell (D-MI), Jim Saxton (R-NJ), and George Miller (D-CA), and representatives of the National Audubon Society, Wildlife Management Institute, International Association of Fish and Wildlife Agencies, and Wildlife Legislative Fund of America to develop alternative legislation. The negotiations resulted in the National Wildlife Refuge System Improvement Act, P.L. 105-57, which was signed into law by President Clinton on October 9, 1997.

Many provisions of P.L. 105-57 coincide with those found in Executive Order 12996. Key legislative provisions mirroring the Executive Order include the Refuge System mission statement, definition of priority public uses, and a requirement that the biological integrity, diversity, and environmental health of the Refuge System be maintained. Citing the Executive Order's provision on priority public uses as the foundation for the direction set in the bill, the legislation defines compatible wildlife-dependent recreation as "a legitimate and appropriate general public use of the [Refuge] System." It establishes certain wildlife-dependent public uses as priority public uses, to receive enhanced consideration over others. These uses are defined as hunting, fishing, wildlife observation and photography, and environmental education and interpretation. The legislation states that these uses should be facilitated when compatible but does not mandate these activities. These uses also were defined as priority public uses in Executive Order 12996.

The Improvement Act retains refuge managers' authority to use their best professional judgment to determine compatible public uses and whether or not they will be permitted. "Compatible use" is defined as one that "will not materially interfere with or detract from the fulfillment of the mission of the [Refuge] System or the purposes of a refuge." This language retains the current regulatory definition of "compatible use" used by the U.S. Fish and Wildlife Service. The new legislation includes provisions requiring that all new public uses and any renewal of existing uses comply with a public involvement process spelled out in the bill. It also requires public involvement in the development of refuge management plans. The plans must identify the purposes of each refuge, data on wildlife populations, archaeological and cultural values, suitable visitor facilities, any problems that affect wildlife and actions to remedy them, and opportunities for compatible wildlife-dependent recreation.

The only legislation defining the Refuge System prior to P.L. 105-57 came in 1966, with passage of the National Wildlife Refuge System Administration Act, which the law amends. This law provided that all of the individual refuges become the National Wildlife Refuge System and established a "compatibility standard" for permitting public uses of individual refuges. However, the 1966 law lacked a unifying purpose or mission for the Refuge System and a specific process by which compatibility determinations should be made. The National Wildlife Refuge System Improvement Act of 1997 is designed to address these issues and, for the first time in its history, provides the Refuge System with an organic act to govern its management and use into the next century.

Expanding the Potential for Partnerships

Providing increased opportunities for wildlife-related recreation on FWS lands in an era of limited budgets requires the agency to work more effectively and efficiently with its non-government partners. A major thrust for the FWS over the coming decade will be to increase the number of partnerships with outside organizations working to reach common conservation goals. As part of its initial efforts to implement President Clinton's executive order on wildlife refuges, the FWS set out to increase the participation of refuge "Friends" groups in providing visitor's services— ranging from environmental education and interpretation to guided tours—on refuge lands. CARE, a coalition of conservation and recreation groups, is also working together with Congress to ensure that the refuge system receives the funding it needs to meet operational needs.

Prior to his Executive Order on refuge management, President Clinton signed Executive Order 12962 on Recreational Fisheries. The executive order required federal agencies to work together to improve recreational fisheries under their existing responsibilities and programs. To guide agencies in improving fishing opportunities, the executive order required agencies to develop a joint comprehensive fisheries conservation plan. To ensure that the plans are implemented and monitored, President Clinton assigned the Sport Fishing and Boating Partnership Council to annually review the progress of each agency represented in the plan.

The Sport Fishing and Boating Partnership Council, made up of representatives of state natural resource agencies and the fishing and boating industries and their trade associations, was formed three years ago to provide guidance and recommendations to the Secretary of the Interior on government policies affecting recreational boating and fishing. In addition to input from the council, the U.S. Fish and Wildlife Service has organized a series of fisheries stakeholder's meetings throughout the nation. These meetings brought together representatives of state, federal and Tribal natural resources agencies; conservation groups; recreational industry representatives and anglers to explore how non-federal and federal organizations can work together more effectively for the benefit of fisheries resources. These initiatives, and related efforts, will play an increasing role in meeting and responding to evolving demands for wildlife-related recreation on FWS lands as the National Wildlife Refuge System moves toward the celebration of its first century in 2003.

Other Federal Land Resources

Two other important federal sources of recreation land are not primarily land managing agencies. These are the U.S. Department of Defense (DoD) and Indian tribal land, administered in part by the Bureau of Indian Affairs (BIA). Both limit public access, and neither is guided by a systematic recreation policy. Each Indian reservation and Defense Department installation is a separate and unique case, thus recreation access and availability varies. Indian land is not federally owned, but is administered with assistance from the federal government.

Indian Land

(By Gary L. Rankel, U. S. Department of the Interior, Bureau of Indian Affairs, Washington, D.C.)

The United States contains approximately 56 million acres of Indian land, an area about the size of Georgia and South Carolina combined. The great majority of this land is on reservations in the Southwest,

Great Plains, and Mountain states. It includes more than 500 federally recognized tribes, most located in the states of Alaska, California, and Oklahoma. Land ownership within reservations ranges from 100 percent tribal to a complex "checkerboarded" pattern involving numerous tribal, individual Indian, and non-Indian owners. Unlike state and federal land management agencies, tribal governments have no mission or charge to provide outdoor recreation or other public use opportunities on Indian land. This land is for exclusive Indian use pursuant to treaties, statutes, and executive orders. As sovereign governments, tribes have the power to make laws, administer justice, manage use, and regulate member and non-member activity on Indian land.

Tribal fish, wildlife, and outdoor recreation operations are funded through the BIA's Fish, Wildlife, and Recreation program. The goal of this program is to fulfill and execute the federal government's trust and rights protection responsibilities relating to fish, wildlife, and recreation resources for the sustenance, cultural enrichment, and economic support of Indians. This goal is carried out through the Indian Self-Determination Act of 1975, which permits tribes to contract with the bureau to carry out programs that would otherwise be performed by federal personnel. More than 95 percent of program resources are contracted to tribes.

Recognizing the potential of their resource bases, many tribal governments have pursued outdoor recreation and tourism as an economic development strategy, establishing programs that account for millions of public-use days annually. Indian pow-wows, fiestas, fairs, and religious ceremonies draw additional millions of visitors, including many from foreign countries. Indian museums, cultural centers, heritage displays, and arts and crafts shops are also popular attractions. In recent years, Indian casinos, bingo halls and other gaming establishments have begun to receive heavy use, boosting many Indian and local economies.

Recreational fishery potentials exist on more than 100 reservations in 23 states containing approximately 750,000 acres of lakes and impoundments, and 10,000 miles of rivers and streams.[7] Of more than 80 recreational fisheries programs conducted on Indian reservations, several are nationally renowned, such as the Cherokee, NC; Leech Lake, MN; and Wind River, WY tribes. Tribal hatcheries in the Pacific Northwest, the Great Lakes states, and other regions create diverse fishing opportunities for a variety of species. Indian reservations offer a host of hunting opportunities and support several tribal programs that are popular for their guided and package hunts featuring elk, bighorn sheep, and other big game. Numerous other tribes offer diverse hunting experiences for bear, javelina, mountain lion, waterfowl, upland birds, and other species. A number of tribes have set aside portions of their reservations as hunting preserves, wildlife refuges, wildlife viewing areas, and wilderness areas. Recently, more than 30 tribes throughout the Plains states created the Intertribal Bison Cooperative to reestablish bison herds for subsistence, cultural, religious, and tourism-related purposes.

Other recreation facilities and opportunities on Indian land include day-use areas, full-convenience RV parks and campgrounds, boating facilities, and water sports activities including whitewater rafting and houseboat rentals. Hiking, horseback riding, biking, off-road motoring, winter sports, spectator sports, and other leisure pursuits are also available.

An especially popular Indian tourism area is the Four Corners region of the Southwest. This area offers numerous major tourist attractions and includes spectacular desert scenery, cliff dwellings, and unique Indian cultural events and religious ceremonies. Alaska Indian tribes—including Eskimos, Aleuts, Athabascans, and others—offer a variety of tourism attractions and services. Other prosperous Indian tourism centers are located throughout Oklahoma and on the eastern band of Cherokee Indians Reservation, which borders the Great Smoky Mountains National Park. Others heavily involved in tourism include the Miccosukee tribe of Florida, the Alabama-Coushatta tribes of Texas, the Flathead and Blackfeet reservations of Montana, and the Penobscot and Passamaquoddy tribes of Maine.

Several tribes maintain tourism offices and visitor centers, and many have produced colorful brochures, maps, and information packages describing attractions, opportunities, and programs on their reservations. Many reservations are posted to facilitate visitor use, and some tribes offer guided tours of reservation landmarks and attractions. Not all tribes promote tourism and public use of reservation resources, however. Of those that do, many prohibit public use of certain land. Some tribes prohibit photography and many Indian people prefer not being photographed. Attendance at religious ceremonies may be off-limits or by invitation only.

---

[7]The BIA does not have an up-to-date brochure or directory which lists recreational opportunities available to the general public on Indian land. The most current centralized information is in a 1991 BIA report titled "Outdoor Recreation on Indian Lands: Opportunities and Contacts." It lists each tribe/reservation and office to contact for more information. The brief information provided lists whether public use is allowed for the eight recreational activities—fishing, hunting, camping, bicycling, boating, hiking, snowmobiling, and auto touring—that were part of the Bush Administration's *Enjoy Outdoors America* initiative in the early 1990s. Zinser (1995) recommends the guidebook, *Discover Indian Reservations USA* by Veronica E. Tiller (Council Publications, 1992, Denver CO), as a source of information on recreational attractions and services on individual reservations.

The proximity of Indian reservations to many national parks and other landmarks and attractions, and the compatibility of low-impact cultural, historic, and ecosystem-based tourism with traditional tribal values and goals make these lands potentially important recreation resources. Implementation of tourism programs for Indian lands will require training of willing tribes in the areas of tourism and concessions management, promotion and marketing, visitor services, facilities management, infrastructure development, and similar related fields. Cooperative efforts involving tribes, other governments, and the private sector could facilitate the development of regional tourism packages.

Department of Defense Land

(By George H. Siehl, Congressional Research Service (retired), Gaithersburg, MD)

The Department of Defense (DoD) is seldom associated with outdoor recreation or natural resources. With about 25 million acres under management throughout the United States, however, DoD ranks as the fifth largest federal property owner. While recreation is not a part of the DoD military mission, that much land cannot be ignored in an assessment of outdoor recreation resources.

Military reservations have long provided for the recreation needs of military personnel and their families and, to a more limited extent, to nonmilitary visitors. Large bases contain playgrounds, playing fields or courts, marinas, golf courses, and extensive open space suitable for biking, hiking, hunting, fishing, or wildlife observation. In short, military bases provide the same kinds of outdoor recreation opportunities that many other communities provide for local residents. For many years, military bases were treated as self-contained communities for a variety of reasons. With the advent of the all-volunteer force, the military increasingly has become family-centered. With these changes, some barriers to interaction with neighboring communities have lessened. More base commanders now welcome area residents to visit and enjoy military land, subject to any constraints caused by their mission.

The Army, in particular, has a long history of protecting natural resources. It administered the battlefield parks of the American Civil War from their founding in the final third of the last century through the 1930s, when management was shifted to the National Park Service. The Army cavalrymen and engineers were the first national park rangers. They were sent to protect early parks prior to establishment of the National Park Service in 1916. In this capacity, they designed and built roads and structures in Yellowstone National Park that remain in service to this day. The Army also administered the 1930s Civilian Conservation Corps camps, whose occupants built many recreation improvements in national parks and forests.

The U.S. Coast Guard, in the Department of Transportation, becomes a military organization in wartime. On a daily basis, however, the Coast Guard is a recreation facilitator. It oversees recreational boating, enforces safety laws, and helps educate boaters. Thus, the military, which at first glance seems to bear little relationship to outdoor recreation, is an important player.

The DoD is in the midst of a massive downsizing that began late in the Reagan administration, accelerated after the Gulf War, and continues in the Clinton years. This decade-long process has shed manpower, ships, planes, vehicles, and hundreds of bases. Within this overall restructuring, recreation is affected most directly by DoD land requirements. In 1988, 1991 to 1993, and 1995, legislation required the DoD to review its needs for bases as the number of troops decreased and to dispose of excess real property. Base closures have benefitted outdoor recreation because some land was transferred to federal, state, and local governments specifically for recreation, conservation, or open-space uses.

The Federal Lands to Parks program, administered by the National Park Service, helped 91 local and state agencies acquire approximately 5,700 acres of transferred properties for park land in the decade 1986 to 1996.[8] Since military base decommissioning began in 1988, the NPS has identified 65 bases with land and facilities appropriate for potential transfer to recreation agencies. As of mid-1996, six of these bases had transferred over 1,000 acres, and an additional 12,000 acres from the remaining bases were pending transfer approval to more than 70 local and state recreation agencies (USDI-NPS, 1996a). In other cases, where decommissioned military land was not transferred directly to recreation and park agencies, recreation was included in a mix of land uses in the base re-use plans which were developed in conjunction with local governments and the private sector.

---

[8]Authorized by the Federal Property and Administrative Services Act of 1949, the Federal Lands to Parks Program has transferred over 1,200 surplus Federal properties totaling more than 142,000 acres to State and local recreation and park agencies since 1949. The properties range from parcels of less than an acre to the 7,000 acre Croft State Park in South Carolina (Kelly, Cornelssen, and Bailey 1996).

Many of the developed recreation facilities on bases are funded through the DoD Morale, Welfare, and Recreation (MWR) program, which is financed not from tax dollars, but from profits from the military commissaries and military user fees for recreation equipment or facilities. Possible limitations on what commissaries can sell could eventually curtail funds available for development and maintenance of recreation opportunities on military land.

A DoD funding source with natural resource significance has been reduced. The Legacy Resources Management program was established by Congress in the 1991 DoD Appropriation Act. That program first received $10 million per year and later $25 million. Funding for fiscal years 1996 and 1997 was $3 million and $10 million, respectively. The money was made available to bases on a competitive basis to inventory, protect, and manage biological, cultural, and geophysical resources on DoD land. Although recreation was not included as a program goal, the improvement of resource management provided indirect benefits to wildlife activities such as observation or hunting. Other conservation funds have been integrated with the service operational programs. In the Army, for instance, resource conservation is now incorporated in the Integrated Training Area Management (ITAM) program. Specific projects under this arrangement tie closely to supporting training and readiness requirements for the Army. Activities include restoration of vegetative cover on tank training ranges.

Looking ahead, recreation interests and initiatives on DoD land will be at the margin, for the most part. Marketing of recreation on military land is likely to come through individual efforts by base commanders to be better neighbors with surrounding communities. Dedication of land on closed bases to recreation and open-space uses is the most likely means of benefiting broad recreation interests in the years ahead. Nonetheless, land remaining under DoD management will be an important reservoir of open space and habitat for wildlife. Already, this land shelters over 400 endangered or candidate species. Continued emphasis on stewardship by DoD is essential to enhancing resource values, but pressures to spend available funds to benefit military readiness will persist.

Since World War II, military technology has contributed much to outdoor recreation. Perhaps the best example of this technology transfer is the rubber life raft. Other outdoor recreation adaptations from military technology and equipment include four-wheel drive vehicles, camouflaged clothing, and more recently, night vision and global positioning devices. Additional ideas will be borrowed and adapted from the military in the years ahead. Similarly, DoD will pick up on improvements in recreation gear. In addition, many bases contain museums or outdoor displays of historic equipment that draw visitors. Also, ceremonies, parades, and demonstrations such as many bases provided on Armed Forces Day bring crowds interested in history, heritage, and patriotism.

The Federal Water Resource Agencies

The remaining three federal land-managing agencies that provide outdoor recreation opportunities in the United States are the U.S. Army Corps of Engineers (CE), the Bureau of Reclamation (BoR) in the Department of the Interior, and the independent Tennessee Valley Authority (TVA). A fourth agency, the National Oceanic and Atmospheric Administration (NOAA) in the Department of Commerce, plays an important indirect role with respect to coastal and marine recreation. The CE, BoR, and TVA each manage federal water resource projects primarily for navigation, flood control, and water supply, but also for outdoor recreation as a secondary responsibility.

Another characteristic common to the CE, BoR, and TVA is that their ratio of developed land—with its infrastructure and facilities—to dispersed land is much larger than the ratios for the FS, NPS, BLM, and FWS. The three water resource agencies do not manage vast tracts of land as the other agencies do. Consequently, their recreation management programs are heavily oriented toward developed facilities, especially those associated with reservoirs.

A third distinguishing trait of these three agencies is the proximity of their areas to population centers. Many reservoirs are on watercourses near cities. Even BoR, a strictly Western agency, has many recreation areas near urban centers such as Denver, Phoenix, Salt Lake City, Sacramento, and cities of California's Central Valley. Over 80 percent of the CE water resource projects are within 50 miles of a metropolitan area, and 40 percent are within 50 miles of two metropolitan statistical areas. The TVA is a regional agency, serving parts of seven Southeastern states. The Tennessee River system extends from western North Carolina and eastern Tennessee west into Mississippi and then northward to Kentucky. The metropolitan areas of Asheville, Knoxville, Nashville, Chattanooga, Huntsville, Birmingham, Atlanta, and Memphis are all close to TVA's water resources.

Bureau of Reclamation

BoR administers 310 recreation areas spread throughout 17 Western states. Overall, BoR land and water cover about 6.5 million acres (Table III.1). Just 11 recreation areas covering about 200,000 acres are outside of the two Western regions. Almost 85 percent of BoR resources are located in the Rocky Mountain region. BoR differs from the other federal agencies in that it does not manage much of its property. Rather, recreation management is often contracted to other federal agencies, state natural resource agencies, and local governments. Only about 14 percent of BoR recreation areas are managed by BoR.

Since BoR was established under the Reclamation Act of 1902, it has been known primarily for developing and managing large-scale agricultural water resource projects. The emphasis on reservoir construction has declined in recent years. Instead, BoR is now concentrating on balanced management of its existing properties for a variety of values. An indication of the importance of recreation in management comes from the 1994 decision to emphasize amenity resource values such as wildlife and recreation at Arizona's Glen Canyon Dam (Zinser, 1995). More details on the trends and issues involved in the BoR's role as an outdoor recreation provider are in the accompanying article, "Outdoor Recreation Trends in the Bureau of Reclamation."

Outdoor Recreation Trends in the Bureau of Reclamation

(By Richard A. Crysdale, Senior Outdoor Recreation Planner [retired], U.S. Bureau of Reclamation, Denver, CO)

One role of the Bureau of Reclamation (BoR) in the U. S. Department of the Interior is providing recreation opportunities in outdoor water settings. The development of its water-based areas are facilitated by legislation which encourages non-federal recreation management of the recreation sites and allows BoR to cost-share the development of facilities. In many cases, recreation development legislation is specific to a given project. The management of these resources is primarily by other federal and non-federal public entities.

Since 1902, BoR has developed water primarily for irrigation, municipal and industrial use, hydroelectric power, and flood control in the 17 western states. In 1965, the Federal Water Project Recreation Act (PL 89-72) recognized fish and wildlife and recreation as purposes for developing water. This meant fish and wildlife and recreation could be included in the analysis for a benefit-cost ratio to determine the feasibility of developing water projects.

Today, BoR has 310 designated recreation areas managed by various federal, state and local public agencies. BoR manages just 48 of these recreation areas which were never transferred to other agencies or were transferred but returned. Water storage developments like reservoirs provide 4.9 million acres of land, 1.7 million surface acres of water, and 13,000 miles of shoreline for recreation. There are over 16,000 miles of water conveyance canals and other facilities, some of which provide fishing, hunting and trail use opportunities.

Visitation at the designated recreation areas reached an estimated 87 million in 1996. BoR and the U.S. Army Corps of Engineers, which develops water primarily for flood control and navigation, administer just two percent of the total federal estate. Nearly one-third of the total visitation to the federal estate occurs on BoR and Corps water developments. The National Park Service and U.S. Forest Service manage nine National Recreation Areas (NRA) on BoR water developments. Tourists from other countries are attracted to these NRAs. Lake Mead NRA in Nevada, for example, has 11 million visitors annually of which an estimated ten percent are from other countries. Over one million visitors tour Hoover Dam every year. Since 1981, visitation to BoR water developments has increased an average of 1.2 million visitors per year.

Since 1987, more people live west of the Mississippi River than east of it. The western states are dominated by arid and semiarid areas, and a rapidly growing urban population concentrated along the west coast, Las Vegas, Phoenix and along the Rocky Mountain Front Range of New Mexico and Colorado. The mountains are a natural reservoir for storing precipitation during the winter. The spring thaw of snow brings about a rapid runoff of water. The urban and rural populations are heavily dependent upon water developments to capture the runoff and supplement it with ground water development to meet their agricultural, municipal-industrial, and hydroelectric power needs throughout the rest of the year.

Water Conservation and Outdoor Recreation

Conservation of water is a major trend driven primarily by various laws passed by Congress. Three major forms of water conservation are: (1) reduce seepage losses in the existing system, (2) change operations of existing systems to meet contemporary needs, and (3) develop multiple-use rather than single purpose facilities. Each has significant implications for the recreation uses and resource management of the water developments. Examples of each follow.

1) Reduce Seepage Losses: Most of the 16,000 miles of BoR water conveyances are not lined by concrete. Canals lose water simply through the saturation of the clay lining which results in establishing riparian habitat and wetlands adjacent to the canals. Such seepage also recharges the groundwater. Lining is essential to deliver the maximum water to its destination.

In the case of lining most of the Coachella Canal in southern California, BoR used modern designs and techniques. Concrete lining was placed without dewatering the canal, interrupting water service, and protecting the canal fishery. A stair step configuration of the lining was placed in the canal to allow deer and other large entrapped mammals to escape the water. Some fishermen trespass on BoR canal right-of-ways and occasionally fall into the canals. On the newly lined Coachella canal, fishermen would be able to use the stair case configuration to escape.

BoR, the Central Valley Irrigation District and Imperial County developed a joint program to establish public fishing in the lined portion of the canal (USDI Bureau of Reclamation, 1993). The program will be managed by the Imperial County Parks Department, which will provide liability insurance. The terminal reservoir for the canal is the 120 surface-acre Lake Cahuilla in which canal entrained fish will end their journey. The lake is also stocked by the State of California. In 1988, 14,958 anglers fished in Lake Cahuilla.

Other BoR canals will be lined to conserve water and provide new and safer fishing opportunities for western anglers. The key to opening up canal rights-of-way for fishing and other recreation uses, such as trails, will be other governmental entities' willingness to assume the recreation management responsibilities. The recreation management entities must also have cooperation from the irrigation districts.

2) Change Operation of Existing Facilities: There are several examples of changing operations primarily brought about by mandates of law and changing uses of water through the market system. Three of these examples are: a) changing hydroelectric operations of the Glen Canyon Dam on the Colorado River in Arizona, b) changing operations of a whole water development system to meet contemporary needs of a region, and c) change in design for dam outlets.

Glen Canyon Dam Operations

The Grand Canyon Protection Act of 1992 requires the Secretary of the Interior "...to protect, mitigate adverse impacts to, and improve the values for which the Grand Canyon National Park and Glen Canyon National Recreation Area were established, including but not limited to natural and cultural resources and visitor use." Glen Canyon Dam, completed in 1964, has historically been used primarily for power generation during periods of peak demand. The reservoir, Lake Powell, is part of the Glen Canyon NRA which annually serves over 3.5 million visitors. Below the dam, the Colorado River flows through Grand Canyon National Park for nearly 300 miles before entering Lake Mead NRA. The stretch through the Grand Canyon is very popular for river running. Concessions serve thousands of visitors with lengthy river running trips, backpacking, and horseback excursions down to and along the Colorado River. The National Park Service has a 10–year waiting list of applicants who want to run the river in their own craft through the Grand Canyon.

Glen Canyon Dam altered the natural flows of the Colorado River, significantly changing the riverine ecosystem vegetation, the stabilization of sandy beaches used for overnight camping, and the well-being of river users. The water level fluctuations would vary from 3 feet to 12 feet overnight. The historical releases ranged from 3,000 cubic feet per second to 44,500 cubic feet within a 24-hour period. After years of comprehensive environmental studies, plus an interim operating schedule which reduced the wide variation of flow releases usually between 6,000 and 8,000 cubic feet, a final operation procedure was established (USDI Bureau of Reclamation, 1995). The new operations are more recreation user and environmentally friendly, and they resemble more closely the historical natural flows of the Colorado River. Recreation users of the Colorado River in the Grand Canyon had a significant influence on passage of the Grand Canyon Protection Act. Recreators will no doubt have a significant influence on the future operations of other water developments.

Changing Operation of Existing Systems

Public Law 101-618, The Fallon Paiute Shoshone Indian Tribes Water Rights Settlement Act of 1990, and Public Law 102-575, the Reclamation Projects Authorization Adjustment Act, with numerous titles for specific directions for each project, are examples of changing water uses and priorities. These laws will significantly affect the long-term trend of water use, priorities, and alter changes of water operations to meet contemporary needs. Recreation, although recognized as a purpose for water development, but not a "beneficial use" of water, has a potential of benefitting from the new operation changes. One of the congressional directives includes the restoration of historic river flows to bring back anadromous fisheries to California. Any time fisheries are improved, recreation users will also benefit from the water system changes that bring back the fish habitat.

Some of the irrigation districts, which sponsored most of the water developments in the western states, are selling their water and water rights to developing urban areas. Water formerly used for irrigation is being converted to municipal and industrial use and low head hydroelectric power. That means projects which have systems of dams and water storage, diversion structures, canals, powerplants and pump-back storage powerplants are altering the schedules of water releases in the system. The urban consumer demands for water are somewhat different than the water demands for irrigating crops. Studies are underway to examine the operation changes and determine the recreation and tourism implications of longer water retention in reservoirs and streams during the prime season. If higher reservoir water levels can be retained during the prime recreation season, the reservoirs may experience greater visitation for longer periods of time.

Changes in Dam Outlet Design

Many times when water is developed prime riparian-habitat is lost. The U. S. Fish and Wildlife Service will recommend mitigation measures to BoR to enhance fish and wildlife. At times when Congress provides funding, BoR will follow the recommendations which result in significant resource enhancement. One of the enhancements is the development of multiple level release capability of dams to tap the stratified water temperatures in the reservoirs. This multi-level release capability and a change in operation of the dam provides favorable fishery habitat for food and reproduction of fish in the river below the dam.

Flaming Gorge Dam in Utah was the first dam with multiple level releases which created a blue ribbon fishery on the Green River below the dam. A water temperature "curtain" to tap the stratified water temperatures was installed at Shasta Dam, California, to enhance the downstream fishery habitat of the Sacramento River. The blended water temperatures will enhance fish growth and reproduction. Any time the fishery is enhanced and fishing improves, recreation users benefit. Fishing opportunities are scarce in the west because of the low number of available streams, lakes and reservoirs. The quality of fishing is significantly improved by the multi-level releases of the dams. More dams will be retrofitted with multi-level capability in the future as funds become available.

3) Develop Multiple Uses: The water conveyances were designed specifically for only transporting water from one place to another. Fish from reservoirs and streams frequently become entrained in the water conveyance flows. Canals have a sterile habitat with little food, cover and opportunities for reproduction, and some of the flows are too swift. Some of the fish in water conveyances die because of the poor habitat conditions.

Fisheries found in conveyance facilities have either been unmanaged or closed to fishing. BoR scientists are exploring the development of favorable fishery habitat in canals to accommodate entrained fish, and provide new fishing opportunities for anglers (Mueller, 1996; Mueller & Liston, 1994). The Arizona Game and Fish Department is promoting a highly successful urban fishery program that accommodated over 225,000 angler trips in 1988 (Agyagos, et al. 1990). Another example of the recreation potential of urban canals is the Salt River Project canals in Phoenix. The canal has the potential to provide an additional 750,000 angler-days and generate $1.5 million annually from the sale of new fishing licenses. Existing water facilities may be pressed into service to meet future fishing needs, especially in the urban areas where such opportunities are scarce.

Summary for Trends in the Bureau of Reclamation

Population growth in the western United States continues to challenge the management of western waters for recreation. Trends in population growth, changes in water needs, and scarcity of water resource recreation opportunities have triggered legislation to explore water conservation methods. Legislation is the driving force to reduce seepage, change operations of water development systems, and invent new technologies for improving downstream fishery habitats. Conversion of single purpose water conveyances to multiple use, and public-friendly access is a trend beginning to meet the urban population's recreation needs. These trends will carry over into the next century.

U.S. Army Corps of Engineers

The CE (or "Corps") has 456 reservoirs and other water projects in 42 states. The CE provides important outdoor recreation opportunities throughout the United States, despite managing only about 11.5 million acres of land and water (Table III.1). This acreage ranks fifth among federal agencies—only about one-seventh the amount of NPS land and well below 10 percent of both FS and BLM land. Two major factors account for the CE's status as a leading outdoor recreation supplier: accessibility and attractiveness. Accessibility is evident in the proximity of many Corps projects to metropolitan areas and the fact that they can accommodate large user populations. Corps recreation areas are attractive because they contain bodies of water, a traditional "magnet" which attracts visitors.

Nearly half of CE land and water in the United States is located in the South. Southern acreage is almost twice that of the next ranking region, the North. The Pacific Coast has many Corps projects, but total land and water area in that region is less than five percent of the U.S. total. Like BoR, the CE leases management of many of its recreation areas, but not to the same extent. According to CE's 1994 Natural Resources Management System (NRMS) database, the agency administers 4,331 developed recreation areas at its projects, about 58 percent of which are managed directly by the CE. The remainder are managed by other federal agencies, concessionaires, state and local governments, and special government districts and associations.

Developed recreation areas administered by the CE cover about 1.7 million acres or about 15 percent of total agency area. Although 9.8 million acres remain "undeveloped," just over 80 percent of Corps recreation use occurs at developed sites. The CE also has a number of developed recreation areas devoted to intensive recreation use. In 1994 these areas covered about 220,000 acres, or 13 percent, of the developed acreage. Facilities offered at developed recreation areas include swimming pools, boat rentals, fishing piers, campsites, picnic sites, boat ramps, swimming areas, and trails.

The Corps of Engineers Recreation Program: Current and Future Trends

(By R. Scott Jackson, Research Biologist, Environmental Laboratory, US Army Corps of Engineers Waterways Experiment Station, Vicksburg, MS; David J. Wahus, Chief, Recreation Programs Section, Natural Resource Management Branch, U.S. Army Corps of Engineers, Washington, D.C.; and H. Roger Hamilton, Chief, Resource Analysis Branch, Environmental Laboratory, US Army Corps of Engineers Waterways Experiment Station, Vicksburg, MS)

Program Overview

The Corps of Engineers is a major command within the Department of the Army providing civil engineering support to the Army and other organizations within the United States and countries worldwide. An important component of the Corps of Engineers (CE) mission is to develop and manage water resources in the United States for a variety of purposes including flood control, navigation, hydropower, water supply, fish and wildlife and recreation. Currently the CE has 456 multiple purpose water resource development projects under its jurisdiction. These projects include reservoirs and navigation systems in 42 states throughout the U.S.

CE projects constitute a nationally significant recreation resource with over 11 million acres of land and water and over 40 thousand miles of shoreline (U.S. Army Corps of Engineers, 1997). Projects range from large remote reservoirs on the Missouri River in the Upper Great Plains to small urban reservoirs in New England. Over 80 percent of CE projects are within fifty miles of a major metropolitan area. These projects received over 375 million visits in 1996 (U.S. Army Corps of Engineers, 1997) and serve one in ten Americans annually. Recreational use of CE projects represents some of the most intense recreational activity within the federal estate. CE projects receive nearly 30 percent of federal recreation use on less than two percent of the federally managed lands and waters. This results in the need for vigilant management of CE resources to maintain high levels of visitor satisfaction and minimize conflicts among user groups. The close proximity of CE projects to metropolitan areas and the water-oriented nature of CE projects influences recreation use patterns. Over 80 percent of the visits to CE projects are day trips with boating, swimming, and sightseeing among the most popular activities.

A major factor in the success of the CE recreation program is the high level of cooperation between the CE and non-federal partners to provide recreation facilities on CE projects. Over 40 percent of the over 4300 recreation areas on CE projects are operated by non-federal partners including other federal agencies, state, county and local units of government and a variety of non-governmental organizations. In addition, 685 commercial concessions provide those services which can be most effectively offered by the private sector. This cooperative approach has provided a wide variety of recreational opportunities on CE projects for the American public.

One of the important motivations for cooperators to participate in the CE recreation program is the significant economic impact of spending by visitors to CE projects. It was estimated that over $12 billion was spent by visitors to CE projects in 1994. This resulted in $5 billion in income and 187,000 jobs in industries directly supplying goods and services to CE visitors. Secondary effects of visitor spending accounted for an additional 410,000 jobs (Jackson, et al., 1996).

Factors Affecting the Future Direction of the CE Recreation Program

Important factors affecting the demand for the Corps recreation program are the multiple purpose nature of CE projects, the close proximity of CE projects to U.S. population centers and the fact that most CE managed recreation resources are associated with lakes and rivers. Taken together, these factors provide a strong indication that demand will continue to be high for recreation opportunities on CE projects. The effects of this high demand can be seen at many lakes where boaters compete with personal watercraft for access to the water on busy summer weekends. These demands have created significant challenges for CE managers. The following are examples of program initiatives which respond to these challenges.

Performance Goals and Measures: The CE recreation program along with most federal programs currently operate under severe financial and manpower constraints at a time when demand for recreation opportunities at CE projects are at their greatest. Many recreation program initiatives have focused on increasing program efficiency and effectiveness. The Government Performance and Results Act of 1992 requires that all federal agencies develop and implement performance goals and measures for agency programs. The recreation program was identified as one of nine major business areas within the CE Civil Works Program. Performance goals and measures are being implemented to guide the evaluation of program efficiency and effectiveness.

Recreational Fisheries: Individual recreation user groups have been successful in influencing the emphasis on federal recreation programs. For instance, Executive Order 12692, signed by the President on 7 June 1995, directed federal agencies to restore and enhance aquatic systems to the extent permitted by law and, where practical, provide for increased recreational fishing opportunities nationwide. This Order has resulted in an evaluation of CE operations to identify opportunities to increase public access and the quality of fisheries resources and the development of a recreational fisheries conservation plan.

CE managed fisheries resources are nationally significant, providing for approximately 25 percent, or 100 million visits, of all U.S. freshwater fishing visits (U.S. Army Corps of Engineers, 1997). Activities initiated in 1996 under this Executive Order include improving over 900,000 surface acres of water for fisheries resources; establishing or restoring 46 populations of fish; conducting over 12,000 public outreach programs for fishing, aquatic resources and boater safety; and establishing 137 partnerships that produced over $3 million in recreational fishing and habitat improvements.

Enhancing Recreation Opportunities: Two pieces of legislation have placed high priority on the identification of opportunities for enhancing recreation programs on CE projects. The Omnibus Parks and Public Land Management Act of 1996 (PL 104-333) calls for the creation of a nine member commission to be appointed by the President to conduct a National Recreation Lakes Review. The purpose is to evaluate the current and anticipated demand for recreation opportunities at federally-managed man-made lakes and reservoirs and develop alternatives for enhanced recreation use of such facilities. In addition Section 208 of the

Water Resources Development Act of 1996 directs the Secretary of the Army to provide increased emphasis and opportunities for recreation at water resources projects operated, maintained or constructed by the Corps of Engineers. Taken together, this legislation provides an opportunity to position the CE recreation program to more effectively respond to rapidly growing and changing recreation demand.

Multiple Use Water Management: Increased demand for CE project resources is not confined to recreation. Changing land use patterns and economic conditions have required that the CE reevaluate water management strategies for many river systems under the agency's jurisdiction. Droughts in the upper Midwest in the late 1980s led to an evaluation of Missouri River water management practices to give greater consideration to the effects of current operations on recreational use of CE reservoirs in Montana, North Dakota and South Dakota (USAE Missouri River Division, 1994). Similar comprehensive evaluation of water management practices associated with the Columbia River System (U.S. Department of Energy et al., 1994), and major river systems in Florida, Alabama and Georgia have focused attention on the implications of water management actions on recreational use of these systems and increased the awareness of the importance of maintaining effective techniques for monitoring recreational use of these systems.

Recreation User Fees: User fees are essential to finance the operation of CE managed recreation areas. Under current policies, fee revenues are used to offset federal operation and maintenance funding. The Omnibus Budget Reconciliation Act of 1993 (PL 103-66) authorized the CE to charge user fees for certain day use facilities. Prior to that time, user fees were confined to camping and group facilities. Fee revenues have increased in the past several years. In Fiscal Year 1996, the CE collected over $34 million, a 26 percent increase over 1995. These funds are returned to the CE for operation and maintenance activities.

Volunteer Program: The public has increasingly demonstrated personal support for the CE–recreation and natural resources program. In 1996 over 70,000 volunteers provided services valued at over $9 million in support of CE management activities. Volunteers participated in wide variety of activities including lake cleanup programs, tree planting, fish habitat, and environmental education projects.

Challenge Cost Share Program: Recent legislation provided an opportunity for the public to participate in support of CE programs. Section 225 of the Water Resource Development Act of 1992 authorized the Secretary of the Army to enter into cooperative agreements with non-federal public and private entities to provide support to CE recreation and natural resource management programs where facilities are being managed at complete federal expense. The policy, known as the A Challenge Cost Share Program, allows the CE to accept contributions of funds, materials, and services in conjunction with its program. By September 1996, 16 agreements had been signed under the program. Cost share partners have provided over $300,000 in funds, materials and services in addition to the $205 thousand contributed by the CE.

Summary for Army Corps of Engineers

Tourism has become a major industry both globally and nationally. Outdoor recreation resource management at Corps of Engineer lakes play a significant role in that industry. Corps lakes form the nucleus of the state park systems in some states. Recreation, a function of multipurpose water resource development which received little consideration a few years ago, is now an important purpose of these lakes. Recreation benefits to the public are now on par with or exceed benefits from the traditional functions of flood control or navigation. Recreation use continues to increase at a dramatic rate on many projects, while the natural resource base which supports it remains constant or slightly diminished as new demands for a variety of uses are placed on it. The CE recreation program faces significant challenges to respond to this intense recreation demand. Most recreation opportunities provided by the CE support water-based recreation activities which are projected to increase in the future. Technological innovations such as the introduction of personal watercraft will increase the complexity of managing recreation use to minimize conflict and maintain visitor safety and satisfaction.

In the future, visitors will continue to demand a high–quality recreation experience and value for the fees they pay. Managers will seek partnerships with public and private organizations to enhance recreation opportunities and increase public participation in the recreation program. Competition for water supplied by multiple–purpose water resource development projects in many parts of the country will increase in the future. This will require that the benefits, both monetary and non-monetary, of the CE recreation program be reassessed periodically in order to provide the information necessary to make tradeoffs between competing uses of water.

Tennessee Valley Authority[9]

The TVA was created in 1933 as one of President Roosevelt's New Deal programs. Its purpose was to improve environmental, social, and economic conditions in the Tennessee River watershed, an area which covers some 41,000 square miles and incorporates portions of seven Southeastern states. The primary mission assigned to TVA was to manage the Tennessee River and its tributaries to provide flood control, improve navigation, and generate hydroelectric power. To meet these three key objectives, TVA has developed a series of 28 multipurpose dams along 650 miles of the Tennessee River and its tributaries. These reservoirs, with a total of over 600,000 acres of surface water and 11,000 miles of shoreline, have become a major source for outdoor recreation in the region.

TVA established its Recreation Resources program in the late 1960s and began providing recreation improvements such as picnic facilities, boat ramps, access roads, and sanitary facilities. TVA's policy for outdoor recreation has been to encourage development by other public agencies and private investors, to reserve some land for wildlife management and hunting, to transfer appropriate forest land to the National Park Service and USDA Forest Service, and to manage its own recreation facilities along reservoir shorelines. TVA's undeveloped land above reservoir shorelines is open for picnicking, walking, and camping unless otherwise posted. The agency is also involved in trail development, mostly near its developed recreation areas and population centers, and operates a number of river access points for whitewater recreation.

All TVA resources are in the South. Overall, the TVA owns slightly more than a million acres of land and water (Table III.1). Approximately 440,000 land acres are open to the public for outdoor recreation, the large majority of this area is undeveloped. Only about 25,000 acres are actually in developed recreation areas, some managed by TVA and some by state and local government agencies. A 1992 TVA inventory showed their 25,000 acres being distributed across 164 recreation areas on 30 reservoirs. These areas provide facilities for boat launching, picnicking, bank fishing, swimming, hiking or walking, and camping. Another 228,000 acres (not shown in Table III.1) are leased to other federal agencies and to state, county, and municipal governments. Group camps, clubs, and an estimated 300 commercial recreation enterprises also lease a substantial portion of TVA land, although acreages are unknown. Further, the 1988 *TVA Handbook* listed 91 public access sites on 24 rivers and streams managed by TVA.

Unique among TVA resources is the 170,000-acre Land Between the Lakes (LBL) national recreation area in Kentucky and Tennessee.[10] LBL differs from other TVA resources in the amount of its natural resources devoted to outdoor recreation and environmental education, as well as in the level of services and facilities provided. LBL is operated under a multiple-use management philosophy. Facilities include a visitor center with planetarium, wildlife interpretive areas, a living history farm, a designated off-highway vehicle area, several campgrounds, lake access areas, and hiking and equestrian trails.

Due to decreases in federal appropriations, TVA has taken steps to reduce the scope of its recreation facilities management program. For example, TVA conveyed 14 of its developed recreation areas to other operators in 1996 to reduce costs. These arrangements are structured to ensure the facilities remain open and available to the general public, while at the same time giving alternative operators flexibility to manage areas to meet their needs and objectives. This situation has occurred at a time when recreation use pressures on the Tennessee River system appear to be increasing. Increases in general boating activity, fishing, informal recreation use of undeveloped TVA shoreline land, and the construction of private water use facilities associated with waterfront residential development are especially prominent trends. TVA strategies and initiatives which address the future of its Recreation Resources program include:

---

[9]Portions of this section were written by Robert A. Marker, Recreation Specialist, Tennessee Valley Authority.

[10]Although called a "National Recreation Area" by the TVA, LBL is not included among the specially designated National Recreation Areas managed by the FS, NPS, and BLM which are described later in this Chapter.

- Decreasing its role as a direct provider of recreation facilities and services. The current trend toward establishing partnerships with others to manage TVA recreation facilities is likely to continue. Establishment of additional user fees may also be considered to increase cost recovery at areas TVA continues to operate.
- Solicitation of new commercial recreation development at selected reservoir sites where recreation needs can be identified and private investment is determined to be feasible.
- A greater focus on the management of recreation use along undeveloped shorelines land to improve their quality and protect the resources. This will involve cooperative partnerships with other public agencies and volunteer groups.
- Increased cooperation with state boating agencies and other organizations to promote safe boating practices.
- Development and implementation of plans for guiding future construction of private residential water use facilities on the reservoir system.
- Seeking a greater degree of public input to ensure that public needs and values are considered in recreation and resource management planning.

National Oceanic and Atmospheric Administration

(By V. Robert Leeworthy, Senior Economist, National Oceanic and Atmospheric Administration, Silver Spring, MD)

NOAA is different from most other agencies that provide outdoor recreation opportunities. NOAA does not own recreation areas; however, the agency does directly manage 12 sites called National Marine Sanctuaries (Table III.3). Generally, NOAA does not provide facilities. Exceptions are the museum at the Monitor National Marine Sanctuary in North Carolina and the aquarium at the Monterey Bay National Marine Sanctuary in California, which NOAA partially funds. NOAA's primary mission is to provide scientific information to support management of the nation's coastal and ocean resources. NOAA's focus is primarily on natural resources that provide outdoor recreation opportunities. The agency directly and indirectly influences management of coastal and ocean resources through several programs described in the following sections. Because NOAA does not own any of the resources it manages, it is pioneering efforts in multi-jurisdictional, integrated management efforts. The National Marine Sanctuaries (NMS) are the only areas NOAA directly manages for outdoor recreation opportunities. The trends, issues, and directions the agency are facing are described with respect to these sanctuaries.

NOAA is organized into three major services: (1) the National Weather Service (NWS), (2) the National Marine Fisheries Service (NMFS), and (3) the National Ocean Service (NOS). Most are familiar with NWS local, regional, and national weather forecasts as well as hurricane tracking. The NWS provides invaluable information for planning outdoor recreation activities. The NMFS manages the nation's marine fisheries in cooperation with the states. NMFS establishes regulations in federal waters and works with the states through regional fishery management councils to develop fishery management plans and consistent regulations across jurisdictions (not always successful). NMFS manages the fishery resources for both commercial and recreational fisheries. The NOS provides both nautical and aeronautical charts that are important for recreational boating and flying. The NOS also houses the Office of Ocean and Coastal Resource Management (OCRM) and the Office of Ocean Resources Conservation and Assessment (ORCA). OCRM administers the Coastal Zone Management program, the National Estuarine Research Reserve System, and the National Marine Sanctuaries program. These programs form the core of NOAA management of coastal and ocean resources that support outdoor recreation. ORCA supports OCRM and other agencies by providing assessment services. For example, ORCA has had an interagency agreement since 1987 with the USDA Forest Service Outdoor Recreation and Wilderness Assessment Group to gather information and conduct economic analyses of outdoor recreational uses in coastal areas.

Table III.3: National Marine Sanctuaries Managed by the National Oceanic and Atmospheric Administration, 1997

Name	State	Area (Sq. Mi.)	Year Designated
Channel Islands	California	1,658	1980
Cordell Bank	California	526	1989
Fagatele Bay	American Samoa	0.25	1986
Florida Keys	Florida	3,674	1990
Flower Garden Banks	Texas/Louisiana	56	1992
Gray's Reef	Georgia	23	1981
Gulf of Farallones	California	1,255	1981
Hawaiian Islands Humpback Whale	Hawaii	1,300	1992
Monitor	North Carolina	1	1975
Monterey Bay	California	5,328	1992
Olympic Coast	Washington	3,310	1994
Jerry E. Studds Stellwagon Bank	Massachusetts	842	1992
Thunder Bay (proposed)	Michigan	—	—
Northwest Straits (proposed)	Washington	—	—
All Sanctuaries		17,973.25	

Source: National Oceanic and Atmospheric Administration. Office of Ocean Resources Conservation and Assessment.

The nation's coastal and ocean areas represent some of the most ecologically and economically important regions of the country. Congress recognized this in 1972 when it passed the Coastal Zone Management Act (CZMA) and the National Marine Sanctuaries Act. The CZMA created a partnership between OCRM and state and territorial governments. Day-to-day management decisions are made at the state level in 30 states and 21 individual national estuarine research reserves. OCRM field staff make day-to-day decisions in the 12 national marine sanctuaries.

These programs are greater than the sum of their parts. They represent national systems for the protection and management of critical coastal and ocean resources. OCRM provides the leadership necessary to support and enhance these national networks.

OCRM supports and encourages research and monitoring to answer management questions through the marine and estuarine protected area systems. OCRM also makes and influences national coastal and ocean policy: advocating for wetlands and coral reef protection, coastal hazard mitigation, nonpoint source pollution control, waterfront revitalization, and public access to the shore. OCRM ensures that federal agency decisions are consistent with state coastal management programs and coordinates with national estuarine research reserves and national marine sanctuaries. OCRM also uses national outreach and education campaigns to enhance public awareness and understanding of coastal and marine issues. Finally, OCRM shares its expertise through direct technical assistance to other countries to foster responsible ocean and coastal management globally.

NOAA's role and status in providing outdoor recreation opportunities is growing through its management of the nation's coastal and ocean resources. The National Marine Sanctuaries program continues to expand. In 1990, the Florida Keys National Marine Sanctuary (FKNMS) was designated. Prior to 1990, the Florida Keys contained two national marine sanctuaries: the Key Largo National Marine Sanctuary and the Looe Key National Marine Sanctuary. The two early sanctuaries existed entirely in federal waters and represented a relatively small portion of the entire Florida Keys. The newly created FKNMS includes all waters surrounding the Florida Keys, an area over 3,600 square miles. Thus, this new sanctuary encompasses multiple governmental jurisdictions requiring an integrated approach to management. Multiple jurisdictional sanctuaries are a new trend. The Monterey Bay National Marine Sanctuary (designated in 1992) and the Olympic Coast National Marine Sanctuary (designated in 1994) are multiple jurisdictional sanctuaries, as are the proposed Thunder Bay, located entirely in the Michigan state waters of Lake Huron, and the Northwest Straits Sanctuaries, located entirely in the Washington state waters of Puget Sound. The proposed Thunder Bay National Marine Sanctuary would be the first freshwater sanctuary. Also, the scope of the proposed Thunder Bay Sanctuary is currently limited to underwater cultural resources. Although this is similar to the Monitor National Marine Sanctuary, it expands the scope and direction of the sanctuary program. The Thunder Bay sanctuary will primarily serve the interests of recreational divers.

Three emerging concepts in natural resource management explain recent changes in the sanctuary program. The concepts of ecosystem management, sustainability or sustainable development, and integrated management have forced the agency into rethinking its management of natural resources. The National Marine Sanctuary program has become a testing ground for integrating these concepts into coherent management strategies. The recently approved management plan for the FKNMS reflects this integration.

Federal Water Resources and Facilities

The BoR, CE, and TVA are the primary federal water resource management agencies. Other federal agencies also have responsibility for a variety of water resources, including streams, rivers, lakes, bays, and estuaries. The FS, in particular, manages numerous streams, rivers, and lakes within its 191-million-acre National Forest System. Most National Wildlife Refuges are around bays, estuaries, rivers, or wetlands. The National Park Service has three types of management units—national rivers, national seashores, and national lakeshores—that focus on water resources, in addition to the multitude of water resources in the National Parks System. Two other types of water areas, National Recreation Areas and National Wild and Scenic Rivers, are also managed by federal agencies. These are covered in more detail in the next section on federal specially designated resources. The BLM has a surprising number of both river miles and water recreation facilities under its management.

Water resource settings attract visitors. Often, land-based recreation facilities, like campgrounds, picnic sites, and trails, are built near water features. A comprehensive inventory of all federal water resources is not available. Thus, it was not possible to assemble a table describing the total water acreage, river mileage, or number of water recreation facilities managed by the U.S. government. Instead, several statistics that serve as proxies are presented in Table III.4.

Table III.4: Acreage and Number of Selected Water-Based Federal Resources by Agency and Region, 1996

AGENCY AND TYPE OF RESOURCE	REGION (ACRES IN 1000S)				
	North	South	Rocky Mountains	Pacific Coast	U.S. Total
ARMY CORPS OF ENGINEERS					
Water acres	1,310.1	2,613.4	1,360.9	299.0	5,583.4
Number of boat ramps	303	1,408	185	87	1,983
Number of swimming areas	107	423	43	36	609
NATIONAL PARK SERVICE					
National River acres[1]	370.7	233.9	0	30.8	635.4
National Seashore/Lakeshore acres	315.3	435.1	0	71.1	821.5
Number units with swimming	35	59	24	38	156
Number units with boating	58	124	32	56	270
BUREAU OF RECLAMATION					
Water acres	0	93.5	1,195.9	395.5	1,684.9
Number sites with swimming[2]	0	11	107	70	188
Number sites with boating[2]	0	11	145	84	240
BUREAU OF LAND MANAGEMENT[3]					
Miles of floatable rivers managed	0	0	*	*	5,400
Boat ramps and access points	0	0	*	*	127
USDA FOREST SERVICE					
Number of boating sites[4]	474	262	385	226	1,347
Number of swimming sites[4]	107	99	66	36	308
FISH AND WILDLIFE SERVICE					
Number of Refuges with boating	35	84	44	31	194
Number of Refuges with fishing	48	83	48	35	214
Number of Refuges with hunting	43	83	67	49	242

Table III.4 Cont.

TENNESSEE VALLEY AUTHORITY					
Number of swimming beaches	0	59	0	0	59
Number of boat ramps	0	160	0	0	160

[1]Includes all NPS river-based units: National River and Recreation Area, Wild River, National Scenic River, National River, Scenic and Recreational River, National Scenic Riverway, National Recreational River, Wild and Scenic River. Only selected Wild and Scenic Rivers managed by the National Park Service are classified as NPS Units. This acreage reflects only those classified units.

[2]Includes all sites administered by BuRec. Only 44 of 308 sites nationally are actually managed by BuRec.

[3]Regional distribution of BLM water resources is not available by region (* denotes a number greater than zero). Except for a very small number of boating sites in the eastern states (shown as 0 in table), all resources are in the Rocky Mountains and Pacific Coast regions.

[4]Includes fee and non-fee sites managed by the Forest Service and its concessionaires.

Sources: Army Corps of Engineers, Natural Resources Management System, 1994.
National Park Service Statistical Abstract. 1995.
Bureau of Reclamation, Recreation Areas on Bureau Projects, 1992.
Bureau of Land Management, Recreation Management Information System, 1996.
USDA Forest Service: Site and Facilities Report, 1996.
U.S. Fish & Wildlife Service, National Wildlife Refuges: A Visitor's Guide, 1995.
Tennessee Valley Authority, "Development of TVA Recreation Facilities Cumulative through September 30, 1992."

U.S. Army Corps of Engineers

Water resources account for about 5.5 million of CE properties, or just under half of the total acreage managed by that agency (Table III.4). Almost half of CE water acreage is in the South. Comparatively few CE water resources are in the Pacific Coast region. Nationally, the Corps manages almost 2,000 boat ramps, most of which are in the South. The South also has almost 70 percent of the Corps' swimming areas. Few CE swimming areas are in the Rocky Mountain or Pacific Coast regions.

National Park Service

Nationwide, about 42 percent of the 369 NPS units provide swimming opportunities (Table III.4). Units with swimming areas are fairly evenly distributed across the four regions, with the most located in the South and the least in the Rocky Mountain region. Considerably more NPS units offer boating. The South region has more than twice as many units as any other region that offer boating opportunities and nearly half of the national total. Significant water resources that support a variety of recreational uses exist in nearly all of the national parks and many other NPS units. Some of the units have special water resource designations.

National rivers, seashores, and lakeshores are water-based outdoor recreation settings. Table III.4 shows the land and water acreage in these units. Almost 1.5 million acres nationwide are classified as national rivers, seashores, or lakeshores.[11] Over 95 percent of the 635,400 acres in 15 national rivers are located in the two Eastern regions. The only Western national river is the Alagnak Wild River in Alaska. Tennessee has the most national river acreage of any state with almost 100,000. Minnesota and Missouri rank next with over 80,000 national river acres each. Two national rivers—the Mississippi and the Big South Fork—are part of joint national river and recreation area units.[12] Only one national river, the Bluestone National River in West Virginia, has been established since 1987.

---

[11]"National River" is used here as a generic term which summarizes a variety of linear water resources in the NPS. These include the following classified units: National River and Recreation Area, Wild River, National Scenic River, National River, Scenic and Recreational River, National Scenic Riverway, National Recreational River, and Wild and Scenic River. Only selected Wild and Scenic Rivers managed by the National Park Service are classified as NPS Units. This acreage reflects only those classified units.

[12]These two areas are included in the National River analysis and not in the National Recreation Area data covered later in this chapter.

National seashore and lakeshore acreage is distributed similarly to national rivers. Thirteen of the 14 national seashore and national lakeshore units, comprising more than 90 percent of the acreage, are in the two Eastern regions. Only Point Reyes National Seashore in California is in the West. All four national lakeshores are in the North region along the Great Lakes. All but two of the Eastern national seashores are in the South, the two largest being the Gulf Islands in Florida and Mississippi, and Padre Island in Texas. The most recent national seashore or lakeshore designation was in 1975.

Bureau of Reclamation

The BoR manages about 1.7 million acres of water, roughly 25 percent of its total area (Table III.4). The large majority (86 percent) of the 308 recreation areas that BoR administers are leased. Even though it does not manage most of the areas, BoR's recreation areas brochure lists information about all sites. About 60 percent of the agency's recreation sites have facilities for swimming, while 78 percent offer boating. For both sets of sites, well over half are in the Rocky Mountain region, where most of the BoR property is located.

The Bureau of Reclamation is a major provider of water-based recreation facilities, including this boat ramp at Lake Berryessa, California.

Bureau of Land Management

The BLM manages a substantial number of river miles, many of which are highly valued for whitewater recreation. The Arkansas Headwaters State Recreation Area in Colorado, jointly managed with the Colorado Division of Parks and Outdoor Recreation, is one example. In total, the BLM manages more than 5,400 miles of floatable rivers and 125 boat access sites (Table III.4). The regional distribution of these resources was not available. The BLM estimates that it manages approximately 174,000 miles of fishable streams and 2.6 million acres of lakes and reservoirs.

USDA Forest Service

Thousands of lakes and numerous river headwaters are in the national forests. The FS keeps data on the number of recreation sites that offer boating and swimming facilities, both those that charge fees and those that do not (Table III.4). More than four times as many areas offer boating than swimming opportunities. These are relatively evenly distributed across the four regions. Of the boating sites, about 35 percent are in the North, followed by 29 percent in the Rocky Mountains. About two-thirds of swimming sites are in the

Eastern regions. The Rocky Mountain region has a relatively smaller share of swimming sites and the Pacific Coast region has just 12 percent of all agency swimming sites. FS data show an 11 percent gain in boating sites since 1992. Swimming areas declined by five percent during the same period.

Dyar Pasture Waterfowl Area in Greene County, Georgia is a migratory bird habitat area sponsored collaboratively by the USDA Forest Service, the Georgia Department of Natural Resources, Ducks Unlimited, and Georgia Power Company. Photo courtesy of Cassandra Y. Johnson.

U.S. Fish and Wildlife Service

The FWS does not keep a database of the water-based sites available for public recreation on national wildlife refuges. However, refuge acreage is an indicator of water-based recreation opportunities, since most refuges are along coastal waters, wetlands, and flyways. Acreage in the National Wildlife Refuge System is presented in Table III.1 (p. 41). Information in the National Wildlife Refuge *Visitor's Guide* indicates whether a refuge is open for boating, fishing, or hunting. Of the 319 refuges open for public use, 61 percent allow boating, two-thirds allow fishing, and three-fourths allow hunting. The two Western regions have more refuges open for hunting than for either boating or fishing. In the North, more refuges are open for fishing. The large majority of Southern refuges allow all three uses.

Tennessee Valley Authority

Most TVA acreage is associated with water-based recreation. A 1992 TVA report indicates the agency has 59 swimming beaches and 160 boat ramps, all in the South (Table III.4). This total includes only a few of the water-based sites leased by the TVA to other government bodies, group camps, clubs, and commercial providers.[13]

---

[13]Some, but only a few, of the recreation areas listed in the TVA report "Development of TVA Recreation Facilities Cumulative Through September 30, 1992" are areas leased to State, county and municipal governments. This list is incomplete compared to information in the 1988 TVA Handbook. The handbook describes 118 public parks, 455 public access areas and roadside parks, 55 group camps and clubs, and 298 commercial recreation areas on land leased from the TVA. Since these data are somewhat dated as of 1997, this situation has undoubtedly changed.

Nationwide Rivers Inventory

The Nationwide Rivers Inventory (NRI) is a listing of free-flowing, undeveloped river segments with outstanding wild, scenic, or recreation potential. Begun in 1982, the NRI database is compiled and maintained by the NPS. As of 1995, there were 3,377 river segments in the NRI totaling almost 85,000 miles (Table III.5).[14] The NRI was developed as a result of the National Wild and Scenic Rivers Act of 1968 and executive directives that require each federal agency to avoid or mitigate adverse effects on rivers identified by the NRI. River segments identified by the NRI do not include designated wild and scenic rivers but represent potential additions.[15] NRI river segments are important resources for whitewater and dispersed recreation. Some 191 river segments were added to the NRI in 1995 from a few state government river assessments. All other segments in the database were identified by the FS, NPS, or BLM.

NRI river segments are identified by their outstanding values. Types of values include scenic, recreational, geologic, fish, wildlife, historic, cultural, and other. Figure III.1 shows U.S. counties with one or more NRI river segments with outstanding resource values. Mileage for all NRI river segments and for each value individually (except 'other') are presented in Table III.5. By comparison, the U.S. total mileage of outstanding river segments identified by the NRI miles is almost eight times the 10,816 river miles formally protected as designated national Wild and Scenic Rivers.

Table III.5: Miles of Outstanding River Segments by Recreational or Amenity Value and Region, 1995

Recreational or Amenity Value	Region				
	North	South	Rocky Mountains	Pacific Coast	U.S. Total
Scenic	15,035	21,491	13,894	8,661	59,081
Recreational	17,227	21,834	10,012	7,458	56,531
Fish	9,405	18,591	10,849	9,857	48,702
Wildlife	5,496	19,225	9,403	5,690	39,814
Geologic	6,672	14,685	8,618	4,585	34,560
Historic	5,606	12,064	4,121	2,795	24,586
Cultural	1,746	9,916	5,389	2,391	19,442
All Values[1]	27,843	24,378	16,631	15,803	84,655

[1]Mileage for the various values is not additive because river segments may have more than one value.

Source: Nationwide Rivers Inventory. National Park Service. 1993. Additional river segments (191) were added to the database in 1995.

[14]Seventy-three river segments are located in two states, with each state having a record for its segment. Therefore, the database actually has 3,450 separate records.

[15]The National Wild and Scenic River System is described in the next section on specially designated federal resource systems.

Figure III.1: Counties with Rivers Having Outstanding Resource Values Identified by the Nationwide Rivers Inventory, 1995[16]

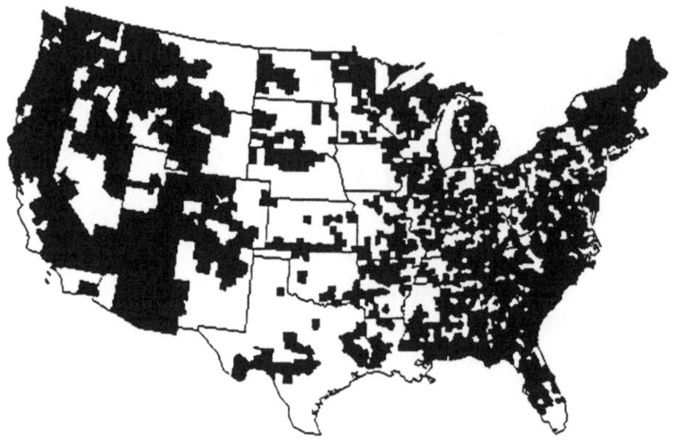

Source: Nationwide Rivers Inventory. National Park Service. 1993. Additional river segments (191) were added to the database in 1995.

There are considerably more NRI miles listed in the two Eastern regions. The North has the most river miles overall (almost one-third of the U.S. total), followed by the South, the Rocky Mountains and the Pacific Coast. Alaska is the leader among the states, with 4,507 miles. Michigan, Washington, Oregon, New York, California, and North Carolina each have more than 3,000 miles of outstanding rivers.

Most rivers listed have more than one outstanding value. Nationally, just under 70 percent of river miles have scenic value, and two-thirds have recreation value. Fish values are attributed to more than half the river miles and wildlife values to just under half. Geologic, historic, and cultural values are relatively less common, both nationally and in each of the four regions. Scenic values are most common for segments in the South and Rocky Mountain regions. Nearly 90 percent of river miles in the South were also classified as having recreation value. In the North, about three-fifths of river miles were judged to be important for recreation. It appears that in the South most river segments were assigned both scenic and recreation values. The South also has the highest percentage of river miles with wildlife values. The Pacific Coast is the only region where the most common value was something other than scenic or recreation. Fish values were present in 62 percent of rivers in this region, reflecting the importance of salmon and other anadromous fish.

Almost 35 percent of the NRI river segments were added to the inventory in either 1993 or 1995, representing just under 20 percent of total miles nationally. This increase probably represents movement toward completing the inventory. While some rivers may have increased in quality enough now to qualify as outstanding, other rivers likely have declined since first inventoried in 1982. Only about 23 percent of the river segments originally cataloged in 1982 were updated for the 1993 database.

Specially Designated Federal Systems

Some federal land is specially designated as part of federal systems with special recreation values. These systems include the National Wilderness Preservation System, National Recreation Areas, National Trails, and National Wild and Scenic Rivers. Wilderness and Wild and Scenic Rivers contain some of America's most wild and undeveloped areas. National Scenic and Historic trails within the National Trails System preserve significant scenic and recreational corridors as well as important parts of the nation's heritage. National Recreation Trails (NRT) are shorter, but significant trail resources, especially near urban areas. National Recreation Areas are a diverse group of resources ranging from pristine areas in Alaska to more developed, urban sites. All NRAs are managed primarily for their recreation and amenity values.

[16]Due to space constraints, none of the U.S. maps depicted in this chapter shows Alaska and Hawaii.

Historians describe a third wave of the conservation movement that commenced in the Kennedy Administration after the Outdoor Recreation Resources Review Commission (ORRRC). The 1962 ORRRC report to Congress spawned a variety of specially designated federal systems. The Wilderness Act (1964), the Wild and Scenic Rivers Act (1968), and the National Trails System Act (1968) were all heavily influenced by the ORRRC findings. National recreation areas (NRA) are technically not a system, but a policy circular written by the Recreation Advisory Council in 1963 spelled out the concept of an NRA and communicated this to Congress and the federal land-managing agencies. As a result, various pieces of legislation were passed in the 1960s and 1970s designating several NRAs.

Wilderness and wild and scenic river designations are governed by special criteria, so their establishment depends on unique natural features. On the other hand, many, if not most,of the NRTs and NRAs have been established under the philosophy of making federal recreation resources available to the general population. Zinser (1995) provided an excellent comprehensive summary of these systems. Here, these four systems and changes since the late 1980s are briefly described. In addition to designated wild and scenic rivers, also described is the Nationwide Whitewater Inventory conducted by the American Whitewater Affiliation.

National Wilderness Preservation System

Upon passage of the Wilderness Act in 1964, 54 Forest Service primitive areas became units of the National Wilderness Preservation System (NWPS). All but four of these areas were in the West. The system quadrupled in size when the Alaska National Interest Lands Conservation Act of 1980 added 56 million acres (Figure III.2). Designated Wilderness is not "new" federal land, rather Wilderness represents redesignation. Since 1980, growth has been modest, except in 1984 and 1994. In 1984, 21 Wilderness bills added 7.3 million acres to the NWPS, many in Eastern states. The California Desert Protection Act of 1994 added nearly 7.5 million acres, split among the NPS, FS, and BLM. Roughly 3.16 million acres were designated as Wilderness in the Death Valley National Park, some transferred from the BLM and the remainder from the former Death Valley National Monument.

Figure III.2: Acreage Added to the National Wilderness Preservation System by Year, 1964-1994

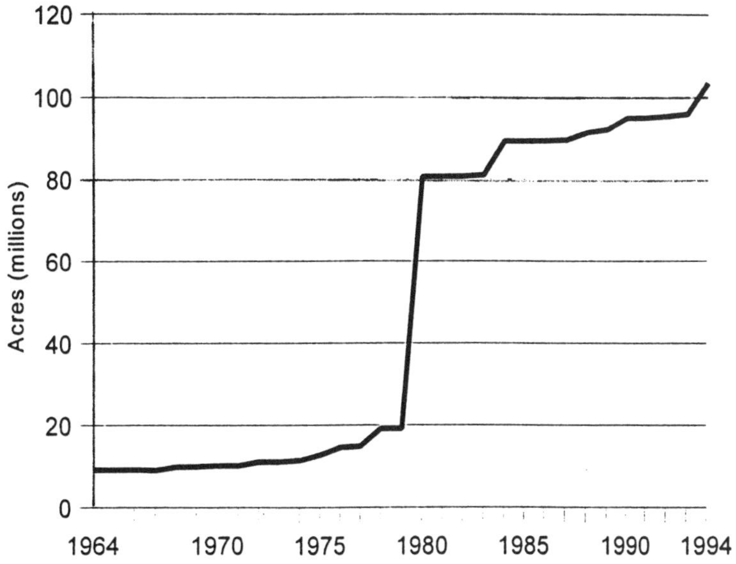

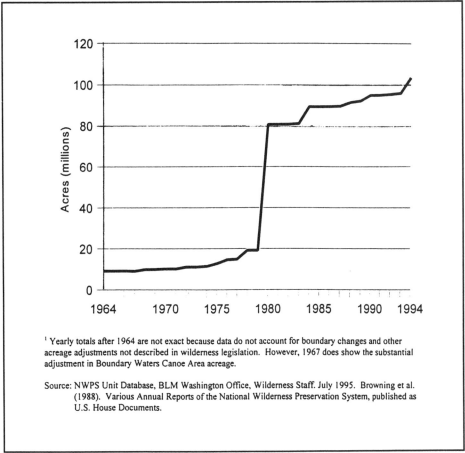

[1] Yearly totals after 1964 are not exact because data do not account for boundary changes and other acreage adjustments not described in wilderness legislation. However, 1967 does show the substantial adjustment in Boundary Waters Canoe Area acreage.

Source: NWPS Unit Database, BLM Washington Office, Wilderness Staff. July 1995. Browning et al. (1988). Various Annual Reports of the National Wilderness Preservation System, published as U.S. House Documents.

In mid-1995, the NWPS consisted of about 103.6 million acres in 630 units, most in the West. Almost one out of six federal acres (16 percent), or about 4.5 percent of the total U.S. land area, is in the NWPS. The two Western regions contain 96 percent of the system with just under 100 million acres (Table III.6). Alaska alone accounts for 57.4 of the 99.5 million Western Wilderness acres. All but about six million acres of Alaska Wilderness is managed by either the NPS or the FWS. Removing Alaska from the analysis, the West still contains over 91 percent of NWPS acreage, or 42.1 of the 46.2 million acres of non-Alaska Wilderness (Figure III.3). This distribution essentially mirrors the distribution of federal land in the United States.

Despite the uneven distribution of Wilderness acreage, only six states—Connecticut, Delaware, Iowa, Kansas, Maryland, and Rhode Island—have no designated Wilderness acreage. California has the most NWPS units of any state (130), followed by Arizona (89), Alaska (49), and Colorado (40). Units range in size from the 9.1-million-acre Wrangell-St. Elias Wilderness in Alaska to the 6-acre Pelican Island Wilderness in Florida and the 6-acre Birch Islands Unit Wilderness in Maine. Upon its 1994 designation, the Death Valley Wilderness in California, with about 3.2 million acres, supplanted the 2.4 million acre Frank Church-River of No Return Wilderness in Idaho as the largest unit in the contiguous States.

The NPS manages the greatest number of Wilderness acres, 43 million, almost 42 percent of the system total (Table III.6). All but 2.3 million of these acres, however, are in Alaska. The FS manages nearly two-thirds of the NWPS acreage outside of Alaska. Currently, there are about 5.2 million acres of BLM wilderness, 90 percent of which has been added since 1987 (Table III.6). The BLM has also recommended that 336 wilderness study areas comprising 9.5 million acres be added to the NWPS (U.S. GAO 1993).

Table III.6: Increase in Designated Area, 1987-1995 and Current Area, 1995, of National Wilderness Preservation System by Federal Agency and Region

Agency	Region (1000 acres)									
	North		South		Rocky Mountains		Pacific Coast[1]		U.S. Total	
	Increase	Current	Increase	Current	Increase	Current	Increase	Current	Increase	Current
USDA Forest Service	40.5	1,307.2	78.4	692.2	1,273.3	17,890.1	830.9	14,780.3	2,223.1	34,669.8
National Park Service	0	133.4	15.0	1,462.8	0	693.2	5,606.2	40,718.0	5,621.2	43,007.4
Fish & Wildlife Service	0	63.5	0	470.2	1,343.4	1,464.8	9.0	18,686.8	1,352.4	20,685.3
Bureau of Land Management	0	0	0	0	1,178.6	1,626.0	3,573.5	3,601.0	4,752.1	5,227.0
All Agencies	40.5	1,504.1	93.4	2,625.2	3,795.3	21,674.1	10,019.6	77,786.1	13,948.8	103,589.5

[1]Alaska accounts for 57.4 million of the Pacific Coast's 77.8 million acres. Agency breakdown is: FS, 5.7 million; NPS, 33.0 million; FWS, 18.7 million.

Source: NWPS Unit Database, BLM Washington Office, Wilderness Staff. July 1995.

Figure III.3: National Wilderness Preservation System Acreage by State, 1995

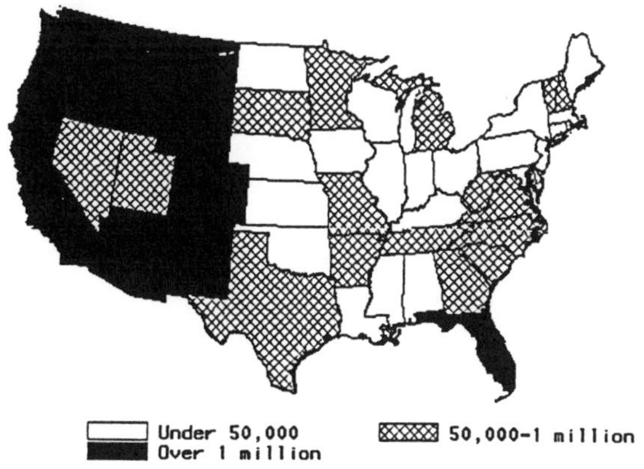

Source: NWPS Unit database, BLM Washington Office, Wilderness Staff. July 1995.

Other changes to the NWPS since 1987 are noted in Table III.6. Nearly 14 million acres have been added, an increase of about 16 percent.[17] The NPS and the BLM accounted for 10.4 of the 14 million added acres. About 7.5 million acres of these additions came in the 1994 California Desert Protection Act. Two other years, 1988 and 1990, also saw substantial additions to the system. In 1988, 1.8 million acres of NPS and FS land were designated, most of it in large parcels in the Mount Ranier, Olympic, and North Cascades National Parks. About 2.8 million acres of FS, BLM, and FWS land were added to the NWPS in 1990. Since 1987, each of the four land-managing agencies has increased its Wilderness acreage by more than 1 million acres. Only about 134,000 acres, one percent of the additions since 1987, occurred in the two Eastern regions (Figure III.4).

Figure III.4: Growth in National Wilderness Preservation System Acreage by State, 1987-1995

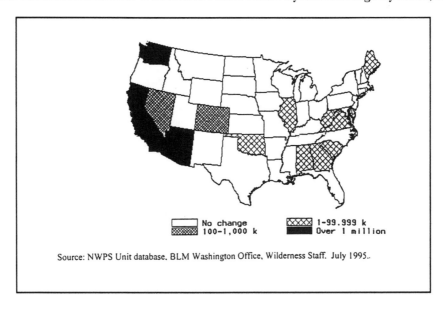

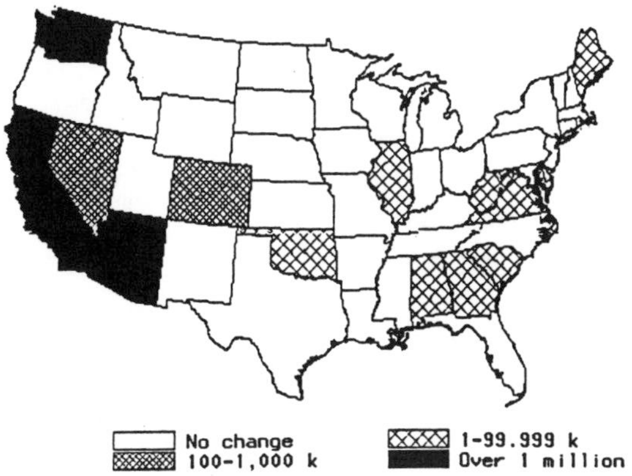

Source: NWPS Unit database, BLM Washington Office, Wilderness Staff. July 1995..

[17]According to David Brown, Executive Director, America Outdoors, there is concern among some outdoor recreation outfitters that recent changes in federal policy have given individual agency managers of Wilderness areas too much autonomy to the extent some are unfairly restricting access to organized outfitters and their expeditions.

National Recreation Areas

National Recreation Areas (NRA) are not a legislatively defined system. Nevertheless, they are very important special federal areas for outdoor recreation. The NRAs are diverse, but their unifying characteristic is that they "warrant management which is clearly *different* from the general thrust of the National Park or National Forest Systems" (Shands, 1990). The NPS focus on preservation and the FS and BLM policies of multiple-use are de-emphasized in NRAs to allow more intensive management for recreation. NRAs are the only category of NPS units, or of specially designated FS and BLM areas, with the word "recreation" in their title.

Most NRAs are primarily water-based. Lake Mead was designated as the first NRA in 1936, followed by Coulee Dam in 1946, and Glen Canyon in 1958. In 1963 the Recreation Advisory Council of the Bureau of Outdoor Recreation wrote executive branch guidelines describing the selection, establishment, and administration of NRAs. Two of the guidelines were that NRAs be located within easy driving distance of large populations and be able to accommodate large numbers of people. Eleven NRAs were established during the 1960s. Starting in 1972, Congress authorized the first urban NRA gateway in New York City. Four more urban NRAs were designated during the 1970s in the Cleveland, Atlanta, San Francisco, and Los Angeles metropolitan areas.

Most of the urban NRAs provide public access to water or, in the case of Los Angeles, water and mountains. Urban NRAs tend to be a mixture of public and private land managed under a federal umbrella by means of easements, land-use controls, and access agreements. For example, the Chattahoochee River NRA in Atlanta is actually 14 separate parks along a 48-mile stretch of river. A 1988 symposium on NRAs sponsored by the NPS and FS suggested this arrangement as a model for future NRAs (USDA Forest Service, 1990). This suggestion appears to have been borne out in the Boston Harbor Islands NRA, designated in 1996. This NRA consists of 31 islands totaling about 1,200 acres, none federally owned. The islands are owned by eight separate entities, and the entire system is to be coordinated under NPS' management. The 13-member Boston Harbor Islands Partnership will include representatives of the NPS, the U.S. Coast Guard, and various state, local, and private agencies. In addition, an even broader-based advisory council will help set management direction and policy (Poole, 1997).

There are 38 NRAs nationwide, 17 managed by the FS, 19 managed by the NPS, one managed by the BLM, and one (Whiskeytown-Shasta-Trinity NRA in California) managed jointly by the NPS and FS. Together, these areas make up over 7.0 million acres of federal land (Table III.7). An additional half-million acres within the NRAs are not federally owned, but much of it is open for public use through agreements with landowners. Most NRAs are located in the western United States. The NPS manages just under half of all NRA acres, most located within the Lake Mead and Glen Canyon NRAs in Nevada, Arizona, and Utah. The only area managed by the BLM is the largely undeveloped one-million-acre White Mountains NRA in Alaska.

Table III.7: Increase in Acreage, 1987-1995 and current acreage, 1995, of Federal Land in National Recreation Areas by Agency and Region

Agency	Region (1000 acres)									
	North		South		Rocky Mountains		Pacific Coast		U.S. Total	
	Increase	Current	Increase	Current	Increase	Current	Increase	Current	Increase	Current
USDA Forest Service	13.0	129.7	49.0	167.6	312.7	1,464.3	305.2	918.3	679.9	2,679.8
National Park Service	2.1	96.3	0	116.4	0	2,773.2	0	366.7	2.1	3,352.7
Bureau of Land Management	0	0	0	0	0	0	0	1,000.0	0	1,000.0
All Agencies	15.1	226.0	49.0	284.0	312.7	4,237.5	305.2	2,285.0	682.0	7,032.5

Source: Land Areas of the National Forest System. As of September 1995.
National Park Service Statistical Abstract. 1995.

Since 1987, about 682,000 acres have been newly designated as NRAs, about an 11 percent increase (Table III.7). All but 2,100 of these acres are managed by the FS. The only new NRA managed by the NPS is the Gauley River NRA in West Virginia. New FS NRAs include Winding Stair Mountain (Oklahoma), Grand Island (Michigan), Smith River (California), Ed Jenkins (Georgia), and Spring Mountain (Nevada). Smith River and Spring Mountain are each larger than 300,000 acres and together make up most of the new NRA acreage since 1987.

Wisconsin's 1,000-mile Ice Age National Scenic Trail winds through terminal moraine left by the great Wisconsin Glacier over 10,000 years ago. Pine trees shroud this section of the trail located in the Chequamegon National Forest. Photo courtesy of Ice Age Park & Trail Foundation.

National Trails System (NTS)

The National Trails System Act was passed by Congress in 1968 to assist the Appalachian Trail and to establish a national system of trails. Most trails on federal land are not officially a part of the NTS.[18] However, trails in the NTS represent significant and special outdoor recreation resources. Three different types of National Trails make up the NTS.[19] *National Historic Trails* help to preserve the nation's heritage by telling the story of exploration, migration, and military action in the United States. Designation of these trails is as much for symbolism as for the limited protection provided for in the Trails Act. National historic trails generally consist of remnant sites and trail segments. They are not continuous paths in the traditional sense. The purpose is to preserve the integrity of significant travel corridors and routes in U.S. history. Of course, historical and cultural interpretation are central to these trail routes. Many related facilities typically surround the historic trails, including visitor centers, walking trails, and water resources.

In 1997 there were 12 designated national historic trails, all but two managed by the NPS. The brochure *National Trails System Map and Guide*, published by the NPS, provides a summary of each trail, its history, and the attractions found along the trail route. Of the 12 trails, four have been authorized since 1990: Juan Bautista de Anza (1990), California (1992), Pony Express (1992), and Selma-to-Montgomery (1996).

National Scenic Trails (NST) provided the impetus for creating the NTS. These trails preserve outstanding recreation opportunities along nationally significant scenic, historic, natural, and cultural corridors. As the name implies, the emphasis is on scenery. Three of the trails follow the ridges of the major U.S.

---

[18]Unfortunately, an accurate inventory of all federal trails is nearly impossible. In fact, most federal agencies struggle to keep their own information centralized and current. Certainly, individual management units such as FS districts or NPS units know what exists within their management areas, but coordinating and updating all of the information into a single Federal trails database has proven to be exceedingly difficult.

[19]This does not include *connecting* or *side trails* which are included in the legislation as eligible to be included in the system. Their purpose is to provide access to the three main designated trail types. *National Historic Trails* were not added to the system until separate legislation was passed in 1978.

mountain ranges. The great length of the NSTs is another important quality, making the trails accessible to millions of people throughout the country. There are currently eight NSTs, three administered by the FS and five by the NPS. Forest Service NSTs include the Continental Divide, Florida, and Pacific Crest. National Park Service NSTs are the Appalachian, Ice Age, Natchez Trace, North Country, and Potomac Heritage.

Only the Appalachian Trail and Pacific Crest Trail are continuous footpaths. The Appalachian Trail totals 2,157 miles, only 44 of which remain unprotected and not publicly owned. Just 30 miles of the Pacific Crest's 2,638 mile length are unprotected. No new NSTs have been designated since 1987, but activity continues on all trails to complete sections and acquire land or easements. For example, a partnership was formed in 1996 between the NPS and the American Hiking Society to strengthen planning and trail development efforts along the Potomac Heritage Trail corridor. Although not continuous, the other six trails have long stretches open to public use, including 795 miles on the Continental Divide trail and the 184-mile Chesapeake and Ohio Canal towpath on the Potomac Heritage Trail. The NTS Map and Guide provides a description of each trail with total miles designated and an approximation of the mileage open for public use.

A significant development in the NTS occurred in 1992 when Congress authorized the secretary of the interior to study the feasibility of adding the *American Discovery Trail* (ADT). Originally conceived in the early 1980s by the American Hiking Society and *Backpacker* magazine, the trail would serve as an East-West connecting link across the United States. The proposed trail would help connect urban and rural areas, increase accessibility to the National Trails System in urban areas, and provide for bicycle and equestrian transportation, in addition to foot travel.

One recommendation to Congress is that the National Trails System Act be amended to create a new trail designation called "National Discovery Trails" (USDI National Park Service, 1996b). This new designation would have the primary purpose of connecting with other trails and would allow the discovery trails to be located alongside roads to preserve their continuity. The proposed general corridor for the ADT would be more than 6,350 miles long, extending from the San Francisco Bay area to coastal Delaware (USDI National Park Service, 1996c). The trail would split into Northern and Southern legs at Denver and rejoin in Cincinnati. American Discovery Trail legislation pased the Senate in July, 1998, but was still awaiting action by the House of Representatives as of that date.

National Recreation Trails (NRT) are by far the most numerous. Their distinction lies in their variety and proximity to urban areas. The Trails Act also allowed designation of NRTs in relatively remote scenic areas. The secretaries of the interior and agriculture were given authority to designate NRTs without congressional approval. Favorable publicity, community benefits, and added protection were three reasons cited by supporters of the act why resource managers might apply for NRT designation. A recent study of NRTs said that it is difficult to assess whether NRT designation has resulted in those intended benefits (Tynon, Chavez, & Harding, 1997).

A total of 821 trails in the United States are currently designated as NRTs, about 65 percent of which are federally managed. The remaining 35 percent are managed by a variety of nonfederal public and private entities. NRTs include river routes, historic tours, and a cave trail, in addition to traditional footpaths. Some urban multi-use trails and heavily-used nature trails are paved. NRTs can accommodate hiking, bicycling, horseback riding, interpretive use, disabled access, snowmobiling, cross-country skiing, and motorized water-based uses.

There are just under 10,000 NRT miles in the United States, fairly evenly distributed nationally (Table III.8). Federal agencies manage over half of the trail mileage with much higher proportions in the West. In the North, more than 80 percent of trail miles are managed by nonfederal entities, and in the South the percentage of nonfederal trails is about 40 percent. Over 1,400 miles have been designated as NRTs since 1987, but 179 trail miles dropped their NRT designation for a net increase of 1,229 miles (Table III.8). More than 70 percent of the net gain occurred in the North. Nearly 800 miles were added between 1993 and late 1995, including a 100-mile trail in Maryland, a 150-mile trail in Washington state, and the 410-mile U.S. Route 6 Grand Army of the Republic highway trail in Pennsylvania.

Table III.8: Net Increase in Miles, 1987-1995, of National Recreation Trails by Type of Managing Agency and Region

Type of Agency	North		South		Rocky Mountains		Pacific Coast		U.S. Total	
	Increase	Current	Increase	Current	Increase	Current	Increase	Current	Increase	Current
Federal	20	539	-74	1,479	33	2,021	128	1,546	107	5,585
State	740	1,016	37	400	5	84	205	286	987	1,786
Local	98	783	0	279	0	192	7	202	105	1,456
Other[1]	25	706	0	304	0	146	5	6	30	1,162
All Agencies	883	3,044	-37	2,462	38	2,443	345	2,040	1,229	9,989

[1]Other includes various private corporations and foundations as well as non-profit and other semi-public organizations and associations.

Source: Register of National Recreation Trails. Washington D.C.: U.S. Department of the Interior. January 1993. Also, Update of National Recreation Trails Designated by the Secretary of the Interior. January 1, 1993 through October 1, 1995.

Walking and hiking are the dominant allowable uses on NRTs (Table III.9). More than 90 percent of trail miles nationwide are suitable for foot travel. The next largest category is horseback riding, which are permitted by 37.5 percent of NRTs. The two Western regions, which are dominated by rural and federal trails, allow considerably more horse use than the more urban Eastern trails. Five times as many miles in the North are designated for bicycle use as in any other region. Only the South has disabled access on more than 10 percent of trail miles. Surprisingly, the South has no NRT miles suitable for motorized use. Interpretive trail uses are very modest in all regions, but they are most common in the North. Winter use trail mileage is most prevalent in the North and Rocky Mountain Regions.

Table III.9: Total Miles and Percentage of National Recreation Trails by Type of Trail Use Allowed and Region, 1993[1]

Type of use allowed[2]	North	South	Rocky Mountains	Pacific Coast	U.S. Total
Foot	2,419 (96.3)	2,218 (88.1)	2,213 (90.7)	1,753 (91.8)	8,603 (91.7)
Bicycling	1,356 (54.0)	199 (7.9)	219 (9.0)	207 (10.9)	1,981 (21.1)
Access for disabled	171 (6.8)	273 (10.8)	105 (4.3)	82 (4.3)	631 (6.7)
Horseback riding	508 (20.2)	259 (10.3)	1,548 (63.5)	1,200 (62.9)	3,515 (37.5)
Interpretive	126 (5.0)	10 (0.4)	24 (1.05)	37 (1.9)	197 (2.1)
Motorized	576 (22.9)	0 (0.0)	641 (26.3)	526 (27.6)	1,743 (18.6)
Water-based	205 (8.1)	291 (11.6)	27 (1.1)	156 (8.2)	679 (7.2)
Snowmobiling	798 (31.7)	34 (1.3)	550 (22.5)	141 (7.4)	1,523 (16.2)
Cross-country skiing	888 (35.3)	38 (1.5)	608 (24.9)	281 (14.7)	1,815 (19.4)

[1]Trail miles are not additive across uses due to multiple uses allowed on most trails. Table does not include 14 new trails designated since 1993 because use information was not available. Percentages are based on regional and national trail miles with known allowable uses: North, 2,512; South, 2,518; Rocky Mountains, 2,439; Pacific Coast, 1910; U.S. Total, 9,378.

[2]One trail, the 1.2 mile Horsethief Cave Trail in Wyoming, is designated for underground use.

Source: Register of National Recreation Trails. Washington, D.C. Department of the Interior. January 1993.

National Wild and Scenic Rivers

The Wild and Scenic Rivers Act passed in Congress on the same day in 1968 as the National Trails System Act. The former act states that certain selected rivers of the United States,

> which with their immediate environments, possess outstandingly remarkable scenic, recreational, geologic, fish and wildlife, historic, cultural, or other similar values, shall be preserved in free-flowing condition, and that they and their immediate environments shall be protected for the benefit and enjoyment of present and future generations.

The act has helped preserve the availability of whitewater recreation resources in many parts of the country. Wild and Scenic River (WSR) segments are classified into one of three types:

(1) *wild*—free of impoundments and generally inaccessible except by trail; shorelines essentially primitive; represent "vestiges of primitive America."

(2) *scenic*—free of impoundments; shorelines largely primitive and undeveloped, but accessible in places by roads.

(3) *recreational*—readily accessible by road or railroad; may have some development along shorelines; may have undergone some impoundment or diversion in the past.

Several rivers in the system have more than one classification type. One WSR may also be managed by more than one agency or managing body. As of November 1996, the WSR system consisted of 154 river segments totaling 10,816 miles (Table III.10). Thirty-seven states throughout the United States have WSR mileage (Figure III.5). Five rivers form the borders between states—St. Croix (MN and WI), Snake (ID and OR), Missouri (NE and SD), Upper Delaware (NY and PA), Middle Delaware (NJ and PA), and Chattooga (SC and GA). The Western regions of the country contain more than 75 percent of the WSR system mileage. Alaska accounts for about 30 percent of the system, followed by California with 17 percent, and Oregon with 16 percent. Together, mileage within these three states comprises almost two-thirds of the WSR system.

Table III.10: Increase in Miles of Rivers in the National Wild and Scenic River System by Agency and Region, 1987-1996

Agency	Region									
	North		South		Rocky Mountains		Pacific Coast		U.S. Total	
	Increase	**Current**	**Increase**	**Current**	**Increase**	**Current**	**Increase**	**Current**	**Increase**	**Current**
USDA Forest Service	687	820	276	377	55	961	939	2,189	1,957	4,347
National Park Service	200	561	0	237	143	214	0	1,434	343	2,446
Fish & Wildlife Service	0	0	0	0	0	0	0	1,043	0	1,043
Bureau of Land Management	0	0	0	0	34	227	621	1,806	655	2,033
State Agencies	146	391	11	45	0	0	0	442	157	878
Other[1]	0	0	5	5	0	0	0	65	5	70
All Agencies	1,033	1,772	292	664	232	1,402	1,560	6,979	3,117	10,817

[1]*Other* includes the U.S. Army Corps of Engineers (1 river segment) and the Hoopa Valley and Round Valley Indian Reservations in California (3 river segments).

Source: River Mileage Classifications For Components of the National Wild and Scenic Rivers System. National Park Service, Division of Park Planning and Special Studies. November 1996.

Figure III.5: Miles of National Wild and Scenic Rivers by State, 1996

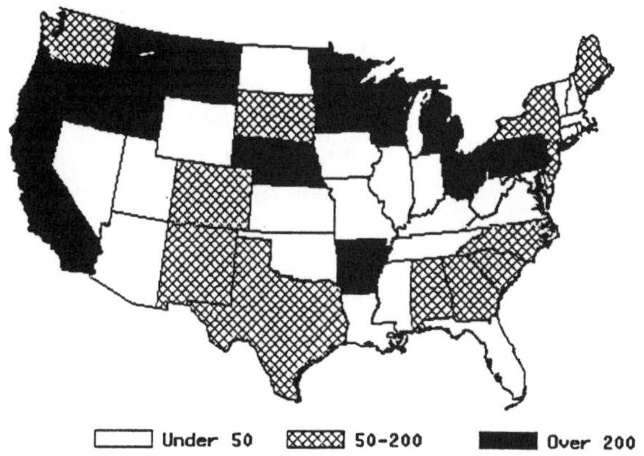

Source: National Park Service. Division of Park Planning and Special Studies. River mileage classifications for components of the National Wild and Scenic Rivers System. November 1996.

More WSR miles are managed by the FS (40 percent of the system total) than any other agency. Next is the NPS with 23 percent and BLM with 19 percent. The FWS, state agencies, the CE, and two Indian tribes also manage WSRs. The system has grown an impressive 40 percent since 1987 (Table III.10). Just under half of this growth was in Oregon. Other states with significant growth since 1987 include Michigan, Arkansas, Nebraska, Pennsylvania, and New Jersey (Figure III.6).

Figure III.6: Miles of National Wild and Scenic Rivers Added Between 1987 and 1996, by State

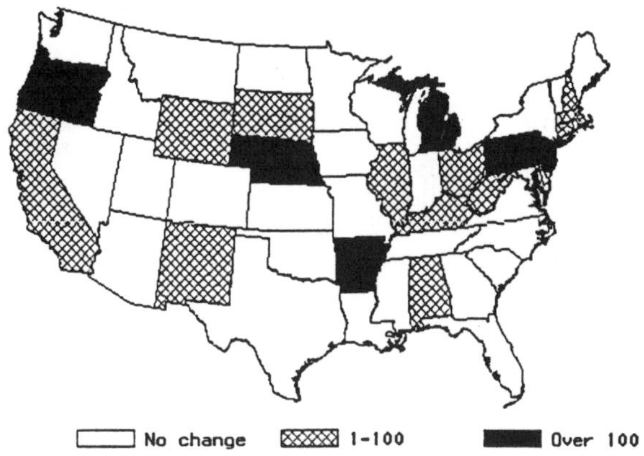

Source: National Park Service. Division of Park Planning and Special Studies. River mileage classifications for components of the National Wild and Scenic Rivers System. November 1996.

Just under half (48 percent) of the WSRs are classified as *wild*, followed by *recreational* (30 percent) and *scenic* rivers (22 percent). Because of Alaska, the large majority of wild rivers (80 percent) are in the Pacific Coast region. Scenic rivers, on the other hand, are nearly as common in the North as in the Pacific Coast. The North has 872 miles of scenic rivers compared to the Pacific Coast's 882 miles. All regions but the South have substantial mileage of recreational rivers. The Rocky Mountain region has two and one-half times as much recreational river mileage as scenic. The North has about 150 more scenic river miles than recreational. Just over half of the South's WSR miles are classified as scenic. The FS manages the majority of scenic and recreational WSR miles, but wild river miles are split fairly evenly among the four federal agencies, with the NPS managing 130 more miles (1,532) than the FS (1,402).

In addition to WSRs, fast-moving rivers in general are highly valued for recreation experiences. Activities usually focus on rafting, kayaking, and canoeing on whitewater rivers. Whitewater recreation has a devoted following and supports a large outfitter and guide industry. The American Whitewater Affiliation (AWA), a conservation group based in suburban Washington, D.C., maintains a *Nationwide Whitewater Inventory* and serves as an advocate for whitewater resources. A principal reason for their database is to provide information about whitewater resources to the Federal Energy Regulatory Commission which relicenses hydroelectric power plants.

In January 1997, the inventory listed 2,297 whitewater river segments totaling almost 31,000 miles (Table III.11). The database covers all eligible whitewater rivers, regardless of managing agency or organization. A single river may be comprised of many segments, and the inventory does not include rivers of class I difficulty (the 'easiest' of six levels in the International Scale of Difficulty). Class I river segments are excluded because they are often indistinguishable from flatwater. AWA has compiled a database of all rivers class II and above, but cautions that included river mileage does not specify the quality of the whitewater recreation experience. A continuous stretch of river with the desired level of difficulty is necessary for a good whitewater experience. But overall quality reflects many variables, including the reliability of flows, water quality, scenic features, boating seasons, and proximity to population.

Table III.11: Miles of Rivers Identified by Nationwide Whitewater Inventory Miles by Level of Difficulty and Region, 1996

Level of Difficulty	Region				
	North	**South**	**Rocky Mountains**	**Pacific Coast**	**U.S. Total**
Class I-III	6,077	4,961	4,387	1,978	17,403
Class IV-VI	318	132	980	1,412	2,842
Variety[1]	3,215	1,625	3,798	1,744	10,382
All Segments[2]	9,610	6,718	9,165	5,134	30,627

[1]This category represents segments with a variety of difficulty levels such that they could not be classified as either easy (Class I-III) or difficult (Class IV-VI) rivers alone. Difficulty levels based on the Whitewater International Scale of Difficulty.

[2]32 river segments totaling 372 miles did not have location information.

Source: American Whitewater Affiliation. Silver Spring, Maryland.

Other than the Plains states, parts of the Midwest, the Mississippi Delta region, and Florida, whitewater rivers are well distributed throughout the United States (Figure III.7). The North and Rocky Mountain regions both have more than 9,000 miles. The majority of the river mileage in the inventory (about 57 percent) might be classified as "easier" (class I-III) in level of difficulty. The "most difficult" river segments (class IV-VI) are concentrated in the West where there are greater elevations (Figure III.8). There are relatively few of the higher difficulty classes in the South, less than half the mileage in the North. Nationwide, the most difficult classes of river mileage accounts for less than 10 percent of all whitewater miles. The third category in Table III.15 shows the mileage of river segments that have a variety of difficulty classes. The Rocky Mountain region has the most miles of these rivers followed by the North. It is difficult to categorize these as either easier or more difficult because a single river segment may range from class I to class VI. That much range is rare, but a lot of these segments can range across two or three classes from I to V, so one might argue that these represent "intermediate" whitewater.

Figure III.7: Counties with Whitewater Rivers, All Difficulty Classes, 1997

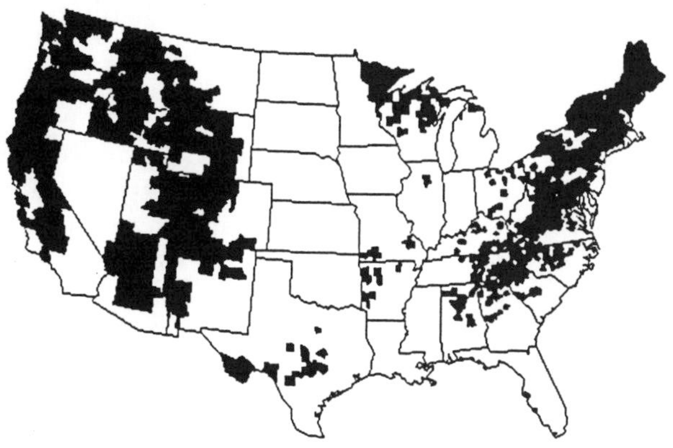

Source: American Whitewater Affiliation, Nationwide Whitewater Inventory, 1997.

Figure III.8: Counties with Whitewater Rivers, Difficulty Classes IV-VI Only, 1997

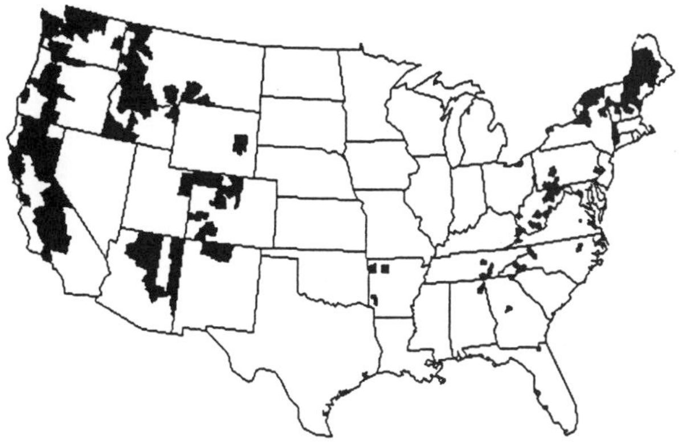

Source: American Whitewater Affiliation, Nationwide Whitewater Inventory, 1997.

Camping Facilities on Public Land

(By Douglas McEwen, Professor, Southern Illinois University, Carbondale, IL)

In the American consciousness, camping is strongly associated with the great outdoors and the tradition of providing public places for camping is firmly established. Because of its status as a favorite tradition, the provision of public camping facilities is examined in detail here. Although it was not possible to separate out the supply of public campgrounds by government provider, it is appropriate that camping is covered in the federal section because of the historical importance of the federal agencies in providing camping opportunities to the public. Private camping facilities are covered later in the chapter.

Camping can probably be traced back to the early 1800s, when Americans began to discover wilderness as a source of scenic beauty and spiritual inspiration. Camping was certainly an early recreation activity in national parks and national forests. The first campgrounds were probably unplanned and visitor-established. However, as visitor numbers grew and impacts increased, public agencies responded by constructing permanent campgrounds (Ibrahim & Cordes, 1993). While records of these early campgrounds are difficult to find, it is safe to state that since the early 1900s there has been a steady expansion of public campgrounds, both at the state and federal levels.

The Woodall Publishing Company has collected information from all public agencies on their campgrounds, and it was selected as the most accurate source available.[20] While public agencies certainly must have records of the numbers of campgrounds operated, these records are not unified in any single source and are very difficult to assemble.

In 1996, Woodall's inventory listed a total of more than 4,000 public (government) campgrounds in the United States (Table III.12). Despite much more federal land in the Western United States, the two Eastern regions have 61 percent of the nation's public campgrounds (Figure III.9), up from 55 percent in 1977. Local and especially state governments are responsible for the majority of eastern public campgrounds. The total number of public campgrounds in the United States has fallen by about 12 percent in the past 20 years. This drop, however, occurred primarily between 1977 and 1987. There was a modest net gain in public campgrounds between 1987 and 1996.

Table III.12: Number of Public Campgrounds and Campsites by Year and Region[1]

Type of Site and Year	Region				
	North	South	Rocky Mountains	Pacific Coast	U.S. Total
Campgrounds					
1977	1,561	1,014	1,264	829	4,668
1987	1,450	993	801	751	3,995
1996	1,409	1,064	826	792	4,091
Campsites					
1977	137,268	63,377	54,081	56,488	311,214
1987	157,190	83,229	58,220	65,011	363,650
1996	149,722	89,636	65,870	65,708	370,936

[1]Public campgrounds and campsites are those provided by Federal, State, and local levels of government.

Source: Woodall Publishing Company campground inventory database. Lake Forest, Illinois.

All regions except the North experienced a decline in public campgrounds between 1977 and 1987 then regained some by 1996. In the North, the net loss of public campgrounds continued into the 1990s. Overall, only the South has shown a net increase in campgrounds since 1977. The Rocky Mountains lost public campgrounds at the dramatic rate of 35 percent between 1977 and 1996. This probably reflects the closure of many scattered, remote federal campgrounds that were costly to maintain and operate. Though such closures have been occurring nationwide, they appear to be greatest in the Rocky Mountain region. Whether this action will impact the overall trend in the public sector to a large degree remains to be seen.

[20]Woodall's does not distinguish among public campgrounds provided by federal, state, and local governments, so this section covers public campgrounds in general, not just federal campgrounds.

Figure III.9: Percentage of Public Campgrounds by Region, 1996

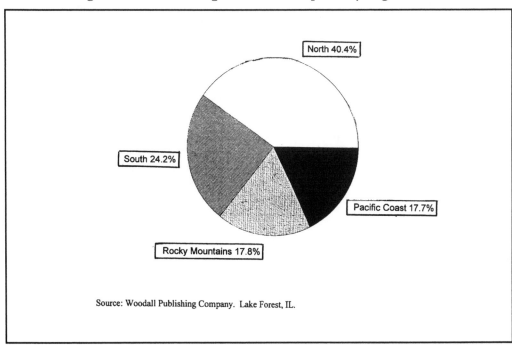

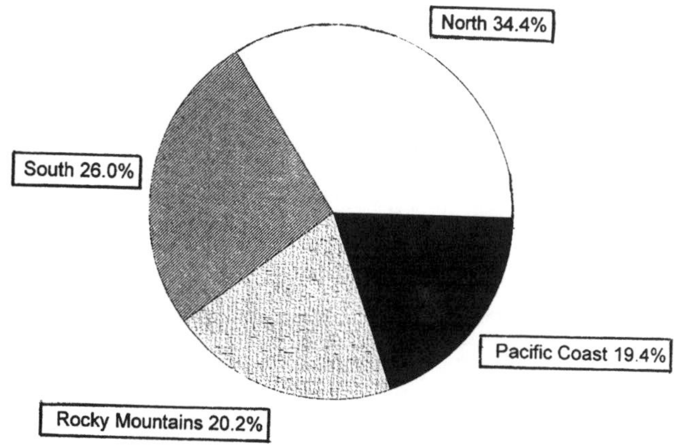

Source: Woodall Publishing Company. Lake Forest, IL.

The public sector has experienced a gain of almost 60,000 campsites (individual units within a campground) since 1977, a 19 percent increase (Table III.12). The number or campsites increased fastest in the first decade and only slightly between 1987 and 1996. It would be reasonable to expect that the new campgrounds added in the past decade are large with a great number of campsites. Just over 64 percent of the campsites are in the North and South, compared to 60 percent of the campgrounds (Figure III.10). All four regions experienced net gains in campsites over the 20 year period since 1977. The fastest growing was the South at 41 percent. The Rocky Mountains also added campsites at a rate above 22 percent. The Pacific Coast grew moderately (16 percent) and the North added only 9 percent more campsites during the 20-year period. Between 1987 and 1966 the North dropped over 7,000 campsites, the only region to register a loss during that period. Comparing the overall trend of decreasing numbers of campground with increasing numbers of campsites from 1977 to 1966 indicates current public campgrounds are larger on the average than in the past.

Figure III.10: Percentage of Public Campsites by Region, 1996

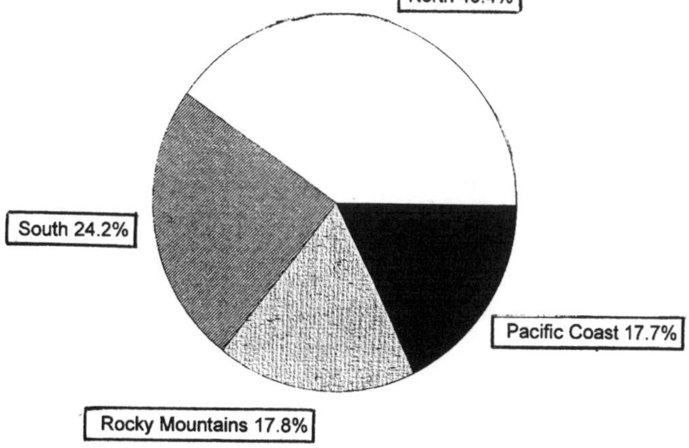

Source: Woodall Publishing Company. Lake Forest, IL.

The public sector, with fewer overall numbers of campsites than the private sector, continues to expand steadily the variety of campsites it provides. Woodall Publishing Company classifies campsites as (1) full hookup with water, sewer, and electricity; (2) water and electricity; (3) electricity only; and (4) no hookups. Between 1977 and 1996, more than 9,300 full hookup sites were added, an 87-percent increase (Table III.13). During the same period, electricity-only campsites experienced a similar growth pattern, an 86-percent increase. From 1977 to 1996, the public sector almost tripled its capacity of improved sites, adding more than 40,000 water and electric sites. On the other hand, the number of no hookup campsites in the public sector continued to steadily decline. The decline was less dramatic than experienced in the private sector and probably reflects the closing of some small, marginal campgrounds as well as conversion to improved sites. The public agencies appear to be moving away from rustic campgrounds to more full-service facilities, but this trend is not as dramatic as in the private sector, and the overall number of campsites is much smaller.

Table III.13: Number of Campsites at Public Campgrounds by Type and Year, 1977-1996[1]

Campsite type	Year		
	1977	1987[2]	1996
Full hookups	10,651	16,356	19,975
Water & electric	22,755	51,060	65,357
Electric only	40,528	71,165	75,279
No hookups	237,280	223,647	210,480
All campsite types	311,214	362,228	371,091

[1]Public campgrounds and campsites are those provided by federal, state, and local levels of government.

[1]Woodall Publishing Company's 1987 data on campsite types do not match exactly the total number of U.S. campsites in 1987 as shown in Table III.16.

Source: Woodall Publishing Company. Lake Forest, IL.

PUBLIC/PRIVATE PARTNERSHIP RESOURCES

A significant trend to emerge, especially in the 1990s, is the abundance of partnerships among the federal, state, and local levels of government, non-profit and non-governmental organizations, and the private sector. Recreation and natural resource managers speak frequently about the advantages of "leveraged" resources, shared advocacy, common interests, and larger constituencies. Partnerships may even be a necessity to bring together a diverse group of individuals and institutions which all share an interest in a given resource. Partnerships no doubt have disadvantages too, but their success and prevalence throughout the outdoor recreation community indicate that the benefits mostly outweigh the costs.

A detailed review of recreation partnerships is beyond the scope of this chapter. However, in two areas—Scenic Byways and Watchable Wildlife programs—partnerships have emerged as major trends in outdoor recreation. Both "Scenic Byways" and "Watchable Wildlife" are umbrella terms developed over the past decade in response to demand for scenic driving and nonconsumptive wildlife recreation. Each is characterized by partnerships involving all levels of government, non-profit organizations, and the commercial sector. Leadership for both is provided by the federal government. Both Scenic Byways and Watchable Wildlife programs depend on the involvement of numerous partners, as described in the following sections.

Scenic Byways

(By Joan W. Tannen, program manager, National Scenic Byways Clearinghouse, Washington, D.C.)

Scenic Byways address the demand for two of the nation's most popular recreational activities, sightseeing and driving for pleasure. Although parkways and other scenic drives have been around in the U.S. for decades, it is only since the late 1980s that formally established Scenic Byway programs proliferated at federal and state government levels. Local and regional governments and the private and non-profit sectors are involved in many scenic byway partnerships as well. The establishment of Scenic Byway programs represents a very important trend in the supply of outdoor recreation opportunities in this country, serving the dual purpose of providing access to desirable areas and providing viewing opportunities.

Sightseeing and driving for pleasure have proven to be two of the most popular leisure activities in national surveys and polls, including the President's Commission on Americans Outdoors. Repeatedly, Americans say they enjoy experiencing the nation's beauty and heritage by driving along its scenic roads. Even though some might argue that roads and highways have been in place for years and that nothing has really changed with respect to outdoor recreation, the simple fact that transportation routes are being recognized for their scenic and recreational values is significant enough. State and federal recognition and promotion of scenic transportation corridors increases the supply of scenic driving opportunities, even with actions as simple as signage, interpretation, and information dissemination.

A scenic byway is a roadway corridor recognized for its outstanding intrinsic qualities. As the name implies, these byways usually have exceptional scenic attributes. However, scenery is not the only recognized quality. These corridors may also be recognized for outstanding historic, cultural, natural, archaeological, or recreational qualities. Scenic byways may wander through quiet rural countrysides or traverse urban areas. They may be spectacular destinations which attract domestic and international visitors, or little-known local routes valued by local communities for weekend driving. They may be called by different names, e.g., scenic or historic byways, rustic roads, back country byways, heritage corridors or all-American roads. Each has in common special or unique features which are, to different degrees, protected and promoted so that they can be appreciated and shared.

A scenic byway roadway corridor is more than the road and its right-of-way. It includes the byway corridor along with corresponding resources that make the byway unique. Scenic byways may take in lakes, mountains, pastoral scenery, cultural or historical features, unique geological formations, or striking vistas that both attract and provide enjoyment for the traveler. Accommodations for picnicking, hiking, camping, and other recreation activities may be available along the route itself or the route may provide a pleasant access to areas offering these activities. Complementary facilities such as rest stops, scenic overlooks, visitor centers, and bicycle and pedestrian trails may further enhance the experience.

Background and History

Driving for pleasure has been a popular form of recreation for as long as Americans have driven automobiles. The first fragmented scenic byway efforts began in the early 1900s, when Americans began relying on motorized transportation. The Bronx River Parkway, built in Westchester County, New York in 1913, is considered to be the first scenic road designed to enhance the drive for travelers (Federal Highway Administration, 1988). This model for future parkways demonstrated new engineering concepts and was beautifully landscaped. The design elements used in constructing the Bronx River Parkway served as a precedent for other scenic parkways and byways that followed, including Virginia's Mount Vernon Memorial Highway, completed in 1932. These parkways were special because they were designed to be driven at moderate speeds to allow travelers to enjoy the scenery and the driving experience.

Some states were also beginning related scenic byway efforts during the 1930s. Scenic preservation in Vermont began in 1937 when the legislature mandated that a scenic route (SR 100) be developed from the Massachusetts border through Vermont to the Canadian border. Oregon's Columbia River Highway in the Columbia River Gorge, built between 1913 and 1922, was constructed to complement the surrounding environment and provide spectacular views of the gorge. Oregon also initiated efforts to protect scenic features of the state with legislation to protect standing timber and to plant trees along state highways. These efforts in Oregon resulted in a new policy for the Bureau of Public Roads (the precursor to the Federal Highway Administration). Beginning in 1934, each state was required to spend at least one percent of its total federal-aid funding for appropriate roadside landscaping (FHWA, 1988).

Construction on many of the National Park Service parkways, including the Blue Ridge Parkway in Virginia and North Carolina, and the Natchez Trace in Mississippi, Alabama and Tennessee, began during the 1930s. During these Depression years, the National Industrial Recovery Act authorized funding for the construction of public highways and parkways to stimulate the economy. The Blue Ridge Parkway was approved as one of these relief projects in 1929. Private contractors and local labor, as well as Civilian Conservation Corps and Emergency Relief Administration crews, participated in the first segments of this multi-million dollar construction project (Jolley, 1969). Similarly, many other scenic roads were built during this era.

In 1958, Congress created the Outdoor Recreation Resources Review Commission (ORRRC) in response to the nation's growing demand for outdoor recreation. ORRRC was charged with determining what facilities, including Scenic Byways and parkways, could best meet demand. In 1962, the results concluded that driving for pleasure and walking were by far the most popular forms of outdoor recreation (FHWA, 1988). With mobility and leisure time increasing, the commission forecasted that more people would travel further and more frequently to enjoy the country's scenic routes.

During the 1960s, a coordinated national scenic byway effort began to evolve. In April, 1964 the Recreation Advisory Council of the Bureau of Outdoor Recreation issued a policy statement recommending that a national program of scenic roads and parkways be developed. During the same period, Congress enacted the Highway Beautification Act of 1965 to provide for scenic development and beautification of the federal highway systems. In 1973, Congress directed the Federal Highway Administration to study the feasibility of developing a national scenic highway system, but most scenic byway initiatives were placed on hold during the Vietnam and War on Poverty era.

Outdoor recreation and Scenic Byways have always gone hand in hand. The President's Commission on American Outdoors (1986) stated in its report: "Americans are at home on the road. Pleasure driving to view the historic, natural, pastoral qualities offered by many of our nation's secondary roads is an important part of recreation for a majority of our population, comprising some 15 percent of all vehicle miles driven." Driving for pleasure continues to rank very highly among America's most popular outdoor recreation activities. In 1990, congressional appropriation legislation for the department of transportation included the following provisions for conducting a national scenic byway study (FHWA, 1991):

- Update a nationwide inventory of existing Scenic Byways.
- Develop guidelines for the establishment of a national scenic byway program, including recommended techniques for maintaining and enhancing scenic byway qualities.
- Conduct case studies on the economic impacts of Scenic Byways on travel and tourism.
- Analyze potential safety problems and associated environmental impacts.

Further broad-based support for Scenic Byways was generated as a result of this study. In 1991, Congress passed the Intermodal Surface Transportation Efficiency Act (ISTEA). The foundations of the National Scenic Byways Program to be administered by the Federal Highway Administration were outlined in Section 1047 of that legislation. Today there are many different scenic byway programs and initiatives across the country at all levels—national, state, local and private. These programs were developed to promote and protect roads under the management of a host of government bodies and public-private partnerships. Different programs have also been designed to meet a variety of objectives.

Federal Programs

The U.S. Departments of Transportation, Agriculture, and Interior are primarily responsible for Scenic Byway initiatives at the federal level. The Federal Highway Administration (FHWA) in the department of transportation administers the Federal-Aid Highway Program. Roads receiving funds from this program are owned and operated by state and local public agencies. While these systems contain only about 22 percent of the nation's total public road mileage, approximately 79 percent of travel in the United States is on these roads (FHWA, 1988).

The FHWA manages the National Scenic Byways Program that was mandated in ISTEA. This legislation charged the secretary of transportation with developing criteria for designating highways having outstanding scenic, historic, recreational, cultural, natural, and/or archaeological qualities as either "national Scenic Byways" or "all-American roads." To be designated as a national scenic byway, a road must meet the criteria for at least one of the six intrinsic qualities. The "best of the best" byways are designated as all-American roads. These all-American roads must meet the criteria for multiple intrinsic qualities so exceptional that these routes are "destinations unto themselves," attracting national and international visitors. As of mid-1997, 20 highway corridors totaling 2,481 miles had been designated under the National Scenic Byways Program. These six all-American roads, (1,078 miles) and 14 National Scenic Byways (1,403 miles) represent roads that are also designated within the National Forest Scenic Byways Program, the Bureau of Land Management Back Country Byways Program, state scenic byway programs, or roads that are under the jurisdiction of the National Park Service and the Bureau of Indian Affairs (FHWA, 1996).

The purpose of the National Scenic Byway Program is to increase tourism, create new jobs and foster economic development, while at the same time preserving and protecting the intrinsic qualities of these roadway corridors. This umbrella program was designed as a voluntary, grass roots initiative to assure community commitment to designation and management of a byway. The nomination process allows state-designated byways or federal agency byways to be nominated for designation as a national scenic byway or all-American road. The program is purely voluntary. A diverse group of interests have come together to support national scenic byway initiatives, including environmental preservationists, tourism advocates, proponents of recreation, land use planners, historians, transportation specialists, educators, and the motoring public (National Scenic Byways Program, 1995).

ISTEA authorized grant funds for the National Scenic Byways Program totaling $50 million for technical and financial assistance to the states for the planning, design, and development of state scenic byway programs. The legislation also established an interim Scenic Byways grant program funded at $30 million for fiscal years 1992 through 1994, to allow states a wide range of scenic byway projects while the national program was being established. A total of 18 states started programs as a result of these federal funds and 11 more states took advantage of scenic byway grants to improve and upgrade their existing programs.[21] National Scenic Byways Program discretionary grants totaling $74.3 million were awarded to 37 states, including the District of Columbia and Puerto Rico, for 552 projects (FHWA, 1997a).

The USDA Forest Service began its National Forest Scenic Byway Program in 1988 as part of its national recreation strategy. This program was established in direct response to the President's Commission on Americans Outdoors findings that listed pleasure driving as the second most popular form of outdoor recreation for most Americans. At that time, scenic stretches of existing national forest roads in 30 states were identified for potential designation.

There are currently 133 National Forest Scenic Byways in 35 states totaling 7,680 miles (USDA Forest Service, 1996). Scenic vistas, and the facilities for enjoying them, are the primary focus. The Forest Service also places emphasis on interpretation of heritage and cultural resources, land management practices, increased accessibility to Forest Service lands and services, and linking the national forests with neighboring communities to provide additional services to travelers. While Forest Service scenic highways are located primarily within the national forests, many also traverse portions of private land. The goals of the Forest Service Scenic Byways Program are to (Robertson, 1988):

- Showcase outstanding national forest scenery.
- Demonstrate the national forests as the major federal provider of outdoor recreation in the U.S.
- Increase public awareness and understanding of Forest Service activities.
- Meet the growing demand of driving for pleasure as a significant recreation use.
- Increase the use of the national forests by non-traditional users.
- Contribute to the nation's overall Scenic Byways effort.

Although the National Park Service (NPS) does not have a formal Scenic Byway program, the roads within national parks are treated as Scenic Byways in design, construction and management. There are nine congressionally designated national parkways including the Blue Ridge parkway in Virginia and North Carolina and the George Washington Memorial parkway in Virginia.[22] These elongated parks were designed for drivers to experience scenic, recreational, or historic features of national significance. Wide rights-of-way and other design techniques are used to protect and enhance scenic views.

Similarly, most roads in national parks are recognized and treated as Scenic Byways. All National Park Service sites encompass unique natural, historic, cultural, and recreational qualities, and the park road system is the principal mode of access to these qualities. Scenic overlooks, recreation centers, and interpretive exhibits are abundant on park roads. Many park roads have even been placed on the National Register of Historic Places in recognition of their historic value. The Mount Vernon Memorial Highway in Virginia, and the Going-to-the-Sun Road in Glacier National Park, Montana, are two such examples. The motorized vehicle is the principal mode of transportation in National Parks, therefore the NPS has recognized how critical it is to design park roads with respect for both the natural resources and the visitor experience.

---

[21]Scenic Byway projects can also be funded through the 10 percent set-aside of ISTEA Surface Transportation Program (STP) funds for enhancement projects.

[22]The George Washington Memorial Parkway includes a portion in Maryland which is called the Clara Barton Parkway.

The Bureau of Indian Affairs (BIA), also in the department of the interior, in cooperation with the Indian Tribal Councils, is responsible for the design, construction and maintenance of an extensive system of roads held in trust for tribal units. Many reservation roads have scenic characteristics and offer unique cultural features. With land use planning and increased attention to design, these roads have potential as Scenic Byways. The BIA recognizes that Scenic Byways have the potential to increase travel and tourism on designated reservation roads and to generate economic development (FHWA, 1991).

Another interior department agency, the Bureau of Land Management (BLM), started its Back Country Byways program in 1989. The objective was to provide visitors with the opportunity to explore some of the BLM's less accessible unique and scenic lands in the West. As of July 1996, 64 back country byways, covering approximately 3,180 miles, were designated by the BLM. Back country byways are classified according to the terrain and the type of vehicle required to accommodate the route. Type I is negotiable by a normal passenger car. Type II requires a two-wheel drive vehicle with high ground clearances. Type III requires a four-wheel drive vehicle. Type IV are single track trails that can accommodate mountain bikes, dirt bikes, snowmobiles, and all-terrain vehicles. Thirty-two of the Back Country Byways are type I, negotiable by a normal passenger car. Ten more have type 1 segments (USDI Bureau of Land Management, 1996). The goals of the BLM Back Country Byway program are to (USDI Bureau of Land Management, 1993):

- Increase the opportunities for the American public to see and enjoy unique scenic and historic resources on public lands.
- Foster partnerships at the local, state, and national levels.
- Contribute to local and regional economies.
- Enhance the visitor recreation experience and multiple use management message through interpretation.
- Manage visitor use of the byway to minimize environmental impacts and to protect the visitor.
- Contribute to the National Scenic Byway Program in a manner that is appropriate for public lands managed by the BLM.

State Programs

Many states have their own Scenic Byway programs. California, Maine, Minnesota, New York, Oregon, Vermont, Virginia, Washington, and Wisconsin in particular have a long history of commitment to development of scenic roads in their states. In some states, such as California and New York, the Scenic Byway program is authorized by legislation and roads are designated in accordance with state-determined standards and procedures. In other states, such as Colorado and Maryland, the Scenic Byway program has administrative authorization under a general or executive authority. Some states, such as Missouri and Illinois, have no formal scenic byway program, but have designated some routes as scenic as part of a special initiative. For example, the Great River Road along the Mississippi River travels through some states that do not have Scenic Byway programs. It is managed by a commission of representatives from the states through which it passes (Mastran, 1992).

Thirty-five states plus the District of Columbia have formal Scenic Byway programs (Table III.14). Another seven States—Illinois, Missouri, Nebraska, Oklahoma, South Carolina, Tennessee, and Texas—are still in the planning stages. Twenty-six of the 35 programs have been created since 1987 and over half of the programs (19) since 1992. Nine of the most recent programs were funded or otherwise supported by ISTEA. About half of the programs were created by state legislatures and the rest by executive authority. These statistics highlight the emerging trend of Scenic Byways in the United States, especially in the 1990s.

Table III.14: Summary of State Scenic Byway Programs, 1996

State	Year Created	Legislative Authority?	Creation Aided by ISTEA?
Alaska	1993	No	No
Arizona	1982	Yes	No
California	1963	Yes	No
Colorado	1989	No	No
Connecticut	1989	Yes	No
Dist. of Columbia	1995	n/a[1]	Yes
Florida	1996	Yes	Yes
Georgia	1992	No	No
Idaho	1977	No	No
Indiana	1994	No	No
Iowa	1993	Yes	Yes
Kansas	1993	No	Yes
Kentucky	1994	No	No
Louisiana	1991	Yes	No
Maine	1979	Yes	No
Maryland	1988	No	No
Massachusetts	n/a	Yes	No
Michigan	1993	Yes	No
Minnesota	1992	No	No
Nevada	1980s	Yes	No
New Hampshire	1992	Yes	No
New Jersey	1993	No	No
New Mexico	1993	Yes	No
New York	1992	Yes	Yes
North Carolina	1990	Yes	No
North Dakota	1996	No	n/a
Ohio	1994	No	Yes
Oregon	1995	No	No
Rhode Island	1985	Yes	n/a
South Dakota	1990	No	n/a
Utah	1989	No	n/a
Vermont	1977 & 1996	Yes	Yes
Virginia	1973	Yes	n/a
Washington	1967 & 1993	Yes	n/a
West Virginia	1995	No	Yes
Wyoming	1994	No	Yes

[1]Information was not available.

Source: American Recreation Coalition, National Trust for Historic Preservation and Scenic America. 1996. Key Findings: 1996 Survey of State Scenic Byways Programs. Washington, D.C.: American Recreation Coalition.

While there are many similarities between the state programs, there can be differences in the philosophies and objectives behind these programs. For example, the California, Oregon, and Vermont programs designate routes primarily on the basis of aesthetics and preservation of resources, while tourism considerations play a more important role in Texas, Tennessee and Maryland (FHWA, 1996). Comparisons between state programs based on this limited amount of information is cautioned, however. Differences in state program criteria, objectives, and philosophies greatly affect the number of byways designated as well as the length of each byway.

Private Sector Programs

The American Automobile Association (AAA) has the only private sector scenic byway program that evaluates routes at a national level. Over the years, AAA received appeals from its members to indicate scenic roads on the AAA maps. AAA's professional road reporters, who drive the country's roadways gathering information for AAA programs, started to evaluate scenic roadways on an ad hoc basis. In the late 1960s and early 1970s, information on scenic roads was included for the first time on each map. AAA started to develop a formal scenic byway program in 1979 when they established five categories of scenic routes: natural beauty, cultural interest, quintessential scenery, unique features, and roads designated in a public lands Scenic Byway program. In 1996, AAA had designated 543 byways totaling 27,375 miles (AAA, 1995). Their program is dynamic, with roads continuously being evaluated for designation or redesignation.

Future Trends

Interest in Scenic Byways and all of the scenic byway programs continues to gain momentum. While scenic byway initiatives have long proven to be popular in the U. S., the initial success of the National Scenic Byways Program has had a significant extended effect. Eighteen states started a program through funding from the national program. Several existing state programs have been improved with national program grants. This seems to be a continuing trend, with additional states currently working on the development of scenic byway programs. Scenic byway grant funds from the National Scenic Byways program have served as seed monies for 552 scenic byway projects at the state and local levels. When combined with other funding and initiatives, these projects have worked to preserve and protect the unique qualities of these special routes while simultaneously promoting them for the enjoyment of the byway traveler.

The Intermodal Surface Transportation Efficiency Act (ISTEA), the enabling legislation for the National Scenic Byways program, comes up for renewal at the end of fiscal year 1997. The administration's proposed new ISTEA legislation, NEXTEA (National Economic Crossroads Transportation Efficiency Act), if it passes, would continue with a fairly consistent treatment of the National Scenic Byways program (FHWA, 1997b). The Scenic Byways program is generally considered to be an ISTEA success story (Schoener, 1997).

The USDA Forest Service's National Forest Scenic Byway program and the BLM's Back Country Byways program have increasing interest that is expected to continue. The Forest Service is currently screening to determine which routes represent the best in their program. Selected byways will be reviewed for potential nomination to the National Scenic Byway program. The Forest Service also plans to work closely with the states to have national forest Scenic Byways considered for designation in state programs. Similarly, the Bureau of Land Management is currently reviewing BLM back country byways to determine which meet the criteria for the National Scenic Byways program.

Partnerships between interested groups have been a key to the success of many scenic byway initiatives. The protection of Scenic Byways as unique national assets have been supported by various government authorities, public and private organizations, and grass roots organizations. These partnerships have created unified attention to the values and benefits of scenic byway initiatives. While it has taken time for partnerships to develop, the long-term viability of scenic byway programs will be better protected in the long run. The increasing emphasis throughout the U.S. on community values, national pride, environmental protection, historic preservation and overall quality of life should continue to complement scenic byway efforts and initiatives.

Watchable Wildlife

(By Kimberly H. Anderson, USDA Forest Service, Rocky Mountain Region, Lakewood, CO)

Numerous national studies, including the President's Commission on Americans Outdoors (PCAO), have identified wildlife-associated recreation as extremely popular for millions of Americans. The PCAO encouraged educators to integrate environmental education into basic school curriculums and federal resource agencies to play a greater role in providing viewing opportunities for people to experience the nation's wildlife resources.

In response to the PCAO, a report entitled "Watchable Wildlife: A New Initiative," was published by Defenders of Wildlife in cooperation with the Bureau of Land Management, U.S. Fish and Wildlife Service, and the USDA Forest Service. This report launched the national Watchable Wildlife effort (Vickerman 1989).[23]

---

[23]"Watchable Wildlife: A New Initiative" is available from Defenders of Wildlife, Portland, OR. (503) 293-1433. $5.00.

The initiative provided a framework for federal and state agencies and private conservation groups to unite a number of scattered efforts to provide new recreational, conservation, and educational opportunities.

A national memorandum of understanding (MOU) for Watchable Wildlife was prepared and signed by the major participants in December, 1990. The purpose was to encourage cooperation among diverse agencies and groups in developing partnerships to establish Watchable Wildlife programs across the country. The MOU outlined five goals for the Watchable Wildlife program: recreation opportunities, economic development, educational programming, conservation, and partnerships. Partnerships are a critical component to strengthen, diversify, and coordinate the variety of efforts already underway to provide quality viewing opportunities. Original participants included 10 federal agencies, a coalition of state agencies represented by the International Association of Fish and Wildlife Agencies and four conservation groups. The MOU has been amended twice, first to extend its life until December 1998, and second to diversify the participation by adding five additional groups.[24] Current participants now include:

American Birding Association
Defender of Wildlife
Ducks Unlimited
Humane Society of the United States
International Association of Fish and Wildlife Agencies
National Fish and Wildlife Foundation
The Izaak Walton League of America, Inc.
Wildlife Forever
Bureau of Land Management
Bureau of Reclamation
Department of the Air Force
Department of the Navy
National Park Service
USDA Forest Service
U.S. Fish and Wildlife Service

The Watchable Wildlife Program

The National Watchable Wildlife program is a cooperative coalition of public and private groups working to meet Americans' interest in wildlife-associated recreation. Some of the activities which fall under the Watchable Wildlife umbrella include observing fish, viewing flowers, general nature study, butterfly gardens, visitor center interpretive displays, aquariums, and fish hatcheries. Watchable wildlife operates on the premise that with ample and accessible opportunities to learn about nature, viewers will become more effective advocates for wildlife, native plants, and aquatic species conservation. The program is implemented through federal and state agencies and non-governmental entities, working in partnership to develop:

- A network of <u>nature (wildlife, fisheries, and wildflower) viewing sites</u>. Sites are selected based on a number of criteria such as ability to withstand public use, accessibility, safety, ecological significance, scenic quality, and viewing probability.

- A wildlife viewing <u>site signing system</u>. The binocular logo was adopted by the Federal Highway Administration to designate viewing areas. Signs featuring the logo identify the sites and are strategically placed along highways and secondary roads to direct viewers to the sites.[25]

---

[24]The MOU for the National Watchable Wildlife Program underwent revision during 1997.

[25]California provides a good example of an extensive system of clearly identified and signed Watchable Wildlife sites, now found in all of the state's counties. The California Division of Tourism is very involved and supportive of the program and has identified viewing sites with the binocular logo in their maps.

- A series of Watchable Wildlife viewing guide books, which include wildlife, wildflower, and fish viewing sites state to state. To date, 34 state wildlife-viewing guides have been published in partnership with the lead organization, Defenders of Wildlife, publisher Falcon Press, dozens of state fish and wildlife agencies, and other national and local partners.[26]

- An increase in the general public awareness and support for the conservation of natural resources. This is accomplished through environmental education programs that promote sound and safe viewing practices, skills to minimize human impacts, a connection to the land, and a fostering of land and water stewardship. These experiential outdoor learning opportunities teach visitors about wildlife, fish, wildflowers, and other natural resources through interpretive signing, guide books, festivals, walks, ranger talks, etc.

Case Study—USDA Forest Service NatureWatch Program

The Forest Service has been a driving force behind development of the National Watchable Wildlife program. In 1988, the agency started "Eyes on Wildlife," its first Watchable Wildlife program which predated the MOU by about a year. Later, as nature viewing activities, opportunities, and interest increased across the wide spectrum of watchable species, a broader scope for the program was desired. In 1994, the Forest Service adopted the term "NatureWatch" for its national viewing, education, and conservation program. The NatureWatch program highlights three areas of outdoor viewing: Eyes on Wildlife (the original emphasis on wildlife), FishWatch (fish and aquatic ecosystems), and Celebrating Wildflowers (native plants and wildflowers). In 1996, there were over 840 nature viewing sites on national forests and grasslands and an additional 285 sites were identified for development (USDA Forest Service, 1997). Further, the Forest Service had established 82 sites for fish viewing.

All three components of the NatureWatch program are cooperative between the Forest Service and its partners. Partners add their perspectives to the diversity of ways to learn about natural resources through educational activities, viewing blinds, boardwalks, festivals, naturalist trails, interactive displays, computer programs, brochures, and classes.[27] Some examples of specific NatureWatch programs follow, including partner commitments and involvement.

Fish Watching, Utah

The Utah Division of Wildlife Resources and the Uinta and Wasatch-Cache National Forest provided opportunities for viewing spawning Bonneville cutthroat trout in the spring and Kokanee salmon in the fall in Utah's Strawberry River, a few footsteps away from the viewing trail. About 500 visitors took part in the spring viewing sessions. The fall viewing sessions had over 5,500 take part, including 460 children in guided school groups.

Conasauga River Snorkeling Trail, Tennessee

Fish watchers snorkel among the 60 colorful and unusual fish species inhabiting the Conasauga State Scenic River through the Cherokee National Forest in Tennessee. Redeye bass and sunfish linger in the deep pools. Alabama hogsuckers, stonerollers and darters flash through shallow riffles. Forest staff lead snorkel tours and give slide shows that help people appreciate the Conasauga River as critical habitat for the Conasauga logperch and other rare and endangered species.

Puget Sound Eyes on Wildlife Partnership Coordinator, Washington

Twenty-six committed partners contributed to the "Puget Sound Eyes on Wildlife" program. Two national forests worked closely with the Pilchuck and Black Hills Audubon Societies, Washington Department of

---

[26] There are now 25 guides in the Falcon Press series, and over 600,000 total units have been sold. Four new guides in the Falcon Press series were published in 1996: Alaska, Maine, Nebraska, and Ohio. Four more were published in 1997: New Hampshire, New Jersey, New York, and West Virginia. Kansas, Wyoming, and Michigan all recently produced independently published guides, bringing that total to nine.

[27] An example of the involvement of NatureWatch's partners is that of the non-governmental organization, Wildlife Forever. Wildlife Forever is active in a number of nature viewing activities and is a lead partner with the Forest Service in matching funds for interpretive NatureWatch signs. They continue to explore different approaches to Watchable Wildlife through radio programs, wildscaping for wildlife, and the production of a 15-lesson wildlife curriculum on CD-ROM. "Getting into Golf" with Jack Nicklaus is a program to help develop an appreciation in golfers for the wildlife with which they share the golfing links.

Fish and Wildlife, the Rocky Mountain Elk Foundation and Trout Unlimited to support a coordinator who delivers NatureWatch to Seattle area residents. Projects ranged from an actual 300-pound bald eagle nest exhibit that attracted 4,000 visitors, to printing 10,000 copies of a bird checklist and developing exhibit materials for the Boyd Creek Riparian Interpretive Trail.

Taylor Creek Viewing Bridge and Stream Profile Chamber, California

Visitors are able to view aquatic life without disturbing them or getting wet when they visit an underground stream profile chamber with a 30-foot window into "Life in the Fast Lane." The salmon viewing bridge, "spawnsored" by the California Tahoe Conservancy and the Lake Tahoe Basin Management Unity, allows visitors to watch spawning salmon without eroding the stream banks, or disturbing the "nesting" fish. Other sights can be seen from the Taylor Creek Meadow Wildlife Viewing Deck including mountain scenery, deer, and osprey, nesting geese, and other mammals. The Kokanee Salmon Education program draws 120,000 people yearly, including thousands of school children to learn about stream ecology.

Celebrating Wildflower Events, Kentucky

The Kentucky Department of Fish and Wildlife and Kentucky Native Plant Society each joined Kentucky state parks and the Daniel Boone National Forest in putting on natural resource weekends at Natural Bridge State Park to promote the enjoyment and education of native plant and herptofauna resources. The annual Wildflowers Weekend attracted 300 people to kickoff Celebrating Wildflower activities on the forest. The annual herpetology weekend attracted 200 visitors. It was also filmed by the outdoor television show *Kentucky Afield* and aired to more than 80,000 Kentucky viewers. Both programs used slide shows, field trips, examples of plants and animals and a photography workshop.

Raptor Festival, Montana

The highest number of golden eagles in North America soar over Montana's Bridger Bowls Ski Area each October. The Bridger Bowl Ski Corporation, HawkWatch International, Montana Department of Fish, Wildlife & Parks, and Wild Birds Unlimited joined with the Bridger National Forest to offer a Raptor Festival, attended by 2,000 people. Participants hiked to the ridge top to identify eagles and hawks and attended raptor education workshops. A new raptor display installed at the ski area provides year-round interpretation of the number one golden eagle flyway in the United States.

"People and the Land: Our Siskiyou Heritage," Oregon

The Siskiyou National Forest and 47 partners sponsored and put on a four-day event titled "People and the Land: Our Siskiyou Heritage" on the 25th anniversary of Earth Day. Their purpose was to interpret the relationship between the inhabitants of the Siskiyou region and their environment, both historically and currently. The booths utilized hands-on exhibits and one on one interaction. Over 5,000 people attended the event, including 2,500 school children. Partners included the Bureau of Land Management, two colleges, two historical societies, National Park Service, Girl Scouts of America, nature organizations, Indian tribes, and others.

Schoolyard Wild Landscaping, Colorado

The National Watchable Wildlife Conference, held in Estes Park, Colorado in 1995, inspired the community, Arapaho-Roosevelt National Forest staff, and many local partners to work with students and teachers to transform the town's schoolyard into a wildland garden. High school students constructed bat houses; first graders hung their handmade birdhouses, and a biology class planted a native garden resistant to drought. The Boy Scouts planted fifty new native tree species. Now teachers are able to step with students into an environmental education classroom through their back door. The school hopes to designate their school site as a NatureWatch site with their own binocular logo.

International Migratory Bird Day, Arizona

In southern Arizona on the Coronado National Forest a fortunate "birder" can find elegant trogons. Newcomers and expert birders are drawn to Sabino Canyon National Recreation Area for birding tours of the sky island ecosystems, backyard landscaping for birds, trogon research and neotropical migratory bird conservation. The 1996 International Migratory Bird Day attracted 750 visitors, of which nearly a quarter were Hispanic. Tucson Audubon Society, Arizona Game and Fish Department, a local raptor group, the Sabino Canyon Volunteer Naturalists, and Forest Service staff all participated in the event.

Wildlife Viewing Guide, Illinois

Efforts by a Shawnee National Forest Watchable Wildlife team led to the inclusion of nine forest sites in the Illinois Wildlife Viewing Guide, published in 1996 in cooperation with the Illinois Department of Natural resources. These nine sites provide some of the best wildlife viewing opportunities in the state.

Other National Non-Consumptive Wildlife Efforts

In addition to the Forest Service's NatureWatch and its partners, and the National Watchable Wildlife Memorandum of Understanding, there are other significant national collaborative efforts toward promoting conservation through viewing. They include:

1. Celebrating Wildflowers

The Native Plant Conservation Initiative is a national consortium of nine federal and nearly 60 non-federal cooperators focusing on the conservation of the Nation's native flora. The group promotes public awareness preserving these natural resources through education, photography, and viewing. They participate in Celebrating Wildflowers Week, the third full week in May, which is the kick off for wildflower events that happen nearly year round. Events include walks, talks, wildflower festivals, displays, brochures, posters, a Celebrating Wildflower events calendar, and a national Celebrating Wildflowers Hotline number to call for bloom reports between April and August. During Autumn, this telephone number then becomes a hotline for Fall Foliage viewing.

2. Fish Watch

In 1996, a session was held at the American Fisheries Society Conference entitled "How to Make Fish As Popular As Dinosaurs." Representatives from most federal and state agency groups attended, as did a variety of conservation and business groups. The purpose of the session was to explore ways to engage the public in conservation of fisheries and aquatic resources. The approach was education and hands-on events for children to learn about fish biology, aquatic species, ecosystem health, clean water, and watersheds. Pathway to Fishing, Adopt a Watershed, and Future Fisherman's Foundation are just a few of the national efforts underway. These groups are committed to the conservation of fisheries and aquatic resources through educational programs, stream profile viewing chambers, over-water platforms, river snorkeling, fish festivals, Fran and Francis fish mascots, fish story telling tents, casting clinics, and fish derbies.

3. Partners in Flight

Public and private organizations and businesses are also taking action to help reverse the decline in many migratory bird populations. Groups involved include Harcourt Brace, Wild Bird Feeding Institute and National Bird Feeding Society, Phillips 66, Swift, Department of Defense, National Fish and Wildlife Foundation, U.S. Fish and Wildlife Service, USDA Forest Service, and others. International Migratory Bird Day is celebrated each May to help conserve migratory birds and their habitats between Canada, the United States, Mexico, the Caribbean, and South America.

STATE LAND AND WATER RESOURCES FOR OUTDOOR RECREATION

State land and water resources are generally somewhere between the mostly resource-oriented opportunities provided by the federal agencies and the facility-oriented opportunities provided by local government and the private sector. State-owned recreation resources cover less area than federal resources. They tend to be somewhat more developed, however, offering more services at locations usually closer to population centers, especially in the eastern United States. On the other hand, State resources are not consistently developed to the degree of most urban and local government parks, and many have significant acreages of wildland. In many ways, though, State land and water resources provide their own spectrum of opportunities similar to what is offered across all levels of government and the private sector. See the accompanying article, "The State Government Role in Outdoor Recreation" for the perspective of a State outdoor recreation professional.

State-owned outdoor recreation resources are dominated by state parks. A detailed report on the 50 state park systems is presented in the next section. A number of other significant state-owned and managed resources, however, also play important roles in outdoor recreation. They include: State trails programs, state forest systems, State Fish and Wildlife land, State-designated wilderness, and State-designated scenic rivers. State resource systems are difficult to summarize because of variation in resources, policies, and definitions. Management styles for fish and wildlife resources vary considerably. State Forest systems range widely in scope and funding. The National Association of State Park Directors (NASPD) produces a summary report of all state park systems. Even this effort suffers from difficulty in controlling data collection over multiple periods of time. The NASPD presents trend data between 1991 and 1995. But trend data were nearly impossible to obtain for forest and fish and game programs.

The State Government Role in Outdoor Recreation

(By James DeLoney, Program Head of Consumer Research, Texas Parks and Wildlife Department, Austin, TX)

In the compendium of outdoor recreation providers there are federal, state, and local governments; the private commercial sector; the quasi-or non-profit sector; and the individual. Twenty-seven of the most recent Statewide Comprehensive Outdoor Recreation Plans (SCORPs) available, dated in the late 1980s and 1990s, served as the primary sources to develop this article on the State role in providing outdoor recreation. SCORPs document issues, actions, programs, and trends occurring in states, and give insights about the diverse roles state governments play in outdoor recreation and tourism. States have been producing SCORPs since the mid 1960s as a requirement to participate in the federal Land and Water Conservation Fund Program. Several examples are given about the experiences of the Texas Parks and Wildlife Department as a state government provider of outdoor recreation.

Over time the desires of the populace shape the role of each level of government, including the roles state governments play in the provision of outdoor recreation and resource-based tourism. Roles of state government are two-fold: (1) to manage, protect, and conserve the state's natural and cultural resources; and (2) to provide outdoor recreation, environmental education, and cultural/historical interpretation. To this end, state agencies:

- Operate and maintain a system of public lands, including state parks and wildlife management areas;
- Monitor, conserve, and enhance the quality of rivers, streams, lakes, public and private lands, coastal marshes, wetlands, bays, beaches, and Gulf waters;
- Manage and regulate fishing, hunting, and boating opportunities and activities;
- Assist public and private entities in providing quality outdoor recreation opportunities;
- Cooperate with other governmental entities in these areas (Texas Parks and Wildlife Department, 1994).

The most visible role that state governments play in the provision of outdoor recreation and resource-based tourism is the operation and maintenance of state park systems. Sites comprising state parks systems range from large natural areas to small historical sites. State park systems range in size from less than 10,000 acres to over 3.2 million acres (National Association of State Park Directors, 1996). Generally, state parks fill a niche between the larger, more significant federal national parks and the smaller, more intensely developed local parks. Results from surveys of Texas citizens reveals that the public prefers state parks that (a) are located outside of cities in a rural natural setting near a freshwater stream or lake; (b) serve as many people as possible, including tourists; (c) are a place where people can feel secure; (d) are properly maintained before the state purchases new park sites; (e) have reasonable entrance fees, but not so high to prohibit access to lower income families. Popular with state park visitors are good, clean restrooms; trails; wilderness or natural areas; abundant wildlife; and camping and fishing facilities, all presented to them by a friendly, informative park staff (Goldbloom 1991; DeLoney, Eley, & Dziekan 1996).

A significant role of state governments is the preservation of natural resources sought by recreationists and tourists, accomplished largely through state parks. State governments also play a significant role in the conservation and management of the state's wildlife populations. Nature tourism, which is dependent on the conservation of natural and wildlife resources, appears to be an international phenomenondestined for greater popularity and economic importance.

State governments regulate many activities which directly or indirectly impact outdoor recreation and tourism. Regulatory functions range from reservoir development, freshwater instream flows, water quality, hunting and fishing for sport and commercial activities, to sand and gravel permits in freshwater streams. These are just a few of the hundreds of licenses and permits controlled by the states.

Current Trends, Issues And Other Forces of Change

Changing Preferences

Public values drive trends in outdoor recreation participation. An example of a current trend in outdoor recreation participation is the shift from consumptive (e.g., hunting) to non-consumptive (e.g., bird watching) uses of wildlife. It is often difficult for state governments to provide outdoor recreation opportunities as quickly as changes in outdoor recreation participation occur. The management of state parks and wildlife management areas in Texas illustrate this point. Visitation to Texas state parks exceeds 20 million annually, while visitation to wildlife management areas remains low, even though non-consumptive uses of wildlife in Texas are popular. The reason is that state parks were designed, developed, and staffed to support visitors, while wildlife management areas were managed from a biological perspective to support wildlife rather than visitors.

Accordingly, state park managers encouraged visitation while wildlife management area managers concentrated on wildlife management. Plans are now underway in the Texas Parks and Wildlife Department to make the wildlife areas more accessible to the public. The planning, development, and staffing of an infrastructure at wildlife management areas to support the rapid increase in the non-consumptive uses of wildlife is a lengthy, expensive process. It will take years before the recreational opportunities on the wildlife management areas can meet the public demands for non-consumptive wildlife opportunities.

Societal Trends

Shifts in values result in state governments having to deal with situations quite different from the past. One of the most dramatic trends has been in the composition of the American family. State park visitation tends to be a predominantly family–oriented activity. In Texas, the individual least likely to visit a state park would be single or a single parent (Goldbloom, 1991). Changing characteristics of the American family present state government outdoor recreation and tourism providers with challenges. How can the increasing numbers of "nontraditional" families be attracted to visit state outdoor recreation and tourism areas? How will state government outdoor recreation providers meet the special needs of such families? For example, the needs of a mother visiting a state park with children may differ from the needs of a family accompanied by a father.

The urbanization of America is another trend which has affected state-provided outdoor recreation opportunities, most notably hunting. In years past, fathers who lived in rural areas taught their sons to hunt. Today, 70 percent of the U.S. population lives in urbanized areas, and fewer fathers live in the same household with their children. Some states, including Texas, are attempting to get women more interested in the outdoors. Since 1993, over 1,500 women in Texas have participated in a workshop titled "Becoming An Outdoors Woman" (Dziekan, DeLoney, & Eley, 1997). Whether or not past levels in hunting participation can be sustained in view of these societal changes remains to be seen.

Research studies have shown correlations between participation in outdoor recreation activities and the age and race of the participant. Continuing shifts in the age, race, and family composition of the population will impact future outdoor recreation participation, particularly at state parks where family visits dominate and certain racial groups have been under represented. While the overall participation can be expected to increase due to the increase in population, increases in non-Caucasian races and the elderly age groups may result in declines in statistics such as the proportions of the population participating in outdoor recreation activities.

Resource Trends

Of the statewide issues identified in the 27 SCORPs reviewed, resource conservation occurred most frequently. A common thread among the states was to ensure the conservation of the natural, cultural, and historical resources upon which outdoor recreation and tourism depend. This finding may indicate to state government planners and managers the most important role for state park systems, a role supported by public values.

Budgets are another strong driving force influencing changes in the role of state governments in outdoor recreation and tourism. In the SCORPs, funding for parks and recreation was cited second most often as a statewide issue. National, state, and local funding for parks and recreation fails to keep pace with public demand for quality outdoor recreation opportunities. Funding has been a perennial statewide issue for years in many states (DeLoney, et al., 1996). The elimination of Federal Land and Water Conservation Fund (LWCF) moneys to states escalated funding problems for state governments. Texas received over $254 million (in 1994 dollars) in LWCF moneys from 1965-1995 (DeLoney, et al., 1996) to fund 923 park projects, 66 of which were state parks (Urbina, 1997). State and local funds have to make up this shortfall at a time when it seems unlikely that governments will raise taxes for the purpose. Further, the Texas Parks and Wildlife Department no longer receives funds from general revenues to operate state parks, and the department is attempting to become self-sufficient at a time when the Texas State Park System faces an estimated $185 million backlog in maintenance and repairs. These trends require the agency to recover a greater portion of operation and maintenance costs from user fees at Texas state parks. Other states report similar trends. The perennial funding issue will continue far into the foreseeable future.

Current Interests, Marketing Initiatives, and Directions

State governments, like other levels of government, are tasked with meeting growing outdoor recreation needs without corresponding increases in budgets. State governments are having to rely more and more on marketing initiatives to meet increasing demands. Since 1991, the Texas Parks and Wildlife Department (TPWD) has worked closely with a Texas A&M University marketing professor to revamp its pricing structure for state parks. Further, the department created its own marketing branch in the agency.

There are two key reasons for state governments' interest in marketing. First is the need to understand their customers from a marketing perspective. Second is the overriding need to improve budget situations to make visitors incur more of the cost of providing the outdoor recreation opportunities. A public opinion survey of visitors to Texas state parks found that 61 percent agreed that "user fees and entrance charges to state parks should be set high enough to cover a park's operating cost" (Wall & Crompton, 1995).

Although state governments have started applying marketing concepts used by the private or commercial sector, there is room for improvement. For example, state parks are designed and developed as a product using master planning concepts which do not conform to current marketing principles. Attempts are then made to attract visitors, or customers, to the product. Current marketing concepts require customers to be involved in determining the product they will be offered (Crompton & Lamb, 1986).

Another marketing initiative taken by state governments is the establishment of 501 (c)(3) foundations. In Texas, donations and sponsorships are channeled through the Texas State Park Foundation. Foundations give the state agencies more flexibility, enabling them to accomplish goals which would be either impossible or difficult for the state agency without the assistance of the foundation. Other initiatives in Texas include the aggressive promotion of state parks, greater emphasis on the TPWD's public image and relationship with the public, and revamping consumer research to address all of the agency's outdoor recreation and tourism customers. Other states have implemented similar changes to place greater emphasis on marketing and customer research. Other marketing initiatives taken by state governments to improve outdoor recreation opportunities and services include centralized reservation systems for visitors; acceptance of credit cards; packaged tours at state managed sites; outreach to under-represented socio-demographic groups such as minorities and women; use of volunteers to supplement full-time staff; and integration of the parks and recreation areas with the local community rather than administering them as islands in local areas.

State governments are very active in tourism. Some states, such as Arkansas, place state parks and tourism in the same agency. Gunn (1994) divides tourism into three sectors: business, nonprofit, and governmental and states that, "Contrary to tourism being an industry or dominated by the business sector, it is developed and managed by another very important sector—government. ...The governmental sector owns and manages much of the infrastructure upon which tourism depends". State governments are rapidly becoming more aware of the importance of the economic impacts of outdoor recreation and tourism. In Texas, tourism was a $23 billion business in 1993 (State Task Force on Texas Nature Tourism, 1994). Visitors to Texas state parks generate an estimated annual economic impact on local communities of over $770 million (DeLoney, et al., 1996). State government outdoor recreation providers are working more closely with the tourism industry and other private or commercial businesses who provide products and the infrastructure needed for people to engage in outdoor recreation and tourism. This cooperative interest is likely to continue.

Future Trends, Issues, and Directions of State Governments

State governments will face future trends similar to current trends. The trend to run state governments more like businesses will continue well into the foreseeable future. State governments have one major complicating factor, however, in trying to run governmental entities like businesses—political considerations. It is doubtful whether a governmental entity can operate entirely like a business given political realities. Elected political officials may not support dedicated funds because they lose the flexibility to react to other priorities in the budgetary process.

Coupled with the issue of dedicated funds is the problem of employee motivation. For any business to prosper, employees must be motivated. To increase state park revenues, park employees responsible for implementing revenue increases must receive benefits from their efforts. They must, for example, see the revenues they generate come back to their park or at least to the state park system. State park visitors are more receptive to higher fees if they see improvements made in the park with the higher fees. If revenues go back to the general treasury for the elected officials to disburse rather than to the park to improve the quality of visitor service, then the quality of service does not improve and the visitors are left dissatisfied.

State governments can expect the quality of the visitor's experience to become more of an issue in the future. As park visitors are charged higher fees, they expect corresponding increases in the quality of service and amenities they receive for the higher prices (More, Dustin, & Knopf, 1996). There appears to be a link between high service quality and long-term customer loyalty (Backman & Veldkamp, 1995). LaPage (1995), a former state parks director, makes the following observation about the quality issue:

> The rewards for failing to improve the quality of public use can only be more restrictions, more deferred maintenance, more loss of heritage, less diversity, and reduced feelings of pride of ownership. Conversely, a commitment to improving the quality of public use and expanding the public's responsibility for its own resources can provide real assurance of park perpetuity.

In the future, the decisions of state government leaders will continue to determine the quality of visitor services and experiences. Decisions such as staff freezes and reductions, budget reductions, park closures, and the operation of parks for political reasons rather than to meet criteria established by the agency may have adverse long-range impacts on the mission and goals of the state agency, particularly the generation of revenues from user fees.

Another issue that state governments must address is unfair competition with the private sector. "Most public park systems have a policy of non-competition with the private sector. Public park pricing practices, however, usually undercut those of close substitutes in the private sector. Public park expansion practices often continue to disregard the private sector's unused capacity..." (LaPage, 1995). Recent price increases in state park fees in Texas have brought prices more in line with prices for similar services in the private sector.

State government entities will face another dimension of this issue in the future. While the private sector challenges state governments to operate more like private business, there is a prevailing sentiment among some in the private sector that any profitable aspects of the operations should be placed in private hands. If the profit–generating aspects of an operation are removed, it is unclear how that entity can continue to operate in a businesslike fashion.

States must deal with one trend both currently and in the future. It is unlikely the federal government will support funding state and local parks from the Federal Land and Water Conservation Fund or urban park spending (Tice, 1997). From 1965-94, LWCF appropriations pumped $6.1 billion (in 1994 dollars) into state and local parks (DeLoney, et al., 1996). This issue is at least two-fold: Where will the money come from to maintain these parks in the future? And how will state and local governments generate sufficient funding over the next 30 years that will not be forthcoming from federal sources? Compounding this issue is the decaying infrastructure which increases maintenance costs (DeLoney, et al., 1996).

The interest of outdoor recreationists and tourists in a diversity of activities will continue into the future. A continuing increase in foreign tourists will add to the diversity of interests. The challenge to the states is how to meet such a wide range of interests in recreational activities and continue to provide opportunities in established but stable activities, such as fishing. The greatest challenge facing state governments in the future may be simply the way they do the business of providing outdoor recreation and tourism opportunities, particularly the integration of revenue generation and business practices with political realities while providing quality visitor experiences. Whoever conducts the business will need to understand outdoor recreation, tourism, economics, politics, business and marketing concepts, and possess the ability to apply these understandings to meet outdoor recreation and tourism demands at the state government level. In the future world economy, outdoor recreation and tourism will become an even bigger business.

State Park Systems in the United States

(By Daniel D. McLean, Associate Professor, Indiana University, Bloomington, IN)

America's state parks and associated areas provide close-to-home outdoor recreation opportunities. The majority of U.S. counties have one or more state park system areas—a sharp contrast to federal land which is primarily in the West (Figure III.11). Many counties that are designated as 'Metropolitan' or are adjacent to Metropolitan counties contain state park areas (Figure III.12).[28] State park systems provide nearby recreation opportunities for metropolitan residents, especially in the Eastern United States where the majority of the population is. The 50 state park systems share many similarities, but each also has uniqueness.

This section focuses on the common attributes of state parks in the United States, examining their current status. It also describes trends and their potential impacts. Also covered are the types of areas and facilities administered within state park systems. In 1924, the first National Conference on State Parks was convened by Stephen Mather. Since then, state park directors have met regularly. The NASPD has provided a forum for discussion, as well as a wealth of statistical information about America's state parks. For the last 20 years, the NASPD has sponsored the "Annual Information Exchange" (AIX), which gathers data related to development and progress of state parks. Since 1991, data collection has become more consistent. The most current data are for the year ending June 30, 1995.

Figure III.11: Counties with State Parks or Recreation Areas, 1995

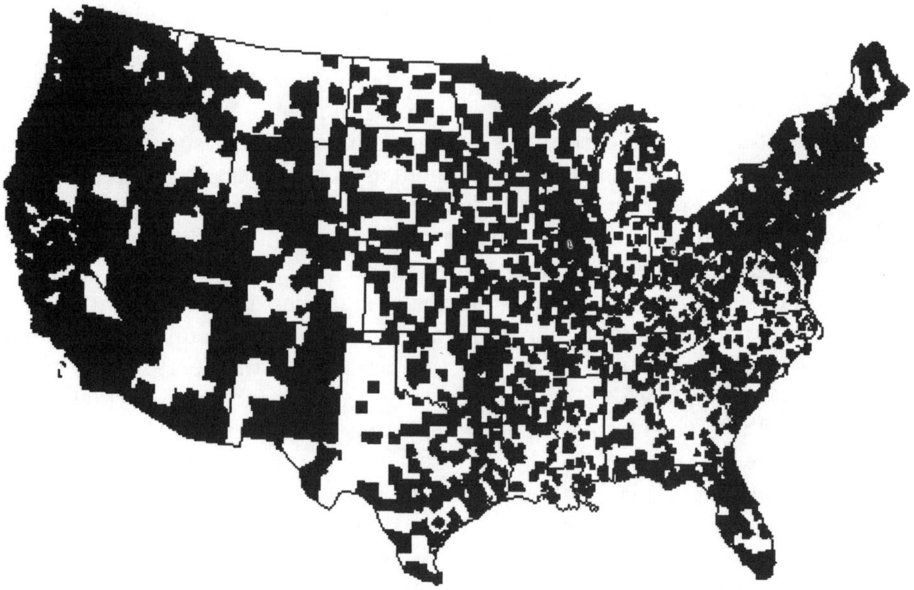

Source: USDA Forest Service. State park database compiled from state DNR literature and brochures. 1995.

[28]Metropolitan designation of U.S. counties was done by the USDA Economic Research Service, Rural Economy Division, Calvin Beale, Demographer, 1993.

Figure III.12: Counties with State Parks or Recreation Areas that Are Either Classified as Metropolitan or Are Adjacent to Metropolitan Counties, 1995

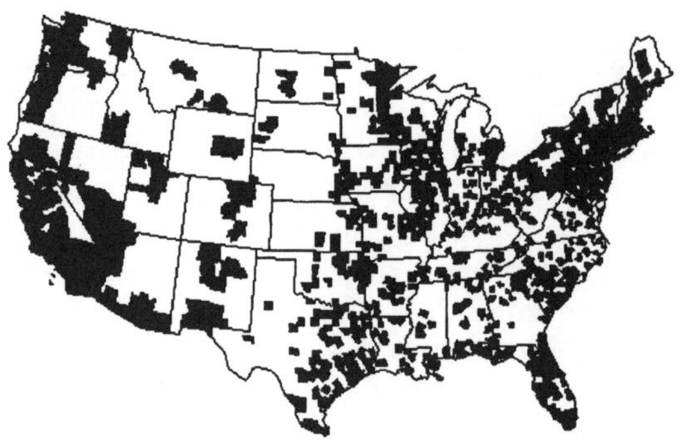

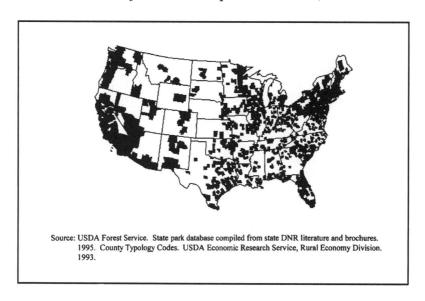

Source: USDA Forest Service. State park database compiled from state DNR literature and brochures. 1995. County Typology Codes. USDA Economic Research Service, Rural Economy Division. 1993.

Inventory of State Park Areas

State park agencies administer a wide variety of areas, eight distinctive and two collective. The categories of areas include state parks, recreation areas, natural areas, historic areas, environmental education areas, scientific areas, state forests, State Fish and Wildlife areas, other areas, and miscellaneous areas. Definitions established by the NASPD insure better consistency in reporting. The inventory makes it clear that state park agencies manage far more than parks.

Trails are a very important recreation resource managed by state park agencies. They are not included among the eight system areas, but are treated separately. The 1996 AIX reports 1,353 state trails totaling 15,390 miles in the United States. These totals do not include trails in state parks or other agency areas. Almost every state park agency or other state government agency manages a program specifically for trails (in some states, more than one). Program functions go beyond managing state trails to statewide trail planning, technical assistance to local governments and other trail groups, grants administration, and a variety of other purposes. State trail programs are covered later in the chapter.

Depending on the legislative mandate of a particular state, most agencies manage a variety of different types of areas. Eight state park agencies administer state forests, but most states have a separate state forestry agency. In contrast, one state reported having no state parks in both the 1992 and the 1996 AIX reports. However, this same state has almost 42,000 acres administered by its "state park agency." State legislative bodies which designate the types of areas in a system impact the agency's ability to report within NASPD predetermined definitions.

The state park estate is quite large, though it is just a fraction of the size of the federal estate. In 1995, state park agencies reported administering more than 5,500 areas (Table III.15). About 92 percent of the areas were open and in operation. The North region has more than twice the number of areas as any other region, and almost half of the national total. From 1991 to 1995, the total number of areas in the system increased by 32 percent, a net gain of 1,267 areas. The number of operating areas increased by 37 percent. As expected, state parks represent the largest single type of area administered with one-third of the total units (Table III.13). Recreation areas, natural areas, historic areas, and "other" areas round out the top five.

Table III.15: Number and Area of State Park System Areas by Type of Area and Region, 1995

Type of Area	Region									
	North		South		Rocky Mountains		Pacific Coast		U.S. Total	
	Number	Area[1]	Number	Area[1]	Number	Area	Number	Area[1]	Number	Area[1]
State Parks	1,023	2,144.8	388	858.6	202	804.2	238	4,018.0	1,851	7,825.6
Recreation Areas	115	179.6	124	106.5	135	193.3	395	764.6	769	1,244.0
Natural Areas	218	115.5	86	622.9	242	191.5	76	98.2	622	1,028.1
Historic Areas	184	15.8	168	29.1	101	26.6	94	17.1	547	88.7
Environmental Education Areas	42	88.6	3	4.7	6	5.9	0	0	51	99.2
Scientific Areas	89	10.6	0	0	0	0	0	0	89	10.6
Forests	274	770.1	0	0	0	0	0	0	274	770.1
Fish and Wildlife Areas	45	102.7	1	0.2	423	307.1	0	0	469	410.1
Other Areas	205	47.5	32	44.8	49	3.4	203	49.1	489	144.8
Miscellaneous Areas	300	178.2	32	8.5	6	2.1	44	1.6	382	190.4
All Areas	2,495	3,653.3	834	1,675.3	1,164	1,534.1	1,050	4,948.6	5,543	11,811.3

[1]Numbers may not sum exactly to totals because of rounding.

Source: National Association of State Park Directors, *Annual Information Exchange*, 1996.

State park system areas totaled approximately 11.8 million acres (Table III.15). The size of the state park estate varies considerably by region and by type of area. The Pacific Coast (including Alaska) has over 40 percent of the total state park system acreage in the United States. Alaska by itself has more than one-fourth of the U.S. acreage, despite having just 2 percent of the areas. Excluding Alaska, the North region dominates acreage as it does areas with about 43 percent of the total land area in the other 49 states. State park system acreage increased by slightly more than 850,000 acres (about 8 percent) between 1991 and 1995. Among the types of areas, state parks dominate in acreage, accounting for just under two-thirds of all acres managed (Table III.15). Recreation areas are a distant second at about 11 percent and natural areas third at about 9 percent of the total estate acres. Even though state park agencies administer a variety of areas, their primary business is state parks. Alaska contains an exceptionally large portion of this land. With respect to state parks proper, Alaska's 2.89 million acres represent 37 percent of the national state park total of 7.83 million acres. Alaska also has almost one-quarter of the nation's 1.24 million acres of State Recreation Areas.

The Rocky Mountain region has the most natural areas, but the South has the most acreage set aside for this type of area. Texas and Florida account for more than 430,000 acres of the South's natural areas. Between 1991 and 1995, there was a 60 percent increase in the number of defined natural areas, but only a 7 percent gain in area. Natural areas in the Rocky Mountain region grew at the rate of 166 percent over that period and the Pacific region reported a 62 percent growth rate. Alaska reported no new natural areas. Colorado reported an increase in the number of natural areas from 70 to 200, and acreage of natural areas increased 31,000 acres. Every region showed some growth in natural areas, but the South reported the slowest growth.

Historic areas are more equally divided among the four regions. The North has the largest number and the South has the most acreage. Among states, California manages the most historic area acreage, over 13,500 acres. Growth in historic areas from 1991 to 1995 has been moderate, a 7 percent increase in areas and a 15 percent gain in acreage. Environmental education and scientific areas are almost exclusively in the North with 82 percent of the classified education areas and 89 percent of the area. The Rocky Mountains and South regions also have environmental education areas, but their numbers are very small. All of the scientific areas are in the North. The growth of environmental education and scientific areas was dramatic between 1991 and 1995. There were 22 environmental education areas reported in 1991 and 51 areas in 1995. Illinois grew fastest, from none in 1991 to 23 in 1995. Growth of scientific areas was even more dramatic, from five areas in 1991 to 89 in 1995. All of the increase occurred in Iowa, which had no scientific areas in 1991.

State forests present somewhat of an anomaly to the reporting process. Most states have their own forest resource management administrative units. Eight state park agencies in the North report having some forest management responsibility. The data do not clarify whether separate forest management units are present in each state. No other region reports having any units designated as forests in their state park systems. Fish and wildlife areas constitute 3.5 percent of the state park estate area. This category also represents a function administered by a separate agency in most states. The Rocky Mountain region has 90 percent of the areas and 75 percent of the acreage. Kansas accounts for 23 percent of fish and wildlife areas and 68 percent of the acreage. West Virginia and Illinois also have a substantial number and size of fish and wildlife areas. Nationwide, fish and wildlife areas managed by state park agencies increased from just 49 in 1991 to 469 in 1996. It is likely that transfers of authority, changes in classification, and varied interpretation of how to report areas accounts for a major portion of the reported change.

State park system areas identified as "Other" are those not previously identified. They are considered special or significant enough in a particular State to warrant separate identification and treatment. "Other" areas account for approximately 9 percent of national state park system areas, but only about 1 percent of acreage. The Rocky Mountain Region has considerably fewer acres in the "other" area category than the other three regions, each of which manages more than 40,000 of these acres.

"Miscellaneous"areas, those that are not easily categorized or distinguished enough to be classified, total 1.6 percent of the state park estate area and just under 7 percent of the areas. The number of miscellaneous areas increased substantially between 1991 and 1995, but the reported acreage decreased. The data do not provide a clear picture as to why this has occurred. It is probable that miscellaneous areas (which are sort of a catch-all "everything else" category) were added mostly as small tracts of land without easy classification while larger tracts received a formal classification. In some cases, the miscellaneous areas may be used as a holding category while the state park agency determines how to classify them.

Inventory of State Park Facilities

State park agencies manage a large variety of facilities. The most popular and common types of facilities are listed in Table III.16. Campsites are the most common facilities found in the state parks systems. Every State manages campsites, which number almost 200,000 improved and primitive campsites in 2,910 areas throughout the United States. Since 1991, the number of improved campsites increased in every region, highest in the Rocky Mountains at 15 percent. The North has more than twice as many improved campsites as any other region and nearly one-half the national total. One interesting trend between 1991 and 1995 is a 3.5 percent decline in the number of year-round improved campsites. The greatest loss of year-round improved campsites was in the North Region, where 7,500 fewer were reported. However, during the same period seasonal improved campsites increased substantially, especially in the North. It seems likely that some year-round improved campsites have been reclassified as seasonal. During the same period, almost all of the improved campsites added in the South were year-round.

Both primitive campsites and state park system areas with primitive campsites suffered a net loss between 1991 and 1995. Nationally, there were approximately 2,100 fewer primitive campsites and 290 fewer primitive camping areas. All of these losses occurred in the South. Excluding the South, the number of primitive campsites actually increased by almost 2,000. Texas accounted for 83 percent of the reported loss of primitive campsites. Beginning with the 1995 AIX, Texas reported no primitive campsites. During the same period, the number of improved campsites increased by almost 2,200, so it is very likely that Texas reclassified most of its primitive campsites and perhaps closed others.

Cabins and cottages represent a significant part of the state park estate. The North and South account for about 87 percent of the more than 6,000 cabins and cottages in the United States. Only seven States do not have cabins or cottages. These facilities are a distinctive feature of state parks. Between 1991 and 1995, the number of cabins and cottages increased a modest 7 percent. The increase in year-round cabins and cottages was 14 percent compared to a decline in seasonal cabins and cottages of about 5 percent. The increase in year-round cabins and cottages signals a trend towards extending use of state parks.

Table III.16: Number of State Park System Facilities and Percent Seasonal by Type of Facility and Region, 1995[1]

Type of Facility	Region				
	North	South	Rocky Mountains	Pacific Coast	U.S. Total
Improved campsites	71,336 (77)	30,706 (14)	18,216 (39)	21,707 (25)	141,965 (49)
Primitive campsites	16,938 (63)	5,153 (2)	18,605 (10)	9,063 (37)	49,759 (32)
Cabin/cottages	2,728 (47)	2,562 (9)	376 (63)	408 (5)	6,074 (29)
Lodges	43 (23)	53 (0)	7 (86)	7 (0)	110 (15)
Lodge rooms	2,648 (16)	2,681 (0)	200 (80)	609 (0)	6,138 (9)
Golf courses	48 (79)	54 (0)	4 (75)	6 (66)	112 (40)
Golf Holes	748 (75)	837 (0)	54 (83)	72 (63)	1,711 (38)
Marinas	98 (93)	82 (5)	55 (25)	11 (45)	246 (46)
Swimming pools	158 (91)	128 (97)	8 (88)	2 (100)	296 (93)
Stables	35 (83)	23 (61)	13 (62)	4 (50)	75 (71)
Ski slopes	25 (100)	0 (0)	0 (0)	4 (100)	29 (100)

[1] Percentage of facilities which are operated on a seasonal basis is given in parentheses.

Source: National Association of State Park Directors, *Annual Information Exchange*, 1996.

Development of lodges as revenue–producing facilities for state parks has increased by 31 percent since 1991. The North Region had the largest growth with 12 new lodge sites, followed by the South (8) and the Pacific (6). There are 110 total lodges in 109 areas throughout the United States. Only 26 of the 50 reporting States have lodges. Kentucky leads the nation with 15, followed by Ohio, Illinois and West Virginia with 8 each. Eight of the reporting States have only one lodge. Most lodges operate year round, but 16 of them are seasonal. Both Missouri and South Dakota report 5 seasonal lodges. In all, a capacity of over 6,000 lodge rooms was reported, an average of more than 55 rooms per lodge. Year-round lodges tend to be larger than seasonal lodges. The number of lodge rooms grew almost 13 percent between 1991 and 1995.

Golfing opportunities in state parks appear to be growing, but the data are somewhat conflicting. Although there was a net decline of three golf courses between 1991 and 1995, the number of year–round golf courses increased by 11 (8 in the North). We suspect that five courses that had been seasonal now operate all year. Golf participation has grown dramatically in the last decade. Not only is the influence of the sport being felt, but also the potential for golf courses to generate revenue. The bulk of the state golf courses are in the South, as are the number of year-round holes. The North has the most seasonal holes. Between 1991 and 1995, the number of year-round holes in the state park estate grew by 42 percent and seasonal holes available for play increased 95 percent. All of the seasonal golfing holes were added in the North.

The presence of marinas in the state park estate has grown only moderately. Between 1991 and 1995, the number of areas with marinas grew by 5 percent, but the number of operating marinas declined. The loss was all in seasonal marinas; the number of year-round marinas increased. Only 10 states report not having a marina in their system. The Pacific Coast Region has the fewest marinas, probably because so many private marinas exist along the Pacific Coast.

Swimming pools are a regional emphasis in the North and South. Of all pools available, 97 percent are in these regions. The data suggest that the bulk of the pools are outdoors and only in operation during the summer. It is also suspected the 20 indoor pools are associated with year-round lodges. For example, seven of the 20 year-round pools are in Ohio, a State with 8 year-round lodges. Swimming pools continue to be built. From 1991 to 1995, the number of seasonal pools increased 56 percent, while the number of year-round pools declined 46 percent.

Stables are present in all of the regions, although less so in the Western regions. Their number has been relatively constant. Between 1991 and 1995 there was no increase in the total number of stables. Seven year-round stables were eliminated, but seven seasonal stables were added. Stables are the only reported state park facility that did not change between the two reporting periods. Ten states report ski slopes. Minnesota has 14, and Massachusetts, New Hampshire, Pennsylvania, and Washington all report two ski slopes each. Clearly, ski slopes are not prominent in the state park estate, and exist only in States with sufficient snow and cold.

A key trend in the facilities provided by state park systems is the move from seasonal to year-round use. With some exceptions, numbers of seasonal facilities are declining and the numbers of year-round facilities are increasing. Many seasonal facilities are either being converted to year-round facilities or are being closed. The reasons for conversion are probably the increased demand by Americans for year-round recreation and increased financial pressure on state parks to produce revenue. Closure of seasonal facilities is attributable to generation of insufficient revenue to cover costs. State parks are more than just areas to view wildlife and enjoy nature. Increasingly, they are destination resorts or camping destinations. The natural beauty and diversity of recreational and educational opportunities that are accessible to large numbers of people assures a strong role for state park systems in the spectrum of outdoor recreation providers.

America's State Parks—An End-of-Century Assessment

(By Ney C. Landrum, Executive Director, National Association of State Park Directors, Tallahassee, FL)

The state parks of the United States have been a major provider of public outdoor recreation for almost a century. Starting with the designation of a few scattered sites in the mid– to late–1800s, the state park movement gained significant momentum in the 1920s and 1930s with establishment of the first real state park *systems.* Today, the 50 state park systems contain almost 12 million acres in some 5,500 individual units, and host about three-quarters of a billion visitors a year (National Association of State Park Directors: *1996 Annual Information Exchange).*Because of their large number and great diversity, it is difficult to generalize about the state parks. For the most part, however, they concentrate on the provision of *resource-based* outdoor recreation—that is, those types of recreational activities that are supported essentially by the resources (which may be either natural or cultural) of the park rather than by man-made facilities. In this respect, the state parks are similar to the national parks, although typically much smaller in size. With their wide distribution, the state parks are easily accessible to prospective users, and have historically catered to the population base within the general vicinity. In some cases, though, the state parks were conceived primarily as an attraction for principally out-of-state tourists, acknowledging their value for economic purposes in addition to the satisfaction of public outdoor recreation needs.

Although the state parks continue to be an important, if not essential, component of state government services, for the past two decades or so they have found themselves less able to compete effectively with other programs for public funding. In this era of increasingly tight budgets and shifting government priorities, state park programs in some extreme cases have not been funded sufficiently to maintain their status quo, much less to expand to meet increasing outdoor recreation demand. This deteriorating financial situation probably has brought about the most momentous change in state park operating philosophy since inception of the movement.

As noted, the state parks have long acknowledged an economic purpose of varying degree, and by virtue of providing popular services for a fee have assumed an entrepreneurial role as well. Thus, it is a simple matter procedurally to generate revenues through many aspects of state park operations: entrance fees, parking fees, camping and other activity fees, sales of goods and services either directly or through concessions, and so forth. Historically, the state parks have offset a significant portion of their operating costs with such revenues. When the effect of serious budget cut-backs first hit the state parks in the early 1970s, the common response was to raise more revenue through new and increased fees to compensate for reductions in general revenue. The relative ease with which this was done resulted in even greater demands for financial self-sufficiency being placed on the state park agencies. From 1975 to 1995, state park revenues increased by 364%, and the degree of operating cost recovery from 35.8% to 43.0% (National Recreation and Park Association: *State Park Statistics—1975,* and National Association of State Park Directors: *1996 Annual Information Exchange).*

Selected State Park Statistics for the 50 State Park Systems of the United States, 1975-1995

	1975#	1980	1985	1990	1995
State park units	3,804	4,512	4,726*	4,599	5,541
Acreage (1000's)	9,838	9,275	10,175	10,346	11,807
Day visitors (1000's)	465,302	467,051	597,669	664,047	686,483
Overnight visitors (1000's)	51,488	68,204	62,572	60,291	59,121
Full-time staff	18,083	11,192	12,950	15,739	18,980
Part-time staff	26,846	21,168	21,032	25,981	29,861
Operating expenditures ($1000's)	322,276	495,378	740,637	1,060,401	1,244,903
Fixed capital outlay ($1000's)	319,704	490,286	275,788	435,051	275,771
Operating revenue ($1000's)	115,406	180,595	284,657	401,800	535,685

1975 data are from *State Park Statistics—1975,* published by the National Recreation and Park Association, 1977. Remaining data are from the appropriate volumes of *Annual Information Exchange,* published by the National Association of State Park Directors. Because of possible differences in methodology, data from the two different sources may not be fully comparable in every respect.

* The actual published figure was adjusted in this one instance to make it more directly comparable with the corresponding figures for the other years.

Although greater emphasis has, perforce, been placed on revenue generation over the last two decades, the state parks have not deviated materially from their central mission of providing resource-based outdoor recreation opportunities to the public at modest cost. In fact, the parks' ability to offset budget shortfalls through self-generation of revenues has in part enabled steady, if not spectacular, growth to continue in park acreage, facilities and visitation—although not always without conflict and controversy over the side-effects of certain of these revenue measures. Questions have been raised, for instance, about fee increases and the possibility of pricing the state parks out of reach of lower-income families, usually considered a major target user group for such public recreation areas. Another frequently expressed concern is the possibility of over-commercialization—changing the character of the parks with too many revenue–producing facilities, such as lodges, restaurants, golf courses and marinas. Fortunately, most state park systems seek to achieve a balance in their programs, using classification, zoning and similar techniques, so that some areas may be identified for intensive development while others are kept in near pristine condition. To juggle all of the demands successfully, state park professionals today must still be qualified resource managers even as they strive to operate their parks in a more business-like manner to "make ends meet."

A generation ago, a state parks staffer would likely refer to park users as "visitors" or "patrons;" today, the term "customer" is more commonly heard. Semantics aside, that seemingly innocuous variation in terminology signifies a different orientation in the operation of state park programs in this day and time. While the state parks have retained their immense popularity with the public, they seem to have lost some of the status as an important public service that provided the momentum for their establishment in years past. State legislatures, confronted by other pressing demands for government funding, have tended to take the route of least resistance where parks are concerned. Although the level of appropriations for state parks nationwide has increased steadily over the years (up 286% since 1975 [op. cit.]), it nevertheless reflects a growing dependence on the ability of the parks to generate a substantial part of their own operating funds. This attitude of more or less letting the parks "fend for themselves" has had the practical effect of changing the way many of the nation's state park programs operate.

In their efforts to become more entrepreneurial, the state parks have experimented with a number of approaches for either raising revenue or cutting costs. Merchandizing activities have been greatly expanded, providing for new lines of goods as well as for innovative sales techniques. Retail outlets for park-related merchandise in off-park locations, such as shopping malls, have been tried, as have mail-order catalog sales of similar items. Subsidies from private businesses, in the form of either cash or goods and services, are being pursued successfully in exchange for licenses to operate in state parks or recognition in state park related contexts. New partnerships have been formed with private enterprise to construct and operate major park facilities and, in some cases, to assume responsibility from the state for operating existing park areas. "Privatization," with its infinite variations, is probably the cost-cutting concept generating the most interest in state park circles today.

State park agencies are also looking increasingly to the nonprofit segment of the private sector for help in dealing with current problems. "Friends" groups, support organizations, and foundations of one kind or another have been established in almost every state. These groups of highly-motivated citizens are called on to provide volunteer help in the parks, to raise funds for various projects, and to lobby state legislatures in support of state park programs. In addition to the direct, more immediate results achieved through these efforts, this type of citizen involvement also helps to create a larger, lasting constituent base for the state parks.

Although state parks have been popular outdoor recreation destinations for many years, the overall rate of visitation increase has been relatively modest—up only 44% from 1975 to 1995 *[op. cit.]*. The unused capacity available in the fifty state park systems is undoubtedly substantial. To take advantage of this situation and, not incidentally, generate additional revenues through increased visitation, state park agencies have become more aggressive in recent years in marketing the recreational opportunities of the parks. Such marketing activities take many forms, and frequently involve cooperative arrangements with state tourism agencies. In fact, state parks programs in several states have actually been housed in the agencies responsible for statewide tourism promotion. While this organizational placement has certain advantages, it also has raised some concern that the resource management responsibility of state parks might be compromised by too much promotion and the resulting need to accommodate artificially–induced levels of use. It is still too early to assess the impact of this factor.

While, from a management standpoint, financial considerations seem to have exerted a major influence over the direction state park programs have taken in recent years, the parks themselves have taken on a new aura of importance in this era of heightened environmental awareness and appreciation for nature. State parks, being much more accessible than the national parks and typically more "green" than the local parks, are ideally situated to serve the "back to nature" needs of the American people. The state parks have responded to this demand by continuing to do what they have always done best: provide traditional forms of resource-based outdoor recreation in an essentially natural setting. As the need has grown, the parks have expanded (total acreage has increased by 20% since 1975 *[op. cit.]*), installed basic facilities for access, safety, and appropriate use, and provided an adequate level of staffing to manage the resources and service the visitors (although the ratio of park acreage to full-time staff personnel increased from 544 to 622 between 1975 and 1995 *[op. cit.]*, suggesting a slight decline in overall staff capability). The parks have also continued to emphasize interpretation as their paramount program offering, recognizing the parity of nature appreciation and environmental education with the more traditional forms of active outdoor recreation: picnicking, swimming, camping, boating, hiking, and the like. The fundamental precept of good state park planning is to provide a *balance* of appropriate resource-based outdoor recreational experiences—not necessarily within each park, but within the system as a whole.

The Future of State Parks

America's state parks—while continuing to grow, adjust, and adapt—have essentially achieved maturity as a comprehensive nationwide movement. They have a clearly definable mission, and have situated themselves well to serve their important purpose. While some further expansion of their resource base can be expected, it probably will be opportunistic, adding a new park here and there as circumstances permit. More likely will be continued development of new facilities—especially of the more up-scale variety—designed to draw additional visitors from farther distances. Private capital will be wooed for joint venture projects of likely increasing magnitude. Further experimentation with various degrees of "privatization" of state park operations will undoubtedly occur over the next decade or so.

The greatest uncertainty facing the state parks in the foreseeable future is the matter of unstable funding. This uncertainty, and the probability that the parks will be required to generate an even larger share of their operating budgets, places an unnatural constraint on the ability of park administrators to plan and carry out their program in a manner purely to fulfill the mission of their state park system. Be that as it may, it is expected that the state parks will, through a variety of innovative measures, obtain the funding necessary to maintain their operations at least a minimally adequate level.

One encouraging aspect of state park operations over the years has been the consistently high level of user satisfaction reflected by in-park surveys and opinion polls. Even today, it is apparent from overall user reaction that the quality of experience in the parks has not suffered appreciably from the vicissitudes of park funding and consequent operational adjustments. Managing assets so as to maintain the quality of outdoor recreational experience while still protecting resources remains a real challenge for state park administrators. Because it is much easier to assess visitor satisfaction than resource condition, there is a danger that—especially in times of budget short-falls and limited management options—the former will be selected over the latter as the sole measure of operational success. Maintaining the right balance between use *and* preservation considerations will therefore continue to be the most fundamental issue with which state park professionals have to deal in the years ahead.

State Trail Programs in the United States

(By Roger L. Moore, Associate Professor, North Carolina State University, Raleigh, NC, and Mark I. Ivy, Graduate Research Assistant, North Carolina State University, Raleigh, NC)

Trails are an integral part of the infrastructure of North America. They have been used for transportation for centuries and recreation for many generations. Trails are still essential for recreation and transportation today, but they are also increasingly valuable for a host of other benefits. They generate significant tourism expenditures, improve health and fitness, attract corporate relocations, increase community pride, facilitate environmental education, provide access to other recreation areas, create a sense of place, motivate conservation, and provide open–space protection and much more. The activities that take place on trails are expanding rapidly as are the types of trails being provided including traditional backcountry trails, rail-trails, surfaced multiple-use trails in suburban and urban areas, and greenways. Trails have been and continue to be built and managed by public, private, and nonprofit organizations as well as less–formal trail user groups. Among the most important providers of trail opportunities in the U.S., however, are states. They manage large areas of public land with large numbers of existing trail miles spread widely across their states and are well positioned to facilitate local trail efforts. This section focuses on the trail programs operated by state governments. The objectives are to describe the current status of these programs and to identify the current trends and future issues they will soon be facing.

Description of State Trail Programs

Not surprisingly, the trail programs of the various states are quite diverse. All of the states responding to a survey conducted by Moore (1994) were involved in some aspect of trail development or management, although the programs are located in various state agencies and some do not consider their trail efforts to constitute a formal trails program. In fact, most states have more than one program relating to trails. Staff size of the state trail programs vary from 0 to 40 full time equivalents (FTE) with an average program staff of 2.7. Only about 35 percent of the 52 trail administrators responding were assigned full time to trails in 1994 (including bicycle and/or pedestrian responsibilities). Those who reported not being assigned to trails full time, spent an average of about half their time on trail issues.

Seventy percent of the trail administrators reported that their states had state trail legislation. Washington passed the earliest trail legislation (1967) and Vermont passed the most recent legislation (1994). Just over half of the legislation was passed during the 1970s. The earliest trail staff was hired by California in 1945 and the most recent in 1992 by several states. Nearly half of the programs hired their first staff during the 1970s as well.

The types of activities carried out by state trail programs are varied, as are the priorities attached to each activity. Of 22 different activities included in the survey, the following five were considered to be the programs' highest priorities on average: "providing trail opportunities close to where people live," "staff support for state trails advisory committee," "awarding grants," "developing trail plans," and "providing an interconnected system of trails in our state."

State Trail Plans and Support Information

Thirty-two programs (66 percent) reported that their state had developed a state trails plan since 1974 and over half of those have been revised since 1990. Thirty-two programs also reported that they had a state trails inventory and 24 said their Statewide Comprehensive Outdoor Recreation Plan (SCORP) included estimates of total trail usage or number of users by activity type for their state. Five others reported that they had such information in planning documents other than their SCORP. In terms of support information, 70 percent of the programs reported having trail construction guidelines for bicycle and pedestrian facilities, while about 60 percent had trail construction guidelines for other types of trails. One-third of the state trails programs reported having estimates of the economic impact of trails or trail use in their states.

Sources and Uses of Funds

Most trail administrators estimated that federal land managing agency budgets and state appropriations were the largest source of planning and maintenance funds being expended on trails in their states in Fiscal Year 1993.[29] Most considered the Intermodal Surface Transportation Efficiency Act (ISTEA) funds to be the largest sources of acquisition and development funding, however. Overall, state trail programs spent the largest portion of their budgets on acquisition and development expenditures and the least for administration and planning. All but two of the programs were active in awarding trail grants within their states. These grant programs included various sources of monies including the state appropriations, the National Recreational Trails Fund (NRTF), Land and Water Conservation Fund (LWCF), registration fees, etc. The supply of grant money was not sufficient to meet the demand. Some states, such as Delaware, have initiated a state version of the Land and Water Conservation Fund to try and fill the void created when funding virtually ceased for the state side of the federal program. Other innovative sources of funding used by trail programs include various forms of taxes, license fees, bond issues, and lottery funds.

Trail Trends and Factors Motivating Trail Development

Trail administrators felt that support for and use of trails had increased in all areas over the past five years. Two-thirds reported that overall use was seeing "significant increases" in their states. Trail use was seen as increasing more than support for trails, however. Of all the types of support examined, administrators felt that public support had increased more than any other kind of support during the past five years. Forty percent reported "significant increases" in public support. Volunteer involvement was reported to have increased at a similar rate. The weakest area of support was state trail program budgets. Although 24 respondents (47 percent) reported increases in their budgets over the past five years, 19 (37 percent) reported no change.

Trail administrators reported that the largest increases in use over the past five years had occurred in suburban areas. Increases there were said to have been "minor" by 42 percent of respondents and "significant" by 52 percent. The smallest increases were reported in backcountry areas. Thirty-one percent felt there had been no change in backcountry trail use in their states and six percent reported that use had actually decreased on their backcounty trails. Trail administrators, on average, reported increases in all 10 activities listed in the survey. Mountain bike use, however, was felt to have increased more than that of any other trail activity. Just under 80 percent said mountain bike use had increased, and 25 percent said the increases had been significant. Motorized types of use were felt to have increased less than nonmotorized uses overall (Table III.17).

Table III.17: State Trends in Trail Use Over the Past Five Years by Location and Type

Use	Mean	Standard Deviation	Number Responding
Location			
Use in Suburban Areas	4.46[1]	.61	50
Use in Urban Areas	4.43	.64	51
Use in Rural Areas	4.02	.68	50
Use in Backcountry Areas	3.84	.90	49

[29]These estimates include all trails in the state, not just those managed by the states.

Table III.17: State Trends in Trail Use Over the Past Five Years by Location and Type

Use	Mean	Standard Deviation	Number Responding
Type			
Use by Mountain Bicyclists	4.86	.46	49
Use by Walkers/Hikers	4.33	.69	49
Use by Other Bicyclists	4.04	.68	48
Use by Equestrians	3.90	.83	41
Use by Runners	3.78	.87	49
Use by Snowmobiles	3.68	.85	41
Use by Cross-Country Skiers	3.67	.75	43
Use by ATVs	3.62	1.01	47
Use by 4-Wheel Drives	3.45	.95	47
Use by Motorcyclists	3.40	.80	47

[1] Means based on a five-point scale with 1 indicating "Significant Decreases" and 5 "Significant Increases."

Source: Moore, R. L. (1994). State trail programs: A survey of state trail administrators. Denver, CO: The National Association of State Trail Administrators. Available c/o Colorado State Trails Program, 1313 Sherman St., Room 618, Denver, CO 80203.

Trail administrators had interesting insights on what was motivating trail development in their states. They were given a list of nine broad public benefits that trails might have and asked to rate each in terms of how much of a factor they felt it was in motivating the development of new trails in their state. The responses indicated that all of the factors were considered to be of at least some importance. "Public recreation opportunities," however, was by far the most important. The second most important motivation, on average, was "tourism and economic development." "Traffic reduction and transportation alternatives" was felt to be the least important motivating factor of the nine examined (Table III.18). Two states considered "natural resources protection" and "preserving railroad rights-of-way" as other motives for trail development.

Table III.18: Factors Motivating Trail Development in State According to State Trail Administrators

Benefit	Mean	Standard Deviation	Number Responding
Public recreation opportunities	6.24[1]	1.03	49
Tourism and economic development	5.45	1.47	51
Health and fitness	5.12	1.31	51
Aesthetic beauty	5.08	1.38	51
Preserving undeveloped open space	4.96	1.70	49
Community pride	4.94	1.45	50
Access for disabled persons	4.78	1.25	51
Public education about nature and the environment	4.61	1.42	51
Traffic reduction and transportation alternatives	4.16	1.68	49

[1]Means based on a seven-point scale with 1 indicating "Not At All Important" and 7 "Extremely Important."

Source: Moore, R. L. 1994. State Trail Programs: A Survey of State Trail Administrators. Denver, CO: The National Association of State Trail Administrators. Available c/o Colorado State Trails Program, 1313 Sherman St., Room 618, Denver, CO 80203.

A final trend identified in the survey was partnerships with volunteers. State trail programs are clearly tapping into this source of labor to provide trail opportunities. Thirty-five states had figures regarding the number of volunteers involved on state land. The two states with the greatest volunteer involvement were Florida, which estimated that 14,000 volunteers had contributed labor worth over $1.1 million in 1993, and New Hampshire where an estimated 80 percent of the trails on state land were adopted by volunteers. Administrators also identified numerous techniques they were using to encourage volunteer involvement on trails such as providing recognition and/or award programs, sponsoring "Adopt-A-Trail" programs, providing stipends, workers' compensation, National Trails Day events, technical assistance, tools, etc.

Current and Future Trail Issues

State programs are currently facing obstacles to their trail efforts and expect to encounter many of these same obstacles as well as new challenges in the future. When asked, "What are the biggest roadblocks to getting and keeping trails on the ground in your state?" over one quarter of the responses identified funding as the biggest roadblock. Various threats to trails and trail lands was the next largest group. A large number of the trail administrators also reported that there was a major problem with lack of awareness of the value of trails and too little support for trails. This roadblock was seen as a problem with government agencies and officials as well as with the general public (Table III.19).

Table III.19: Biggest Roadblocks to Getting and Keeping State Trails on the Ground in State

Item	Number Responding	Percent
Funding	30	27.5
Threats to Trails and Trail Lands	24	22.0
Lack of Awareness and Support	20	18.3
Funding Maintenance	10	9.2
Interagency Coordination	6	5.5
Trail Program	3	2.8
Leadership	3	2.8
Federal Legislation	3	2.8
State Legislation	2	1.8
Conflict/Multiple Use	2	1.8
Motorized Use	2	1.8
Maintenance	1	0.9
Technical Assistance	1	0.9
Volunteers	1	0.9
Use Trends	1	0.9
Total	109	100.0

Source: Moore, R. L. 1994. State Trail Programs: A Survey of State Trail Administrators. Denver, CO: The National Association of State Trail Administrators. Available c/o Colorado State Trails Program, 1313 Sherman St., Room 618, Denver, CO 80203.

When asked to identify the most pressing issues currently facing trails in their states, the most frequent responses related to specific threats to trails and trail lands. Many of these concerns involved landowner opposition and development obliterating existing trails and potential trail locations. Lack of funding and concerns about trail conflict and other issues related to multiple use were the next most pressing issues identified. Other issues currently of concern to the states are listed in Table III.20.

Table III.20 also presents a summary of the responses to a question which asked respondents to identify the most pressing issues they felt were currently facing trails nationally. The concerns identified were similar to the ones expressed for the state level with an even greater concern about funding. Administrators saw funding to be the most pressing issue nationwide, apparently even more pressing than funding in their home states. Specific threats to trails and trail lands was their second greatest type of concern followed by conflict and multiple use. Funding for the National Recreational Trails Fund was specifically mentioned by eight of the programs making it the fourth most frequently expressed issue.

Table III.20: Most Pressing Issues Facing Trails Now and Five-10 Years from Now

	Currently In Your State		Currently In the Nation		In the Future Nationally	
	Number Responding	Percent	Number Responding	Percent	Number Responding	Percent
Threats to Trails and Trail Lands	29	15.5	18	15.3	18	15.3
Funding	25	13.4	30	25.4	13	11.1
Conflict/Multiple Use	22	11.8	11	9.3	21	17.8
Funding Maintenance	14	7.5	7	5.9	6	5.1
Trail Plans	13	7.0	0	0.0	2	1.7
Motorized Use	10	5.3	3	2.5	5	4.2
Interagency Coordination	9	4.8	6	5.1	2	1.7
Funding Development	8	4.3	0	0.0	0	0.0
Providing Trails Close to Where People Live	8	4.3	2	1.7	6	5.1
Trail Program	7	3.7	2	1.7	1	0.8
Maintenance	6	3.2	4	3.4	2	1.7
Technical Assistance	5	2.7	7	5.9	2	1.7
Promoting Trails and Trail Issues	5	2.7	5	4.2	3	2.5
Federal Legislation	5	2.7	0	0.0	4	3.4
Staffing	4	2.1	0	0.0	0	0.0
Leadership	4	2.1	5	4.2	2	1.7
Trail Development	4	2.1	0	0.0	0	0.0
Trail Safety	3	1.6	2	1.7	5	4.2
Non-Motorized Use	3	1.6	0	0.0	0	0.0
Rail-Trails	2	1.1	1	0.8	3	2.5
Volunteers	1	0.5	2	1.7	0	0.0
Funding NRTF	0	0.0	8	6.8	0	0.0
Long Distance Trails	0	0.0	3	2.5	3	2.5
Use Trends	0	0.0	2	1.7	2	1.7
Liability	0	0.0	0	0.0	4	3.4
Other Legislation	0	0.0	0	0.0	4	3.4
Trails for Transportation	0	0.0	0	0.0	4	3.4
Resource Management	0	0.0	0	0.0	3	2.5
User Fees	0	0.0	0	0.0	2	1.7
Mountain Bike Use	0	0.0	0	0.0	1	0.8
Total	187	100.0	118	99.8	118	99.8

Source: Moore, R. L. 1994. State Trail Programs: A Survey of State Trail Administrators. Denver, CO: The National Association of State Trail Administrators. Available c/o Colorado State Trails Program, 1313 Sherman St., Room 618, Denver, CO 80203.

Trail administrators were then asked to speculate about what they expected to be the most important new issues trails would be facing in the next 5-10 years. Conflict and multiple use were the biggest concerns trail administrators saw on the horizon followed by threats to trails and trail lands. They still expected funding and funding for maintenance to be major concerns, however. Providing trails close to where people live was the fifth most frequently mentioned issue trail administrators felt they would be facing in the next decade.

Respondents also identified the new or emerging user groups they felt would be important in 10 years. Mountain biking was the response of nearly 26 percent of the trail administrators. It was mentioned more than twice as often as the next most frequent response of walking and hiking (12.1 percent). Other emerging user groups identified were motorized use (10.6 percent), bicycling (10.6 percent), roller blading/in-line skating (9.1 percent), and commuting (7.8 percent). Various trail interest groups were also noted as new or emerging. These included "groups with political power," "wise land use groups," "trails planning groups," "trail advisory groups," "trail advocacy groups," and groups promoting "interagency cooperation." Various segments of the population were also considered to be new or emerging user groups. Foremost among these were the physically challenged and seniors.

Conclusion of State Trail Programs

What is the current status of state trail programs in the United States? Almost every state is involved in the trail development and management business, and no state has the resources to meet the public demands for trails. ISTEA, the National Recreational Trails Fund Act and state level programs that were developed to augment the Land and Water Conservation Fund have become the primary sources of funding for trail planning and development. Trail maintenance and management tasks have increasingly been assumed by volunteers. Public demand for trails continues to increase and technology is providing recreationists with new ways to enjoy trails. Mountain bikes and in-line skates are two recent inventions that have drastically changed the mix of users on trails. The increasing number of users and types of use on finite trail systems make the potential for conflict high and call for proactive planning and management at all levels.

The states are in a strong position to guide the development of trails into the next century. Not only do they manage extensive trail networks, states also manage federal grant funds and often provide state funds for trail purposes as well. States are frequently more in touch with local issues and organizations than are federal agencies. States can encourage the development of trails as part of the infrastructure of communities and can encourage the development of trail networks as opposed to isolated trail segments. Overall, state trail programs play a vital role in coordinating and providing trail opportunities both in communities and throughout the states.

Other State Resource Systems

State Forests

State forests offer outdoor recreation opportunities in nearly every state. They offer an alternative to the more developed state parks in the form of more primitive and dispersed recreation. They often resemble federal backcountry land more so than state parks, which usually are designed to serve large numbers of visitors. Typical activities at state forests include camping, hiking, nature study, picnicking, horseback riding, fishing, and hunting. In some Northeastern states, there are few distinctions among state forests, state parks, and State Fish and Wildlife Areas, but that is not the case in most other states (Knudson, 1984). Many state forests are little known because their recreational opportunities are not publicized. The focus in state forests often is on timber production and forest management demonstrations. Some state forests, however, have set aside areas for intensive recreation use.

Among the 50 States, only Nevada did not list state-owned forest land in the 1996 "State Forestry Statistics Report." This report is an unpublished document summarizing the annual survey of state foresters done by the National Association of State Foresters (NASF). Even the Great Plains states of Kansas, Nebraska, and the Dakotas reported some state-owned forest land. The report notes that there are over 50 million acres of state–owned forest land in the United States (Table III.21), but it is unclear whether all tracts referenced are designated as "state forests." By contrast, Jensen (1995) and Cordell et al. (1990) both estimated that there are approximately 26 million acres of designated state forests in the country.

A more meaningful statistic is acreage of state forests in states with a forest recreation program. This figure amounts to almost 23 million acres nationally. The North has 76 percent of this acreage. By comparison, the 1989 Forest Service Resources Planning Act Assessment reported 26.2 million acres of state forests open to recreation, regardless of whether the state operated a formal recreation program. Since these numbers do not measure the same thing, the comparison is somewhat tenuous. States that do not have a formal state forest recreation program undoubtedly offer some recreation opportunities indicating that the 1996 estimate of 22.8 million acres likely underestimates actual recreation acreage.

Table III.21: Total Area, Area in Recreation Programs, and Recreation Budgets of State Forest Programs by Region, 1996[1]

	Region				
	North	South	Rocky Mountains	Pacific Coast	U.S. Total
State Forest acreage[2]	18.58	3.59	3.61	24.50	50.28
State Forest acreage in states with forest recreation program	17.40	2.37	0.03	3.00	22.80
Total budget of state forest recreation programs[3]	9,546	842	12	3,442	13,842

[1]All acreages are in millions.

[2]Does not include Arizona, Hawaii, and California, states which did not respond to NASF State Forestry statistics study. Acreage estimates for these states from the 1992 National Resources Inventory: Arizona—462,700; California—435,000; Hawaii—718,900.

[3]Dollars are in thousands.

Source: 1996 State Forestry Statistics Report. National Association of State Foresters. Washington, D.C. USDA Forest Service. 1989 Resources Planning Act Assessment of Outdoor Recreation and Wilderness.

The share of state forest recreation land in the two eastern regions is larger than in the West. Half of the 50 states have a forest recreation program, according to the NASF, and 22 of these 25 states are in the East. Fifteen of the 20 Northern states and seven of the 13 Southern states reported having a forest recreation program within their state forest agency. Just one of 12 Rocky Mountain states and two of the five Pacific Coast states have a recreation program.

Alaska has about 43 percent of all state forest acreage in the United States (21.5 of the 50.3 million), but it does not have a forest recreation program. Washington has nearly all of the forest recreation program funding spent in the Pacific Coast. Washington trailed only Michigan in the amount of annual expenditures. Oregon also has a state forest recreation program, but it did not report expenditures. After Michigan and Washington, the states with the largest program budgets were Maryland, New York, and Pennsylvania. Also, New York, Michigan, Minnesota, and Pennsylvania are the leaders in state forest acreage among the lower 48 states.

State Wilderness

Several states manage designated wilderness through formal wilderness programs similar to the National Wilderness Preservation System (NWPS). Eight states—six in the East and two in the West—had such programs in 1995, all established during the 1970s (Figure III.13). These areas complement the NWPS by protecting some ecosystems not found on federal land. Further, they provide opportunities for primitive and dispersed recreation, especially in the East where such opportunities are relatively scarce. Stankey (1984) conducted the first overview of state wilderness programs in the early 1980s. He found that nine states managed a total of 48 areas comprising approximately 1.67 million acres. The following criteria defined an established State Wilderness program: (1) statutory or administrative recognition; (2) goals for preserving natural qualities and allowing primitive recreational opportunities; (3) prohibition of development activities; (4) minimum areas size criteria; (5) recognition of other values compatible with wilderness management (e.g., historic, scientific, educational, and scenic).

Figure III.13: Acreage in State Wilderness Porgrams, 1996[1]

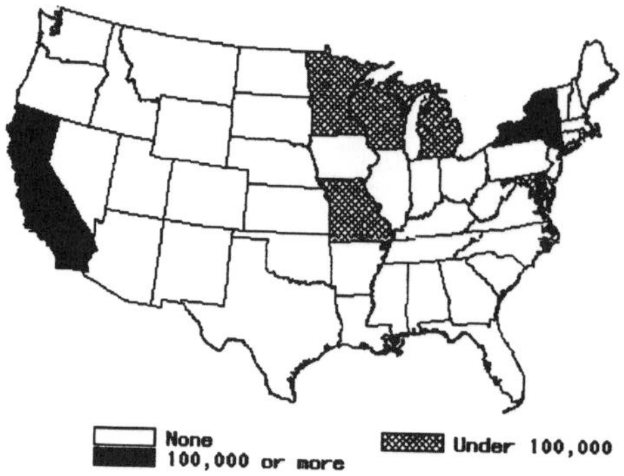

[1]Alaska, not shown, has a State Wilderness program with 5 areas covering 1.36 million acres.

Source: Peterson, M. R. 1996. Wilderness by state mandate: a survey of state-designated wilderness areas. Natural Areas Journal. 16(3): 192-197.

Peterson (1996) did a follow-up survey of State Wilderness programs in the mid-1990s. His research showed that one state program was eliminated (Florida in 1989), but that the protected acreage in the remaining eight state programs almost doubled to 3.11 million acres.[30] The number of state Wilderness areas also increased from 48 to 58 by the mid-1990s, with one new area pending approval in Missouri. Ten of the original 48 areas were in Florida, so the increase in the number of areas in the remaining eight states amounts to a 53 percent gain in those states. Ten of the areas in three states (Alaska, New York, and California) are also quite large, averaging 100,000 acres. These same three states make up 94 percent of state wilderness systems with 2.92 million acres. The other five states, all in the East, have 185,000 acres of state Wilderness in 26 units. When combined with New York, these states account for 42 percent of the acreage and 79 percent of the 58 units. Remove Alaska, however, and the Eastern states make up three-fourths of the state Wilderness acres. Other states have designated individual areas as "wilderness," e.g., Baxter State Park in Maine and McCurtain County Wilderness Area in Oklahoma, but have not established formal wilderness systems.

State Fish and Wildlife Land

State governments also manage wildlife and fish resources. Every state has an agency or commission of some form responsible for wildlife and fish management and regulation. Operations of these agencies usually include three functions (Knudson, 1984): (1) regulation of hunting and fishing; (2) assistance to landowners, including public agencies, on habitat management and wildlife population manipulation; and (3) management of public land habitat.

The authorization and administrative functions of wildlife and fish agencies vary by state. Some operate as divisions in state departments of natural resources and others operate as independent government commissions with political appointments. Whatever the case, state fish and wildlife agencies own some tracts and manage others through lease agreements with various public and private property owners. In most states, state fish and wildlife tracts are called "Wildlife Management Areas" or "State Fish and Game Lands." Similar to state forests, they tend to offer primitive opportunities and more dispersed settings than are found in state parks. Besides hunting and fishing, other popular activities include camping, picnicking, hiking, and nature study. Knudson (1984) notes that these recreational activities are more popular than fishing and hunting on state fish and wildlife land because they are not constrained by seasons.

---

[30]The 1996 NASF State Forestry Statistics Report also lists eight states having a "Wilderness Management" program within their state forestry divisions. However, these are evidently not the same as the authorized State wilderness programs since only three states are present on both lists. No further details are provided about the duties and responsibilities of these management programs located within state divisions of forestry.

Unfortunately, there is no current inventory of state fish and wildlife land in the United States. Jensen (1995) described 9.3 million state fish and wildlife acres in the United States based on a BLM report, but the source could not be confirmed. The 1980 RPA Assessment also estimated about 9 million acres of state wildlife areas, but the 1989 RPA Assessment estimated approximately 14 million acres. These inventories probably did not measure the same resources. One current estimate of state fish and wildlife land comes from the 1992 National Resources Inventory (NRI) conducted by the USDA Natural Resources Conservation Service. The measure, however, is not well defined. The NRI refers to "state-owned land with primary use reserved-dedicated to wildlife." The national total from this measure, excluding Alaska, is 5.7 million acres. That total, even without Alaska, is probably too small to cover all state fish and wildlife land. For example, a recent article noted that fish and wildlife land in California had tripled since 1970, and the current amount in that state alone is 825,000 acres (Jacobs, 1997).

State Scenic Rivers

The National Wild and Scenic River System and designated units in the National Park System such as "National River" or "National Scenic Riverway" are two primary ways that rivers are protected by the federal government. A total of 32 state governments also have river protection programs covering approximately 300 rivers and 13,500 river miles (Table III.22). The five largest state systems are in Michigan, Maine, California, Louisiana, and New York and represent over half of the river miles protected by states. Thirteen of the 32 states have completed inventories of their rivers, and three have not protected any river miles despite having an established program. Most of the programs were started in the 1960s and 1970s in the wake of the Wild and Scenic Rivers Act of 1968. Seven programs were established in the 1980s, with Idaho's and New Hampshire's being as late as 1988.

State-sanctioned river protection is largely an eastern–U.S. phenomenon. Eighty-four percent of rivers and 78 percent of river miles are in the East. Further, 26 of the 32 states with programs are located in the North and South regions. Similar to state wilderness, this pattern is because most western rivers of outstanding quality are under federal protection. State programs vary in types of designations and the level of protection. In any event, state scenic rivers represent a significant resource for undeveloped water-based recreation, especially in the East.

Table III.22: Number and Miles of State-Designed Scenic Rivers by Region, 1993

Number and Mileage	Region				
	North	South	Rocky Mountains	Pacific Coast	U.S. Total
Number of rivers	156	99	13	35	303
River mileage	8,114	2,488	581	2,369	13,552

Source: Palmer, Tim. 1993. *The Wild and Scenic Rivers of America*. Washington, D.C.: Island Press.

LOCAL GOVERNMENT RESOURCES FOR OUTDOOR RECREATION

A recurring theme in nearly every assessment of outdoor recreation in the United States has been the need for recreation opportunities close to where most people live. This need will accelerate as America becomes an increasingly urban nation. The large majority of states added developed land (defined as urban and built-up land plus rural transportation infrastructure) at a rate of 10 percent or more during the 1982 to 1992 decade (Figure III.14). Increases were especially large in the Southeast, Southwest, and New England states. Local government agencies, more than any other provider, supply many of the opportunities demanded by urban and suburban dwellers. The President's Commission on Americans Outdoors estimated in 1987 that 60 percent of recreation areas nationwide are provided by local government, most of which are highly developed and managed for intensive use. This has been the traditional emphasis of local government since the origins of the "recreation movement" in crowded urban areas in the late 19th century.

Much of what local governments provide is geared toward indoor, rather than outdoor, recreation.[31] However, the green spaces and athletic fields that local governments provide are highly valued for outdoor recreation. In addition, many local governments—especially in larger cities, county governments, and special recreation and park districts—also manage natural areas, trails, and less developed open space. Local governments, therefore, provide a wide variety of opportunities for outdoor recreation and serve more people than any other provider by virtue of their location.

Because summary data on the types and amounts of outdoor recreation resources managed by local governments are limited, this section presents a combination of survey results, case studies, anecdotal information, and other observations about the local recreation and park situation. First, we look at local government recreation and park agencies, drawing inferences about local resources for outdoor recreation from information about the agencies that provide them. Second, we discuss outdoor recreation in urban areas, including the settings, infrastructure, management, and issues that affect individuals' experiences with nature in the city. Third, we examine the phenomena of greenways, rail-trails, and other linear recreation paths. The development of these natural corridors for recreation and transportation may be one of the most significant trends in outdoor recreation supply in the past decade.

Figure III.14: Percent Increase in Developed Land by State, 1982-1992[1]

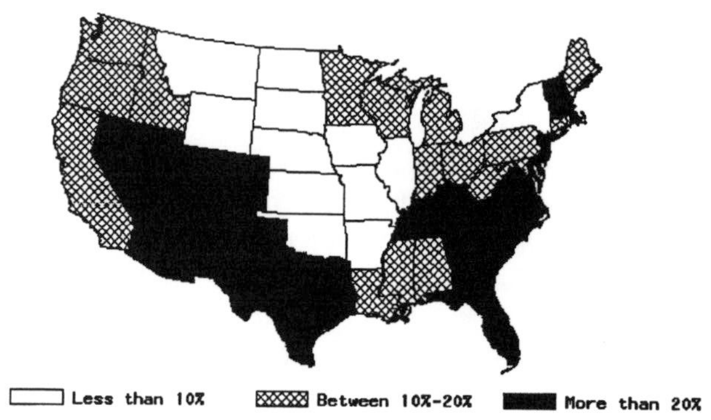

[1] Developed land includes urban and built-up land plus rural transportation infrastructure.

Source: 1992 National Resources Inventory, USDA Natural Resources Conservation Service.

Recreation and Park Agencies

(By Cheryl S. Beeler, Associate Professor, Florida State University, Tallahassee, Florida)

Local governments in the United States have long provided recreation and park services. Management ranges from informal and unpaid park committees in unincorporated communities (of perhaps just one person) to bureaucracies of several hundred employees in large cities. The common bond between all local providers is that most offer both (1) recreation programming and services and (2) facilities and parks. The National Recreation and Park Association (NRPA) sponsored a study in 1993 to learn more about the local government agencies that manage recreation and parks (Beeler, 1993). The criterion that defined an "agency" was a minimum of one full-time professional staff person. This eliminated very small communities without a formal structure for recreation and parks management. Working with state recreation associations, university researchers, and other knowledgeable sources from each state, a total of 4,528 local government departments were identified. From this list, a stratified sample (by geographic region, population served, and type of local

---

[31]Some of the larger local recreation and parks departments have expanded to cover zoos, stadiums, civic centers, libraries, tourism promotion, cultural arts, historic sites, and cemeteries.

government jurisdiction) of 1,500 departments was selected for the survey on organization, structure, finance, and budgets. A total of 967 departments (65 percent) responded.

Municipal Recreation and Parks

Just under three-fourths of the local park and recreation agencies are municipal departments (Table III.23). Municipalities, including cities, villages, boroughs, and towns, receive legal authority to establish park and recreation services through state laws, either through recreation enabling acts, special laws, or local charter provisions. The type of park and recreation services offered by a municipality varies depending on the number and type of people served. For example, in communities of less than 2,500 people, the park and recreation department may operate with only one full-time professional. The number of areas and facilities owned and operated is typically limited, and may only include one site, such as a multipurpose park or a small community center. In most cases, small cities and towns depend heavily on joint-use agreements with local schools for ballfields, courts, gymnasiums, and meeting rooms.

Table III.23: Number of Local Government Park and Recreation Departments by Type and Region, 1993

Type of local government	Region				
	North	South	Rocky Mountains	Pacific Coast	U.S. Total
Municipal	1,621	896	307	465	3,289
County	333	416	38	93	880
Special District	214	9	0	93	316
Other	3	40	0	0	43
All Types	2,171	1,361	345	651	4,528

Source: Beeler, Cheryl S. (1993). *National Comprehensive Salary and Benefits Study*. Arlington, VA: National Recreation and Park Association.

Most small park and recreation departments rely on community volunteers to coach and officiate sports leagues, as well as to organize and run youth recreation programs. It is also common to find many recreation programs and community-wide special events cosponsored by schools, local church groups, civic and fraternal organizations, and local businesses.

In contrast, municipalities of more than 250,000 may have 50 or more full-time employees. The type of areas and facilities acquired, developed, and operated may be diverse, including not only multipurpose parks, playgrounds, community centers, sports fields and courts, and swimming pools, but also facilities for performing arts, golf, ice skating, camping, and the enjoyment of nature. Marinas, zoos, aquariums, gardens, museums and galleries, libraries, and cemeteries may also be provided. Street and area beautification is often a responsibility.

Programs may include team sports (softball, baseball, basketball, volleyball, soccer, football, and hockey); individual sports (tennis, golf, aerobics, swimming, and gymnastics); outdoor recreation (picnicking, boating, fishing, hunting, skiing, swimming, biking, walking/hiking, and nature study); summer recreation programs and camps; before-school and after-school programs; instructional classes (arts and crafts, music, dancing, drama, and martial arts); concert, cultural exhibits; special events; and special programs for people with disabilities. As in small departments, most large municipal park and recreation departments work closely with voluntary agencies, schools and colleges, church groups, business, and industry in offering programs, services, and community-wide special events.

City parks and recreation areas like Atlanta's Bessie Branham Park offer inner-city residents an opportuniy to experience "green space" close to home.

County Recreation and Parks

Not quite one-fifth of the departments offering park and recreation services at the local level are connected to county governments (Table III.23). In contrast to municipalities, county governments are legally established as subdivisions of the state. Of the 880 county governments offering park and recreation services in the United States, approximately 85 percent are in the East.

Early in the 20th century, county departments were primarily responsible for large parks for passive recreation. At that time, very few county departments provided active programs and services. However, times changed and more county park and recreation departments assumed responsibility for active recreation and direct service programs and activities. Today, county park and recreation systems are highly diverse. Some are similar to systems in small cities or rural towns, employing only one full-time professional, operating one or two areas and facilities, and focusing on youth programs. Others operate like large municipal departments with large staffs offering an array of programs and services and operating a network of parks and facilities for active recreation.

Special Park Districts

About 7 percent of local park and recreation organizations are special districts (Table III.24). In several states, especially Illinois and California, state legislation authorized establishment of recreation and park districts. Special park districts are independent of other units of local government, but can be likened to political subdivisions of states, such as cities and counties. Since special districts have taxing authority, their programs are better funded than those of municipalities and counties. As with municipalities and counties, the programs and services of special districts vary with number and type of people served.

Organization, Financing, and Budgeting

In the 1993 NRPA nationwide study, department organization, structure, funding, and compensation of employees were addressed. The data from the 967 responding departments help describe the current status of local government parks and recreation service. Local government parks and recreation departments are typically organized in one of three ways: (1) to provide a combination of parks and recreation services; (2) to provide recreation services only; or (3) to provide park services only. Early in this century, most local governments organized separate departments for recreation services and for parks. More recently, this organizational pattern has changed. The large majority of local government departments (81 percent) are organized to provide a combination of park and recreation services. Fifteen percent of the responding departments provided recreation services only, and only 4 percent provided park services only.

Financing of parks and recreation varies by size and type of local government. Obviously, financing of parks and recreation in a city of 1,000,000 is more complex than in a city of less than 2,500. The bulk of local revenue for operating parks and recreation departments comes from general property taxes, fees, and charges. For major capital outlays, most local parks and recreation departments rely on a combination of revenue sources, including general obligation and revenue bonds, federal and state grants, and special tax assessments.

In her NRPA study of local parks and recreation departments, Beeler (1993) collected data on current operating budgets, which covered employee salaries and benefits, routine supplies, materials, and contractual services but not capital outlays. Based on population size of the communities, annual operating budgets for parks and recreation departments ranged from under $35,000 to over $70 million. The median budget for the 945 responding departments was $700,000. The number of full-time, permanent staff in these departments ranged from 1 to 1,127; the median number of employees was eight. Local departments in the western United States tended to operate with larger budgets and more employees than the other regions.

Issues and Trends

Local recreation and park administrators face many challenging issues and trends. Many have persisted over a number of years and will likely continue into the future. We discuss five major issues.

1) Accountability and Justification of Services

A major issue for all providers of local government services is the mounting pressure to become more business-like and account for costs of services. Today's local administrators must explicitly justify their programs and services in terms of benefits to the public. Godbey, Graefe, and James (1992) found that 75 percent of respondents to a national telephone survey of 1,305 Americans used local parks and playgrounds, 51 percent occasionally, and 24 percent frequently. The most frequently mentioned benefits that people received from use of local recreation resources were personal benefits (such as exercise, fitness, conditioning, relaxation, and peace) and social benefits (such as competition, cooperation, and sense of community).

2) Financing Capital Improvements

A second issue impacting local recreation and park administration is financing capital improvements, including land acquisition, facility development, and facility renovation. Over the past 10 years, major cutbacks have been made in federal, state, and local funding. At the same time, the American public has asked for more local park areas and facilities, more recreation programs, and increased services. Today's administrators face inadequate levels of funding to satisfy growing public demands.

3) Operating Budgets

Closely related is the issue of adequate financing for staffing, operating, and maintaining new developed areas and facilities. Rarely are operating budgets appropriately increased for staffing and maintenance of new areas. Once capital projects receive funding, administrators must immediately begin searching for creative revenue sources to operate and maintain them.[32] If administrators are not successful in identifying alternative resources, they must staff and operate new areas and facilities with current budgets.

4) Spending Priorities

A fourth issue facing local parks and recreation is spending priorities. Like most government services at the local level, parks and recreation departments have limited funding to meet growing needs of culturally diverse communities. Local departments are finding it more difficult to provide equal opportunity for leisure experiences to all people. Often they sacrifice majority needs to meet minority needs, such as offering programs for people with disabilities, "at-risk" teens, or the homeless. Today's local departments must make difficult choices for the use of their limited public financial resources.

5) Crime and Violence

The last issue is crime and violence. Almost every local community in America has been impacted by crimes, including vandalism, gang-related activity, and substance abuse. Unfortunately, many crimes occur in public parks and recreation areas. Local parks and recreation officials must continuously look for sensible ways to keep parks safe.

---

[32]A current example of a creative funding source is the sale of licensing rights by cities to corporate sponsors, currently underway in Los Angeles and Buffalo, and proposed in New York City (Hurt 1997). In Los Angeles, county lifeguards all wear the same official swimwear. In New York one official said, "There's no reason why all the trash cans in New York City parks can't bear the same logo, but we're not going to put a [corporate sponsor] name on Central Park."

Local Recreation Facilities and Sites

Following the Beeler study, the NRPA sponsored another project to study the amounts and types of recreation facilities and sites provided by local governments (PKF Consulting, 1995). The purpose was to gather baseline data against which local departments could compare themselves for planning purposes. The study design was to sample the same 1,500 recreation and park agencies as in the Beeler study. The stratified sample assured representation from agencies serving both large and small populations, from four regions of the United States, and from a variety of municipal, county, and special district governments. The 12-page questionnaire was returned by 520 agencies, a 35 percent response rate. One section of the questionnaire was devoted to inventory of facilities, fields and courts, passive recreation space, and park areas. The specific items identified under these four headings give a good indication of the diversity of resources provided by local governments:[33]

1. Facilities—Amphitheater, archery range (outdoor), badminton court, skeet and trap range, golf driving range, miniature golf course, Par-3 9-hole golf course, Par-3 18-hole golf course, 9-hole standard golf course, 18-hole standard golf course, equestrian center, ice rink (outdoor/convertible), swimming pool (outdoor), waterparks, 1/4 miles/meter running track, marina, boat ramp, camping areas (overnight, RV, and tent), historical/cultural sites.

2. Fields/Courts—Little League baseball fields, adult baseball/softball fields, basketball courts (outdoor), field hockey fields, soccer fields, football fields, handball courts (outdoor), tennis courts, sand volleyball courts, outdoor multiple recreation courts (basketball, volleyball, tennis, soccer).

3. Passive recreation space—beach areas, lakes, jogging/bicycling trails, hiking/equestrian trails, snowmobile and cross-country ski trails.

4. Park areas—Mini-park (servicing a limited number of streets in a neighborhood), neighborhood park (servicing several small clusters of residential areas), community park (servicing an identifiable group of neighborhoods equating to a community area), metro/regional park (servicing a region or metropolitan area).

Table III.24 shows the percentages of agencies by region, serving fewer than 50,000 people, that provided different types of outdoor recreation resources. Table III.25 does the same for agencies serving 50,000 or more people.[34] The proportion of agencies providing passive recreation space and four kinds of park areas is evidence of the role of local government in outdoor recreation resources. Larger agencies (Table III.25) were more likely than the smaller agencies to provide all five kinds of passive recreation spaces. For example, nationwide, large agencies are more than twice as likely as smaller ones to provide hiking and equestrian trails and almost three times as likely to provide snowmobile and cross-country ski trails. The difference does not necessarily reflect a lower demand for these resources in smaller cities and counties, but indicates better ability by larger agencies to provide more recreation resources.

---

[33]The questionnaire listed a variety of indoor and outdoor resources, but only outdoor facilities and courts are included in here.

[34]The NRPA study actually broke population into 10 separate categories, but low numbers in many categories left many proportions statistically unreliable. Fifty-thousand is a good dividing point between 'large' and 'small' populations and is the number traditionally used by the Census Bureau to define metropolitan areas.

Table III.24: Estimated Percentage of Local Government Agencies Serving Populations Under 50,000 that Provided Selected Outdoor Recreation Resources by National Recreation and Park Association Region, 1994

	NRPA Region[1]				
Type of Recreation Resource	Northeast (n=80)[2]	North Central (n=114)	South (n=111)	West (n=66)	U.S. Total (n=371)
Passive Recreation Space					
Beach areas	41.3	22.8	18.0	19.7	24.8
Lakes	37.5	45.6	31.5	36.4	38.0
Jogging/Bicycling trails	41.3	59.6	54.0	60.6	54.2
Hiking/Equestrian trails	18.8	24.6	16.2	34.8	22.6
Snowmobile and Cross-country trails	8.8	17.5	0.0	3.0	7.8
Park Areas					
Mini	58.8	70.2	55.0	71.2	63.3
Neighborhood	68.8	78.1	63.1	83.3	72.5
Community	78.8	89.5	79.3	81.1	82.7
Metro/Regional	16.3	31.6	27.9	31.8	27.2

[1]The NRPA regions used in this study are different from the regions reported elsewhere in this book. See Appendix III.4 for a list of states comprising the NRPA regions.

[2]Sample size of local recreation and park agencies.

Source: PKF Consulting. (1995). *Local Park and Recreation Facilities and Sites*. Arlington, VA: National Recreation and Park Association.

Table III.25: Estimated Percentage of Local Government Agencies Serving Populations 50,000 and Over that Provided Selected Outdoor Recreation Resources by National Recreation and Park Association Region, 1994

	NRPA Region[1]				
Type of Recreation Resource	Northeast (n=22)[2]	North Central (n=40)	South (n=47)	West (n=40)	U.S. Total (n=149)
Passive Recreation Space					
Beach areas	50.0	32.5	29.8	37.5	35.5
Lakes	59.1	47.5	66.0	57.7	57.7
Jogging/Bicycling trails	63.6	65.0	74.5	72.5	69.8
Hiking/Equestrian trails	36.4	60.0	34.0	70.0	51.0
Snowmobile and Cross-country trails	27.3	42.5	4.3	15.0	20.8
Park Areas					
Mini	50.0	55.0	63.8	77.5	63.1
Neighborhood	68.2	60.0	74.5	75.0	69.8
Community	72.7	75.0	93.6	82.5	82.6
Metro/Regional	40.9	65.0	78.7	75.0	68.5

[1]The NRPA regions used in this study are different from the regions reported elsewhere in this book. See Appendix III.4 for a list of states comprising the NRPA regions.

[2]Sample size of local recreation and park agencies.

Source: PKF Consulting. (1995). *Local Park and Recreation Facilities and Sites*. Arlington, VA: National Recreation and Park Association.

Jogging and bicycling trails are the most common resource for both small and large agencies in all regions. Lakes are also common among large agencies, but less so among small agencies. Hiking and equestrian trails are less common in the South for both small and large agencies, but more common in the West. Beaches managed by both small and large local agencies are more common by a considerable margin in the Northeast. As expected, snowmobiling and cross-country ski trails are much more common in the Northeast and North Central Regions and almost nonexistent in the South. Most snowmobile and ski trails in the West tend to be on federal and state, rather than local government lands.

Except for Metro/Regional Parks, the park areas are very similar for small and large agencies. About 63 percent of agencies have mini-parks, 70 percent have neighborhood parks, and 82 percent have community parks. A much higher percentage of large agencies manage metro/regional parks, both nationally and in each region. More agencies, both small and large, manage community parks than neighborhood parks, although this may be a matter of nomenclature change.

The NRPA study also examined general trends in additions of facilities and sites in the previous five years. The report mentions that fields and courts, passive recreation space, and park areas have been added to local agencies at a greater rate than both recreation facilities and water-related facilities. Added passive recreation space and park areas included, but were not limited to: trails, conservation areas, open space, playgrounds, tot land, mini-parks, neighborhood parks, multi-parks, and waterfront passive green-span (PKF Consulting, 1995).

The NRPA study conducted by Godbey, Graefe, and James (1992) reported that 72 percent of the 1,305 respondents to a nationwide telephone survey said they lived within walking distance of a public park. Further, 79 percent said they had used either recreation or park services in the past 12 months. Most of these individuals said they used only parks (49 percent), while a very small percentage said they used only recreation services (4 percent). The remainder said they used both parks and recreation services within the last year. When the question was altered to include participation by a member of the household, the proportion using local recreation and park resources rose to 88 percent.

Outdoor Recreation in Urban Areas

Recreation in urban areas is typically characterized by highly developed parks, athletic fields, playgrounds, golf courses, tennis courts, and the like. But most local government recreation and park agencies also manage open space or undeveloped areas for passive outdoor recreation. Much of this land is preserved in greenway corridors or trails corridors. Often, urban recreation and park agencies provide a balance between highly developed areas and quieter, more natural areas. No one has inventoried the amount of natural or undeveloped land managed by local government. Local recreation and park agencies that are managed as Special Districts, rather than as municipal or county departments, frequently emphasize natural resources and conservation over more intensive recreation. Special districts are authorized in several states, but most notably in Illinois, Ohio, California, and Michigan.

The following two articles overview outdoor recreation in urban and metropolitan America. The first, "Urban Outdoor Recreation," discusses issues and trends based on the work of the USDA Forest Service research unit, Managing Forest Environments for Urbanites, based in Chicago. The second article, "Outdoor Recreation in a Special Recreation District: Cleveland Metroparks," is a case study of one of the premier special districts in the United States.

Urban Outdoor Recreation

(By John F. Dwyer, Research Forester, USDA Forest Service, Evanston IL)

Introduction

"Urban outdoor recreation" often conjures up singular images of sports in an urban park. More careful study reveals a wide spectrum of settings and experiences, and strong interrelationships between recreation resources and other important components of the urban system.

Significance

Opportunities for outdoor recreation in urban areas are critical to the health and well-being of urban residents. The high value that urban residents place on urban outdoor recreation is partly due to the sharp contrast that it offers to other aspects of urban life. A wide cross-section of the urban population takes advantage of these opportunities, including many individuals who do not visit more remote park and forest settings. While it is difficult to estimate the amount of outdoor recreation that takes place in urban areas; with 80 percent of the U.S. population living, working, and spending most of its leisure time in urban areas; it is clear that the vast majority of outdoor recreation in the U.S. occurs in urban areas.

Settings

Outdoor recreation settings in urban areas range from backyards, streets, and sidewalks in the central-city to greenways on the urban fringe (Dwyer, 1990; Gobster & Dickhut, 1995; Gobster, 1995). All are key components of the intricate network of urban greenspace. Urban parks are often a setting for historical, architectural, and cultural attractions. From symphony concerts and museum exhibits to sculpture and murals to drama and dance, urban parks are showcases for the cultural treasures of the city. Urban parks also serve as "free" space—one of the few places in a city where access and use are not tightly controlled.

Experiences

Urban outdoor recreation experiences are diverse, from extensive hiking and nature study to brief outings for fitness. Close proximity allows outings to be woven into the daily routine, such as early morning, lunchtime, or after-work walks in a nearby park. Frequent use of the urban outdoor environment is often an important component of everyday life. Urban outdoor settings may also host large group outings, including extended family, neighborhood, business, and other groups who are able to assemble because of short travel distances and the availability of large areas with which they are familiar. Opportunities for solitude may also be found in many urban areas in the form of quiet places to walk, bicycle, fish, or observe nature. Urban recreation areas introduce people to natural settings, allowing them to observe and learn about nature.

Management

Management and use of urban outdoor recreation resources are linked to a complex and interrelated matrix of diverse urban land uses, ownerships, and infrastructure. Recreation resources are often integral components of a wide range of efforts to improve the quality of urban life, particularly health (Hull & Ulrich, 1992), environmental quality (Dwyer, et al., 1992), and education (Simmons, 1996).

Forces For Change

Change is the hallmark of all systems, but it is especially pervasive in the urban environment where there is so much interrelated activity. Of particular significance for urban recreation are changes in land use and management, infrastructure, populations, recreation resource use, scientific knowledge, underserved populations, concern for personal safety, fiscal constraints, and partnerships and collaboration.

Land Use and Management

Changes in the use and management of land throughout urban systems have important implications for urban outdoor recreation opportunities. Land and water resources no longer needed for other uses are becoming available for recreation. Examples include river corridors, railroad rights of way, and former manufacturing sites. Improvements in air and water quality, as well as cleanup of open spaces (including "brownfields") are also creating new or enhanced recreation opportunities. These physical changes in the urban landscape are changing public perceptions about recreation opportunities in the city. For example, rivers and steams that were formerly regarded as open sewers (e.g., sections of the Chicago River) are becoming popular locations for boating and fishing, and riverbanks are becoming favored locations for bird watching and hiking (Westphal & Gobster 1995). At the same time, expanding needs for a wide range of land uses in the urban environment often threaten to displace recreation resources.

Infrastructure

Urban outdoor recreation resources and associated greenspaces are increasingly seen by urban planners as critical components of the urban infrastructure with important implications for transportation (bicycle trails), health, air quality, stormwater management, microclimate, noise abatement, and visual quality (Dwyer, et al., 1992). Aging infrastructure in parks, transportation, utilities, and other resources is creating significant challenges for managers and planners. The rebuilding of infrastructure is creating new opportunities for partnerships and shared responsibilities that can enhance recreation. Bicycle trails, for example, are being built along new roads. Bridge construction is providing opportunities for accommodating trails above, alongside, or under new or renovated structures. In many of America's large cities in the Northeast and Midwest, much infrastructure was constructed 50 to 100 years ago. Life spans of this infrastructure are being exceeded. For example, in Chicago's lakefront park system, which includes nearly one-half of the city's park land, is built on filled areas of Lake Michigan. Over eight miles of the shoreline revetment that holds this land in place is predicted to fail in the next 10 years. The estimated cost for reconstruction is nearly $300 million.

Populations

Changes in the character and location of the urban population are bringing important changes in urban outdoor recreation. Increased aging and racial and ethnic diversity are influencing the outdoor recreation activities, settings, and programs that urban residents want (Dwyer 1994, 1995b). Immigrants continue to settle first in urban centers, bringing in a constant flow of new ideas and practices to urban recreation areas. Population shifts with having important implications for management of recreation resources include movement of people out of some areas, gentrification, changing composition of neighborhoods, and expansion of the population on the urban fringe. With these changes, managers of recreation sites are finding that the number, character, preferences, and needs of the people they serve continue to change.

Recreation Resource Use

Public interest is increasing in the environment, physical fitness, volunteerism (Westphal, 1993), and preservation and restoration of historic, cultural, and natural resources (Dwyer & Stewart, 1995). Results include new and sometimes conflicting demands for recreation resources. Increasing demands and conflicts are also being generated by the growing popularity of new recreation equipment, such as in–line skates, mountain bicycles, climbing walls, and facilities for indoor golf, indoor skiing, and indoor surfing.

Scientific Knowledge

As more is learned about the contribution of recreation to health and well-being (Driver, Brown, & Peterson, 1991; Hull & Ulrich, 1992), public, private, and not-for-profit groups are giving increased attention to providing urban recreation opportunities. As people appreciate the benefits of recreation and other resources, more cooperative efforts are undertaken. Recreation is included with education, environmental quality, and public health as a significant urban activity. New knowledge about the role of greenspace in improving the quality of the urban environment is also bringing increased attention to the contribution of urban outdoor recreation areas to air and water quality (Dwyer, et al., 1992). At the same time, urban ecosystems are beginning to contribute to scientific knowledge as laboratories for understanding how a diverse cross section of people interact with forest resources (Dwyer & Schroeder, 1994).

Underserved Populations

Public programs are focusing on providing recreation and other important services to people who are currently "underserved." Such people include urban residents, and particularly those living in inner-cities. Increased public concern over "environmental justice" is helping to place a high priority on efforts to overcome physical, economic, and social barriers to participation in outdoor recreation.

Safety

Concerns about personal safety in urban parks are being addressed. Solutions are reflected in site location, design (Schroeder & Anderson, 1984), management, programming, and neighborhood involvement. "Park Watch" programs are becoming popular.

Fiscal Restraints

Limited funds make it increasingly difficult to establish and maintain urban outdoor recreation resources (Dwyer, 1995c; Stewart, 1995). Results include limited land acquisitions and developments, heavy backlogs of maintenance, and searches for more cost effective ways to provide urban outdoor recreation opportunities. One strategy is to provide greenway linkages to existing park and recreation resources. Another is to recycle land in existing government inventories. Parking lots, schoolyard, public grounds, and vacant lots are being "greened" with the combined assistance of volunteer groups and government resources. Shortfalls of public funds for operating outdoor recreation areas are generating significant interest in more and higher fees, concession operations, and privatization of facilities and programs.

Partnerships and Collaborative Efforts

Greenways, rivers, and trails are being given increased attention as ecologists highlight their role in connecting otherwise fragmented landscapes (Gobster, 1995). Management of the urban landscape calls for collaborative planning across metropolitan areas and focuses attention on the coordinated management of interrelated resources among urban, suburban, exurban, and rural areas. Scarcities of fiscal resources and staff are often stimulating collaboration.

The Years Ahead

Urban outdoor recreation managers are witnessing and leading exciting changes and urban recreation is getting increasing attention. Significant changes in the urban environment have created difficult challenges, and new partnerships and other collaborative approaches are being created to enhance recreation opportunities across the urban landscape.

Increased Emphasis

Public, private, and not-for-profit groups will increase their efforts to provide urban recreation because they know that outdoor recreation can enhance the quality of urban life. Many people are strongly committed to serve the "underserved" urban populations, and increased attention is focused on the wide range of physical, biological, and social benefits provided by urban greenspace.

The Changing Urban Environment

Changes in the urban infrastructure, land use, distribution of the people over the landscape, and "new" recreation activities and technologies will continue to be important forces for change in recreation resources. New recreation opportunities will become available in conjunction with improvements in the quality of the urban environment (air, water, and land). Opportunities also will arise as land and water resources previously used for commercial and industrial purposes become available for public use.

The Challenges

The most difficult issues will often center on: (1) allocation of resources among various outdoor recreation opportunities across the urban system, (2) serving increasingly diverse populations, and (3) the relative emphasis to place on natural resources, facilities, physical fitness, historic preservation, education, and other components of recreation resource management in a particular area.

Collaborative Planning

Recreation resources will be managed in context with other important resources in the urban system. Bicycle and walking paths will be included in plans for streets and highways. Offices and factories will incorporate fitness trails and active and passive recreation areas in their site plans. Schools and colleges will make more extensive use of outdoor campuses for their activities. Neighborhood groups will play an increasingly significant role in planning for and management of local resources. Urban greenspace will be an integral part of comprehensive strategies to manage stormwater, air quality, microclimate, and esthetic quality. We will see increased public involvement in resource planning, management, and day-to-day activities. Collaborative partnerships will multiply. Many of the partnerships will involve public, private, and not-for-profit groups at the federal, state, and local levels working to develop cost-effective strategies to enhance opportunities for outdoor recreation across the urban landscape.

Outdoor Recreation in a Special Recreation District: Cleveland Metroparks

(By Robert D. Bixler, Research and Program Evaluation Manager, Cleveland Metroparks, Cleveland, OH)

Cleveland Metroparks is composed of 14 reservations situated in the densely populated metropolitan area of northeastern Ohio with 2.5 million residents. Its largely undeveloped woodland reservations total 19,650 acres and receive over 40 million visits a year. Cleveland Metroparks provides opportunities for traditional outdoor recreation activities such as hiking, picnicking, nature study, fishing, swimming, nonmotorized boating and canoeing, horseback riding, sledding, cross country skiing and scenic driving. Other popular recreation activities provided by the park district include golfing, bicycling on paved trails, and physical fitness trails. The park district has a strong educational emphasis providing nature center exhibits, environmental education and outdoor skills programs to over 400,000 children and adults annually. Since 1975, Cleveland Metroparks has also operated Cleveland Metroparks Zoo.

Established in 1917, the park district is an independent government agency operating as a separate political subdivision of the state of Ohio. The mission of the park district, which is defined by the state law that provides for its existence, is the conservation of the natural resources. The annual budget of 45 million dollars comes primarily from property taxes, although 32 percent is generated by user fees and federal, state and local grants. Approximately every 10 years, residents of the tax district have the opportunity to support property tax levies that exclusively support the park district.

Typically, in large metropolitan areas, there are an immense number of choices of leisure activities. Cleveland Metroparks competes for attention with several distinguished museums, recreation and fitness centers, and an array of private amusement parks, golf courses and other educational and recreation facilities. Aggressive marketing of facilities and programs serves to constantly remind area residents that the park district is one of their recreation options. Public service announcements, paid advertising, and special event promotions have become a routine part of marketing Cleveland Metroparks, along with nontraditional promotional methods that target users who do not pay attention to mass media. Special events, particularly weekend festivals, have provided incentive for many infrequent users of the park district to choose to visit again.

Urban Green Space

Parks are becoming increasingly landlocked and urban open space for new reservations is difficult to acquire. In Cleveland, regional parks are needed to better serve tax payers living in areas that are not near existing open space. Similarly, with development encroaching on the reservations, protecting water quality and natural resources is becoming difficult. Since 1985, the park district has acquired two large parks from the city of Cleveland in under served communities. Another strategy for establishing parks is negotiation of recreation easements with industry and private landowners either near existing reservations or to create new parks. Cleveland Metroparks has recently developed a new 350-acre Ohio and Erie Canal Reservation, with the cooperation of American Steel and Wire, BP Oil, ALCOA, Centerior Energy, and the Ohio Department of Natural Resources. Additionally, partnerships between private landowners and Cleveland Metroparks have provided opportunities to acquire important conservation easements in existing parks at minimal cost, providing additional protection of water quality and wildlife.

Outdoor Recreation

New high-tech recreation activities like mountain biking, rock climbing and in-line skating provide opportunities for serving new outdoor enthusiasts, but also require new management strategies. Historically, introduction to wildland recreation activities and traditions has been passed from parent to child. These new high-tech activities are promoted by product manufacturers of the recreation technology, rather than through traditional family socialization. Because Cleveland Metroparks is within a large urban area, the park district is often where novices try these new activities for the first time. Due to inexperience, these new outdoor recreationists tend to be accident–prone and are a source of conflict with traditional park users. In some instances, the activity may increase natural resource impacts. With mountain bikes, Cleveland Metroparks has taken a wait–and–see approach, asking clubs and organizations promoting mountain biking to first establish codes of conduct and a land ethic among their members, before these activities are allowed in the park district. Through its Institute of the Great Outdoors, the park district does provide opportunities for recreationists to learn the techniques and ethics of both new and traditional wildland recreation activities.

Like many park facilities established in the early part of the 20th century, much of the infrastructure was built by the Civilian Conservation Corp in a short period of time during the Great Depression. Many of these structures are now showing signs of wear and must be replaced or rehabilitated. Over half the bridges as well as a system of river fords in the Park District need immediate renovation. The costs of infrastructure repair and replacement will impact capital budgets for many years.

The park district is often called the Emerald Necklace because of its striking scenery, fauna and flora, and historical and cultural attractions. Though often described as "state park" quality, Cleveland Metroparks has initiated a weekend festival program to entice people to visit reservations further from their homes. These substantial educational and outdoor recreation festivals attract large crowds, up to 20,000 people. Festival participants range from 30 to 50 percent first-time visitors. These events have increased the number of reservations area residents regularly visit.

Twenty years ago, sightings of wildlife such as wild turkey and deer were infrequent. Viewing wildlife, particularly deer, has become a major motive for scenic driving through the reservations. But with no hunting, a lack of large predators and optimal wildlife habitat, populations of racoon, deer, and other wildlife are at an all-time high. Picnickers report being surrounded at their tables by racoons begging for food. Car collisions with deer have increased, and some reservations in the park district are almost devoid of ground plants and understory trees from overgrazing by deer. Cleveland Metroparks has changed its management of refuse, established "no feeding of wildlife policies," and implemented a multi-strategy education program to alter visitor/wildlife interactions. The park district may need to begin culling deer to adequately protect park flora.

Cleveland Metroparks has increased the level of services provided, at little additional cost, through hosting not-for-profit agencies operations on Park District property. For example, Girl Scout cabins, camps for children with disabilities, historic preservation societies, a performing arts theater, a nature center and planetarium, and a fine arts and crafts exhibition and education center are all facilities and programs provided on Cleveland Metroparks properties. These organizations provide high quality services to approximately 275,000 people each year. Cleveland Metroparks has established a planning position to develop a Geographic Information System (GIS) for northeastern Ohio. This sophisticated computer mapping function provides opportunities to simultaneously evaluate all aspects of land planning, including transportation systems, natural resources, and recreational use. This capability, combined with a research staff focusing on evaluation of services and regional recreation demand, provides a systematic base of information that contributes to responsible decision making.

Trends

Over the next 10 to 15 years, national and regional trends will have an impact on Cleveland Metroparks service to area residents. Effectively responding to changing demands requires careful planning and foresight. A trend that could negatively impact Cleveland Metroparks ability to provide high quality service is the decreasing population in the tax district. Urban sprawl is resulting in current residents of the service area moving to adjoining counties. Many of these people will continue to use Cleveland Metroparks, since many of the reservations are near the outer boundaries of the tax district. However, these enthusiastic users will no longer be able to vote in support of tax levies or directly contribute to the cost of maintaining the parks through property taxes. Alternative revenue sources will need to be evaluated. The population in the tax district is expected to increasingly reflect larger percentages of minorities. Current usage levels of Cleveland Metroparks facilities by minority populations is low relative to their proportion in the general population. This is a function of most of the reservations not being close to urban centers where many minorities reside. Also, minority participation rates in outdoor recreation activities have been extremely low.

Two strategies for involving more minorities in outdoor recreation activities are being implemented; the impact of these initiatives will become apparent within the next generation. First, new reservations are being established closer to urban areas to make parklands more accessible on a daily basis. Frequent visitation will help to establish patterns of regular park usage among greater numbers of urbanites. Second, programs for urban youth are being started that introduce them to outdoor recreation activities in meaningful ways. No longer is the park district satisfied with short, one-contact programs that superficially teach a single skill. Programs that introduce children and youth to outdoor recreation focus on more than the obvious psychomotor skills necessary to participate in an activity. Park district staff strive for multiple contacts with the same youth, and are aware that there are many peripheral attitudes and skills needed to successfully carry out an activity after the initial introduction. Staff are increasingly aware of the need of these youths for a supportive social group that shares interest in the outdoor recreation activity. The park district even has a social scientist working on identifying key socialization forces among families active in wildland recreation. These socialization forces will be mimicked in programs for youth from families uninvolved in outdoor recreation.

Changes in work schedules and year-round school may require changes in schedules of programming and staff deployment. The park district is already seeing significantly heavier visitation on Fridays than other weekdays. This is probably due to four-day work weeks and eight-days on, four-days off work patterns. Nontraditional work schedules and changes in school calendars may create a different yearly visitation profile, with decreasing activity in the summer and increased activity in the other seasons. Changes in school year calendars, in which students go to school longer or have long breaks scattered throughout the year, will result in the need to redistribute programming that was traditionally offered only during the summer and often by seasonal staff. Major changes in staffing may be required to meet increased demands in traditionally low visitation periods of the year. The possibilities for serving school-age students, who will have large numbers of shorter breaks from school rather than one long break, will provide a welcome challenge. Changes in the region will require a responsive management style to continue to provide quality outdoor recreation experiences for area residents while protecting natural resources. Cleveland Metroparks must respond to trends, but as a major recreation and educational provider in northeastern Ohio serving nearly 80 percent of area residents, it will also shape recreation demand.

Greenways

Greenways, broadly defined as open-space corridors serving recreation and conservation purposes, may be the most significant trend affecting local outdoor recreation in the United States over the past decade. The term "greenway" was recently coined, but the concepts and ideas go back to Olmsted and the mid-19th century (Little, 1990). It was not until the recommendations of the President's Commission on Americans Outdoors in 1987, however, that the concept developed into a widely-recognized "movement."

The greenway movement springs from local, ground-up, grass-roots efforts of citizens and community activists to protect linear green spaces close to where they live. The President's Commission spoke about "lighting a prairie fire of local action" for greenways. One conservative estimate referred to over 500 active greenway projects in the United States in the mid-1990s (Searns, 1995). Another trait of the movement is its emergence because of, not in spite of, the lack of government funds devoted to open space protection (Little, 1990). The decline of the Land and Water Conservation Fund starting in the early 1980s, and other cutbacks at federal and state levels, necessitated local approaches to land conservation and recreation planning. Federal, state, and regional government agencies typically provide expertise, coordination, and incentives to local groups (Hardt & Hastings, 1995).

An important appeal of greenways is their multipurpose nature (Fabos, 1995). In addition to providing recreation opportunities (walking, jogging, bicycling, nature study, and other activities), greenways protect nature, provide environmental benefits, and protect historic and cultural heritage. Fabos (1995) notes that greenways are one solution to the recreational needs of our increasingly dispersed and decentralized metropolitan populations.

Because of urban sprawl, large parks are not as effective in serving the local population as they used to be. Greenways are more effective at serving large, spatially distributed populations because of their linear nature. This advantage is summarized by two characteristics: linkages and "edge" (Little, 1990). Linkages represent the connections greenways provide between places and edge is the increased perimeter, and thus access, that a linear space provides over a more compact space with the same area. The linear nature of greenways highlights the importance of coordination and partnerships between various landowners and constituencies. Outspoken local leadership often is necessary to bring diverse groups together and build advocacy and political support (Hardt & Hastings, 1995).

The growth and popularity of greenways are among the most significant trends in outdoor recreation in the 1990s. Photo courtesy of Carter J. Betz.

A number of national, regional, and grass-roots organizations have assumed leadership roles working together and with local citizen and government groups to develop and protect greenways. One prominent national group is The Conservation Fund, which operates the American Greenways Program, an umbrella organization promoting greenways at the national, state, regional, and local levels. This program provides professional and technical assistance to citizens, private landowners, nonprofit, and for-profit organizations, and government agencies. It also administers a grants program with single awards up to $2,500 to local greenway projects.

Greenways: America's Natural Connections

(By Edward T. McMahon, American Greenways Program Director, The Conservation Fund, Arlington, VA)

"A connected system of parks is manifestly far more complete and useful than a series of isolated parks."

—Frederick Law Olmsted, 1903

Introduction

Over the past century, America has invested large sums of money in our federal and state parks, forests, and preserves. While we have the finest national park system in the world, most of these parks tend to be far from where people live and are limited in their ability to meet the growing diversity of America's recreation and conservation needs. Increasingly, outdoor recreation occurs close to home, in or near the cities and suburbs where 80 percent of Americans live and work. As a result, in 1987, the President's Commission on Americans Outdoors recommended the establishment of a national "network of greenways to provide people with access to open space close to where they live, and to link together the rural and urban open space in the American landscape." The Commission also called for a "prairie fire of local action" to implement the greenway concept. Today, this prairie fire has ignited, and greenways are being developed in thousands of communities across the country.

Defining Greenways

greenway (gren'-wa) n. 1. A linear open space established along either a natural corridor, such as a riverfront, stream valley, or ridgeline, or overland along a railroad right-of-way converted to recreational use, a canal, a scenic road, or other route. 2. Any natural or landscaped course for pedestrian or bicycle passage. 3. An open-space connector linking parks, nature reserves, cultural features, or historic sites with each other and with populated areas. 4. Locally, certain strip or linear parks designated as a parkway or greenbelt. [American neologism: green + way; origin obscure]

—Charles Little, *Greenways for America,* 1990

Greenways are *corridors* of protected open space managed for conservation and recreation purposes. Greenways typically follow linear landscape features such as rivers, streams, and ridgelines. They are also being created along canals, abandoned railroad lines, utility corridors, country roads, and other man–made features. Greenways are, of course, not new. The concept grew out of the work of landscape architect Frederick Law Olmstead, who was the designer of some of the nation's first linear parks. In 1869, Olmstead designed a plan for Riverside, Illinois that incorporated an extensive greenbelt along the Des Plaines River. Olmstead felt that the river structure provided a better entry into this Chicago suburb than the highway. He later created the "emerald necklace" in Boston which was a series of parks connected by wetlands, streams, and parks. The concept evolved with the development of the Appalachian Trail in 1921, the urban parkways of the 1930s, and the post-World War II greenbelt concept. The term itself was not used until at least 1959 and did not come into widespread use until the 1970s. In his book, *Greenways for America,* author Charles Little identifies five major types of greenways:

1. Urban riverside greenways, usually created as part of (or instead of) a redevelopment program along neglected, often run-down, city waterfronts.

2. Recreational greenways, featuring paths and trails of various kinds, often of relatively long distance, based on natural corridors, as well as man-made features such as abandoned rail lines, canals, or other public rights-of-way.

3. Ecologically significant natural corridors, usually along rivers and streams and sometimes ridgelines, to provide for wildlife migration and habitat protection as well as nature study.

4. Scenic and historic routes, usually along a road or highway (or sometimes a waterway), the most representative of which make an effort to provide pedestrian access along the route or at least places to alight from a car.

5. Comprehensive greenway systems or networks, usually based on natural landforms such as valleys and ridges, but sometimes simply an opportunistic assemblage of greenways and open spaces of various kinds to create a regional green infrastructure.

Benefits of Greenways

Greenways provide a multitude of benefits for people, wildlife, and the economy. More expansive and flexible than traditional, more confirmed parks, greenways can provide a community trail system for linear forms of outdoor recreation such as hiking, jogging, bicycling, rollerblading, horseback riding, cross country skiing, or just plain strolling. Further, greenways provide lifelines for wildlife moving from one isolated natural area to another. They can help to preserve biodiversity and wildlife habitat by protecting environmentally–sensitive land along rivers, streams, and wetlands. They can protect water quality by providing a buffer against urban run-off and non-point source pollution. Greenways can soften and direct urban growth, and they can act as outdoor classrooms—a close–to–home way to get children out of school and into nature.

Greenways can also stimulate the economy by providing an array of economic and quality of life benefits. Numerous studies demonstrate that linear parks can increase nearby property values, which can in turn increase local tax revenues. Spending by residents on greenway-related activities helps support recreation-oriented businesses and employment, as well as other businesses that are patronized by greenway users. Greenways often provide new business opportunities and locations for commercial activities like bed and breakfast establishments, and bicycle and canoe rental shops. Greenways are often major tourist attractions that generate expenditures on lodging, food, and recreation-oriented services. Finally, greenways can reduce public expenditures by lowering the costs associated with flooding, storm water management, and other natural hazards.

In summary, greenways are a cost-effective, multi-purpose concept that allows public agencies to link existing parks, historic sites, and natural areas into a network of green space with numerous environmental, recreational, and economic benefits.

Current Situation

Greenways can be found in all states and regions of the country. Today there are an estimated 5,000 greenways already in existence across the United States. These vary from large multi-state greenways like the Appalachian Trail or Blue Ridge Parkway, to extensive riverfront promenades like the Riverfront Park in Battle Creek, Michigan or the American River Parkway in Sacramento, California, to small streamside parks like the Happy Creek Greenway in Front Royal, Virginia.

Greenways vary in size, scope, and nature. Some are ecological corridors with little or no public access, like the Pinhook Swamp Wildlife Movement Corridor in Florida; others, like the Minute Man Trail in Boston, Massachusetts, attract millions of visitors each year. The scope and widespread nature of greenways is illustrated by the following statistics.

Rail-Trails—The Rails-to-Trails Conservancy reports that, nationwide, more than 900 abandoned railroad lines totaling almost 9,500 linear miles have been converted into multi-purpose linear parks. These trails now receive more than 100 million users each year, including cyclists and pedestrians. Michigan has the most miles of rail trail. Florida has the greatest number of urban rail trails. Washington has the most suburban mileage. The longest rail trail is Missouri's Katy Trail at almost 200 miles. When completed, Nebraska's Cowboy Line Trail will be the longest at 321 miles.

Waterfronts—The Waterfront Center maintains files on over 1,000 waterfront promenades and linear parks located along rivers, streams, and harbors in the United States. Many of these waterfront parks are known for their role in attracting tourists and fostering related economic development. For example, the San Antonio Riverwalk is the leading tourist attraction in the state of Texas. The Augusta, Georgia Canal Project has leveraged more than $100 million in new waterfront development from a public investment of $8 million in a riverfront walkway and park.

Save Our Streams—The Izaak Walton League reports that there are over 2,000 Save Our Streams projects around the country involving streamside restoration, water quality monitoring, and riverside clean-up.

ISTEA—The Intermodal Surface Transportation Efficiency Act (ISTEA) is the first federal transportation law that explicitly acknowledges bicycling and walking as viable modes of transportation. This landmark legislation has led to a dramatic increase in funding for greenway related projects including rail trails and other bicycle and pedestrian facilities. The Surface Transportation Policy Project reports that over $1 billion has been spent in the last six years on more than 3,000 projects involving greenways, railtrails, and other bicycle and pedestrian facilities around the country.

National ISTEA Enhancement Funding for Non-motorized Transportation Facilities

Type of Facility	Federal Share (Millions $)	Number of Projects
Rails-Trails	385	814
Greenway Trails*	562	1,073
Other Bicycle and Pedestrian facilities**	253	1,443
Total	1,200	3,330

*Greenway trails includes sidepaths and off-road trail and bikeway facilities that are not rail-trails.
**Other bicycle & pedestrian facilities includes on-road bicycle facilities, overpasses, underpasses, pedestrian sidewalks, plazas, etc.

National Park Service—In 1996, the Rivers, Trails, and Conservation Assistance Program of the National Park Service provided technical assistance to 130 greenway projects in 46 states. These projects ranged from the development of a regional bikeway system for Cape Cod, Massachusetts, to creating 280 miles of trails and seven new riverfront parks in the state of New York.

State and Regional Greenway Systems

Since 1990, more than a dozen states have embarked on efforts to plan, design, and implement statewide systems of greenways. For example, in Maryland the program is directed by a Maryland Greenways Commission made up of civic, business, and government leaders appointed by the governor. The commission has identified more than 900 miles of existing and 1,000 miles of proposed greenways. The program has an active land acquisition component and the state has developed a Greenways Atlas that identifies existing and potential greenway corridors in every county. Similar efforts have been initiated in Florida, Connecticut, Rhode Island, Massachusetts, Pennsylvania, Illinois, Ohio, South Carolina, and Tennessee. At the regional level, a majority of the nation's major metropolitan areas have also embarked on the development of regional, multi-jurisdictional greenway systems. Some of the most advanced are in Portland, Chicago, Indianapolis, Kansas City, Chattanooga, Denver, and Boston.

New Directions and Future Trends

A number of factors are combining to give great impetus to the greenway movement. These factors include watershed planning and whole ecosystem management, increased federal funding for bicycle and pedestrian facilities, the shift from an industrially–based economy to a service and higher tech economy that places more emphasis on quality of life factors in corporate facility siting decisions, a growing concern about the negative impacts of sprawl, the increased demand for close-to-home outdoor recreation facilities, the search for cost effective approaches for dealing with flood control, stormwater management and non-point source pollution, and finally a shift in consumer preferences regarding desired amenities in new home communities.

The greenway concept is a relatively new idea that integrates many established conservation, land use planning, urban design and landscape architectural ideas, concepts and strategies. If all of the greenway projects that are currently planned or envisioned were completed, almost a third of the nation's landscape would be incorporated into an enormous system of greenways and natural infrastructure. Clearly greenways are an idea that has caught the imagination of citizens and officials all over the nation. This is primarily because greenway planning is a multi-purpose, multi-objective process that addresses concerns of ecologists, wildlife biologists, recreation planners and enthusiasts, tourism officials, as well as historic preservation and community revitalization advocates.

Rails-to-Trails

(By Hugh Morris, Rails-to-Trails Conservancy, Washington, D.C.)

The Rails-to-Trails Conservancy (RTC) is another major organization deeply involved in the development and protection of greenways in the United States. Founded in 1986, RTC's mission is to protect America's railroad corridors which were, and still are, being abandoned at the rate of about 2,000 miles per year. This rate has remained fairly constant for several years. The recent mergers of several of the nation's largest rail companies may accelerate the abandonment of rail lines in the near future as the companies strive to establish the most efficient networks for their business.

Rail infrastructure in the United States peaked in 1930 at about 300,000 miles. Today only half of that remains in active use. Many of the corridors that have been abandoned are lost forever because the land has reverted back to adjacent landowners. Railroads remain one of the most efficient ways to transport people and goods. However, reassembling these corridors for future rail use would be prohibitively expensive and time consuming. Demand for rail transport on currently inactive corridors may reemerge in the future. Thus, preservation of the corridor may have long-term national benefits. Using corridors as trails keeps them intact and provides interim benefits to users.

The creation of rail-trails is primarily due to the efforts of local trail enthusiasts, citizens, local politicians, and business leaders who see an opportunity for a trail in their community and work to make it a reality. RTC does not own any of the rail-trails, but supports the local trail development process by providing technical, legal, and policy assistance. RTC also safeguards and expands federal policies in support of rail-trails, such as the Railbanking Act of 1986 (Section 8(d) of the National Trails System Act), which allows rail corridors to be "banked" for future rail use. Another federal program that aids trail development is the Transportation Enhancements funding from ISTEA, which funneled $1 billion to bicycle and pedestrian projects, including trails, between 1992 and 1997.

The number of rail-trails in the United States has grown tremendously since RTC's founding. Many rail-trails predate the organization, but RTC now documents more than 900 rail-trails covering over 9,300 miles (Table III.26). This mileage is equivalent to nearly one-fourth the length of the U.S. Interstate Highway System. The pace of trail development shows no signs of slowing. RTC is currently tracking more than 1,100 rail-trail projects nationwide, representing nearly 18,000 more miles of trail (Table III.26). Further, RTC has assisted with the development of 41 trails alongside historic canals covering 685 miles (not included in the rail-trail statistics).

Table III.26: Number and Miles of Rail-Trails by Status, Allowable Uses, and Region, 1997

Rail-Trail Status and Allowable Uses	Number and Miles	Region North	South	Rocky Mountains	Pacific Coast	U.S. Total
Status						
Open for Public Use	Number	622	101	70	110	903
	Miles	7,361	669	455	824	9,308
Trail Projects	Number	634	241	124	139	1,138
Underway	Miles	8,250	3,560	3,318	2,660	17,789
Allowable Uses						
Walking	Number	544	90	64	102	800
	Miles	6,178	636	438	769	8,021
Horseback Riding	Number	228	20	27	53	328
	Miles	3,699	354.8	290	620	4,963
Bicycling	Number	259	48	39	61	407
	Miles	3,106	328	274	280	3,988
In–line Skating	Number	131	38	28	50	247
	Miles	1,200	266	167	251	1,884
Mountain Biking	Number	236	16	25	29	306
	Miles	3,218	248	171	457	4,094
Fishing	Number	183	15	15	28	241
	Miles	2,268	196	70	408	2,942
Cross-Country Skiing	Number	414	10	41	21	486
	Miles	4,808	163	347	420	5,737
Snowmobiling	Number	193	0	12	2	207
	Miles	4,081	0	176	38	4,294
Wheelchair Accessible	Number	245	49	38	61	393
	Miles	3,031	362	279	309	3,982

Source: Rails-to-Trails Conservancy Trails Database. May, 1997.

The North region dominates the supply of existing rail-trails in the United States (Figure III.15). The North accounts for 80 percent of the total rail-trail mileage and 70 percent of the trails. The states of Michigan, Minnesota, Wisconsin, and Pennsylvania alone make up almost half of the national trail mileage (48 percent) and nearly one-third of the trails. The North also has the nation's longest rail-trail (Missouri's Katy Trail, 185 miles and still developing) and its busiest (Boston's Minuteman Trail, used by more than two million people annually). The Rocky Mountain region has the fewest trails and least trail mileage. Rail-trail projects that are not currently open to public use are also dominated by the North, but are much more evenly distributed than existing rail-trails (Figure III.16). The same is true for their mileage.

Figure III.15: Counties with Existing Rail-Trails, 1997

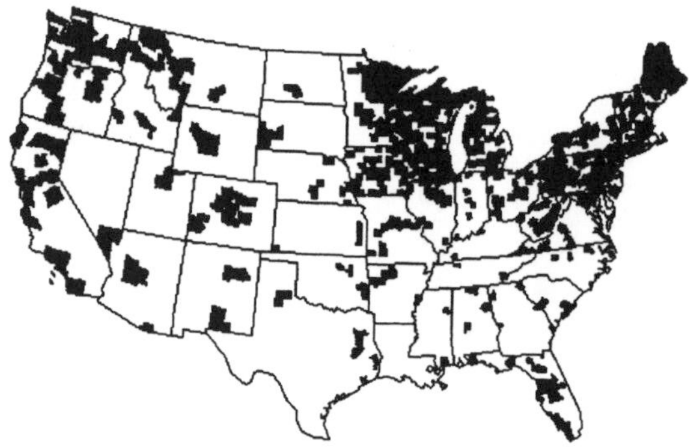

Source: Rails-to-Trails Conservancy trails database. 1997.

Figure III.16: Counties with Rail-Trail Projects Not Yet Open for Public Use, 1997

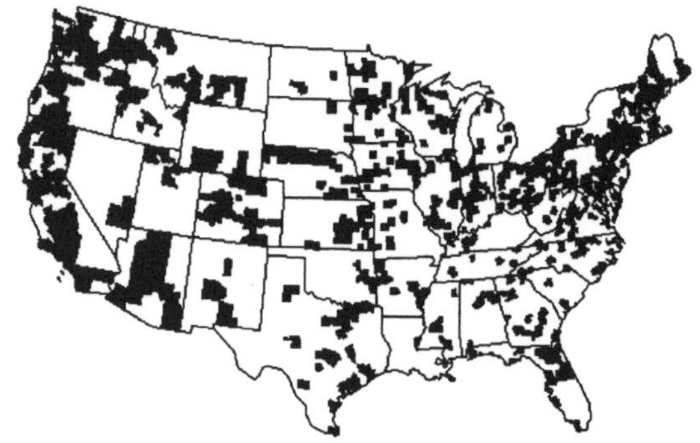

Source: Rails-to-Trails Conservancy trails database. 1997.

As expected, walking is the most prevalent use, occurring on almost 90 percent of the trails (Table III.26). The next most common use is cross-country skiing, allowed on more than half of the trails nationwide, although most are in the North. Among types of trail use, snowmobiling is allowed (or suitable) on the least number of trails, but the mileage of snowmobile trails is substantial, particularly in the North. There are no suitable snowmobile trails in the South and only two in the Pacific Coast region.

Bicycling is also a popular and common use, but mountain biking is not allowed on as many trails. Mountain biking trails do comprise more mileage, however, which probably reflects the longer lengths of these mostly unpaved, overland trails. The relatively small amount of trail mileage on which in-line skating is allowed probably reflects the limited number of paved trails, as much as it does use restrictions. Only about one-third of trails are either asphalt or concrete and they make up less than one-fourth of the mileage. Fishing and horseback riding are other recognized uses for which many trails are not appropriate or suitable due to their location or surface. Wheelchairs are accommodated on about 44 percent of trails. Many unpaved trails, therefore, are classified as wheelchair accessible.

RTC recently shifted its strategic focus from corridor preservation and individual trail development to connecting rail-trails into a nationwide system of trails and greenways. Of particular interest and concern is the need to develop and expand trails in urban areas. Trails can play an important role in developing sustainable communities by preserving green infrastructure, providing alternative transportation routes for non-motorized roads, and promoting economic development. Many urban areas now have the beginnings of trail systems. The St. Louis region, for example, has a burgeoning trail network on both sides of the Missouri River that is made up of 20 different trails, both short and long, urban and rural. Likewise, the Washington, D.C. area has several trails that originate in various suburbs and, like spokes on a wheel, connect those suburbs to the city center. These trails are used by commuters as well as for recreation.

Nationally, the most significant development affecting rail-trails is the renewal of the federal transportation legislation that has provided funds for more than 750 trails and trail projects. ISTEA was adopted in 1991 and has provided significant funding for trails through the Transportation Enhancements and other programs. The Enhancements program set aside more than $1 billion for projects that enhanced the nation's transportation facilities for non-motorized vehicle modes, such as pedestrians and bicycles. The reauthorization of this legislation occurred in October 1997.

On the legal front, *Preseault vs. the State of Vermont* is challenging the viability of the federal railbanking statute. While railbanking is a useful method for facilitating the preservation of a rail corridor, only about five percent of rail-trails are railbanked. The U.S. Supreme Court upheld the constitutionality of the railbanking statute, but it remanded the decision of the land takings issue back to a lower court. This court recently ruled that the railbanking law caused a land taking from the Preseaults and that they are entitled to compensation for that taking. The next step is for the court to assess the damages due to the Preseaults.

While the outcome of ISTEA reauthorization and the Preseault case will have some bearing on the development of rail-trails, the number of rail-trails already in the project stage ensures that a steady stream of new trails will be opening all over the United States well into the future. Together, open and projected trail miles sum to over 27,000 miles of (expected) trails in the United States. RTC's database also contains an additional 2,850 miles of trail that are connected to rail-trails but are not part of the abandoned rail lines (not included in Table III.26). Although a comprehensive database of all greenway miles—including other types in addition to rail-trails—does not exist, the number is easily in the tens of thousands of miles currently. With proposed greenways of all types included, the total length of U.S. greenways probably approaches 100,000 miles. These numbers tell only the statistical part of the story of greenways, much of which has occurred since the late 1980s. Clearly, greenways are one of the most significant developments in outdoor recreation in the United States over the past decade.

PRIVATE SECTOR RESOURCES FOR OUTDOOR RECREATION

The private sector is the fourth major provider of outdoor recreation resources in addition to the federal, state, and local levels of government. Private land (including water) and businesses play a critical role in supplying outdoor recreation opportunities, especially in regions of the country with relatively little public land. Private land provides a variety of settings for outdoor recreation, from the highly developed to the primitive. Some recreation activities like gardening and family gatherings, not to mention informal relaxation and sunbathing, occur predominantly on private land.

Recreation businesses provide many of the necessary inputs that consumers need for satisfying recreation experiences. Businesses manage natural resources, provide facilities and equipment, and offer leadership and other services to individuals or groups that recreate outdoors. In addition, semiprivate, not-for-profit groups, including land trusts, conservancies and the like, manage resources and make some available to the public for recreation. In this section, we look broadly at private recreation resources in two general categories: land and recreation businesses.

Private Recreation Land

National Private Landowners Study

The National Private Landowners Study (NPLOS) was conducted by the FS, USDA Natural Resources Conservation Service, and the University of Georgia in 1975, 1985, and again in 1995.[35] A major purpose was to investigate private landowner practices with respect to recreation and accessibility. Private land was classified into one of five categories: (1) closed to public access, (2) leased to individuals or groups for recreation, (3) reserved for family and friends' recreational use only, (4) open to the general public for recreation, and (5) undesignated. An estimate of the amount of land in each of these categories was calculated for every county in the coterminous United States. Two of the categories, open and leased land, indicate accessibility of private land to the public for recreation, both with and without a price.

The 1992 National Resources Inventory estimated a total of about 1.3 billion acres of nonfederal forest and agricultural land in the United States, excluding Alaska. Roughly 181.1 million of these acres (14 percent) are nonindustrial private land available for outdoor recreation (Table III.27). Most of these 181 million acres are open to the general public (72 percent); the remainder are leased to either individuals or groups (28 percent). The South, with about 64.2 million acres either open or leased, has over one-third of the U.S. private land that is available for recreation. Next is the Rocky Mountains (56.3 million acres), followed by the North (47.1 million) and Pacific Coast (13.5 million).

Table III.27: Area of Private Land Open and Leased for Outdoor Recreation by Region, 1995

Availability of Private Land	Region (1000 acres)				
	North	South	Rocky Mountains	Pacific Coast	U.S. Total
Open to general public	42,105.8	30,262.1	45,882.5	12,233.8	130,484.2
Leased to individuals and groups	5,028.8	33,906.8	10,404.7	1,231.8	50,572.1
Either open or leased	47,134.6	64,168.9	56,287.2	13,465.6	181,056.3

Private land available in the South is about evenly split between open and leased, but in all other regions the amount of leased land is relatively minor. In the North and Pacific Coast, the ratio of open to leased land is about nine to one. Land open to the general public for outdoor recreation in the North makes up 89 percent of available private nonindustrial land versus 11 percent that is leased. In the Pacific Coast, open land accounts for 91 percent of the available land and leased land the remaining 9 percent. The Rocky Mountains are somewhat less dominated by open land, with leased land comprising 19 percent of the regional total available for recreation. The South has more than three times as much leased land as any other region and accounts for two-thirds of all leased land in the United States. The Rocky Mountains have the most open land acreage (45.8 million), followed closely by the North (42.1 million acres).

The 1985 NPLOS also estimated acreages of private nonindustrial land in each of the five access categories, but methodological differences between the two studies make comparisons difficult. Considering this caveat, the trend between the two surveys indicates an estimated 35 percent decline in amount of land available for public outdoor recreation, down from 278 million total acres in 1985. The most pronounced change was in the amount of open land in the Rocky Mountains, which fell by an estimated 43 million acres. In addition, open land in North declined by 39.6 million acres. Leased acreage actually increased slightly overall nationwide by less than a million acres. Both the South and Rocky Mountains showed significant gains in leased land, the North only a modest loss, but the Pacific Coast showed a substantial loss of about 10 million acres.

---

[35]See Chapter IV for thorough coverage of the results and findings of the 1995 NPLOS.

Outdoor Recreation on Private Land in the Northeast: Case Briefs

(By Wilfred E. Richard, Outdoor Ventures North, Inc., Georgetown, ME, and Lloyd C. Irland, The Irland Group Forestry Consultants, Winthrop, ME)

Introduction

This article describes four examples of how the private sector and public/private partnerships have responded to provide outdoor recreation opportunities on private land in the northeastern United States. Just under 94 percent of the land area of Maine, New Hampshire, and Vermont is in private ownership. In Pennsylvania, hunting is a major activity requiring extensive blocks of land. Thus, the importance of privately owned resources for outdoor recreation is obvious (Northern Forest Lands Council, 1994). Also important is the economic issue of supplementary income for the landowner.

Private land available for public recreation is declining due to a number of factors, including the purchase of second homes by nonresidents and the associated fragmentation of the landscape, urban development, and the increased posting of land. Also affecting recreational access to private land are concerns about landowner liability, perceptions of government interference and 'takings,' and state regulations that inhibit recreational development. It is generally agreed that "... in the best interest of forest conservation, large industrial holdings [should] remain under the stability of forest industry ownership" (Brown, 1993a, p. 14). However, if public use of private land is to be achieved in an emerging multiuse and multi–owner landscape, outdoor recreationists must be perceived as legitimate users and responsible users.

As population and the demand for outdoor recreation continue to increase, there is a growing need to develop more access to privately forested land and to enhance the amenities of that land. Because of technological advances in outdoor recreation gear and equipment, demand has not only grown but is also becoming increasingly diverse with activities for every season. An increasingly differentiated market has developed in both mechanized (e.g., snowmobiles, ATVs, dirt bikes, jet skis) and nonmechanized (e.g., sea kayaking, whitewater rafting, nordic skiing, winter hiking, nature photography) recreation. Case briefs presented below describe a variety of recreation activities and resources provided on private land: a winter recreation program in Maine, an innovative backcountry lease agreement in New Hampshire, a general state strategy for assuring private land access in Vermont, and a statewide hunting lease program in Pennsylvania.

Maine Snowmobile Program

Maine has about 11,000 miles of snowmobile trails that are managed through the state's snowmobile program. Involved in this cooperative program are two partners: the Snowmobile Program of the Maine Bureau of Parks and Lands, and organized snowmobile clubs. This program is funded by the state of Maine through a dedicated account that is supported by a percentage of snowmobile registration fees and snowmobile gasoline taxes. The clubs initiate the approach to landowners for trail use and/or development rights. If the clubs do not work with the respective landowners, the state will not fund development or maintenance of a trail.

If issues do arise between owners and users, the state steps in to serve as mediator. Though snowmobile clubs make the initial time and financial commitment to develop a new trail, they are then reimbursed through the dedicated funds. According to the state administrator of the program, reimbursement is through a grant application process which is based on "a great deal of trust" between clubs and the state. This trust involves two key elements: that permission has been extended by a landowner to a club and that claimed expenses for development and maintenance are genuine. Capital equipment purchases (e.g., trail grooming machines) with these dedicated funds are not allowed. However, this prohibition is currently being reviewed.

In terms of liability, the state avails itself of "common law liability," referred to as the "landowner liability" law and the "recreational use" statute that guards against liability for recreational and harvesting activities (Title 14, M.R.S.A. Section 159-A). Under this protection, whether a landowner gives permission or not, the landowner is protected:

> If someone uses your land or passes through your land for outdoor recreation or harvesting, you assume no responsibility and incur no liability for injuries to that person or that person's property. You are protected whether or not you give permission to use your land (Androscoggin Land Trust, 1996).

In addition, the state's Bureau of Parks and Recreation maintains a $300,000 liability policy. To date, even in the light of many fatal accidents over the 20-plus year history of the state snowmobile program, there has not been one instance of legal action being brought against the state.

In terms of land easements, the program does not grant easements, per se. What the Bureau of Parks and Recreation of the Department of Conservation does, though, is to purchase or lease abandoned railroad beds and convert them into multiuse trails. Finally, there are cross-border trail linkages known as the "Interstate Trail System."

Phillips Brook Backcountry Recreation Area

Mountain Recreation, a company based in Conway, New Hampshire, has designed an innovative strategy for developing and managing recreational land while not actually owning the land itself. Conducting operations as a subsidiary, Timberland Trails, Inc. (TT), Mountain Recreation has a three-year "recreation rights" contract with International Paper Timberlands Operating Company. TT is developing and managing the Phillips Brook Backcountry Recreation Area on International Paper–owned land in northern New Hampshire. Opened in the summer of 1997, it offers backcountry lodging and trail facilities on 24,000 acres of wildlands. Through this arrangement, a "flexible trail system" has been developed, one that uses existing skid roads as trails; conversely, trails may be used as skid roads as circumstances require. The private timber company's interest in the project is summed up by Duane Nadeau, timberlands manager for International Paper (Jimenez, 1997):

> To the best of our knowledge, this will be the first time in the United States that a private professional recreation company will be co-managed with industrial forestry on private lands. The way things are right now, the forest owner has nothing but the income from timber to support the property. The costs of road building, insurance, managing land, and all other costs continue to rise, but the trees can only give you so much. It's reached the point where there has to be some other revenue source for land to remain commercial forest, and recreation is an obvious place to look.

In terms of liability, TT maintains a management program for risk reduction. All risk factors are examined and subsequently reduced through a management plan. For example, TT field representatives review waiver agreements with clients who choose to visit Phillips Brook. In this fashion, clients are made fully aware, in writing, of the risk associated with a back country adventure. TT has essentially a two-track strategy. First, as New Hampshire state limited liability protection applies to non-fee recreation, the public is invited to bike, hike, and ski on Phillips Brook trails at no charge. By not charging the public for use of land or trails, the issue of liability is resolved. Instead, fees are charged for lodging and meals. Second, an agreement is maintained that names the landowner, International Paper Timberlands Operating Company, as co-insurers and includes a hold-harmless agreement for TT. This agreement is substantively similar to Maine's landowner liability law.

Under the direction of Mountain Recreation President Bill Altenburg, TT serves as an interface between the public and the landowners. There is no threat that the public will become a landowner through imposition of eminent domain under the National Trail Systems Act of 1968—which provides for taking up to a 1,000 foot corridor along a trail—or through any other federal or state regulatory entity. Through this land management method, landowners are protected from "creeping corridors" that may interfere with an owner's use of the land. But, at the same time, the land is made available to the public. The local press has written many positive stories about Phillips Brook with headlines such as "use of trails is free" (Tetreault, 1997), "have fun on paper company land" (Marvel, 1997), and "new rec area is paradise" (Tracy, 1997).

Additionally, one of Altenburg's missions is to educate the public about the concept of an industrial forest. Strategically, the goal is a multiuse forest as recreational and industrial land in which both industry and the public have a stake. Apparently, consideration is being given by other paper companies in both New Hampshire and Maine to utilize the Mountain Recreation approach as a model. Mountain Recreation is also negotiating for similar projects in Montana, Idaho, Washington, and New York. The usual approach to recreation by paper and land management companies, who own much of the industrial forest, is to basically monitor use.

Vermont Private Lands Task Group

In Vermont, as in Maine and New Hampshire, the amount of private land available for public recreation is declining due to a number of factors including rural migration and increased levels of litigation. The incidence of posting is increasing, particularly as parcels of land become fragmented into vacation or second-home sized lots, usually of a few acres (Brown 1993b). This fragmentation has resulted in the Vermont Private Lands Task Group designing a strategy to slow the downward spiral of land available to the public. With approximately 90 percent of its total land in private ownership (not just forested land) and with an important recreation–based tourism sector, the state of Vermont has taken policy and program action to encourage maintenance of the traditional use of private land by the public. As a result of this effort, two publications have been produced. The first was written by the "Public Outdoor Recreation on Privately-Owned Lands Task Force" released as a report by that title (Vermont Agency of Natural Resources, 1994). While the report lists 10 issues, goals, and actions that it identifies as requiring action, two in particular stand out:

- Landowners may face the threat or loss of their traditional uses when recreational groups have access and rights to their land. Suggested goal and associated actions involves working together to communicate that traditional uses of land, such as forestry, constitutes a legitimate use of the land. This corresponds with one of the missions of the Phillips Brook Backcountry Recreation Area, which is to educate the public on the legitimacy and economic value of an industrial forest.
- Some landowners fear the threat of takings (including regulatory, eminent domain, and adverse possession) of private property due to recreational use. While recreationists should be allowed use of land, it should not come at the price of reducing the landowner's ability to make a profit or to otherwise use the land. Landowners would be involved in any planning process for recreational use and in education of the public about the negative affects of "taking" land.

Following publication of the task force report, a booklet entitled "Public Recreation on Private Land: A Landowner's Guide" was released (Vermont Agency of Natural Resources, 1997). That document lists guidelines that are clearly codified here. For example, in the discussion of the responsibilities of recreational organizations, it states that:

- The organization must have the means to educate visitors about allowed uses and proper care of the land.
- The organization must contact the landowner at least annually (or at some other agree-upon interval) to check on his/her satisfaction, problems, and intentions for continued use.

Elsewhere, the guide addresses a specific provision that has been made in Vermont statutes (10 V.S.A. Section 448) for protecting the rights of landowners whose land is crossed by the Vermont Trail System. No public or private owner is liable for injury or damage (p.8). Neither Maine nor New Hampshire specifically limits liability associated with hiking. As with Maine and New Hampshire statutes, Vermont statute (10 V.S.A. Section 5212) releases a landowner from liability for recreational use when a fee is not charged (p.7). The intent is to encourage open access to recreational use by the public, while reassuring the owner that he or she is not incurring great personal risk.

Public Hunting on Private Land in Pennsylvania

Pennsylvania is a major hunting state, with some 2.3 million hunting licenses sold each year. Since the 1930s, its Game Commission has managed a program of arrangements for hunter access to privately–owned land. While often described as a "leasing" program, it involves some minor incentives for the landowners but no cash rental payment. Agreements signed under the program have five–year terms.

Under these programs, hunting access to 4.5 million acres of private land is assured. This is an area equal to 16 percent of the commonwealth's entire land area. This is in addition to the significant amount of state forest and game land that is also available. The program involves about 30,000 individual landowners as cooperators, so it is a major administrative task to operate the program. The total area under the program has been roughly stable in recent years, but this masks considerable dynamism as some owners drop out and are replaced by others.

There are three related programs, one for farms, one for commercially managed timberlands, and one for small tracts. Cooperating land is marked, and rules for using it are taught in hunter safety courses and in information materials for hunters. No survey has been conducted to determine the amount of hunting activity supported by this land, but it is clearly a huge number. Much of this land is relatively close to cities so it offers a significant improvement in access for many hunters. Hunters must gain the landowner's permission to use the land under the program.

National Private Forest Land Study

The National Private Forest Land Study, conducted by the FS Northeastern Forest Experiment Station in 1994, sought to learn more about the management practices and ownership objectives of private forest owners. Scientists estimated a total of 9.91 million owners and 393.5 million acres of privately–owned forest (Table III.28).[36] The private forest estate is important because so many recreation activities occur there. More than four out of every five private forest acres are in the eastern United States (Figure III.17). An even higher proportion of private forest land owners are in the East.

Table III.28: Estimated Number of Owners and Acreage of Private Forest Land by Year and Region, 1978 and 1994

Owners and Acres	Year	Region				
		North	South	Rocky Mountains	Pacific Coast	U.S. Total
Owners (1000s)	1978	3,289.5	3,850.4	131.7	486.3	7,757.9
	1994	3,940.1	4,940.2	385.7	644.6	9,910.6
Acres (1000s)	1978	114,054.0	173,133.0	16,135.0	29,771.0	333,093.0
	1994	129,491.9	187,781.8	30,354.7	45,832.6	393,461.0

Source: Birch, Thomas W. 1996. *Private Forest-land Owners of the United States, 1994.* USDA Forest Service, Northeastern Forest Experiment Station, Resource Bulletin, NE-134.

Figure III.17: Percentage of Private Forest Land Acreage by Region, 1994

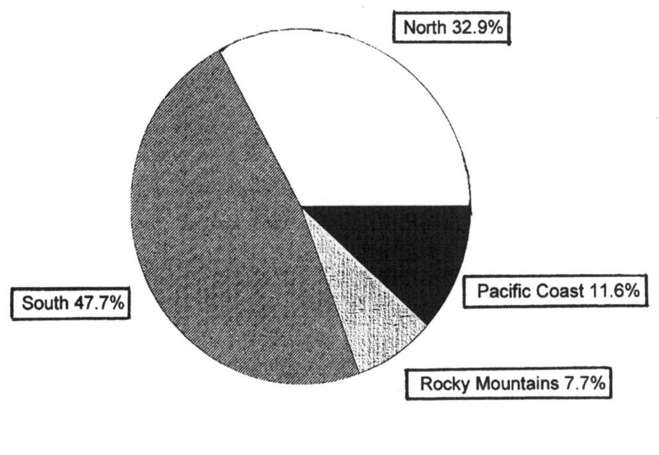

Source: Birch, Thomas W. 1996. *Private Forest-land Owners of the United States, 1994.* USDA Forest Service, Northeastern Forest Experiment Station, Resource Bulletin, NE-134.

Estimated private forest acreage and ownership units increased considerably between 1978 and 1994, about 18 percent. Ownership units increased even more, at the rate of 28 percent. Size of the average ownership unit stayed about the same in the West (74.2 acres in 1978 versus 73.9 acres in 1994), but declined

[36]This compares to the national total of 394.5 million acres of private forest estimated by the 1992 National Resources inventory.

somewhat in the East (40.2 acres in 1978 versus 35.7 acres in 1994). Individually–owned forest land accounted for about three-fifths of the total in 1994 (Table III.29). Most of the rest is owned by corporations, with the remainder belonging to partnerships and other owners. The share of individual and other owner acreage increased between 1978 and 1994 while those of partnerships and corporations dropped from 41 percent of forest land to 35 percent. Corporate acreage still increased, however, and comprises more than one of every four private forest acres in the United States. This is especially true in the Pacific Coast and South, where 52 and 28 percent of private forest acres, respectively, are owned by corporations. The North and Rocky Mountains are both around 20 percent.

Table III.29: Estimated Number of Acres of Forest Land in Private Ownership by Type of Ownership, United States, 1978 and 1994

Type of ownership	1978		1994	
	Millions	Percent	Millions	Percent[1]
Individual	183.5	55.1	232.3	59.0
Partnership	35.8	10.7	29.7	7.5
Corporation	101.1	30.4	107.1	27.2
Other	12.7	3.8	24.3	6.2
All Ownerships	333.1	100.0	393.4	100.0

[1]Numbers may not sum exactly to totals because of rounding.

Source: Birch, Thomas W. 1996. Private Forest-Land Owners of the United States. USDA Forest Service, Northeastern Forest Experiment State, Resource Bulletin NE-134.

The "other" category of forest land ownership includes recreation and sport clubs, undivided estates, trusts, and Indian tribal land. Of the U.S. total of 24.3 million acres in this category, almost one-third are owned by recreation or sport clubs (Table III.30). In the North, 3.77 of 3.93 million 'other' acres (96 percent) are owned by recreation or sport clubs. Recreation clubs are also prevalent in the South, with 2.86 of 5.27 million acres (54 percent) of 'other' private land. In the Rocky Mountains, just five percent of 'other' private land is owned by recreation/sport clubs and in the Pacific Coast, the figure is 14 percent.

Table III.30: Acres of Recreational Uses and Benefits of Private Forest Land by Region, 1994

Use/Benefit	Region (1000 acres)				
	North	South	Rocky Mountains	Pacific Coast	U.S. Total
Recreation/sport club or association	3,776.5	2,857.2	638.5	491.2	7,763.4
Recreation as one of top two reasons for owning woodland	34,347.0	32,832.2	6,009.6	5,649.7	78,838.5
Recreation as one of top two expected future benefits of owning woodland	41,931.6	44,251.5	8,991.9	7,772.3	102,947.3

Source: Birch, Thomas W. 1996. Private Forest-Land Owners of the United States. USDA Forest Service, Northeastern Forest Experiment State, Resource Bulletin NE-134.

Two other indicators of outdoor recreation use and benefit are shown in Table III.26. Private forest land owners were asked to list the reasons they own woodland and the benefits they expect to derive during the next 10 years. Respondents who rated recreation as one of the top two reasons for owning their land own 78.8 million of the 393.5 million acres (20.0 percent) of private forest. The proportion who listed recreation as a primary objective was highest in the North (27 percent) and lowest in the Pacific Coast (12 percent). A little more than one-fourth (26 percent) of respondents nationally said that they expect recreation to be one of the top two benefits they derive from their land during the next 10 years. They own about 103 million acres of forest. Again, a larger proportion of forest owners in the North Region expect these benefits. They own about 32 percent of private forest land in the North. The Rocky Mountains follows closely with 30 percent of the acres expected to provide future recreational benefits. Percentages in the South and Pacific Coast are also higher for expected benefits than for stated ownership reasons. In the South, 24 percent expect future benefits from recreation and in the Pacific Coast, 17 percent.

Nature Conservancy Land

Another type of land with significant outdoor recreation value is the semiprivate land managed by land trusts and conservancies. The largest and best known of these is The Nature Conservancy (TNC). Their land is classified as 'semiprivate,' but while most of it is owned by the conservancies or other private owners, a large percentage is open for recreation. TNC maintains a comprehensive database of tracts it has identified as having significant natural values, as well as properties it owns or manages. For the latter, TNC describes public access allowed and resource protection status.

Visitors examine wetlands at the Nature Conservancy's Cape May Migratory Bird Refuge in New Jersey. Photo courtesy of the Nature Conservancy. Photograph by Connie Gelb.

TNC's database consists of 7,159 tracts totaling 3.33 million acres. A little over half of this land (1.71 million acres in 5,165 tracts) is designated as part of a "Managed Area." Managed Areas are defined by management, not ownership, and are created to characterize natural areas under protective management. The remaining 1,994 tracts totaling 1.62 million acres are not part of a designated Managed Area. They have been identified as having significant ecological values worthy of preservation. Little additional information is available on these undesignated tracts. Once the tract owner agrees to protect certain site values or characteristics, the tract is reclassified as a Managed Area.

The 1.71 million acres of Managed Areas are fairly evenly distributed between the eastern and western United States, with the most in the Rocky Mountains (35 percent) and North (29 percent), and the least in the Pacific Coast (20 percent) and South (16 percent) (Table III.31). About 1.2 million acres of the Managed Areas are managed as Nature Conservancy Preserves. More preserves are located in the Rocky Mountains (43 percent of preserve acreage) than in any other region. In 1987, Nature Conservancy Preserves totaled about 823,000 acres. The increase of 387,000 plus acres represents a 47.0 percent gain in preserve resources.

Table III.31: Acres of Land Managed by the Nature Conservacy by Classification, Access, and Region, 1997

Classification and Access	Region (1000 acres)				
	North	South	Rocky Mountains	Pacific Coast	U.S. Total
Managed Areas	493.4	272.8	595.5	346.1	1,707.8
Open to public access[1]	237.5	101.5	391.2	74.5	804.7
Restricted public access	105.3	51.8	27.7	146.4	331.2
Closed to public access	34.8	11.5	14.3	9.1	69.7
Preserves[2]	225.1	175.1	517.1	292.9	1,210.2

[1]Open, restricted and closed public access do not sum to Managed Area acres because 502,200 acres did not have public access information.

[2]Preserves are part of the Managed Areas. The approximately 500,000 acres of Managed Areas that are not Preserves are either resources managed by other organizations or resources managed by The Nature Conservancy, but not established as Preserves.

Source: The Nature Conservancy. Managed Area Basic Record file.

Just under half of the Managed Areas (804,700 acres) are open to the public and another 19 percent of Managed Area acres have restricted public access. Further information about the recreation on these areas is not available, but it is fairly safe to assume that the permitted types of recreation must have low impact. Nature study and wildlife observation are undoubtedly the most common form of recreation that occurs on the Managed Areas. Nearly half of the open acres are in the Rocky Mountains, while under 10 percent are in the Pacific Coast. No information was available about public access to just under 30 percent of the Managed Areas.

Private Recreation Businesses

Campgrounds

(By Douglas McEwen, Professor, Southern Illinois University, Carbondale, Illinois)

Privately–owned campgrounds have been in existence since the early 1930s, when they were first chronicled in the Woodall Publishing Company's 1937 edition of "Trailering Parks and Campgrounds." During World War II many of these campgrounds were converted to emergency housing, and then became mobile home parks. Private campgrounds became an important sector of the outdoor recreation supply system in the mid-1950s, when many private landowners started operating small campgrounds. Later, many additional campgrounds were developed along interstate highways to serve the traveling camper (McEwen & Profaizer, 1989).

Although most Americans associate the term campground with a rustic, tree-shaded area, the word has also been used to describe sites with a half-dozen recreational vehicle (RV) gravel parking spaces attached to a truck stop or mobile home park. On the other hand, luxurious RV parks with manicured sites, full-service bathrooms, and numerous recreation amenities have too been called campgrounds. Since differences between the types of campgrounds are great, the National Association of RV Parks and Campgrounds generally recognizes luxury RV parks where visitors live for two to 12 months per year as being distinct from campgrounds where visitors stay for shorter periods and receive fewer amenities. Still, the range in campground conditions is great and presents difficulties in deciding which units to include in a national inventory.

Woodall Publishing Company, which has been conducting in-depth analyses of its campground national inventories just since 1987, annually reviews its listing of campgrounds and RV parks, deleting between three and five percent each year because of poor quality. This inventory, conducted in conjunction with the publication of their campground directory, is the best and most consistent source of data on private campgrounds in the United States. The word "campgrounds," as defined by Woodall's inventory, includes both RV parks and campgrounds.

In 1996, the Woodall Publishing Company inventory listed a total of 6,900 private campgrounds (Table III.32). The two eastern regions account for 53 percent of private campgrounds nationwide, the North leading all regions with 36 percent. In 1977, there were 8,164 campgrounds with 68 percent in the East. The national net loss of 1,264 private campgrounds occurred primarily in the East, and especially the North, which lost more than 1,000 campgrounds, a 29 percent drop in the past 20 years.

Nationally, the total number of private campgrounds has shrunk by 15 percent since 1977. Many of the closed campgrounds were probably small, inefficient, and unprofitable. The trend seems to be accelerating in the private campground sector. Between 1977 and 1987, only about one percent of the private campgrounds were closed, but between 1987 and 1996 the decline was 14 percent. Patterns differ somewhat among regions. The rate of decline between 1977 and 1996 was much less in the South and Rocky Mountains. Meanwhile, the Pacific Coast essentially stayed the same with a net loss of only seven campgrounds.

Table III.32: Number of Private Campgrounds and Campsites by Year and Region

Type of Site and Year	Region				
	North	South	Rocky Mountains	Pacific Coast	U.S. Total
Campgrounds					
1977	3,515	2,058	1,393	1,198	8,164
1987	3,174	2,114	1,431	1,343	8,062
1996	2,504	1,850	1,355	1,191	6,900
Campsites					
1977	352,933	202,496	88,740	72,553	716,722
1987	409,196	280,046	144,499	113,969	947,710
1996	334,847	233,724	139,783	103,319	811,673

Source: Woodall Publishing Company campground inventory database. Lake Forest, Illinois.

The trend of decreasing private campgrounds in the North seems to be accelerating. The 10 percent drop from 1977 to 1987 increased to 21 percent between 1987 and 1996. The other three regions gained campgrounds during the first decade and lost in the second. The South increased slightly between 1977 and 1987, but then dropped 12 percent between 1987 and 1996. Private campgrounds in the Rocky Mountain region increased slightly between 1977 and 1987, but then declined during the 1987 to 1996 period resulting in a net loss of 38 units. In the Pacific Coast, a 12 percent increase in the first decade was followed by an 11 percent loss in the second decade.

In 1996, there were a reported 811,673 private campsites in the United States (Table III.28). Distribution of campsites is similar to that of campgrounds; 86 percent of all sites are in the East. The North contained almost one-half (49 percent) of all campsites. During the 1977 to 1996 period, there was a 13 percent increase in the number of campsites nationally, but this figure masks a mixed pattern. Between 1977 and 1987 there was a 32 percent increase in the numbers of campsites, followed by a 14 percent decrease between 1987 and 1996. In all regions, campsite numbers grew substantially between 1977 and 1987, but then declined between 1987 and 1996. The net result, except in the North, was an increase in the number of campsites over the 20-year period. In the North, however, overall campsite numbers decreased five percent from 1977 to 1996. In the South, the total number of campsites grew 15 percent from 1977 to 1996. The growth was fueled by a vigorous 38 percent increase of private campsites between 1977 and 1986, but was tempered by a 17 percent decline between 1987 and 1996.

In the western regions, percentage growth rates were strong, but the base number of campsites is much smaller than in the East. The Rocky Mountain region experienced a 58 percent gain in private campsites between 1977 and 1996. The Pacific Coast Region grew at the rate of 42 percent during the same period. Both western regions also experienced gains in the first decade followed by losses in the second. The Rocky Mountains added campsites at the rate of 63 percent between 1977 and 1987, then lost at the much smaller rate of three percent between 1987 and 1996. The situation was similar in the Pacific Coast: a 57 percent increase between 1977 and 1987 followed by a nine percent decline between 1987 and 1996.

Large increases in the number of campsites between 1977 and 1987 (especially in the South, Rocky Mountains, and Pacific Coast), combined with a decrease in the total number of campgrounds during the same period, indicate a trend toward larger campgrounds. This change could indicate that large numbers of small, unprofitable campgrounds closed during that period.

Woodall Publishing Company classifies campsites as: (1) full hookup with water, sewer, and electricity, as well as television and cable service in some cases; (2) water and electricity; (3) electricity only; and (4) no hookups. In 1996, 59 percent of private campsites in the United States had full hookups; 27 percent had water and electricity; just two percent had electricity only; and 12 percent had no hookups (Table III.33). As in previous years, the private sector accounted for the vast majority of all full hookup sites, about 480,000 compared to just under 20,000 in the public sector. A similar pattern holds for water and electricity campsites, though not to the same extent as full hookup sites. The public sector has traditionally provided rustic, no-hookup campsites and accounts for 69 percent of these sites nationwide. The same pattern was also true for the electricity–only sites, with 81 percent provided by the public sector.

Table III.33: Number of Campsites at Private Campgrounds by Type of Amenity and Year, 1977-1996

Type of Amenity	Year		
	1977	1987[1]	1996[1]
Full hookup	285,532	483,672	480,783
Water & electricity	269,551	310,066	220,521
Electricity only	47,752	30,900	17,689
No hookups	113,887	122,585	94,667
All sites	716,722	947,223	813,660

[1]Woodall Publishing Company's 1987 and 1996 data on campsite types do not match exactly the total number of U.S. campsites as shown in Table III.33.

Source: Woodall Publishing Company campground inventory database. Lake Forest, Illinois.

Between 1977 and 1987, over 198,000 full hookup campsites were constructed in the private sector, a 69 percent increase. During that same period, there were modest increases in water and electric sites, up 15 percent, and no-hookup sites, up eight percent. However, during the 1987 to 1996 period, the number of water and electric, electric only, and no-hookup sites declined substantially. The net results over the 20-year span was an 18 percent drop in the number of water and electric sites, a 17 percent drop in no-hookup sites, and a dramatic 63 percent drop in electric only sites. While many private campgrounds still maintain a number of no-hookup campsites in tenting or overflow areas, the great momentum is toward full-hookup sites. Since most customers demand water as well as electricity, providing only the latter is a fading venture. Indeed, only about two percent of all commercial campsites are electricity only.

Woodall's inventory lists a wide variety of private campground facilities and services ranging from laundry to recreation programs. About 58 percent of the campgrounds are open year round and 61 percent lease sites to campers on an annual basis. The number of sites leased on a seasonal basis grew substantially between 1977 and 1987 (62 percent), but then slowed between 1987 and 1996. It appears that more of the private campgrounds remaining in business are offering seasonal leases, a trend that is likely to continue into the future. Approximately one-third of the campgrounds offer cable TV and phone hookups. Between 1987 and 1996, the number of campgrounds offering these communication services almost doubled, another trend likely to continue.

Private campgrounds offer a variety of recreation facilities, with horseshoes being the most popular. Over 64 percent of the campgrounds have horseshoe pits, probably because this is a very inexpensive facility to build and maintain. About 44 percent of private campgrounds provide playgrounds. This proportion is slightly lower than in previous years. Federal consumer product safety standards have been published for playgrounds, and owners can be held liable if playgrounds do not meet these strict standards. Retrofitting or replacing playgrounds is expensive, and it is possible that owners are removing these structures rather than face increased liability risks.

Also declining are the numbers of swimming pools, down 35 percent between 1977 and 1987 and 11 percent between 1987 and 1996. Overall, there has been a 42 percent decrease in the number of campgrounds with swimming pools over the last 19 years. Reasons for this drop are unclear, but the number of smaller campgrounds dropping out of the market might explain the decline. In general, the larger, luxurious campgrounds have swimming pools.

Finally, the number of campgrounds offering boating declined by 27 percent between 1977 and 1996. The decline could be explained by the closing of smaller, rural campgrounds that usually had a small lake or pond for boating. Unfortunately, comprehensive data on campground facilities and programs are not available from the public sector for a comparison. With regard to restrictions, the number of private campgrounds excluding tents seems to be slowly rising. Now, 20 percent exclude tents. It is unlikely that any public campgrounds exclude tents.

A major recreation resource somewhat related to private campgrounds yet unique in its own right is the "Organized Camp." They are similar in that both provide access to camping opportunities, but organized camps are very much program–oriented and mostly geared toward youth. About one-quarter of U.S. organized camps are for-profit businesses, so they do not necessarily belong in the same category as private campgrounds or other recreation businesses. However, they are not exactly public resources either, since the majority are operated by youth agencies and religious organizations. They are often referred to as "semi-private" resources because most do not exclude people as private firms do, but they are not supported by public tax dollars. In any event, organized camps are a significant outdoor recreation resource that introduces thousands of young Americans to the outdoors. Data are not available on the amount of land and water resources that make up organized camps in this country, but the large number of camps assures that it is not inconsequential.

Organized Camps in the United States

(By Connie Coutellier, Professional Development Director, American Camping Association, Martinsville, IN)

Philosophy and Management of Organized Camps

More than 8,500 day and resident camps of varying types, lengths, and sponsorships flourish throughout the United States. Camps provide a sustained, group living experience in an outdoor setting and utilize the resources of the natural surroundings to contribute to each camper's mental, physical, social, and spiritual growth. Each summer, more than six million children and adults take advantage of these organized recreational and educational opportunities. In a 1996 American Camping Association (ACA) survey of organized camps, over 50 percent of the respondents reported an increase in enrollment of 15 percent over the 1995 figures.

Today, the management of camps requires skill, vision, and innovative strategies for success. ACA is a nonprofit educational organization representing all segments of the camp profession including agencies serving youth, independent camps, religious and fraternal organizations, and municipal government operated camps. Approximately 6,200 camps are operated by nonprofit groups including youth agencies and religious organizations, and 2,300 by privately owned independent for-profit operators. The most popular session length is one week to two weeks, although the majority of independent camp operators offer four, six, and eight week sessions. Summer camps for children, adults, families, and seniors operate under trained professionals and have volunteer or paid staff to work with their special client groups. Camps may be found in rural, suburban or urban communities, operate on several thousand back country acres, or in city parks.

Camps are designed in a variety of styles and formats and provide activities that vary to meet many interests. Most camps offer a general program of outdoor activities such as hiking, swimming, sports and games, arts and crafts, and nature awareness. Some camps have special emphasis on programs such as horseback riding, water sports, music, or adventure challenge activities. While camps provide facilities and services for a broad range of children, youth, and adults, some camps provide services to special groups. There are programs for seniors, families, campers with cancer, gifted and talented children, youth at risk, diabetics, asthmatics, or persons with disabilities.

Summer camps employ more than 500,000 adults to work as counselors, program or activity leaders, unit and program directors or supervisors, and in support–services roles such as maintenance, administration, food service, and health care. Most camps average from 40 to 50 percent returning staff. In the past 10 years there has been an increase in the use of international staff to expose campers to different cultures.

Types of Camps

Of the estimated 8,500 American camps, approximately 5,500 are resident camps and 3,000 are day camps. Resident camps are designed for campers staying at camp from several days to eight weeks. They sleep overnight in cabins, tents, tepees, or other forms of shelter, and participate in a variety of supervised activities. Having grown by nearly 90 percent in the past 20 years, day camps offer sessions and age-appropriate programs similar to resident camps. Campers are often transported to camp by bus or van, and return home each day in the late afternoon. Trip camps provide programs where participants transport themselves to different sites by backpacking, riding, or canoeing. Travel camps often transport campers by car or bus to geographic and topographic places of interest. Family camps offer cross-generational activities on weekends throughout the year, as well as family sessions during the summer. Family camps have increased more than 500 percent in the past 12 years.

A number of resident camps offer licensed child care and day camps on their sites for the benefit of their neighboring communities. In addition to the increase of children with disabilities being mainstreamed into camps, many new camps have opened to provide specialized services to children with special medical needs. Camps are also recruiting and serving more international campers.

Year-round use of camp facilities is a growing trend. Programs are evolving from spring and fall ancillary weekends to winterized full–service operations seven days a week. Many camps work with schools to provide environmental education during the school year, provide year–round program and food services and have some year–round staff. Camps can often be rented to other groups wishing to provide camping services to their constituents. With meeting rooms, sleeping and eating accommodations readily available, many facilities are both camps and year–round conference or retreat centers.

Accredited Camps

As the accrediting body for the camp profession, the American Camping Association is an advocate for the accredited-camp experience. ACA Standards are continually revised and updated to reflect the needs of camps, the public and the changing body of laws and regulations. Although many state and federal laws and regulations address basic sanitation and food service concerns, ACA standards go a step further in addressing the specific areas of programming, personnel, health care, and management practices. Separate standards are applied to activities such as aquatics, horseback riding, adventure challenge activities, and travel and trip programs. ACA publishes a *Guide to ACA-Accredited Camps* available from their bookstore and in libraries. It provides camp listings and program information for parents and for those seeking summer employment in a day or resident camp.

While fees to attend camp vary, they generally range from $15 to $100 per day for resident camps and from $10 to $50 per day for day camps. Nearly 85 percent of ACA-accredited camps offer some level of financial assistance to more than one million children from economically–deprived families, or to those who may have special medical needs or are in special situations that might preclude them from attending camp. The need, however, far outweighs the ability of camps to provide assistance. Camps securing assistance for children with medical needs have more success in fund–raising efforts than those serving at-risk youth. The challenge for the camping industry is to make the camp experience financially available for all children.

Program Trends

A particular emphasis of organized camp programming is building the self-confidence, independence, and self-reliance of each individual camper. In an ACA survey, about 60 percent of the directors reported adding new activities and programs over the last few years. The most common program trends in camps are challenging and adventurous activities, including high and low ropes courses, climbing walls, zip lines, backpacking and mountain biking, and cave exploring. There is also an increased emphasis on performing arts and fine arts such as dance, theater, ceramics, leather crafts, woodworking, photography, etc.

The ACA is committed to minimum impact camping and has an *Outdoor Living Skills* training program that teaches children how to visit nature "softly." This is a response to the industry's interest in conservation and appropriate land use issues and is consistent with the USDA Forest Service *Leave No Trace* program. ACA has signed a "Memorandum of Understanding" with the Forest Service and many summer camps have long-term contracts to build and operate facilities on Forest Service lands. National Parks and Forest Service lands are often used for hiking, backpacking, and tripping programs.

Expected Future Trends

Camp Operations

- Acquiring funding to deal with *aging property and non-winterized facilities* is one of the most pressing property management concerns. New government regulations are requiring heavy investment in new *infrastructure*, especially water, sewer, and cleanup of any buried toxic hazards on camp property.
- Year-round school is still under debate in many communities. Nearly four percent of all students attend year-round schools. Camps are *extending the season and diversifying their services*. The ACA accreditation program is changing from accrediting only summer programs to accrediting year-round operations.
- *Technology* has drastically changed the business aspects of marketing and operating a camp. Use of the Internet as a marketing tool continues to increase. Computers are used not only for registration and financial records but also for program scheduling and client data. Communication expectations of parents have changed with available technology. Cellular phones are common on outdoors trips. Campers often receive letters via fax and E-mail. Over the next five years, the use of technology, combined with other measures, will dramatically change the nature of the teaching/learning process. ACA and camps will need to diversify methods for training directors and staff.
- Acquiring, training, and maintaining adequate *employed and volunteer staff* is a significant challenge. In fact, 40 percent of ACA's membership has joined in the past five years without a significant change in the total membership. More professionals are choosing to use the camp director experience as a stepping stone to other agency management positions. While the number of potential summer staff from ages 18 to 24 will continue to grow through 2010 based on Census projections, they will likely have less experience in working with children, especially in an outdoor setting.
- Increasing *regulatory requirements* at the county, state, and federal levels are another issue that will affect camp operations. Camp directors must comply with and maintain records for a wide variety of laws and regulations including: Child Labor, OSHA (programs for hazardous materials, blood-born pathogens, lockout/tag out), EEOC, Americans with Disabilities Act, Civil Rights, Fair Labor, Criminal Records Act, food and drug laws, copyright laws, Child Protection Act, etc.

Meeting the Needs of Campers and the Public

- More leisure time options in American society have resulted in increased competition for children's time in the summer months. Increasingly, school years are longer and greater numbers of working parents mean that vacation time is often tightly scheduled. The number of school–aged children ages five to 14 will continue to grow and peak in 2003. After that, the Census Bureau projects a decline through 2010. Camps are currently operating at an average capacity of 91 percent. Camps offering six– and eight–week sessions may need to offer *shorter sessions* and recruit more campers or have more *flexible schedules* to meet parent needs.
- Parents expect more of camps. Research on youth development outcomes and training for directors must reflect systematic ways to *measure the outcomes* promised. Parents also have greater expectations of camps for providing a safe environment and qualified staff and security for their children.
- The cost of operating camp has continually increased. Making a camp experience *affordable for everyone* is a major challenge especially as many families have less discretionary income and are losing ground in overall family income.
- Camp directors will also need to recognize the impact of changing demographics in their communities and be proactive in attracting and keeping a *diverse constituency*.
- Another issue involves the rising rates of *youth violence* in the United States. Camps will need additional resources and training to help prepare staff to deal with problem behaviors in camp.
- Still another issue is the *influence of technology* and the entertainment industry on American youth. Children today are the video generation. Television viewing continues to consume a lot of children's discretionary time and the amount of time children spend on the Internet is increasing at a very rapid rate. Camps will need to design programs that attract this generation.
- More children are coming to camp with *medications and allergies*. The rates of asthma and chronic bronchitis in children are increasing in this country. Attention Deficit Hyperactivity Disorder (ADAD) affects three to five percent of the U.S. children. Camp infirmaries are evolving into health and wellness centers to educate campers and staff on safety and prevention, monitor risks and manage treatment and medications.

Downhill Skiing

Downhill ski areas are located, not surprisingly, in the cold-weather states of the North and throughout the mountainous West (Figure III.18). The number of areas in the United States increased 14 percent between 1987 and 1996, for a total of 449 (Table III.34). Most of the growth occurred in the North, where nearly two-thirds of downhill ski areas are located. The number of ski areas in the North increased faster (25 percent) than the national rate. The South, with only four percent of U.S. ski areas, had a net loss of one ski area between 1987 and 1996, while the Rocky Mountains, with 21 percent of the ski areas, gained one. The Pacific Coast added eight ski areas to the 46 that existed in 1987, a 17 percent increase.

Figure III.18: Counties with Downhill Ski Areas, 1996

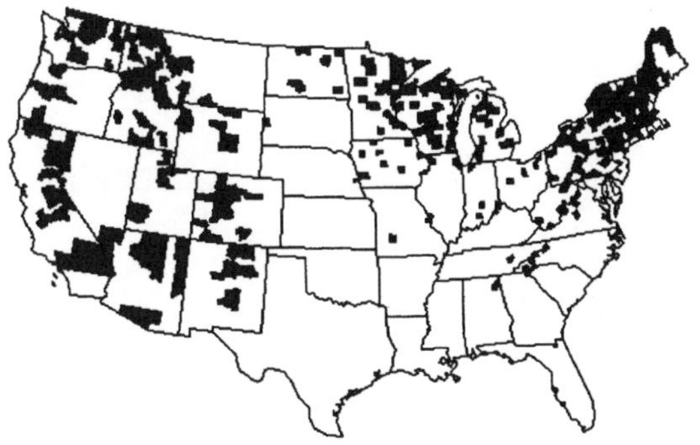

Source: Interski Services, Inc. *The White Book: Industry Edition.* Washington, DC. 1996.

Table III.34: Number of Downhill Ski Areas, Lift Capacity per Hour and Vertical Transfer Feet, and Number of Cross Country Ski Areas by Region, 1996 and 1987[1]

Ski Area Statistic	Year	Region				
		North	South	Rocky Mountains	Pacific Coast	U.S. Total
Downhill Skiing						
Number of Areas	1996	287	16	92	54	449
	1987	230	17	91	46	384
Lift capacity per hour (1000s)	1996	1,698.1	64.4	787.5	528.1	3,078.1
	1987	1,251.2	60.7	532.2	376.5	2,220.6
Vertical transfer feet[2] (millions)	1996	826.49	26.73	836.09	395.76	2,085.07
Cross-Country Skiing						
Number of Areas	1996	424	3	141	68	636
	1987	285	1	90	45	421

[1]Figures may not sum exactly to totals because of rounding.

[2]Vertical transfer feet is the sum of the product of vertical rise times lift capacity per hour for each lift at a ski area. Comparable data were not available for 1987.

Source: *The White Book of Ski Areas, Industry Edition*. 1996. Cross Country Ski Areas Association. Ski area database. 1996. National Outdoor Recreation Supply Information System. 1987. USDA Forest Service, Southern Research Station.

Total skier lift capacity per hour is probably a better indicator of the increase in the supply of downhill skiing resources. Nationally, downhill ski areas have the capability of accommodating over three million skiers per hour, an increase of 39 percent since 1987. Regional totals are the sum of lift capacity per hour for each ski area. The North had a lower proportion (55 percent) of lift capacity than it did ski areas in 1996, but still led the Rocky Mountain region, which had 26 percent of the national lift capacity, by a wide margin. The South had only about two percent of U.S. lift capacity. Another useful statistic to describe downhill skiing supply is vertical transfer feet per hour (VTFH). The VTFH is the sum of lift capacity times vertical rise for all lifts at a ski area. Because it has much greater elevation gains, the Rocky Mountain Region just surpasses the North in total VTFH. The Rocky Mountains had 836 million VTFH compared to the North's 826 million, despite having less than one-third the number of areas as the North. Together, the Rocky Mountain and the North regions account for 80 percent of the national total of VTFH. The South has only one percent of total VTFH.

Downhill Ski Area Trends in the United States

(By Stacy Gardner, Communications Director, National Ski Areas Association, Lakewood, CO)

Ski Area and Skier Trends

The 1995-96 season marked 54 million downhill skiing visits, up 2.5 percent from the prior season, but down slightly from the record number of 54.6 million skier/snowboarder visits during the 1993-94 season. Although the number of resorts nationwide has shrunk from more than 700 in 1986 to 519 in 1996, the number of skier/snowboarder visits has remained relatively stable. What this means is that the surviving resorts are getting bigger; they have been able to meet consumers' needs and expectations. According to data gathered for the National Ski Areas Association's Economic Analysis of United States Ski Areas (1996), which provides an in-depth review of resort financial data, U.S. resorts' operating profits increased an average of 10 percent during the past three seasons, based on a sampling of 95 resorts. Although weather will always remain a factor, resorts today are financially more stable and better equipped to deal with the future.

According to the National Sporting Goods Association, 9.3 million skiers and 2.2 million snowboarders were on the slopes in 1995. Although that represents only five percent of the U.S. population, these individuals are financially secure Americans who have a disposable income to enjoy this type of recreation. According to *American Demographics*, future U.S. population trends favor growth in the ski industry. There are 78 million baby boomers (born 1946-1964), 44 million Generation Xers (born 1965-1977), and 72 million echo boomers, the children of baby boomers, (born 1978-1994). The fact that visits to resorts in the recent past have remained stable is significant considering the 24– to 34–year–old segment represents about 25 percent of the customer base, the greatest percentage of all ages. Most of these individuals are part of the Generation X population, which is about 30 percent less than the number of baby boomers. Children are a critical market for the ski industry because these echo boomers will replace the Generation Xers on the slopes, and their numbers are nearly the same as the baby boomers.

The trend of mountain resort consolidation continues to increase in the 1990s. The ski industry is no different from others like banking, publishing, or cable broadcasting. A number of key industry leaders—e.g., the former owner of Vail Associates and the chairman of the American Ski Company—have purchased numerous resorts all over the country, which is a sign that they are confident the echo boomer population will take to the slopes soon.

Future of the Ski Industry

The National Ski Areas Association's 1997 Future of the Industry Summit provided a forum for mountain resort owners and operators to gain insight into future sociological, economic, and demographic trends. For example, white males, who historically have made up the majority of customers, are shrinking as a demographic group. Resorts are exploring strategies to reach nontraditional markets. Strategies such as relationship marketing, strategic alliances, and business re-engineering are becoming integral components of a resort's marketing plans. For example, one major ski company has built strategic alliances with international beverage, energy, automobile, and credit card companies to support their efforts in increasing the skier/snowboarder market and retaining customers. The most powerful undercurrents driving the mountain recreation industry into the future are a combination of economic forces, changing customer values and demographics, and technological opportunities.

Cross-Country Skiing

Despite a decline in the number of Nordic skiers since the 1980s boom years, the number of commercial cross country ski areas in the United States increased 51 percent between 1987 and 1996 (Table III.34). The distribution of U.S. cross country ski areas is very similar to that of downhill ski areas (Figure III.19). Sites are scattered throughout the West, but there appears to be an especially heavy concentration in New England and the Northeast. The 636 commercial ski areas nationwide are defined by the following characteristics: (1) professional ski school and staff, (2) ski shops with rental equipment, (3) groomed and marked trails, and (4) base lodging with amenities. Most of these areas are operated as private businesses that must offer these services to attract consumers. Only a handful of the areas are managed by local governments.

Figure III.19: Counties with Commercial Cross Country Ski Areas, 1996

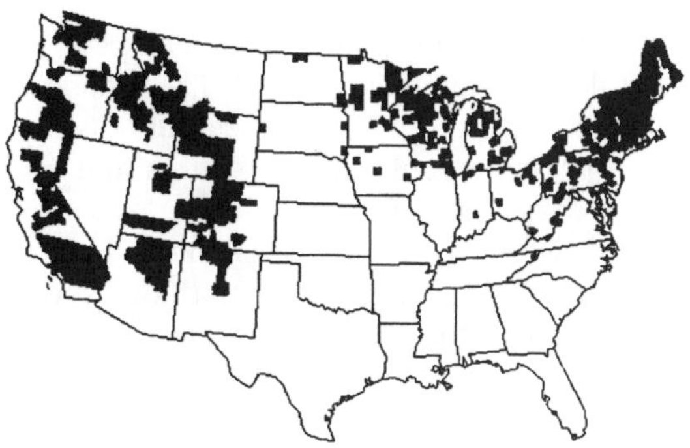

Source: Cross-Country Ski Areas Association ski area database. 1996.

Approximately two-thirds of cross country ski areas are in the North. Ski areas in the North grew at about the same rate as nationally, a 49 percent increase since 1987. The Rocky Mountain region is a distant second with 22 percent of the U.S. ski areas. This region's areas grew 57 percent between 1987 and 1996. The Pacific Coast added ski areas at a 51 percent rate. The South added two cross country ski areas to its 1987 total of just one.

Of course, cross country skiing is not limited to established commercial areas. Often, it is done on trails in public parks and forests, golf courses, private land, and even city streets and sidewalks. Conclusive data do not exist, but it is believed that a relatively small percentage of all cross country skiing in the United States occurs at the established commercial areas. The cross country ski industry is a major advocate of skiing at commercial centers, however, because of the instruction, service, and improved conditions that make for satisfying skiing experiences.

In recent years, some nontraditional winter activities have gained popularity and begun to use the same resources that support downhill and cross-country skiing (Newman, 1997). Three popular activities use what might be called "sliding" devices. Snowboards are shorter and wider than regular skis and thus easier to control. Other innovative products are snow skates, which emulate in-line skates on snow, and snow bikes, which are not new but are gaining in popularity. Also prominent at ski areas and other winter sports centers are more traditional activities such as snowshoeing, tubing, and sledding.

Cross Country Skiing Trends in the United States

(By Chris Frado, President, Cross Country Ski Areas Association[38])

Cross country skiing, Nordic skiing, ski touring, ski skating, track skiing, backcountry skiing, and telemark skiing are the names that distinguish "free-heel" skiing from "fixed-heel" skiing, better known as alpine or downhill skiing. Certainly, skiing downhill is part of cross country skiing but unlike the downhill or alpine skiers, cross country skiers also ski up hills and across flat and rolling terrain. Cross country ski boots are only attached to the ski at the toe of the boot and the heels are free to move up off the ski. This allows the skier to walk uphill on cross country skis, classically glide along in a diagonal (walking or running) stride, and execute the graceful telemark turn when descending a slope. The information in this article relates primarily to recreational cross country skiing on marked, groomed trails at both commercial ski centers and noncommercial trail systems as well as backyard, park, and golf course skiing.[39]

Cross Country Skiing in the United States

The cross country ski industry represents some 3.5 million recreational enthusiasts, 500 commercial cross country ski centers, and 19 ski equipment suppliers.[40] The industry is served by several organizations: a) Cross Country Ski Areas Association represents the ski centers that operate commercial trail systems; b) SnowSports Industries America represents equipment suppliers and hosts the largest national ski buyers show; c) National Ski Patrol provides training and certification for safety patrollers; d) Professional Ski Instructors of America provides training and certification for individuals teaching skiing; and e) U.S. Skiing governs and sanctions Nordic ski racing, ski jumping, and biathlon events.

The cross country skiing industry in the U.S. dates back to the 1960s, became organized in the early 1970s, and enjoyed a boom in the 1980s when the number of users approached 6.5 million. This number leveled off in the 1990s to about half as many users. Not surprisingly, weather plays a major role in the participation level of skiing. Changes in snowfall and associated weather patterns have contributed to a decline in the popularity of cross country skiing. Additionally, what was once sold as an advantage has evolved into disadvantage. The industry was launched with the rallying phrase, "If you can walk, you can cross country ski." This lured millions of Americans to try it in the 1970s and 1980s.

For thousands of Americans, however, walking on skis slogging through the snow without the benefit of a ski lesson or a groomed trail often left them tired and frustrated. Skis were tough to turn or control and often delaminated, boots were cold and nonsupportive, bindings were functional but not comfortable, and bamboo poles broke easily. If a person kept at it, usually it was due to his or her love of the outdoors. Self teaching is not a recommended way to learn skiing. Proper instruction on groomed trails shortens the beginner's learning curve and increases his or her enjoyment. To further challenge industry growth, the accessibility of free places to ski without developed facilities perpetuates an attitude that lessons or groomed trails are not necessarily desirable. Further, by not using developed skiing facilities, the skier's exposure to advances in ski equipment, clothing, technique, and professional instruction are limited.

Today technological advancements in ski equipment are at an all–time high. Commercial trail operators use sophisticated machine grooming methods to prepare the snow surface for ideal ski conditions. Initial ski instruction on a machine groomed trail surface helps considerably in making cross country skiing a rewarding experience in the long run. With skiing skills, confidence, and preparedness, the cross country skier is much more likely to enjoy the experience.

---

[38]John Frado, consultant with Nordic Group International, a land planning firm specializing in trail-based recreation facilities, assisted in preparing this article.

[39]Similar to the downhill skiing article, this article also does not agree with Table III.35 about the number of commercial cross country ski areas nationwide, even though the data came from the same source. It is likely that the article does not include public sector cross country ski areas in its count, for example, those operated by local parks and recreation departments. The Table III.35 data may also include some ski area lodges or resorts that were subsequently deleted from the ski area list upon closer inspection.

[40]Extreme backcountry skiing and lift-serviced telemark skiing are not covered in this article.

Cross Country Skiing Trends

Forces that are driving changes that significantly affect cross country skiing are global warming, inconsistent weather patterns, people's desire for health and fitness, value, the popularity of ski skating and the need for family recreation opportunities. As winter snowfall becomes less predictable in regions that were once guaranteed reliable snow coverage, it becomes harder to sustain skiers' interests. Many people have taken up other winter activities to replace cross country skiing when snow is doubtful or non-existent. Cross country skiing remains an excellent means for individuals seeking to improve their health and fitness. Most experts agree that there is no better fitness activity than cross country skiing because it is both an aerobic activity and uses all the major muscle groups while not stressing the body's joints.

With respect to value, cross country skiing is an affordable activity requiring an initial investment in the range of $300 to $600 for skis, poles, boots, and a compatible binding system. On average, a trail ticket at a cross country ski area for a weekend day of skiing on a machine groomed trail system with marked trails and a map costs $7 to $15. A group ski lesson adds approximately $10 to $15 to the cost of a day of recreation at a professional Nordic ski center. Ski centers add value to the trail ticket by providing restrooms, a heated lounge area, and/or warming huts on the trails, food service, and a trained staff to answer questions and offer advice on the trails best suited for the individual skier.

The majority of cross country skiers tend to be middle-aged males and females in the mid-to-upper level income categories. As this demographic group brings young children with them skiing, the Nordic centers have responded by becoming increasingly family-friendly. Special sleds with a waist harness for the skier to easily pull children on the trails have replaced backpack child carriers on ski trails. Children's terrain gardens offer kids a visually exciting area to ski around colorful fairyland creatures that invite play on humps, bumps, tunnels, and small hills. Most ski centers offer children's ski rentals as well as adult sizes.

The popularity of ski skating has affected cross country skiing by requiring wider trails and smooth or crowned trail surfaces.[41] Additionally, because tracks are undesirable to the ski skater, trails must be groomed differently. The usual solution seen at ski centers is to widen the groomed trail surface to 16-18 feet and place the tracks on the sides leaving a center skating lane, or place double tracks on one side with the other side for skating. Also seen, though not as common, is a restriction on skating to designated trails.

Current Issues

To promote growth, the cross country ski industry is promoting lessons on groomed trails as the most productive way to learn and enjoy skiing. It is assumed, as has been demonstrated in other activities, that a lesson and optimum learning conditions will contribute to a higher level of capture and retention of lifelong skiers. Skiers can choose from developed cross country ski areas, many at downhill ski resorts, county and state parks, golf courses that permit skiers and snowmobilers, open fields, pastures, and forested trails. The ease of access to these resources poses some problems in addition to current policies that favor multiple-use trails.

While many snowmobile trails present an attractive machine-packed ski trail, a cross country skier on a snowmobile trail becomes a hazard to the snow machine operator. Further, with the speeds that ski skaters are capable of and the quiet movement of a skier, collisions at intersections and around corners are of growing concern. Perhaps the greatest conflict between skiers and snowmobilers on the same trail is an inequity in responsibility. Generally, the snowmobile user has received permission for use of the trail and contributed in some fashion (i.e., volunteer labor and/or licensing fees) to the trail maintenance. The skier, on the other hand, may be regarded as a trespasser using the trail without permission or investment. Snowmobile trails should be marked to exclude skiers or clearly marked and designated for joint use. Compatible off–season uses of ski trails are mountain biking, hiking, walking, and horseback riding.

Shared trail use with snowshoers is appropriate when there is respect for the machine prepared ski track (grooves in the snow) in the trail. The industry is working to develop trail courtesies and educate users so that snowshoers and cross country skiers can enjoy the same trails. More than half of the nation's ski centers welcome snowshoers and are inviting their skiing customers to also rent and try snowshoeing. The recent popularity of snowshoeing is an opportunity for cross country ski trail providers to reach out to other trail users.

---

[41] Ski skating is a relatively new ski technique mimicking ice skating; the skis and arms are thrust out to either side in a V shape. Most skiers find skating more thrilling than the traditional forward movement of diagonal striding that resembles walking or jogging. Skating is a considerably fast and physically demanding ski technique favored by racers and fitness skiers.

In some places commercial cross country ski areas are threatened by government agencies and municipalities that provide groomed ski trails without an associated user fee. This policy makes it more difficult for private business to compete in the marketplace, perpetuates an attitude that cross country ski trails should be free, and discourages beginning skiers from taking a lesson at a ski area. It creates an interesting dilemma. Access to many places to ski is one of the attractions of cross country skiing, but experiences on free trails without instruction or groomed trails can contribute to unrewarding experiences and high drop-out rates. To promote the benefits of ski lessons and groomed trails, the cross country ski industry conducts a nationwide celebration of cross country skiing, Ski Fest, the second Sunday in January. Ski areas across the country and in selected cities offer free cross country ski lessons on groomed trails to beginners. The annual event has introduced more than 12,000 people to cross country skiing the past three years.

Statistics on cross country skiing use and related revenues are lacking. Demographic information on the users is readily available and unlike many sports shows strong participation (49 percent) by women. Equipment sales are well documented by SnowSports Industries America, but unfortunately many types of skiing are included in the cross country category: track, touring, and backcountry.[42] It is unclear whether telemark skiing is included in the cross country ski statistics. The industry has been negligent in collecting skier visit data and measuring itself. Beginning in the 1997-1998 season, the Cross Country Ski Areas Association will collect skier visit data from its more than 200 member ski centers in the United States. Then an analysis will be done to determine local revenues generated by skiers on lodging, meals, and associated services.

Consumers are demonstrating a desire for variety and choices while recreating. Field studies indicate Nordic skiers are more inclined to ski at a variety of areas than are downhill skiers. Ski areas find that their customers want recommendations of other places where they can cross country ski. In response, some Nordic ski areas have adopted sister areas to cross promote, put out brochures from other ski areas, and have staff members share their personal favorites with customers. Not all ski areas are participating in these measures. To add value and choice, most Nordic centers are expanding their menu of winter recreational opportunities. Snowshoeing is a widely favored alternative activity. Other options include kicksleds, tubing hills, dogsledding, ice skating, sleigh rides and nature interpretive programs. The most requested, but least offered, activity are package programs for skiers which include an orientation, an educational component, food and beverage, and a recreational activity with a leader offering guidance. There is currently much interest in women's programming and some interest in longer programs along the lines of a ski camp for several days.

Future Trends

Based on current issues and trends, as well as observations of the industry, we expect the following future trends for cross country skiing in the United States:

- There will be *fewer small cross country ski centers*. Smaller businesses will face escalating operating costs and will be unable to compete with the more sophisticated Nordic centers, which have expanded their recreational menu and upgraded facilities.
- *Snowmaking* at cross country ski areas will become more commonplace. With guarantees of reliable snow coverage and consistent ski conditions, participation levels will increase.
- Manufacturers will simplify ski choices by *consolidating ski types* and offering simpler, one– or two–choice sizing of skis.
- Economics will force government agencies and municipalities to implement *competitive user fees* for sophisticated machine-groomed cross country ski trails or privatize those areas.
- As the current population of downhill skiers age, there will likely be an *increase in cross-overs to Nordic skiing*. The sport is more forgiving on the joints yet offers much of the same outdoor winter experience that downhill skiers enjoy. In addition, since so many downhill ski resorts have a Nordic center, the cross-over skier will be able to patronize a familiar ski area while cross country skiing. It will be to the advantage of downhill ski areas to promote cross country skiing.
- The importance of *weather* on the future of cross country skiing cannot be minimized. However, changes in global weather patterns, perhaps due to global warming, might be contributing to reduced snow precipitation at some ski areas.

---

[42]Track skiing includes recreational groomed trail skiing and performance skiing—racing and fitness skiing—on groomed trails. Touring includes recreational backyard and ungroomed trail skiing on easy to moderate terrain. Backcountry skiing is done off trail, usually while carrying gear and often involving challenging and extreme terrain.

- Continuing medical research on the *health benefits* of reducing stress and increasing fitness could lead to more interest in winter fitness activities. Cross country skiing could benefit from renewed concern for personal fitness and stress reduction.

Other Recreation Businesses

American Business Information, Inc. (ABI) keeps a database of firms in the United States that advertise in yellow page telephone directories. Firms are identified by their four-digit Standard Industrial Classification (SIC) codes and ABI adds two more digits for further detail. Among the businesses that advertise are numerous land and water-based recreation businesses, most of which are in the 7,000 Services series of the SIC. The most valuable information from ABI is a list of the number of firms and their locations for each six-digit specialized type of business.

An increase or decrease in the number of firms providing a particular service or product is an indicator of a change in the private sector. A change in the number of firms can reflect an increase or decrease in willingness to advertise, but changes in advertising behavior alone certainly cannot explain most changes in the number of listed firms. The numbers of listed firms nationally and by region in 1995 and 1996 were tallied for: marinas, boat rentals, bicycle tours and rentals, organized camps, golf courses (public), golf courses (private), archery ranges, guide and outfitter services, and rifle and pistol ranges.

Table III.35: Number of Selected Recreation Buisnesses by Region, 1985-1996

Type of Business	Year	Region				
		North	South	Rocky Mountains	Pacific Coast	U.S. Total
Marinas	1985	2,348	1,964	157	539	5,008
	1996	2,822	2,236	161	552	5,771
Boat rental	1985	1,782	1,732	173	1,148	4,835
	1996	1,602	2,054	239	907	4,802
Bicycle rental and tours	1985	245	179	76	54	554
	1996	218	266	264	190	938
Organized camp	1985	5,165	1,838	577	1,050	8,630
	1996	3,737	1,722	476	790	6,725
Public golf courses[1]	1985	3,406	1,369	638	748	6,161
	1996	4,576	2,353	1,020	949	8,898
Private golf courses[2]	1985	932	921	246	288	2,387
	1996	1,117	1,267	282	335	3,001
Archery range	1985	152	26	31	17	226
	1996	291	69	53	27	440
Guide and outfitter service	1985	83	93	397	325	898
	1996	190	361	527	252	1,330
Rifle and pistol range	1985	126	130	38	57	351
	1996	182	206	51	118	557

[1]Golf courses open to the public, but not necessarily owned by a public agency.

[2]Golf courses open to members only, e.g., country clubs.

Source: American Business Information, Inc. (ABI). Omaha, Nebraska. 1985 and 1996.

Numbers of firms of most types increased between 1985 and 1996. One exception was organized camps, which declined 22 percent nationally (Table III.35).[43] The number of camps decreased at the highest rates in the North and Pacific Coast. Boat rental firms essentially stayed the same, registering a drop of less than one percent. Gains in the South and Rocky Mountains were offset by losses in the North and Pacific Coast.

Except for guides and outfitters and bicycle tours and rentals, there were more businesses in both years in the more populated eastern regions. Gains for all other businesses were 25 percent or more. The number of archery ranges nearly doubled. Bicycle tours and rentals grew 69 percent, undoubtedly reflecting the growing popularity of mountain bikes over the past decade. Rifle and pistol ranges grew 59 percent, but each started with a relatively low number of firms in 1985 (as did archery ranges). Guide and outfitter services (48 percent) also increased nearly 50 percent, despite a decline in the number of firms in the Pacific Coast. The number of these businesses more than doubled in the North and nearly tripled in the South to offset that loss. Golf courses, both of those open to the public and those open only to members, also grew. Courses open to the public grew especially fast in the South (72 percent) and Rocky Mountains (60 percent). Private golf courses also grew fastest in the South, with an increase of 38 percent.

A few other recreation businesses for which data were not available in 1985 (not shown in Table III.35) are tennis clubs open to the public and to members only, tourist attractions, and canoe rental/outfitter services. In 1996, there were 1,252 private tennis clubs listed and 816 public tennis clubs in the United States. Over two-thirds (68 percent) of the private clubs are in the eastern regions, led by the North with 36 percent. Over half (56 percent) of public tennis clubs are in the North. The North and South together have 80 percent of tennis clubs open to the public. Probably due to the influence of Florida, over half (55 percent) of the listed tourist attractions are in the South. These attractions include a variety of businesses, ranging from amusement and entertainment places to museums and natural resource-based attractions. Also included are historical sites and other public attractions. The two eastern regions have just under three-fourths (74 percent) of the listed tourist attractions in 1996. The ABI database also listed 430 canoe rental and outfitter firms in 1996, the large majority (76 percent) located in the North. A very small percentage of these firms (three percent) are in the two Western regions. It is probably safe to say that canoeing is largely an eastern activity, whereas whitewater rafting is popular throughout the United States wherever adequate streams are located.

A major recreation industry which scarcely existed 10 years ago in the United States is in–line skating. Rentals and especially sales of in–line skates have emerged as perhaps one of the biggest recreation businesses, and certainly the fastest growing. Further, in–line skating has gone well beyond fad status to become a significant influence on American culture, especially among youth. Influence is also being felt on the way recreation spaces are being planned and managed, in particular popular urban parks and linear paths.

The In–line Skating Industry: Trends, Issues, and Futures

(By Gilbert M. Clark, Executive Director, International In–line Skating Association, Kensington, MD)

In–line skating is the fastest growing recreational activity in the United States. It also is growing at a very rapid pace internationally. This outcome could not have been predicted in 1980 when a young hockey player named Scott Olson, looking for a way to practice his skills during the Minnesota summers, came across an old pair of skates in a sporting goods store in Minneapolis. The skates had four wheels aligned in a row, rather than in the traditional four corner arrangement associated with roller skates. In fact, in–line skates are not new; they were used by 19th century thespians to duplicate onstage the effect of ice skating. Their usage by everyday folks would have to wait until outdoor pavement was common. Olson saw these possibilities and was soon duplicating the old skates in his basement for his friends. From that inauspicious beginning has arisen a $1 billion industry in the United States alone.

Olson sold his business, which he named Rollerblade, to a local businessman who was able to bring resources to the venture that led to the company's further growth. During the early 1980s, Rollerblade continued to refine the product and added recreational and fitness skates. Today, about 85 percent of in–line skaters use fitness or recreational skates. As in–line skating began to gain public acceptance, other companies entered the market. Typically, these companies had extensive related experience, such as making ice skates, roller skates, and ski products or were involved in the in–line industry as suppliers to in–line skate manufac-

---

[43]According to the American Camping Association (ACA), the number of organized camps in the United States has *not* declined as the ABI data on advertising firms indicates. The ACA says there are approximately 8,500 organized camps in the country in 1997, which is closer to ABI's 1985 figure (see the accompanying article written by the ACA). Thus, the ABI data may not be a reliable indicator of the number or organized camps, especially since most camps are non-profit organizations and may have chosen not to advertise.

turers. By the end of the decade, there were about 10 skate companies. There also were a number of wheel and bearing manufacturers making both original equipment manufacturer (OEM) and replacement parts. The industry was showing signs of maturing.

A key development during this period was the recognition that in–line skating was an activity that no one had learned—like they had bicycling—as a child. Adults brought concerns about safety that had to be addressed if the sport were to grow beyond a child-based market. This meant developing safety and education programs. Several manufacturers developed innovative programs, including one to train and certify in–line skate instructors. The industry was quick to develop and advocate the use of protective gear and safe skating behavior. These programs were assumed by the International In–line Skating Association (IISA), which was formed in 1991 by the existing members of the industry. The most recent phase of this industry's growth has seen the entry into the market of a second wave of shoe and ski companies seeking to use their particular expertise to gain a foothold in the very competitive marketplace. Their success is uncertain because the existing companies have a decade or more of experience and knowledge in the market.

Today, the industry is comprised of over 200 companies in the U.S. alone, and many others in Canada, Europe, and Asia, which manufacture boots, wheels, bearings, hockey equipment, playing surfaces, and protective gear used by an estimated 50 million people or more worldwide. Participation in in–line competitive sports is also growing, led by in–line hockey's popularity, and includes stunt skating and in–line racing.

Recent Trends

While the industry grew around 30 percent a year during the early 1990s, 1996 saw a slowing of this rapid growth. Subsequent analysis indicates that this flattening of the growth curve was precipitated by a poor Christmas selling season in 1995 and a buildup of inventory that subsequently was affected by poor spring weather in 1996. In addition, there was a disruption at the retail level when a number of large sporting goods chain outlets went out of business and disposed of existing inventory at rock bottom prices. In fact, while shipments from skate companies were down in 1 996, according to one research firm, participation in the sport grew during the same period by 19 percent. It is expected that these problems have resolved themselves and that 1997 will see an improved climate for skate sales.

The acceptance of in–line skating as a legitimate recreational and sporting activity by nearly 31 million Americans in 1996 has generated concerns about health and safety. The rapid increase in the number of skaters saw a concomitant increase in injuries associated with the activity. In 1995, about 100,000 in–line skaters were admitted to emergency rooms, according to the Consumer Product Safety Commission. This number, while unacceptably large because protective gear could have prevented most of these injuries, nevertheless produced an injury rate less than that of traditional sports such as basketball and baseball, and much less than that of bicycling. The in–line industry has clearly been able to demonstrate that in–line skating is a safe activity, particularly when protective gear is worn and the skater has taken a lesson.

As a fitness activity, there are few things better than in–line skating. Numerous scientific studies demonstrate that in–line skating produces an aerobic and exercise benefit equivalent to running. This benefit is generated without the joint and impact damage associated with running, and comes at a modest cost compared to exercise equipment and health club memberships. Again, the industry sees the fitness benefits as attractive to older Americans who are looking for a way to stay in shape while enjoying the outdoors.

In–line skates are used in a wide variety of competitive sports, which underscores the amazing versatility of this product. In–line hockey is the fastest growing sport in America, with about three million participants in 1995. It is played at every level, by men and women, children and adults, and has spawned a professional league. Stunt or aggressive skating is also growing rapidly, but is basically a sport for youth and young adults. It has proven to be a very popular spectator sport as part of the "extreme games" phenomenon. In–line racing has been slower to develop although it is practiced by a dedicated group of athletes, and efforts are underway to open this exciting sport to recreational skaters. Altogether, it is estimated that competitive sport activities make up 15 percent of the in–line market.

Current Issues and Outlook

There are several issues that confront the in–line industry at this time. Maintaining access to outdoor venues and facilities is a principle concern. Another is expanding the market for in–line skates by educating the general adult population that skating is safe and easily learned. A third is adjusting and responding to changes inevitably wrought by the continued growth of the category.

In–line skaters are unique in that they have attributes of both a vehicle and pedestrian. To be enjoyed fully, in–line skating requires smooth pavement. Generally this is found on roads or bike paths. Experienced skaters view themselves as vehicles, capable of skating on roads with the same rights and responsibilities as bicyclists. Many skaters however, feel more comfortable skating on sidewalks or recreational paths. Fortunately, such paths have proliferated under the federal transportation law enacted in 1991, The Intermodal Surface Transportation Efficiency Act (ISTEA).

ISTEA, up for renewal in 1997, has generated thousands of miles of paved surfaces, thus helping to stimulate the growth of in–line skating. A key issue will be the continuation of the Transportation Enhancements section of the law, which has generated funds for non-highway construction projects. This provision will be opposed by highway lobbies. The bicycle and in–line industries will vigorously advocate its renewal, and thus far have found support from the Clinton Administration.

Access to the roads is also extremely important. Unfortunately, many localities have determined that in–line skating should be banned from their streets. This has been done with little thought to the effect on adults and others who need access to streets for transportation and fitness skating. Generally, these bans have been prompted by reactions to skating in congested areas or other inappropriate locations rather than by actual accidents to skaters. To protect skaters' access, the industry has taken the initiative in promoting the construction of skate parks. Such parks contain a variety of facilities, including ramps and rails for aggressive skaters, and hockey rinks.

The perception that in–line skating is just for kids prevents millions of adults from taking up an activity that is both fun and healthful. The in–line industry has addressed this by emphasizing the benefits of instruction. The IISA Instructor Certification Program has trained thousands of people to teach skating. A single lesson can help overcome fear and reduce the potential of falling. IISA also promotes the use of protective gear. Studies have shown that 90 percent of in–line injuries can be prevented by the use of wrist guards, knee and elbow pads, and helmets. In many large cities, the IISA sponsors National Skate Patrol units, which consist of volunteers who keep others from skating dangerously and help new skaters with basic skills such as stopping. Skate patrols help keep conflicts from arising with bicyclists and pedestrians in crowded venues such as New York's Central Park.

The in–line skating industry has seen several predictable stages of growth and is likely to see several more. The flattening of the sales growth curve in 1996 resulted in economic loss for some players, particularly those in the low-end segment of the market. Sales in large discount chains were particularly affected in 1996. There has been some fallout as a result. At the same time, new companies are entering the market. Some are well financed and are likely to help create additional exposure for the industry through their marketing efforts. The upshot may be that they will help grow the industry; that is, they will increase the size of the pie, rather than take shares from the existing pie.

In the past few years the industry has also seen the entrance of many small companies that produce peripheral equipment such as clothing, special wheels, and other gadgets. This is typical of a growing industry. These companies provide innovation and enthusiasm and some may eventually grow into very big companies.

It is expected that there will be continued growth in the number of in–line skating participants in the United States in the next five years. The number of skaters could approach 50 million if current trends continue. In addition, there will be at least that number of in–line skaters in Europe, Asia, and South America. U.S. companies and foreign company subsidiaries located in the United States will play a significant role in this expansion. In–line skate retailers will be better prepared to sell skate fit and performance that meet customer needs and expectations. At present, in–line skate specialty stores account for about 23 percent of all sales. This segment likely will grow as customers seek better advice and service.

There will be a continued need to stress safety issues and to have available professional instruction for novices. This will inevitably be integrated into any marketing campaigns aimed at adults. As the years pass there will be millions of adults who learned how to skate as children. At this point, skating will be viewed as a normal lifetime activity, like bicycling.

Product innovation, always a strong point of this industry, will continue. Advanced materials such as titanium, magnesium, metal composites, and graphite will continue to be used in a variety of applications. In addition to making skates lighter and stronger, manufacturers will look for ways to make them as user-friendly as possible. Replacing laces with buckles is one example that has been met with consumer approval. Click-off frames and wheels, frames that are easily aligned to compensate for the user's unique physical attributes, braking systems, and removable frames that attach to walkable boots are all examples of ideas under constant refinement by skate manufacturers.

The future of the in–line skating industry is bright, but not without challenges. Questions concerning access to streets and paths are the ones of greatest concern to the industry. These questions should be answered in the next five years. The goal of the IISA is that they be answered in an affirmative manner, thus removing any roadblocks to in–line skating's growth and popularity for many years to come.

SUPPLY INDEX FOR OUTDOOR RECREATION

Agencies that manage public land often need to summarize the availability of recreation opportunities, and compare availability over time or locations. Evaluation of the adequacy of recreation opportunities has been an important part of many state and national assessments of outdoor recreation (Outdoor Recreation Resources Review Commission, 1962; Bureau of Outdoor Recreation, 1973; California Department of Parks and Recreation, 1989; Cordell, et al., 1990). Summaries can help planners and policymakers to visualize and understand trends in resource availability. So far, this Chapter has presented information on a wide array of separate recreation resources. In this section, we summarize the spatial distributions of the most significant resources and the people who use them.

We selected 50 resource variables from which to develop summary measures. First, resources with similar variation in abundance across counties were identified. These resource measures were then linearly combined into one value. That value represents an index of the availability of that set of recreation resources.

Fourteen types of recreation resources with distinct patterns of distribution were identified. Two of these types describe urban, developed resources that are often associated with population centers. Six describe resources associated with dispersed or 'great outdoors' activities. Four types describe the distribution of water-related resources, and two types describe the distribution of winter-related resources. Table III.36 provides a summary of the specific recreation resources that relate to each resource type.

Table III.36: Interpretation of Retained Factors for Outdoor Recreation Supply Index

Factor	Interpretation
Local Facilities	Developed, local use facilities, closely tied to population growth. Associated with local park and recreation departments.
Open Space	Fairgrounds, greenways, rail-trails.
Great Outdoors	Great outdoors resources. Mountains, wilderness, Forest Service and National Park Service land, and outfitter and guide services.
Wildlife Land	Land set aside for habitat and wildlife: primarily owned by Fish and Wildlife Service and The Nature Conservancy.
State and Private Forests	State parks and privately–owned forest land.
Western Land	Western agricultural land, mostly Bureau of Land Management and private agricultural acres.
Camping Areas	Camping areas (public and private), and hunting/fishing opportunities.
Other Federal Land	Other federal recreation land (mostly TVA, COE, BuRec), and public camping opportunities.
Large Water Bodies	Coastal and large water body resources: marinas, fishing, other boating opportunities.
Whitewater	Wild, scenic, and whitewater river opportunities.
Flatwater	Flatwater and wetlands areas.
Lowland Rivers	Lowland river resources, especially rivers near wetlands or coasts.
Developed Winter	Developed winter (i.e., ski) opportunities, and forest land.
Undeveloped Winter	Undeveloped agricultural and public recreation land in mountains.

These summary measures permit regional and county-level assessments of major types of recreation resources. To evaluate how well off one county is with respect to any type of recreation resource, one must look not only at the resources and user population in that county, but also at the resources and population in surrounding counties. In the following series of maps, counties that have above-average availability of resources per capita relative to other counties within a 200-mile radius are shown.

Figure III.20: Counties with Above-Average Per Capita Availability of Local Facilities

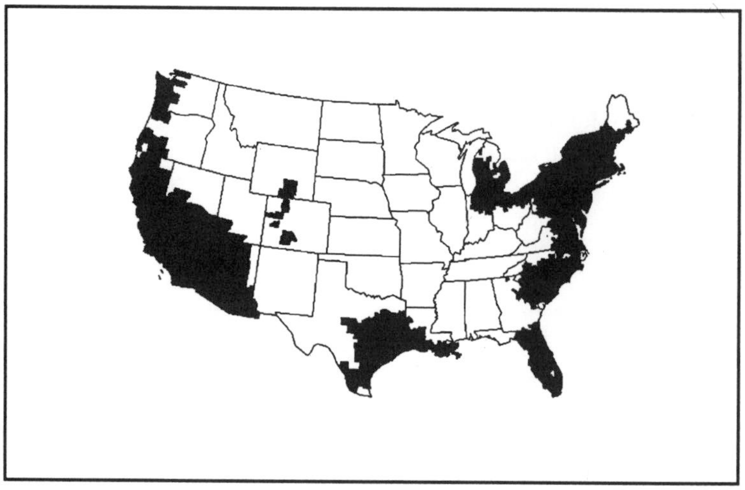

Mapping Counties with Resource Abundance

Counties with greater-than-average per capita availability of local facilities (henceforth, resource summaries or factors are denoted in uppercase as in Table III.32), the first urban abundance factor, are mostly along the Eastern Seaboard and Piedmont, the western Gulf Coast, the shores of Lakes Huron, Erie, and Ontario, and in portions of Florida, California, Arizona, and Washington (Figure III.20). In essence, these resources are close to the highly urbanized areas in the East, on the Gulf of Mexico, and on the West Coast. In addition, retirement areas in Florida, Arizona, and South Carolina have above-average availability for these resources.

Figure III.21: Counties with Above-Average Per Capita Availability of Open Space

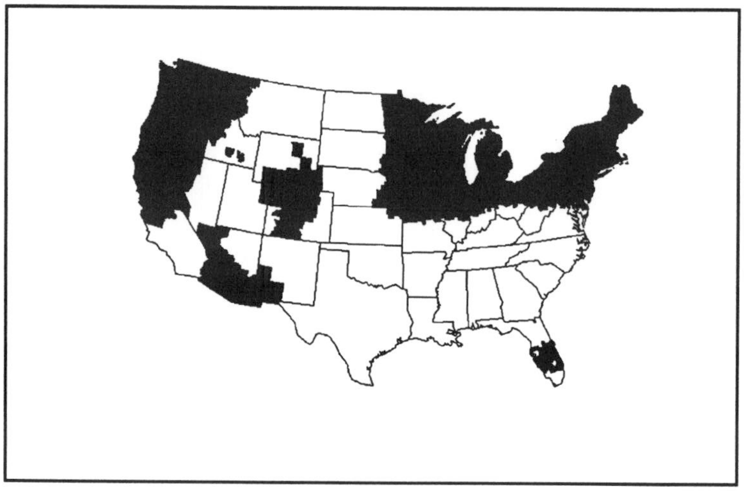

Open space, the second urban factor, is found mostly in the Pacific Northwest, the Northeast, the upper Midwest, and in the central Rockies (Figure III.21). Smaller pockets of availability are found in central Florida and southern Arizona. Rather than being tied to population centers, these resources are tied to transportation corridors, including areas that have or have had extensive rail networks. The tie between these networks and fairgrounds may come from the agricultural heritage of these areas. Fairgrounds in the Midwest were often centered in county seats, which had rail lines to transport crops and livestock to market centers.

Figure III.22: Counties with Above-Average Per Capita Availability of Great Outdoors Resources

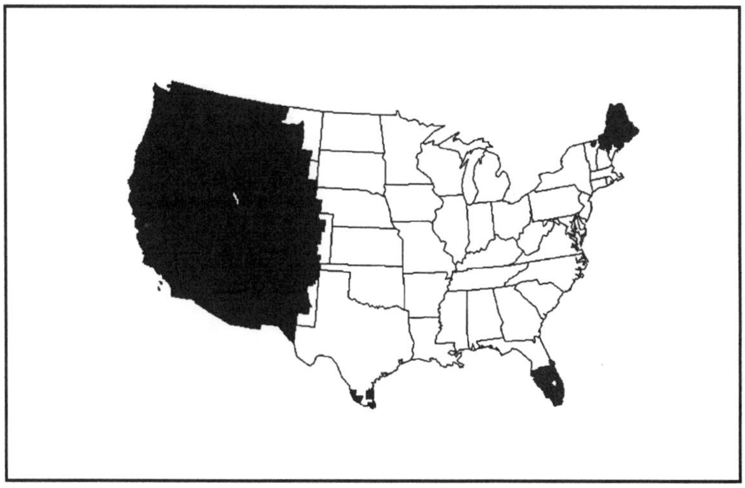

Not surprisingly, the greatest concentrations of the first land-based factor, Great Outdoors, are in the 11 westernmost states (Figure III.22). Almost no counties east of the 105th meridian have above-average availability of these resources, except for southern Florida, extreme southern Texas, and the northern reaches of New England. These pockets of resource abundance are due to areas such as Everglades NP, Acadia NP, and the Green and White Mountain National Forests. The Appalachian Mountains contain some of these types of resources. However, their size and concentration is generally insufficient to compare with the relative availability in the Western states.

Preserved habitat areas or Wildlife Land, the second land factor, is available to residents in most counties in the East, from Louisiana to Maine. In addition, relative abundance of resources exists for populations near arid areas in the West and in the northern portions of Michigan, Montana, and Wisconsin. These areas are especially important in offering opportunities for viewing wildlife, nature study, and outdoor photography.

Figure III.23: Counties with Above-Average Per Capita Availability of Wildlife Land

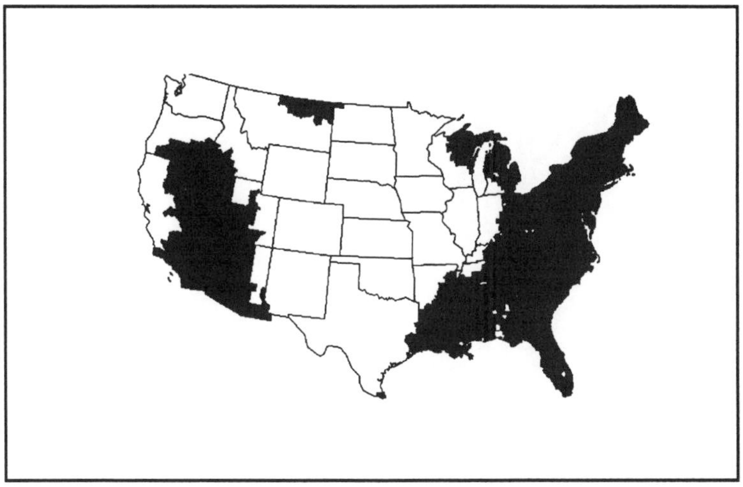

State park and private forest acres make up the third land factor, labeled *state* and *private forests*. These resources are relatively plentiful in the Middle Atlantic and New England states, in much of the Deep South, the Upper Lake states, the Four Corners region, and the Pacific Northwest (Figure III.24). In the West, state parks are a greater contributor than private forests. In the Deep South, the opposite is true. In the Northeast and Upper Lake states, both contribute approximately equally.

Figure III.24: Counties with Above-Average Per Capita Availability of State and Private Forests

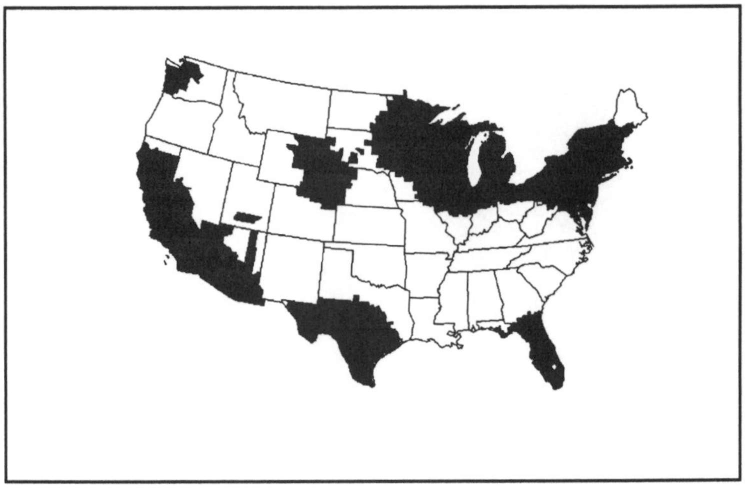

The fourth land factor, Western land, describes privately owned crop, pasture, and range land and public range land like that managed by the BLM. The availability of these resources per capita is greatest in counties west of the 96th meridian, except for western Washington and northwestern Oregon (Figure III.25). The pattern of above-average availability is strongly influenced by the location of large BLM holdings. The area of relative abundance looks much like that in Figure III.22, the first land factor describing great outdoors resources, but extends further eastward into the Great Plains states, including Texas, Oklahoma, Kansas, Nebraska, and the Dakotas.

Figure III.25: Counties with Above-Average Per Capita Availability of Western Land

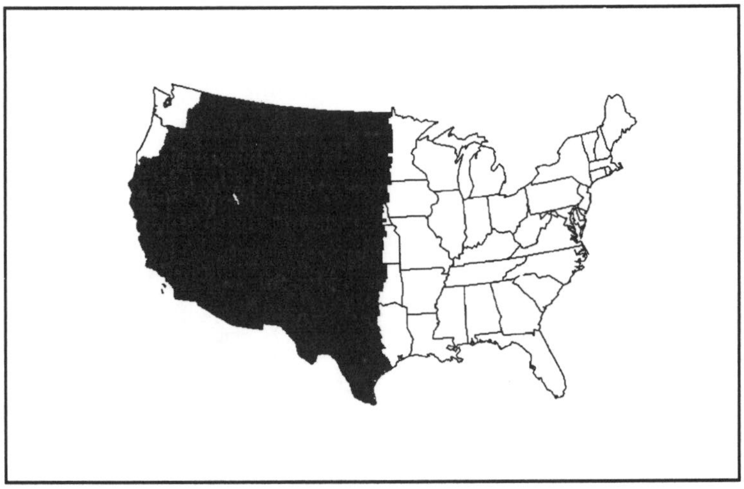

The fifth land-based factor, *camping areas*, describes mostly developed camping opportunities. The greatest concentration of these opportunities per capita are in parts of the Middle Atlantic and New England states, the Upper Midwest, including Minnesota, Michigan, and Wisconsin, southern Texas and Florida, California and Arizona, and the area in and around the Nebraska Panhandle (Figure III.26).

Figure III.26: Counties with Above-Average Per Capita Availability of Camping Areas

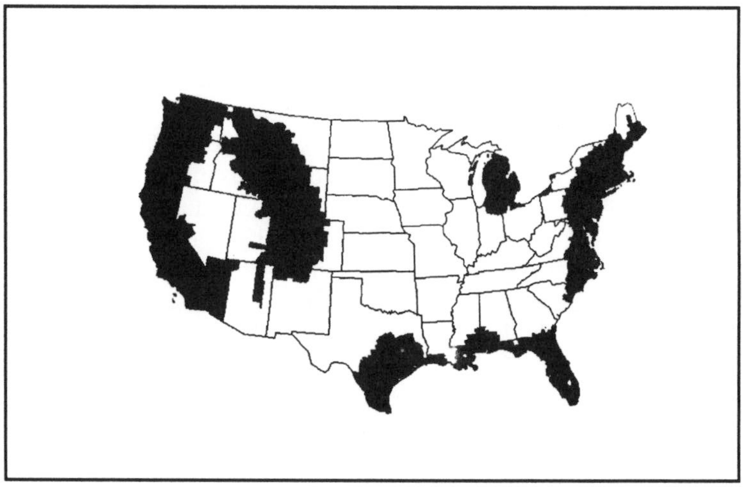

Resources related to the last of the land-based factors, Other federal land, primarily include federal land managed by the Tennessee Valley Authority (TVA), the Army Corps of Engineers (CE), and the Bureau of Reclamation (BoR). Counties that have above-average access to this factor are located in several regions (Figure III.27). Near the Mississippi and Missouri Rivers from Louisiana northward, high availability is due to CE land. For counties in the western portion of the Tennessee River basin, both TVA and CE resources are available. In Pacific Coast states and Arizona, BR areas are available.

Figure III.27: Counties with Above-Average Per Capita Availability of Other Federal Land

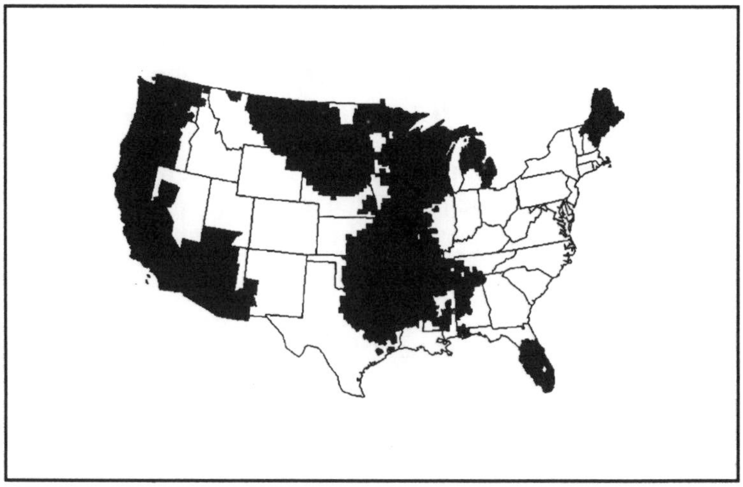

Large water bodies, the first factor for water-based recreation resources, includes marinas and other private sector enterprises found along coasts and large water bodies. Counties with higher-than-average access to these resources are mostly along the coasts (Table III.37). In addition, most counties in Michigan fall into the above-average category, due to proximity to several Great Lakes. Large national recreation areas, including Flaming Gorge, Lake Mead, Glen Canyon, and large reservoirs in the West account for the inland portion of the map shading.

Whitewater river opportunities make up the second water-based resource factor. These opportunities are available to most counties in the West, due to relatively large numbers of wild and scenic rivers in the

Rockies, Cascades, and Sierras (Figure III.27). In the East, availability is greatest for counties that are close to the Appalachian Mountains. The portions of Minnesota, Michigan, and Wisconsin that are close to Lake Superior and several Texas counties along the Rio Grande also have above-average access to these types of opportunities.

The third water-related factor, flatwater, describes co-existent flatwater (lakes, ponds, and reservoirs) and wetland resources. To a noticeable extent, private firms that rent or livery canoes are also tied to this resource type. There appear to be five geographic clusters of counties with above-average access to these types of water resources (Figure III.28). In the Southeast, these resources occur in counties in the Coastal Plain and in the western portion of the Mississippi River drainage through Louisiana and Arkansas. Another cluster appears in northern New York and New England. The abundance of lakes in the upper Midwest is evident in a cluster of counties that spreads across the northern tier of the country from Michigan to eastern Montana. The same large reservoirs that contribute to the large water bodies and coastal resources factor also contribute to an area of availability in the West that stretches from southwestern Wyoming though most of Utah, and into southern Arizona and California. Finally, several large lakes, including Chelan, Priest, and Ross, contribute strongly to higher availability scores for the northernmost counties in Washington and Idaho.

The last water-resource factor, lowland rivers, describes rivers that are near wetlands or coastal areas (Figure III.29). Essentially all of the eastern Coastal Plain, despite its large population, has above-average availability of this type of resource. In addition, portions of several states in the Mississippi River Basin near its southern end (Arkansas, Mississippi, Louisiana), and several hundred miles north (Iowa, Illinois, Wisconsin) have relatively greater access to these resources. Other clusters of counties occur along the Canadian border from Minnesota to Washington, portions of Washington around the Puget Sound, and northern California and western Oregon.

Developed winter resources, the first snow factor, are most available to people living in the Middle-Atlantic and New England states, the upper lake states (Michigan, Wisconsin, Minnesota), and the mountainous areas of the West (Figure III.30). Availability of public land and agricultural land that can be used for winter sports (the second winter resource factor, undeveloped winter resources) is above average in the West, starting as far east as the Dakotas, western Nebraska, Colorado, and New Mexico, but not including the southwestern portion of California (Figure III.31). The only other county with above-average abundance of these resources is Aroostook County at the very northern end of Maine.

About one-third of counties have an above-average availability measure for not more than two resource factors. These counties are clustered in an arc that extends from northern Texas, through most of Oklahoma and Kansas, eastern Nebraska, most of Missouri, the southern portions of Illinois, Indiana, and Ohio, most of Kentucky and Tennessee, and into northeastern Alabama and the northern half of Georgia.

In contrast, only about 210 counties have above-average availability for 10 or more resource factors. These counties are in three separate groupings. One group is a crescent starting in northwestern New Mexico, and continuing west and north through Arizona to include most of California and most of the western halves of Oregon and Washington. Another cluster contains the Catskills and Adirondacks in New York, and most of the New England region that lies to the east and north of there. The smallest cluster of these counties occurs in a band of central Florida counties, that run across the peninsula roughly from Tampa to Orlando and Cape Canaveral.

Regional Comparisons

In this section, we compare percentages of counties in various geographic regions that are above the national average in resource availability for each resource type. More importantly, we look at the proportion of the population in each region that lives in counties that have above-average resource availability.

The resource types that are most geographically concentrated across the United States are the first land-based factor, great outdoors, and the second winter resource factor, undeveloped winter resources (Table III.37). Fewer than 20 percent of counties have above-average access to these types of resources. Conversely, over 40 percent of counties in the United States have above average availability to three resource types: state and private forests and other federal land.

Table III.37: Percentage of Counties with Above Average Recreation Availability Index Values by Recreation Resource Type and Region

Recreation Resource Type	North	South	Region Rocky Mountain	Pacific Coast	U.S. Total
Local Facilities	34.4	29.3	6.0	64.7	28.1
Open Space	79.6	1.6	24.1	91.0	35.8
Great Outdoors	1.3	2.2	42.5	100.0	13.8
Wildlife Land	47.2	69.2	10.2	16.5	48.2
State & Private Forests	49.5	43.3	15.1	97.7	42.3
Western Land	3.8	17.6	93.5	69.2	29.6
Camping Areas	68.2	15.4	17.8	54.9	35.1
Other Federal Land	44.7	29.7	44.0	95.5	40.2
Large Water Bodies	26.9	25.2	22.7	93.2	28.2
Whitewater	26.4	8.5	40.0	99.3	24.4
Flatwater	31.3	32.3	30.8	19.6	31.1
Lowland Rivers	30.5	42.2	18.4	69.9	34.9
Developed Winter	50.8	0.3	30.9	100.0	27.3
Undeveloped Winter	1.8	0.1	68.9	96.2	18.0

However, just looking at the number of counties that are located near these resource types can be misleading. Of greater interest is the proportion of the regional population that lives in these counties. Table III.38 shows that for the United States as a whole, only about five percent of the population lives in areas that have above–average access to public wildlands (great outdoors) or undeveloped winter areas. Only about 10 percent live in those primarily western counties with relatively abundant opportunities for open agricultural and nonforest public land (western land). Conversely, nearly two-thirds of the U.S. population lives in areas with above-average access to land set aside for habitat preservation (Wildlife Land), and just over half live in counties with better-than-average availability of state park and privately–owned forests (state and private forests).

Table III.38: Percentage of Regional Population Living in Counties with Above Average Recreation Availability Index Values by Recreation Resource Type and Region

Recreation Resource Type	North	South	Region Rocky Mountain	Pacific Coast	U.S. Total
Local Facilities	54.7	35.0	11.0	81.5	45.5
Open Space	83.5	1.9	33.8	78.9	47.7
Great Outdoors	0.4	1.8	37.7	100.0	5.6
Wildlife Land	62.7	79.2	11.6	24.9	66.1
State & Private Forests	58.0	44.9	15.9	94.7	51.9
Western Land	0.8	9.0	83.2	78.1	10.1
Camping Areas	76.5	12.3	20.6	75.9	47.7
Other Federal Land	24.9	24.6	50.2	99.0	28.1
Large Water Bodies	42.9	25.6	22.4	98.4	36.6
Whitewater	34.1	11.9	35.2	98.3	27.0
Flatwater	23.9	26.1	23.5	25.9	24.8
Lowland Rivers	41.2	41.4	8.8	67.2	40.6
Developed Winter	57.0	0.7	29.4	100.0	34.0
Undeveloped Winter	0.3	0.0	52.5	91.3	5.2

In the North, open space, the resource type that relates to greenways, rail-trails, and fairgrounds, is available to over four-fifths of the region's population. In addition, three-fourths of the regional population has high levels of access to camping, hunting, and fishing opportunities (camping areas), and between 55 and 60 percent have access to developed urban facilities (local facilities), skiing opportunities (developed winter), and state parks and private forest opportunities (state and private forests). However, less than one percent of the population in this region has above-average access to three of the resource types: FS/NPS/wilderness (great outdoors), large agricultural or public range tracts (western land), or winter access to undeveloped range and agricultural acres (undeveloped winter).

Not surprisingly, only a very small proportion of residents of the South live in areas where winter recreation resources are relatively abundant. In addition, only about two percent of the residents of this region live in counties where either NPS/FS/wilderness (great outdoors) or greenways and rail-trails (open space) are abundant. However, nearly 80 percent of the population in this region lives in areas where there are relatively high amounts of land set aside for habitat preservation (wildlife land).

In the Rocky Mountain region, over 80 percent of the population lives in areas with above-average availability of private agricultural, range, and BLM land (western land). Perhaps this is not surprising, given the regional concentration of BLM land. About half of the region's population has above-average availability of undeveloped winter resources. Only for flatwater and wetland resources is less than 10 percent of the population better situated than the national average.

The Pacific Coast region has by far the greatest access to recreation resources. For seven of the 14 resource types, over 90 percent of the population in this region lives in areas with availability above the national average. In fact, for skiing opportunities (developed winter) and for public wildland opportunities (great outdoors), all of the population in the Pacific Coast does better than the national average. In addition, over two-thirds of the population has above-average access to five other resource types. Less than half of the region's population lives in areas with comparatively high access for only for two resource types, land set aside for habitat preservation (wildlife land) and flatwater/wetland resources (flatwater). Even for these two, about one-fourth of the regional population is better off than the national average.

Table III.39: Percent of Regional Population Living in Counties with Stable or Increasing Recreation Availability Index Values by Recreation Resource Type and Region, 1987-1997

Recreation Resource Type	North	South	Region Rocky Mountain	Pacific Coast	U.S. Total
Local Facilities	41.3	94.6	1.7	6.8	57.6
Open Space	100.0	99.8	100.0	100.0	99.9
Great Outdoors	2.3	72.8	28.0	22.3	28.8
Wildlife Land	69.7	52.3	61.4	82.6	66.1
State & Private Forests	100.0	69.0	48.9	45.9	74.2
Western Land	26.3	42.3	3.8	2.0	26.3
Camping Areas	9.6	36.3	43.3	2.4	19.5
Other Federal Land	0.7	46.6	9.6	0.0	15.4
Large Water Bodies	1.4	31.9	67.1	4.0	16.2
Whitewater	35.8	88.1	50.9	40.6	54.0
Flatwater	0.7	10.1	5.4	55.4	8.5
Lowland Rivers	100.0	98.3	98.4	99.8	99.3
Developed Winter	100.0	91.8	72.0	29.9	85.7
Undeveloped Winter	12.9	91.4	15.5	20.8	38.7

Changes since 1987

To examine the changes over the last 10 years in the availability of the 14 resource types, index values were calculated using resource counts and population that existed about 10 years ago. We examine the portion of the population that had stable or increasing per-capita resource availability over the 10 years (Table III.39). Where the population percentage shown in Table III.39 is low, most of the population lives in areas where the per-capita resource availability declined. Thus, we also highlight resource types for which per-capita availability is worsening. These declines may or may not signify reductions in the resource base. Per-capita availability can decline if growth in resources does not keep pace with growth in population. On the other hand, increases in per-capita availability can only occur when resource growth is greater than population growth. Population has been growing in almost all counties in the United States.

Virtually all of the population in all of the regions have seen increases in greenways and rail-trails (open space). Organizations promoting trail and greenway development have become much more prominent in the last 10 years. Government funding to develop these types of resources also has increased, notably via ISTEA legislation. All regions also had increases in lowland river resources. However, given the definition of this resource type, we think this increase reflects more of a change in resource definition, such as reclassification of acres from lowland rivers to wetlands, than an actual increase in resources.

All of the population of the North region saw stable to increased availability of state parks and private forests (state and private forests), and of developed winter resources. These trends are consistent with findings in the earlier portion of this chapter that indicated increases in state park land, and increases in capacity of ski areas. Over two-thirds of the people in the North region live in counties that had stable or increased availability of land protected for wildlife habitat (wildlife land). In contrast, more than 90 percent of the population in the North lived in areas that had declining per-capita availability for five of the resource types: (1) great outdoors resources that include FS, NPS, and designated wilderness areas, (2) camping opportunities (camping areas), (3) recreation opportunities on federal water-managing agency land (other federal land), (4) coastal resources and associated private businesses (large water bodies), and (5) flatwater and wetland resources.

Despite relatively large population increases in the last 10 years, resource availability growth was more consistent in the South than in any other region. Over 90 percent of the population lived in areas with stable or increasing recreation supply for five of the resource types, including both types of urban resources (local facilities and open space), both types of winter resources, and lowland river opportunities. The stability of winter resources is misleading. Many people in the South live where there were no opportunities 10 years ago, and there still are no opportunities for winter recreation. For all of the land resource types, at least 36 percent of the South's population lived in areas that had stable or increasing per capita resource availability. The South was the only region where more than half of the population lived in areas with increases in the Great Outdoors resources—FS, NPS, and Wilderness (73 percent). The only resource factor for which over 90 percent of the South's population had declining per-capita availability was flatwater and wetland resources.

The majority of the population in the Rocky Mountain region lived in areas with increasing or stable per capita resource availability for six of the 14 resource types. The six types are: open space (greenways/trails, 100 percent), wildlife land (land set aside for habitat preservation, 61 percent), large water bodies and boating opportunities (67 percent), whitewater and wild river resources (51 percent), lowland river resources (98 percent), and developed winter skiing resources (72 percent). Because of stability in the federal resource base and increasing population, there was a decline for almost all residents of this region for three resource types: great outdoors (FS, NPS, and Wilderness land); Western land (BLM and private agricultural land); and other federal land (land managed by federal water agencies). In addition, more than 90 percent of residents experienced reduced per-capita availability for flatwater and wetland resources.

The Pacific Coast Region was the only one where a majority of people lived in areas that had increases in per capita availability of Flatwater and wetland recreation opportunities (55 percent). Other resource types for which a majority of the regional population had availability increases included: open space (greenway and trail opportunities, 100 percent), wildlife land (habitat preservation land, 83 percent), and lowland river resources (effectively 100 percent). On the other hand, this region was the only one in which less than half of the population had per capita increases in the availability of developed winter opportunities. Five resource types had declining availability for over 90 percent of the population: local facilities (developed urban resources); western land (BLM and agricultural land); camping areas (camping opportunities); other federal land (BR and CE); and whitewater and wild river opportunities.

In general, opportunities for factors that relate to developed resources are increasing or at least keeping pace with population growth in most regions of the country. Developed camping opportunities appear to be an exception. Here, population growth has exceeded resource growth, especially in the Northeast and along the Pacific Coast. In addition, resource types centered on land, water, and river resources that receive preservation protection from conservation groups, state park systems, or the federal government also have had stable or growing levels of availability for many Americans.

Per-capita availability of several types of resources is declining. For some of them, the reduction stems from a fixed resource base coupled with an increasing population. Examples include beaches and coastal areas, and opportunities provided at small federal land-managing agencies, such as TVA or CE. For other resource types, the cause of decline is shrinkage in the resource base. Examples here include private agricultural land, fee areas for hunting and fishing, and wetlands in some areas.

CONCLUSION

Across all levels of government, there appears to be a noticeable trend toward increasing the number, quality, and scope of developed land-based facilities. This trend includes increased service levels at both public and private campgrounds, more resort-like character at both federal and state recreation facilities, and closures of small, lower quality areas. Federal agencies have increasingly adopted a customer orientation in the way they provide services. Meanwhile, sustainability and ecosystem health continue to receive heavy emphasis. Similarly, state park agencies work to strike the proper balance between providing services and protecting their resources. There have been increases in the number of private businesses that provide access to and services on public land. At the same time, there has been continued pressure to preserve the wild areas that remain. Federal and state Wilderness holdings and land owned by conservation groups have grown in the last 10 years.

Growth in trail resources has been substantial, especially in the North. Most states have established formal trails programs. Rail-trail conversions, and growth in the National Recreation Trail System have been concentrated in the North Region. Greenway development is prevalent in the North and throughout the country. The fact that many greenways are developed in and around cities increases their significance. Local initiatives in combination with ISTEA Transportation Enhancement funds were responsible for much of this activity. Compared to the situation a decade ago, the development of greenways and other linear recreation paths must rank as one of the most significant outdoor recreation trends in the United States.

Another significant trend has been the rise of two umbrella programs that have emphasized partnerships, namely the Watchable Wildlife and Scenic Byway programs that have sprouted across the country in the past 10 years. Their emphasis has been to involve all levels of government, the private sector, and citizens' groups to increase the accessibility of wildlife viewing and scenic driving opportunities. Just as important is the goal of protecting and appreciating the resources and relaying that message through education and interpretation.

In general, the U.S. water resource base has been stable. Acreage in lakes and reservoirs has increased slightly, but this growth has closely paralleled population growth. We presume most of these increases are tied to reservoirs supplying water for residential use. The trend to increase the amount of and level of protection of river resources has continued, as indicated by increases in both state and federal designations of important river segments, and by increases in National Recreation Areas, which often include water features.

Developed facilities for winter recreation have increased across the country. Downhill ski areas have increased their capacity in all regions. Opportunities for cross country skiing and snowmobiling on trails and parkland have grown especially in the North, and the number of cross-country areas has grown. However, private forest and agricultural land, which supported much of this activity in the past has continued to be converted to other uses or it has been closed to the public.

REFERENCES

Agyagos, F., Watt, B., & Persons, W. R. (1990). *Urban lake compliance survey—Phoenix Metropolitan Area*. Phoenix, AZ: Arizona Game and Fish Department.

American Automobile Association. (1995). *Scenic byways of the United States and Canada*. Heathrow, FL: Author.

Androscoggin Land Trust. (1996, September). Maine Landowner Liability Explained.

Backman, S. J., & Veldkamp, C. (1995). Examination of the relationship between service quality and user loyalty. *Journal of Park and Recreation Administration, 13*(2), 29-41.

Beeler, C. S. (1993). *National comprehensive salary and benefits study*. Arlington, VA: National Recreation and Park Association.

Brown, T. L. (1993a). *Forest conservation, forest recreation and tourism and the forest industry: Interrelationships and compatibility.* A Briefing Paper to the Northern Forest Lands Council. October 7, 1993.

Brown, T. L. (1993b). *Outdoor recreation and tourism studies applied to the northern forest lands: Literature review and analysis.* Northern Forest Lands Council, Recreation and Tourism Subcommittee.

Browning, J. A., Hendee, J. C., & Roggenbuck, J. W. (1988). *103 wilderness laws: Milestones and management direction in wilderness legislation, 1964-1987.* Station Bulletin 51. Moscow, ID: University of Idaho.

Bureau of Outdoor Recreation. (1973). *Outdoor recreation - a legacy for America.* Appendix A: An economic analysis. Washington, D.C.: U.S. Government Printing Office.

California Department of Parks and Recreation. (1989). SCORP planning in review: A compendium and analysis of current statewide comprehensive outdoor recreation planning documents. Sacramento, CA: Author.

Cordell, H. K., Bergstrom, J. C., Hartmann, L. A., & English, D. B. K. (1990). *An analysis outdoor recreation and wilderness situation in the United States: 1989-2040* (General Technical Report RM-189). Fort Collins, CO: USDA Forest Service, Rocky Mountain Forest and Range Experiment Station.

Crompton, J., & Lamb, C., Jr. (1986). *Marketing government and social services*. New York: John Wiley and Sons.

DeLoney, J., Eley, R., & Dziekan, K. (1996). *1995 Texas outdoor recreation plan—assessment and policy plan*. Austin, TX: Texas Parks and Wildlife Department.

Driver, B. L., Brown, P. J., & Peterson, G. L. (Eds.), (1991). *Benefits of leisure*. State College, PA: Venture.

Dwyer, J. F. (1990). Wildland management near large urban centers: The need for diversity. In D. Lime (Ed.), *Proceedings of managing America's enduring wilderness resource* (pp. 318-324). Minneapolis, MN: University of Minnesota Press.

Dwyer, J. F. (1994). *Customer diversity and the future demand for outdoor recreation* (General Technical Report RM-252). Fort Collins, CO: USDA Forest Service Rocky Mountain Forest and Range Experiment Station.

Dwyer, J. F. (1995a). Multicultural values: Responding to cultural diversity. In J. L. Thompson, D. W. Lime, B. Gartner, & W. M. Sames (Comps.), *Proceedings of the Fourth International Outdoor Recreation and Tourism Trends Symposium and the 1995 National Recreation Resource Planning Conference* (pp. 227-230). St. Paul, MN: University of Minnesota.

Dwyer, J. F. (1995b). Changing population demographics: Implications for recreation resources management. In J. L. Thompson, D. W. Lime, B. Gartner, & W. M. Sames (Comps.), *Proceedings of the Fourth International Outdoor Recreation and Tourism Trends Symposium and the 1995 National Recreation Resource Planning Conference* (pp. 245-248). St. Paul, MN: University of Minnesota.

Dwyer, J. F. (1995c). Challenges in meeting urban and near-urban recreation needs with limited resources: An overview. In J. L. Thompson, D. W. Lime, B. Gartner, & W. M. Sames (Comps.), *Proceedings of the Fourth International Outdoor Recreation and Tourism Trends Symposium and the 1995 National Recreation Resource Planning Conference* (pp. 599-602). St. Paul, MN: University of Minnesota.

Dwyer, J. F., McPherson, E. G., Schroeder, H. W., & Rowntree, R. A. (1992). Assessing the benefits and costs of the urban forest. *Journal of Arboriculture, 18*(5), 227-234.

Dwyer, J. F. & Schroeder, H. W. (1994). The human dimensions of urban forestry. *Journal of Forestry, 92*(10), 12-15.

Dwyer, J. F. & Stewart, S. I. (1995). Restoring urban recreation opportunities: An overview with illustrations. In J. L. Thompson, D. W. Lime, B. Gartner, & W. M. Sames (Comps.), *Proceedings of the Fourth International Outdoor Recreation and Tourism Trends Symposium and the 1995 National Recreation Resource Planning Conference* (pp. 606-609). St. Paul MN: University of Minnesota.

Dziekan, K., DeLoney, J., & Eley, R. (1997). *Becoming an outdoors-woman: Socio-demographic profile of workshop participants*. Workshops held October 1993-February 1997. Austin, TX: Consumer Research Program Area, Communications Division, Texas Parks and Wildlife Department.

Fabos, J. G. (1995). Introduction and overview: The greenway movement, uses and potentials of greenways. *Landscape and Urban Planning, 33*(1), 1-13.

Federal Highway Administration (FHWA). (1988). *Scenic byways*. Washington, D.C.: US Department of Transportation.

Federal Highway Administration. (1991). *National scenic byways study*. Washington, D.C.: US Department of Transportation.

Federal Highway Administration. (1996). *Scenic byways*. Washington, D.C.: US Department of Transportation.

Federal Highway Administration. (1997a). *The National Scenic Byways Program: FY92-97 in Review*. Washington, D.C.: US Department of Transportation.

Federal Highway Administration. (1997b). *National Economic Crossroads Transportation Efficiency Act: Key information*. Washington, D.C.: US Department of Transportation.

Gobster, P. H. (1995). Perceptions and use of a metropolitan greenway system for recreation. *Landscape and Urban Planning, 33*, 401-413.

Gobster, P. H. & Dickhut, K. R. (1995). Exploring interspace: Open space opportunities in dense urban areas. In C. Kollin and M. Barratt (Eds.), *Inside urban ecosystems: Proceedings of the Seventh National Urban Forestry Conference* (pp. 70-73). Washington D.C.: American Forests.

Godbey, G., Graefe, A., & James, S. W. (1992). *The benefits of local recreation and park services: A nationwide study of the perceptions of the American public*. Arlington, VA: National Recreation and Park Association.

Goldbloom, A. (1991). *1991 Citizen survey on Texas state parks*. Austin, TX: Statewide Planning and Research, Public Lands Division, Texas Parks and Wildlife Department.

Gunn, C. (1994). *Tourism planning—basics, concepts, cases*. Washington, D.C.: Taylor & Francis.

Hardt, M. M., & Hastings, W. (1995). Local, metropolitan, and regional greenways. In J. L. Thompson, et al. (comp.), (1995, May 14-17), *Proceedings of the Fourth International Outdoor Recreation and Tourism Trends Symposium and the 1995 National Recreation Resource Planning Conference*, St. Paul, MN.

Henson, L. D. (1988). Memo to regional foresters regarding fiscal year 1988 accomplishment. Washington, D.C.: USDA Forest Service.

Hull, R. B. IV, & Ulrich, R. (1992). Health benefits and costs of urban forests. In P. Rodbell (Ed.), *Alliances for community trees: Proceedings of the Fifth National Urban Forestry Conference* (pp. 69-72). Washington D.C.: American Forestry Association.

Hurt, H. III. (1997, August 11). Parks brought to you by... *U.S. News & World Report, 123*(6), 42-45.

Ibrahim, H., & Cordes, K. A. (1993). *Outdoor recreation*. Dubuque, IA: Brown and Benchmark.

Jackson, R. S., Stynes, D. J., Propst, D. B., & Carlson, B. D. (1996). *A summary of the national and state economic effects of the 1994 U.S. Army Corps of Engineer Recreation Program* (Technical Report, R-96-1). Vicksburg, MS: U.S. Army Engineer Waterways Experiment Station.

Jacobs, P. (1997, April 28). Boom in holdings puts wildlife agency to test. *Los Angeles Times*, pp. 1-4.

Jensen, C. R. (1995). *Outdoor recreation in America* (5th ed.). Champaign, IL: Human Kinetics Press.

Jimenez, R. (1997, April 20). An experiment in backcountry. *Boston Globe*, pp. NHI, NH7.

Jolley, H. (1969). *The Blue Ridge Parkway.* Knoxville, TN: The University of Tennessee Press.

Kelly, J. T., Cornelssen, C., & Bailey, M. (1996). Military base closures can change lands to parks. *Parks and Recreation, 31*(1), 70-76.

Knudson, D. M. (1984). *Outdoor recreation* (Rev. ed.). New York: MacMillan.

LaPage, W. F. (1995). Parklands as paradox: The search for logic in the public's parklands. *Journal of Park and Recreation Administration, 13*(4), 1-12.

Little, C. E. (1990). *Greenways for America*. Baltimore: Johns Hopkins University Press.

Maine Snowmobile Program. (1997, March 3). Communication.

Marvel, W. (1997, June 7). Have fun on paper company land. *The Conway Daily Sun*, pp. 1, 16.

Mastran, S. (1992). *The protection of America's scenic byways.* Information Series No. 68, 1992. Washington, D.C.: National Trust for Historic Preservation.

McEwen, D., & Profaizer, L. (1989). Trends in private and public campgrounds, 1978-1987. *Trends, 26*(2), 24-29.

Moore, R. L. (1994). *State trail programs: A survey of state trail administrators*. Denver, CO: The National Association of State Trail Administrators.

More, T. A., Dustin, D. L., & Knopf, R.C. (1996). Behavioral consequences of campground user fees. *Journal of Park and Recreation Administration, 14*(1), 81-93.

Mueller, G. (1996). Establishment of a fish community in the Hayden-Rhodes and Salt-Gila Aqueducts, Arizona. *North American Journal of Fisheries Management,16*(4), American Fisheries Society.

Mueller, G., & Liston, C. R. (1994). Evaluation of tire reefs for enhancing aquatic communities in concrete-lined canals. *North American Journal of Fisheries Management, 14*(3), American Fisheries Society.

National Access and Travel Management Strategy Team. (1992). *Travel management: Bringing people and places together*. Report of the National Access and Travel Management Strategy Team. Washington D.C.: USDA Forest Service.

National Association of State Park Directors. (1996). *1996 annual information exchange: State park statistical data for the year ending June 30, 1995.* Tallahassee, FL: Author.

National Forest Scenic Byways Inventory (database). (1996). Washington, D.C.: USDA Forest Service.

National Scenic Byways Program. (1995, May 18). *Federal Register: 60*(96), 26759-26762. Washington, D.C.: Office of the Federal Register, National Archives and Records Administration.

Newman, R. J. (1997, February 24). Who needs skis? *U.S. News & World Report, 122*(7), 58-60.

Northern Forest Lands Council. (1994, September). *Finding common ground: Conserving the northern forest.* Portsmouth, NH: Northern Forest Lands Council.

Outdoor Recreation Resources Review Commission (1962). *Economic studies of outdoor recreation* (ORRRC Report 24). Washington, D.C.: U.S. Government Printing Office.

Overbay, J. (1993). Statement of James Overbay, Deputy Chief, Forest Service, United States Department of Agriculture before the Subcommittee on National Parks, Forest and Public Lands Committee on Natural resources, United States House of Representatives, Concerning Problems with Access to Public Lands. (November 9).

Peterson, M. R. (1996). Wilderness by state mandate: A survey of state-designated wilderness areas. *Natural Areas Journal, 16(3)*, 192-197.

PKF Consulting. (1995). *Local park and recreation facilities and sites*. Arlington, VA: National Recreation and Park Association.

Poole, W. (1997). Window on the wilderness. *Land and People, 9*(1), 2-6.

President's Commission on Americans Outdoors. (1986). *Report and recommendations to the President of the United States*. Washington, D.C.: U.S. Government Printing Office.

Reynolds, G. R. (1996). Memo to Regional Foresters regarding FY 96 Rights-of way Acquisition Accomplishment. Washington, D.C.: USDA Forest Service.

Robertson, D. (1988, August 29). *Memo to regional foresters* (Memorandum). Washington, D.C.: USDA Forest Service.

Robertson, F. D. (1992). Memo in the National Access and Travel Management Conference, August, 1991. Denver, CO: USDA Forest Service.

Satchell, M. (1997a, January 20). Clinton's 'mother of all land-grabs.' *U.S. News & World Report, 122*(2), 42-44.

Satchell, M. (1997b, July 21). Parks in peril. *U.S. News & World Report, 123*(6), 22-28.

Schoener, G. (1997, May 13). *ISTEA: Where it stands: Where it's headed*. Paper presented at the Scenic America National Training Conference, Baltimore, MD.

Schroeder, H. W. & Anderson, L. M. (1984). Perception of personal safety in urban recreation sites. *Journal of Leisure Research, 16*(2), 178-194.

Searns, R. M. (1995). The evolution of greenways as an adaptive urban landscape form. *Landscape and Urban Planning, 33*(1), 65-80.

Shands, W. (1990). Showcases of excellence. In *National Recreation Areas: A Showcase For Excellence*, FS-442. Washington, D.C.: USDA Forest Service.

Simmons, D. (1996). Teaching in natural areas: What urban teachers feel is most appropriate. *Environmental Education Research, 2*(2), 149-157.

Stankey, G. H. (1984). Wilderness preservation activity at the state level: A national review. *Natural Areas Journal, 4*(4), 20-28.

State Task Force on Texas Nature Tourism. (1994). *Nature tourism in the Lone Star State: Economic opportunities in nature*. Report submitted by the Texas Parks and Wildlife Department and the Texas Department of Commerce. Austin, Texas.

Stewart, S. I. (1995). Challenges in meeting urban and near-urban needs with limited resources: A summary of the workshop discussion. In J. L. Thompson, D. W. Lime, B. Gartner, & W. M. Sames (Comps.), *Proceedings of the Fourth International Outdoor Recreation and Tourism Trends Symposium and the 1995 National Recreation Resource Planning Conference* (pp. 603-605). St. Paul MN: University of Minnesota.

Tennessee Valley Authority. (1988). *The TVA Handbook*. Knoxville, TN: Tennessee Valley Authority.

Tetreault, B. (1997, June 9). Opening ceremonies held for Phillips Brook Recreation Area. *The Berlin Daily Sun*, pp. 1, 7.

Texas Parks and Wildlife Department. (1994). *Natural agenda—a strategic plan for Texas Parks and Wildlife 1995-1999*. Austin, TX: Author.

Tice, R. D. (1997, April 1997). Letter to Secretary of the Interior Bruce Babbitt from R. Dean Tice, Executive Director, National Recreation and Park Association, dated March 12, 1997, in *Parks and Recreation*, p. 8.

Tracy, P. (1997, June 6). New rec area is paradise. *The Union Leader*, p. B3.

Times Mirror Magazines, Inc. (no date). Locked Out: How private owners are turning public lands—your lands, your constituents' lands—into their own private property by seizing control of access roads and locking the gates. Washington, D.C.: Times Mirror Magazines, Inc., 1705 DeSales St, NW, Suite 801, 20036.

Tynon, J. F., Harding, J. A., & Chavez, D. J. (1998). *National recreation trails: An overview*. Paper presented at 1997 Northeastern Recreation Research Conference, April 6-8, Bolton Landing, NY, pp. 225-227.

United States Army Corps of Engineers. (1997). *Natural resource management system*. Washington, D.C.: U.S. Army Corps of Engineers Headquarters.

United States Army Engineer Missouri River Division. (1994). *Master water control manual, Missouri River review: Review and update, Volume 6c: Economic studies, recreation economics*. Omaha, NE: Author.

United States Department of Agriculture Forest Service. (1990). *National recreation areas: A showcase for excellence*. FS-442. Washington, D.C.: Author.

United States Department of Agriculture Forest Service. (1997). *Wildlife opportunities report*. Unpublished document. Washington, D.C.: Wildlife, Fish, and Rare Plants Program.

United States Department of Energy, Bonneville Power Administration, US. Army Engineer, North Pacific Division, & U.S. Bureau of Reclamation. (1994). *Columbia River system operation review draft environmental impact statement, Appendix J: Recreation*. Portland, OR: Authors.

United States Department of the Interior, Bureau of Land Management. (1993, December 17). *BLM handbook 8357-1—byways*. Washington, D.C.

United States Department of the Interior, Bureau of Land Management. (1996, July 29). *BLM back country byways master list*. Washington, D.C.

United States Department of the Interior, Bureau of Reclamation (1993). Draft Environmental Impact Statement/ Environmental Impact Report. Denver, CO: Bureau of Reclamation.

United States Department of the Interior, Bureau of Reclamation (1995). *Operation of Glen Canyon Dam final environmental impact statement*. Denver, CO: Bureau of Reclamation.

United States Department of the Interior, National Park Service. (1987-1996, Annual). *National Park Service statistical abstract*. Denver, CO: Author, Public Use Statistics Program Center.

United States Department of the Interior, National Park Service. (1995). *The national parks: Index 1995*. Washington, D.C.: Author.

United States Department of the Interior, National Park Service. (1996a). *Federal lands-to-parks program: Base closure status list by state*. Unpublished report.

United States Department of the Interior, National Park Service. (1996b). *American discovery trail. National trail feasibility study, Vol. 1: Environmental assessment*. Denver, CO: Denver Service Center.

United States Department of the Interior, National Park Service. (1996c). *American discovery trail. National trail feasibility study. Vol. 2: Description of the trail corridor*. Denver, CO: Denver Service Center.

United States Department of the Interior, National Park Service. (1997). *1997 National Park Service strategic plan*. Washington, D.C.: Author.

United States General Accounting Office. (1992, April). *Federal lands: Reasons for and effects of inadequate public access*. Briefing report to the chairman, Subcommittee on National Parks and Public Lands, Committee on Interior and Insular Affairs, House of Representatives. GAO/RCED-92-116BR. Washington, D.C.

United States General Accounting Office. (1993). *Federal land management: Status and uses of wilderness study areas*. Report to the Chairman, Subcommittee on National Parks, Forests, and Public Lands, Committee on Natural Resources, House of Representatives. GAO/RCED-93-151.

Urbina, R. (1997). *TPWD recreation grants tracking system*. Austin, TX: Texas Parks and Wildlife Department, Statewide Comprehensive Outdoor Recreation Plans.

Vermont Agency of Natural Resources, Department of Forests, Parks, and Recreation. (1994, March.) Chapter 3: "Public outdoor recreation on privately-owned Lands Task Group Report." In *Vermont recreation plan: Task group report.* Montpelier, VT: Author.

Vermont Agency of Natural Resources, Department of Forests, Parks, and Recreation. (1997). *Public recreation on private land: A landowner's guide.* Draft. Montpelier, VT: Author.

Vickerman, S. (1989). *Watchable wildlife: A new Initiative*. Portland, OR: Defenders of Wildlife.

Wall, K., & Crompton, J. (1995). *The revenue implications of changing daily entrance fees to per-person pricing at Texas state parks*. College Station, TX: Texas A&M University.

Westphal, L. M. (1993). Why trees? Urban forestry volunteers values and motivations. In. P. H. Gobster (Ed.), *Managing urban and high use recreation settings*. Selected papers from the Urban Forestry and Ethnic Minorities and the Environment Paper Sessions at the 4th North American Symposium on Society and Resource Management (General Technical Report NC-163), (pp. 19-23). St. Paul MN: USDA Forest Service North Central Forest Experiment Station.

Westphal, L. M. & Gobster, P. H. (1995). Legacy of the Clean Water Act: Impacts of water quality on urban river recreation. In J. L. Thompson, D. W. Lime, B. Gartner, & W. M. Sames (Comps.), *Proceedings of the Fourth International Outdoor Recreation and Tourism Trends Symposium and the 1995 National Recreation Resource Planning Conference* (pp. 620-624). St. Paul MN: University of Minnesota.

Zinser, C. I. (1995). *Outdoor recreation: United States national parks, forests, and public lands*. New York: John Wiley and Sons.

Statewide Comprehensive Outdoor Recreation Plans

Arizona State Parks Board. (1994). *1994 Arizona statewide comprehensive outdoor recreation plan*. Phoenix, AZ.

Center for Policy Research and Planning, Mississippi Institutions of Higher Learning. (1990). *1990 Mississippi statewide comprehensive outdoor recreation plan*. Jackson, MS.

California Resources Agency, Department of Parks and Recreation. (1994). *California outdoor recreation plan 1993.* Sacramento, CA.

Delaware Department of Natural Resources and Environmental Control. (1990). *Delaware outdoors 1990*. Dover, DE.

Florida Department of Environmental Protection, Division of Recreation and Parks. (1994). *Outdoor recreation in Florida 1994.* Tallahassee, FL.

Georgia Department of Natural Resources, Parks Recreation, and Historic Sites Division. (1995). *1995 Georgia statewide comprehensive outdoor recreation plan*. Atlanta, GA.

Idaho Parks and Recreation Board. (1989) *1990 Centennial Edition: Idaho Outdoor Recreation Plan*. Boise, ID.

Illinois Department of Conservation. (1989). *The Illinois outdoor recreation plan 1988-1993*. Springfield, IL.

Indiana Department of Natural Resources. (1994). *1994-1999 Indiana statewide comprehensive outdoor recreation plan*. Indianapolis, IN.

Kentucky Department of Local Government. (1989). *1989 Assessment and policy plan for outdoor recreation.* Commonwealth of Kentucky. Frankfort, KY.

Louisiana Department of Culture, Recreation, and Tourism, Office of State Parks. (1995). *Louisiana statewide comprehensive outdoor recreation plan*. Baton Rouge, LA.

Minnesota Departments of Natural Resources and Trade and Economic Development. (1989). *Minnesota's outdoor legacy: Strategies for the 90s statewide comprehensive outdoor recreation plan for 1990-1994.* St. Paul, MN.

Missouri Department of Natural Resources, Division of State Parks. (1996). *Missouri statewide comprehensive outdoor recreation plan 1996 to 2001*. Jefferson City, MO.

Nebraska Game and Parks Commission, Planning and Programming Division. (1991). *Nebraska statewide comprehensive outdoor recreation plan: Assessment and policy plan 1991-1995.* Lincoln, NE.

New Hampshire Office of State Planning. (1994). *New Hampshire outdoors 1994-1999: Statewide comprehensive outdoor recreation plan*. Concord, NH.

New Jersey Department of Environmental Protection. (1989). *The Commonwealth of New Jersey: Outdoor recreation resources plan summary*. Trenton, NJ.

New Mexico Energy, Minerals and Natural Resources Department, Parks and Recreation Division. (1991). *Statewide comprehensive outdoor recreation plan for New Mexico*. Santa Fe, NM.

New York Office of Parks, Recreation and Historic Preservation. (1994). *1994 New York statewide comprehensive outdoor recreation plan: People, resources, recreation*. Albany, NY.

North Dakota Parks and Recreation Department. (1996). *North Dakota 1996-2000 statewide comprehensive outdoor recreation plan*. Bismarck, ND.

Oklahoma Tourism and Recreation Department, Division of Planning and Development. (1992). *Oklahoma outdoor recreation assessment and planning 1992*. Oklahoma City, OK.

Oregon Parks and Recreation Department, Policy and Planning Division. (1995). *Oregon outdoor recreation plan 1994-1999*. Salem, OR.

Rhode Island Department of Administration and Department of Environmental Management, Division of Planning. (1992). *Ocean State outdoors: Rhode Island's comprehensive outdoor recreation plan*. Providence, RI.

South Carolina Department of Parks, Recreation and Tourism. (1996). *1995 South Carolina statewide comprehensive outdoor recreation plan*. Columbia, SC.

Texas Parks and Wildlife Department. (1996). *1995 Texas outdoor recreation plan—assessment and policy plan*. Austin, TX.

Utah Department of Natural Resources, Division of Parks and Recreation. (1992). *1992 Utah statewide comprehensive outdoor recreation plan*. Salt Lake City, UT.

Vermont Agency of Natural Resources, Department of Forests, Parks and Recreation. (1993). *Vermont recreation plan: Assessment and policy plan 1993*. Montpelier, VT: Author.

West Virginia Development Office. (1993). *West Virginia statewide comprehensive outdoor recreation plan 1993-1997*. Charleston, WV.

CHAPTER IV

PRIVATE LANDS AND OUTDOOR RECREATION IN THE UNITED STATES

. . . .

R. Jeff Teasley[1]
John C. Bergstrom
H. Ken Cordell
Stanley J. Zarnoch
Paul Gentle

Acknowledgments:
We gratefully acknowledge Carter Betz of the USDA Forest Service, Southern Research Station, for his work in helping to develop and test the sampling plan that supported the National Private Landowners Survey (NPLOS). In addition, we thank Mr. Betz for executing the plan for sampling local tax rolls over the United States. We would also like to thank Gary Jann of the USDA Natural Resources Conservation Service for his effort in the coordination and assistance of over 700 NRCS field agents who visited local tax offices in the lower 48 states to choose our samples. We would also like to thank Ms. Jo Anne Norris for her support before and during the NPLOS surveying process. Last, but not least, we would like to thank Ms. Janet Lee for her exemplary performance as project supervisor. Her excellent supervision of the large student worker staff as well as her superb handling of the tremendous burden of the day-to-day management and database updating for such a large mail survey were key to the overall success of the project.

INTRODUCTION

Outdoor recreation on private lands is influenced by myriad factors. To provide background and context on these factors, this chapter first overviews the private land situation in the United States and provides general information and discussion related to ownership and tenure, land-use patterns, legal restrictions, and economic conditions, including taxation issues. Implications of these factors with respect to use of private land for outdoor recreation are also discussed.

Overall, there is little extant information on recreational use and access to private land. To help fill this information gap, the National Private Landowners Survey (NPLOS) was recently conducted (1995-96). A major focus of NPLOS was to obtain data for estimating the amount of private land open for outdoor recreation in the United States and landowner practices and attitudes related to access to their lands for outdoor recreation.

---

[1]R. Jeff Teasley is a Research Coordinator, John C. Bergstrom is a Professor, and Paul Gentle is a Post Doctoral Associate, University of Georgia, Athens, GA; H. Ken Cordell is a Research Forester and Project Leader, USDA Forest Service, Athens, GA; and Stanley Zarnoch is a Statistician, USDA Forest Service, Asheville, NC.

The NPLOS methodology, results, and the implications of these results are discussed after a brief review of recreation use of private land. This chapter ends by offering general conclusions about outdoor recreational use of private lands in the United States.

Outdoor Recreational Use of Private Lands

An important reason for increasing recreational pursuits on private lands has to do with the inability of public lands to meet all of the nation's recreational needs. In 1962, the Outdoor Recreation Resources Review Commission projected that by the year 2000 there would be a tripling of recreational land demand. However, that mark was surpassed in 1983. As a result, public park visitation resulted in "overuse and degradation of natural resources" in some areas (Wright & Kaiser, 1986). There will be increasing importance for private, rural land to be able to add to the supply of outdoor recreational opportunities (Wright & Fesenmaier, 1988; Wright, Cordell, & Brown, 1988; Cordell, English, & Randall, 1993).

The most comprehensive research program for collecting data on the supply of private, nonindustrial lands available is the National Private Landownership Survey (NPLOS), conducted every 10 years. The NPLOS collects information on the amount of land available for various uses, as well as access policies that different landowners stipulate for recreationists (Wright, Cordell, Brown, & Rowell, 1988).

Posting by private landowners is a means of restricting public access. Despite particular attitudes of owners, socioeconomic differences, or differences in rural versus urban settings, it has been "clearly shown that most landowner characteristics are poor predictors of posting behavior" (Brown, Decker, & Kelly, 1984). Rather, the most important factor in a landowner's decision to post is when a landowner has had "unpleasant experiences with recreationists" (Brown, Decker, & Kelly, 1984).

Of course, private land use brings with it the issue of liability. American law gives landowners some protection from liability. The "mere ownership of land and the fact that a visitor was injured on that land does not presume liability for the injury;" only when a landowner "fails to fulfill the legal duty to act" is the landowner liable for visitor's injuries (Kaiser & Wright, 1985).

Laws concerning liability vary from state to state (Wright & Kaiser, 1986). The increasing demand for outdoor recreation in America brings into play the question of liability. Recreational use statutes have reduced landowner liability through the creation of a category of entrant on private land. That type of entrant is known as a "constructive trespasser." Landowners cannot "maliciously injure a trespasser." This would preclude the setting of traps, such as "stringing barbed wire across known dirt bike trails." The law also allows for differences in liability between the individual who has "permission" to use land and an individual who enters into a business agreement with the landowner (Wright, 1986).

In a study by Wright, Kaiser, and Fletcher (1988), landowners were divided into five groups, depending on the strictness of access rules. Prohibitive land owners allowed no one access to their land and used it solely for their own benefit. Exclusionists limited hunting to themselves and family members. Restrictionists were much like exclusionists but also allowed friends and employees to use their land. Landowners who allowed public access to their properties were termed open landowners. It was found that exclusionists and prohibitionists expressed negative attitudes toward hunter behavior-related problems and liability, whereas restrictionists and open landowners were the most agreeable about access to public hunting. Wright and Fesenmaier (1990) state that landowners who were "anti-hunting" had that viewpoint due to their perception that hunting is "an anachronism" because it is no longer a necessity in order to survive. Perhaps more importantly, it was found that "an important aspect that distinguishes these landowners is their belief that by permitting access, they are better able to control the actions of hunters" (Wright & Fesenmaier, 1990).

Tindall (1990) notes the rise of a public land tenure category known as the "recreation estate." Due to increasing recreational demand for public land, as indicated both in national opinion polls and actual user visits to National Park Service facilities, the President's Commission on Americans Outdoors made important recommendations in 1988 (Geisler, 1993). The report recognized the role private land must play in satisfying both current and future demand for outdoor recreation opportunities. Furthermore, the commission called for new public-private partnerships and an approximate $1 billion per annum trust fund to aid in the attainment of recreational facility/opportunity goals (Madison, 1988). Though no law has materialized, there have been signs in the last quarter of this century of bipartisan support in the area of new tenure allocations and designations.

The role of private land in providing recreation opportunities is also influenced by occupational restructuring. Occupational restructuring creates a new definition of land-use needs and ethics. When service-sector employment grows at the expense of manufacturing and more basic extractive employment, the domestic importance of land-based occupations lessens, with a parallel decline in the "significance of land as a factor of production, social status, and basis of wealth." At this point, land assumes different importance as a recreational and aesthetic good, reinforcing a service relationship between people and the land in lieu of an active, material-based, sustenance relationship (Geisler, 1993).

As population grows, the demand for leisure space and recreational opportunities will increase, causing the national per capita availability of public recreation land to shrink (Geisler, 1993). Perhaps more than any other factor, this shrinking public recreation land base will steadily increase demand and interest in the use of private lands for outdoor recreation. Due to the increasing importance of private land as a recreational resource, there is increasing interest in the outdoor recreational use of private land. Currently, however, available data describing recreational use of private land and landowner attitudes toward this use are relatively sparse. To help fill this gap, another National Private Landowners Survey (NPLOS) was recently conducted. The survey and its results are discussed in the next section.

THE NATIONAL PRIVATE LANDOWNERS SURVEY

NPLOS Background

The National Private Landowner Survey (NPLOS), initiated in early 1994, was a cooperative effort of the USDA National Resource Conservation Service (NRCS), formerly the Soil Conservation Service, the USDA Forest Service's Southern Research Station (USFS), and the University of Georgia's Department of Agricultural and Applied Economics (UGA).[2] The project originated from the NRCS and USFS. The NRCS needed information about landowners and their tracts to improve service to them. The USFS needed data for the Renewable Resources Planning Act Assessment of the supply of and demand for outdoor recreation, which is the basic purpose for this book.

Throughout the nation, outdoor recreation is widespread and growing. The 1994-95 National Survey on Recreation and the Environment (Cordell, McDonald, Briggs, Teasley, Biesterfeldt, Bergstrom, & Mou, 1997) estimates the types and quantities of activities occurring in the U.S., but it does not say where this recreation is taking place. Sources such as the CUSTOMER onsite visitor surveys conducted by the USFS in the late 1980s and early 1990s provide some data about recreation that occurs on national forests and other public lands. Some data are gathered by government agencies and some private businesses administering recreation sites around the nation. However, there is little information on the amount of recreation occurring on private land in the United States or on landowners' attitudes about it. The intent of the NPLOS was to help fill this void.

Sampling Plan and Survey Methods

The objective of NPLOS was to survey a representative national sample of owners of rural, private tracts of at least 10 acres. Sampling design was in two stages. The first or primary sampling units were U.S. counties (excluding Alaska and Hawaii) and the second, or secondary, sampling units were landowners within the counties.

It was believed that 12,500 completed questionnaires were needed to adequately describe the U.S. rural private landowner situation. Hence, assuming a questionnaire return rate of 50 percent based on the Dillman survey research method (Dillman, 1978) and allowing for about 1,000 unusable returns, a sample size of 26,000 private landowners was targeted.

Through the cooperation of NRCS District Conservationists, a sample was drawn from county landholding records throughout the nation. Tracts sampled were rural and primarily privately owned. Strict instructions were devised for the random selection of the sample and were communicated to the NRCS agents accordingly.

The number of sample counties (primary units) was determined by dividing 26,000 by the number of tracts to be sampled per county, 35, which yielded 743 counties nationwide. That number was rounded up to 750. To ensure that sampled tracts were not all of a similar size, four tract size strata were defined: 10-19 acres, 20-99 acres, 100-499 acres, and 500 or more acres. The first three strata had a sample of 10 tracts each per county. Given their relative scarcity, the 500+ acres stratum had a maximum of five tracts per county. In many counties, that number was smaller. Many counties had no tracts larger than 500 acres.

---

[2] The University of Georgia, Department of Agricultural & Applied Economic and the U.S. Forest Service, Southern Research Experiment Station have a cooperative research group, the Environmental Resources Assessment Group, that forms the basis of their relationship.

Two criteria were used for selecting the 750 counties for the sample: low population density and level of private ownership. Counties that did not have the kinds of rural, private ownerships that NPLOS sought for the survey were removed from consideration. These counties were primarily urbanized, highly–developed counties or those dominated by public land. Using U.S. Census data, urban or metropolitan counties were identified as those with a population density of 400 or more persons per square mile. Counties were also excluded from sampling if the density was between 300 and 400 persons per square mile, *or* if the county's land base was 70 percent or more public land (federal or state) or urban "built up" land, *unless* the county had a sufficiently large amount of rural, private acres—140,000 in the eastern U.S. or 250,000 acres in the western United States.[3] These types of counties (220 out of 3,082) were excluded because they did not meet the objective of sampling counties with a high percentage of rural, private, and undeveloped tracts. A sample of 750 from 2,862 eligible counties yielded a probability of selection of about one in four (26.2 percent). A goal was to distribute the sample equally across the 48 contiguous states. A simple random sample might have caused some states to have a disproportionate number of counties selected, while other states had none selected at all. A similar concern was that some regions within states would be oversampled at the expense of other regions. Rather than divide each state into geographic quartiles, the decision was made to sample proportionally based upon ecoregions in each state (Bailey's Ecoregions of the United States, 1976). Therefore, strata were formed based on each ecoregion in every state. Roughly one-fourth of the eligible counties were then randomly selected from each ecoregion.

The initial questionnaire (over 30 pages) had 10 sections dealing with different aspects of private land use and ownership. After attempts to make it shorter, it was decided that two versions of the questionnaire were needed.[4] Each version contained identical core questions in each of its sections so that the two databases could be combined. Each version also concentrated on different areas in detail so that all questions from the original version could be included in either of the two questionnaires. To achieve random sampling, addresses were assigned alternately between the two versions. Due to obvious errors in the address database (such as no street address or box, no identifying name, etc.), there were approximately 23,000 valid addresses to be assigned a survey version.

The first section of the questionnaire covered general landowner and tract information. The second section covered changes in the land, such as additions or sales of acreage. Section three inquired about the owners' reasons for owning the land, ways in which they might use their land, and the types of land management practices they have applied to the land. The next section inquired about the accessibility of the land as well as posting practices and any problems the landowner had with other people's use of their land. Section five asked questions about the recreational use of the land by friends and family members. The sixth section inquired about any leasing that had occurred on the land. Section seven asked briefly about the use the land gets from the general population. The eighth section, also brief, inquired about parts of the land that might be closed to all outside use. The ninth section asked some theoretical questions about access for the general population in the future as well as plans the landowner might have to manage his or her tract. Section 10 was a general demographic section that asked for information on age, race, gender, income, employment, education, etc.

Questionnaire mailing began in early August, 1995. Because of the samples' size, groups of states were identified in order to break up the mailings. Large states with many counties represented a substantial block of the sample and were therefore grouped together with only one other state. Surveying began in states on the East Coast and progressed westward. Respondents were mailed one of the two versions of the questionnaire. If no reply had been received in approximately three weeks, respondents were mailed a postcard reminder. If respondents did not return the questionnaire within another three weeks, they were sent another complete survey package. The second survey marked the end of our attempts to get respondents to reply. The last mailings occurred in mid-July, 1996. The above procedure constitutes a modified Dillman method for mail surveys.

---

[3] The eastern and western acreage figures represented the 95th percentile of rural, private, undeveloped acres among counties in those regions.

[4] Actually three versions of the NPLOS questionnaire were developed and implemented. The third is a 'corporate version,' which will not be treated in this report.

Survey Results

The response rate for the NPLOS questionnaire for both versions was slightly above 30 percent. The results reported in this chapter are presented for the nation in the aggregate and for the four assessment regions (Table IV.1). Approximately 13,500 respondents in our sample did not reply with any type of information. Of these 13,500, a semi-random sample of 3,000 was drawn to attempt a very condensed phone questionnaire, which asked key questions designed to allow testing for non-response bias. The results of this phone questionnaire compared well to the questionnaire data, and it was decided that adjustments for non-response bias were not required.

Table IV.1: Regional Definitions used in NPLOS Analysis, 1995-96

Region	States Included in Region
North	Connecticut, Delaware, District of Columbia, Illinois, Indiana, Iowa, Maine, Maryland, Massachusetts, Michigan, Minnesota, Missouri, New Hampshire, New Jersey, New York, Ohio, Pennsylvania, Rhode Island, Vermont, West Virginia, Wisconsin
South	Alabama, Arkansas, Florida, Georgia, Kentucky, Louisiana, Mississippi, North Carolina, Oklahoma, South Carolina, Tennessee, Texas, Virginia
Rocky Mountains and Great Plains	Arizona, Colorado, Idaho, Kansas, Montana, Nebraska, Nevada, New Mexico, North Dakota, South Dakota, Utah, Wyoming
Pacific Coast	California, Oregon, Washington

Source: National Private Landowners Survey (NPLOS), Environmental Resource Assessment Group, Athens, Ga.

Tract size across the United States for the NPLOS varied from a low of 10 acres (which was set as a lower bound for the sampling) to a high of 39,000 acres. Tracts in the western U.S. had slightly higher mean tract sizes. Proportions of private tracts in the four acreage categories (10-19, 20-99, 100-499, and 500+ acres) across the four regions were fairly uniform, except that 15 percent of all private tracts in the Pacific Coast region were in the 500+ acre category (Table IV.2). The number of years the tract was owned was also fairly uniform across regions, with the exception of the Pacific Coast, where landowners seemed more likely to own their land for 10 years or less than landowners in other regions (Figure IV.1). Approximately 45 percent of landowners in the nation own more than one tract of land, while almost the same percentage (47 percent) have their primary residence located on the tract chosen for the survey (Table IV.). Landowners are more likely to live on the sampled tract in the North than anywhere else in the U.S. Of those who do not live on their land, the proportion of owners, by the distance they live from their land, is presented in Figure IV.2. Across all regions of the U.S., more than half of landowners who did not live on their land lived within 50 miles of the sampled tract (Figure IV.2). Mean driving distances in the Rocky Mountain region and the Northern region were noticeably higher than the other two regions.

Table IV.2: Proportion of Owners by Tract Size Category and Region, 1995-96

Tract size category	U.S. overall	Region			
		North	South	Pacific Coast	Rocky Mountains
10-19 acres	29.2	32.2	27.5	26.1	25.7
20-99 acres	34.4	34.2	33.8	36.4	35.5
100-499 acres	29.8	29.3	31.6	22.7	28.9
500 + acres	6.7	4.3	7.1	14.8	9.9

Source: National Private Landowners Survey (NPLOS), Environmental Resource Assessment Group, Athens, Ga.

Table IV.3: Percentage of Landowners by Owner Characteristic and Region, 1995-96

Owner Characteristic	U.S. Overall	Region			
		North	South	Pacific Coast	Rocky Mountains
Own other tracts	44.7	40.3	45.9	63.2	48.6
Live on land	46.9	55.0	42.7	45.6	34.6

Source: National Private Landowners Survey (NPLOS), Environmental Resource Assessment Group, Athens, Ga.

Figure IV.1: Proportion of Landowners by the Number of Years They Have Owned Their Tracts and by Region, 1995-96

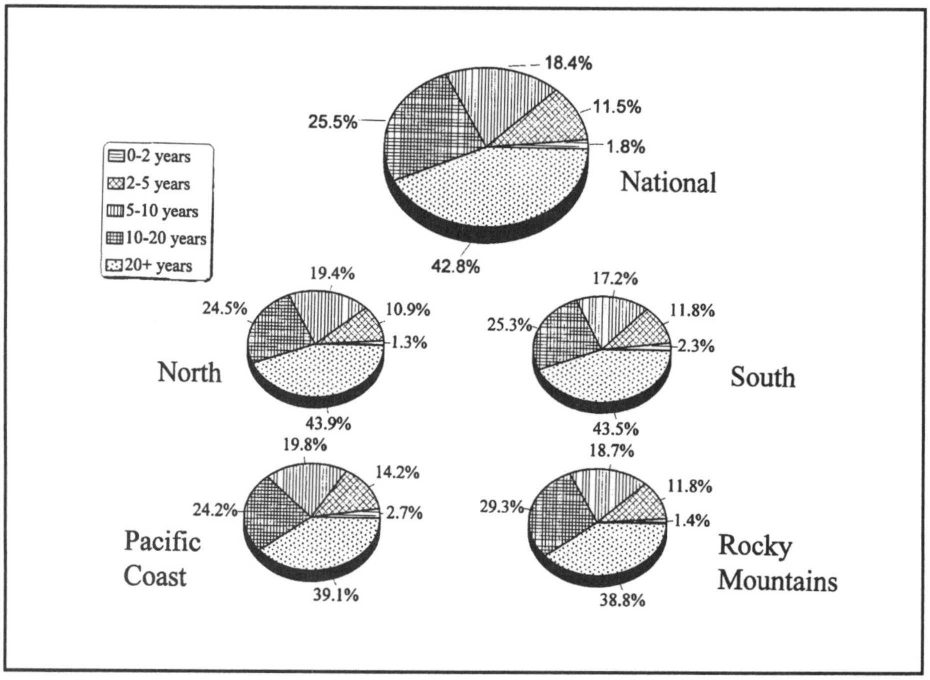

Figure IV.2: Proportion of Absentee Owners by Driving Distance to Tract from Residence and Region, 1995-96

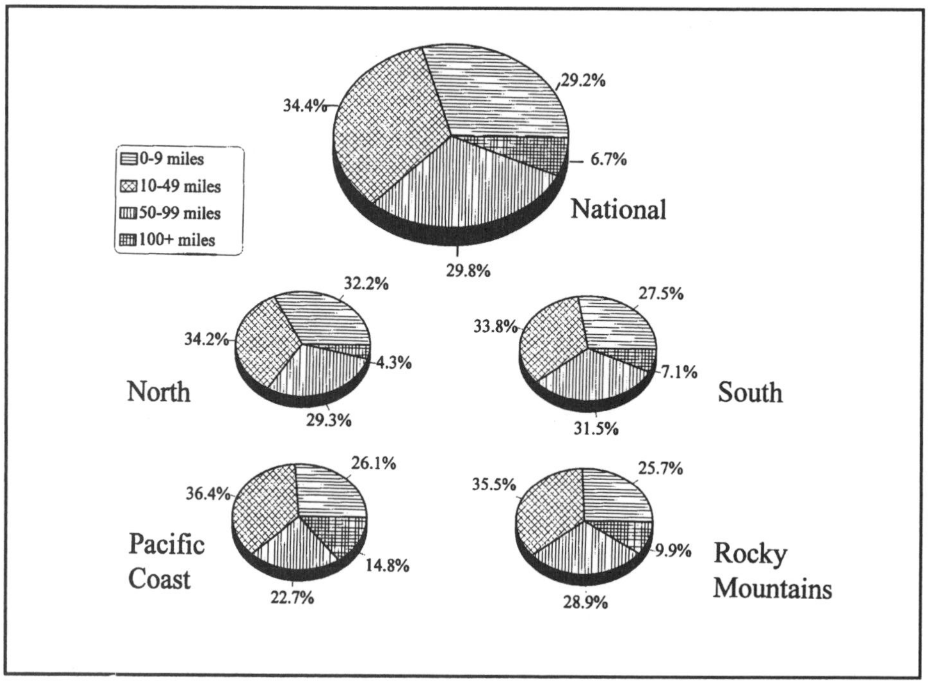

Landowners were also asked about the land surrounding their tracts (Table IV.6), since in many instances this affects land use and management practices. A surprising proportion of owners (14 percent) listed their land as either sharing a border with or being surrounded by government land. With the exception of the Rocky Mountain region, well over 50 percent of landowners said their land was next to a paved public road. Tracts with streams or rivers running through them were more common in the East. Roughly 46 percent of tracts in the North and South had a stream or river running through the land.

Table IV.4: Percent of Responding Owners by Description of Land and Region, 1995-96

Description of Land	U.S. Overall	Region			
		North	South	Pacific Coast	Rocky Mountains
Adjoins government or public land	13.8	12.9	11.7	25.6	18.8
Next to or within a short walk of a large river, lake, or reservoir	15.6	16.9	14.2	23.1	13.1
Land around mine is a state or federal designated wildlife management area	5.1	5.3	4.1	8.6	6.2
Next to or short walk to a residential subdivision	15.4	15.6	16.3	17.6	11.7
Next to a paved public road or highway	55.8	55.8	62.5	63.2	35.2
Land is more hilly and steep than flat	37.8	43.1	33.5	43.0	32.1
Has one or more streams or rivers running through it	42.7	45.9	45.9	34.3	26.8

Source: National Private Landowners Survey (NPLOS), Environmental Resource Assessment Group, Athens, Ga.

Many landowners reported changes in their land holding since they first purchased the sampled tracts (Table IV.5). A roughly equal number of landowners bought and sold land either adjoining or nearby the sample tracts. One point to note is the difference between averages of land bought and sold. The mean acreage added is substantially higher than that sold for the North and South, whereas the trend is reversed for the Rocky Mountain and Pacific Coast regions. Acreage bought and sold in the last five years differs somewhat from this trend. Only in the North and Rocky Mountain regions does the acreage bought exceed the acreage sold.

Table IV.5: Percentage of Private Tracts that Have Changed Status and Average Acreage by Type of Change and Region, 1995-96

Type of Change	U.S. Overall	Region			
		North	South	Pacific Coast	Rocky Mountains
Added Acreage? (% Yes)	15.6	16.3	14.1	15.2	17.9
Average Acreage Added	159.16	89.1	313.7	170.5	368.4
Amount of Acreage Added in last five years	44.0	21.8	43.8	18.3	114.3
Sold Acreage? (% Yes)	13.9	15.2	14.5	12.2	9.3
Average Acreage Sold	113.87	37.2	127.3	211.2	453.2
Amount of Acreage Sold in last five years	52.9	8.5	106.7	209.3	25.0

Source: National Private Landowners Survey (NPLOS), Environmental Resource Assessment Group, Athens, Ga.

The entire sample of landowners was asked about reasons they might consider selling some or all of their land. The most frequent reasons given were either they were "approached with a good offer" or that they "needed the money" (Figure IV..3). Again, landowners checked an average of just over one of the reasons provided.

Figure IV.3: Percent of Reasons Checked by Private Landowners as Reasons They Might Consider Selling All or a Part of Their Land, 1995-96

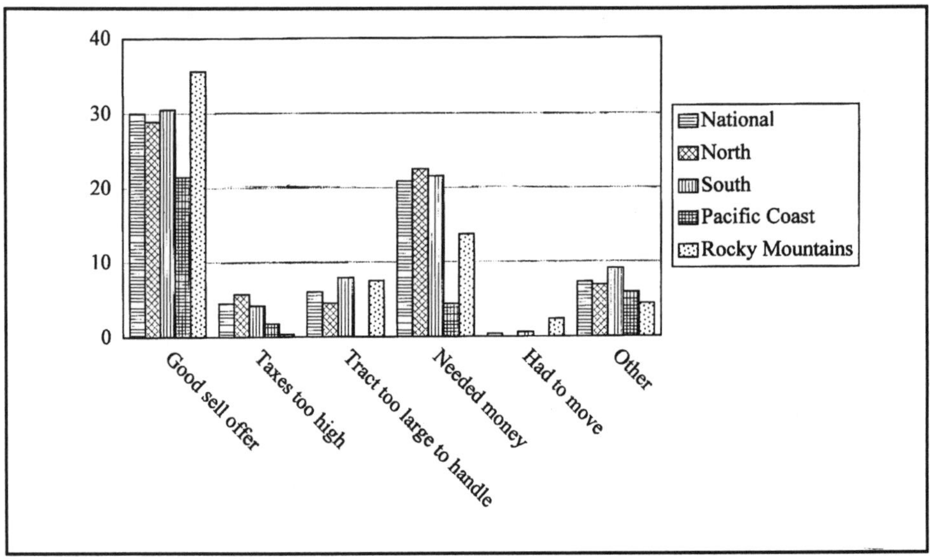

There was very little difference across regions for average miles of maintained roads and trails on private land and little difference in the amount of either that were open to outside use (Table 4.6). The amount of roads and trails open to outside use does not necessarily reflect roads and trails open for people who do not have permission to use the landowners' land.

Table IV.6: Average Mileage of Roads or Trails per Tract by Type of Road or Trail and Region, 1995-96

Type of Road or Trail	U.S. Overall	Region: North	South	Pacific Coast	Rocky Mountains
Maintained road	.5	.4	.6	1.0	.6
Maintained open roads	.4	.4	.5	1.0	.3
Maintained trails	.4	.3	.4	.3	.3
Maintained open trails	.3	.3	.4	.3	.2

Source: National Private Landowners Survey (NPLOS), Environmental Resource Assessment Group, Athens, Ga.

Owning Rural Land

Of the many reasons why people own land, some are easily expressed and others are not. We were interested not only in the objective facts related to private land, but also in owners' subjective perceptions of rural land use issues. Figure IV.4 presents some of the reasons landowners expressed for owning rural land. Note that the three most frequently listed reasons were ones tied more to emotions than objective reasons: "enjoying my own green-space," "living in a rural environment," and "making an estate for heirs." On average, landowners checked more than four of the 17 reasons for owning land.

Figure IV.4: Percent Landowners by Reasons for Owning Land and Region, 1995-96

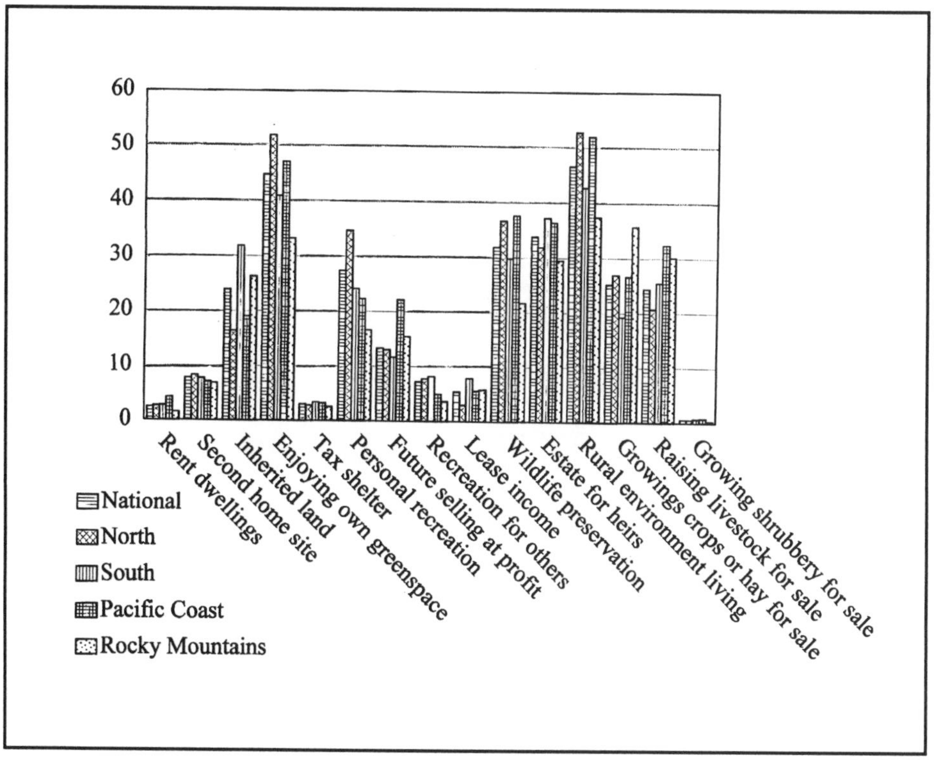

The questions leading to Figures IV.5-9 further delve into the way owners feel about their land and how their management actions might interact with the environment. The statements presented to them were worded such that we could distinguish between the environmental and utilitarian motives for using the land. It is interesting to note the differences between the different regions of the country in answering this question.

Figure IV.5: Percentage of Landowners Agreeing that People Must Rule Over Nature; Plants and Animals Are for Our Use by Region, 1995-96

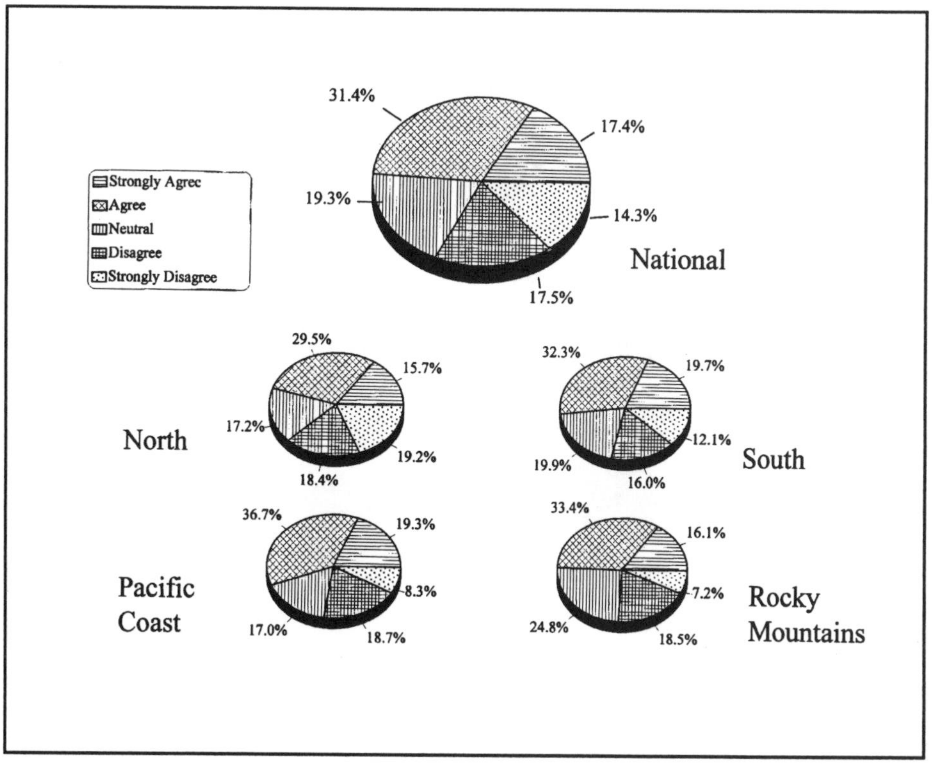

Figure IV.6: Percentage of Landowners Agreeing that the Balance of Nature Is Very Delicate, So We Must Try to Limit Economic Growth that Exploits Nature by Region, 1995-96

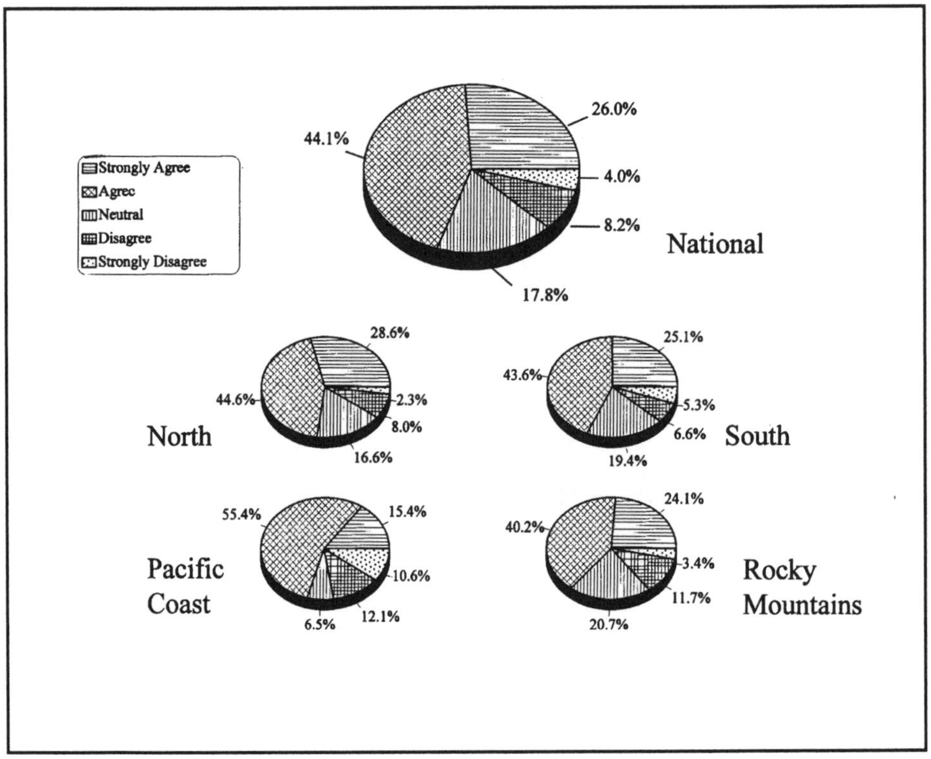

Figure IV.7: Percentage of Landowners Agreeing that Private Landowners Have the Right to Do as They Please with Their Lands Regardless of What It Does to the Environment by Region, 1995-96

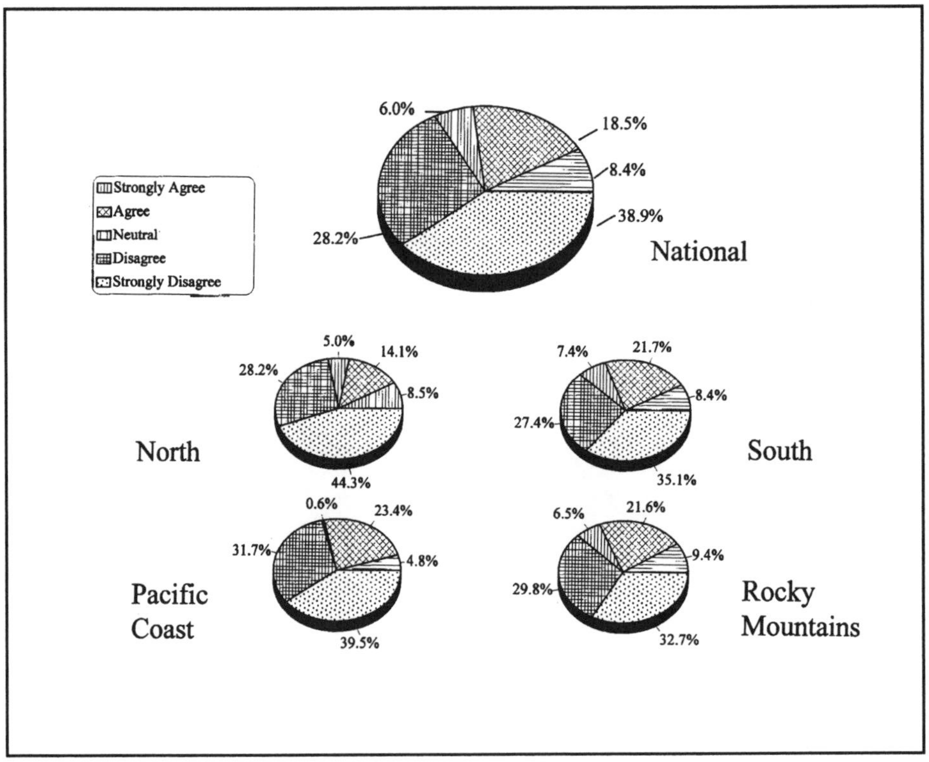

Figure IV.8: Percentage of Landowners Agreeing that Private Property Rights are Important, but Only if They Don't Hurt the Environment by Region, 1995-96

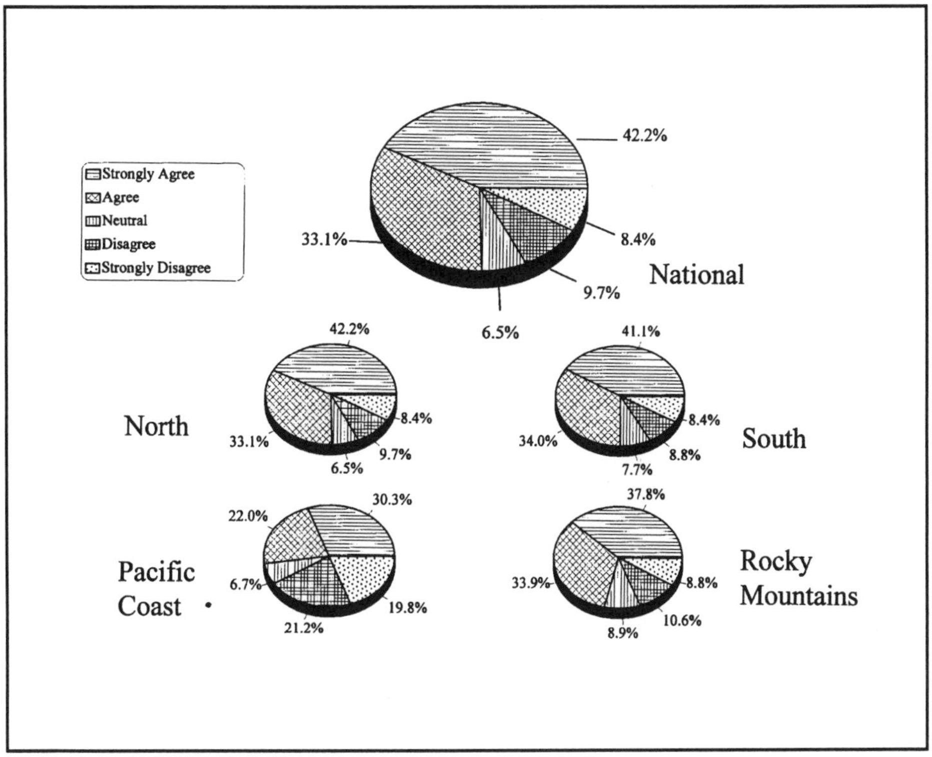

Figure IV.9: Percentage of Landowners Agreeing that Private Property Rights Should Be Limited, if Necessary, to Protect the Environment by Region, 1995-96

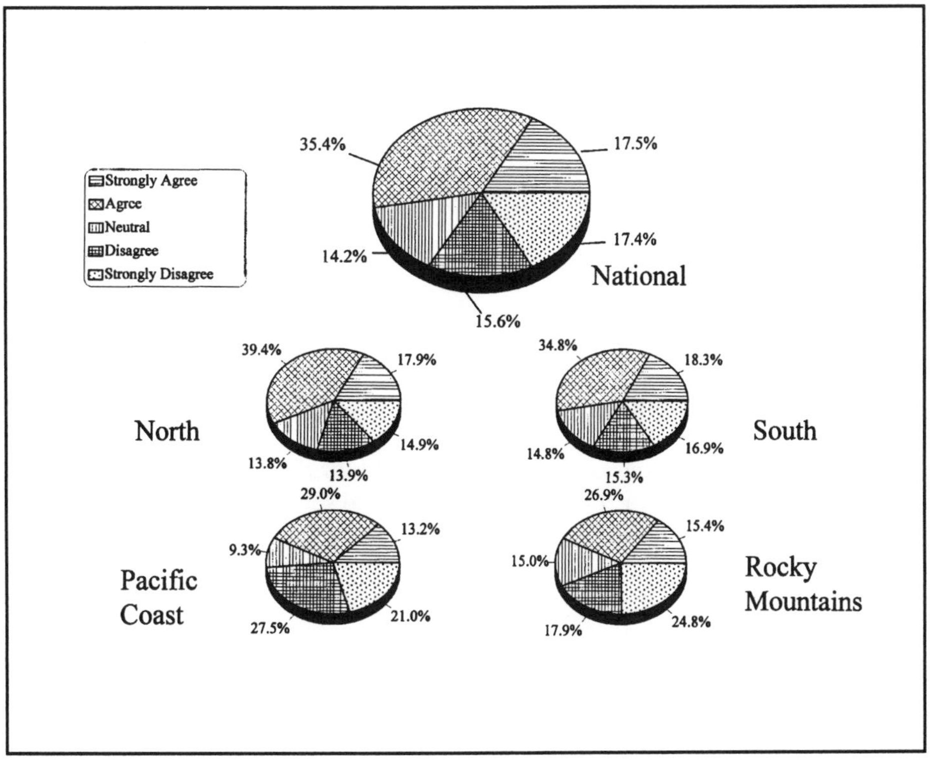

Landowners were also asked about their plans for making money from or for improving the natural aspects of their land. Although responses across regions varied some, in general they were very close. One exception is the Northern response to improving wildlife, water, aesthetics, or other natural components of land. Landowners in this region seemed less likely to use their land for making money. Most landowners fall into the middle, "cross-use," categories. A surprising number of respondents refused to answer this question—30 percent on average.

Table IV.7–Percentage of Owners Indicating Primary Emphasis for Managing Their Lands by Type of Management Emphasis and Region, 1995-96

Method of Management	U.S. Overall	North	South	Pacific Coast	Rocky Mountains
		Region			
I will emphasize improving wildlife, water, aesthetics, or other natural components and do not intend to grow timber, raise livestock, or similarly use my land to make money	14.8	21.4	10.3	10.6	8.8
I will emphasize improving the natural components of my land, but I also plan to use my land to make money	24.4	23.1	26.8	25.6	21.3
I will emphasize using my land to make money, but I will also put some effort into maintaining the natural components	22.3	20.2	21.8	29.5	27.5
I will mostly use my land just to make money	8.7	7.6	7.2	13.0	14.5
Don't know/not applicable	29.8	27.7	33.9	21.3	27.9

Source: National Private Landowners Survey (NPLOS), Environmental Resource Assessment Group, Athens, Ga.

Ways to Use Land and Perceptions

The possession of land represents many things in the lives of rural landowners. To many, owning land provides a means for garnering income. The following tables present some of the ways rural owners use their land to produce income and some of the future plans they hold for their land.

Rural owners have many plans for their land. Some plan to sell or buy additional acreage (Table IV.8). A large percentage across the regions have "other" plans for their land. Nationally, 9.7 percent of owners said they would sell because taxes are too high (Table IV.9).

Rural owners produce income from their land in a variety of ways. Nationally, the majority of ways are "grazing cattle and other livestock," "sharecropping with someone," and "harvesting timber or pulpwood" (Figure IV.10). There are, of course, regional variations among the activities. Most notable is the seemingly high "harvest of timber" in the South, "leasing to a business interest and renting a dwelling" on the Pacific Coast, and "sharecropping" in the Rocky Mountain region.

Table IV.8: Percentage of Owners Indicating Plans for the Land by Type of Plan and Region, 1995-96

Plans for land	U.S. Overall	Region: North	South	Pacific Coast	Rocky Mountains
Sell all the land	15.1	15.0	12.9	21.9	19.3
Sell part of the land	6.0	7.3	5.0	7.3	4.7
Add adjoining acreage	12.0	12.7	11.9	9.9	11.1
Other	52.2	50.7	56.5	60.9	42.2

Source: National Private Landowners Survey (NPLOS), Environmental Resource Assessment Group, Athens, Ga.

Table IV.9: Percentage of Listed Reasons for Selling Land, by Reason and Region, 1995-96

Reasons for selling land	U.S. Overall	Region: North	South	Pacific Coast	Rocky Mountains
Taxes are too high	9.7	12.7	6.5	14.4	7.8
Tract is too large to keep up	3.5	3.5	3.7	6.8	1.7
I need money	5.5	5.3	5.5	9.0	4.8
I will be moving	2.9	3.4	2.2	1.8	3.7
Land prices are high/ good time to sell	4.3	4.4	3.8	3.9	5.6
Other	12.1	11.5	11.6	17.1	13.7

Source: National Private Landowners Survey (NPLOS), Environmental Resource Assessment Group, Athens, Ga.

Figure IV.10: Percent of Different Ways that Landowners Earn Income from Their Land by Region, 1995-96

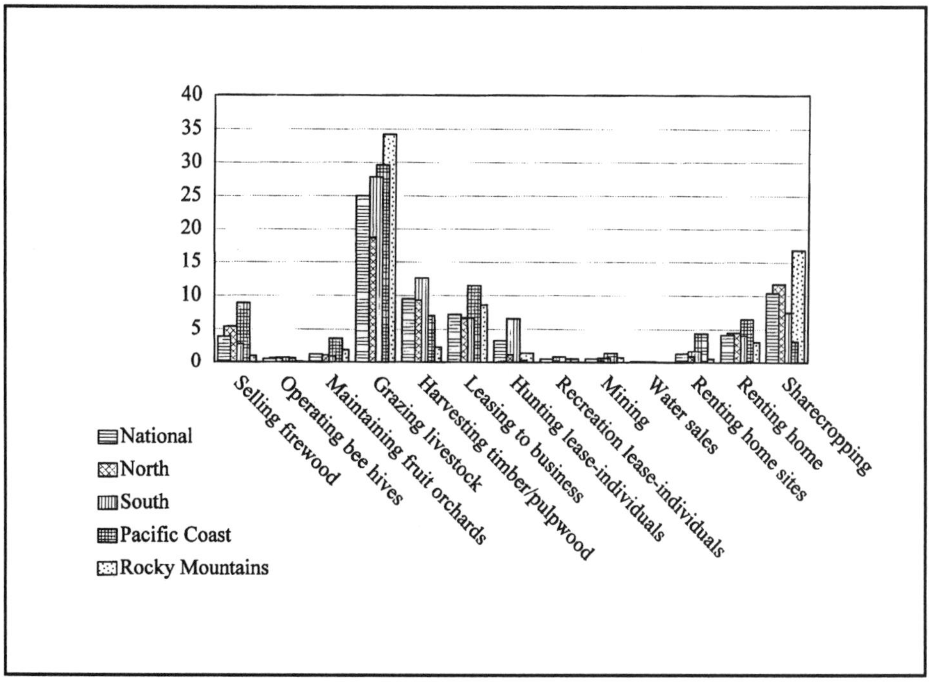

Table IV.10 breaks out the types of forestry products that were harvested from landowners' tracts. Across all owners, the number of products harvested off their land in the past year (bottom of Table IV.10) is fewer than one.

Table IV.10: Percentage of Owners Having Harvested Wood Products in Last Year by Type of Wood Product and Region, 1995-96

Type of Wood Product Harvested	U.S. Overall	Region			
		North	South	Pacific Coast	Rocky Mountains
Firewood for your or others' personal use, but not for sale	26.6	32.4	25.0	24.5	14.5
Fence posts, lumber, or other products for own use, but not for sale	6.1	6.7	6.5	6.3	2.9
Firewood for sale	2.8	3.4	1.5	14.0	1.1
Posts, poles, or pilings for sale	0.6	0.8	0.3	3.1	0
Christmas trees for sale	0.4	0.9	0.2	0	0
Pinestraw, bark, or other mulch for sale	0.3	0.1	0.6	0	0
Other products	3.4	4.2	2.9	7.8	1.3
Don't know what was harvested	1.3	0.6	1.8	1.3	2.0
Mean number of products harvested	0.4	0.5	0.4	0.6	0.2

Source: National Private Landowners Survey (NPLOS), Environmental Resource Assessment Group, Athens, Ga.

Nationally, 9.7 percent of landowners use, or have used, some type of forestry incentive program (Table IV.11). For farm and forestry operations information, many sources were used. At the national level, an average of two of the listed sources were used to help provide the owner with useful information about practices carried out on their land. The Cooperative Extension Service and the Natural Resources Conservation Service were two of the main sources listed.

Table IV.11: Percentage of Rural Landowners Using Forestry Incentive Programs Information Sources for Farm and Forestry Practices, by Source and Region, 1995-96

Use of Forestry Incentive Program or Information Source	U.S. Overall	Region			
		North	South	Pacific Coast	Rocky Mountains
Used forestry incentive program	9.7	9.3	12.7	9.1	3.0
Cooperative Extension Service	37.4	38.4	36.5	31.2	38.8
Natural Resources Conservation Service	29.3	30.5	27.0	20.3	34.6
State Forestry Commission	13.0	10.9	17.0	25.2	4.7
Farm or forestry suppliers	9.5	8.2	10.5	15.3	9.0
Farm, forestry, or other magazines or newsletters	21.8	21.5	20.1	44.0	20.2
Radio and/or television	14.7	13.1	14.1	18.0	19.6
Friends, neighbors, or colleagues	32.8	29.6	33.7	37.5	38.3
Other	9.1	9.3	9.0	16.7	6.7
Average number of items checked	1.7	1.6	1.7	2.1	1.7

Source: National Private Landowners Survey (NPLOS), Environmental Resource Assessment Group, Athens, Ga.

Protecting Land

For many rural owners, protection, conservation, and thoughtful use of their land are prime considerations. Three of the top management practices included planting trees, improving habitat for wildlife, and using controlled burns to help keep down undesirable vegetation (Table IV.12).

Table IV.12: Percentage of Landowners Using Management Practices by Type of Practice and Region, 1995-96

Type of Management Practice	U.S. Overall	Region			
		North	South	Pacific Coast	Rocky Mountains
Cleared woodland or natural rangeland for crops, pasture or development	5.1	5.1	6.2	6.6	1.9
Harvested mature timber	8.4	10.3	8.5	5.9	2.8
Thinned trees for better timber growth	8.2	12.5	6.0	5.6	2.4
Planted trees	12.3	14.2	9.5	19.5	12.3
Improved habitat for wildlife	12.1	14.8	10.9	11.3	7.5
Provided habitat and/or protection for songbirds	7.7	10.2	6.0	5.9	5.5
Developed ponds or lakes	5.4	4.9	6.1	9.6	3.8
Stocked fish in streams, ponds, or lakes	5.0	2.4	4.0	6.3	1.9
Developed roads	3.1	0.6	1.6	1.1	1.4
Developed boat ramp, beach, or other access to a river or lake	4.8	6.4	4.6	1.9	1.4
Applied fertilizer to range or woodlands	0.5	0.5	0.6	0.6	0.1
Used fire to control undesirable vegetation	10.8	10.2	13.5	9.3	5.5
Controlled a wildfire that broke out	3.4	2.0	4.5	6..4	3.8
Other	1.1	4.4	3.1	1.9	8.0

Source: National Private Landowners Survey (NPLOS), Environmental Resource Assessment Group, Athens, Ga.

Because wetland management practices are so important in maintaining waterfowl habitat and the general health of the land, landowners were asked whether they undertook any wetland conservation practices. Table IV.13 shows the wetland practices employed by landowners across the nation. Application of such practices varied by region. Participation among landowners in the Pacific Coast were generally the highest among regions for these practices, although owners in the North also preserved wetlands at a comparatively high rate. For landowners who applied some type of wetland conservation practice, the average number of acres involved is shown at the bottom of Table IV.13.

Table IV.13: Percentage of Landowners Using Wetland Conservation Practices by Type of Practice and Region, 1995-96

Type of Wetland Conservation Practice	U.S. Overall	Region			
		North	South	Pacific Coast	Rocky Mountains
Preserving wetlands, such as marshes, swamps, etc.	6.5	8.4	4.4	7.5	6.1
Restoring wetlands by closing drainage systems	1.0	0.7	0.9	4.7	1.2
Creating wetlands through dams or water diversion	3.5	2.9	3.6	8.1	3.7
Receiving state or federal assistance for protecting wetlands	0.6	0.3	0.7	0.0	1.0
I have not undertaken any wetland activities	69.4	71.5	69.6	60.5	65.1
Mean acres practice of those who apply	47.1	41.5	40.1	25.2	105.5

Source: National Private Landowners Survey (NPLOS), Environmental Resource Assessment Group, Athens, Ga.

Another way that owners try to protect and manage their land is by limiting access to people outside their households. Table IV.14 presents some methods of controlling access. The major method is by requiring verbal permission to gain access. Between the high rankings of "getting verbal permission" and having "no requirements for access," there would seem to be low-cost access for public use of private land over most of the nation.

Table IV.14: Percentage of Landowners Who Lease by Type of Agreement Used and Region, 1995-96

Type of Agreement	U.S. Overall	Region			
		North	South	Pacific Coast	Rocky Mountains
Sign a lease agreement	3.1	1.0	5.6	4.6	2.4
Get written permission only, no fee	8.6	8.1	9.8	6.5	7.2
Get written permission AND pay a fee	1.6	0.8	2.6	1.0	1.6
Get verbal permission, no fee	47.0	51.2	42.8	48.8	44.9
Get verbal permission AND pay a fee	1.5	1.1	2.1	1.8	1.3
I have no requirements	15.0	16.8	11.9	18.5	16.8
Other	13.9	13.9	14.8	13.8	11.4

Source: National Private Landowners Survey (NPLOS), Environmental Resource Assessment Group, Athens, Ga.

Posting is a popular way to prevent or control access. Throughout the NPLOS questionnaire, questions pertaining to posting were posed to the landowner. The following tables present the results of this questioning, some of the reasons landowners gave for posting, and some of the problems they have experienced that may have led to posting.

Table IV.15 shows the percentage of owners across the country who post some or all of their land and the average acreage posted. Nationally, 40 percent of landowners post at least some of their land. The reader will note that all but the North reported acreages larger than the earlier reported mean tract sizes. This may be a result of larger tract landowners reporting posted acres and smaller tract landowners abstaining from answering the question, whether or not they posted.

Table IV.15: Percentage of Tracts and Acreage Posted by Region, 1995-96

Posting Attribute	U.S. Overall	North	Region South	Pacific Coast	Rocky Mountains
Percentage who post	40.5	42.2	41.0	46.7	31.9
Average acres posted	205.7	108.8	238.4	298.0	397.4

Source: National Private Landowners Survey (NPLOS), Environmental Resource Assessment Group, Athens, Ga.

Many owners have experienced problems from time to time with outside people's use of their land, these problems may be a cause for much of the posting that occurs today. This finding is consistent with the previous research on recreational access to private lands reported earlier in this chapter. Figure IV.11 lists problems experienced by regions of the country. Across regions, most owners have dealt with two or more of the listed problems. Some of the top problems listed nationally are littering or garbage dumping, poaching of wildlife (illegal hunting), and damaged fences or gates. Looking at the Pacific Coast region, greater percentages of landowners reported problems more frequently than landowners in the rest of the country.

Table IV.16, as a follow-up to the above, lists reasons landowners gave for posting their land. For the most part, it seems that landowners want to know who is on their land in order to keep out persons they do not know.

Figure IV.11: Percentage of Landowner Problems that Have Been Encountered with Outside Person Usage of Their Land, by Region, 1995-96

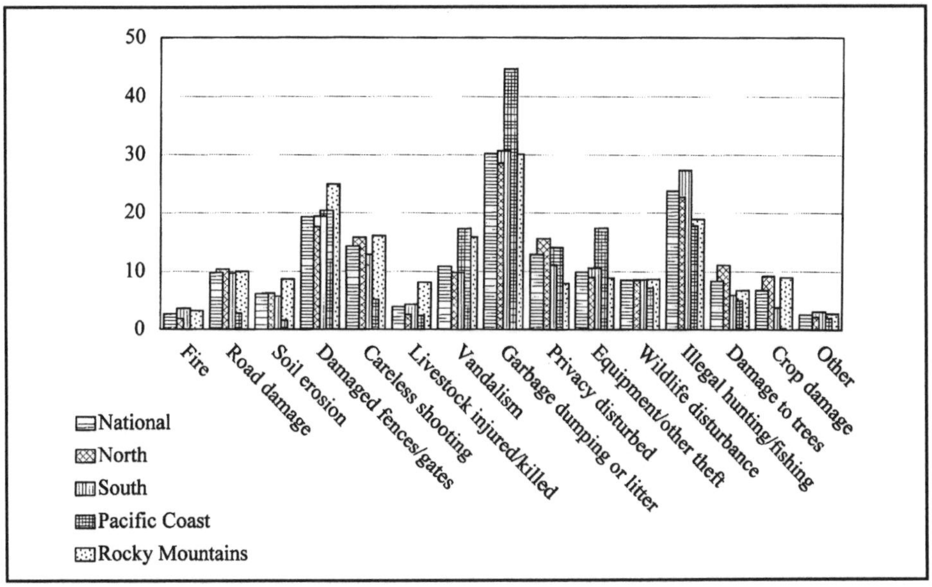

Table IV.16: Percentage of Landowner Who Post Their Land by Reason for Posting and Region, 1995-96

Reason for Posting	U.S. Overall	North	South	Pacific Coast	Rocky Mountains
		Region			
Know who is on the property	39.1	40.2	39.5	41.6	33.7
Keep hunters out	29.3	29.2	32.3	37.9	18.5
Keep motor vehicles out	27.5	28.3	26.7	43.5	22.2
Keep out people I don't know	33.8	33.2	36.8	44.0	24.6
Keep out people who don't have permission	37.7	37.6	39.5	45.0	30.5
Keep everyone out	9.1	7.6	10.4	19.3	6.8
To ensure privacy	20.4	20.1	22.0	25.8	15.4
To prevent littering	27.9	26.4	30.2	38.7	22.5
To prevent damage to property or livestock	30.9	27.4	33.7	43.7	29.3
To be safe from hunters	20.6	22.4	22.1	23.5	10.2
To protect me from lawsuits	28.2	28.5	29.8	37.0	20.4
To prevent fires	20.2	16.3	25.9	28.3	14.0
Other	5.1	5.9	4.8	5.0	3.9

Source: National Private Landowners Survey (NPLOS), Environmental Resource Assessment Group, Athens, Ga.

Table IV.17 summarizes the degree to which landowners post the different types of land they own. As one can see from Table IV.17, lands that are leased for hunting and/or other recreational pursuits are much more likely to be posted. This is often the result of the club or individual leasing taking responsibility for posting.

Judging by the results presented in Table IV.18, most owners do not expect to post much more land than they presently post, although on average 15 percent say they will post more. A small percentage (two percent nationally) plan to decrease the acreage they presently have posted.

Table IV.17: Percentage of Landowners Who Post by Land Access Classification and Region, 1995-96

Land Access Classification	U.S. Overall	North	South	Pacific Coast	Rocky Mountains
		Region			
Land reserved only for household	45.3	47.1	44.0	51.6	40.4
Land leased to a club or individual for hunting	79.0	74.1	84.3	28.2	60.6
Land open to people landowner does not know	28.7	26.4	29.1	50.5	28.9
Land closed to all but household	53.3	56.0	55.3	49.3	39.2

Source: National Private Landowners Survey (NPLOS), Environmental Resource Assessment Group, Athens, Ga.

Table IV.18: Percentage of Owners Expecting to Post in the Future by Level of Posting and Region, 1995-96

Expected Level of Posting	U.S. Overall	Region			
		North	South	Pacific Coast	Rocky Mountains
More	15.4	15.0	15.8	16.5	15.1
Same	82.4	83.0	81.3	82.8	83.1
Less	2.2	2.0	2.8	0.7	1.8

Source: National Private Landowners Survey (NPLOS), Environmental Resource Assessment Group, Athens, Ga.

Recreational Use and Access

A major purpose for the NPLOS project was to identify and quantify recreation use that occurs on private land in the U.S. One component of that recreational use is landowners' personal use, including family use. Another is the use by persons outside the family. This section will examine various types of recreational use and access.

Table IV.19 shows the percentage of owners who have acreage "closed" to all outsiders (outside the household) and the average number of closed acres per tract for those having closed land, nationally and regionally. While the percentage reporting closed land is fairly equal across regions, the mean acreage varies mostly because of differences in average tract sizes across the regions, with western tracts being larger.

Table IV.20 shows the percentage of landowners who recreate on their own land. Such personal recreation might include taking walks or big game hunting.

Table IV.19: Percentage of Ownerships and Average Acreage Closed to Recreation Except for Family Members by Land Closure Attribute and Region, 1995-96

Land Closure Attribute	U.S. Overall	Region			
		North	South	Pacific Coast	Rocky Mountains
Percentage of ownerships having closed land	28.5	27.7	30.2	31.2	25.8
Mean number of acres closed for those who said they had closed land	96.4	71.1	94.7	196.3	148.6

Source: National Private Landowners Survey (NPLOS), Environmental Resource Assessment Group, Athens, Ga.

Table IV.20: Percentage of Landowners Who Personally Participate in Recreation on Their Lands and Landowners who Permit Access for Recreation by Persons Outside their Family by Region, 1995-96

Group	U.S. Overall	Region			
		North	South	Pacific Coast	Rocky Mountains
Participate in recreation on their land (Percent)					
Landowners	70.7	77.3	66.2	65.0	52.1
Permit access for recreation by persons outside their family (Percent)					
Landowners	47.9	55.2	42.5	45.9	41.5

Table IV.20 also shows the percentage, by region, of owners allowing access to people outside their household. The influence of long-standing open access in the North is evident. Roughly half of landowners across the nation allow persons outside their household to recreate on their land. Most of those given access were known personally by the landowner (Table IV.27). The percentage of "outside groups not known personally by the landowner," curiously, was higher than for "people in no way connected with clubs and organizations" for all regions of the country but the South. These percentages were highest in the North where more private land is open to outside use than in any other portion of the country.

Table IV.21: Proportion of Landowners Who Open Access to Outside People by Persons Permitted Access and Region, 1995-96

Persons Permitted Access	U.S. Overall	Region North	South	Pacific Coast	Rocky Mountains
Members of your immediate family who do not live with you	49.4	53.6	48.2	52.3	39.5
People outside your immediate family or household who you know personally	49.3	55.2	45.3	60.8	39.3
Individuals or members of clubs, organizations, or groups who lease your land	5.1	4.2	7.4	4.5	2.1
Outside persons who you may or may not know and with whom you have no personal connections	11.9	16.0	6.5	11.0	14.1

Source: National Private Landowners Survey (NPLOS), Environmental Resource Assessment Group, Athens, Ga.

Approximately 15 percent of owners permit access to some of their land for recreation (Table IV.22). For those who have open acreage, averages are reported. Average open acreage is largest in the Western regions of the country. Table IV.22 also presents estimated average number of 'outsiders' who used the open acreage, as well as the average number of times per year each person used the land.

Table IV.23 also presents percentages of ownerships by type of persons permitted access. The estimated average number of people who used the landowner's land in the East is almost double that of the West.

Table IV. 22: Percentage of Owners, Acreages and Use of Open Private Land by Region, 1995-96

	U.S. Overall	Region North	South	Pacific Coast	Rocky Mountains
Percentage having some land completely open	14.5	19.5	8.4	14.2	16.6
Average number of acres per open tract	238.7	130.4	220.1	327.2	942.8
Average numbers of people using the tract	28	27.7	35.0	10.7	23.0
Average number of times tract used per person	5.2	4.8	7.4	3.1	3.0
Average annual use	158.5	176.8	174.2	29.4	119.6

Source: National Private Landowners Survey (NPLOS), Environmental Resource Assessment Group, Athens, Ga.

Table IV.23: Percentage of Ownerships by Categories of Persons Having Access to Land and Number of Users, 1995-96

Persons Having Access	U.S. Overall	Region North	South	Pacific Coast	Rocky Mountains
Percent Response					
Landowner and members of their family who live with owner	66.5	59.4	69.4	95.1	54.6
Members of family who do not live with owner	51.6	36.7	56.3	95.1	51.7
Others owner know	32.5	42.0	29.7	0.0	31.5
Others owners don't know	8.8	3.1	12.2	4.9	0.0
Number					
Number of people who used the land in the last year	13.9	14.2	14.6	7.3	7.3

Source: National Private Landowners Survey (NPLOS), Environmental Resource Assessment Group, Athens, Ga.

Table IV.24 presents the results of the question of how many of the people who had explicit permission to use the private land for recreation did so and the average number of times they recreated on the land in the past year. The bottom section of the table provides an estimate of total use. With the exception of the Pacific Coast, most of the use seems to be by people from outside the family.

In this study, we were interested not only in the amount of recreation that was occurring on private land, but also in the types of recreation. Figure IV.12 summarizes the types of recreational activities that landowners reported as occurring on their lands in the past year. A number of the activities listed occur frequently on private lands, with some variation among activities by region. Small game hunting is reported as the most popular activity nationally especially in the North and South.

Table IV.24: People with Explicit Permission to Use Private Land and the Average Number of Times that Right Was Exercised 1995-96

People and Use by Group	U.S. Overall	Region North	South	Pacific Coast	Rocky Mountains
Number of people with permission					
Household	1.7	1.8	1.4	2.2	1.7
Family not living with you	4.7	4.9	4.7	5.9	4.1
Others	6.7	7.2	6.1	6.6	7.0
Number of times in past year people went					
Household	31.8	40.1	26.2	39.1	17.9
Family not living with you	9.8	8.7	11.9	15.4	4.8
Others	8.7	9.4	8.3	9.2	7.1
Total use per year					
Household	92.6	113.7	64.7	187.1	71.8
Family not living with you	97.9	95.9	94.4	324.6	30.3
Others	140.8	172.5	113.3	75.2	142.3

Source: National Private Landowners Survey (NPLOS), Environmental Resource Assessment Group, Athens, Ga.

Figure IV.12: Percentage of Recreational Activities Occurring on Land, by Region, 1995-96

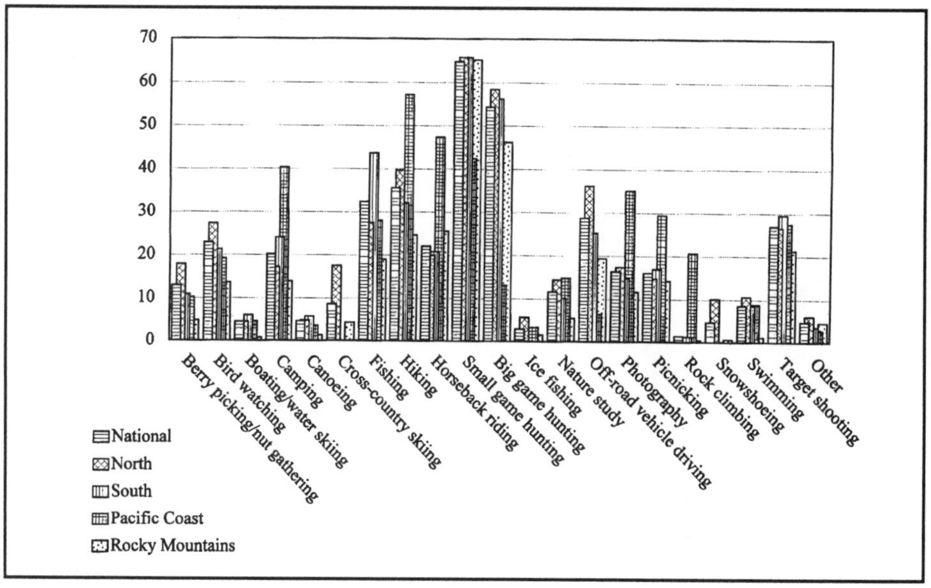

For various reasons, landowners allow their land to be used by people outside of their own family (Table IV.25). Overwhelmingly, "maintaining goodwill with their neighbors and others" is the primary reason for allowing access. This percentage drops noticeably in the Pacific Coast and Rocky Mountain regions, but is still ranked as the number one reason for allowing access in these regions.

Responses of landowners to questions about past access to their land suggest that the access situation is about the same now as it was five years ago (Table IV.26). Although the most frequent response was that access will remain the same, there is a noticeable trend toward closing more land to outside recreation in the future in all regions.

Table IV.25: Percentage of Landowners by Reasons for Allowing Recreation on Their Land and by Region, 1995-96

Reasons for Recreation		Region			
	U.S. Overall	North	South	Pacific Coast	Rocky Mountains
Primary source of income	0.6	0.3	0.9	0.0	0.6
Helps pay the taxes	2.9	1.2	5.0	9.4	0.6
Extra income	0.0	0.0	0.0	0.0	0.0
Help care for and protect my land	3.7	2.0	6.2	4.3	1.8
Help control trespassing	8.4	7.1	11.2	4.0	5.6
Maintain goodwill with neighbors and others	41.2	44.8	40.0	26.9	37.9
Other reasons	15.5	16.7	14.8	15.7	13.7

Source: National Private Landowners Survey (NPLOS), Environmental Resource Assessment Group, Athens, Ga.

Table IV.26: Percent of Owners Indicating More, Same, or Less Land Open to Recreation for Non-Family Members by Time Period and Region, 1995-96

		Region			
	U.S. Overall	North	South	Pacific Coast	Rocky Mountains
Five years ago					
More	5.0	4.9	5.3	6.2	4.2
Same	88.2	89.1	86.1	88.4	91.0
Less	6.8	6.0	8.6	5.5	4.8
Five years from now					
More	3.0	1.8	4.2	2.0	3.9
Same	83.7	85.8	81.7	85.8	82.1
Less	13.3	12.4	14.1	12.2	14.0

Source: National Private Landowners Survey (NPLOS), Environmental Resource Assessment Group, Athens, Ga.

Leasing and Access Rules

Another type of access to private lands is conveyed by a lease agreement. Because leasing can be an important income source to the owner as well as a means of protecting the land, it was given detailed treatment in the NPLOS.

Table IV.27 presents several reasons why landowners might want to lease their land. There was not enough data to support analysis of the Pacific Coast region for leasing, and no column is presented for that region. Nationally and regionally the two major reasons landowners gave for leasing their land are to help pay property taxes and to help control trespassing or unwanted use.

Table IV.28 presents some general information about leasing, the average numbers of people involved in leases, as well as the amount of recreational use that occurs on tracts. The first row, "mean acres leased for recreation," reflects the average acreage leased across all landowners nationally and regionally. This average includes many zeroes for those who do not lease. The second row, "mean acres leased for recreation," summarizes the average acres leased among those owners who had a lease agreement.

Table IV.27: Percentage of Landowners by Reasons for Leasing Land and Region, 1995-96

Reason		Region		
	U.S. Overall	North	South	Rocky Mountains
Source of income	14.8	6.3	16.6	25.1
Helps pay property taxes	74.5	61.5	80.5	42.2
Extra income	39.4	30.0	39.3	82.9
Control trespassing or unwanted use	60.7	29.6	70.2	53.8
Maintain goodwill	25.3	17.5	27.5	26.7
Help care for and protect land	52.0	27.0	60.7	31.1
Other	0.1	0.0	0.2	0.0
Mean number of above reasons checked	2.7	1.8	3.0	2.6

Source: National Private Landowners Survey (NPLOS), Environmental Resource Assessment Group, Athens, Ga.

Table IV.28: Number of Acres, Leases, and Use of Leased Private Land, by Region, 1995-96

Acres, Leases, and Use per Tract	U.S. Overall	Region North	South	Rocky Mountains
Mean acres per tract leased for recreation across all landowners	14.9	3.7	32.4	5.2
Mean acres leased for recreation by landowners	338.0	183.0	418.4	341.5
Number of different leases per tract	1.0	0.8	1.0	1.4
Number of different people covered by leases per tract	12.4	9.4	14.1	8.5
Average number of times used per tract, per year	32.8	22.6	37.9	15.8
Mean "person trips" per year to lease	586.0	192.3	750.5	262.0

Source: National Private Landowners Survey (NPLOS), Environmental Resource Assessment Group, Athens, Ga.

Table IV.29 shows the different types of lease agreements across regions. For the most part, these are written agreements with fees, though a substantial number are verbal with a fee. The verbal agreement seems more prevalent in the North.

The percentage of owners leasing by different types of leasing groups is shown in Table IV.30. Clubs are the most common of lessees, especially in the South. In the Rocky Mountain region, different proportions among group types are evident with more individual leasing being reported. The number of people who live within 50 miles of the leased tract is higher in the South than in other regions.

Table IV.29: Percentage of Owners Who Lease by Type of Agreement and Region, 1995-96

Type of Lease Agreement	U.S. Overall	Region North	South	Rocky Mountains
Verbal agreement with no fee	2.4	4.1	2.0	0.0
Verbal agreement with fee	23.4	47.3	15.4	32.3
Written agreement with no fee	5.3	8.4	4.8	0.0
Written agreement with fee	68.6	40.2	77.3	67.7
Other	0.3	0.0	0.5	0.0

Source: National Private Landowners Survey (NPLOS), Environmental Resource Assessment Group, Athens, Ga.

Table IV.30: Percentage of Landowners by Different Types of Individuals or Groups Who Lease Land and by Region, 1995-96

To Whom the Respondent Leases	U.S. Overall	Region North	South	Rocky Mountains
Individual	16.9	11.4	15.9	31.7
Group of individuals, but not a club	25.2	25.1	24.6	31.1
A club	32.0	21.1	39.6	16.8
Business or corporation	5.2	12.1	1.9	10.3
Government agency	0.3	0.0	0.4	0.0
Others	0.4	0.3	0.7	0.4
Mean number of people leasing who live within 50 miles	6.0	1.6	7.5	2.0

Source: National Private Landowners Survey (NPLOS), Environmental Resource Assessment Group, Athens, Ga.

Table IV.31 shows the results of questions about method and time period by which they leased their land. The most prevalent time period is the annual lease, which is most likely the least confusing leasing approach. "By the lease"[5] also is a popular way of leasing and seems to be increasing as a result of specialization. Length of leases also reflects how the owner manages his/her leasing strategy. The bottom of Table IV.31 indicates that "yearly" leasing is most popular nationally, with leasing "by the season" falling second. In Rocky Mountain regions, however, this relationship is reversed.

Table IV.32 presents strategies for owners for leasing with fees. The highest percentages of landowners choose charging a fee slightly lower than the "going rate" in order to lease to someone whom they trust will take care of their land (42.2 percent). An exception to this leasing practice is in the Rocky Mountain region, where 63 percent lease at the "going rate." Nationally, leasing at the going rate is second at 30 percent, while almost 20 percent lease at a rate much lower than the going rate in order to get someone they trust. A little over eight percent lease to the highest bidder.

Table IV.31: Percentage of Landowners Who Lease by Method for Charging and Tenure of Lease and by Region, 1995-96

Method for Charging and Tenure	U.S. Overall	Region North	South	Rocky Mountains
Method of Charging				
By the year	67.6	39.5	79.3	60.7
By the season	13.2	17.3	10.9	25.4
By the person	7.9	9.6	6.4	5.2
By the lease	9.8	5.3	11.6	18.7
Other	0.5	0.2	0.8	0.4
Tenure of lease				
Season	36.2	43.3	34.7	49.2
Combination	5.2	10.8	1.9	6.4
Other, less than a year	8.3	18.0	1.4	15.0
Yearly	50.3	27.8	62.0	29.4

Source: National Private Landowners Survey (NPLOS), Environmental Resource Assessment Group, Athens, Ga.

[5] By the Lease' is somewhat of a specialized term that basically means the lessee's pay by the type of recreation activity. For example, a landowner might offer a lease to hunt turkeys AND a lease for big game hunting.

Table IV.32: Percentage Landowners by Strategies for Choosing the Lessee and by Region, 1995-96

Leasing Strategies with Fee	U.S. Overall	Region North	South	Rocky Mountains
Lease to highest bidder	8.1	26.8	3.6	0.0
Lease at the going rate	30.0	19.1	30.6	63.3
Lease at slightly lower rate in order to get someone I trust to take care of the land	42.2	36.2	46.0	10.0
Lease at a much lower rate in order to get someone I trust to take care of the land	19.8	17.9	19.8	26.7

Source: National Private Landowners Survey (NPLOS), Environmental Resource Assessment Group, Athens, Ga.

Another strategy for capturing revenue from recreation on private lands that is similar to a lease is "pay-as-you-go." The landowner charges an access fee to people who use their land on each occasion of use. This would probably be most effective when some type of "special attribute" exists on the land. Examples of such attributes are: a section of whitewater on a river, a scenic hiking trail, a pay fishing pond, or a strategically located boat ramp providing access to a lake or canal. There are, however, very few owners across the nation who practice a pay-as-you-go policy (Table 4.33). However, it seems to be most prevalent in the South, where approximately eight percent of owners reported charging a fee for the use of their land for recreation. Almost 80 percent of these owners charged a "per person" fee.

Table IV.33: Percentage Charging Fees and Amount for Recreation Access to Private Land by Region, 1995-96

	U.S. Overall	Region South	Rocky Mountains
Do you charge fees for people, in general, to use your land? (% Yes)	2.7	8.1	1.9
What is the charge?	$30.24	$30.48	$18.14
Is fee:			
per person	74.6	79.3	100.0
per group	35.3	33.2	0
per vehicle	13.4	17.0	0
other	0.1	0.2	0.1
Is charge per day? (% Yes)	94.6	97.7	69.6

Source: National Private Landowners Survey (NPLOS), Environmental Resource Assessment Group, Athens, Ga.

One aspect of leasing that has been a long-standing concern to owners is liability. Table 4.34 shows the different ways landowners handle liability. Carrying insurance, both by the landowner and lessee, is the most popular way of handling liability concerns. Other ways a landowner addresses liability may be a waiver of injury signed by the lessee or removal of all hazards. Finally, approximately 15 percent of owners say they do nothing to address the prospect of liability.

Figure IV.13 presents results of a question asking whether the owners would be willing to lease or allow an individual to recreate on that part of their land they considered closed. The question probed willingness under the condition that interested individuals personally contact the landowner, demonstrating honesty and trustworthiness. Over half of owners in all regions replied negatively to this question. Roughly 40 percent indicated willingness to consider this type of access and five percent said they did not know.

Table IV.34: Percentage of Landowners by Method for Handling Leasing and Liability and by Region, 1995-96

Liability Handling	U.S. Overall	Region: North	Region: South	Region: Rocky Mountains
I carry insurance	44.1	73.6	36.0	36.7
Lessee carries insurance	48.8	53.5	49.0	25.1
Lessee signs a waiver	26.5	27.2	26.9	17.1
All known hazards removed	20.9	18.6	22.9	0.0
Do nothing about liability	14.8	5.3	16.8	25.1

Source: National Private Landowners Survey (NPLOS), Environmental Resource Assessment Group, Athens, Ga.

Figure IV.13: Percentage of Landowners Who Would Consider Letting Outside People Recreate on Land that Is Completely Closed, by Region, 1995-96

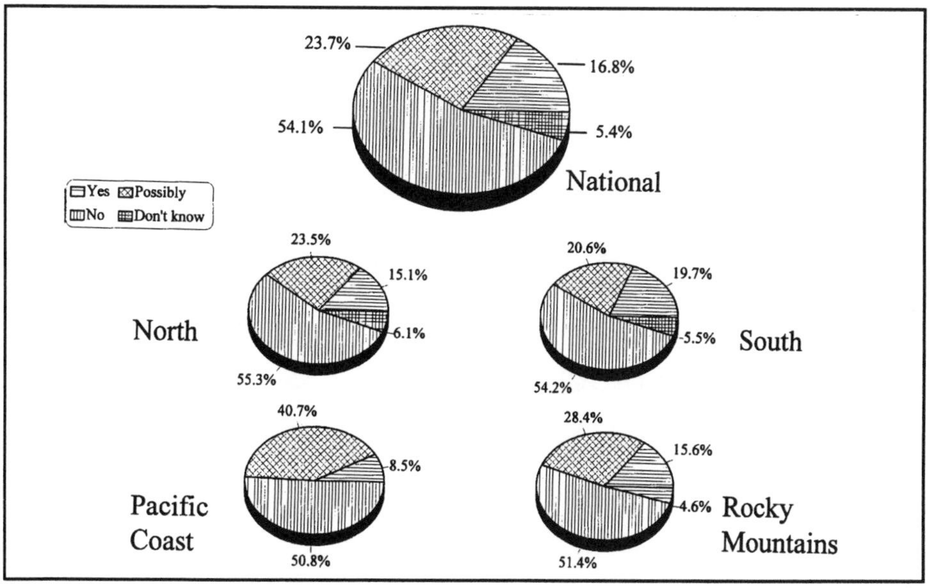

Finally, owners were asked what it would take in the future for a group or individual to lease their land for recreation (Table IV.35). "Verbal permission with no fee" was the highest response category, with over 55 percent of owners indicating their consent. Almost 20 percent of owners would require a fee with some type of agreement and 12 percent would have no requirements whatsoever.

Table IV.35: Percentage of Landowners by Type of Access Arrangement and Region, 1995-96

Types of Access Arrangement	U.S. Overall	Region North	South	Pacific Coast	Rocky Mountains
Obtain lease agreement and pay fee	11.1	7.1	15.4	5.1	13.5
Obtain lease agreement, no fee	0.4	0.0	0.7	0.9	0.5
Written permission only	13.6	12.7	14.8	19.3	11.3
Fee only	0.6	0.4	0.5	3.4	0.6
Written permission and a fee	4.1	2.3	5.1	9.5	5.3
Verbal permission and a fee	2.7	2.6	2.9	2.6	2.8
Verbal permission, no fee	55.8	62.6	50.4	49.8	551.5
No requirements	11.7	12.3	10.2	9.4	14.4

Source: National Private Landowners Survey (NPLOS), Environmental Resource Assessment Group, Athens, Ga.

Landowner Demographics

Almost 85 percent of private landowners across the nation classify themselves as full-time employed and 15 percent as part-time employed (Figure IV.14). Thirty percent of owners reported being self-employed (Table IV.36). Approximately 40 percent across the country have completed no more than high school, while 33 percent had received a bachelor's or higher degree from college (Table IV.37). Ninety-three percent of the landowner population is white, the average age was 60, and three quarters were male (Table IV.38). Almost 60 percent of all private landowners lived on a farm in what they consider to be a rural area, while almost 12 percent reported living in a large to very large city (Figure IV.15). Almost all private owners said they were citizens of the U.S. and 98.3 percent said they were born in the U.S. (Table IV.39). Mean household size of the owners was just under two (Table IV.40). Average annual family income at the national level was about $55,000, 13.6 percent made over $100,000 and three percent made less than $5,000 (Figure IV.16).

Table IV.36: Percent of Landowners by Type of Employment and by Region, 1995-96

Employment	U.S. Overall	Region North	South	Pacific Coast	Rocky Mountains
Retired	38.8	36.6	42.7	27.6	38.4
Unemployed and actively looking for work	0.4	0.6	0.3	1.0	0.2
Unemployed but not actively looking for work	0.4	0.5	0.6	0.0	0.1
Federal, state, or local government employee	8.0	7.8	8.4	9.3	7.1
Employee of private business or corporation	18.8	20.8	18.4	17.9	13.8
Self-employed	30.1	30.5	25.4	43.2	37.4
Housewife or househusband	3.4	3.2	4.0	1.0	3.0
Other	0.1	0.0	0.2	0.0	0.0

Source: National Private Landowners Survey (NPLOS), Environmental Resource Assessment Group, Athens, Ga.

Table IV.37: Percent of Landowners by Education Level and by Region, 1995-96

Education Level	U.S. Overall	North	Region South	Pacific Coast	Rocky Mountains
Grades 1 to 8	5.4	4.7	6.5	3.3	5.0
Some high school	6.2	6.4	6.9	3.9	4.6
Graduate high school	27.9	33.6	23.6	17.6	25.6
Some college	21.4	19.5	22.4	22.7	23.9
Completed an associates degree	7.1	6.9	6.5	13.1	7.4
Graduate undergraduate college	16.9	14.3	19.1	20.8	17.3
Completed a master's degree	9.3	8.8	9.4	8.0	11.2
Completed a doctorate degree	5.8	5.8	5.5	10.6	5.0
Other	0.0	0.0	0.1	0.0	0.0

Source: National Private Landowners Survey (NPLOS), Environmental Resource Assessment Group, Athens, Ga.

Table IV.38: Percent of Landowners by Race, Age and Sex and by Region, 1995-96

Owner Characteristic	U.S. Overall	North	Region South	Pacific Coast	Rocky Mountains
White, not of Hispanic origin	92.5	93.9	89.9	92.1	95.6
Hispanic or Latino	1.4	0.9	1.1	5.1	2.6
African American	1.5	0.2	3.8	0.0	0.1
Native American	4.5	4.9	5.2	2.1	1.7
Asian or Pacific Islander	0.1	0.1	0.0	0.7	0.0
Other	0.0	0.0	0.0	0.0	0.0
Mean Age	59.5	58.6	60.6	57.6	60.1
Male	76.1	80.8	71.1	80.3	74.6
Female	23.9	19.2	28.9	19.7	25.4

Source: National Private Landowners Survey (NPLOS), Environmental Resource Assessment Group, Athens, Ga.

Figure IV.14: Percentage by Employment Type of Rural Private Landowners, by Region, 1995-96

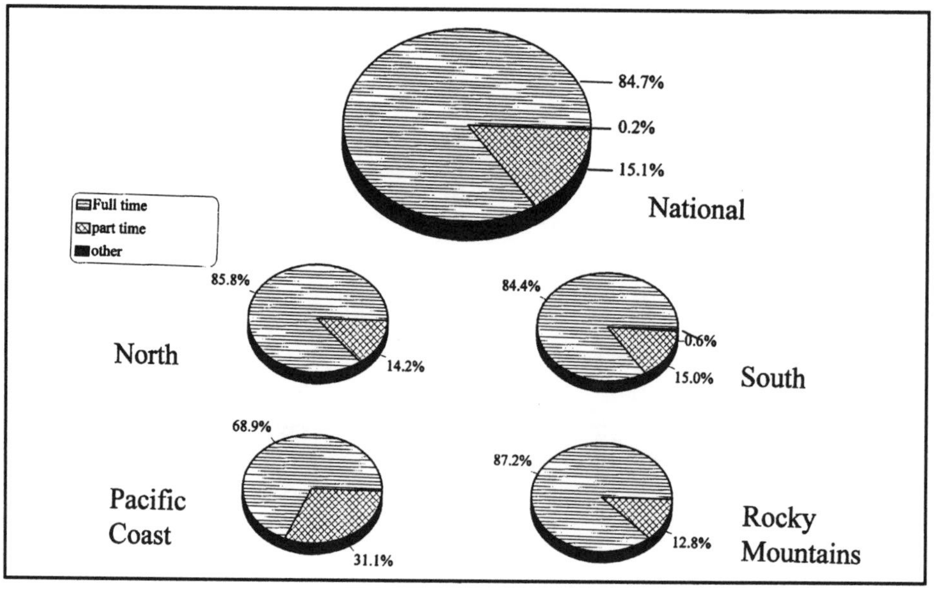

Figure IV.15: Percentage Classification of Where Rural Landowners Reside, by Region, 1995-96

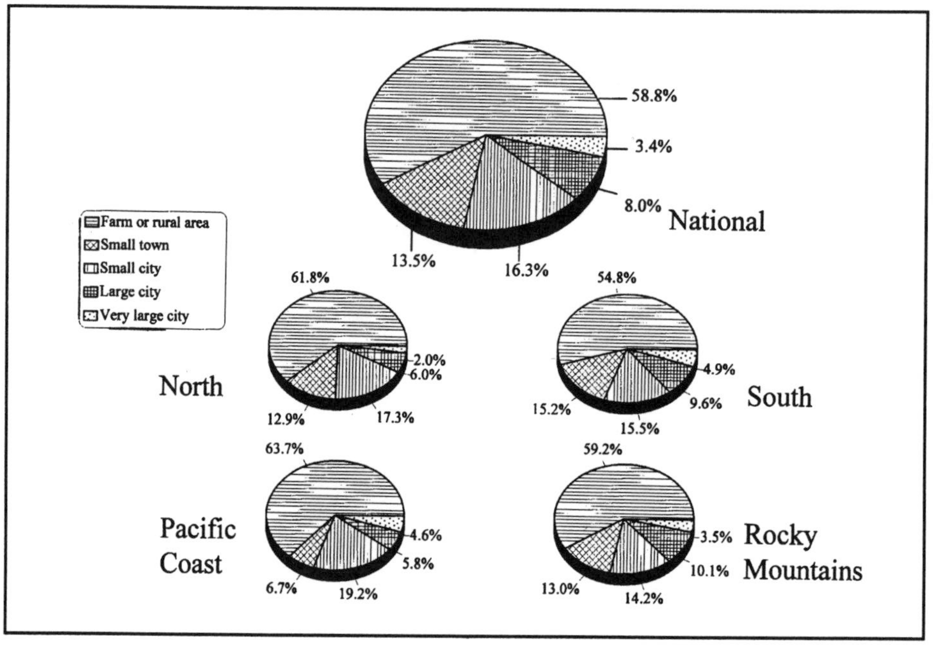

Figure IV.16: Percent of Household Income Categories of Rural Private Landowners, by Region, 1995-96

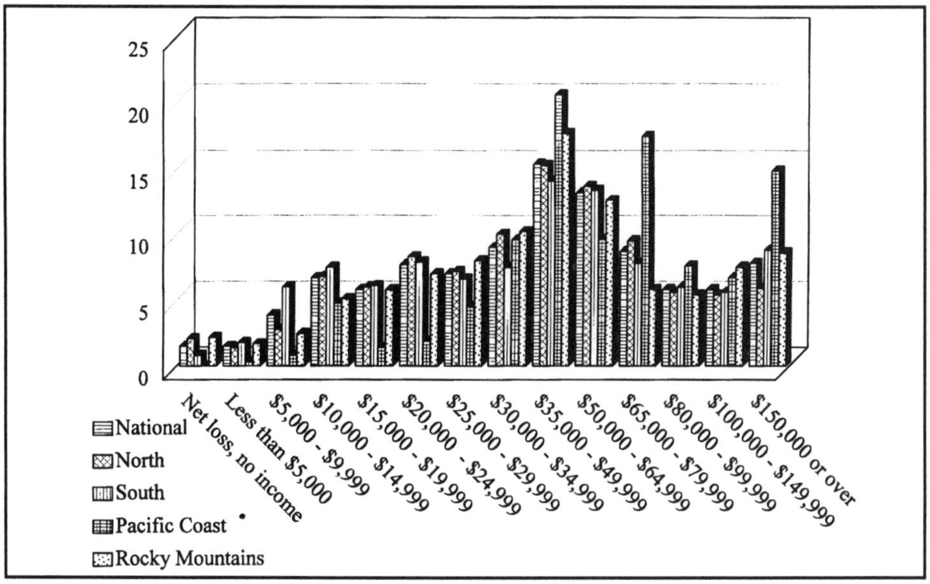

Table IV.39: Percent of Landowners by Citizenship and Birthplace and by Region, 1995-96

Citizenship and Birthplace	U.S. Overall	Region North	South	Pacific Coast	Rocky Mountains
U.S. Citizen	99.7	99.9	99.9	95.3	100.0
Born in U.S.	98.3	97.4	99.4	97.3	98.7

Source: National Private Landowners Survey (NPLOS), Environmental Resource Assessment Group, Athens, Ga.

Table IV.40: Mean Number in Household Members by Region, 1995-96

Number in Household	U.S. Overall	Region North	South	Pacific Coast	Rocky Mountains
Mean number of children	0.6	0.6	0.5	0.7	0.5
Mean number of relatives	0.1	0.1	0.2	0.03	0.1
Mean number of unrelated others	0.1	0.1	0.1	0.1	0.1
Mean household size	1.8	1.8	1.7	1.8	1.7

Source: National Private Landowners Survey (NPLOS), Environmental Resource Assessment Group, Athens, Ga.

Summary

The majority of rural landowners in the U.S. are white and over 60 years of age. They have owned their land for more than 20 years. The national average tract size, as indicated by the NPLOS, is almost 140 acres. The range of tract size observed in the NPLOS was from 10 to almost 40,000 acres. Almost half of the total hold other tracts of land and live on the tract asked about in our questionnaire. Of those who do not live on the land, 60 percent live within 20 miles. However, among those who do not live on their land, almost 30 percent have a residence over 100 miles away.

A substantial percentage of private lands border public lands, especially in the West. Also, many tracts adjoin a paved public road and have streams or rivers running through them. Only a small proportion of owners have added to or sold any of their land. Those who have tended to add more than they sold for a net gain in average tract size. Most of those who did sell some of their land did so because they got a good offer when they needed the money and sold to someone they knew, either a family member, friend, relative, or someone local. Many rural landowners said they own their land primarily for aesthetic reasons such as, "enjoying their own green space," "providing a place for wildlife," and just "living in a rural environment." More landowners feel that "people should rule over nature", but also feel rather strongly that there must be a "balance between human use of the environment and its maintenance." Over 70 percent of rural landowners expect to use their land for making money, but they also plan to put some effort into maintaining the natural components of the land. While it seems that rural landowners believe the environment needs to be protected, at the same time they are leery of private property rights being limited by an outside agency.

Rural landowners have definite plans for the land they own. Some of the plans listed include selling all or part of their land to make a profit, but 12 percent of owners indicated plans to add land to their existing holdings. They use a variety of ways to earn income from their land, including grazing cattle, sharecropping and leasing to outside interests. Harvesting timber products seems to be one of the major commercial uses of rural land. The last wood product harvesting, including firewood, pulpwood, and lumber, as a national average, was about nine years ago for most owners. This reflects the rotating nature of growing trees for sale. Only 10 percent of landowners used any kind of forestry incentive program, and their major sources of information for farm or forestry operations are the Cooperative Extension Service or the Natural Resources Conservation Service. Many landowners have engaged in conservation practices, including planting trees, improving habitat for wildlife, and using burns to control unwanted vegetation. Some owners are consciously using wetland conservation practices.

Protecting their land seemed of great importance to most owners. One way of doing this is through posting. Approximately 40 percent of landowners reported posting their property, and of those who post, the average acreage per tract is 200 acres. Some of the more significant problems landowners have had, which may have led them to take protective measures, were destruction of property, littering, poaching, and disruption of privacy. Landowners said they began posting so they would know who was on their property and when, to prevent damage to property and livestock, and to be safe. The percentage of reserved land that was posted closely parallels that percentage of the overall acreage owners typically post. Close to 80 percent of the land leased to clubs or individuals for recreation has been posted, either by the club or by the owner. Ninety-eight percent of landowners said they would post the same or even more of their acreage in the future.

Learning more about recreation on private land was one of the main reasons for undertaking NPLOS. A major determinant of the amount of recreation that occurs on private lands is accessibility of the land to outsiders. One-third of rural owners said portions of their tract were completely closed to all people outside their family. Nationally, owners said they kept a private reserve of land equal to about 65 acres for their use only. Over 70 percent of landowners across the U.S. reported that they engaged in recreational activities on their own land, and almost 50 percent said they had allowed access to people outside their family. Only 15 percent of rural landowners said they made some option of their land available to access by outside people. The largest percentage of landowners allowed only family, friends, and other people they knew personally. Landowners who allowed use reported the average number of people using their land as 14 per year. Of the different categories of people who recreated on private land, the number of times family members used the land per year was approximately 95, and use by people outside the family was well over 100 times per year.

Many types of recreational activities were pursued on private land. Hunting, fishing, hiking, and camping were among the top activities listed. Activities less frequently mentioned were swimming, nature study, and target shooting. When landowners were asked why they allowed access to their land for recreation, most said it was to maintain good will with their neighbors and others, and a notable percentage said it helped to pay taxes and provided income. Rural owners reported that they have changed little on the issue of access in the past five years, although there does seem to be a trend to limit more land in the future.

Some landowners get income by granting access to groups outside their family. By and large they use this income to help pay taxes, but they also see other benefits, such as help from clubs and individuals who lease protecting their land. Typically, a landowner leases to only one group. For the most part, this lease is a written agreement with a fee. Three-quarters of leasing owners charged by the year or hunting season, and close to 90 percent said the lease covered a "season or year." Many owners said they leased at a rate slightly lower than the going rate to entice lessees who they felt they could trust take care of the land. Aside from leasing, few landowners seem to be using daily or other pay-as-you-go fees as a source of income. Such fees probably are a viable alternative only if the land has notable and saleable recreational attributes. According to most landowners, outside people will be permitted to use their land in the future if they obtain verbal permission, and there will be no fee.

The concern about liability is always an issue for landowners. The primary way landowners manage liability is by having the club or individual who is leasing carry insurance or by carrying insurance themselves.

Almost 40 percent of rural landowners listed themselves as retired and almost 50 percent reported being self-employed or employed by a private business or corporation. A little over 10 percent of private owners said they had not completed high school and 28 percent said they had no more than high school. Six percent of landowners across the U.S. said they had completed a doctoral degree. Outside of whites, who represent the overwhelming majority of rural owners, the largest racial group owning rural land was Native Americans. They make up 4.5 percent of the landowner population. The most common single household income category reported was $35,000 to $50,000 per year. Households reporting incomes over $100,000 represented 13.6 percent of landowners across the country. The Pacific Coast had the highest concentration of those high-income households.

TRENDS

Comparing the 1996 NPLOS to the 1986 NPLOS (Wright, et al., 1988) we see several notable differences, but also many similarities. Landowner demographics seem to be changing slightly. There is a drop in white ownership from 96 percent in the 1986 NPLOS to 93 percent in the 1996 NPLOS. There are slightly more female landowners (80 percent male in 1986, vs. 76 percent male in 1996) and the average age of owners in the U.S. has risen almost two years to 60. Family size has dropped by approximately one person per household and there are fewer self-classified retirees as owners. The largest change demographically between the two studies is in household income and education level. Reported household incomes have risen from an average of just over $35,300 in 1986 to approximately $55,500 in the 1996 study. Educationally, there is a percentage decline in the category of "high school graduates only" but the percentage is picked up in the greater number of landowners who reported finishing a college degree, either an associate's or bachelor's. The percentage of owners claiming a graduate degree has changed little and is still approximately 15 percent.

Ownership patterns also seem to have changed somewhat. Forty-seven percent of landowners in the 1996 study said they lived on their land, whereas only 38 percent responded the same for the 1986 survey. However, where 90 percent of landowners said they lived within 20 miles of their land in 1986, only 50 percent indicated the same in 1996. The number of years owners have had their tracts has dropped somewhat from 23.3 to 21.3 years in the 10 years between surveys. Average reported tract size has decreased from 183 acres in 1986 to 138 in 1996.[6] Hunting remains the most popular recreational activity pursued on private lands, although a number of other activities are gaining in popularity and are higher on the list reported by the landowner. The percentage of owners who post at least some portion of their lands has risen from 33 percent in 1986 to 41 percent in 1996. The average number of acres owners posted per tract has decreased slightly from 232 acres to 206.

Though the way in which the questions were worded to respondents were slightly different between the surveys, it seems that access for recreation to individuals who the landowner does not know (open land) has decreased from 25 percent to 15 percent. Access to private land by individuals known by the landowner has remained close to the same (47 percent in 1986 and 50 percent in 1996). Leasing of land by landowners for recreation has also remained close to the same, with only three percent of landowners reporting they leased land in 1996 and slightly less than four percent responding the same in 1986.

---

[6] More investigation needs to be done on acreage comparison between the two studies, however, for the 1986 NPLOS limited its sample to tracts larger than 20 acres and the 1996 cutoff was 10 acres. Using the 1996 data but increasing the lower limit to 20 acres gives a mean tract size of approximately 186.

DISCUSSION

The right to own land, especially rural land, is an important part of our heritage as Americans. Rural landowners are seen by many as the backbone of our society. As farm acreage is taken out of agricultural production, either by urban sprawl or the ravages of the agricultural market, it drives rural owners to find other values and ways of using their lands. Because recreation is a major part of American lifestyles, access to private rural land is critical in assessing outdoor recreation opportunities in the United States.

Nearly 60 percent of all land in the U.S. is privately owned. The rural private portion of this "estate" supports a large number of recreational activities. A small portion of private land is open to recreation without any restriction. Other, larger portions are available through leasing or by asking permission from the owners.

Rural private owners are very interested in the management of their land. Because most owners live on or within 50 miles of it, they are able to watch the effects of their land management closely. A number of owners take part in wetland conservation practices and even more use local Cooperative Extension Service and Natural Resource Conservation Service field offices as sources of information about farm and forestry practices. Landowners seemed to be aware of environmental situations that may affect their land as well. However, the thought of an outside entity exercising control over their land uses is not an acceptable approach.

Overall, landowners seem to make quite a bit of their land available for recreation outside of their own family, with approximately half allowing people outside their family to recreate on their land as long as they know them. Private land, therefore, provides substantial recreation opportunities. In many cases, the accessibility to private lands may be somewhat greater than accessibility to public lands. This is especially true if one looks at public access in terms of the distance the majority of the population lives from the land. Centers of population are quite a bit further from public land in the North and South than they are in the West, where most of the public land exists.

Landowners seem much more comfortable with use of their land by people they know than by people outside their family or circle of friends. This tendency was evidenced both by the percentages of owners allowing certain group classifications to use their land and by the responses given for posting lands.

Liability issues are persistent and of increasing concern to rural landowners, but few take actions to limit their liability. An exception is in the North, where the majority of landowners have insurance. However, given the prevalence of litigation in the U.S., the issue of granting access and risking a lawsuit seems a major influence on the availability of private land for public recreational use. This possibility is reinforced by landowner predictions that they will make less land available in the future.

Despite liability problems, most landowners seemed open to the possibility of providing some form of public access to their lands. For example, when answering the question of why they allow outside access, owners overwhelmingly said it was to maintain goodwill with their neighbors and others.

Generally, limited public access to private land in the U.S. has been, and is expected to remain, fairly stable. Access is for the most part dictated by location. Without potentially large incomes to support leasing, most urbanites will not be able to require access to private land. Landowners usually grant permission to use their lands based mainly on their familiarity with the recreationist or the trustworthiness of the lessee.

However, because many urban dwellers do not participate in the types of recreational activities that occur on rural private land, limited access for these activities found in the NPLOS may not constrain the overall availability of appropriate recreational opportunities much. Referring back to the 1994-95 NSRE study (Cordell, et al., 1997), we see high rates of participation in many activities that are either land attribute intensive (e.g., caving, rock climbing, downhill skiing, etc.) or facility intensive (e.g., visiting nature centers, team sports, camping, etc.). For the most part, these types of activities do not occur on private rural land. Also, from a review of associated literature, it seems that most city dwellers do not have the means or the time to spend traveling past urban areas to take advantage of recreational opportunities on private land, even if those opportunities are available.

Recreation activities with the greatest potential for future demand on private land include hunting and fishing, wildlife observation, and hiking. According to NPLOS, hunting was the number one activity pursued on private land. Even though NSRE results (Cordell, et al., 1997) suggest reduced participation in hunting, it is expected that demand for high-quality lease hunting on private land will remain high. Trends also suggest there may be increased opportunity for leasing private land for warm and cold water fishing, as well as for camping.

Trends also suggest growing opportunities to lease private land for non-consumptive recreation activities. For example, NPLOS showed that hiking was a major use of private lands in the Pacific Coast. This result suggests the possibility of leasing land, for example, to private hiking clubs. Also, NSRE results (Cordell, et al., 1997) show very high participation in wildlife observation. This result suggests opportunities for leasing private land for wildlife observation. Private land may also be made available without a fee to individuals and groups engaging in wildlife observation.

Some type of intermediary brokerage service could perhaps give landowners and potential urban users a communication link to help in expanding the recreation market for private land. Given the propensity of landowners to allow access mostly to those they know personally and the potential demand for outdoor recreation that exists in urban areas, a service that would screen potential users for the landowner and make opportunities on private land available to urbanites could increase the utilization of and income from private lands for recreation. This approach could benefit private rural landowners while providing high-quality, low-cost recreation to segments of the population that otherwise might never go past the urban fringe.

REFERENCES

Alig, R. J. (1986). Econometric analysis of forest acreage trends in the Southeast. *Forest Science, 32*(1), 119-134.

Alig, R. J., & Healy, R. (1987). Urban and built-up land area changes in the United States: An empirical investigation of determinants. *Land Economics, 63*(3), 215-226.

Houghton Mifflin Company. (1994). *American heritage college dictionary*. New York: Author.

Barlowe, R. (1986). *Land resource economics: The economics of real estate*. Englewood Cliffs, NJ: Prentice-Hall.

Brown, J. L., Decker, D. J., & Kelley, J. W. (1984). Access to private lands for hunting in New York: 1963-1980. *Wildlife Society Bulletin, 12*, 344-349.

Brueckner, J. K., & Fangler, D. A. (1983). The economics of urban sprawl: Theory and evidence on the spatial sizes of cities. *Review of Economics and Statistics, 50*, 479-482.

Cordell, H. K., English, D. B., & Randall, S. (1993). *Effects of subdivision and access restrictions on private land recreation opportunities.* Athens, GA: U.S. Department of Agriculture, Forestry Service, Southern Research Station.

Cordell, H. K., McDonald, B. L., Briggs, J. A., Teasley, R. J., Biesterfeldt, R., Bergstrom, J., & Mou, S. (1997). *Emerging markets for outdoor recreation in the United States*. Athens, GA: U.S. Department of Agriculture, Forest Service, Southern Research Station.

Dillman, D. A. (1978). *Mail and telephone surveys.* New York: John Wiley & Sons.

Geisler, Charles. (1993). Ownership: An overview. *Rural Sociology, 58*(4), 532-546.

Kaiser, R. A., & Wright, B. A. (1985, November-December). Recreational access to private lands: Beyond the liability hurdle. *Journal of Soil and Water Conservation*, 478-481.

Madison, C. (1988). The land and water conservation fund: Paying for a nation's playground. *Nature Conservancy Magazine, 38*(5), 4-7.

Meyer, P. (1979, January). Land rush. *Harper's Magazine, 258*, 45-60.

Tindall, B. (1990). Reflections on the past, perspectives on the future. *America's heritage. Proceedings of a symposium on the 25th anniversary of the Land and Water Conservation Fund.* Arlington, VA: National Recreation and Parks Association.

Wright, B. A. (1986, Summer). Recreational access and landowner liability in Virginia: Protection for landowners. *Virginia Forests*, 14-15.

Wright, B. A., & Fesenmaier, D. R. (1988). Modeling rural landowners' hunter access policies in east Texas, USA. *Environmental Management, 12*(2), 229-236.

Wright, B. A., & Fesenmaier, D. R. (1990). A factor analytic study of attitudinal structure and its impact on rural landowners' access policies. *Environmental Management, 14*(2), 269-277.

Wright, B. A., Cordell, H. K., & Brown, T. L. (1988). Recreational access to non-industrial private lands in the U.S. In B. A. Wright, H. K. Cordell, T. L. Brown, & B. Sales (Eds.), *Proceedings of Society of American Foresters annual conference* (1-25). Bethesda, MD: Society of American Foresters.

Wright, B. A., Kaiser, R., & Fletcher, J. (1988). Hunter access decisions by rural landowners: An east Texas example. *Wildlife Society Bulletin, 16*(2), 152-158.

Wright, B. A., & Kaiser, R. A. (1986). Wildlife administrators' perceptions of hunter access problems: A national overview. *Wildlife Society Bulletin, 14*(1), 30-34.

Wright, B. A., Cordell, H. K., Brown, T. L., & Rowell, A. L. (1988). The national private land ownership study: Establishing the benchmark. In A. H. Watson (Comp.), *Outdoor recreation benchmark 1988: Proceedings of the National Outdoor Recreation Forum* (33-50). Asheville, NC: U.S. Department of Agriculture, Forest Service, Southern Research Station.

Wunderlich, G. (1993). The land question: Are there answers? *Rural Sociology, 58*(4), 547-559.

Additional Readings

Harris, Marshall. (1953). *Origin of the land tenure system.* Ames, IA: Iowa State College Press.

CHAPTER V

OUTDOOR RECREATION PARTICIPATION TRENDS

. . . .

H. Ken Cordell[1]
Barbara L. McDonald
R. Jeff Teasley
John C. Bergstrom
Jack Martin
Jim Bason
Vernon R. Leeworthy

Invited Papers:

Deborah J. Chavez, USDA Forest Service
Richard J. Bowers & Richard R. Hoffman, American Whitewater Affiliation
Paul J. Baicich, Gregory S. Butcher, & Paul Green, American Birding Association
Cassandra Johnson, USDA Forest Service
Patricia L. Winter & Deborah J. Chavez, USDA Forest Service
J.M. Bowker, D.B.K. English, & G. Bhat, USDA Forest Service & University of Georgia
Richard Stenger, Free Lance Journalist
Daniel McLean, Indiana University
D.B.K. English & D. Marcoullier, USDA Forest Service & University of Wisconsin
Joseph O'Leary, Purdue University
Elwood Shafer, Pennsylvania State University
David J. Humphreys, Recreation Vehicle Industry Association
Alan Lane, United Four Wheel Drive Association
Jeffrey A. Yeager, American Canoe Association
Molly Chaffinch, American Horse Council
Gary MacFadden, Adventure Cycling Association
Barbara J. Turner
Celeste McCaleb and BASS Inc. Staff, Bass Anglers Sportsman Society
Adena Cook, BlueRibbon Coalition
Sally Moser and Sam Davidson, The Access Fund
Eric J. Lundquist, American Motorcyclist Association

Acknowledgments:
The National Survey on Recreation and the Environment (NSRE) has been a collaborative effort involving many along the way. This chapter is intended as the final national summary report on findings from the NSRE. Sponsoring organizations include:

---

[1]H. Ken Cordell is a research forester and project leader, USDA Forest Service, Athens, GA; Barbara L. McDonald is a research scientist, USDA Forest Service, Washington, D.C.; R. Jeff Teasley is a research coordinator, John C. Bergstrom is a professor, Jack Martin is an administrative director, and Jim Bason is a research coordinator, University of Georgia, Athens, GA; and Vernon R. Leeworthy is chief economist, National Oceanic and Atmospheric Administration, Washington, D.C.

USDA Forest Service (Research, RPA Recreation and Wildlife Divisions) (FS)
The University of Georgia (UGA)
USDI Bureau of Land Management (BLM)
DOD Corps of Engineers (COE)
The Sporting Goods Manufacturers Association (SGMA)
The Environmental Protection Agency (EPA)
DOC National Oceanic and Atmospheric Administration (NOAA)
USDA Economic Research Service (ERS)
USDI National Park Service (NPS)

Key individuals contributing (in addition to the authors) include:

Sandy Briggs, SGMA
Burt Lewis, Mt. Olive College
Morgan Miles, Georgia Southern University
Bill Hausen, COE
Jay McConnell, FS (retired)
Greg Super, FS
Merle Van Horne, NPS
Alan Watson, FS
Mary Jo Keely, (formerly EPA)
Dan Hellerstein, ERS
Del Price, BLM (retired)
Hal Hallett, BLM
Andrew Schretter, Duke University
Rita Peacock, UGA
Shela Mou, FS
Bob Leeworthy, NOAA
Ed Hamilton, Indiana University
Cindy Swanson, FS

INTRODUCTION

As part of this national assessment of outdoor recreation trends, we have taken a look at participation patterns and levels of participation across activities and across segments of our society. The primary source of data is the National Survey on Recreation and the Environment (NSRE). The NSRE is the latest in the continuing series of National Recreation Surveys conducted by the federal government since 1960 (Cordell, 1995). The NSRE covers participation in over 80 activities, ranging from casual walking outdoors to more challenging activities such as rock climbing and white water canoeing.

This chapter on outdoor recreation participation first looks at national participation in land-, water-, and snow- and ice-based recreation activities. Long-term trends are covered, tracking some activities back to the original national survey done in 1960. To examine geographic patterns, differences in population percentages across Census regions and divisions are explored, with a focus on activities with the greatest differences. To further explore geographic patterns, selected activities are mapped at county scale to show more detailed patterns of participation across and within regions. Intensity of participation is described using days and trips away from home as the measure of involvement in outdoor activities. Participation differences among social groups in American society are examined, and constraints to participation described.

The closing sections of this chapter include descriptions of visits to federal and state recreation areas, international tourism in the United States, outdoor recreation consumer spending trends, and economic effects of outdoor recreationists' spending.

NATIONAL PARTICIPATION ESTIMATES

Design, collection, and analysis of data for the National Survey on Recreation and the Environment are covered in Technical Appendix V.[2] Generally, the raw data from the survey were weighted to adjust for disproportionate representation of people 16 years old or older in the NSRE sample relative to the distribution in the population by age, sex, and racial stratum as estimated in the 1990 Census of U.S. Population and Housing.

General Types of Participation

Thirteen basic types of outdoor recreation participation were surveyed (Table V.1). An estimated 94.5 percent of the population reported that during the 12 months just prior to their interview for the NSRE in 1994-95, they participated in one or more of the activities included in the survey activity list. This percentage, referred to as "global" participation, amounts to over 189 million people age 16 or older. Level of participation and activities pursued, as would be expected, varied greatly among different social strata within the sample. In the 1982-83 National Recreation Survey, 89 percent indicated participation in one of more of the 36 activities listed in that survey (Van Horne, Szwak, & Randall, 1986). While it appears that participation in the U.S. overall has been increasing in recent years, one suspected reason for the magnitude of difference between the global estimates in 1982-83 and 1994-95 is the longer list of activities used in the more recent survey.

Across all of the 13 types of participation, the four most popular single activities were:

Walking	66.7 percent
Viewing a beach or waterside	62.1 percent
Family gatherings outdoors	61.8 percent
Sightseeing	56.6 percent

The most popular types of outdoor participation, as measured by the number of people reporting they had participated in one or more of the activities of those types, include viewing- and learning-oriented activities, such as bird watching (almost 153 million participants); trail, street, and road activities such as biking (nearly 137 million participants); social activities such as picnicking (136 million); spectator activities outdoors such as attending an outdoor concert (118 million); and swimming in pools and natural waters, sometimes with a snorkel or scuba gear (approaching 109 million). For the most part, these types of activities are relatively low cost, can be pursued without a great deal of physical exertion, and do not require special equipment or skills. Most of these types of activities remain popular among Americans past the age of 60.

Table V.1: Percent and Number of People 16 Years and Older in the U.S. Participating in 13 Types of Outdoor Recreational Activities, 1994-95

Type of outdoor activity	Percent of population 16 or older	Number in millions
Participated in any type of activity	94.5	189.3
Trail/street/road activities	68.3	136.9
Individual sports	22.0	44.1
Team sports	26.4	53.0
Spectator activities	58.7	117.6
Viewing/learning activities	76.2	152.6
Snow and ice activities	18.1	36.3

[2]This technical appendix is available in table form from the USDA Forest Service, Outdoor Recreation and Wilderness Assessment Group, 320 Green Street, Athens, GA 30602-2044. Herein all references to Technical Appendices shall be abbreviated as TAs.

Table V.1 Cont.

Type of outdoor activity	Percent of population 16 or older	Number in millions
Camping (all overnight)	26.3	52.8
Hunting	9.3	18.6
Fishing	28.9	57.9
Boating/floating	29.0	58.1
Swimming	54.2	108.6
Outdoor adventure activities	36.8	73.6
Social activities	67.8	135.9

Source: 1994-95 National Survey on Recreation and the Environment, USDA Forest Service and the University of Georgia, Athens, Georgia. The NSRE is the most recent of the series of National Recreation Surveys begun nationally in 1960.

Individual and team sports constitute another category of participation. Team sports, including baseball, football, and soccer, are participated in at least once annually by 53 million people. Soccer is a particularly fast-growing sport, but many of the players are less than 16 years old—too young to be included in our sample. Individual sports include tennis and golf. Just over 44 million people are estimated to have participated at least once in the past 12 months in individual sports. Both individual and team sports typically require some sort of specially designed site for participation, such as tennis courts or baseball fields. Most of these facilities are provided by local government or the private sector.

Camping is a traditional form of outdoor recreation. In the U.S. during the 1994-95 survey period, an estimated 52.8 million people 16 or older went camping overnight at least once. This number is just over one fourth of the population of that age. Camping includes staying overnight near roads in developed campgrounds such as those provided on national forests or national parks, and especially those in state parks. Camping also includes staying overnight in more primitive settings lacking most of the amenities of a developed campground. For most primitive camping, one must carry water and provide all camping facilities, such as a table.

Consumptive wildlife (terrestrial) or fish activities include various forms of hunting or fishing. Hunting, as will be shown later, is one of the few steadily declining activities in this country. Cultural shifts and the difficulty of finding places to hunt seem to be the primary reasons for this decline. Just over nine percent of the U.S. population over 15 participates in this seasonal activity, mostly in the middle to late fall of the year. Fishing is much more popular, and opportunities to do it are more abundant because many lakes, rivers, and ocean fronts have numerous boat ramps and fishing piers for public access. Fishing includes saltwater and warm and cold freshwater settings. Coldwater fishing includes fishing for salmon and other anadromous (migratory) species.

Motorized and nonmotorized boating and floating on water are participated in by just over 58 million people. Introduction of jet skis has dramatically changed the nature of boating in America since the last national survey done in the early 1980s. Floating includes tubing (inner tubes or manufactured floating tubes) and rafting, where oars or paddles are used mainly for steering. Commercial floating outfitters are becoming more numerous.

When the phrase "outdoor recreation" is mentioned, many think of activities like mountain climbing and backpacking in remote areas. We have classed these more challenging activities as outdoor adventure. They generally involve physically challenging settings away from roads and developed sites. Nearly 74 million, over one-third of the population, participate in outdoor adventure activities.

Land-Based Activities

Activities that occur primarily on land, rather than on water or snow and ice, constitute the largest single category of outdoor recreational participation in the country. Trail, street, and road activities; viewing and learning activities; camping of various forms; hunting; outdoor adventure; and a limited number of social activities are discussed below as they occur primarily on land.

Trail, Street, and Road Activities

By far the single most popular activity in the United States is walking outdoors. An estimated 133.7 million, two thirds of all of the 200 million people in the U. S. 16 or older (at time of survey), participated one or more times per year (Table V.2). Participation can occur on neighborhood streets and walking trails, as well as in more remote settings such as at Bureau of Land Management recreation sites. Biking is the next most popular trail, street, and road activity with over 57 million participants. Of people who bike, an estimated 6.4 million bike long distances and participate in bike touring. This activity occurs on roads and highways all across the United States. Running and jogging has over 52 million participants, over 26 percent of the population 16 and older. Serious runners make up a much smaller proportion than this percentage, which includes many who are casual joggers putting in a mile or two once every few days.

Table V.2: Percent and Number of People 16 Years and Older in the U.S. Participating in Land-Resource-Based Outdoor Activities, 1994-95

Type of outdoor activity	Percent of population 16 or older	Number in millions
Trail/Street/Road Activities		
Running/jogging	26.2	52.5
Biking	28.6	57.4
Long distance biking	3.2	6.4
Walking	66.7	133.7
Viewing/Learning Activities		
Visiting a nature center	46.4	93.1
Visiting a visitor center	34.6	69.4
Visit a prehistoric site	17.4	34.9
Visit a historic site	44.1	88.4
Bird-watching	27.0	54.1
Wildlife viewing	31.2	62.6
Other wildlife viewing	13.8	27.5
Sightseeing	56.6	113.4
Camping		
Developed area	20.7	41.5
RV developed camping	8.6	17.3
Tent developed camping	14.6	29.4
Primitive area	14.0	28.0
RV primitive camping	3.5	7.1
Tent primitive camping	10.7	21.5
Other camping	2.1	4.2
Hunting		
Big game	7.1	14.2
Small game	6.5	13.0
Migratory bird	2.1	4.3
Outdoor Adventure		
Hiking	23.8	47.8
Hiking to a summit	8.3	16.6
Orienteering	2.4	4.8

Table V.2 Cont.

Type of outdoor activity	Percent of population 16 or older	Number in millions
Backpacking	7.6	15.2
Backpacking to a summit	3.3	6.6
Mountain climbing	4.5	9.0
Rock climbing	3.7	7.5
Caving	4.7	9.5
Off-road driving	13.9	27.9
Horseback riding	7.1	14.3
Horseback riding on trails	5.2	10.4
Social Activities		
Picnicking	49.1	98.3
Family gathering	61.8	123.8

Source: 1994-95 National Survey on Recreation and the Environment, USDA Forest Service and the University of Georgia, Athens, Georgia. The NSRE is the most recent of the series of National Recreation Surveys begun nationally in 1960.

Viewing and Learning Activities

Visiting sites of interest and viewing wildlife are rapidly growing types of land-based outdoor recreation. Sightseeing, a loosely defined activity, is also a part of this type of participation, and it is the most popular of viewing and learning activities. As an outdoor activity, sightseeing is usually thought of as driving to interesting places to see whatever is there or whatever is going on. Sightseeing might include driving along the Blue Ridge Parkway in western North Carolina or driving the coast of Oregon when the fog is in, always with the hope of seeing seals or whales. Sightseeing can also include driving in cities or other highly–developed settings to see the sights, for example, azaleas in bloom in the spring in Madison, Georgia.

Nature centers, visitor centers, and other outdoor-oriented education facilities are popular in the United States. Over 93 million visit nature centers, many of which are local to most people's communities, and almost 70 million visit visitor centers, such as the Mt. St. Helens Visitor Center on the Mt. Baker-Snoqualmie National Forest in Washington. In addition, over 88 million visit historic sites, designated and undesignated. Historic sites might include a national battlefield, a preserved settler's cabin, or the Liberty Bell. Nearly 35 million are estimated to visit prehistoric sites such as Pueblo ruins or some of the Native American mounds in the eastern part of the country. Learning about the culture, natural environment, and history of sites is a significant outdoor recreation motivation if participation estimates are any evidence.

Fort Point National Historic Site, constructed in 1861 to guard the entrance to San Francisco Bay, is dwarfed by the Golden Gate Bridge. The Civil War fortress is a national historic site and is part of the Golden Gate National Recreation Area. Photo courtesy of USDI National Park Service. Photo by Richard Frear.

Viewing, feeding, and photographing birds and other wildlife have long been popular across all ages and social strata. Almost 63 million people in the U.S. over the age of 15 view mammals and reptiles. Just over 54 million watch birds, including song birds, raptors, sea birds, and waders. As will be shown later, appreciation of wildlife is one of the most rapidly growing forms of outdoor recreation.

Camping

Camping is something that quickly comes to mind when one is thinking about outdoor recreation trips. Most people have camped at one time or another in their lives. As shown in Table V.2, camping can occur in a variety of ways. In developed campgrounds, the most distinguishing characteristic is whether it involves an RV (recreational vehicle) or a tent. Across the country, over 41 million people camp at least once a year in a developed campground that includes restrooms, showers (usually), a campsite with table and fireplace, water, paved or gravel roads, and individual parking spaces. Over 17 million people camp in an RV, many of which are quite large and require hookups for electricity, water, and increasingly, phone and cable TV. See contributed paper by Humphreys on RV market at the end of this chapter. More people, over 29 million in 1994-95, however, pitch tents in campgrounds. By nearly a ratio of two to one, tent campers outnumber RV campers.

Camping in primitive settings is an activity of 28 million people, about 14 percent of Americans age 16 or older. These areas usually lack restrooms, hookups, and most facilities and services. Much primitive camping occurs along forest roads, at secondary road pulloffs, or at other places where access is possible. By a ratio of three to one, primitive campers use tents rather than RVs. This preference is of course to be expected since most RVs require hookups and nearly level parking.

Hunting

Three types of hunting are listed in Table V.2: big game, small game, and migratory birds. An estimated 14 million people hunt big game species, including deer, turkey, elk, and other large birds or mammals. Some 13 million hunt small game species, including squirrels, rabbits, and other small mammals. Just over four million hunt migratory birds, primarily ducks and geese. Overall, hunting is a declining activity in the United States.

Outdoor Adventure

Among the outdoor adventure types of activities shown in Table V.2, hiking is the most popular in terms of number of participants on an annual basis. Almost 24 percent of the population 16 years and older, about 48 million people, went hiking once or more during the 1994-95 survey period. Among hikers, over 16 million took their hike to reach a summit. Hiking is one of the principal uses of the massive system of trails in the United States. Backpacking differs from hiking in that it involves one or more nights camping on a trail and the need to carry food, shelter and utensils in a backpack. Over 15 million went backpacking; nearly seven million of those backpacking had a summit as a destination. Backpacking is one of the major uses of trails into remote public land.

Along with hiking and backpacking, many also use trails or go cross-country on horseback (over 14 million) or using off-road vehicles, such as motorcycles, four-wheel drive vehicles, or three-wheel ATVs (almost 28 million). Of the 14 million who went horseback riding, over 10 million did so on trails. Road shoulders, pastures, and rinks are also used for horseback riding. Off-road driving can be done in specially designated areas on public or private land, often where there are challenging hills and uneven terrain, or it can occur on the cleared rights-of-way along highways, on private cleared land, in power-line rights-of-way, or in many other venues. (See contributed paper on four-wheel recreation by Alan Lane at the end of this chapter.)

Social Activities

Table V.2 shows participation in outdoor picnics and family gatherings. Nearly half of the 200 million people 16 or older in the U.S. participate in picnicking. This experience can be as casual as a single person taking lunch in the nearby local park, or as elaborate as a full gourmet spread of cheeses, wines, pickles, and breads among friends. Often associated with picnicking are family gatherings outdoors. Throughout this country, group shelters and multiple family picnic sites have been developed to facilitate this very popular activity—124 million, or 62 percent of the population. Family gatherings frequently involve annual or less frequent reunions of relatives. Almost always they involve cooking outside, covered dishes brought from home, and sharing of memories.

Water-Based Activities

Boating and floating, fishing, swimming, and viewing activities are the types of water-based activities summarized in Table V.3.

Boating

By far the most popular boating activity is motor boating with 47 million participants, nearly 24 percent of the population 16 and older. Motor boats have gotten larger and more powerful engines in excess of 200 horsepower, often driving boats ranging well over 20 feet in length. Motor boating is very popular on Corps of Engineers, Bureau of Reclamation, and Tennessee Valley Authority reservoirs; on large rivers and in sounds; and on the ocean. Associated with motor boating is waterskiing, in which almost 18 million participate. Jet skiing is another form of engine-powered boating. Jet skiing is a relatively new activity brought about by jet water propulsion technology that has been marketed for fewer than 20 years. Its popularity has reached almost 10 million participants already. Jet skis and jet boats can be used in water not formerly accessible to conventional propeller-driven boats, such as river rapids, ocean surf, shallows, and narrow reaches of rivers and reservoirs.

Wind-powered boating (including sailboarding and windsurfing) is less popular than motorized forms of boating. Almost 10 million people sail and 2.2 million sailboard or windsurf. Sailing using a yacht can be very expensive, but it also can be done at relatively low cost (by renting or using smaller craft). Sailing usually requires large bodies of water with stretches that are not limited by low bridges or shallow water. Along with sailboarding and windsurfing, sailing a boat requires a relatively high amount of skill.

Muscle-powered boating and floating activities include canoeing, kayaking, rowing, and floating or rafting. Most of the 14 million canoeing participants use open-top canoes (13.5 million). Fewer than one million use closed-top canoes, typically designed and used for running stretches of whitewater rivers. Used almost exclusively for whitewater and ocean use, kayaks are used by 2.6 million. Kayaks are favored typically because of their maneuverability in confined places and in steering a course through rapids. (See contributed paper on paddlesports by Yeager at the end of this chapter.) A significant industry has developed to facilitate rafting and other floating on whitewater and other fast-moving streams. Raft rentals, shuttle services, and river guides are services provided mostly by the private sector on many popular stretches of rivers. Some outfitters have begun renting tubes for floating less dangerous stretches of rivers. This form of recreation outfitting seems to be growing rapidly.

Table V.3: Percent and Number of People 16 Years and Older in the U.S. Participating in Water-Resource-Based Outdoor Activities, 1994-95

Type of outdoor activity	Percent of population 16 or older	Number in millions
Boating/Floating		
Sailing	4.8	9.6
Canoeing	7.0	14.1
Open-top canoeing	6.8	13.5
Closed-top canoeing	0.4	0.8
Kayaking	1.3	2.6
Rowing	4.2	8.4
Floating, rafting	7.6	15.2
Motor-boating	23.5	47.0
Water skiing	8.9	17.9
Jet skiing	4.7	9.5
Sailboarding/windsurfing	1.1	2.2
Fishing		
Freshwater	24.4	48.8
Saltwater	9.5	19.0
Warmwater	20.4	40.8
Coldwater	10.4	20.8
Ice	2.0	4.0
Anadromous	4.5	9.1
Catch and release	7.7	15.5

Table V.3 Cont.

Type of outdoor activity	Percent of population 16 or older	Number in millions
Swimming		
Surfing	1.3	2.6
Swimming/pool	44.2	88.5
Swimming/non-pool	39.0	78.1
Snorkeling/scuba	7.2	14.5
Viewing Activities		
Fish viewing	13.7	27.4
Visiting a beach or waterside	62.1	124.4
Studying nature near water	27.6	55.4

Source: 1994-95 National Survey on Recreation and the Environment, USDA Forest Service and the University of Georgia, Athens, Georgia. The NSRE is the most recent of the series of National Recreation Surveys begun nationally in 1960.

Fishing

Fishing remains popular throughout the country. Sale of boats, fishing gear, bait and other related fishing supplies is an important source of revenue for many small stores as well as for numerous large-scale equipment manufacturing companies.

Fishing occurs in lakes, streams, and oceans. The type of water determines, in large part, the species sought and thus the type of fishing pursued. Of the nearly 58 million people in the U. S. who fish, nearly 49 million fish in fresh water. Among those who fish in fresh water, most, about 41 million, fish in warm water, a category of water bodies that includes most lakes, reservoirs, large rivers, and ponds. Bass, crappie, and other species are the most familiar and sought after. About 21 million age 16 and older fish for coldwater species, such as trout and northern pike. A special category of coldwater fishing is anadromous fishing for migratory species such as salmon. Just over nine million people fish for anadromous species.

It is further estimated that 19 million people fish in salt water including oceans (from shore and by boat), ocean inlets and sounds, tidal estuaries, and inland saltwater lakes. Along ocean saltwater shorelines, many private and public fishing piers have been constructed, and a large number of fishing guide and excursion businesses are in operation. In northern reaches of the country where lakes, rivers, and saltwater bodies freeze over in winter, ice fishing is enjoyed by an estimated four million people.

Fishing has long been a favorite American leisure time activity. This photo shows recreationists near East Point, Georgia, circa 1930s. Photo courtesy of the Hargrett Rare Book and Manuscript Library, University of Georgia Libraries.

In saltwater and freshwater, by choice or by state regulation, an estimated 15.5 million people fish by the catch-and-release method. Catch and release is regulated both by species and by size.

Swimming

Of the estimated 109 million people who swim out of doors, over 88 million are estimated to do at least some portion of their swimming in pools. Just over 78 million swim in "natural" waters such as streams, lakes, ponds, and oceans. Over 14 million are estimated to go snorkeling or scuba diving one or more times over the course of a year, and 2.6 million surf on conventional surfboards.

Viewing and Learning

Over three quarters of people over 15 participate in some form of viewing or learning activities. Water-related viewing or learning is an important part of this pursuit. Over 124 million people visit a beach or other waterside during the course of a year. For many, these visits are numerous. Studying nature near water is also popular, with over 55 million people participating. An activity just recently included in recreation participation studies is fish viewing. Over 27 million participate in some form of fish viewing, from watching trout in alpine lakes to observing fish in outdoor aquariums and fish hatcheries.

Snow–and Ice–Based Activities

Skiing, skating, and snowmobiling are the three types of snow and ice activities presented in Table V.4. Of the 36 million who participate in some form of snow and ice activity(ies), nearly 17 million ski, over 20 million sled, and 4.5 million snowboard downhill. Snowboarding is a relatively new activity that is rapidly growing in popularity. Snowboards are similar to skateboards or surfboards in concept. Snowboards afford a great deal more maneuverability than traditional long skis. Snowboarding and sledding do not require as much maintenance as downhill skiing slopes, but snowboarders benefit greatly from use of the lifts at skiing areas.

Table V.4: Percent and Number of People 16 Years and Older in the U.S. Participating in Snow- and Ice-Based Outdoor Activities, 1994-95

Type of outdoor activity	Percent of population 16 or older	Number in millions
Downhill Skiing		
Snowboarding	2.3	4.5
Sledding	10.2	20.5
Downhill skiing	8.4	16.8
Cross Country Skiing		
On groomed trails	2.7	5.4
On ungroomed trails	2.8	5.7
Back country	1.9	3.7
All forms	3.3	6.5
Ice skating	5.2	10.5
Snowmobiling	3.6	7.1

Source: 1994-95 National Survey on Recreation and the Environment, USDA Forest Service and the University of Georgia, Athens, Georgia. The NSRE is the most recent of the series of National Recreation Surveys begun nationally in 1960.

Cross-country skiing occurs on or off trails and can be on either groomed or ungroomed trails. Overall, 6.5 million people ski cross country, most of them in a variety of venues. An estimated 3.7 million ski cross-country in backcountry areas (self-defined), 5.7 million ski on ungroomed trails, and 5.4 million ski on groomed trails. Some 10.5 million ice skate and over 7 million snowmobile.

Days and Trips Taken for Recreational Activities

In addition to the percentages and numbers in the population who participate, it is highly useful to know how much participation is involved. In the NSRE, participants were asked how many trips 15 or more minutes away from home were taken for the primary purpose of participating in outdoor recreation and how many different days during the year participants engaged in various activities. In the sections that follow, recreation trips away from home and participation days are reported by the activity that was the primary motivation for participation. In addition to the mean number of trips and days on which participation occurred, estimates of total trips and days by activity are provided.

Land-Based Participation

Land-based recreational trips and days are shown in Table V.6. Mean number of trips specifically for participating in the activities listed range from a low of 1.7 for caving to a high of 13.2 for ORV driving. Most are in the range of four to eight trips per year to participate in the activities covered. Just behind off-road driving in mean number of trips per person per year are wildlife viewing (10.7), biking (9.6), sightseeing (9.1), and hiking (9.1).

Table V.6: Mean and Total Trips and Days per Year During that People 16 Years Older in the U.S. Participated in Land-Resource-Based Activities, 1994-95

Activity	Mean number of trips per participant per year[1]	Total trips per year for the U.S. (millions)	Mean number of days per participant per year[1]	Total days per year for the U.S. (millions)
Trail/Street/Road Activities				
Biking	9.6	553.02	39.0	2237.0
Bike touring	—[2]	—[2]	19.6	126.0
Walking	—[2]	—[2]	107.6	14381.4
Viewing/Learning Activities				
Visit a prehistoric site	2.8	96.13	5.0	175.6
Visit a historic site	3.0	264.31	5.5	482.4
Bird-watching	7.1	385.51	87.8	4749.2
Wildlife viewing	10.7	670.74	36.9	2307.9
Sightseeing	9.1	1036.90	18.0	2036.3
Camping				
Developed area	4.7	196.78	10.7	442.4
Primitive area	4.8	134.50	9.2	258.6
Hunting				
Big game	8.1	115.72	14.3	204.0
Small game	8.8	113.79	13.8	178.8
Migratory bird	5.7	24.44	7.8	33.5
Outdoor Adventure Activities				
Hiking	9.1	434.23	16.8	804.7
Orienteering	—[2]	—[2]	6.3	30.6
Backpacking	4.5	68.47	8.6	129.7
Mountain climbing	3.0	27.25	4.4	39.8
Rock climbing	3.5	26.10	5.1	37.7
Caving	1.7	15.83	2.4	22.3
Off-Road driving	13.2	368.83	24.6	685.5
Horseback riding	8.7	124.32	23.6	336.3
Social Activities				
Picnicking	5.3	518.74	8.8	861.9
Family gathering	6.3	778.45	8.8	1084.5

[1] Means for trips and days include only participants in the activity and are not computed on the basis of total population count.
[2] Trips were not asked in the National Survey on Recreation and the Environment for some activities.

Because some activities have large numbers of participants (see Table V.2), total trips per year across all participants is a very large number for some activities. From highest to lowest, the five activities with the most total trips include:

Sightseeing	1,037 million
Family Gatherings	778 million
Wildlife viewing	671 million
Biking	553 million
Picnicking	519 million.

Viewing and learning activities, such as visiting historic sites, wildlife viewing, and sightseeing, are among the nation's highest participation activities in terms of total number of trips taken to enjoy them. Many outdoor adventure activities, such as rock climbing, are among the lowest in total number of trips per year. These activities require either skill, specialized equipment, physical exertion, or all of the above.

The number of different days during which participants engaged in each activity is another measure of activity popularity. As referenced in the NSRE, days of participation are defined as the number of different days on which the activity was done, whether that participation was only for a few minutes or for the entire day.

The activity with the highest mean number of days was walking for exercise or pleasure, with nearly 108 days per person per year. Next were bird watching (88 days), biking (39), wildlife viewing (37), off-road driving (25), and horseback riding (24). (See contributed paper on the horse industry by Chaffinch at the end of this chapter.) The activities with the lowest mean number of days per participant per year were caving (just over two days) and mountain climbing (four). Among activities typically occurring on trails, streets, and roads, viewing and learning have the greatest mean numbers of days per participant per year.

Across all participants in the activities listed in Table V.6, large numbers of total days of participation are shown to have occurred during the 1994-95 survey period. The six activities with over one billion activity days during that period include:

Walking	14.4 billion
Bird watching	4.7 billion
Wildlife viewing	2.3 billion
Biking	2.2 billion
Sightseeing	2.0 billion
Family gathering	1.1 billion.

The activities with the lowest total days of participation are the outdoor adventure activities, which have both lower numbers of participants and lower average days of participation per person per year.

Trips and days of participation in water-based activities are shown in Table V.7. Although the number of participants is relatively small, number of trips per participant is highest for surfing at almost 22 trips per year. Next highest in trips per participant per year is freshwater fishing (12 trips), warm water fishing (12), and visiting a beach or waterside (12). Lowest in number of trips is rowing, with just over 2 trips per year. Participants tend to take more trips for fishing, swimming, and viewing and learning activities than they take for boating and floating.

Table V.7: Mean and Total Trips and Days per Year During Which People 16 Years Older in the U.S. Participated in Water-Resource-Based Activities, 1994-95

Activity	Mean number of trips per participant per year[1]	Total trips per year for the U.S. (millions)	Mean number of days per participant per year[1]	Total days per year for the U.S. (millions)
Boating/Floating				
Sailing	5.0	48.37	8.1	77.8
Canoeing	2.8	38.95	5.3	74.6
Kayaking	3.0	8.02	7.3	19.3
Rowing	2.3	19.45	5.3	45.0
Floating, Rafting	3.1	47.10	5.1	77.3
Motorboating	7.3	344.53	14.9	699.9
Waterskiing	5.4	95.97	9.7	173.1
Jet Skiing	3.1	29.33	7.6	72.3
Sailboarding/windsurfing	2.7	5.91	6.1	13.5
Fishing				
Freshwater	12.4	606.17	18.1	886.1
Saltwater	8.7	165.32	13.1	249.3
Warmwater	12.0	487.65	17.8	725.8
Coldwater	7.7	160.28	11.3	234.5
Anadromous	7.7	69.41	9.4	85.1
Catch and release	—[2]	—[2]	18.40	284.7
Swimming Activities				
Surfing	21.8	56.93	30.5	79.5
Swimming/pool	8.0	710.31	27.6	2438.9
Swimming/non-pool	6.9	542.08	15.9	1241.4
Snorkeling/Scuba	3.9	57.19	7.2	105.1
Viewing Activities				
Fish viewing	—[2]	—[2]	17.30	475.4
Visiting a beach or waterside	11.6	1438.11	25.6	3187.9
Studying nature near water	5.8	322.12	24.4	1352.9

[1] Means for trips and days include only participants in the activity and are not computed on the basis of total population count.
[2] Trips were not asked in the National Survey on Recreation and the Environment for some activities.

Because of large numbers of participants and high mean numbers of trips per year, estimated total number of trips for water-based activities shows four water-based activities with over 500 million trips per year:

Visiting a beach or waterside	1,438 million
Swimming in a pool	710 million
Freshwater fishing	606 million
Swimming in lakes or streams	542 million.

As with trips, the activity with the highest mean number of days per participant is surfing with over 30 days per year. Nearly as many days per participant are associated with pool swimming (28 days), visiting a beach or waterside (26 days), and studying nature near water (24). These high levels of participation resulted in these three activities being the most popular water-based activities surveyed based on total days of participation, with swimming in rivers, lakes, and oceans following as the fourth most popular activity as follows:

Visiting a beach or waterside	3.2 billion
Swimming in pools	2.4 billion
Studying nature near water	1.4 billion
Swimming in rivers, lakes	1.2 billion.

Participants devote many fewer days to boating and floating than to fishing, swimming, and viewing.

Snow and Ice Participation

For snow and ice activities, modest mean and total numbers of trips and days are shown in Table V.8. While mean trips and days are of similar magnitude among the activities of downhill skiing, cross-country skiing, and snowmobiling, totals are much different, with downhill skiing generating about three times as many trips and over two times as many days of participation per year.

Table V.8: Mean and Total Trips and Days per Year During Which People 16 Years Older in the U.S. Participated in Snow/Ice-Resource-Based Activities, 1994-95

Activity	Mean number of trips per participant per year[1]	Total trips per year for the U.S. (millions)	Mean number of days per participant per year[1]	Total days per year for the U.S. (millions)
Snow and Ice Activities				
Downhill skiing	4.5	75.47	7.5	126.5
Cross-country skiing	3.8	24.64	7.5	49.0
Snowmobiling	3.2	23.06	9.3	65.8

[1] Means for trips and days include only participants in the activity and are not computed on the basis of total population count.
[2] Trips were not asked in the National Survey on Recreation and the Environment for some activities.

The Most Active Participants

While over 94 percent of the U.S. population participates in some form of outdoor recreation over the course of a year, a group that we term *enthusiasts* accounts for most of the participation days. In Table V.9, participation days for enthusiasts, the one third of participants for each activity who are most active, are summarized. In column one, the percentages of the population 16 years and older who are the enthusiasts are shown. These percentages range from a low of 0.2 percent for kayaking to a high of 21.4 percent for walking. Even though these percentages are small relative to the whole population, column three indicates that enthusiasts account for most of the total participation days across all participants. Percentage of total participation days accounted for by enthusiasts ranges from a low of 58 percent for caving to a high of 94 percent for horseback riding.

Table V.9: Percent of Population, Days Annually and Percent of Total Days by the One-Third of Participants Who Are the Most Active by Activity and Age Group, 1994-95

Activity[1]	Percent of U.S. population classified as enthusiasts	To be classified as an enthusiast, an individual had to participate at least this number of days annually	Percent of total participation days by enthusiasts	Percent of enthusiasts by Age Group 16-24	25-49	50 and over
Fitness Activities						
Biking	7.4	30	80	24.4	56.9	18.7
Walking	21.4	112	76	15	45.4	39.6
Viewing Activities						
Visit a prehistoric site	4.3	3	75	17.2	53.1	29.7
Visit a historic site	11.8	4	72	14.7	55.9	29.4
Bird-watching	9.1	50	91	4.9	44.3	50.8
Wildlife viewing	9.6	12	92	10.6	57.7	31.8
Fish viewing	3.7	10	85	9.5	58.3	32.2
Sightseeing	17.4	12	78	13.1	50.5	36.4
Visiting a beach or waterside	19.7	15	84	20.4	57.6	22.0
Studying nature near water	8.5	10	89	12.3	58.8	28.8
Snow and Ice Activities						
Downhill skiing	2.6	6	74	35.8	53.6	10.6
Cross-country skiing	0.9	6	73	16.8	54.4	28.8
Snowmobiling	1.1	5	84	22	62.6	15.5
Camping (overall)						
Developed area	6.3	8	76	15	59.7	25.2
Primitive area	4.1	7	76	24.2	60	15.9
Hunting						
Big game	2.4	12	74	20.8	64.6	14.6
Small game	1.9	10	77	18.6	64.6	16.8
Migratory bird	0.6	7	71	20.2	57.1	22.8
Fishing						
Freshwater	7.1	15	79	16.5	55.7	27.7
Saltwater	2.6	7	85	17.2	57.4	25.4
Warmwater	6.2	14	82	18.7	54.7	26.5
Coldwater	2.3	10	76	13.2	55.9	30.9
Anadromous	1.0	6	80	16.6	57.2	26.2
Catch and release	3.9	15	80	19.3	58.2	22.5
Boating						
Sailing	1.4	5	81	23.4	49.8	26.8
Canoeing	1.8	4	73	27.6	49.4	23.1
Kayaking	0.2	5	78	22.5	71.3	6.2
Rowing	1.1	3	79	15.5	51.3	33.1
Floating, Rafting	1.9	4	75	37.1	55.5	7.5
Sailboard/windsurfing	0.3	4	81	24.5	56.6	18.8

Table V.9 Cont.

Swimming Activities						
Surfing	0.3	15	89	54.2	38.6	7.1
Swimming/pool	13.0	25	80	26.9	55	18.1
Swimming/non-pool	11.9	13	78	27	58.7	14.3
Snorkeling/Scuba	1.8	5	77	20.2	68	11.9
Outdoor Adventure Activities						
Hiking	7.1	10	83	24.4	58.3	17.3
Orienteering	0.6	5	75	32.2	55	12.8
Backpacking	2.4	5	81	33.4	56	10.7
Mountain climbing	1.3	3	74	29.5	55.6	14.8
Rock climbing	1.0	3	78	45.5	48.4	6.2
Caving	1.1	2	58	34.4	54.6	11
Off-road driving	4.5	14	87	25.6	57	17.3
Horseback riding	2.3	6	94	36.8	52.6	10.5
Social Activities						
Picnicking	15.0	7	73	13.5	64.0	22.6

[1]This table includes only activities for which the number of days participated was asked.

Enthusiasts account for 70 to 89 percent of total participation days for individual activities. These percentages tend to be highest for viewing and learning, fishing, and outdoor adventure activities. The activities for which enthusiasts are most likely to be between the ages of 16 to 24 are downhill skiing, canoeing, floating and rafting, surfing, swimming, orienteering, backpacking, mountain climbing, rock climbing, caving, off-road driving, and horseback riding. (See contributed paper on main streaming of rock climbing by Moser and Davidson at the end of this chapter.) Activities for which enthusiasts are most likely to be over the age of 50 include walking, bird watching, wildlife viewing, fish viewing, sightseeing, and coldwater fishing.

NATIONAL TRENDS IN PARTICIPATION

The primary measures of outdoor recreation market shifts include trends in percentages and numbers of participants in activities, as well as in number of days during which people pursue those activities. Analysts often focus on the percentages of people who report participation. While this information is important, this chapter focuses on trends in numbers of people who participate as the more telling growth indicator. Numbers of participants account for both general popularity shifts (changes in the percentage of the population who participate) and changes in the population base, which has grown over 65 percent since the first national recreation survey in 1960.

Below are the estimated millions of people 12 years old or older in the United States during annual periods covered by the four National Recreation Surveys for the United States:

1960	131 million
1965	144 million (10 percent more than 1960)
1982-83	188 million (44 percent more than 1960)
1994-95	216 million (65 percent more than 1960).

The following sections examine long-term trends in number and percentage of participants since 1960 for activities common to the 1960, 1965, 1982-83, and 1994-95 national surveys. Recent trends for a larger set of activities common to the 1982-83 and 1994-95 surveys also are presented.

Long-Term Trends

Land-Based Activities

Four land-based activities have been tracked since the original National Recreation Survey (Figure V.1). For two of these activities, bicycling and camping, there has been growth in numbers of people who participate. It is obvious when visiting a bicycle shop that the technology for biking has changed dramatically over the 35 years spanning the first and last surveys. The days of the large balloon-tired Schwinn single speed with Bendix brakes have passed. The ones that remain are mounted on the walls of nostalgia-themed restaurants. When the 1960 survey was being conducted, 10-speed bikes were just beginning to appear. In 1960, about 13 million people 12 years or older reported that they had gone bicycling one or more times during the past year. By 1965, that number had jumped to nearly 26 million 12 years or older—a doubling of the number participating. The increase was driven partly by the improvements in technology represented by the 10-speed bike. (See contributed paper by MacFadden on cycling issues at the end of this chapter.)

Figure V.1: Long-Term Trends in Millions and Percent of Population 12 Years and Older Participating Annually in Four Representative Land-Resource-Based Activities, 1960-1995

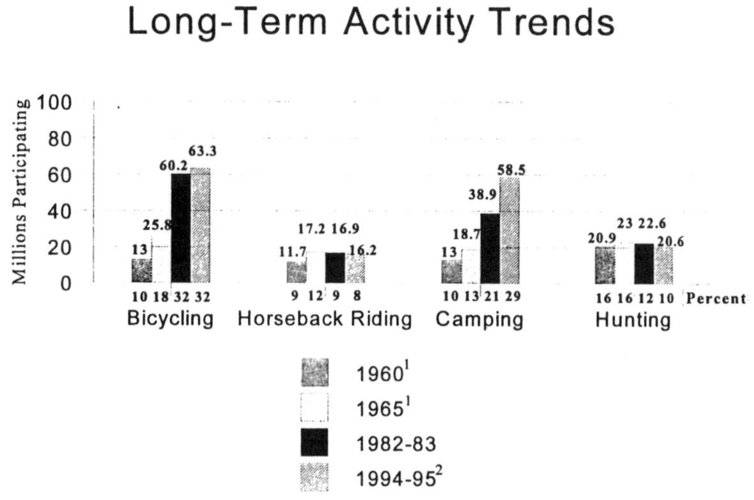

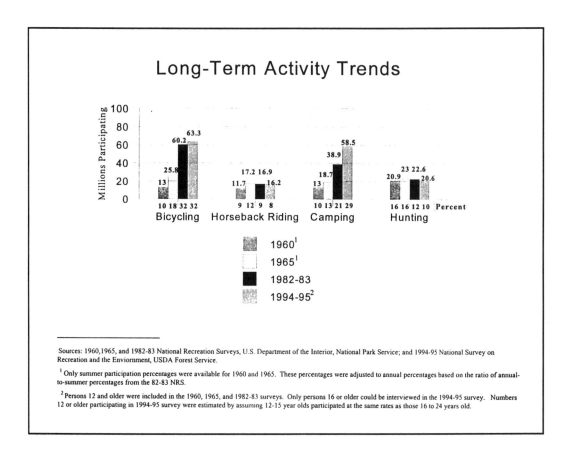

Sources: 1960,1965, and 1982-83 National Recreation Surveys, U.S. Department of the Interior, National Park Service; and 1994-95 National Survey on Recreation and the Enviornment, USDA Forest Service.

[1] Only summer participation percentages were available for 1960 and 1965. These percentages were adjusted to annual percentages based on the ratio of annual-to-summer percentages from the 82-83 NRS.

[2] Persons 12 and older were included in the 1960, 1965, and 1982-83 surveys. Only persons 16 or older could be interviewed in the 1994-95 survey. Numbers 12 or older participating in 1994-95 survey were estimated by assuming 12-15 year olds participated at the same rates as those 16 to 24 years old.

In 1982-83, just over 60 million reported they had participated in bicycling, over $3^1/_2$ times as many as in 1960. During the 1980s and especially in the 1990s, technology has transformed biking into a recreational pursuit as diverse as the people who ride those bicycles. Mountain bikes are among the more notable advancements. Mountain bikes with their lightweight but rugged construction and all terrain tires enable riders both to traverse very difficult and challenging terrain and to commute to class on university campuses (see feature article by Chavez that follows later in this chapter). Mountain bikes, lightweight racing bikes with 20 or more speeds, and many other variations of bike designs have helped stimulate an increase to nearly 63 million biking participants at the time of the 1994-95 survey. An estimated 6.9 million people (3.2 percent of the population) reported that some of their biking activity was long-distance touring.

While the most recent survey indicates a constant percentage of people who participate in some form of biking between the 1980s and 1990s, the increase in numbers of participants driven by population growth and new technology translates into continued slow growth in this market. In the early 1980s, the bicycle riding craze was at its height, and the high level of participation observed at that time may be more a reflection of a fad than a true long-term growth trend.

Camping is another activity with long-term growth. The character of camping, like bicycling, has changed noticeably over the 35 years covered by the national surveys. In the 1960s, much of the camping was in developed campgrounds set up to accommodate families, most of whom were camping in tents. In the 1960s there would have been some, but relatively few, pop-up tent trailers and pickup trucks with camper inserts. There would have been even fewer car-towed, rigid-construction trailers, such as the famous Air Stream, which now is considered by many to be among the elite of camping trailers.

In 1960 about 13 million people 12 or older reported camping one or more times during the previous 12 months. In 1965, the equipment and options for camping were largely unchanged from 1960, but camping was drawing nearly 19 million participants, a 44-percent increase. By 1982-83, camping had more than tripled in numbers of people participating and more than doubled in the percentage of the population reporting one or more camping trips during the year.

In 1994-95, over 58 million people 12 or older had participated in camping in the previous 12 months. This number is about 350 percent growth in 35 years since the first national survey in 1960. The nature of camping, like bicycling, has changed as much as the numbers in that time span. While camping with the family is still popular, few camping parties anymore are families with young children. Now there are many more retirees with expensive motor homes, many more singles traveling with friends and camping to keep lodging costs down, and groups camping together as a way of gaining access to other recreational opportunities or unique features, such as the Devil's Tower in South Dakota. All of these increasingly diverse groups are to be found in increasing numbers in the 1990s.

In addition to camping in developed campgrounds, both public (government managed) and commercial, many are choosing to camp in more primitive settings, where few if any facilities and amenities are provided. Primitive camping is more convenient and comfortable in the 1990s than it was even as recently as the early 1980s. Better and more weather-resistant tents, recreation vehicles that are easier to set up and much more self-contained, and more functional camping equipment (such as gas–cook stoves) can make primitive camping nearly as comfortable as developed site camping. Below are the participation statistics for people 12 or older for 1982-83 and 1994-95 for developed and primitive camping:

	1982-83		1994-95	
Activity	Percent	Millions	Percent	Millions
Developed (all)	17	33	21	47
With an RV	—	—	9	20
Tent camping	—	—	15	34
Primitive	10	18	14	31
With an RV	—	—	4	8
Tent camping	—	—	11	24
Other camping	4	8	2	4

While developed camping grew about 42 percent, primitive camping grew by about 72 percent. The "other camping" category is ill-defined, but it is important because it includes camping styles that respondents feel did not fit the offered categories. Other camping includes activities like group camping and canoe camping. The "other camping" category has shown a decrease over the survey periods.

The other two activities that could be compared back to the 1960 survey were horseback riding and hunting. Both of these activities require access to relatively large areas of land and trails. Horseback riding has decreased in both percentage of the population and number of people participating. The number of horseback riding participants peaked in the 1960s. Since then it has decreased steadily to its current level of just over 16 million participants. An estimated 5.2 percent of the population—69 percent of horseback riders—does some of their riding on trails.

Hunting also is a declining activity. The estimated number who hunted in 1994-95 is less than the estimated number in the 1960s. The proportion of the population that hunts decreased in these 35 years from 16 percent in 1960 to 10 percent in the 1990s. Over seven percent of the population 12 or older hunts big game, 6.5 percent hunts small game, and 2.1 percent hunts migratory bird species, mainly ducks and geese. Obviously, many hunters participate in all three of the forms of hunting just mentioned.

Gaining access to land or water areas for hunting is becoming increasingly difficult. In the 1960s there was more undeveloped land area in the country and fewer people to compete for its use. In many rural areas, permission was not needed to hunt on someone else's land. In the 1990s, the undeveloped land area is smaller, while the population is much larger. In addition, social pressures against hunting are rising, and increasing numbers of people have grown up totally in an urban environment where hunting was never introduced to them. These and many other factors are the likely contributors to the decline in the popularity of hunting in the United States.

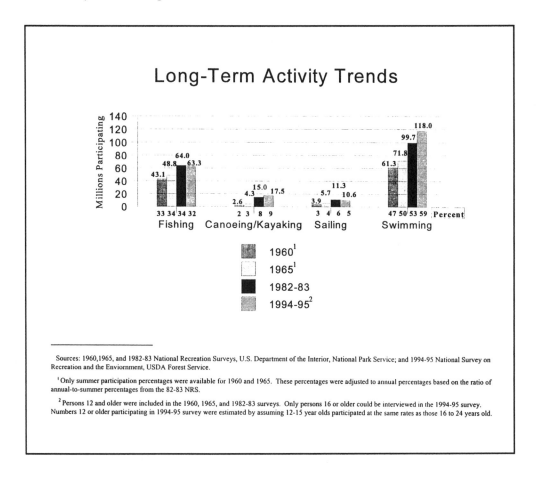

Long-Term Trends—Water-Based Activities

Among the four water-based activities with comparable statistics in the four National Recreation Surveys, two have decreased in numbers of participants and two have increased (Figure V.2). Numbers of participants and percentages of the population who fish and sail decreased between 1982 and 1994. The percentage of the population that fishes was between 33 and 34 percent in 1960, 1965, and 1982-83; the percentage dropped somewhat to 32 percent in 1994-95. This percentage decrease was large enough to affect a decrease in the number of people 12 and older participating in fishing, even though population increased nearly 15 percent during that 13-year period. (See contributed paper by McCaleb on fishing trends at the end of this chapter.)

Figure V.2: Long-Term Trends in Millions and Percent of Population 12 Years and Older Participating Annually in Four Representative Water-Resource-Based Activities, 1960-1995

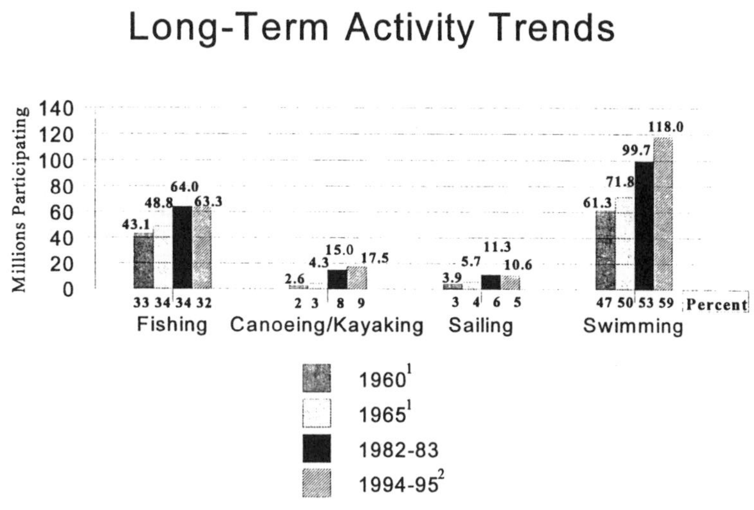

Sources: 1960,1965, and 1982-83 National Recreation Surveys, U.S. Department of the Interior, National Park Service; and 1994-95 National Survey on Recreation and the Enviornment, USDA Forest Service.

[1] Only summer participation percentages were available for 1960 and 1965. These percentages were adjusted to annual percentages based on the ratio of annual-to-summer percentages from the 82-83 NRS.

[2] Persons 12 and older were included in the 1960, 1965, and 1982-83 surveys. Only persons 16 or older could be interviewed in the 1994-95 survey. Numbers 12 or older participating in 1994-95 survey were estimated by assuming 12-15 year olds participated at the same rates as those 16 to 24 years old.

Sailing increased substantially between 1960 and the 1980s from nearly four million to over 11 million participants. During this period, the percentage of the population participating nearly doubled. Between the 1982-83 survey and the 1994-95 survey, however, estimates of both the percentage and number of participants decreased.

Participation increased in the more physically active water activities of canoeing and kayaking and swimming. Canoeing and kayaking can be done on still water or white water. Participants in canoeing and kayaking grew from an estimated 2.6 million in 1960 to approximately 15 million in 1982-83. The estimated number of participants in 1994-95 was 17.5 million. Of those reporting participation, 91 percent went canoeing, 20 percent went kayaking, and 11 percent went both canoeing and kayaking during 1994-95. The estimated percentage of canoeists and kayakers who used their boats in white water in 1994-95 was 21.1. Canoeing and kayaking were not treated as separate activities in previous surveys.

White water activities have been supported by advancements in the technology of the equipment, boats as well as paddles, floatation inserts, spray aprons, and other items. From the aluminum and wooden boats in the 1960s and before, the new equipment has evolved rapidly toward more durable plastic boats that can withstand impacts from obstacles and torque from twisting through rapids. New hull designs make these boats more maneuverable as well as durable.

Swimming was enjoyed by almost one-half the population in 1960, and its popularity has continued to grow. In 1960, swimming was an activity of 47 percent of people 12 and older; currently the estimated percentage participating is 59 percent. The growth of this percentage combined with population expansion has resulted in a near doubling of numbers of participants in just over 35 years, from 61 million in 1960 to 118 million in 1994-95. In 1982-83, 80 million went swimming in a pool and 59 million went swimming in a lake, pond, stream, or ocean. In 1994-95, 96 million went pool swimming and 85 million went swimming in an impoundment, river, or ocean.

Long-Term Trends—Snow Skiing

In the 1960 and 1965 national surveys, downhill and cross-country skiing were not distinguished as separate activities. In the five years separating these surveys, the estimated percentage participating in snow skiing grew from two to four percent (Figure V.3). This use represented an increase of over three million participants from 2.6 to 5.7 million. In the 17 years up to the 1982-83 survey, numbers of skiers rose to almost 17 million, nearly a threefold increase. In 1982-83, an estimated nine percent of the population participated in some form of skiing—2 million downhill and six million cross-country. By the 1994-95 survey, over 26 million participated in skiing, 19 million downhill, and seven million cross-country. Between 1982-83 and 1994-95 there was a 50–percent increase in downhill skiing participants and a 176–percent increase in cross–country participants.

Figure V.3: Long-Term Trends in Millions and Percent of Population 12 Years and Older Participating Annually in Snow Skiing, 1960-1995

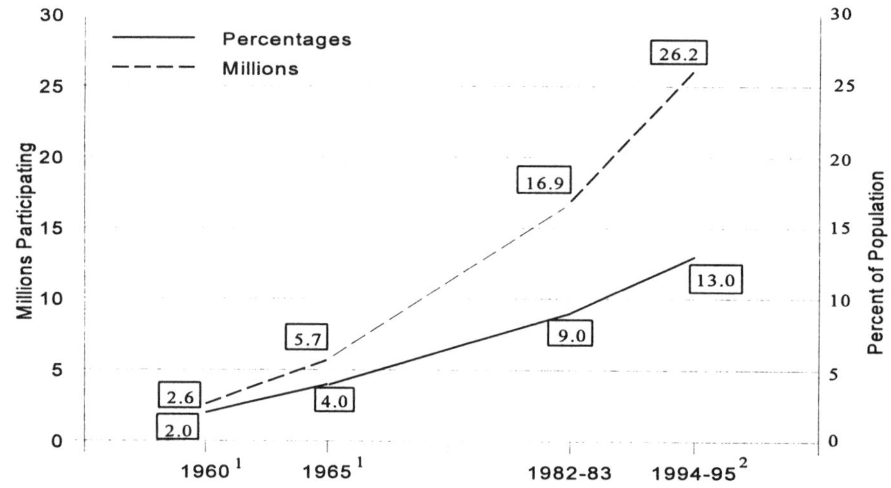

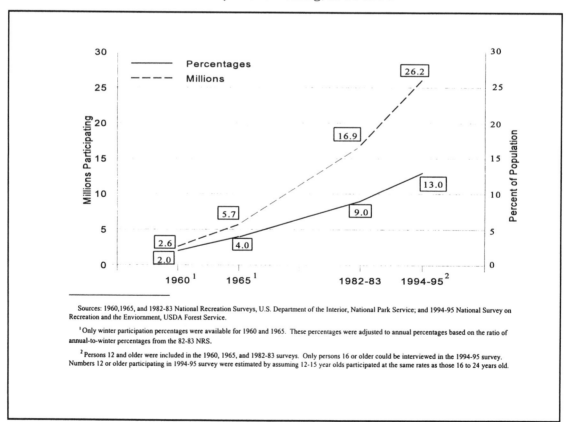

Sources: 1960,1965, and 1982-83 National Recreation Surveys, U.S. Department of the Interior, National Park Service; and 1994-95 National Survey on Recreation and the Enviornment, USDA Forest Service.

[1] Only winter participation percentages were available for 1960 and 1965. These percentages were adjusted to annual percentages based on the ratio of annual-to-winter percentages from the 82-83 NRS.

[2] Persons 12 and older were included in the 1960, 1965, and 1982-83 surveys. Only persons 16 or older could be interviewed in the 1994-95 survey. Numbers 12 or older participating in 1994-95 survey were estimated by assuming 12-15 year olds participated at the same rates as those 16 to 24 years old.

Recent Trends

Table V.10 shows recent trends in 29 activities common to both the 1982-83 and 1994-95 surveys. Because the most recent survey focused on people 16 years and older, estimates of the numbers of participants for each of the two time periods covered do not include people 12 to 15 years old. Activities are grouped by the type of resource involved (land, water, etc.) and ranked from highest to lowest percentage growth in numbers of participants within each resource type.

Of the 13 land-resource-based activities in Table V.10, 11 show increases in numbers of participants. Only horseback riding and hunting decreased. Bird watching, by casual as well as by avid participants, has the highest percentage growth rate of any activity listed (an increase of over 155 percent). Bird watching also had one of the highest rises in millions of participants (32 million), second only to walking, which had an increase of 40 million.

Table V.10: Millions and Percentage Change of Persons 16 Years or Older Participating at Least Once in 12 Months in Land, Water, Snow/Ice, and Other Activities in the United States, 1982-83 and 1994-95

Resource Base and Activity	Number in Millions		Percent Change
	1982-83	1994-95	
Land-resource-based activities			
Bird watching	21.2	54.1	+155.2
Hiking	24.7	47.8	+93.5
Backpacking	8.8	15.2	+72.7
Primitive area camping	17.7	28.0	+58.2
Off-road driving	19.4	27.9	+43.8
Walking	93.6	133.7	+42.8
Sightseeing	81.3	113.4	+39.5
Developed area camping	30.0	41.5	+38.3
Picnicking	84.8	98.3	+15.9
Running/jogging	45.9	52.5	+14.4
Bicycling	56.5	57.4	+1.6
Horseback riding	15.9	14.3	-10.1
Hunting	21.2	18.6	-12.3
Water-resource-based activities			
Motorboating	33.6	47.0	+39.9
Swimming/river, lake, or ocean	56.5	78.1	+38.2
Swimming/pool	76.0	88.5	+16.4
Water skiing	15.9	17.9	+12.6
Fishing	60.1	57.8	-3.8
Sailing	10.6	9.6	-9.4
Snow & ice-resource-based activities			
Downhill skiing	10.6	16.8	+58.5
Snowmobiling	5.3	7.1	+34.0
Cross-country skiing	5.3	6.5	+22.6
Sledding	17.7	20.5	+15.8
Ice skating	10.6	10.5	-0.9
Outdoor sports & spectator activities			
Attending an outdoor concert or play	44.2	68.4	+54.7
Attending a sports event	70.7	95.2	+34.7
Golf	23.0	29.7	+29.1
Outdoor team sports	42.4	53.0	+25.0
Tennis	30.0	21.2	-29.3

Sources: 1982-83 National Recreation Survey, U.S. Department of the Interior and 1994-95 National Survey on Recreation and the Environment, USDA Forest Service.

The next four activities after bird watching are hiking, backpacking, primitive area camping, and off-road vehicle driving. All of these activities occur on trails or in other settings that lack developed facilities and amenities. The number of hiking participants 16 or older nearly doubled in the 13 years between the surveys, reaching nearly 50 million who participated one or more times per year by 1995. The number of backpackers increased to over 15 million in this period, and for the first time surpassed the number of horseback riders. Hiking and backpacking are the two primary on-foot recreational uses of trails.

Primitive area camping grew nearly as much as developed camping in millions of new participants 16 or older. As mentioned earlier, improvements in camping equipment have made camping outside of developed campgrounds more convenient and comfortable. Off-road driving of vehicles ranging from dune buggies and all-terrain vehicles (ATVs) to dirt bikes and trail motorcycles increased by more than eight million participants in the 13 years between surveys. Difficulty in finding appropriate places to ride these vehicles may have limited growth in this activity. ATVs are also increasingly used for work purposes, such as herding, inspecting fence lines, and accessing remote work sites without roads. (See contributed paper on motorized vehicles by Cook and the paper on motorcycling by Lundquist at the end of this chapter.)

The remaining six land-based activities that grew in numbers of participants occur mostly on streets and trails near the homes of the participants or near roadways or developed recreation sites. While bird watching, hiking, backpacking, and primitive camping grew at faster rates, some of these more slowly growing land-based activities expanded more in absolute numbers of participants because the base number of participants in 1982-83 was much larger than for other activities. Walking participants, for example, increased by about 43 percent, but this use represented over 40 million added participants. Sightseeing grew by nearly 40 percent, but this growth added 32 million participants. Picnicking grew by nearly 14 million. These activities are low cost and require little skill, but they appeal to a broad range of people.

Developed camping and picnicking are traditional family activities that, because of changes in the structure of our society, are becoming somewhat less family oriented. Increasingly, the participants in camping and picnicking include greater proportions of singles and groups of unrelated individuals. Running, jogging, or bicycling are more physically demanding than camping and picnicking and often are fitness-motivated activities. They are participated in by roughly one-quarter of the population.

When ranked by increase in numbers of participants, walking, bird watching, sightseeing, hiking, picnicking, and developed camping grew more than other activities. These activities utilize facilities and spaces that are easily accessible to most people.

There are, of course, many more land-based activities than the 13 discussed above. Unfortunately, these 13 are the only ones available for direct comparison between 1982-83 and the most recent 1994-95 survey. However, they do represent a spectrum of activities from ones enjoyed mainly in developed settings to those enjoyed mainly in backcountry settings. They also cut across the activity types from very passive to highly active.

There are six water-resource-based activities that are comparable between the surveys. Among these, motorboating grew by the largest percentage between surveys, followed by swimming and water skiing. Fishing and sailing both decreased in numbers of participants. Swimming in rivers, lakes, or oceans and swimming in pools grew by almost 22 million and by over 12 million participants, respectively. Across all forms of outdoor recreation, swimming ranks among the top five in overall popularity. Swimming is obviously a lifetime activity that need not be abandoned with age.

Both hunting and fishing are classified as consumptive activities, i.e., where something is physically removed or "harvested" from the site of participation. These forms of outdoor recreation are becoming less popular in American society. In fact, hunting, is protested by some organizations and individuals. While harder-to-gain access is one of the reasons for declining hunting, fishing access has remained about constant. Popularity of wildlife and fish viewing is increasing. These may be among the activities former hunters and anglers are moving toward.

Snow– and ice–based activities generally involve relatively small percentages of the country's population. Of the five activities shown in Table V.10, all but ice skating increased. Downhill skiing was the fastest growing of these activities, increasing over 58 percent in the number of participants. The estimated increases in the number of participants may not result in overall greater revenues at ski slopes because new skiers may not be skiing as often as experienced skiers. In a section presented later, it is shown that the estimated percentages of downhill skiers who ski 11 or more days per year dropped between 1982 and 1995.

Snowmobiling and cross-country skiing each had about 5.3 million participants in 1982-83. By 1995, those numbers had increased to 7.1 million for snowmobiling and 6.5 million for cross-country skiing. Both of these activities may take place on the same backcountry roads and trails. At times there may be conflicts between these different users of roads and trails in winter, as there are between motorized users and hikers in summer. Increasingly, cross-country skiing occurs on trails groomed specifically for this activity. Participation in ice skating remained nearly constant between the two surveys at between 10 and 11 million participants.

Five outdoor sports or spectator activities were comparable between the 1980s and 1990s surveys. Attending outdoor concerts or plays and attending outdoor sports events increased at more than twice the rate of population growth during that period. These activities also had some of the largest growth in absolute numbers of participants–over 24 million people each. The percentage of the population that attends outdoor sporting events is nearing 50 percent.

Golf grew in participation by just over 29 percent and participation in outdoor team sports grew 25 percent. Only tennis showed a decline in participation since the 1980s, from an estimated 30 million in 1982-83 to just over 21 million in 1994-95.

Trends in Participation Days

Trends in percentages of people who choose various activities and numbers of participants are important indicators of change in outdoor recreation participation. However, these indicators tell only part of the story. Presented below are estimated percentages of participants in selected activities by the number of days per year during which they participated in 1982-83 and in 1994-95. Only activities for which there has been a four-percent or greater shift in number of participation-days are included in Figure V.4.

Figure V.4: Percentages of Participants in Eight Outdoor Recreational Activities by Number of Days of Participation and Year of Survey, 1982-83 and 1994-95

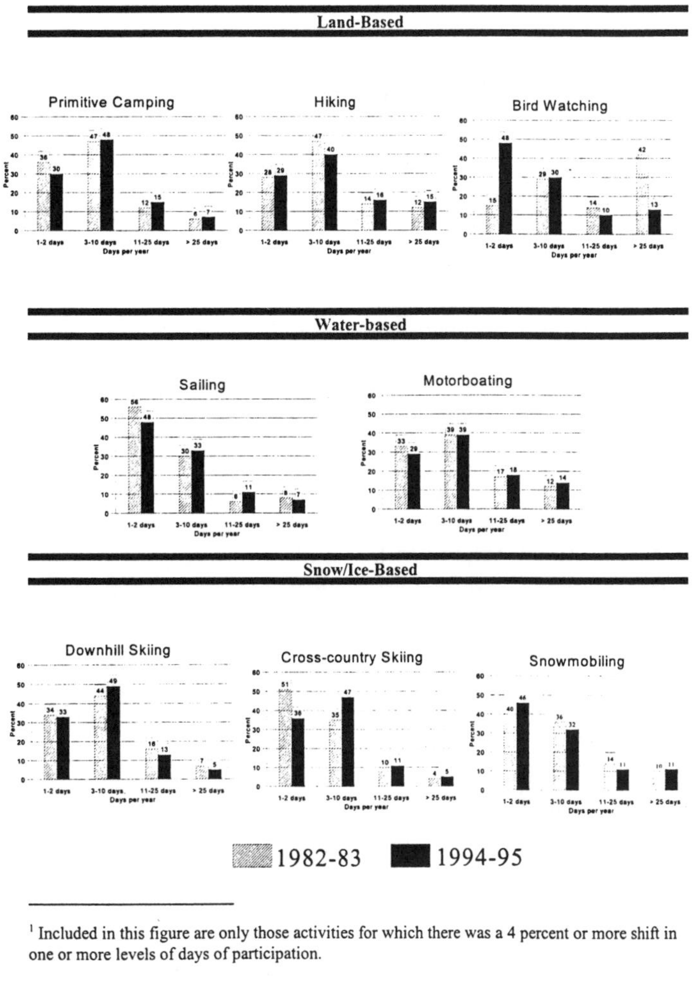

[1] Included in this figure are only those activities for which there was a 4 percent or more shift in one or more levels of days of participation.

Activities that did not have a four-percent shift included bicycling, horseback riding, pool swimming, swimming in natural waters, canoeing or kayaking, backpacking, developed camping, and off-road vehicle driving. Among these activities, proportions of participants by the number of days on which they participated remained fairly constant, meaning that numbers of people by days of participation has increased or decreased at each level of participation roughly proportionate to the overall increase or decrease of participants in the activity.

Among the land-based activities, the greatest shift in participation days was for bird–watching. Compared with number of people participating at the time of the 1982-83 survey, over 33 million people added bird watching on one or more days per year to their outdoor activity agenda. From the estimates of the percentages of bird–watching participants among the four levels of participation days, it is obvious that most of the 20 million "new" bird watching participants engaged in the activity infrequently, on less than three days per year. As the percentages of bird–watchers participating for one-two and three-10 days per year grew, the percentage participating over 11 days per year decreased. The percentage participating 25 or more days per year fell from 42 percent in 1982-83 to 13 percent in 1994-95.

For primitive camping, the shifts were in the opposite direction, with a smaller percentage camping one-two days and a larger percentage camping 11 or more days. A similar pattern occurred with hiking, for which the shift was from fewer to more days per year. This pattern also held true for the water-based activities of sailing and motorboating.

Shifts in percentages of participants between levels of participation per year were mixed for snow and ice activities (Figure V.3). Percentages of participants downhill skiing 11-25 days and more than 25 days per year dropped, while the percentage of skiing three-10 days rose. The percentage cross-country skiing just one-two days per year dropped dramatically, while the percentage doing so for three-10 days rose. The opposite pattern occurred for snowmobiling with decreases in percentages participating three to 25 days and an increase in percentage snowmobiling only one-two days. The percentage of participants snowmobiling more than 25 days per year remained about the same.

FROM CITIES TO WHITEWATER ADVENTURE: THREE FEATURE ARTICLES

The following articles were invited from national experts to cover in more depth a range of recreation interests from passive to active participation.

Trends and Issues in Birding

(By Paul J. Baicich, Gregory S. Butcher, and Paul Green, American Birding Association, Colorado Springs, CO)

From the mid-1980s to the mid-1990s, the numbers of people actively watching birds increased 155.2 percent, outstripping the second and third fastest growing activities in the same category—hiking (up 93 percent) and backpacking (up 72.7 percent). Just how many birders are there in the U.S. today? Annually, those with an interest in birds spend $2.5 billion on bird seed, feeders, baths, and nest boxes (USDI, 1993). These backyard birders may not step beyond their own yard fence to look at birds. Still, we know that an estimated 24.7 million people annually take trips to watch wild birds (USDI, 1993). Winnowing down these numbers certainly means getting closer to some better, more accurate figure for the numbers of serious birders in the U.S. Kellert (1985) estimated that 0.5 percent of the people with feeders in their yards could identify at least 100 bird species. If that figure were applied to the 63.1 million residential bird feeders, the number of skilled backyard birdwatchers would be 315,500. If one took that same figure of 0.5 percent and applied it to the 24.7 million "traveling birdwatchers," one could reasonably reach the figure of 123,500 serious birders, a figure that corresponds closely with our estimate of the total number of members of local bird clubs.

We know that "committed birders" annually spend on average $2,000 each year on birdwatching, with half that amount on travel (Wiedner & Kerlinger, 1990). If that $2,000 figure were applied to the 123,500 dedicated birders, it would yield a minimum "dedicated birder GNP" of $247 million. Moreover, birder spending, or so-called "avitourism," is only recently being appreciated. Part of what it reveals is that refuges and parks cannot be perceived as economic sinks, since they often stimulate local economies (Kerlinger & Eubanks, 1995). For example, at Cape May, New Jersey, more than 100,000 birders visit the area, contributing a cumulative impact of nearly $10 million (Kerlinger & Wiedner, 1991). During a five-week spring migration period, High Island, Texas, had more than 6,000 birders visit in 1992, spending $2.5 million in the area surrounding the isolated Gulf Coast town (Eubanks, Kerlinger, & Payne, 1993). About 50,000 people visit the raptor migration "hotspot" every year at Hawk Mountain, Pennsylvania, directly spending about $4 million in the local economy (Kerlinger & Brett, 1994). The mecca for crane watchers is the area around Grand Island,

Birdwatchers view waterfowl at Delaware Bayshores Bioreserve in New Jersey. Photo courtesy of the Nature Conservancy. Photo by Connie Gelb.

Nebraska, on the Platte River, where at least 80,000 avitourists visit annually. They spend more than $15 million, which has been estimated to stimulate as much as $40 million in overall business activity (Lingle, 1991).

Another measure of the growth of relatively skilled birders can be found through the numbers of participants in the annual National Audubon Society Christmas Bird Counts (CBCs). As Figure V.5 indicates, CBC participants have increased dramatically over the past few decades.

Birders are a heterogenous group seeking a wide range of experiences. Scott, Thigpen, Kim, and Kim's (1996) analysis of birders who visited the 1995 Rockport Hummerbird Festival revealed four groups that differed significantly in terms of their "behavioral involvement." Ordered in declining behavioral involvement, they named their four groups as "undifferentiated birders," "outdoor recreationists," "generalists and water seekers," and "heritage recreationists and comfort seekers." The members of each group had distinct characteristics. Members of the first two groups owned more field guides and bird books, belonged to more organizations, could identify more birds by sight and sound, owned more birding equipment, went on more birding trips within and beyond the state, traveled more miles to go birding, and spent more money on birding trips.

Figure V.5: Change in the Number of National Audubon Society Christmas Bird Counts from 1900-1990

Christmas Bird Counts

✔ 1900	27 participants
✔ 1930	679 participants
✔ 1940	2,100 participants
✔ 1950	4,600 participants
✔ 1960	8,100 participants
✔ 1970	15,000 participants
✔ 1980	32,000 participants
✔ 1990	43,000 participants

Source: Winging It, October 1996, Greg Butcher (author).

In terms of future behavior, comparisons between "undifferentiated birders" and "generalists and water seekers" revealed extreme differences. Members of the first group predicted that they would, on average, go birding 53 days in 1996, compared with 15 days for the second group. One reason for these studies was to understand what facilities Texas Parks and Wildlife should be providing to encourage birding as an economic activity. Because this study was an analysis of people visiting a festival, it does not include one other economically important group, namely the garden bird feeders.

We expect the growth in birding to continue in the near and distant future as baby boomers grow older. Besides the NSRE figures, we can see some important shifts in the past decade and a half. Three examples include the growth of birding specialty stores, birding magazines, and birding festivals. Figure V.6 provides details of these shifts, including starting dates for bird franchise stores and for popular birding magazines.

Figure V.6: Birding Festivals from 1993-1997

Birding Festivals -- a new avitourism development

The first ones appear in the 1980s

1993	approximately 12 festivals
1994	approximately 18 festivals
1995	approximately 23 festivals
1996	approximately 48 festivals
1997	approximately 70 festivals

Source: National Fish & Wildlife Foundation and American Birding Association.

To make a wildlife or bird-viewing area attractive to birders, land managers, businesses, and conservationists are beginning to better understand the constituency they are attempting to reach. Many surveys have indicated that the birders are overwhelmingly middle class, well educated, and highly motivated (Payne, 1991; Kerlinger, 1993; Kerlinger & Eubanks, 1995). One recent survey (Scott, Stewart, & Cole, 1997) revealed that 27 percent of a sample of the American Birding Association (ABA) members had annual household incomes of over $100,000, and 42 percent had graduate or advanced degrees. These findings are generally in line with an earlier, more extensive membership survey that showed 32 percent had annual household incomes of over $75,000 and 43 percent had a postgraduate degree (Bartels, 1994). Fourteen per cent of the springtime birding visitors to High Island, Texas, had an annual family income of $120,000 or more (Eubanks, Kerlinger, & Payne, 1993).

There is consideration of creating a new funding base, possibly modeled after the 60-year-old Pittman-Robertson Act authorizing a user-based excise tax for conservation uses. An excise tax on the manufacturers' price of binoculars, birdseed, feeders, bird houses, bird baths, spotting scopes, field guides, and other outdoor equipment, including camping equipment, is currently identified with the campaign "Teaming with Wildlife." This campaign is aimed at providing a coordinated network of projects and goals, such as "Partners in Flight," which is designed to reverse the decline in migratory bird species. The Partners in Flight conservation effort addresses multiple needs in bird conservation as identified by experienced birders, ornithologists, conservationists, and land managers, but as yet has no formal funding mechanism.

New and recent technologies have an increasing impact on personal activities of birders. Listers and rarity seekers now have beepers to tell them where the next interesting bird can be seen. Local and national list-servers e-mail the latest bird news to subscribers, and provide forums for discussions of birding issues. Interactive data-gathering computer systems, such as Bird Source and Bird Net are being developed by the National Audubon Society, the Cornell Lab for Ornithology, and others. These systems may soon allow individuals to submit their observations and to view group results on their screen, such as patterns of migration.

There is a perceived need for increased access to appropriate habitats and locations so that recreational birders can see more birds. The more popular "hotspots" in North American birding are becoming crowded at specific times of year, for example, Cape May, Point Pelee, Madera Canyon, and High Island. Improving access and providing facilities is one way to accommodate the growing number of birders while protecting the birds themselves.

The promotion of birding festivals (Figure V.6) is linked to the popularization of birding as a pastime. Studies have estimated that 260,000 participated in less than three dozen birding festivals in 1996 (Romero & Stangel, 1997). As the number of such events grows (to more than 60 in 1997) and link up with communities near birding "hotspots," the link between the growing ranks of birders and the preservation of bird habitat will become clearer. Expressed simply, "more habitat means more birds means more birders spending more money in the local community" (Romero & Stangel, 1997).

There is continuing growth in interest in birding. Many more people are becoming birders as they reach their 40s, 50s, and 60s, as their children grow older and as they start looking for new hobbies. Indeed, with baby boomers nearing retirement, increases may be quite large. Adult education and Elderhostel courses have been successful in reaching out to people in older age groups as well as to their grandchildren. Birding vacations become much more affordable to people in their 40s, 50s, and 60s as they reach the peak of their earning power.

In the last *Analysis of the Outdoor Recreation and Wilderness Situation in the United States 1989-2040* (Cordell, Bergstrom, Hartmann, & English, 1990), it was predicted that "wildlife observation and photography" (including birding) was going to increase by an estimated 82 percent by 2040, with trips afield increasing substantially. This assessment predicts a rise by 61 percent of participants in wildlife observation and a rise of 97 percent in participation days by 2050 (Chapter VI).

Mountain Biking—A Rapidly Growing Sport

(By Deborah J. Chavez, Research Social Scientist, USDA Forest Service, Riverside, CA)

Statistics on mountain biking indicate strong growth in participation (Sporting Goods Manufacturing Association [SGMA], 1991), intensified sales (Bicycle Institute of America, 1993; Keller, 1990), and the accelerated use of mountain bikes off-road (Brown, 1988). The SGMA estimated that participation levels for mountain biking increased over 100 percent between 1987 and 1989, from 1.5 million to 3.2 million total days. Additionally, frequent participation (52 or more days per year) rose by over 150 percent during that time. While use occurs nationwide, most is in the western United States with California and Colorado in the lead (SGMA, 1991).

Managers from the Bureau of Land Management (Chavez, Winter, & Baas, 1993a), the Forest Service (Chavez, et al., 1993a; Chavez, 1996a), and the National Park Service (Tilmant, 1991) have all noted that mountain biking use is increasing on their trails. In one study, managers who had only minimal to moderate use stated that the popularity of the sport was growing (Chavez, et al., 1993a). In another study, about half of Forest Service managers reported that mountain biking is a growth sport (Chavez, 1996a).

Studies of mountain bike riders (Hollenhorst, Schuett, Olson, & Chavez, 1995; Hollenhorst, Schuett, Olson, Chavez, & Mainieri, 1995) show patterns that indicate the growth of the sport, especially on trails. Data collected in 1992 from riders at six national forests in the United States indicated an average of 10 years experience bicycling and four years of mountain bike riding experience, with an average 67 rides per year. The same people reported that they rode most often on forest trails and abandoned roads. A study of members of the International Mountain Biking Association (IMBA) in 1994 indicated they had been mountain bike riding for an average of six years, and averaged 95 rides per year. These riders also expressed a desire for trail riding and felt that the trails should be shared with hikers and equestrians.

Profiles of mountain bike riders suggest the riders are most often Anglo/European males. Most riders are 30 or more years of age, have some college education, and earn above $30,000 per year. For most, mountain biking is a day-use activity. This finding may have implications for local economies if they can provide services and amenities for mountain bike riders before and after their rides.

Mountain Bike Rider Studies

Mountain bike riders appear to be a committed group. Various measures indicate that these riders often own more than one bike, and that they have invested sizable amounts of money and time in their sport. Most of the mountain bike riders contacted rode their mountain bike for enjoyment, fun, a love of mountain biking, or for exercise. Many riders reported that mountain biking was one of the most important things they did and that mountain bike riding "said a lot about who they were" and even that their life was "organized around" mountain bike riding. Most rode with their friends, but many belonged to groups, either local or national, and many riders took part in mountain biking events. Nonetheless, these riders also recognized some of the issues associated with their sport. Several reported that the major issues for trail riding included access to trails, impacts to natural resources, conflicts with other groups, trail etiquette, and safety.

Studies of various forest users by Chase (1987), Chavez et al. (1993a), Jacoby (1990), Tilmant (1991), Viehman (1990), and Watson, Williams, and Daigle (1991) found that conflict related to mountain bike use was an important issue. Often, the mountain bike riders are seen as interlopers on trails that were previously used by others. Watson et al. (1991) found evidence of asymmetrical conflict: although one-quarter of the mountain bike riders viewed hikers as a problem, almost two-thirds of the hikers viewed mountain bikers as a problem. Tilmant (1991) found that hiker complaints about mountain bike riders included esthetics, personal beliefs, and desire for solitude. Equestrian groups raised concerns related to safety.

Likely Trends in Mountain Biking

Studies of mountain biking on public land predict expansion of the sport (Chavez, et al., 1993a; Chavez, 1996a; Tilmant, 1991). This expansion can take several directions. It appears that mountain bike riders are committed to the sport and will continue to participate. While the number of mountain bike riders may eventually peak, those who ride may do so more often and go to more places for new recreational experiences.

Many recreation sites that had been traditionally used for other activities are now also used for mountain biking. The best example is the move to use downhill skiing sites for mountain bike riding in the non-snow months. This use can have positive economic impacts for these areas in the "off season." Also, some mountain bike riders are participating in snow-related events such as mountain bike snow races. Thus, mountain bikes are being used in new places and ways.

Many mountain biking events have been held in the past few years, and they are drawing hundreds of participants and thousands of viewers. Since many of these events are held in natural environments, there are implications for the management of those events as well as for local economies.

Mountain bikers who belong to clubs and organizations plan to continue their membership and participation in those groups, in part because these groups have assisted in gaining access to sites and are perceived as giving a collective voice for the rights of mountain bike riders.

Management appears to rely mostly on indirect strategies of getting information to the riders (signs, posters). These techniques will continue to be utilized, because resources for managing natural sites are decreasing. Another tool—bridge building—may become increasingly important. This strategy includes personal involvement by managers and site users.

Whitewater Recreation Trends in the United States

(By Richard J. Bowers and Richard R. Hoffman, American Whitewater Affiliation, Silver Spring, MD)

Reflective of larger societal trends, interest in outdoor recreation across the U.S. is growing and changing as well (ORCA, 1997). In the era of downsizing, global markets and the information superhighway, today's workforce is required to do more with less and must manage increasing amounts of information. Hectic work schedules and stress have created a greater demand for recreational pursuits and more challenging sports that provide excitement, community, and some degree of risk (Hart, 1991).

Whitewater boating is one of the fastest growing human-powered outdoor recreation sports (President's Commission on the Outdoors, 1987), (*Canoe Magazine*, 1993) and is attracting new participants because it incorporates many skills and needs. Whitewater boating allows for both individual accomplishment as well as companionship. While challenging the physical and mental skills of the individual, river running also takes place in groups and helps build teamwork and friendship. Since good paddling depends more on technique than strength, it also attracts more women and young adults.

Whitewater boaters can experience solitude. Even on urban rivers, they can quickly become removed from crowds once on the water. Whitewater is also a sport with some degree of risk characterized by personal achievement and freedom, which often are popular attributes for a recreation activity.

Changes Affecting Whitewater Rivers and Access

Like other outdoor recreation interests, whitewater boating depends on the quality and quantity of available opportunities. Our legacy of heavy development of river resources for hydropower, water supply, and flood control has taken a toll on river resources. In addition to altering habitat and restricting free flowing rivers, this development has reduced the number of river miles available for swimming, boating, fishing, and other human use. Today, less than one percent of the river miles in the United States has whitewater rapids rated at Class II or better (American Whitewater Affiliation, 1990). Often, these are the upstream, headwater portions of our rivers, and some of the most sensitive, critical, and visually appealing of riverine environments.

Obtaining public access to whitewater rivers continues to be a challenge. Legal issues such as access across private land to reach the rivers and the right to travel downstream, in addition to concerns about liability for accidents or injuries, affect the availability of both private and public rivers for recreation. Even where access is not denied outright, rules and regulations have resulted in restrictions on some whitewater rivers, especially on public land. For example, whitewater boaters are banned from all rivers in Yellowstone National Park. In the Grand Canyon National Park, perhaps the premier whitewater destination in the United States, noncommercial boaters must wait up to 10 years for a permit. On the "numbers" section of the Arkansas River in Colorado, the most heavily used whitewater river in the nation, there has been no legal public access in recent years. Increased fees are now being proposed for a host of other rivers, including the Chattooga, Middle Ocoee, and Nantahala in the Southeast, the Rogue and South Fork American in California, and the Upper Youghiogheny in Maryland. Access to rivers is often restricted by the federal government, state agencies, local counties, and private landowners as well.

Increasingly, the supply of quality whitewater opportunities can be attributed in part to the whitewater sport itself. Overcrowding is a concern on popular whitewater rivers like the Ocoee (TN), the Lower Youghiogheny (PA), and the South Fork American (CA). Overcrowding often results in use quotas and lowered experience quality.

Issues and Direction

Seeking to conserve whitewater opportunities, American Whitewater has worked on the following programs:

- The *conservation* of scarce river resources is a high priority. Recreational users are playing a greater role in river conservation as the economic, social, and environmental benefits of whitewater boating are becoming more visible. Whitewater boating will benefit from the permanent protection of nationally significant whitewater rivers like the Clavey in California and the Blackwater in West Virginia.
- A significant opportunity exists to restore whitewater resources through *relicensing of hundreds of existing privately-owned hydropower dams*. Hydro relicensing offers the unique chance to open up whitewater rivers that have been dry for decades. Over the last five years, the dam relicensing process has successfully restored and improved over 80 miles of whitewater. This number includes rivers such as the Black and Beaver (NY), Kern (CA), Nisqually (WA), Tallulah (GA), Pemigewasset (NH), Deerfield (MA/VT), and many others. Between now and the year 2015, another 515 dam projects will also seek new licenses, providing further opportunities to restore river flows.
- Whitewater-related user groups, like paddlers, anglers, and climbers, are working together to negotiate *access and fee policies* with federal, state, and local land managers, and to improve state laws on landowner liability. For example, American Whitewater Affiliation (AWA) works to improve access at regulated hydropower projects, to obtain fair allocations of use between commercial and private boaters on newly regulated rivers, and to cooperate with national, regional, and local land trusts, canoe clubs, and statewide river organizations to acquire rights to streamside lands. Recently, AWA purchased critical access lands to the Blackwater (WV) and Watauga (NC).
- Whitewater user groups are pursuing the right to travel and to portage around obstacles in canoes, kayaks, and other recreational water craft on the waters of rivers that can be navigated by small recreational craft. Confusion about the respective rights of riparian landowners and recreationists has caused conflict in many states with outstanding whitewater.
- *Educating whitewater boaters* about personal responsibility, special hazards, and safety techniques is important. The American Whitewater Safety Code is the most comprehensive and widely distributed source of safety information for whitewater boaters and has been published widely in guidebooks and instructional books around the U.S. and the world. To maintain an "institutional knowledge" base for whitewater safety, AWA provides a database of serious whitewater-related accidents. Maintenance of these data has become difficult due to growth of the sport and the present legal climate. AWA also produces waterproof flash cards that serve as refresher courses on rescue and safety techniques.
- Whitewater groups have organized a variety of *river celebrations* across the country such as whitewater rodeos, new kinds of races, and film festivals. One example is the Gauley River Festival (WV), the largest collection of whitewater boaters in the country outside of racing and Olympic events. There are more than 20 whitewater rodeo events around the nation that emphasize local river conservation and access issues and include local boaters in these issues.

The Future of Whitewater Recreation

Whitewater boating, and indeed all outdoor recreation, will be pressured in the future by declining access and resources and increased demand. Perhaps less obvious, but equally critical, are changes in fees, rules, and regulations. While less tangible than dams or barbed wire fences, these issues are highly significant.

The allocation of access and use rights among competing uses will also be a key discussion point in the future. Besides various forms of human-powered whitewater boating, the wildest rivers are increasingly attracting new user groups, and the most obvious groups are jet boats and jet skis (The Water Skier, 1996). Motorized use in whitewater recreation is already prominent on the Lower Gauley and New River (WV), the Upper Kern (CA), Hells Canyon (ID), and the Skagit (WA). River resources should be available to a wide variety of users, but there are several reasons why motorized use is a problem in whitewater recreation. First, it detracts from the solitude sought by muscle-powered boaters on wild and wilderness rivers. Second, it poses safety hazards to human-powered recreationists. There is little concern over the noise levels of jet boats and jet skis, since it is almost impossible to hear them over large waves and through protective helmets. There is concern for safety of motorized operators as well in that some 2,500 collisions (almost half of all reported water crashes) were attributed to jet-skies in 1994.

Only one percent of our nation's rivers contain Class 2 and above whitewater, including rivers affected by dams, pollution, and other development. This one percent also includes many rivers that have sufficient water flow for boating only a few days per year. Compared to the estimated 2,100 man-made lakes managed and owned by the federal government (National Recreation Lakes Study, 1996), whitewater is a small and declining resource.

PARTICIPATION DIFFERENCES AMONG SOCIAL GROUPS

(By Cassandra Johnson, Social Scientist, USDA Forest Service, Athens, GA)

Population experts predict that the demographic composition of the U.S. population will change significantly over the next 30 years. One of the most notable changes will be a general aging of the population. Trends have already shown that median population age has been steadily increasing since the turn of the century. In 1900, the median age was 24. By 1980, it was 30 and is expected to increase to 36 by the year 2000 and to 41 by 2025 (USDA Forest Service, 1994).

These changes in the age structure have implications for outdoor recreation managers because participation by older individuals tend to increase with successive generations. While participation generally decreases with advancing age, English and Cordell (1985) report that age alone does not sufficiently explain changes in participation. Cohort and period effects should also be considered. For example, the much discussed baby boomers, those born between 1946 and 1964, were introduced at a young age to a wider array of outdoor recreation opportunities than were their parents. Most experts agree that as baby boomers age, they will maintain an interest in many outdoor recreation activities, such as sightseeing, walking for pleasure, and picnicking (Cordell, et al., 1990). The full impact of this maturing generation on outdoor recreation supply has yet to be felt. Moreover, the coming baby bust cohort, those born between 1965 and 1976, and the baby boomlet generation, born between 1977 and 1995, are expected to introduce increasing demands for relatively new activities such as mountain biking, ORV use, rollerblading, snowboarding, and other activities not yet envisioned.

The population is also expected to diversify even more with respect to ethnic and racial background. In 1995, the racial and ethnic composition of the U.S. was estimated at 74 percent white; 12 percent African American; 10 percent Hispanic; three percent Asian/Pacific Islander; and less than one percent American Indian (U.S. Census Bureau, 1994). However, projections of demographic trends indicate that populations of racial and ethnic minorities are growing faster than the U.S. population as a whole. Consider the following: the overall U.S. population is predicted to increase by 70 million between 1980 and 2025, with about 25 million coming from Hispanic groups, 17 million from African Americans, and 14 million from other ethnic groups. Thus, 80 percent of the growth is expected to come from groups that are currently minority populations (Murdock, Backman, Colberg, Hoque, & Hamm, 1990; USDA Forest Service, 1994).

Natural resource management policies could be impacted by these cultural and ethnic changes. It may be that recent Hispanic and Asian/Pacific Islander immigrant groups, as well as some racial and ethnic groups that have been in the U.S. for generations, hold an environmental ethic or orientation different from the North American model based on resource conservation (Simcox, 1993; Hutchison, 1993; Woo, 1996). Resource management agencies, such as the USDA Forest Service, are responding to some of these demographic changes by initiating research to learn more about ethnic recreation behaviors. These initiatives are raising

Snowboarding is gaining popularity among post-baby boom snow and ice recreationists. Photo courtesy of the National Ski Areas Association.

questions about forest use among different racial/ethnic and immigrant groups and about why some of these groups make relatively little use of national forests. For example, studies have established that African Americans are less likely than European Americans to recreate in dispersed settings or to travel to regional recreation areas. Also, Hispanic visitors tend to be more family- and group-oriented when visiting outdoor recreation areas (Dwyer, 1994).

The following sections describe the influences of age, race, sex, income, household size, and education level on outdoor recreation participation. The data source is the 1994-1995 NSRE.[3]

Participation Among Sociodemographic Groups by Types of Activities

Fitness Activities: Running or jogging, biking, walking

Approximately 77 percent of Americans in the 16-24 age group participate in fitness activities (Table V.11). This rate remains fairly constant over the next several age categories, but decreases substantially for the 60-and-over age group. Even for this oldest age group, about 50 percent reported participation. There is virtually no difference in fitness participation for younger groups (16-24 and 25-29) and those in their thirties and forties. Data show that roughly 70 percent of whites participated in fitness activities, compared to about 60 percent for African Americans and other racial and ethnic groups. Walking was most popular for all three racial or ethnic groups.[3] Running or jogging was the second most popular activity for African Americans and others, and biking was the second most frequently mentioned activity for whites.

Men and women participated to a similar extent in fitness activities, 70 percent and 67 percent, respectively.[3] Walking was mentioned most often by both sexes, followed by biking and running or jogging. Participation in most fitness activities also increased with rising income.[3] The only exception was walking. Respondents with annual incomes more than $100,000 were slightly less likely than those with incomes between $75,000 and $100,000 to participate in walking. Participation in fitness activities also varied by number of people in the household. As the number of household members increased, participation increased as well.[3] However, with five or more household members, participation decreased. This value was true for both biking and walking. People with more education tended to participate more in fitness activities.[3] Participation declined, however, for running or jogging among high school graduates and those with some college or technical school training and then increased again for respondents who had completed college.

---

[3]This information is available in table form from the USDA Forest Service, Outdoor Recreation, 320 Green Street, Athens, GA 30602-2044.

Table V.11: Percent of U.S. Population Participating in Fitness Activities by Age Group, 1994-95

Activity	16-24	25-29	30-39	40-49	50-59	Over 60
Fitness Activities	77.2	74.7	76.1	72.0	64.0	49.7
Running/Jogging	50.4	33.2	28.3	23.3	17.4	8.1
Biking	37.9	36.2	37.4	30.7	21.9	10.6
Walking	68.1	72.4	74.6	71.9	64.0	49.7

Source: 1994-95 National Survey on Recreation and the Environment, USDA Forest Service and the University of Georgia, Athens, Georgia. The NSRE is the most recent of the series of National Recreation Surveys begun nationally in 1960.

Individual Sport Activities

About 32 percent of people 16 to 24 years old participated in individual sport activities such as golf and tennis. Participation decreased steadily for the remaining age categories. Golf was the most frequently mentioned individual sport activity for whites (17 percent), and tennis was mentioned more often by African Americans (7.8 percent) and others (12.8 percent). Men were more likely than women to participate in individual sport activities. Golf was mentioned more often by men, and women and men were about as equally likely to participate in tennis. As with fitness activities, participation in individual sports also increased with income. Respondents with annual earnings more than $100,000 participated four times as much as respondents earning less than $15,000 per year. Golf participation, in particular, increased dramatically with rising income. As with fitness activities, participation increased steadily up to four household members and then declined for households with five or more members. This value was also true for both golf and tennis. Roughly 18 percent of those with some high school education participated in individual sports. This rate dropped to about 16 percent for those who had completed high school, and increased again for those with college-level education.

Outdoor Team Sport Activities: Baseball, softball, football, basketball, soccer, volleyball, handball

For these generally vigorous activities, participation was highest for the youngest age cohort. About 40 percent of the 25-29 age group participated, 33 percent of the 30-39 group, and 22 of the 40-44 cohort. One-quarter of whites participated in outdoor team sport activities, one-third of African Americans did so, and about 30 percent of others participated in these activities. Volleyball and softball were mentioned most often by whites, and basketball and volleyball were the two most popular outdoor team sports for African Americans and others. Again, men were more active than women in outdoor team sports. Basketball and softball were most popular among males, and volleyball and softball were most popular for females.

Participation in outdoor team sports increased steadily for household incomes up to $74,999 per year and then remained constant for the $75,000 to $99,999 income group and increased again for the $100,000 plus income groups. Basketball, softball, and volleyball participation actually decreased for the highest income category (over $100,000). Participation increased steadily with increasing income. This trend was true for all activities within outdoor team sports. For many of these activities, the educational group with highest participation was the group with less than high school education. This finding is probably due in part to the greater prevalence of such activities among adolescent groups involved in high school and community sports activities.

Outdoor Spectator Activities

Participation in outdoor spectator activities, such as outdoor concerts and sporting events followed a pattern similar to those of most other activities. The youngest age cohort reported the greatest amount of participation, followed in decreasing order by older groups. Within categories of outdoor spectator activities, just over 40 percent of the youngest age cohorts attended concerts. This rate decreased to about 36 percent for those aged 30-49. Attendance at sporting events was fairly high for all categories except the over-60 group. Males were more likely than females to engage in all kinds of outdoor spectator activities (Table V.12). Attending sporting events was the type of outdoor spectator activity mentioned most often by all three racial and ethnic groups and by men and women. Participation in outdoor spectator activities also increased steadily with rising income. Participation in individual spectator activities increased steadily up to four household members and then either declined or remained constant for households with five or more members. More highly educated respondents also tended to participate more in outdoor spectator activities.

Table V.12: Percent of U.S. Population Participating in Outdoor Spectator Activities by Sex, 1994-95

Activity	Male	Female
Outdoor spectator activities	63.8	54.0
Concerts	35.7	32.8
Attending sporting events	53.6	41.9

Source: 1994-95 National Survey on Recreation and the Environment, USDA Forest Service and the University of Georgia, Athens, Georgia. The NSRE is the most recent of the series of National Recreation Surveys begun nationally in 1960.

Viewing Activities: Nature and visitor centers, prehistoric and historic sites, birdwatching, wildlife and fish viewing, sightseeing, beach or waterside, water-based nature study

About 80 percent of respondents in the first four age cohorts said they participated in a viewing activity.[4] This rate decreased to 56 percent for those over 60. For many of these less strenuous activities, such as bird watching, wildlife viewing, and sightseeing, participation increased with advancing age, but then declined for the last two age categories. Approximately 80 percent of whites reported participating in viewing activities. Sixty-two percent of African Americans and about 67 percent of other groups did so. Visiting a beach or waterside was the most frequently mentioned viewing activity for all racial and ethnic groups, and viewing activities were just about as popular for men as for women.

Income generally had a positive influence on participation in most viewing activities. Participation in bird watching, however, was less affected by income. About 20 percent of those earning less than $15,000 per year reported bird–watching activities. The rate increased to 30 percent for those in the next highest income category and was constant over higher income groups. Participation in viewing activities increased for all household sizes up to five members. As with other activities, participation increased steadily up to four household members and then declined for households with five or more members. This was the case for all viewing activities. Viewing activities also varied positively with increasing education.

Snow and Ice Activities: Ice skating, snowboarding, sledding, downhill skiing, cross-country skiing, snowmobiling

About 25 percent of the 16-24, 25-29, and 30-39 age cohorts reported participation in snow and ice activities. Participation decreased steadily for the remaining age groups. Sledding and downhill skiing were the most frequently mentioned activities in this category. Whites were much more likely than either African Americans or others to engage in snow and ice activities. This is a typical pattern reported in the recreation literature (Dwyer, 1994). While whites reported greater participation than blacks in snow and ice activities, they were similar to African Americans in terms of participation patterns. For example, sledding was the most frequently mentioned activity in this category by both whites and blacks. Downhill skiing was reported most often for other groups. Men were more likely than women to participate in snow and ice activities, and sledding and downhill skiing were the top two activities for both men and women.

Annual income also affected participation in snow-related activities. Downhill skiing increased the most with rising income. Again, participation varied positively with increasing household members up to four and then declined for households with five or more members. About 15 percent of those with the least amount of education reported participation in these activities. The rate decreased slightly for those with a high school diploma, and increased again for respondents with some college or a college degree.

Camping: Developed and primitive camping

Roughly 37 percent of respondents in the 16 to 24 age group participated in some kind of camping. Approximately 33 percent of respondents in the next two age groups participated in camping activities; 28 percent of those age 40-49 did so; 19 percent of those age 50-59; and about 11 percent of those 60 and over participated in camping. Higher proportions of respondents engaged in developed, rather than in primitive, camping. Whites and others camped more frequently than African Americans. Men were also more likely than women to camp, particularly in primitive settings. Camping increased with income up to the middle-income

[4]This information is available in table form from the USDA Forest Service, Outdoor Recreation, 320 Green Street, Athens, GA 30602-2044.

groups, then decreased for the two highest income categories. Participation varied positively with number of people in the household, and a greater education level was associated with increasing participation in camping, except for those with a college degree.

Hunting: Big game, small game, migratory bird

Hunting was more popular for younger age groups, and big and small game hunting were the most popular forms. Hunting was also more popular with whites than either African Americans or others, and all forms of hunting were predominantly male activities. Overall, hunting participation for the highest income group was nearly twice the rate for the lowest income group. Hunting also varied positively with number of household members. However, for households of five or more, participation decreased somewhat for migratory bird hunting. Overall, hunting declined after the high school level of education. The only exception was for migratory bird hunting.

Fishing: Freshwater, saltwater, warmwater, coldwater, ice, anadromous, catch and release

Participation in fishing remained fairly steady over the first four age groups (between 31 percent and 35 percent) and then dropped to about 25 and 17 percent, respectively, for the last two categories. Freshwater and warmwater fishing were the two most popular forms for all age groups. Ice fishing was reported least. Fishing was reported by about 31 percent of whites, about 19 percent of African Americans, and roughly 24 percent of others. Freshwater fishing was the most popular kind of fishing for each racial or ethnic group (Table V.13). A much greater proportion of women participated in fishing than in hunting. Like men, women were more likely to engage in freshwater and warmwater fishing.

Table V.13: Percent of U.S. Population Participating in Fishing Activities by Race/Ethnicity, 1994-95

Activity	White	African-American	Other (including Hispanic)
Fishing	30.6	19.1	49.7
Freshwater fishing	26.3	15.0	16.8
Warmwater fishing	21.9	12.8	13.6
Ice fishing	2.3	0.3	0.6
Anadromous fihsing	4.8	3.2	3.1
Catch and release fishing	8.5	3.9	5.2

Source: 1994-95 National Survey on Recreation and the Environment, USDA Forest Service and the University of Georgia, Athens, Georgia. The NSRE is the most recent of the series of National Recreation Surveys begun nationally in 1960.

As with most other activities, fishing participation also increased with rising income. However, for three kinds of fishing—warmwater, ice, and catch and release, participation either declined or remained constant for the highest income group. The number of people in the household influenced fishing participation as well. For many of the activities within this category, participation increased for households with four or fewer members and then decreased for households with five or more people. All kinds of fishing decreased for people with a college degree.

Boating, sailing, canoeing, kayaking, rowing, floating and rafting, motorboating, water skiing, jet skiing, sailboarding, and windsurfing

Overall, boating activities were reported most often by the 25-29 and 16-24 age groups. Motorboating was the most popular form for all age and ethnic groups, followed by waterskiing and canoeing. Boating activities were more popular among whites than African Americans and others. Roughly one-quarter of women, compared to about one-third of men, reported participation in some form of boating activity. Motorboating was the most popular boating activity for both males and females.

Boating participation was affected greatly by level of income (Table V.14). This relationship is not surprising given that equipment and storage for such activities can be quite costly. Sailing and waterskiing were about four times higher for the highest as for the lowest income group; and canoeing and motorboating were about three times higher. Jet skiing increased most dramatically from two percent participation for persons earning less than $15,000 per annum to 13 percent for those earning over $100,000 per year. All income groups reported the greater levels of participation in motorboating than in other activities.

Overall boating participation is lower for households with five or more members; however, canoeing, kayaking, and rowing participation steadily increased over household size. Also, more educated Americans tended to engage more in boating activities.

Table V.14: Percent of U.S. Population Participating in Boating Activities by Household Income, 1994-95

Activity	<$15,000	$15,000-24,999	$25,000-49,999	$50,000-74,999	$75,000 or more
Boating	19.0	29.0	39.0	48.0	52.0
Sailing	3.0	3.0	5.0	9.0	12.0
Canoeing	4.0	6.0	9.0	14.0	13.0
Motorboating	15.0	23.0	33.0	39.0	43.0
Waterskiing	5.0	8.0	12.0	15.0	18.0
Jet skiing	2.0	4.0	6.0	8.0	12.0

Source: 1994-95 National Survey on Recreation and the Environment, USDA Forest Service and the University of Georgia, Athens, Georgia. The NSRE is the most recent of the series of National Recreation Surveys begun nationally in 1960.

Swimming activities: Surfing, pool swimming, lakes, rivers, and ocean swimming, snorkeling and scuba diving

Over one-half of all Americans engage in some type of swimming. These activities were among the most popular activities for all age groups. Close to 70 percent of the younger groups participated in some kind of swimming activity. Pools and lakes, rivers, and ocean swimming are the most popular forms of swimming activity for all age, racial, and ethnic groups. Both males and females report high participation in swimming.

Generally, higher income groups reported greater participation in swimming than lower income groups. This value was true for all swimming activities except pool swimming, where the highest income group reported slightly less participation than the second highest group. Income varied most with snorkeling and scuba activities. Nearly seven times as many in the highest, compared to the lowest income group, participated in snorkeling and scuba diving. Swimming participation also decreased for households with five or more members, and swimming participation increased steadily with increasing levels of education.

Outdoor adventure activities: Hiking, orienteering, backpacking, mountain climbing, rock climbing, caving, off-road driving, horseback riding

About half of all respondents in the 16-24 and 25-29 age groups participated in outdoor adventure activities. Participation rates were approximately 44 percent for the 30-39 age group; 40 percent for the 40-49 year-olds; 30 percent for the 50-59 year-olds; and just over 15 percent of those 60 and over. Hiking was the most popular outdoor activity for all age groups followed by off-road driving. Outdoor adventure activities were more popular among whites and Asian-Americans than among African Americans. Hiking, in particular, was cited more frequently by whites than other racial and ethnic groups. Outdoor activities were somewhat more popular for men than for women. Hiking and off-road driving were mentioned most often by both sexes. More highly educated Americans were also more likely to participate in these activities.

Income was also positively correlated with outdoor adventure activities. Horseback riding showed the greatest increase with rising income. Only five percent of those in the lowest income groups participated in horseback riding, while 16 percent of those earning over $100,000 per annum did so. Participation in outdoor adventure activities also increased steadily across all household sizes. Table V.15 shows the same was true for education levels.

Table V.15: Percent of U.S. Population Participating in Outdoor Adventure Activities by Household Education Level, 1994-95

Activity	Some High School	High School	Some College	Completed College
Outdoor Adventure Activities				
Hiking	29.8	31.2	40.1	42.4
Backpacking	18.3	17.5	25.8	31.1
Mountain climbing	4.6	3.5	4.9	4.9
Rock climbing	3.9	3.3	3.7	4.0
Off-road driving	14.1	14.2	16.6	11.0
Horseback riding	7.6	6.0	7.6	7.8

Source: 1994-95 National Survey on Recreation and the Environment, USDA Forest Service and the University of Georgia, Athens, Georgia. The NSRE is the most recent of the series of National Recreation Survey series begun nationally in 1960.

Social activities: Yard games, picnicking, family gathering

Participation was at least 70 percent in every age category except the 50-59 and 60 and older groups. Family gathering was the most popular of these activities for all ages. Social activity participation was also high for all three racial or ethnic groups, with family gatherings again being the most popular activity, followed by picnicking and yard games. All forms of social activities were popular for males and females. Participation in social activities increased steadily with income up to the middle income range of $25,000 to $49,999 per year. Thereafter, participation remained steady at 85 percent for the three highest income groups. As earlier noted, outdoor activity participation tended to increase for one to four member households and then decrease for households with five or more members. Also, as education level increased, so did participation in social activities. This was particularly true for picnicking and family gathering.

Participation Trends Among Demographic Groups

In examining participation, it is informative to look at the changes in participation rates for different groups across time. Information on participation trends can indicate possible future trends in demand for outdoor recreation activities. Figures V.7 through V.9 compare average number of activities per year by people age 16 or older by age, sex, race, household income, education level, and size of place of residence. These estimates are from the 1982-1983 National Recreation Survey (NRS) (which included persons 12 or older) and 1994-95 National Survey on Recreation and the Environment. Comparisons show that average number of activities people engaged in over the past 12 months increased across all demographic groups during the 12–year period between surveys.

Figure V.7: Average Number of Activities by Age, 1982-83 and 1994-95

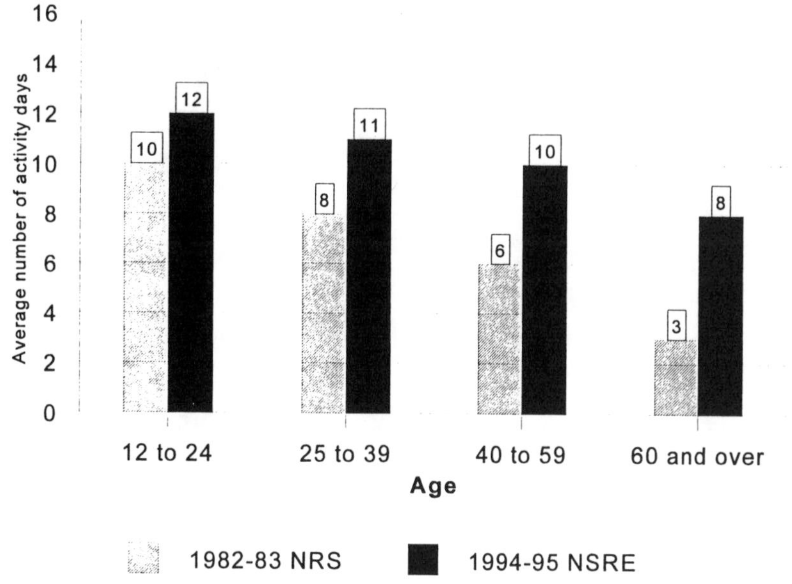

Source: 1994-95 National Survey on Recreation and the Environment (NSRE), USDA Forest Service and the University of Georgia, Athens, Georgia, and National Recreation Survey (NRS), 1982-1983.

Figure V.8: Average Number of Activities by Race, 1982-83 and 1994-95

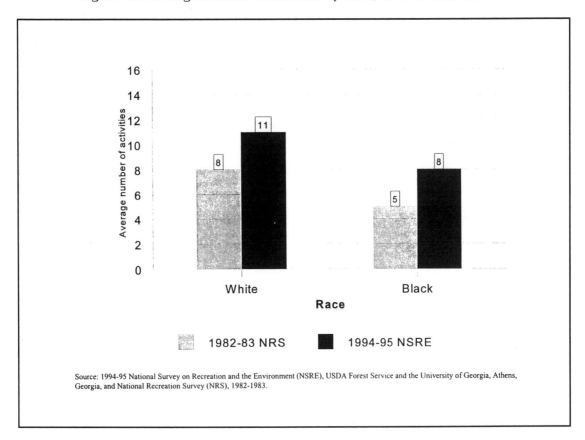

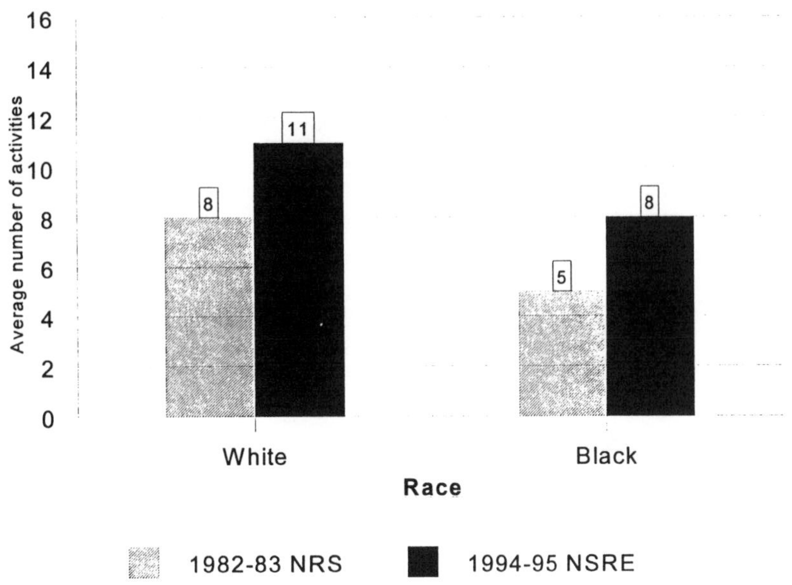

Source: 1994-95 National Survey on Recreation and the Environment (NSRE), USDA Forest Service and the University of Georgia, Athens, Georgia, and National Recreation Survey (NRS), 1982-1983.

Figure V.9: Average Number of Activities by Household Income, 1982-83 and 1994-95

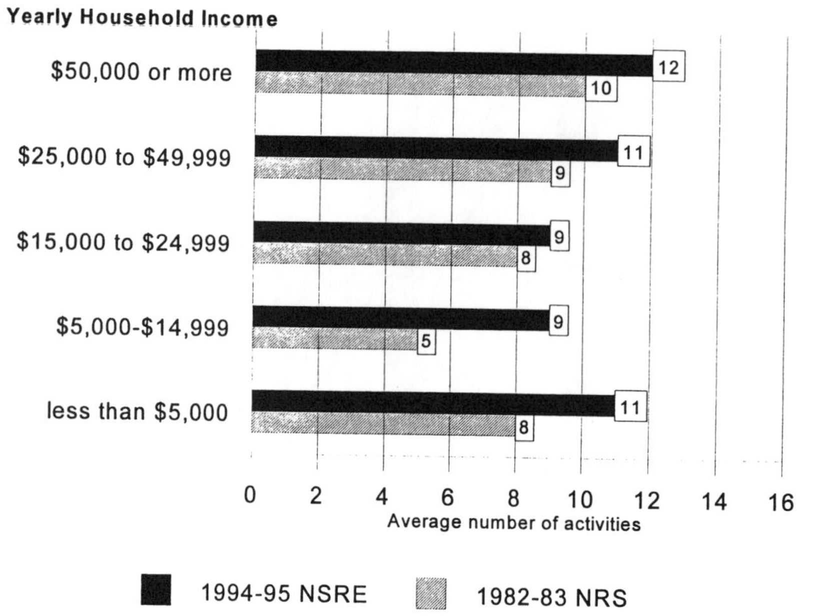

Source: 1994-95 National Survey on Recreation and the Environment (NSRE), USDA Forest Service and the University of Georgia, Athens, Georgia, and National Recreation Survey (NRS), 1982-1983.

Tables V.16 and V.17 present demographic breakdowns of average numbers of activity days and average numbers of trips, respectively, for bicycling, outdoor non-pool swimming, freshwater fishing, developed camping, and picnicking by age, sex, race, household income, education level, number of cars in household, and size of place of residence. These estimates are based on activity days and trips per year by participants.

Table V.16: Average Number of Participation Days by Social Characteristic for Bicycling, Non-Pool Swimming, Freshwater Fishing, Developed Camping, and Picnicking

Social Characteristic	Average Number of Trips				
	Bicycling	Non-pool swimming	Freshwater fishing	Developed camping	Picnicking
Sex					
Male	42	16	21	10	8
Female	36	16	14	11	10
Age					
16-24	40	19	16	8	8
25-39	37	15	17	9	10
40-59	38	14	21	11	9
60 & over	48	15	19	25	7
Race					
White	38	17	18	11	9
Black	42	8	19	7	7
Income					
less than$5,000	24	16	11	5	8
$5,000-$14,999	52	14	17	8	10
$15,000- $24,999	47	16	23	12	10
$25,000- $49,999	34	15	19	10	9
$50,000 or more	40	17	15	10	9
Education					
less than high school	41	15	16	9	10
high school	39	16	22	12	9
less than college	38	17	18	11	9
college or more	39	15	15	9	8
Car Ownership					
0 cars	50	15	20	11	7
1 car	44	15	18	8	9
2 cars	37	15	17	10	9
3 cars	36	17	20	14	8
4 or more cars	39	18	20	11	9
Size of Residence					
less than 5,000	33	9	17	10	12
5,000-24,999	30	16	25	13	9
25,000-49,999	41	14	20	10	7
50,000-999,999	40	16	18	11	9
1 million or more	39	16	11	9	9

Source: 1994-95 National Survey on Recreation and the Environment, USDA Forest Service and University of Georgia, Athens, GA. The NSRE is the most recent of the series of National Recreation Survey series begun nationally in 1960.

Table V.17: Average Number of Trips by Social Characteristic for Bicycling, Non-Pool Swimming, Freshwater Fishing, Developed Camping, and Picnicking

Social Characteristic	Average Number of Trips				
	Non-pool Bicycling	Freshwater swimming	Developed fishing	camping	Picnicking
Sex					
Male	27	11	11	5	6
Female	21	11	11	5	7
Age					
16-24	20	12	11	4	6
25-39	20	11	16	5	7
40-59	32	10	17	51	7
60 & over	47	85	12	85	6
Race					
White	23	11	15	5	7
Black	28	7	18	2	5
Income					
less than $5,000	11	16	9	5	8
$5,000-$14,999	18	11	15	4	7
$15,000- $24,999	27	11	19	52	8
$25,000- $49,999	20	10	16	40	7
$50,000 or more	25	11	12	60	7
Education					
less than high school	23	10	12	4	7
high school	31	11	18	62	7
less than college	22	12	15	6	7
college or more	20	10	16	4	7
Car Ownership					
0 cars	11	11	20	5	6
1 car	25	11	16	4	7
2 cars	27	10	14	5	7
3 cars	21	11	16	6	6
4 or more cars	22	11	15	6	7
Size of residence					
less than 5,000	17	7	14	60	8
5,000-24,999	20	13	19	53	6
25,000-49,999	16	11	16	6	6
50,000-999,999	24	10	16	5	7
1 million or more	29	12	71	3	7

Source: 1994-95 National Survey on Recreation and the Environment, USDA Forest Service and University of Georgia, Athens, GA. The NSRE is the most recent of the series of National Recreation Survey series begun nationally in 1960.

Eleven high-profile activities were also chosen to compare participant composition across time. These activities included bicycling, walking, outdoor swimming, attending outdoor sports, boating, fishing, hunting, developed camping, hiking, bird watching, and picnicking for the 1982-1983 NRS and 1995 NSRE, respectively.[5] The data address the question of the types of people who participate in a given activity, for example, "What kinds of people engage in walking for pleasure, developed camping, or picnicking in 1995?" This information was obtained by first identifying the respondents who said they participated in an activity and then determining what percentage were between the ages of 16-24; what percentage were women or men; or what proportion had less than high school education, etc. Generally, activity participation increased between the two time periods for each demographic category although there were some notable exceptions. For instance, 40 percent of walkers in 1982-83 were male. This rate increased to 47 percent in the 1994-95 NSRE. The proportion of walkers who were female decreased from 60 to 53 percent.

[5]This information is available in table form from the USDA Forest Service, Outdoor Recreation, 320 Green Street, Athens, GA 30602-2044.

Participation in Outdoor Recreation Activities by Hispanic Americans, American Indians, and Asian Americans

We also looked more closely at the "other" racial category to determine what, if any, differences existed among Americans of Hispanic, American Indian (Native Americans), and Asian/Pacific Islander heritage. Hispanic Americans comprised about five percent (n=797) of the respondents to the NSRE and American Indians 155 and Asian Americans 240 respondents or about one percent each. This more in-depth analysis is important because much of the population increase over the next 50 years will come from these groups, particularly Hispanic Americans. Though there are readily identifiable cultural differences among groups within each of these categories, e.g, Mexican-Americans and Puerto Rican Americans, Japanese Americans and Korean Americans, and Plains Indians compared to Eastern Indian nations, we could not examine differences within each of these groups because of limited sample sizes.

Hispanic American visitors complete a Forest Service questionnaire on visitor use at the San Bernadino National Forest in southern California. Photo courtesy of USDA Forest Service. Photo by Deborah Chavez.

Fitness Activities

Table V.18 shows the proportion of Hispanic Americans, American Indians, and Asian Americans who participated in 25 outdoor recreation activities. Roughly one-third of all Hispanic Americans and close to 40 percent of Asian Americans participated in running or jogging, compared to about 27 percent of American Indians. Roughly one-third of Hispanic Americans, American Indians, and Asian Americans reported biking activities, and about 60 percent of each racial or ethnic group participated in walking.

Individual Sport and Outdoor Team Sports

Asian Americans were more likely than either Hispanic Americans or American Indians to participate in either golf or tennis. Asian Americans were also twice as likely as Hispanic Americans to participate in tennis and four times as likely as American Indians to report tennis participation. In fact, tennis was the most popular sport for Asian Americans. Basketball was mentioned most frequently by Hispanic Americans, while American Indians were more likely to participate in volleyball.

Outdoor Spectator and Viewing Activities

Each racial group participated to a similar extent in concert going (between 31 and 34 percent). Roughly equal proportions also attended sporting events (between 40 and 45 percent). About 47 percent of Asian/Pacific Islanders visited nature centers and zoos. Slightly less participation was reported by American Indians (43 percent), and about 41 percent of Hispanic Americans visited nature centers and zoos. American Indians were more likely than the other two groups to bird watch, and Asian Americans and American Indians were more likely than Hispanic Americans to sightsee.

Camping, Hunting, Fishing, Boating, and Swimming

About 28 percent of American Indians participated in developed camping; about 21 percent of Hispanic Americans and 18 percent Asian Americans did so as well. American Indians (21 percent) were also more than three times as likely as Hispanic Americans to participate in any kind of hunting activity, and about four times as likely as Asian Americans to hunt. Forty-three percent of American Indians participated in fishing, compared to 29 percent for Asian Americans, and 25 percent for Hispanic American groups. Twenty-nine percent of American Indians engaged in boating, and roughly one-quarter of Asian Americans and Hispanic Americans did so. All groups participated to a similar extent in both pool and non-pool swimming.

Outdoor Adventure and Social Activities

American Indians and Hispanic Americans were somewhat more likely than Asian Americans to day hike, and off-road driving was more popular among American Indians. Participation in social activities was very popular. American Indians were more likely than either Hispanic Americans or Asian Americans to participate in yard games. Americans Indians and Asian Americans were also more likely than Hispanic Americans to picnic, and Hispanic Americans reported slightly less participation than the other two groups in family gathering activities.

Table V.18: Percent of Hispanic American, American Indian, and Asian Americans Participating in Outdoor Recreation Activities, 1994-95

Activity	Ethnic Group		
	Hispanic American	American Indian	Asian American
Fitness			
Running/Jogging	33.5	26.5	37.5
Bicycling	35.0	33.3	36.1
Walking	57.0	60.2	64.4
Individual Sport Activities and Outdoor Team Sports			
Golf	6.9	8.3	10.2
Tennis	12.2	6.4	24.2
Basketball	18.4	12.6	14.3
Soccer	11.0	3.5	7.0
Volleyball	16.2	23.8	14.7
Handball	17.4	10.2	7.2
Outdoor Spectator and Viewing Activities			
Concerts	30.5	34.0	33.0
Attending sporting events	43.0	44.5	39.7
Visiting nature center	40.6	42.9	47.3
Bird watching	19.0	36.5	19.5
Sightseeing	40.6	54.4	58.3
Camping, Hunting, Fishing, and Boating			
Developed camping	21.1	27.7	18.6
Hunting	6.4	21.1	4.6
Fishing	24.9	43.1	29.2
Boating	23.3	29.1	25.6
Swimming			
Pool swimming	42.1	38.3	39.1
Non-pool swimming	35.8	38.3	35.5
Outdoor Adventure Activities			
Hiking	27.0	30.0	24.3
Off-road driving	18.3	33.2	13.5
Social Activities			
Yard games	29.3	44.0	25.7
Picnicking	50.8	61.2	60.0
Family gathering	56.0	60.0	61.0

Source: 1994-95 National Survey on Recreation and the Environment, USDA Forest Service and the University of Georgia, Athens, Georgia. The NSRE is the most recent of the series of National Recreation Surveys begun nationally in 1960.

Americans with Disabilities and Outdoor Activities

The number of Americans with physical or mental disabilities is estimated at more than 43 million. In 1990 Congress passed the Americans with Disabilities Act (42 U.S.C. 12101 [note]), which prohibits public entities from discriminating against individuals with physical or mental disabilities. The act also prohibits private entities from discriminating against this segment of the American population if any part of their operations involve commercial trade. Private concerns that provide recreation services are included.

The NSRE included questions about various kinds of disabilities, ranging from physical and mental challenges to chemical dependency. Roughly seven percent of respondents indicated some type of disability. We selected 21 activities covering a range of outdoor activity types to compare participation by people who identified themselves as disabled and those who did not indicate a disability. Table V.19 shows walking was the most popular activity for both disabled and nondisabled respondents, followed by family gathering and sightseeing.

Table V.19: Percent of Disabled and Able-Bodied Americans Participating in Outdoor Recreation Activities, 1994-95

Activity	Disabled	Nondisabled
Running/Jogging	12.0	26.2
Basketball	7.0	12.8
Tennis	6.1	10.6
Concerts	32.2	34.2
Attending Sporting events	40.3	47.5
Visiting nature center	44.1	46.4
Hunting	8.5	9.3
Yard games	33.2	36.7
Fishing	31.1	28.9
Team sport	15.5	26.4
Biking	25.8	28.7
Walking	59.7	66.7
Bird watching	34.4	27.0
Sightseeing	56.2	56.6
Developed camping	20.1	20.7
Boating	31.8	29.0
Pool swimming	38.2	44.2
Non-pool swimming	34.2	39.2
Hiking	19.2	23.8
Picnicking	53.0	49.1
Family gathering	59.5	61.8

Source: 1994-95 National Survey on Recreation and the Environment, USDA Forest Service and the University of Georgia, Athens, Georgia. The NSRE is the most recent of the series of National Recreation Surveys begun nationally in 1960.

Generations of Outdoor Recreationists

(Portions of this section were reprinted by permission of B. McDonald and M. Van Horne, 1995.)

The determinants of outdoor recreation behavior are varied and multifaceted. One determinant overlooked in the literature is that of generational roles and personalities. Strauss and Howe (1991), in a comprehensive historical social analysis of American life since the late 1500s, uncovered four such generational roles and personalities that act, interact, and respond differently from one another during periods of social upheaval. These generational personalities occur in a fixed and cyclical order, and each influences the others in predictable ways that keep the cycle turning. For example, the oldest living American age cohort is the *GI generation*, those born between 1901 and 1924. The *silent generation* encompasses Americans born between

1925 and 1942. These are mostly Depression–era babies who lived during World War II. They have been described as restrained, deliberate, and conservative; and those in the workforce are considered to be loyal company employees who appreciate the job security offered by large business concerns.

Strauss and Howe (1991, pp. 299-316) also describe the *boom generation* (roughly equivalent to baby boomers) as that generation born between 1943 and 1960. The older members of this cohort were the radical college students of the 1960s who were pivotal in ushering in the new social movements centered around civil rights, women's rights, anti-war sentiments, and environmental ethics. In contrast, the group Strauss and Howe (1991, pp. 317-334) label as the *thirteenth generation* (born between 1961-1981) is depicted as politically apathetic, narcissistic, and without sincere direction. Members of this generation are much more likely than members of older generations to have been reared in a single parent home and are also more likely than prior generations to be "latchkey" kids. This cohort has also been referred to as *Generation X*, another title which alludes to the ill-defined character of this younger group of Americans (Coupland, 1991; Spiegler, 1996).

Strauss and Howe (1991) describe the *millennial generation* as children born between 1982 and 2004 (roughly). Some of these are today's children, a group that will have considerable social influence for the first half of the twenty-first century. The type of outdoor recreation these children learn as children and young adults will affect both outdoor recreation policy and natural resource policy into the 22nd century. A surprising number of outdoor interests and skills are acquired only, or mainly, in childhood. Certainly, many outdoor-related values are learned during youth. The kind of childhood the *millennial generation* experiences will profoundly impact their later outdoor recreation choices, as well as the way in which outdoor recreation resources are valued and managed.

We examined participation in a selected number of outdoor recreation activities for the *GI, silent, boom*, and *thirteenth generations* (Table V.20). We also looked at indirect participation in these activities for the *millennial generation*, that is, for families with children under six years of age. If we assume the activities to which these young children are exposed in their early, formative years will influence their choices for outdoor recreation as adolescents and adults, then we have an indication of the types of outdoor recreation that may be in demand in the next century.

Table V.20 shows that participation increased for most activities for each successive generation from *GI* to *thirteenth*. Some of this trend is undoubtedly attributed to age differences among generations. To get a better idea of generational effects, we compared the *thirteenth generation* or young adult cohort (16-34) from the 1994-95 NSRE with that of a similarly defined age group (18-44) in the 1960 National Recreation Survey (ORRRC 1962). The latter group is roughly equivalent to Strauss and Howe's *silent generation*. Percent of respondents from the two time periods participating in bicycling, walking, sightseeing, camping, hunting, fishing, boating, swimming, hiking, and picnicking were compared. Table V.21 shows participation increased markedly for each activity over the 35-year period. For instance, only six percent of young adults in 1960 reported biking. This compares with 51 percent in 1995. Moreover, 73 percent of today's young adults reported walking, whereas only 34 percent reported participation in 1960. These differences over time, while holding age group approximately equal, suggest that generational or societal changes, such as greater access to transportation and information and changing ideas about health and physical fitness over the past 37 years, have significantly influenced Americans' participation in outdoor recreation activities.

Table V.20: Percent of Generations Participating in Outdoor Recreation Activities, 1994-95

	Generations of Outdoor Recreationists				
Activity	GI	Silent	Boom	Thirteenth	Millennial
Running/Jogging	5.0	12.6	26.2	43.0	29.9
Bicycling	7.3	21.7	43.4	50.5	33.9
Walking	43.6	61.7	74.8	73.2	72.2
Tennis	2.0	6.0	13.2	21.6	10.7
Baseball	<1.0	2.4	7.7	12.7	9.1
Basketball	<1.0	3.3	11.5	27.4	17.2
Soccer	<1.0	<1.0	4.4	10.4	6.2
Concert going	17.4	26.5	36.6	42.6	32.5
Attending sporting events	21.2	37.2	54.2	56.9	51.0
Bird watching	22.8	32.0	32.7	20.6	24.5

Table V.20 Cont.

Activity	GI	Silent	Boom	Thirteenth	Millennial
	Generations of Outdoor Recreationists				
Sightseeing	34.6	55.4	66.3	58.6	57.7
Downhill skiing	<1.0	2.7	10.8	18.7	8.2
Snowmobiling	<1.0	2.0	4.5	7.5	4.7
Camping	6.2	17.4	33.1	39.1	30.8
Hunting	3.5	7.5	13.3	16.6	11.3
Fishing	13.8	25.7	38.4	41.7	33.7
Boating	14.3	28.5	40.2	45.9	30.6
Swimming	16.1	31.7	52.4	63.0	63.9
Hiking	6..3	14.6	31.1	33.5	25.6
Driving ORV	5.4	9.9	16.4	25.9	16.1
Yard Games	12.1	28.7	48.6	53.6	45.6
Picnicking	30.0	48.3	64.2	58.2	59.2
Family gathering	35.5	54.4	68.0	71.1	69.6

Source: 1994-95 National Survey on Recreation and the Environment, USDA Forest Service and the University of Georgia, Athens, Georgia. The NSRE is the most recent of the series of National Recreation Surveys begun nationally in 1960.

Table V.21: Percent of Persons Participating in Selected Activities by 18-44 Year-Olds in 1960 and 16-34 Year-Olds in 1994-95

Activity	1960 (18-44 year-olds)	1994-95 (16-34 year-olds)
Bicycling	6	51
Walking	34	73
Sightseeing	46	59
Camping	8	39
Hunting	4	17
Fishing	32	42
Boating	25	46
Swimming	57	63
Hiking	5	34
Picnicking	64	58

Source: 1994-95 National Survey on Recreation and the Environment, USDA Forest Service and the University of Georgia, Athens, Georgia, and ORRRC 1960.

Inner-city Poor

(Portions of this section were adapted from an Urban Policy Brief issued from the Office of Policy Development and Research, U.S. Department of Housing and Urban Development, 1994.)

Having the opportunity to recreate has been said to be one of the best predictors of recreation participation (Lindsey & Ogle, 1972). It follows logically that most people would engage in most recreation activities if provided the services and facilities for doing so. However, such facilities and services are not equally distributed among various segments of American society. Americans who live in economically depressed inner-city settings may be at a particular disadvantage in terms of organized, outdoor recreation opportunities because agencies and services are sometimes reluctant to locate in these areas for fear of crime (Wilson, 1980; 1987). The plight of poor minority neighborhoods can be compounded if institutional practices fail to provide them opportunities and resources. Minority neighborhoods without government and business assistance can face further problems of deteriorated housing, inferior schools, inadequate access to services, crumbling infrastructure, frayed social institutions, a lack of local employment opportunities, and civil unrest. For instance, the Kerner Commission Report (National Advisory Commission on Civil Disorders, 1968) on race riots in urban ghettos during the 1960s cited inadequate recreation facilities and programs as one of the major grievances of rioters.

According to reports from the Department of Housing and Urban Development, the dire situation in many inner-city areas has not improved much since the 1960s. The past two decades have witnessed an explosive growth in the number of areas of extreme poverty at the heart of most large cities. By 1990, approximately one in seven census tracts in the nation's 100 largest cities was classified as an area of extreme poverty (an area where at least 40 percent of the residents were poor). In cities such as Detroit and Miami, the percentage of these poverty tracts was much higher. Minorities, for whom residential choice is more likely to be constrained by racial segregation and housing discrimination, are invariably over-represented in these areas. One in four black residents of large cities lives in a high-poverty area. In these areas, black residents make up almost three-fifths of the population. Hispanic Americans are the fastest-growing group in these poor urban neighborhoods. They represented 24 percent of the local population in 1990, compared with less than 20 percent in 1980.

The Urban Tree House program is an example of "reinvestment" efforts in inner-city neighborhoods. The Tree House is an Atlanta-based community project designed to bring an understanding of forestry concepts and careers to inner-city children. Neighborhood children participate in lessons that include storytelling and lectures by natural resource managers and researchers.

Table V.22: Percent of Inner-City Poor, Metropolitan, and Nonmetropolitan Respondents Participating in Outdoor Recreation Activities, 1994-95

Residence and Outdoor Recreation			
Activity	**Inner-City Poor**	**Metropolitan**	**Nonmetropolitan**
Running/jogging	13.2	29.1	25.1
Bicycling	15.5	39.8	34.8
Walking	40.7	69.3	67.4
Tennis	3.1	14.9	10.9
Baseball	1.7	7.9	8.3
Basketball	3.1	15.2	14.6
Soccer	1.8	6.1	3.8
Concert going	14.3	37.2	28.3
Attending Sporting Events	16.6	49.2	48.2
Bird watching	17.5	26.6	28.6
Sightseeing	22.1	59.3	55.3
Downhill skiing	1.1	12.2	8.4

Table V.22 Cont.

Residence and Outdoor Recreation			
Activity	**Inner-City Poor**	**Metropolitan**	**Nonmetropolitan**
Snowmobiling	1.0	4.2	6.9
Camping	8.9	28.8	34.4
Hunting	4.1	9.6	22.8
Fishing	13.3	32.6	43.3
Boating	12.6	37.7	38.5
Pool swimming	15.6	51.2	42.5
Hiking	14.3	27.2	24.8
Driving ORV	5.9	16.4	23.0
Yard Games	12.5	43.2	44.3
Picnicking	28.3	55.8	55.6
Family Gathering	29.9	63.3	64.1

Source: 1994-95 National Survey on Recreation and the Environment, USDA Forest Service and the University of Georgia, Athens, Georgia. The NSRE is the most recent of the series of National Recreation Surveys begun nationally in 1960.

We constructed the category "inner-city poor" by restricting the analyses to individual respondents living in metropolitan counties where: (1) population was at least one million, (2) family income was less than $10,000 per year, (3) the education of the respondent was high school or less, and (4) the respondent was 25 or older. By these criteria, approximately two percent of NSRE respondents could be classified as inner-city poor. Table V.22 compares participation in 23 activities for inner-city poor, metropolitan, and non-metropolitan respondents. Results show that inner-city poor respondents are less likely than either metropolitan or non-metropolitan dwellers to participate in the 23 activities listed. For instance, metropolitan respondents are more than three times as likely as poor city dwellers to engage in a relatively inexpensive activity like pool swimming. This result suggests a lack of swimming facilities in inner-city areas. Participation in the most frequently mentioned activities (walking, picnicking, and family gathering) were the same for inner-city poor, other metropolitan dwellers, and nonmetropolitan dwellers.

Metropolitan and Nonmetropolitan Populations

A review of sociology literature suggests that differences in the attitudes of urban and rural people are diminishing due to factors such mass communication, an increase in nonagricultural industries, and the reorganization and merger of rural governments (Rogers, Burdge, Korshing, & Donnermeyer, 1988). However, Rogers et. al. (1988) also insist that "important rural-urban value differences still exist. These differences stem from historical, occupational, and ecological differences" (p. 12). For instance, studies have shown that rural and urban populations differ in their opinions about familial institutions and environmental pollutants (Lieberson & Wilkinson, 1976). Tremblay and Dunlap (1978) found that rural residents were less concerned than urban residents about environmental issues on the state or national level. Proshansky, Fabian, and Kaminoff (1983) also argue that one's *physical* environment (i.e., place-identity) is just as important a socialization agent in shaping one's self-identity as are intangible norms, values, and beliefs.

We examined participation by size of residence. The categories *metropolitan* and *nonmetropolitan* were more useful for our analyses than *urban* or *rural*. *Metropolitan* refers to counties with populations of at least 250,000. *Nonmetropolitan* counties have populations of 20,000 or less, either adjacent to a metropolitan county or in a rural area not adjacent to a metropolitan area (Butler, 1990). Table V.22 shows that walking for pleasure was the most popular activity for both metropolitan and nonmetropolitan populations. Similar to other groups, family gathering and sightseeing were also among the most popular activities. Not surprisingly, dispersed setting activities like hunting, fishing, and camping were more popular activities for nonmetropolitan than for metropolitan populations.

Participation Barriers

Despite rapid advances in technology, many people still find that they have relatively little time or energy for recreation. We asked NSRE respondents who reported not engaging in recreation activities to tell us what factors prohibited their participation. Table V.23 shows the primary participation barriers for the general population to be not enough time and money, personal health limitations, not having a companion, and outdoor pests. About 20 percent cited inadequate information about outdoor recreation opportunities and crowding as constraining factors. Seventeen percent did not participate because of inadequate site facilities. Inadequate transportation, concerns about personal safety, and poorly maintained areas were a problem for about 14 percent of those who reported they do not recreate.

This urban fishing program in Washington, D.C., sponsored by the U.S. Fish and Wildlife Service, introduces urban youth to nature-based recreation. Photo courtesy of the U.S. Fish and Wildlife Service.

Table V.23: Participation Barriers for the General Population, Whites, African Americans, Hispanic Americans, and Asian Americans, 1994-95

Barriers	General Population	White	African American	Hispanic	Asian
Lack of time	63.8	62.5	65.4	77.1	70.9
Lack of money	42.5	40.8	49.8	49.1	33.9
Personal health	28.2	29.3	26.5	23.5	10.5
No companion	28.1	27.6	30.8	26.8	26.9
Inadequate transportation	14.8	12.1	24.3	31.3	11.4
Crowded activity areas	20.5	19.7	21.9	30.4	16.1
Personal safety concerns	14.0	11.6	23.5	21.1	13.3
Inadequate facilities	16.8	15.3	21.0	25.5	25.6
Poorly maintained areas	14.0	11.5	22.1	27.8	18.8
Pollution problems	13.0	11.1	19.2	23.1	11.0
Inadequate information	21.1	18.6	30.7	34.1	14.2
No assistance for physical condition	13.7	13.4	17.4	11.8	14.3
Household member with disability	6.0	13.4	5.5	5.4	<1.0
Outdoor pests	27.7	26.7	35.6	21.5	19.2
Other reason	19.4	20.5	12.8	21.5	23.6

Source: 1994-95 National Survey on Recreation and the Environment, USDA Forest Service and the University of Georgia, Athens, Georgia. The NSRE is the most recent of the series of National Recreation Survey s begun nationally in 1960.

Insufficient time was the greatest barrier to participation for all racial groups, particularly Hispanic Americans and Asian Americans (Table V.23). A lack of money for recreation was cited by about one-half of African Americans and Hispanic Americans, compared to about 41 percent of whites and 34 percent of Asian Americans. Hispanic Americans and African Americans were more than twice as likely as either whites or Asian Americans to cite inadequate transportation. Also, Hispanic Americans and African Americans were hampered more than other groups by crowded activity areas.

Personal safety was much more of a constraint for African Americans and Hispanic Americans than for either whites or Asian Americans. Whites were less likely than the other racial or ethnic groups to cite inadequate facilities as a barrier. This result probably can be attributed in part to place of residence. African Americans and Hispanic Americans also are more likely than other racial or ethnic groups to live in inner-city areas or rural areas that lack adequate recreation facilities. Furthermore, Hispanic Americans and African Americans were also more likely than either whites or Asian Americans to cite poorly maintained areas as barriers to participation, and pollution is more of a problem for Hispanic Americans and African Americans.

Environmental justice and environmental racism have become major concerns to minority groups, which charge that hazardous waste and garbage disposal sites are located primarily in areas adjacent to low-income populations and populations with relatively little political clout (Bullard, 1995). More Hispanic and African Americans, compared to whites or Asian Americans, were constrained by lack of information about facilities and resources. Whites were more likely than the other groups to be constrained by a household member's physical disability, and outdoor pests were most limiting to African Americans.

Participation barriers for Hispanic and African Americans were more likely than for either whites or Asian Americans to include structural factors, such as pollution, lack of adequate transportation, safety, inadequate information, and poorly maintained facilities. This observation was also made by Washburne (1978), who wrote that minority "underparticipation" may be influenced to a great degree by barriers such as lack of discretionary funds, lack of transportation, and inadequate information about facilities. He referred to it as "marginalization theory." The theory asserts that marginal societal status experienced by racial minorities in America, particularly by African Americans, is largely responsible for the differences between white and nonwhite outdoor recreation participation.

Table V.24 shows constraints on visits by disabled respondents, inner-city poor, and metropolitan and nonmetropolitan populations. Not surprisingly, personal health limitations were the greatest constraint for disabled respondents (75 percent), followed by lack of assistance for physical limitations (54 percent). Just over 40 percent of disabled were constrained by money, and 33 percent did not recreate because of lack of time. About one-quarter of disabled respondents said they were hampered by either personal safety concerns, inadequate facilities, inadequate information, no companions, or annoying pests.

In addition to these more general recreation barriers, people with physical disabilities must also concern themselves with the degree to which recreation facilities are physically accessible to those using assistance devices such as wheelchairs and motorized scooters. Forty-two percent of those indicating some type of disability said physical barriers either limited or prevented their recreation participation. Approximately 37 percent said it is necessary for them to know in advance whether a site or activity is accessible, and about 43 percent said they would participate more in activities if those sponsoring such services would develop universal symbols indicating accessibility. About one-quarter said having either a wheelchair or power scooter at the site would enhance their recreation experience, and 20 percent indicated that large-print signs were helpful. Thirteen percent favored captioning in films or videos, and about 10 percent felt having braille signs and assisted-listening systems would enhance their recreation experiences.

The most frequently mentioned participation barrier for low-income, inner-city people was not enough money. Sixty percent of the respondents cited this factor as a hindrance to greater outdoor recreation participation. This response is not at all surprising given the population. In comparison, 43 percent of the general population cited money as a barrier to participation (Table V.23), and 41 percent of metro respondents did not visit for this reason. Personal health limitations were the second most often-mentioned participation constraint among inner-city respondents (50 percent), followed by inadequate transportation and personal safety concerns (37 percent). In comparison, safety concerns were mentioned by only 14 percent in the general population (Table V.23) and 15 and 12 percent, respectively, of metro and non-metro populations. Approximately 33 percent of inner-city poor did not visit because of outdoor pests, and roughly 30 percent were constrained by inadequate information or no assistance for physical condition. This compares with only 13 and 15 percent, respectively, for metro and nonmetro populations. Lack of time was the greatest constraint for both metropolitan and nonmetropolitan respondents, followed by lack of money, personal health concerns, and outdoor pests.

Table V.24: Percentage of Disabled, Inner-City Poor, Metro, and Nonmetro Populations by Participation Barriers, 1994-95

Barriers	Disabled	Inner-city poor	Metro	Nonmetro
Lack of time	33.2	29.6	64.4	61.7
Lack of money	44.1	60.0	41.4	46.2
Personal health	74.5	50.3	27.0	31.7
No companion	27.1	26.9	28.2	27.8
Inadequate transportation	20.6	37.1	15.2	13.1
Crowded activity areas	22.1	21.8	21.5	17.5
Personal safety concerns	24.3	36.9	14.7	11.7
Inadequate facilities	24.2	17.2	16.4	18.7
Poorly maintained areas	20.2	13.9	14.4	12.8
Pollution problems	19.9	16.2	13.9	9.8
Inadequate information	25.3	28.7	21.5	19.5
No assistance for physical condition	54.0	31.9	13.1	15.3
Household member with disability	6.9	10.0	5.7	7.4
Outdoor pests	25.3	33.2	25.9	33.4
Other reason	17.9	11.8	19.7	18.8

Source: 1994-95 National Survey on Recreation and the Environment, USDA Forest Service and the University of Georgia, Athens, Georgia. The NSRE is the most recent of the series of National Recreation Surveys begun nationally in 1960.

RECREATION IN URBAN-PROXIMATE NATURAL AREAS

(By Patricia L. Winter, Ph.D. and Deborah J. Chavez, Ph.D., USDA Forest Service, Riverside, CA.)

Recreation in urban proximate wildland and wilderness areas and resulting management concerns and challenges have proven a fertile ground for social science research. As the demand for recreation opportunities adjacent to large urban centers has increased, so has the variety of recreational interests, patterns, and preferences, a reflection of the diverse recreationists visiting such areas.

Diversity of Recreationists

Of interest is the degree to which ethnic and racial diversity in the United States is reflected among recreationists, particularly in urban-proximate recreation areas. Studies of day use on the San Bernardino, Angeles, and Los Padres National Forests, each within a one- to two-hour drive for over one million people, provide an opportunity to examine this question. On-site, self-administered questionnaires were provided to recreationists at day-use areas on each of the forests. Of the 168 respondents on the Angeles National Forest, 51 percent identified themselves as Anglo American, 15 percent as Mexican American, 15 percent at Hispanic American, nine percent as Asian American, and fewer than five percent each identified themselves as Central American, African American, or Native American (Chavez, Winter, & Mainieri, 1994). The second most diverse group was found on the Los Padres National Forest where, of the 159 respondents, 64 percent were Anglo, 22 percent were Hispanic, and fewer than five percent each identified themselves as either Asian American, African American, Native American or European (Chavez, et al., 1995). The San Bernardino National Forest had slightly less diversity of recreationists with 65 percent Anglo, 10 percent Mexican American, 10 percent Hispanic American, and fewer than five percent each of Central American, Asian American, African American, and American Indian descent (Chavez & Mainieri, 1994).

Site Variations

Ethnic and racial diversity across the urban-proximate forests varies greatly between sites within a single forest. For example, at the Applewhite picnic area on the San Bernardino National Forest, more than three-quarters (78 percent) of the visitors were of Hispanic descent, while only seven percent were Anglo (Chavez & Winter, 1993). In contrast, respondents contacted at the Children's Forest were mostly Anglo (87 percent) (Chavez & Mainieri, 1994).

Similar types of sites may have a pattern of diversity, such as riparian or water-based recreation studied by Chavez (1992, 1993b), Chavez and Mainieri (1994), and Simcox and Pfister (1990). There is also some suggested variability around accessibility or proximity to the urban center, as seen in trailhead variations on the Angeles National Forest in Parker and Winter (1996). Less accessible wildernesses show very little ethnic and racial diversity (Chavez, 1993a; Winter, 1996). Recreation areas within the urban setting may offer even more ethnic and racial diversity, such as that found by Winter's study of recreationists' land ethics at state park, city park, and Forest Service sites. In this study, Anglos represented approximately 45 percent of the visitor population across all three site types. However, African Americans were only encountered at the city parks, and not at state park and Forest Service sites. Hispanics were the second largest majority at all three site types (Winter, 1996).

Variations can also be seasonal. At the Mecca Hills Recreation Area in the southern California desert, non-holiday visitors were primarily Anglo (64.1 percent), while holiday weekend visitors were primarily Hispanic (76.4 percent) (Chavez, Baas, & Winter, 1993). Each of these variations serves as a demonstration of the complexity of resource management and customer service. This complexity has importance in its implications for differences in perceptions of place, recreational activities, communication patterns and preferences, development preferences, and spill-over of city-based problems into the recreation setting. Each of these is addressed in the following sections. It is important to note, however, that variations in ethnicity and race are not the only socio-demographic considerations in customer service. Culture has a strong linkage to ethnicity and race, and many differences may be explained by culture rather than ethnicity or race. Geographic variation is another important consideration, in that recreation and its many corresponding variables may differ by region, state, or larger community. Finally, level of attachment or identification with culture and community may also serve to explain some of the variability seen within a specific subgroup. Degree of acculturation has been shown to be an important covariate in many ethnic and racial inquiries within the field of recreation (Baas, Ewert, & Chavez, 1993; Caro & Ewert, 1995; Simcox & Pfister, 1990).

Perceptions of Place

Two studies revealed the special meaning that recreational places can have to individuals from Central America (Carr & Chavez, 1993) and Mexico (Chavez, 1996b), wherein an area was cited as reminding recreationists of their homeland. A single place may be viewed in many different ways and have varying expectations for activities that should be acceptable there, as well as services that might be offered. For example, Taylor and Winter (1994) found that respondents to a mailed recreation survey disagreed about whether an area was wilderness, national park, national forest, or city park. These place perceptions were correlated with expected degrees of development, perceptions of acceptable on-site activities, and perceptions of acceptable penalties for depreciative acts. Race and ethnicity were important covariates in these place perception interactions. Variations in place perceptions were also reported by Absher and Winter (1997), although in-depth analyses of these data remain incomplete.

Place perceptions may have some shared meanings when it comes to behavioral conventions or norms, as discussed by Heywood (1993). In his exploration of behavioral expectations at the Applewhite picnic area on the San Bernardino National Forest, people passing through someone's immediate picnic area, playing loud music, and the number of times such potential intrusions could occur before being perceived as bothersome varied by acculturation level of the respondent. Overall, Spanish-speaking recreationists appeared more tolerant of people passing through their picnic site, for example, but if they were English speaking their attitudes more closely emulated Anglo respondents.

Recreational Activities

Recreational activity patterns and interests show similarities and differences among ethnic groups. While the majority of visitors to the Applewhite picnic area were there to picnic (79 percent) or relax (78 percent), how those activities were actually carried out varied (Chavez & Winter, 1993). An indicated interest in group activities, reflecting the larger group sizes within which they have been found to recreate, was expressed at the Mecca Hills and at Applewhite (Chavez, et al., 1993; Chavez & Winter, 1993). Larger group size may be a reflection of cultural differences focusing greater importance on family and extended family (Chavez, 1996b; Chavez & Winter, 1994). While there are some significant differences in types of activities undertaken and those of interest, there are also many similarities (Chavez, 1995). An examination of the meaning of recreation itself reveals significant differences contrasting Anglos with Native Americans (McDonald & McAvoy, 1996).

Communication Patterns and Preferences

Diversity among recreation site visitors is represented in the primary languages they read and speak. While approximately half of the visitors to the Applewhite picnic area read English most of the time, approximately one third reported speaking English, Spanish, or English and Spanish each (Chavez & Winter, 1993). Such variations affect management approaches to communication through signing and face-to-face contacts. Cultural differences add further challenges to the agency-visitor interaction, and are more critical than basic translation issues (Magill, 1995). While a majority of visitors to an area tend to learn about it through informal sources, such as family or friends, this trend is even more true for Hispanics than Anglos (Chavez, et al., 1993, Parker & Winter, 1996), and Anglos are more likely to contact the managing agency for information than are Hispanics (Parker & Winter, 1996). Hispanics have demonstrated a greater interest in information than Anglos (Parker & Winter, 1996), particularly in printed form. Topics of information that the agency deems most important, such as area rules, regulations, and safety messages, appear to be of less interest than other topics. On the Los Padres National Forest, respondents were much more interested in the forest's natural features (79 percent), other sites that were similar (74 percent), and things to see and do at the site (71 percent) than they were in area rules and regulations (48 percent) or safety messages (51 percent) (Chavez, Winter, & Mainieri, 1995). Hispanic visitors may have more interest in information about area rules and regulations (Parker & Winter, 1996). The type of site where recreation is occurring may have some influence on information interest levels, however. At the Imperial Sand Dunes in the southern California desert, OHVers were more interested in safety (50.7 percent) and area rules and regulations (44.6 percent) than they were in things to see and do (30.5 percent) (Chavez, Winter, & Bass, 1993b).

Development Preferences

Variations in recreational patterns and activities, with Hispanics typically recreating in larger family groups, also play out in expressed preferences for degree of site development. At the Mecca Hills recreation area, Anglos indicated significantly greater importance of 10 of the 17 site items listed, including a picnic area, parking spaces, and toilets (Chavez, et al., 1993). A similar finding was revealed in the Applewhite study conducted by Chavez and Winter (1993), where the majority of recreationists were Hispanic and expressed a clear preference for the site rendering the most site development, approximating the characteristics of a regional park. A query of development preferences along the Sacramento River and Shasta Lake Recreation Areas (Winter, 1995) showed that very few additional site amenities were desired, and the majority visitor to these areas was Anglo (approximately 70 to 75 percent). When few additions are desired, water may still be listed as a desirable amenity, even by those expecting little else in site development (Chavez, et al., 1993b; Winter, 1995).

The Spill-Over of Urban Problems into the Recreational Setting

Urban-proximate recreation areas show signs of urban-spillover, affecting recreationists' experience on-site. In one study conducted by Taylor and Winter (1994), a majority of visitors to day use areas reported seeing or experiencing litter (83 percent), carvings on trees (75 percent), other people making loud noises (71 percent), or playing loud music (68 percent) and seeing graffiti on natural or built features (66 percent). The majority of visitors were most bothered by spray paint and litter (between 86 to 90 percent). Although many reported picking up litter, very few reported taking any other intervention steps to end depreciative activities on-site.

Conflict between groups is rarely reported (Chavez, 1993b; Winter, 1995), although multiple use of trails presents an exception, as in the case of conflicts between mountain bikers and other users (Chavez, 1996a). It may be that norms for an area, or behavioral conventions, preclude many of the potential conflicts that could occur in an area (Heywood, 1993), or that individuals have already excluded themselves from recreating in an area because of the fear of conflict (McDonald & McAvoy, 1997).

Resulting Management Strategies

The diversity in ethnic, cultural, and recreational interest revealed in urban-proximate wildland areas has led to innovative management strategies. Forest Service managers are beginning to rely on collaborative efforts, or bridge-building methods, to ameliorate conflicts between various user groups (Chavez, 1996a). Communication complexities, as well as the desire to decrease environmentally depreciative acts, led resource managers to partner with the California Environmental Project to establish an on-site, face-to-face program involving urban youth as the messengers (Absher & Winter, 1997). Areas have been renovated, based on user interests and preferences collected through on-site studies (Chavez, Winter, & Larson, 1995). Diversity may add complexity to understanding the recreational experience and how to best serve customers, but it also provides an incredible learning environment that challenges us to take care in understanding the differences, similarities, and interests of our present and future customers.

PARTICIPATION DIFFERENCES AMONG REGIONS

This section presents percentages of the population 16 years and older and mean numbers of trips and days per participant per year for four assessment regions and for nine forest regions in the United States. Total numbers of participants and total trips and participation-days per year for the four assessment regions are shown in Technical Appendix Table V.7. Percentages of population participating and millions of participants by activity for each of the nine forest regions are shown in Technical Appendix Table V.8.

Comparisons Across Four Assessment Regions

The four assessment regions across which recreation participation is compared include the Pacific Coast states of Alaska, Washington, Oregon, Hawaii, and California; the 12 Rocky Mountain/Great Plains states from Nevada east to Kansas; the South, including 13 states from Texas to Virginia; and the North from Missouri to Maine (see Figure II.1 in Chapter II). These regions are the assessment regions used by the USDA Forest Service for this 10-year Forest and Rangeland Renewable Resources Assessment (see Foreword).

In Table V.25, the first level of comparisons across Assessment Regions is shown for 13 general types of recreation activities. Across the four regions, and relative to national percentages, few differences exist for trail, street, and road activities, individual sports, team sports, spectator sports, boating, swimming, and social activities. Regardless of differences in climate, landscapes, the nature of opportunities, and population size and culture, participation percentages are similar across regions. Numbers of participant are greatest for viewing and learning activities; trail, street, and road activities; social activities; spectator sports; and swimming. Smaller percentages participate in individual and outdoor team sports.

Table V.25: Percentage of Population 16 Years and Older Participating Across 13 Types of Outdoor Activities by Assessment Region of the U.S., 1994-95

Type of Activity	Assessment Region[1]				
	North	South	Rocky Mountain/ Great Plains	Pacific Coast	National
Land					
Trail/street/road	69.2	65.9	69.9	69.7	68.3
Viewing/learning	76.7	73.8	79.8	77.7	76.2
Camping	24.3	22.6	37.8	34.4	26.4
Hunting	9.1	10.5	13.3	5.5	9.3
Outdoor adventure	34.8	32.9	47.5	45.1	36.8
Water					
Boating/floating	30.1	29.1	26.1	26.9	29.0
Fishing	27.9	32.4	31.0	23.9	28.9
Swimming	55.8	53.6	49.8	53.0	54.2

Table V.25 Cont.

Type of Activity	Assessment Region[1] North	South	Rocky Mountain/ Great Plains	Pacific Coast	National
Snow/ice					
Skiing/sledding/ snowmobiling	23.8	8.6	21.7	18.5	18.1
Other					
Individual sport	23.1	20.4	22.5	21.7	22.0
Outdoor team sport	27.3	26.1	24.8	25.3	26.4
Outdoor spectator	59.8	57.2	59.8	57.8	58.7
Social activities	69.3	64.8	71.3	68.0	67.8

[1]The North includes Connecticut, Deleware, Illinois, Indiana, Iowa, Maine, Maryland, Massachusetts, Michigan, Minnesota, Missouri, New York, New Jersey, New Hampshire, Ohio, Pennsylvania, Rhode Island, Vermont, West Virginia, and Wisconsin; the South includes Alabama, Arkansas, Florida, Georgia, Kentucky, Louisiana, Mississippi, North Carolina, Oklahoma, South Carolina, Tennessee, Texas, and Virginia; the Rocky Mountains/Great Plains include Arizona, Colorado, Idaho, Kansas, Montana, Nebraska, Nevada, New Mexico, North Dakota, South Dakota, Utah, and Wyoming; and the Pacific Coast includes Alaska, California, Haiwaii, Oregon, and Washington.

The activity types for which there are evident regional differences include viewing and learning activities, snow and ice activities, camping, hunting, fishing, and outdoor adventure activities. Differences in participation percentages are especially pronounced for snow and ice activities, camping, and outdoor adventure activities (Figure V.10). For snow and ice activities, the highest participation percentage in activities such as skiing is in the North; the second highest is in the Rocky Mountain/Great Plains region. As would be expected, the lowest is in the South where snow and ice activities are mostly restricted to the southern Appalachian Mountains in northern Georgia, western North Carolina, southwestern Virginia, and eastern Tennessee.

Figure V.10: Regional Comparisons of Percentage of Population 16 Years and Older Participating in Snow/Ice, Camping, and Outdoor Adventure Activities, 1994-95

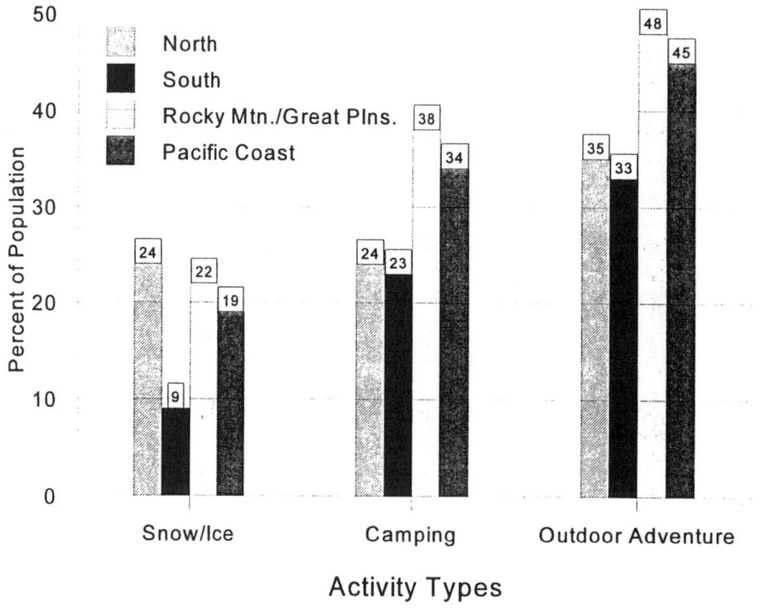

Source: 1994-95 National Survey on Recreation and the Environment (NSRE), USDA Forest Service and the University of Georgia, Athens, Georgia.

Camping participation (Figure V.10) differs between the eastern and western regions. The North and South have 24 and 23 percent of their respective populations 16 or older participating, while the Rocky Mountain/Great Plains and Pacific Coast regions have 38 and 34 percent, respectively. The regional differences in participation in outdoor adventure activities are very similar to those for camping, with the two western regions having 48 and 45 percent of the population participating, while the eastern regions have 35 and 33 percent participating. These regional differences in participation can be attributed at least in part to differences in availability of natural resource opportunities for these activities between the West and the East.

Smaller regional differences were found for viewing, hunting, and fishing. For viewing activities, the region with the smallest percentage of people 16 or older participating is the South at 74 percent; the highest is the Rocky Mountain/Great Plains region with 80 percent. Hunting participation differences are most pronounced between the Rocky Mountain/Great Plains region at 13 percent, and the Pacific Coast region at six percent. For fishing, the region with the highest percentage is the South (32 percent), and the region with the lowest is the Pacific Coast (24 percent). Estimated numbers of participants for each of the four assessment regions by type of recreational activity are shown in Table V.26.

Table V.26: Number of Persons 16 Years and Older Participating Across 13 Types of Outdoor Activities by Assessment Region of the U.S., 1994-95

Type of Activity	Assessment Region[1]				
	North	South	Rocky Mountain/ Great Plains	Pacific Coast	National
Land					
Trail/street/road	63.6	41.0	10.4	21.8	136.9
Viewing/learning	70.5	46.0	11.9	24.3	152.6
Camping	22.4	14.1	5.6	10.8	52.8
Hunting	8.4	6.5	2.0	1.7	18.6
Outdoor adventure	32.0	20.5	7.1	14.1	73.7
Water					
Boating/floating	27.6	18.1	3.9	8.4	58.1
Fishing	25.6	20.2	4.6	7.5	57.9
Swimming	51.2	33.4	7.4	16.6	108.6
Snow/ice					
Skiing/sledding/ snowmobiling	21.9	5.4	3.2	5.8	36.3
Other					
Individual sport	21.2	12.7	3.3	6.8	44.1
Outdoor team sport	25.1	16.3	3.7	7.9	53.0
Outdoor spectator	55.0	35.6	8.9	18.1	117.6
Social activities	63.6	40.4	10.6	21.3	135.9

[1]The North includes Connecticut, Deleware, Illinois, Indiana, Iowa, Maine, Maryland, Massachusetts, Michigan, Minnesota, Missouri, New York, New Jersey, New Hampshire, Ohio, Pennsylvania, Rhode Island, Vermont, West Virginia, and Wisconsin; the South includes Alabama, Arkansas, Florida, Georgia, Kentucky, Louisiana, Mississippi, North Carolina, Oklahoma, South Carolina, Tennessee, Texas, and Virginia; the Rocky Mountains/Great Plains include Arizona, Colorado, Idaho, Kansas, Montana, Nebraska, Nevada, New Mexico, North Dakota, South Dakota, Utah, and Wyoming; and the Pacific Coast includes Alaska, California, Haiwaii, Oregon, and Washington.

Tables V.27 through V.29 compare percentages of population participating, mean numbers of trips away from home, and participation days per person per year in specific activities among the four assessment regions. Across these regions, there are many notable differences across the three measures of participation. For land-based activities, the smallest differences are among activities that are least dependent on specific natural settings or features (Table V.27). Examples include running or jogging, biking, walking, visiting a visitor center, visiting a historic site, sightseeing, horseback riding, and picnicking.

Table V.27: Percentage of Population Participating and Mean Trips and Days per Participant 16 years or Older per Year by Assessment Region for Land-Resource-Based Activities, 1994-95

ACTIVITY	NORTH			SOUTH			ROCKY MOUNTAINS			PACIFIC COAST			NATIONAL		
		Mean			Mean			Mean			Mean			Mean	
	Percent	Trips	Days	Percent	Trips	Days	Percent	Trips	Days	Percent	Trips	Days	Percent	Trips	Days
Trail/Street/Road															
Running/Jogging	24.2	—[1]	—[1]	27.6	—[1]	—[1]	27.5	—[1]	—[1]	28.5	—[1]	—[1]	26.2	—[1]	—[1]
Biking	30.3	9.5	37.9	24.4	8.5	39.5	30.5	10.0	39.8	31.4	11.6	40.8	28.6	9.6	39.0
Long Distance Biking	3.4	—[1]	22.5	2.4	—[1]	15.7	3.1	—[1]	17.9	4.4	—[1]	16.8	3.2	—[1]	19.6
Walking	68.1	—[1]	104.9	64.2	—[1]	109.8	67.2	—[1]	107.8	67.4	—[1]	111.0	66.7	—[1]	107.6
Viewing Activities															
Visiting a Nature Center	47.3	3.6	—[1]	42.8	3.3	—[1]	49.6	3.4	—[1]	49.7	3.7	—[1]	46.4	3.5	—[1]
Visiting a Visitor Center	34.8	—[1]	—[1]	33.1	—[1]	—[1]	36.9	—[1]	—[1]	36.1	—[1]	—[1]	34.6	—[1]	—[1]
Visit a Prehistoric Site	16.1	2.2	3.6	16.1	3.4	6.7	27.1	3.3	5.3	19.2	2.8	6.0	17.4	2.8	5.0
Visit a Historic Site	44.4	2.9	5.0	43.2	3.2	6.4	46.1	3.2	5.6	44.2	2.8	4.9	44.1	3.0	5.5
Bird-Watching	28.5	7.1	84.8	26.4	7.6	97.5	27.8	7.6	92.2	23.5	5.7	74.6	27.0	7.1	87.8
Wildlife Viewing	32.4	11.0	36.9	28.6	12.7	40.4	37.0	10.0	35.9	30.1	6.8	30.8	31.2	10.7	36.9
Other Wildlife Viewing	14.0	—[1]	—[1]	11.9	—[1]	—[1]	13.1	—[1]	—[1]	17.0	—[1]	—[1]	13.8	—[1]	—[1]
Sightseeing	57.0	8.4	17.3	54.4	9.5	17.9	58.3	9.3	18.8	59.3	10.4	19.6	56.6	9.1	18.0
Camping															
Developed Area	19.6	4.6	10.8	17.2	5.0	10.8	27.0	4.4	9.8	28.0	4.8	10.6	20.7	4.7	10.7
RV Developed Camping	8.4	—[1]	—[1]	6.86	—[1]	—[1]	12.08	—[1]	—[1]	11.4	—[1]	—[1]	8.6	—[1]	—[1]
Tent Developed Camping	13.7	—[1]	—[1]	12.1	—[1]	—[1]	18.9	—[1]	—[1]	20.7	—[1]	—[1]	14.6	—[1]	—[1]
Primitive Area	11.8	4.0	7.9	12.8	5.8	10.1	24.2	5.5	9.6	17.8	4.7	10.3	14.0	4.8	9.2
RV Primitive Camping	2.7	—[1]	—[1]	2.9	—[1]	—[1]	7.4	—[1]	—[1]	5.5	—[1]	—[1]	3.5	—[1]	—[1]
Tent Primitive Camping	9.5	—[1]	—[1]	9.9	—[1]	—[1]	17.1	—[1]	—[1]	12.8	—[1]	—[1]	10.7	—[1]	—[1]
Other Camping	2.0	—[1]	—[1]	1.7	—[1]	—[1]	3.0	—[1]	—[1]	2.8	—[1]	—[1]	2.1	—[1]	—[1]
Hunting															
Big game	7.2	7.7	14.5	7.8	9.5	15.7	10.3	5.5	9.5	3.7	7.7	13.7	7.1	8.1	14.3
Small game	6.3	9.4	14.8	7.8	7.7	13.0	8.5	9.0	12.1	3.4	10.2	13.6	6.5	8.8	13.8
Migratory bird	1.7	5.4	7.6	2.6	5.2	7.0	3.8	6.6	8.2	1.8	7.0	10.2	2.1	5.7	7.8

Table V.27 Cont.

ACTIVITY	NORTH			SOUTH			ROCKY MOUNTAINS			PACIFIC COAST			NATIONAL		
		Mean			Mean			Mean			Mean			Mean	
	Percent	Trips	Days	Percent	Trips	Days	Percent	Trips	Days	Percent	Trips	Days	Percent	Trips	Days
Outdoor Adventure Activities															
Hiking	22.5	9.0	16.0	18.1	7.9	17.2	33.4	9.7	17.7	34.8	10.3	17.7	23.8	9.1	16.8
Hiking to a Summit	7.2	—[1]	—[1]	5.7	—[1]	—[1]	13.9	—[1]	—[1]	14.2	—[1]	—[1]	8.3	—[1]	—[1]
Orienteering	2.4	—[1]	4.8	2.1	—[1]	5.9	3.0	—[1]	6.5	2.7	—[1]	10.1	2.4	—[1]	6.3
Backpacking	6.5	5.0	9.0	5.8	3.7	6.9	11.8	4.3	8.2	12.1	4.6	9.6	7.6	4.5	8.6
Backpacking to a Summit	2.8	—[1]	—[1]	2.4	—[1]	—[1]	5.3	—[1]	—[1]	5.4	—[1]	—[1]	3.3	—[1]	—[1]
Mountain Climbing	3.4	2.9	3.8	3.6	2.3	3.3	9.8	4.2	6.5	6.9	3.2	5.2	4.5	3.0	4.4
Rock Climbing	3.2	2.8	4.5	2.8	2.6	3.5	6.5	7.0	8.6	5.5	3.5	5.7	3.7	3.5	5.1
Caving	4.4	1.3	1.7	4.4	2.0	2.9	6.2	1.6	2.6	5.7	2.2	3.0	4.7	1.7	2.4
Off-Road Driving	12.2	13.3	27.6	14.5	15.6	24.3	20.4	11.3	18.9	14.9	9.6	21.2	13.9	13.2	24.6
Horseback Riding	6.1	8.3	19.4	7.5	7.7	22.3	11.2	9.5	28.9	7.5	10.9	32.6	7.1	8.7	23.6
Horseback Riding on Trails	4.7	—[1]	—[1]	5.1	—[1]	—[1]	7.7	—[1]	—[1]	5.8	—[1]	—[1]	5.2	—[1]	—[1]
Social Activities															
Yard Games	40.9	—[1]	—[1]	34.1	—[1]	—[1]	35.1	—[1]	—[1]	30.5	—[1]	—[1]	36.7	—[1]	—[1]
Picnicking	51.2	5.1	8.6	44.0	5.1	8.6	54.6	5.5	8.8	50.4	6.0	9.5	49.1	5.3	8.8
Family Gathering	63.2	6.3	8.6	59.5	5.9	8.4	62.9	6.8	9.9	61.6	6.8	9.4	61.8	6.3	8.8

[1] Trips and days were not asked in the National Survey on Recreation and the Environment for some activities.

Source: 1994-95 National Survey on Recreation and the Environment, USDA Forest Service and the University of Georgia, Athens, Georgia.

Table V.28: Percentage of Population Participating and Mean Trips and Days per Participant 16 years or Older per Year by Assessment Region for Water-Resource-Based Activities, 1994-95

ACTIVITY	NORTH			SOUTH			ROCKY MOUNTAINS			PACIFIC COAST			NATIONAL		
		Mean			Mean			Mean			Mean			Mean	
	Percent	Trips	Days	Percent	Trips	Days	Percent	Trips	Days	Percent	Trips	Days	Percent	Trips	Days
Viewing Activities															
Fish Viewing	13.0	—[1]	16.	13.8	—[1]	19.7	12.6	—[1]	13.9	16.0	—[1]	17.0	13.7	—[1]	17.3
Visiting a Beach or Waterside	62.8	10.2	22.9	60.6	12.2	27.5	55.7	8.1	15.5	66.1	15.6	34.2	62.1	11.6	25.6
Studying Nature near Water	27.3	5.1	21.7	26.6	6.9	29.2	25.1	5.2	18.5	31.9	6.4	26.2	27.6	5.8	24.4
Fishing															
Freshwater	24.1	12.1	18.1	26.7	13.8	20.4	29.0	12.0	17.2	18.4	9.8	12.9	24.4	12.4	18.1
Saltwater	7.5	5.1	7.4	13.4	12.0	18.3	2.9	2.2	4.4	10.6	9.0	13.6	9.5	8.7	13.1
Warmwater	21.2	11.8	17.0	24.9	12.9	20.2	17.8	10.1	14.8	9.9	9.8	13.2	20.4	12.0	17.8
Coldwater	10.0	8.2	12.4	7.4	6.0	9.2	18.7	9.9	13.7	13.4	6.9	9.4	10.4	7.7	11.3
Ice	3.4	—[1]	—[1]	0.3	—[1]	—[1]	3.8	—[1]	—[1]	0.4	—[1]	—[1]	2.0	—[1]	—[1]
Anadromous	4.6	8.0	9.4	3.7	5.7	7.2	3.2	6.1	9.4	6.5	9.4	11.5	4.5	7.7	9.4
Catch and Release	6.8	—[1]	18.1	9.2	—[1]	20.3	11.8	—[1]	16.4	5.8	—[1]	13.5	7.7	—[1]	18.4
Boating															
Sailing	5.2	5.0	8.7	3.7	3.8	7.2	3.1	2.6	4.5	6.7	7.0	8.6	4.8	5.0	8.1
Canoeing	8.7	2.4	5.6	6.7	2.8	4.2	4.9	2.2	4.0	3.9	5.0	7.9	7.0	2.8	5.3
Open-top Canoeing	8.5	—[1]	—[1]	6.3	—[1]	—[1]	4.6	—[1]	—[1]	3.5	—[1]	—[1]	6.8	—[1]	—[1]
Closed-top Canoeing	0.3	—[1]	—[1]	0.5	—[1]	—[1]	0.3	—[1]	—[1]	0.5	—[1]	—[1]	0.4	—[1]	—[1]
Kayaking	1.2	1.6	6.2	1.1	3.2	8.8	0.7	10.1	11.2	2.3	3.6	6.7	1.3	3.0	7.3
Rowing	5.7	2.1	5.0	3.0	3.1	5.4	2.2	2.8	6.4	3.2	2.2	6.4	4.2	2.3	5.3
Floating, Rafting	7.5	2.9	5.1	7.9	3.2	4.9	7.7	3.9	5.8	7.5	2.9	4.9	7.6	3.1	5.1
Motor-boating	24.0	6.7	13.3	24.8	8.6	19.0	21.5	5.7	9.7	20.1	7.3	13.1	23.5	7.3	14.9
Water Skiing	8.2	4.3	9.1	9.7	6.8	10.9	10.2	5.4	8.3	8.9	5.3	9.2	8.9	5.4	9.7
Jet Skiing	4.0	3.8	7.6	5.7	2.1	8.3	4.2	4.5	7.3	4.5	3.2	6.0	4.7	3.1	7.6
Sailboarding/windsurfing	1.1	3.7	8.4	1.0	1.0	4.2	0.8	3.5	4.4	1.5	2.5	4.2	1.1	2.7	6.1
Swimming Activities															
Surfing	0.8	13.1	18.3	1.3	25.6	34.6	0.6	1.7	3.7	3.1	26.9	38.5	1.3	21.8	30.5
Swimming/pool	45.0	7.6	24.7	45.2	8.6	31.3	38.8	8.4	28.2	42.5	8.0	28.3	44.2	8.0	27.6
Swimming/non-pool	41.8	6.7	15.1	37.4	7.2	17.6	32.0	4.9	11.8	37.0	8.2	17.0	39.0	6.9	15.9
Snorkeling/Scuba	6.4	2.3	5.5	7.6	5.6	9.0	5.6	2.8	5.3	9.7	4.7	8.2	7.2	3.9	7.2

[1] Trips and days were not asked in the National Survey on Recreation and the Environment for some activities.
Source: 1994-95 National Survey on Recreation and the Environment, USDA Forest Service and the University of Georgia, Athens, Georgia.

Table V.29: Percentage of Population Participating and Mean Trips and Days per Participant 16 years or Older per Year by Assessment Region for Snow/Ice-Resource-Based Activities, 1994-95

ACTIVITY	NORTH			SOUTH			ROCKY MOUNTAINS			PACIFIC COAST			NATIONAL		
		Mean			Mean			Mean			Mean			Mean	
	Percent	Trips	Days	Percent	Trips	Days	Percent	Trips	Days	Percent	Trips	Days	Percent	Trips	Days
Snow and Ice Activities															
Ice Skating	8.7	—[1]	—[1]	1.5	—[1]	—[1]	4.7	—[1]	—[1]	2.8	—[1]	—[1]	5.2	—[1]	—[1]
Snowboarding	2.7	—[1]	—[1]	1.1	—[1]	—[1]	2.4	—[1]	—[1]	3.2	—[1]	—[1]	2.3	—[1]	—[1]
Sledding	14.7	—[1]	—[1]	4.3	—[1]	—[1]	11.5	—[1]	—[1]	8.1	—[1]	—[1]	10.2	—[1]	—[1]
Downhill Skiing	9.1	4.7	8.0	5.0	1.9	4.2	11.6	5.9	8.6	11.6	5.6	8.7	8.4	4.5	7.5
Cross-Country Skiing	4.8	3.7	8.1	0.6	1.6	4.0	4.4	4.2	6.4	3.5	4.8	7.1	3.3	3.8	7.5
Cross Country Skiing on Groomed Trails	4.0	—[1]	—[1]	0.4	—[1]	—[1]	3.5	—[1]	—[1]	2.9	—[1]	—[1]	2.7	—[1]	—[1]
Cross Country Skiing on Ungroomed Trails	4.2	—[1]	—[1]	0.4	—[1]	—[1]	3.8	—[1]	—[1]	3.1	—[1]	—[1]	2.8	—[1]	—[1]
Backcountry Cross country Skiing	2.7	—[1]	—[1]	0.3	—[1]	—[1]	3.0	—[1]	—[1]	2.1	—[1]	—[1]	1.9	—[1]	—[1]
Snowmobiling	5.4	3.1	10.3	1.2	1.1	3.1	5.1	4.2	8.9	2.1	5.3	8.2	3.6	3.2	9.3

[1] Trips and days were not asked in the National Survey on Recreation and the Environment for some activities.
Source: 1994-95 National Survey on Recreation and the Environment, USDA Forest Service and the University of Georgia, Athens, Georgia.

Prominent examples of activities with substantial differences in regional participation include visiting prehistoric sites, primitive area camping, hiking, backpacking, mountain climbing, and off-road vehicle driving. A regional difference pattern for specific activities emerges that is very similar to that summarized above for aggregations of activities by type. Generally, participation percentages are higher in the two western regions and lower in the two eastern regions. However, comparing number of trips per year across the highly resource-dependent activities reveals relatively little difference between regions in number of trips participants take away from home to pursue their chosen activities. Mean number of days during which participants engaged in the activities is mixed in order of magnitude across regions, except that the most general observation for many of the land-based activities is that participation days are somewhat lower in the eastern than in the western regions.

Percentages of population and mean trips and days per participant per year for water-based activities are presented in Table V.28. As a generalization, participation percentages are lower in the drier western regions. An exception is surfing in the Pacific Coast region. Whether viewing, fishing, boating or swimming, percentages of the population participating is higher in the East. Between the eastern regions, participation in viewing activities is greater in the North, fishing participation is greater in the South, non-motorized boating is greater in the North, motorized boating is greater in the South, and swimming is about the same for the two eastern regions.

Differences in mean trips per year across regions are very mixed and difficult to generalize. Except for stream-based activities, trips per year are generally lowest in the Rocky Mountain and Great Plains region and highest in the North and South regions. Ocean and saltwater trips are obviously lowest in the Rocky Mountain and Great Plains region. Number of warmwater fishing trips is higher in the North and South, while mean number of coldwater fishing trips is greater in the Rocky Mountains. More participation days generally are devoted to water-based activities in the North and South than in the other regions. Notable exceptions are greater mean participation days for coldwater fishing in the Rocky Mountain and Great Plains region, greater anadromous fishing in the Pacific Coast, greater kayaking participation days in the Rocky Mountains, and much higher participation days of surfing in the Pacific Coast.

Participation in snow and ice activities is shown in Table V.29. As noted earlier, percentages of the population are lowest in the South and greatest in the North. Between the western regions, participation percentages are greater in the Rocky Mountain and Great Plains than in the Pacific Coast region. Residents of the two western regions, however, tend to take more activity trips away from home for downhill skiing, cross-country skiing, and snowmobiling than residents of the North. Residents of these two western regions also devote more days to downhill skiing than the residents of the North. However, more participation days are devoted to cross-country skiing and snowmobiling in the North than in the two western regions.

Comparison Across Nine Forest Regions

There are nine forest regions in the United States, which coincide with the nine administrative regions of the National Forest System of the U.S. Forest Service. Percentages of the population, number of participants, and numbers of trips and days for some of the 13 activity types discussed earlier in this chapter and for individual activities vary substantially across the nine forest regions (Appendix Table V.8). Activity types for which forest regional differences vary relatively little include fitness, individual sports, outdoor team sports, outdoor spectator sports, and social activities. Participation in these activity types is not as dependent on access to and the character of the local natural landscape.

Activity types that are heavily dependent on the natural landscape and access to it are listed below. Shown also is the name of the forest region with the lowest participation percentage, the national participation percentage (a measure of the overall interregional participation mode), and the name of the forest region with the highest participation percentage.

Types of Activities	Lowest Region	National Percentages	Highest Region
Viewing	South	76.2	Pac. NW
Snow and Ice	South	18.1	Alaska
Camping	South	26.4	Alaska
Hunting	Pac. SW	9.3	N. Rockies
Fishing	Pac. SW	28.9	Alaska
Boating	S. Western	29.0	Alaska
Swimming	Alaska	54.2	S. Western
Outdoor Adventure	South	36.8	Alaska

Across activity types, percentages of the population participating appear to be lower in the South than in other regions. Participation percentages are highest for Alaska for five of the activity types.

COUNTY PARTICIPATION PATTERNS FOR LAND, WINTER, AND WATER-BASED ACTIVITIES

(By J. M. Bowker, D. B. K. English, and G. Bhat, USDA Forest Service, Athens, GA)

In this section we illustrate national patterns of participants per square mile for three broad types of outdoor recreation–land-based, winter-based, and water-based activities. As the names indicate, these types are determined by resource setting.

The procedure used to estimate county participation per square mile involved multiple steps. First, logistic models (Greene, 1993) were developed for each activity aggregate in each of the four assessment regions. The models extend concepts used in earlier RPA assessments (Hof & Kaiser, 1983; Walsh, Jon, McKean, & Hof, 1992) to the regional level. For each regional cross-sectional model, participation in an aggregate activity by an individual aged 16 or older was modeled as a function of age, age squared, household income, race, gender, population density, and a relevant index of the available supply of the resource supporting the activity (see Chapter VI for a more detailed description of the models and variables). Models were estimated using the NSRE data set (Cordell, McDonald, Lewis, Miles, Martin, & Bason, 1996) and the NORSIS Data Base (see Chapter IV).

Next, county-level estimates of total participation for each activity aggregate were obtained by combining parameter estimates for each regional participation model with county-level demographic data (Woods & Poole, 1997; USDA Forest Service, 1996) and county population totals for residents 16 years and older. These estimates were in turn divided by county area to obtain estimates of participants per square mile.

Maps are presented for each of the activity aggregates with county and state boundaries. Each county is shaded according to estimated participants per square mile. For clarity, counties are classified as falling into one of three participant-per-square-mile intervals based on the estimated distribution for all counties. The intervals are the bottom 25 percent, the middle 50 percent, and the top 25 percent. The distribution of county-level estimates for participants per square mile is different for each activity aggregate, thus the numbers delineating the above percentiles differ.

Land-Based Recreation Activities

The land-based activity type consisted of participation in any of the following specific outdoor activities: biking, horseback riding, picnicking, family gathering, dayhiking, orienteering, backpacking, developed camping, primitive camping, mountain climbing, rock climbing, caving, birdwatching, wildlife viewing, other nature study, big game hunting, small game hunting, migratory bird hunting and visiting a zoo, interpretation center, historic site, or archeological site.

Across all four regions, participation in land-based outdoor recreation was positively influenced by income and relative availability of public and private land suitable for recreation. Race and gender were also important factors in explaining participation, with whites and males being more likely to engage in the recreation forms listed above. Population density had mixed effects across the regions. In the more rural South and Rocky Mountain regions, population density had a positive effect, suggesting that those living in and immediately around metropolitan centers were the most likely participants, while in the more densely populated North and Pacific regions, the effect was opposite. Age and age squared had mixed effects across regions.

The national map for land-based activity participation per square mile shown in Figure V.11. Estimated participants per square mile ranged from almost zero to over 1000. One fourth of the counties had fewer than 14 participants per square mile. For the most part, these counties are in the sparsely populated parts of the Rocky Mountains and the Great Plains, although sections of Northern Minnesota, Michigan, and Maine, along with pockets in the South, also fall into this category.

Figure V.11: Participants per Square Mile for All Land-Based Outdoor Recreation Activities by County, 1995

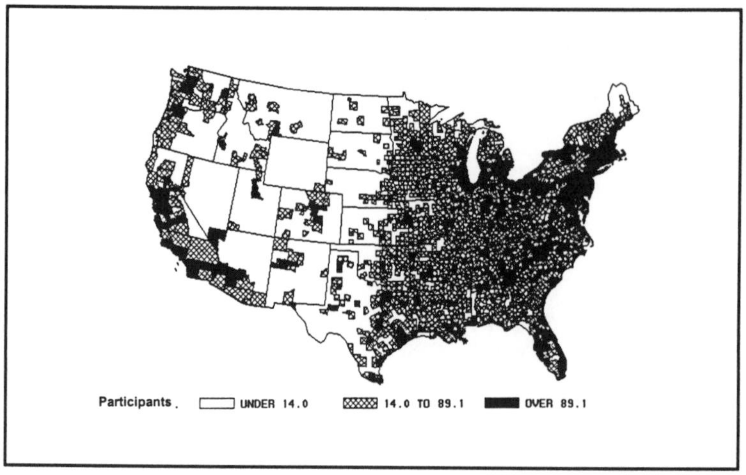

The middle 50 percent of all counties fall into a participant-per-square-mile range of 14.0 to 89.1. These counties are represented by the cross-hatched areas in Figure V.11. Generally, these counties are considered rural and often have significant agricultural or forestry sectors in their economies.

The upper 25 percent of the counties, represented by the blackened areas, are those with more than 89.1 participants per square mile. These counties envelop major metropolitan centers around the country along with densely populated suburban areas. Not surprisingly, these are the areas from which most of the recreation-use pressure on natural resources originates.

Winter-Based Recreation Activities

Winter-based activities are ice-skating, snowboarding, downhill skiing, cross-country skiing, snowmobiling, and sledding. Unlike some of the general land-based activities above, participation in any of the winter-based activities requires a fair amount of physical exertion. This fact, coupled with the seasonal and geographic constraints, leads to a national distribution of county-level participants per square mile in winter-based activities, which is much lower than the very broad land-based activity aggregate.

We estimate that 25 percent of the nation's counties produce fewer than two participants per square mile, while the middle 50 percent of the counties represent between two and 22.4 participants per square mile. The remaining 25 percent of the counties produce more than 22.4 participants per square mile. The pattern for participation in the winter-based activity aggregate is presented in Figure V.12.

Figure V.12: Participants per Square Mile for Snow- and Ice-Based Outdoor Recreation Activities by County, 1995

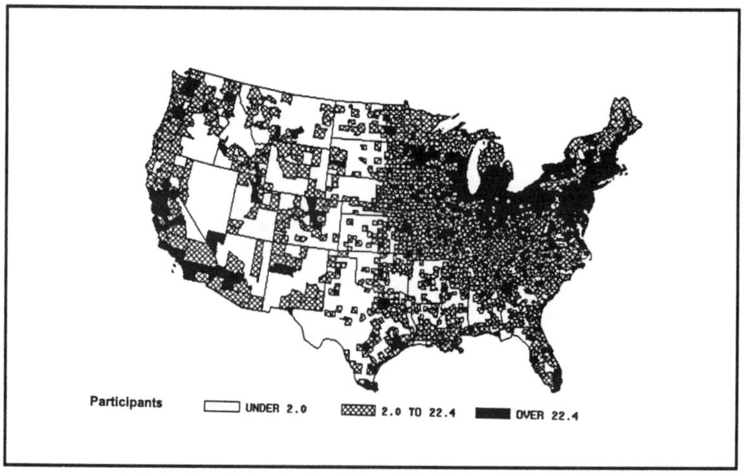

The top 25 percent of the counties in this activity type are similar to the top 25 percent for the land-based activity type. Notable exceptions can be found in the upper Midwest and northern New England. Because the measure used in this section is unaffected by frequency of participants, most population centers around the country fall into the top 25 percent.

A noticeable difference between the winter-based and land-based participation patterns occurs for the middle 50 percent to the counties in each category. For example, considerably more counties in the Great Plains and Rocky Mountain regions fall into the middle of the county-level distribution for the winter-based activities. Correspondingly, fewer rural Southern counties fall into the mid-range of winter-based activities than for land-based activities.

Among the factors influencing participation, income has a strong positive influence as does relative availability of winter-sport opportunities. Race and sex are also important factors with nonwhites less likely to participate and females less likely to participate. Unlike general land-based sports, age is a more prominent factor in explaining participation. Participation initially increases with age and then after peaking begins to decline. This trend is probably due to the physical nature of most sports in this activity type.

Water-Based Activities

The water-based activity type includes participation in any of the following activities: visiting a beach or waterside, freshwater fishing (including warmwater, coldwater, catch and release), saltwater fishing, motorboating, sailing, canoeing, kayaking, rowing, floating, water skiing, jet skiing, rafting, windsurfing, surfing, nonpool swimming, and scuba diving.

Participation patterns for water-based activities are very similar to those for the land-based activities. One-fourth of the nation's counties produce fewer than 12.7 participants per square mile in any water-based activity, while 50 percent fall between 12.7 and 77.7 participants per square mile (Figure V.13). Twenty-five percent of the counties produce in excess of 77.7 participants per square mile, extending up to a maximum of over 3000 participants per square mile.

Figure V.13: Participants per Square Mile for Water-Based Outdoor Recreation Activities by County, 1995

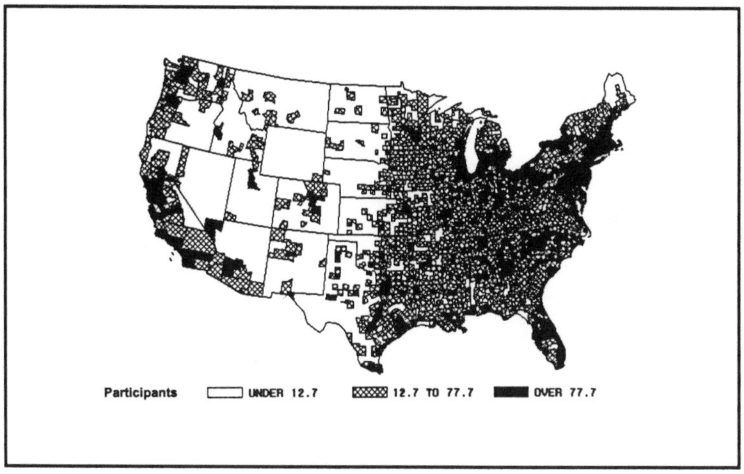

Income, race, and gender are important factors explaining participation in water-based activity participation. As with other activity types, income had a positive influence on participation, while nonwhites and females were in general less likely to participate. Population density adversely affected participation in the North, but it had no effect in the other regions. In the North, participation diminished with age while in the other regions, age had no significant effect on participation. Finally, the index of relative water availability had no significant effect in any region. This relationship is most likely due to the fact that annual participation, irrespective of the intensity, was assessed.

Overall, for land and water-based recreation activities, it appears that pressure on the resources in the form of the number of annual participants emanates from the nation's population centers. This is not surprising. For winter-based activities, pressure per square mile across the country is notably less with 75 percent of the counties producing fewer than 22.4 participants per square mile annually. As expected, participation is noticeably more sparse in the rural South.

Across all regions and activities, income, race, and gender affected participation. Holding other factors constant, nonwhites were less likely to participate in any of the activity types. The same is true for females. If this trend continues into the future it will mitigate, to a certain extent, pressure on resources as the proportion of nonwhites in the population increases. However, if nonwhites and females develop a greater affinity for the outdoor recreation activities included in the categories above, then the pressure on resources supporting these activities could be substantially more than that brought on by population growth alone.

TRENDS IN VISITS TO FEDERAL AREAS

(By Richard Stenger, freelance journalist, Athens, GA)

The former annual Federal Recreation Fee Report (USDI, 1974-1992) tabulated and described public recreation visits to land and recreation sites under the jurisdiction of the seven federal land managing agencies. These agencies include the Tennessee Valley Authority, Fish and Wildlife Service, Bureau of Reclamation, Bureau of Land Management, National Park Service, Corps of Engineers, and Forest Service. Since the Annual Fee Report was discontinued in fiscal year 1993, some of these agencies have continued to compile statistics on visits. Others, for example the Tennessee Valley Authority and the Bureau of Reclamation, have discontinued visit reporting due to budget constraints or shifting priorities. Others, for example the Corps of Engineers and Bureau of Land Management, have revised their methods of collecting and reporting visit statistics, making comparisons with data from previous years difficult. Visitations are typically reported as visitor days and visits. A visitor day is simply an accumulated 12 hours of recreation use by one or more people and may be reported by activity or across all activities. A visit is entrance into and use of an area under agency jurisdiction or into a specifically designated recreation site for any amount of time. For this outdoor recreation assessment, visitor days and visits have been adjusted where possible to account for changes in counting methods among the agencies for the years shown.

For some agencies, like the TVA and Forest Service, trends show significant annual increases in both visitor days and visits (Tables V.30 and V.31). For other agencies, such as the National Park Service and the Bureau of Reclamation, reported visits fluctuated between 1986 and 1996. Overall, visits to federal sites and areas increased by over 40 percent (Figure V.14). The bulk of this increase (some 222 million visitor days) occurred on Forest Service, Corps of Engineers, and Bureau of Land Management land and water areas.

Table V.30: Thousands of Visitor Days of Recreation Use to Federal Recreation Sites by Year and Agency and Growth Index (in Parentheses) from Base Year 1986

	Fiscal Year (October to September)					
Agency	1986	1988	1990	1992	1994	1996
Tennessee Valley Authority	599.3	768.4	826.2	1,136.8	1,161.2	1,207.6
	(100)	(128)	(138)	(190)	(194)	(202)
Fish and Wildlife Service	5,558.6	6,734.3	4,410.3	N/A	N/A	N/A
	(100)	(121)	(79)			
Bureau of Reclamation	24,705.8	24,470.2	23,365.2	22,427.2	22,298.0[b]	27,342.9
	(100)	(99)	(95)	(91)	(90)	(111)
Bureau of Land Management	23,678.5	38,447.4	43,171.8	46,939.5	40,196.3	72,793.7
	(100)	(162)	(182)	(198)	(170)	(307)
National Park Service	111,013.5	114,849.7	110,203.5	115,847.1	111,196.9	104,286.2
	(100)	(103)	(99)	(104)	(100)	(94)
Corps of Engineers	144,170.2	197,795.0	189,820.7	203,434.0	204,905.4	212,008.7
	(100)	(137)	(132)	(141)	(142)	(147)
Forest Service	226,532.7	242,315.7	263,050.6	287,690.6	330,348.4	341,204.0
	(100)	(107)	(116)	(127)	(146)	(151)
Totals	536,258.6	625,380.7	634,848.3	677,475.2	710,106.2	758,843.1
	(100)	(117)	(118)	(126)	(132)	(142)

Source: Federal Recreation Fee Reports and the Respective Agencies.
BLM changes from FY94 to 96 may not reflect differences in visitation, but new counting methods.
BOR statistics for FY93 and 96 are unofficial estimates and exclude BOR units managed by other federal agencies.
TVA figures are for fee-charging areas only and are calender years.
[b]FY93 figures.

Table V.31: Thousands of Visits to Federal Recreation Sites (and Index to 1988) by Agency and Year, 1988-1996

Agency	Fiscal Year 1988	1990	1992	1994	1996
Tennessee Valley Authority	411.5	447.1	568.4	580.6	603.8
	(100)	(116)	(138)	(141)	(147)
Fish and Wildlife Service	25,307.5	27,878.9	29,964.6	27,091.7	29,468.1
	(100)	(110)	(118)	(107)	(116)
Bureau of Reclamation	41,833.4	40,736.4	38,583.7	38,242.0[b]	38,280.0
	(100)	(97)	(92)	(91)	(92)
Bureau of Land Management	57,841.5	71,821.0	69,418.0	50,743.0	58,922.9
	(100)	(124)	(120)	(88)	(102)
National Park Service	286,160.7	259,767.9	273,298.1	268,636.2	265,796.2
	(100)	(91)	(96)	(94)	(93)
Corps of Engineers	N/A	396,157.9	413,456.2	380,357.7	375,722.3
		(100)[c]	(104)	(96)	(95)
Forest Service	N/A	597,609.9[a]	691,180.5	829,839.8	859,210.0
		(100)[c]	(116)	(139)	(144)
Totals	411,554.6	1,394,419.1	1,516,469.5	1,595,491.0	1,628,003.3
		(100)[c]	(109)	(114)	(117)

Source: Federal Recreation Fee Reports and the Respective Agencies.
BLM changes from FY94 to 96 may not reflect differences in visitation, but new counting methods; BOR statistics for FY93 and 96 are unofficial estimates and exclude BOR units managed by other federal agencies; TVA figures are for fee-charging areas only and are calender years.
[a]FY91 figures.
[b]FY93 figures.

Figure V.14: Visitation Trends at Areas Managed by Federal Agencies by Agency and Year, 1986-1996

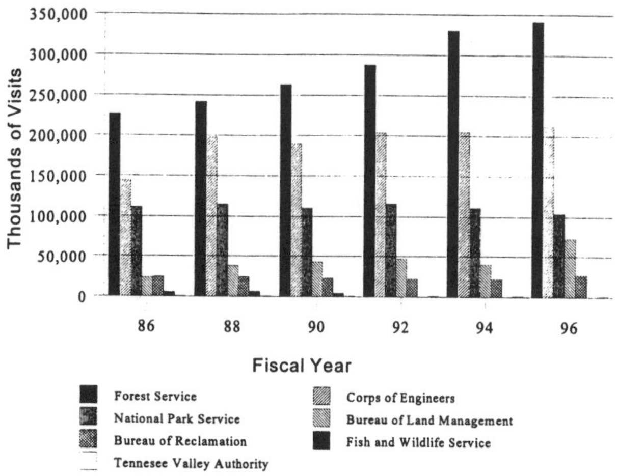

Source: Federal Recreation Fee Reports and the Respective Agencies

1996.

Since the last national assessment in 1987, the status of outdoor recreation on federal land has become uncertain. Reduction of the federal deficit, shifting of priorities for federal funding, and reductions of agency staffing have all contributed to an increase in the difficulty of maintaining federal statistics. While uncertainty still exists about the future role of federal land and of management for outdoor recreation on this land, there has been a recent resurgence of interest in and commitment to improving data and information about federal outdoor recreation. For example, the Forest Service is currently conducting a national pilot of sampling approaches for improving estimates of recreation visits across a variety of recreational settings. The Bureau of Land Management is expected to join in that pilot project in 1998. Reports from local management units upward to national offices have proven very uneven for the agencies, and different approaches are being attempted.

Aside from questions about the quality and completeness of recreation reporting, there are many additional indications that public recreation interest in federal land continues to be strong. Local managers typically report that visitor pressures are continuing to mount. At some popular destinations, visits are rising more rapidly than the services and capacity can be expanded. At some of the more popular national parks, fees have been increased and mass transit and visitor load limits are being instituted.

TRENDS IN VISITS TO STATE PARKS

(By Daniel McLean, Indiana University, Bloomington, IN)

State Park visits, traditionally termed attendance, are reported separately for day and overnight use and for fee and non-fee areas. These reporting categories are not the same as those for federal areas. The day vs. overnight and fee vs. non-fee distinctions are important. Day use includes outings by individuals arriving and departing from a state park the same day. Overnight use involves a stay of at least one night and may be indoors (lodges, cabins, etc.) or outdoors (camping).

Overnight visitation is reported by the type of overnight accommodations used: campsites, cabins and cottages, lodges, group facilities, and other. The extent to which overnight accommodations are used is measured by "rental nights" and reported separately for campsites, cabins and cottages and lodge rooms. A rental night is a single night's use of a single rental unit of a given overnight facility, regardless of the size of the party occupying that rental unit. Thus, a party occupying a campsite for a full week would represent seven "rental nights."

Fee areas refer to parks where entrance fees are charged. Estimates of visits to fee areas are usually quite reliable because entrance to the park is tied to fee collection. Not included in these estimates of visits are persons paying fees for services or special sites within state parks, e.g., restaurant or campsite use. Non-fee areas are parks or other managed areas where no general entrance fee is charged. At these parks, attendance must be estimated through sampling or other means—even though such parks and other similar areas may contain facilities (such as golf courses or riding trails) that do require specific use charges.

Visits to State Parks

Tables V.32 through V.35 report total visits to state park-administered areas by assessment region. One of the most difficult issues to deal with in summarizing visits to state parks is compiling attendance data collected using different methods and assumptions. Some states provide data that are consistent from year to year. Others may have measured use by a variety of methods over time for estimating visits.

Indications are that visits to state parks are increasing. Between 1992 and 1996 there was a modest increase nationally in the number of visits, averaging 1.4 percent, or 10 million new visits annually. Only the Pacific region showed a decline in attendance between 1992 and 1996. The variability of the reporting and attendance estimates across state parks is high. While the five-year report shows an increase, the year with the most visits was in 1995 (see Table V.32). The five-year mean for attendance was 730 million visits annually, with the high occurring in 1995. There was less than a one percent drop between 1995 and 1996, and that drop was the first one in the five-year reporting cycle. The overall reported trend, however, has been steady growth in visits to state parks. Unusually hot or wet summers can account for small changes. It appears that 1996 may have been an anomaly, or it may be a result of adjustments in counting systems in individual states.

Day use is much greater than overnight use in state parks (Table V.33). Of all visits in 1996, only 7.9 percent were overnight. In 1992, the percent of visits that were overnight was 8.0 percent, suggesting a

Golfing and sightseeing are two of the many outdoor activities available in the Georgia State Park system. Photos courtesy of Georgia State Parks and Historic Sites.

consistency over time in the share of overnight visits who spent the night. The actual number of visits overnight, however, has increased over the five-year period as overall visits have increased. Data are not available on occupancy rates of state park campgrounds, cabins, or group sites, nor are data available to indicate whether the level of use of lodges is exceeding the capacity of those lodges.

Fee area visits accounted for 40 percent of the use of state parks in 1996 (Table V.34). At fee areas, 15.2 percent of the visitors stayed overnight, as opposed to only three percent in non-fee areas. The proportions of all areas that do and do not charge fees are not known at the national level. Only seven states report not having any type of entrance fee. It appears, however, that there are a number of additional areas not accounted for in reporting of visits because they do not have entrance fees. Twelve states reported not having any non-fee area visitors, implying that 38 states have some non-fee areas.

Growth in visits to state park fee areas grew 8.2 percent between 1992 and 1996, while visits to non-fee areas grew 6.1 percent. It appears that fee areas are becoming somewhat more heavily used, but reasons for these increases are difficult to ascertain without better information. One statistic that is somewhat revealing is that in 1996 there were a reported 1,998 areas with some type of entrance fee among an overall total of 5,091 operated areas. If accurate, these totals indicate that about 39 percent of state parks charge some type of fee. It should be noted that the estimate of 1,998 areas charging fees is a composite of data reported for individual and vehicle entrance fees. In instances where both fees exist, there may be some double counting. Table V.35 shows the regional distribution of day and overnight visits by assessment region. Day use of non-fee areas is approximately 32 times greater than overnight use in such areas.

Table V.36 presents the number of overnight visits to state parks by type of facilities used. Campers, as previously reported, make up 85.5 percent of overnight visitors. Actual reported camping visits decreased by 1.4 percent between 1992 and 1996, and visits to lodges decreased 11.6 percent. A number of factors can mitigate these findings, including weather, cost, andquality of the experience. Overall there was less than one percent growth in use of overnight facilities between 1992 and 1996.

Table V.32: Number of Visits to State Park Systems by Year and by Region 1992-1996

Region	Year					
	1992	1993	1994	1995	1996	5-Yr. Avg.
Western	48,993,133	52,563,543	54,270,796	58,920,897	58,817,036	54,713,081
Pacific	179,632,907	182,500,018	174,251,064	173,109,546	176,034,153	177,105,538
Southern	162,928,762	164,129,174	167,731,504	168,974,442	152,267,607	163,206,298
Northern	312,219,684	325,606,818	329,270,357	351,261,412	358,482,921	335,368,238
Total	703,774,486	724,799,553	725,523,721	752,266,297	745,601,717	730,393,155
Percent Change from Previous Year		2.99%	0.10%	3.69%	-0.89%	1.47%

Table V.33: Day, Overnight, and Total Number of Visits to State Park Systems by Region, 1996

Region	Visits		
	Day	Overnight	Total
Western	47,163,798	11,653,238	58,817,036
Pacific	164,906,658	11,157,003	176,034,153
Southern	139,505,878	12,734,445	152,267,607
Northern	334,906,223	23,576,653	358,482,921
Total	686,482,557	59,121,339	745,601,717

Table V.34: Number of Visits to Areas Charging Fees for Use by Region. 1996

Region	Visits		
	Day	Overnight	Total
Western	42,136,123	10,597,620	52,733,743
Pacific	22,931,911	8,562,111	31,494,022
Southern	63,216,832	8,450,833	71,667,665
Northern	124,853,618	17,863,676	143,317,294
Total	253,138,484	45,474,240	299,212,724

Table V.35: Day, Overnight, and Total Number of Visits to State Park Systems by Region, 1996

Region	Visits		
	Day	Overnight	Total
Western	5,027,675	1,055,618	11,593,948
Pacific	141,974,747	2,594,892	144,569,639
Southern	76,289,046	4,283,612	80,572,658
Northern	210,052,605	5,712,977	215,765,582
Total	433,344,073	13,647,099	452,501,827

Table V.36: Number of Visits by Type of Accommodation Used at State Parks by Region, 1996

Region	Type of accommodation					
	Campers	Cabins	Lodges	Group Facilities	Other	Total
Western	10,571,514	265,259	110,042	50,224	649,037	11,916,076
Pacific	10,480,919	20,770	109,802	507,676	37,836	11,157,003
Southern	7,237,853	1,399,408	1,114,118	491,725	0	10,243,101
Northern	20,391,952	1,594,524	896,896	664,084	100,439	23,647,635
Total	48,682,238	3,279,961	2,230,858	1,713,709	787,312	56,963,815

The available data indicate steady but modest growth in visits to state parks. Too little data are present to determine if 1996 attendance is an aberration or if it signals a downward trend. Some adjustments can always be anticipated in the data. However, whether the trend is up modestly or more, it remains apparent that recreational use of state parks is extremely important to many Americans. Total number of visits to state parks is three times that to the National Park System, even though the overall area in state parks is substantially less. The availability of natural resources with a variety of activities close to people's homes is obviously important and attractive to many.

RECENT TRENDS IN CONSUMER SPENDING AND INDUSTRY SALES

(By Richard Stenger, Freelance Journalist, Athens, GA)

Estimating spending by Americans on outdoor recreation is difficult for several reasons. First, isolating spending that is specifically for outdoor recreation is subjective. For example, how does one count a trip to the local supermarket before a summer vacation? Second, there are few sources of adequate consumer spending data, especially sources that are specific to outdoor recreation and that are not proprietary information held by industry. Some recent industry statistics are on target, but they are far from complete and generally do not go back many years. A third difficulty is that different economic studies use different computational methods and accounting stances, even though they investigate nearly identical consumer markets. Interest in better data on consumer spending on outdoor recreation is rising, however, and this interest seems to be leading to development of better data sources.

Some of the key estimates of expenditures in specific segments of the outdoor recreation market are summarized below:

- $67.9 billion spent by hunters and anglers in 1996 (U.S. Fish and Wildlife Service, National Survey on Fishing, Hunting, and Wildlife-Related Expenditures)
- $29 billion spent by bird watchers in 1996 (U.S. Fish and Wildlife Service, National Survey on Fishing, Hunting and Wildlife-Related Expenditures)
- $25.3 billion spent by the horse industry primarily for recreation and showing annually (American Horse Council)
- $24 billion spent on fishing annually (Bassmaster Magazine, 1997)
- $17.8 billion retail spending on new and used boats and related goods and services in 1996 (National Marine Manufacturers Association)
- $15.8 billion spent for shipments of recreational vehicles (new, used, rental) to retailers in 1995 (Recreational Vehicle Association)
- $12 billion spent by recreationists at U.S. Corps of Engineers projects for trip-related items in 1995 (Tourism Works for America, 1997)
- $9.4 billion spent on snow sport-related expenditures, such as skiing, snowboarding, travel, entertainment, equipment, accessories, and real estate during the 1994-1995 season (National Ski Areas Association)
- $6.5 billion spent on food and lodging while visiting national wildlife refuges yearly (Tourism Works for America, 1997)
- $6.4 billion spent while on visits to national parks in 1995 (National Park Service, Tourism Works for America, 1997)
- $3.25 billion total expenditures (equipment, clothing, accessories, lodging, food, and fuel) for snowmobiling in 1996 (International Manufacturers Association)
- $2.0 billion spent for rentals at commercial campgrounds in 1995 (National Association of RV Parks and Campgrounds)
- $1.8 billion retail spending for sailboats and related equipment and services in 1996 (Inter/port, 1997)
- $532 million in revenues by state parks in 1994 (National Association of State Park Directors)

The above are taken from a number of different sources and cover different activities. Thus, they cannot be summed to look at the overall magnitude of consumer spending on outdoor recreation in this country. There are several recent industry studies, however, that have provided estimates of total annual expenditures on at least some segments of outdoor recreation-related goods retailing.

First, the Outdoor Recreation Coalition of America estimated that, in 1996, a total of $4.3 billion was spent on retail sales for human-powered outdoor recreation equipment, apparel, and accessories (Table V.37).

The survey involved interviews of 634 randomly selected retailers across all 50 states. Recreation was narrowly defined to include only hiking, camping, backpacking, mountain biking, and in-line skating. Snowboarding and skiing, which in a strict sense do not rely on human power, were not included in the study.

Other findings from this study indicated that sales were growing vigorously. Sales for 1996 were $400 million higher than in 1995. Fifty-seven percent of responding retailers indicated sales were up an average of 16.9 percent. Overall sales were up in each region of the country, including associated consumer spending for items such as travel, permits, fees, outfitters, and guides that reached $35 billion.

Table V.37: Annual Total Spending for Human Powered Recreational Equipment by Type of Equipment, 1997

Type of Equipment	$ Millions	Type of Equipment	$ Millions
Land-based activities		**Rock/Ice/Snow-based activities**	
Apparel	1600.0	Rock/Ice Climbing Equipment	108.2
Footwear	1200.0	Skiing/Snowboard Equipment	2100.0
Backpacks	222.5	Total	2208.2
Camping	299.6	**Geographic Region**	
Tents	180.5	Northeast	971.8
Sleeping Bags	183.3	South	1000.0
Total	3685.9	North Central	954.6
Water-based activities		Rockies	602.0
Paddle Sports	200.1	Far West	752.5
		Total	4280.9

Source: Leisure Trends Group, Boulder, CO, and ORCA, 1997.Table V.38–Wholesale value of annual manufacturers' shipments in the United States by type of equipment and year (in millions of dollars).

The Sporting Goods Manufacturing Association (SGMA) produced a Recreation Market Report for 1994/95 in which it estimated industry-wide sales for outdoor leisure products at the wholesale level. In addition to covering human-powered products, SGMA also covered motorized recreation vehicles like motorcycles, boats, snowmobiles, and goods and equipment used for organized amateur sports. Based on information from sporting goods companies, trade associations, and market research, SGMA concluded that the wholesale value of manufacturer's shipments for all sporting goods and equipment in the United States totaled $57 billion in 1995, a $2.9 billion increase over 1994.

By removing indoor recreation categories such as aerobics, bowling, and ice hockey equipment, the total was $51.0 billion, a $3.3 billion rise over the wholesale total for the same goods and equipment in the previous year (Table V.38). During 1995 and 1994, respectively, wholesale values for outdoor-recreation-related sports equipment were $9.2 and $8.8 billion, for sports apparel $16.2 and $15.4 billion, for athletic footwear $7.9 and $7.1 billion, and recreational transport $17.8 and $16.5 billion.

Table V.38: Wholesale Value of Annual Manufacturers' Shipments in the United States by Type of Equipment and Year (in Millions of Dollars)

Type Sports Equipment	1995	1994	Type Sports Apparel	1995	1994
Baseball/Softball	348	348	Socks	933	875
Camping	1508	1375	Swimwear	1235	1118
Footballs & Sets	125	125	Sports Shirts	4790	4280
Firearms & Hunting	1675	1781	Shorts	1632	1569
Total Golf	2130	1993	Ski	358	327
In-line skates & accessories	725	605	Sweat Pants	970	962
Skateboards	63	60	Sweat Shirts	1905	1845
Scuba & Skin Diving	298	274	Sweat Suits	800	931
Snow Skiing, Alpine	347	359	Parkas/Jackets, Non-Ski	680	627
Snow Skiing, X-Country	37	36	Team	475	475

Table V.38 Cont.

Type	1995	1994	Type	1995	1994
Sports Equipment			**Sports Apparrel**		
Soccer, Balls/Accessories	40	45	Miscellaneous	2375	2375
Fishing	1500	1400	Total Sports Apparel	16153	15384
Tennis	235	259			
Water Sports	140	127			
Total Sports Equipment	9171	8787			
Athletic Footwear			**Recreational Transport**		
Basketball	1825	1725	Bicycle & Accessories	1813	1800
Cross-Training/Fitness	1450	1325	Motorcycles & ATVs	1300	1320
Golf	230	230	Pleasure Boats and Motors	6292	5125
Cleated	300	285	Recreational Vehicles	7032	7249
Running/Jogging	615	685	Snowmobiles	290	300
Tennis	470	52	Water Scooters	1068	675
Other Court	35	40	Total	17795	16469
Walking	1075	900	**All Categories**		
Other	240	300	Sports Equipment	9171	8787
Hiking/Outdoor	625	485	Sports Apparel	16153	15384
Children	1020	1120	Athletic Footwear	7885	7147
Total Athletic Footwear	7885	7147	Recreational Transport	17795	16469
			Total	51004	47787

Source: Sporting Goods Manufacturing Association, 1996.

Besides goods and equipment, travel expenses make up a major part of outdoor recreation-related expenditures. However, this category of spending is the most elusive to quantify because of a lack of explicit accounting for recreation-related travel. For example, what portion of expenses associated with a business trip should be counted as outdoor recreation expenses if the business traveler rents a car to visit a national park?

Based on findings from travel researchers, a rough estimate is provided for travel expenses related to outdoor recreation. Overall, during 1995 domestic and foreign travelers spent $421.5 billion for travel in the United States, a 5.8 percent increase over the 1994 total of $398 billion. Using the estimate that 11.04 percent of all travel in the U.S. in 1995 was for outdoor recreation (Travel Industries Association, Research Department, International Trade Administration and Tourism Industries, 1996), and assuming that total spending per recreation traveler is the same as for all other travelers, a total of $46.53 billion for recreation travel was estimated for 1995.

Determining long-term trends in outdoor recreation spending also is constrained by the small number of studies that have been done in the recent past. Propst, Gavrilis, Dimitris, Cordell, and Hansen (1985) examined outdoor recreation-related expenditures for much of the 1970s and early 1980s, in part relying on the landmark work Outdoor Recreation Statistics (Clawson & Van Doren, 1984). Other more recent studies comparable to this one are not available.

The U.S. Bureau of Economic Analysis (BEA) compiles data summarizing recreation and other spending in its Personal Consumer Expenditures survey. The report, however, relies in large part on estimates provided by the industries themselves. The Consumer Expenditures Survey from the U.S. Bureau of Labor Statistics, which compiles similar statistics on spending patterns in America, uses information directly from consumers. Its total spending estimates tend to be about one third less than those from the BEA's Personal Consumer Expenditures report.

With some exceptions, total consumer spending on goods and services related to outdoor recreation increased steadily in the 10-year period beginning in 1985 (Table V.39). In 1995, the figure stood at $35.6 billion dollars, an $8.1 billion increase over the $27.4 billion in 1985. After 1985, every year selected for this review experienced a spending increase until 1995, in which spending fell slightly from $36.3 billion in 1993.

From $455 million in 1985, the annual amount spent on winter sports equipment rose to as high as $529 million in 1987 before falling to $389.4 million in 1995. The total for water-related expenditures also dropped over the same decade, from $8.4 billion to $7.5 billion. Such variations may not accurately reflect changes in spending because of the risk of sampling errors—the total figures are official projections based on interviews with a limited number of consumers—and because the Bureau of Labor Statistics periodically revises how it classifies expenditures.

Adjusted for inflation using the Consumer's Price Index for sporting goods and equipment, outdoor recreation expenditures still demonstrated a general rise between 1985 and 1995. Based on the Consumer Price Index section dealing with recreation, and inflating all figures to 1995 dollars, $32.4 billion were spent on outdoor recreation related items in 1985, $33.4 billion in 1987, $36.7 billion in 1990, $37.3 billion in 1993, and $35.6 billion in 1995.

Table V.39: Consumer Spending on Outdoor Recreation in Millions of Dollars from 1985 to 1995

Type of Spending	1995	1993	1990	1987	1985
Men's active sportswear	1,044.7	1,159.6	1,080.2	966.9	846.9
Boy's active sportswear	231.8	659.3	572.1	413.3	409.3
Women's active sportswear	2,801.2	2,299.1	2,108.1	2,307.6	1,391.7
Girl's active sportswear	1,173.4	824.4	723.4	510.3	549.4
Recreation expenses, out of town trips	2,185.1	2,052.0	1,708.6	1,505.5	1,328.5
Fees for recreational lessons	5,966.1	5,466.7	4,744.6	3,992.9	3,815.3
Trailer and other attachable campers	2,514.8	2,579.3	2,777.2	1,680.6	2,503.3
Purchase of recreation vehicles	3,407.0	4,882.4	6,110.0	1,795.4	2,012.5
Rental of recreational vehicles	149.4	122.1	225.9	81.9	54.9
Athletic gear	5,185.2	4,729.3	3,521.9	2,988.3	2,820.0
Bicycles	1,297.1	1,491.7	1,199.5	1,287.0	935.7
Camping equipment	670.7	458.2	392.7	349.3	332.4
Hunting equipment	875.7	699.3	846.0	772.0	1,378.0
Rental, repair of misc. sports equipment	169.0	156.1	175.5	220.3	203.3
Land subtotal	27,671.2	27,579.5	26,185.7	18,871.4	18,581.2
Outboard motors	37.1	121.1	290.9	316.3	311.3
Boat without motor and boat trailers	380.2	1,762.9	1,207.3	515.9	321.4
Purchase of boat with motor	4,568.1	3,654.8	3,508.3	5,615.1	4,907.6
Boat and trailer rental, out of town trips	203.0	151.1	109.6	107.3	162.1
Docking and landing fees	462.6	802.4	387.9	505.6	417.5
Fishing equipment	875.7	699.3	846.0	772.0	1,378.0
Water sports equipment	975.6	1,059.5	1,110.3	953.7	913.8
Water subtotal	7,502.2	8,251.0	7,460.2	8,786.1	8,411.6
Winter sports equipment	389.4	475.2	500.4	529.1	455.1
Totals	35,562.9	36,305.8	34,146.3	28,186.6	27,447.9
Totals adjusted to 1995 dollars*	35,562.9	37,322.4	36,707.3	33,372.9	32,416.0

Fishing and Hunting figures are unofficial estimates. The land subtotal, in categories like active sportswear, most likely includes some spending in other subtotals, but could not be broken out from that classification.
Source: U.S. Bureau of Labor Statisics, Consumer Expenditure Surveys
*based on relevent subsets of the BLS's annual Consumer Price Index.

LOCAL JOBS AND INCOME FROM OUTDOOR RECREATION

(By D. B. K. English and D. Marcoullier, USDA Forest Service and University of Wisconsin, respectively, Athens, GA, and Madison, WI)

Introduction

A key issue in natural resource management concerns the number and types of jobs that are associated with various uses of the resources being managed. This issue is especially important for publicly owned resources. Many public agencies, such as the Forest Service, now include the effects of management decisions on resource-dependent rural communities as an explicit consideration in their planning processes (USDA Forest Service, 1995).

With regard to recreational use of these natural resources, jobs and income accrue primarily from the expenditures made by nonresident visitors who come to use the resources as a place to engage in recreation activities (English & Bergstrom, 1994). The majority of the expenditures made by recreation visitors falls into one of four economic sectors: lodging (including hotels, motels, campgrounds, and inns), food (mostly restaurants, rather than grocery stores), retail stores, and recreation/amusement services. In rural areas near large public land holdings, it is not uncommon for a large portion of the economic activity in these sectors to be caused by tourists and other visitors to the area. However, some of the jobs and income in these sectors is caused by local residents' spending. Some is also caused by visitors on trips for purposes other than outdoor recreation, such as for business, or for family matters. It is not always easy to determine what portion is due to recreation visitation, especially since visitation figures are often unavailable.

Our task was to develop an estimate of the amount of recreation-related jobs (both full-time and part-time) and income for the four economic sectors listed above for each of the 2260 nonmetropolitan counties in the continental United States. In doing so, we follow the procedures of published research in the fields of regional science and rural development. Nonmetropolitan counties were excluded to simplify the analysis and to be able to focus more closely on the types of areas where recreation-related tourism is likely to be tied most directly to natural resources.

We performed the analysis separately for each region. The idea behind this method was to allow the greatest flexibility in accounting for differences in visitation and economic structure patterns across the country. However, there were only 78 nonmetropolitan counties in the Pacific Coast region, too few for a separate analysis. We combined these with the Rocky Mountain region and analyzed the Western region.

Methods

Our analysis consisted of four steps, each described briefly. Greater detail can be found in the technical appendix available from the author.[6] Our first step was to summarize a large number of variables that describe the natural resource base or recreation facilities in a county into a smaller set of comprehensive yet distinct variables using a technique called *principal components analysis*. A *principal component* is a summary measure that is a linear combination of resource measures that are correlated across counties. The components are statistically independent of each other and are interpreted as representing distinct types of rural resource-dependent tourism. These components were needed in a later portion of the analysis. The interested reader can find more information on the types of components that were defined for each region in the technical appendix.

The second step was to group counties in each region that were similar in their population density, distance from metropolitan areas, and percentage of land area in forests, cropland, mountains, and pasture/rangeland. This process was done through a technique called cluster analysis. Counties are assigned to a group, or cluster, according to their values on the set of important measures. Clusters are defined in such a way as to minimize the differences among members of a single group, while maximizing differences between groups. Eight clusters resulted for each region (see maps in the technical appendix), which included between 12 and 374 counties.

The next step in moving toward an estimate of recreation-related economic activity was to account for the proportion of activity that was due to local residents' spending. Economic theory indicates that spending by local residents in tourism sectors is not usually considered when defining the amount of activity that is associated with recreation visitation. We chose to do this following the minimum requirements technique (Leatherman & Marcouiller, 1996). In essence, this method determines the minimum amount of activity needed to support the county's population and subtracts that from the total activity in each sector. The remainder is assumed to be attributable to nonresidents.

Some of the nonresident-caused economic activity in tourism sectors is due to nonrecreation travelers. Business and family visits are presumed to be the primary reasons underlying this nonrecreation travel. We assume that the amount of these types of travel in a county is directly proportional to the county's population. We developed an estimate of the recreation-related portion through a regression analysis, where population is

[6]This technical appendix is available in table form from the USDA Forest Service, Outdoor Recreation and Wilderness Assessment Group, 320 Green Street, Athens, GA 30602-2044. Herein all references to Technical Appendices shall be abbreviated as TAs.

used to represent the nonrecreation portion of export activity, and recreation components developed in the first step represent the recreation-related portion.

Results

According to our estimates, there are approximately 300,000 jobs in eating and drinking establishments in nonmetropolitan counties across the country that result from outdoor recreation trips (Table V.40). Somewhat more than 40 percent of these are in rural counties in the North, and about 27 percent in the South and Rocky Mountains region. About five percent of the jobs are in the 78 rural counties in the Pacific Coast. Overall, these jobs generate almost $3.5 billion in employee and proprietor earnings. This income is distributed across the regions roughly equal to the number of jobs, with somewhat less than 40 percent in the North, and about 27 percent each in the South and Rocky Mountains regions. Our estimates indicate that about 23 percent of all jobs in eating and drinking establishments in rural counties are due to nonlocal recreation visits.

Table V.40: Jobs (1000's) and Income ($ Millions) Generated by Non-Local Recreation Visitation, by Region and Sector

Sector	Region				
	North	South	Rocky Mountain	Pacific Coast	U.S. Total
Eating/Drinking					
Jobs	126	78	82	14	300
Income	1333	981	944	197	3455
Accommodations					
Jobs	61	24	67	19	171
Income	1098	484	1474	422	3478
Retail Trade					
Jobs	65	53	47	6	171
Income	944	781	552	89	2366
Recreation Services					
Jobs	51	23	44	7	125
Income	833	404	1099	175	2511
Total, Recreation Sectors					
Jobs	303	178	240	46	767
Income	4208	2650	4069	883	11810
Recreation Total as % of region total for all economic sectors					
Jobs	3	1.8	6.2	3.4	3.1
Income	1.3	0.8	3.3	1.9	1.5

About 171,000 jobs in lodging businesses can be attributed to outdoor recreation by nonlocal visitors. This number represents just over 46 percent of all jobs in lodging businesses. Nearly forty percent (about 67,000) of the recreation-related jobs are in rural counties in the Rocky Mountain region. Undoubtedly, the concentration of recreation resources, especially those owned by federal agencies, accounts for that high proportion. Another 35 percent are in rural counties in the North. About 14 percent (24,000) are in the South and the remaining 11 percent (19,000 jobs) are in the Pacific Coast region. Recreation-related jobs in this sector account for almost $3.5 billion in income to employees and business owners, or about 46 percent of all income generated in this sector in rural counties across the country. Income is distributed across the regions in much the same proportions as are the jobs.

In the retail trade sector, about 171,000 jobs and $2.3 billion in income are attributable to recreation-related visitation. These estimates represent roughly 23 percent of all jobs and income in retail trade in rural counties across the United States. Of the recreation-related jobs, about 39 percent of both are in the North and about 31 percent of both are in the South. The Rocky Mountain region accounts for slightly more than 27 percent of the jobs, but only about 23 percent of the income. The Pacific Coast contains just under four percent of both jobs and income.

Nationally, about 39 percent of all jobs and about 41 percent of income in rural counties in the recreation services sector are attributable to nonresident recreation visitation. The South accounts for about 17 percent of both the rural recreation-related jobs and income in this sector. Although over 41 percent (51,000) of the recreation-related jobs in rural counties are located in the North, these jobs account for only one-third of the income. Relatively higher paying jobs are found in the Rocky Mountain region, where 44,000 jobs (about 35 percent of the recreation related total) account for over 44 percent of the income.

Across all four sectors, we estimate that there are 767,000 jobs that result from recreation trips made by nonresident visitors to the rural counties. These jobs add some $11.8 billion in income to employees and business owners in these counties. Over $4 billion in income accrues to people in rural counties in both the North and Rocky Mountain region, about $2.6 billion in the South, and only $0.9 billion for people in the Pacific Coast.

For two of the sectors, Eating/Drinking and Retail Trade, recreation "exports" (the purchase of recreation-related services by nonresidents) account for approximately one-quarter of the economic activity in each sector. Although recreation can be an important force in generating jobs and income in these sectors, it appears that other factors, including demand by residents, are more important determinants. For these two sectors, each job generates about $12,000 in income. The level of income per job is low most likely because a significant proportion of these types of jobs are part-time and/or seasonal. In the Accommodation and Recreation Services sectors, recreation 'exports' account for almost twice as high a proportion of the total activity, over 40 percent. In addition, income per job is over $20,000 in these sectors.

In some rural counties, there is not enough nonresident recreation visitation to have any economic effect. In others, more than half of all jobs and income are tied to the recreation industry. Across the country, jobs and income generated by recreation 'exports' make up about 3.1 percent and 1.5 percent, respectively, of all jobs and income in nonmetropolitan counties. However, these percentages are not the same for all four regions. In the South, fewer than two percent of all jobs in nonmetropolitan counties serve nonresident recreation visitors. In addition, fewer than one percent of all employee and proprietor income in the rural South is due to nonresident recreation visitation. Rural counties in the Rocky Mountain region are far more dependent on recreation visitation. The jobs that serve the needs of nonresident recreation visitors make up over six percent of all jobs in rural counties in this region. That number is over twice the national percentage, and over three times the proportion for the South. Over three percent of income comes from serving these visitors, also more than twice the national average and over four times the proportion found in the South.

There were 472 rural counties (about 21 percent of the total) wherein over six percent (double the national average) of the total number of jobs were due to nonresident recreation visitation. In 372 counties (about 16 percent of the total) the percentage of income due to nonresident recreation visitation was at least three percent of the total income, or at least double the national average. As one could expect, many of these counties (338) were more than double the national percentage for both jobs and income. These are the counties that are most dependent on recreation. The majority of these recreation-dependent counties are located in mountainous portions of the West (Figure V.15). Other concentrations occur in coastal areas, and near Forest Service, National Park Service, or other large public landholdings in the eastern half of the country.

Figure V.15: Rural Counties Where the Percentage of Both Income and Jobs from Recreation Visitation Are at Least Twice the National Average

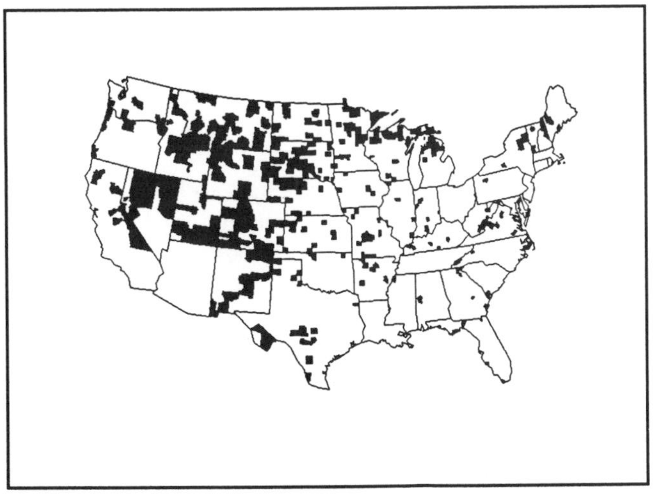

The figures presented here only reflect our estimates of the jobs and income *directly related* to nonresident visitation in the sectors most closely tied to that activity. Visitors also affect other types of businesses, such as gas stations, travel agents, real estate services, and grocery stores, although to a lesser extent than for the sectors examined here. In addition, there can be other types of businesses that support those that are directly tied to recreation. Examples could include laundry or cleaning services for hotels or restaurants, insurance services, or wholesale suppliers. Jobs and income in these types of businesses can also be wholly or partly due to nonresident recreation visitors. As a result, the figures presented here are likely a conservative baseline estimate of the economic effects of recreation in rural counties in the United States.

INTERNATIONAL TOURISM IN THE UNITED STATES

(By Joseph O'Leary, Purdue University, W. Lafayette, IN)

Tourism is a major economic activity throughout the United States and the world. There are literally millions throughout the world who choose to take a pleasure trip or to visit friends and family and pursue resource-based recreation activities. Their travel creates significant economic activity to the point that many international tourism experts suggest that tourism is the largest industry in the world. The U.S. Department of Commerce currently identifies tourism as the third largest industry in the United States.

Many of the resource-based recreation areas that are managed by resource agencies at every level represent the important "pull factors" that influence traveler choices of destinations. Thus, resource agencies that provide resource-based recreation opportunities are in the tourism business and will increasingly be concerned about current and changing travel patterns of tourists.

Recent Trends

In the last ten years international tourism to the United States has grown about 66 percent, going from 27.8 million visitors in 1987 to an estimated 46.2 million in 1997 (Table V.41). Receipts from travel to the United States also grew significantly during this period, expanding from $30.5 billion in 1987 to a projected $88.9 billion in 1997 (Table V.42) (International Trade Administration, 1996). In the United States these numbers have created quite a stir since they represent a positive balance of trade.

Canada leads the 1996 international arrivals to the United States with 15.3 million. Following are Mexico (8.5 million), Japan (5.0 million), the United Kingdom (3.1 million), and Germany (1.9 million), which complete the "top five" countries of origin for international travel to the U.S. This visitation is distributed at varying levels across states (Table V.43). Coastal and border states rank highest in the number of arriving international visitors.

Current Situation and New Developments

Travel is changing. In the U.S., international travel slowed in the mid-1990s, but now appears to be increasing again primarily driven by overseas visitors. U.S. visits from Canada appeared to have reached a peak in 1991 and then declined. At the same time this trend was occurring, Mexican travel to the U.S. also grew sharply and then declined. For Canadians, many trips were to border states with some shift away from travel to states farther away.

In the 1990s, travel to the U.S. from overseas countries has generally grown with only one year of decline, 1994. This growth seems to be related to the economy of these various countries and exchange rates. Economic changes throughout the world have caused a slowdown in travel from major international markets like Germany and Japan.

The leading edge of growth in travel in the world appears to be in Asia, certainly in terms of interregional activity. However, new destination areas have also emerged in the region that are providing competition for North American destinations. The U.S. also appears to be the first choice of Asian travelers when they look outside their own region for a place to visit. Between 1995-96, international travel from Asia increased by 12.2 percent to 7.4 million arrivals.

The International Pleasure Travel Market Studies, jointly sponsored by the Canadian Tourism Commission and the U.S. International Trade Administration, has conducted interviews in 24 countries throughout the world since 1986. This research is designed to gather information on actual and planned long-distance travel in terms of demographics, trip characteristics, psychographic profiles, comparative advantages, activities, and expenditures. We have done analysis on all surveys that have been completed to determine how travelers view forests, parks, and recreation-related activities in the U.S. Part of the interest is exploring the role parks and forests play as an attribute people think about when contemplating travel to the United States. Almost without regard to where travelers come from, outdoor-related activities, and particularly visiting parks and forests, are important for participation and in terms of why visitors want to come to the U.S. (O'Leary & Lang, 1994; Lang & O'Leary, 1990; Lang, 1996; Hsieh, O'Leary, & Morrison, 1994). When travelers are asked about important items they thought about when planning their trips, parks, forest, and historic places emerged as being very important. The importance of forests and parks in the decision process ranged from 91 percent for travelers from Venezuela to 70 percent for Japan. This intense interest in natural environments and outdoor recreation activities has persisted in the 10 years these studies have been conducted.

Future Trends

The 1997 prediction by the Department of Commerce's Tourism Industries Group shows that travel to the United States will grow three to four percent over the next four years. Most of this change will occur as a result of travel from Asia (double-digit percentage growth) and South America (between six and nine percent increases). Canada and Mexico will also increase, but at a relatively modest two percent rate. Within the next two years, travel spending in the U.S. is expected to reach and possibly exceed the $100 billion mark. Natural resource management will be challenged in a number of ways.

There are two key issues that emerge from the investigations of international travelers. First, there are significant changes occurring in the origin, destination, and characteristics of travelers from other parts of the world. This is strongly evident in the increase expected from Asia and South America relative to the stability of the traditional European visitor market. These changes imply that there are new and changing markets that organizations in both the public and private sector will need to address. Addressing these changes can occur independently or as a partnership. In general, it seems that natural resource management will continue to be more influenced by greater numbers of visitors from other countries. Addressing this change is obviously best done collaboratively.

Natural resources and outdoor recreation play a major role in tourism in that they provide the settings and infrastructure for travel activities, experiences, and products. Perceptions about how this role should be handled ebb and flow depending on the leadership, and are made more difficult when organization and budgetary changes encounter new, growing demands for service and partnering.

Natural resource and cultural agencies in the United States have been uncertain in terms of defining their roles in tourism. Their role has seemed to vacillate between one of marketing to one of protectionism. The pattern exhibited is first interest in the international visitor as a customer and developing market research projects, followed by backing away entirely.

Oscillations toward and away from marketing have limited the ability of agencies to deal effectively with the tourist industry. As domestic North American travel markets change toward more fragmentation and diversity, with higher service requirements, agencies already strained by downsizing, reinvention, and policy shifts will be further strained.

Since advertising influences expectations, cooperative linkages between tourism, marketing, park, natural, and cultural resource agencies are essential. It is important to reach the international audience in advance to create appropriate expectations for all involved, including the visitor or guest, the marketer, the eventual host, and the destinations of choice.

Creation of better partnerships to address the changes in travelers will become a critical issue. First, it is clear that international visitors will create special communication challenges. In addition, for both international and domestic visitors, and for different reasons, there will be demands for special requirements from a nonuniform array of visitors that will stretch the talents of virtually all organizations and agencies. The activities international visitors will pursue will only rarely be within the purview of only one group.

Understanding the visitor and the nuances associated with travel behavior are critical. For example, research has been done on repeat travelers. People's perceptions of the country were different if they had been there once or more than once. These differences affect knowledge and experience, how people organize their trips, how they manage information, and what activities they choose. Although some of these issues make intuitive sense, the nature and directions of the changes make thinking about how to respond more complex.

The second issue of concern is better application and sharing of information. Many organizations are outside the "loop" of tourism information, particularly at the international level. In an effort to "engage the public," recreation groups, agencies, and destinations must expand their levels of communication beyond their organizational boundaries. Private and public tourism groups will need to reciprocate exchanges.

Changes that influence travel can have profound impacts on regions, states, and local communities. Natural resources often represent major attractions for tourists throughout North America and result in jobs for people in the local area. If travel behavior changes, the economic flows will also change. Understanding travel behavior is therefore critical to considering how to sustain local, tourism-based economies. A good example has been the reported decline in visitation to some natural parks during summer, 1997. Part of this visitation decline seems due to decreases in the number of international visitors. These types of shifts can profoundly change local economic conditions.

Although there is evidence that cooperation has occurred between heritage-related groups and the tourism industry, it seems more the exception than the rule. Organizations and agencies haven't always known whom to communicate with or what programs and products are being offered. For cooperative efforts to bear fruit, communication and information sharing must be the watchword for the day.

Table V.41: Total Inbound International Arrivals in Thousands and Percentage Change to the United States by Year and by Origin, 1987-1997

Total arrivals and origin	Year 1987	1988	1989	1990	1991	1992	1993	1994	1995	1996e[1]	1997p[1]
Inbound Totals	27834	33942	36365	39363	42674	47261	45779	44753	43318	44791	46216
% Change	7.6	21.9	7.1	8.2	8.4	10.7	-3.1	-2.2	-3.2	3.4	3.2
Overseas	10534	12512	13999	15059	16155	17791	18662	18458	20639	22072	23371
% Change	18.9	18.8	11.9	7.6	7.3	10.1	4.9	-1.1	11.8	6.9	5.9
Canada	12253	13700	15325	17263	19113	18598	17293	14974	14663	14713	15007
% Change	13.5	11.8	11.9	12.6	10.7	-2.7	-7	-13.4	-2.1	-0.3	2
Mexico	5047	7730	7041	7041	7406	10872	9824	11321	8016	8008	7838
% Change	-18.9	53.2	-8.9	0	5.2	46.7	-9.6	15.2	-29.2	-0.1	-2.1

[1] e=estimated; p=projected.
Source: U.S. Dept. of Commerce Tourism Industries, International Trade Administration; Secretaria de Turismo (Mexico); Statistics Canada; Canadian Tourism Research Institute

Table V.42: International Receipts and Percentage Change for All Travel to the United States by Year, 1987-1997

Travel Receipts	Year 1987	1988	1989	1990	1991	1992	1993	1994	1995	1996e[1]	1997p[1]
$ in Millions	30566	38409	46863	58305	64237	71359	74486	75500	79671	84133	88928
% Change	17.7	25.7	22	24.4	10.2	11.1	4.4	1.4	5.5	5.6	5.7

[1] e=estimated; p=projected.
Source: U.S. Dept. of Commerce Tourism Industries, International Trade Administration, Bureau of Economic Analysis

Table V.43: International Arrivals (in Thousands) to the United States by State and by Origin, 1995

States visited (Thousands)	Canada [1] (All Modes)	Canada Rank	Mexico [2] (Air Travel)	Overseas [3] (All Modes)	Overseas Rank	Total [4] Arrivals	Total Rank
Alabama	49	45	*	83	35	134	42
Alaska	63	42	*	62 [5]	38	129	43
Arizona	243	27	46	887	9	1,176	12
Arkansas	24 [5]	50	*	41 [5]	46	68	50
California	827	5	256	5,304	2	6,837	3
Colorado	111	36	37 [5]	433	15	581	26
Connecticut	128	34	9 [5]	227	25	368	32
Delaware	21 [5]	51	*	62 [5]	38	89 [5]	48
Dist. of Columbia (DC)	119	N/A	35 [5]	1,486	N/A	1,640	N/A
Florida	1,729	3	149	5,345	1	7,223	1
Georgia	396	18	15 [5]	599	11	1,010	13
Hawaiian Islands	253	24	*	2,910	4	3,168	4
Idaho	224	28	*	62 [5]	38	287	35
Illinois	391	19	71	1,115	7	1,577	8
Indiana	183	32	*	144	29	334	34
Iowa	80	40	*	62 [5]	38	149	40
Kansas	36 [5]	48	6 [5]	62 [5]	38	113	45
Kentucky	298	23	*	83	35	394	31
Louisiana	85	39	9 [5]	413	17	507	29
Maine	797	6	*	103	33	901	14
Maryland	189	30	*	248	23	447	30
Massachusetts	499	14	24 [5]	1,053	8	1,576	9
Michigan	1,432	4	15 [5]	372	18	1,819	7
Minnesota	574	11	*	206	27	784	19
Mississippi	39 [5]	47	*	62 [5]	38	102 [5]	46
Missouri	105	37	*	144	29	254	36
Montana	623	9	*	41 [5]	40	666	21
Nebraska	58	43	*	21 [5]	46	81	49
Nevada	632	8	62	1,858	5	2,552	5
New Hampshire	418	17	*	103	33	524	27
New Jersey	251	26	9 [5]	599	11	859	17
New Mexico	40	46	*	144	29	193	39
New York	2,552	1	91	4,479	3	7,122	2
North Carolina	329	21	*	310	21	651	22
North Dakota	501	13	*	21 [5]	50	522	27
Ohio	502	12	11 [5]	351	19	865	16
Oklahoma	30 [5]	49	7 [5]	62 [5]	38	103 [5]	47
Oregon	311	22	13 [5]	248	23	578	25
Pennsylvania	588	10	11 [5]	599	11	1,198	11
Rhode Island	51 [5]	44	*	62 [5]	38	117	44
South Carolina	452	16	*	227	25	680	20
South Dakota	99	38	*	41 [5]	46	140	41
Tennessee	336	20	*	268	22	608	23
Texas	253	25	213	867	10	1,333	10
Utah	130	33	12 [5]	433	15	575	24
Vermont	786	7	*	83	35	875	15
Virginia	463	15	*	351	19	822	18
Washington	1,856	2	13 [5]	599	11	2,468	6

Table V.43 Cont.

States visited (Thousands)	Canada [1] (All Modes)	Canada Rank	Mexico [2] (Air Travel)	Overseas [3] (All Modes)	Overseas Rank	Total [4] Arrivals	Total Rank
West Virginia	188	31	*	41 [5]	46	229	38
Wisconsin	193	29	7 [5]	144	29	344	33
Wyoming	65	41	*	165	28	230	37
Guam	N/A	N/A	*	1,238	N/A	N/A	N/A
Puerto Rico	N/A	N/A	16 [5]	103	N/A	N/A	N/A
Total Travel AIR ONLY	3,712		889	N/A		N/A	
Total Travel ALL MODES	14,663		8,016 [6]	20,639		43,318	

Source: Tourism: Tourism Industries (TI), International Trade Administration (ITA)
Note:*Estimates are not provided due to low sample size. N/A = Not Applicable

[1] Data were obtained from *Statistics Canada* and compiled from their International Travel Survey. All Canadian travelers to the U.S. for one night or longer are reported in these estimates.

[2] Visitation estimates only reflect the number of air travelers from Mexico to the U.S. These figures were obtained from the Tourism Industries report *In-Flight Survey of Mexican Air Travelers*, 1995, except where INS I-94 "first intended address" figures are greater than IFS. The total number of air travelers from Mexico to the U.S. in 1995 was 889,000. This total was obtained from the Tourism Industries report Summary of International Travelers to the U.S., 1995.

[3] Data were obtained from the Tourism Industries report *In-Flight Survey of International Travelers to the U.S.*, 1995. All overseas travelers to the U.S. for one night or longer are reported in these estimates.

[4] Data were obtained by totaling the Canadian, Air Travelers from Mexico, first intended address where applicable, estimates not provided due to low sample size, and Overseas arrivals.

[5] Reflects statistical instability due to very small sample size (less than 3%). Data should be used with caution.

[6] This figure was estimated from Banco de Mexico data and represents all Mexican arrivals to the U.S. including air travelers, and those traveling within the 40 kilometer frontier zone, for one or more nights. These estimates are also subject to yearly revisions.

ECOTOURISM IN THE UNITED STATES

(By Elwood Shafer, Pennsylvania State University, College Station, PA)

Ecotourism is a relatively small but growing component of the total nature-based tourism industry in the United States. Nature tourism is travel and recreation for the appreciation of nature and the outdoors. Areas that attract nature tourists range from pristine wilderness to community parks.

Ecotourism has received much attention in recent years and there is considerable debate over what the term means or should mean (Western, 1993). Ecotourism is generally defined as travel and recreation that contributes substantially to a natural area's conservation and protection through education and the dedication of tourism dollars (Environmental Protection Agency, 1996). Most definitions of ecotourism involve the sustainable management of ecosystems with tourist attractions that draw tourist trade, which benefits local communities and interests. At times, these benefits may be substantial enough for local communities, conservation groups, and public or private interests to willingly comanage the ecosystem to maintain and perhaps improve its integrity as a natural system and its attractiveness as a tourist resource (Fennell & Smale, 1992; Go, Milne, & Whittles, 1992).

The concept of ecotourism probably stems from the widespread and growing interest in natural environments and a corresponding recognition of the importance of conserving them. The idea of visiting and experiencing high quality natural environments and also protecting them from harmful impacts is now an acceptable and marketable one.

As a result, ecotourism is among the travel industry's most explosive of growth areas. Within the next decade, tourism will likely become the world's largest industry. Ecotourism never will generate as much profit as traditional tourism, but it appears that it will become an increasingly important niche. In today's tourism market it is nearly impossible to pinpoint how many tourism dollars are spent on ecotourism (Boyd & Butler, 1996).

Current Situation

Sustainable ecotourism depends primarily on sound ecosystem management (EM). But despite intense interest and activity in EM by the federal land management agencies, the problems that ecosystem management are supposed to solve are not clear. "Environmental problems are often framed narrowly in ecological terms, and social and cultural dimensions are mentioned only in passing" (Gerlach & Bengston, 1994). This seeming confusion about what ecosystem management is supposed to do has hampered this natural resource management paradigm.

On one hand, for example, Gordon (1994) proposed that EM "requires that all known contents of an ecosystem be included and considered when decisions and manipulations are made" in land management. On the other hand, Wenger (1997) stressed that "the first step in EM must be a specific description of the land to be managed. The land must be dealt with separately from the ecosystem concept," and for EM purposes, "inventories of natural environments should include only the plants and animals that can be manipulated economically." Trying to inventory the many species of plants and animals "down to bacteria and protozoa that occupy forest land would be extremely expensive and of no utility." (Wenger, 1997).

Despite the many articles that have been written on ecosystem management and ecotourism, there is no consensus in the natural resources community on the identity of the strategies most appropriate in ecosystem management. Nonetheless, generally there seems to be a fair amount of agreement on the following points:

- Resource management for ecotourism activities must be accomplished in such a manner as to assure the economic viability of an ecotourism experience. In this regard, local and legislative requirements affecting resource management may be essential for encouraging ecotourism economic activity within ecologically safe limits.
- Current livelihoods and customs of the human communities in areas with viable ecotourism markets must be sustained, including the aesthetic qualities of landscapes, cultural legacies, and townscapes of those local communities.
- Sustainable ecotourism management must include consideration of the limitations of health of the ecosystem(s) to satisfy both human and natural needs.
- Local ecological processes and interdependencies need to be clearly understood so that ecotourism activities are consistent with the resource's capacity. However, the difficulty of applying capacity concepts is that all changes have some effect that eventually may be detrimental to the ecosystem. Capacity is usually a supply-side consideration, but if ecotourism is to be successful, it must also be based on the perceptions and preferences of ecotourists.
- The need to maintain biological diversity is essential if a tourism destination is to appeal to the average ecotourist. Greater natural variation in the flora and fauna in the destination area is more likely to appeal to ecotourists.

Examples

Ecotourism involves a wide range of environmental conditions and management strategies. Here are three brief examples in Pennsylvania that underscore ecotourism's heterogeneous characteristics (Shafer, Carline, Guldin, & Cordell, 1993).

Hawk Mountain

The Hawk Mountain Sanctuary is a promontory atop the Kittatinny Ridge of the Appalachian Mountains. This 2,000-acre, private, member supported, nonprofit sanctuary is the world's first refuge created to protect and observe raptors. From mid-August through November, large numbers of raptors (hawks, falcons, ospreys, and eagles) migrate south above the mountain ridges. An average total count of raptors during the fall season is about 20,000 birds. Located on the common borders of Berks and Schuylkill Counties, the area is internationally known as a year-round conservation, education, and research center. Membership is about 6,700, and annual total travel to the site by visitors generates approximately $365,000 (1997 dollars) in spending in the local area.

Middle Creek Wildlife Management Area

The Middle Creek Wildlife Management Area is a 5,200-acre state gameland in Lebanon and Lancaster Counties where visitors can observe 238 species of native and migratory waterfowl. Even though fees from hunting license sales are the source of funding for maintaining this area, the Pennsylvania Game Commission provides other recreational opportunities such as hiking, bird watching, and wildlife photography. A visitor center features mounted waterfowl and displays of natural history, ecology, wildlife habitats, and wildlife management practices. The annual total travel expenditures by visitors is about $235,000 (1997 dollars).

Elk Viewing

Elk viewing opportunities cover a 144-square-mile area of state forest and state game lands in Cameron and Elk Counties, where the public can observe from roadsides and trials the only elk herd in the state. It is the only area east of the Mississippi River where elk roam unrestricted. To maintain an annual herd of 130 to 140 elk and to help keep them away from adjoining agricultural areas, the Pennsylvania Game Commission and the Bureau of Forestry engage in special resource management activities, including periodically clear-cutting small patches to stimulate growth of woody browse, maintaining grassy open areas for grazing, and planting selected trees and shrubs to increase food variety. Annual total travel expenditures by visitors are approximately $116,000 (1997 dollars).

Future Issues

Despite the interest in ecotourism by many local communities, state governments, and regional partnerships, many remain unconvinced that it will be a panacea that both protects the environment and supports local economic health. Considerable debate exists over whether ecotourism can be sustainable and which management strategies will minimize the negative impacts associated with human uses in natural ecosystems (Cater, 1993).

Ecosystem planning and development, and thus ecotourism, are usually evolutionary, not revolutionary (Orams, 1995). Integrating ecosystem management and ecotourism cannot be a static process with a definite beginning and ending; rather it must involve continuous evolution of concepts and principles through experience and science that are adaptive to changes in political, economic, and social conditions.

Funding for the maintenance, repair, and construction of the necessary infrastructure for ecotourism may not keep pace with increasing demand for quality experiences without concerted effort to strengthen old and build new public/private partnerships. Effective partnerships will be

A youngster plants and tags a tree in Kern River, California (right), while a Nature Conservancy site visitor in Sycan Marsh, Oregon, records plant species (left). Photos courtesy of the Nature Conservancy. Photos by Rick Hewett (right) and Alan D. St. John (left).

necessary for generating support and funding for expensive, environmentally sensitive construction and maintenance of infrastructure to accommodate, transport, and satisfy ecotourists.

Definitions and interpretations of ecosystem management abound, as do different perspectives on whether and how it will work. Many believe that ecosystem management, even though based on ecological principles, is primarily about people and their choices.

The most challenging aspect of ecotourism management will continue to be the creation of the appropriate coalitions of diverse interests and views such that problems of communication and understanding are overcome and collective needs are met. Sustainable ecosystem management can be better assured if stakeholders have a common understanding of what ecosystems are and common sense of how they are a part of those systems. "Humans interact with nature most significantly through culture, in symbolic ways not comprehended by biological or physical ecosystem models" (Gerlack & Bengston, 1994). Although it is recognized that ecotourism management aims to help sustain economies and other aspects of human welfare, it is concern also for the long-term integrity of ecosystems that will be necessary truly to achieve sustainable ecotourism. Innovative, sustainable development strategies that promote ecotourism will continue to be difficult and politically sensitive.

REFLECTIONS

Across American communities and groups within society, outdoor recreation has remained enormously popular over the years. Although new forms of participating have appeared, an underlying, basic motivation for outdoor recreation participation still is to have the opportunity to experience nature by viewing it, traveling through it, and for a short time at least, living it.

Outdoor recreation is a basic part of our lifestyles that most of us as Americans have come to expect. The National Survey on Recreation and the Environment has shown that almost all in American society participate at some level in some form of outdoor pursuit. Traditional land, water, snow, and ice settings are very much in demand to satisfy the growing appetite both for traditional outdoor recreational activities as well as to serve demand for a growing list of new activities driven by better access and by rapidly evolving technology and information availability.

Over the years and still today, most in demand are places for casual activities such as walking, family gatherings, sightseeing, and visiting beaches, historic sites, and other sites of interest. These activities appeal to a wide spectrum of people from inner cities, the suburbs, and rural countrysides alike. Often, entertainment, fun, learning, and seeing are motivations for these activities. Viewing and learning, socially oriented activities outdoors, and swimming are the most popular forms of participation where natural and historical settings are significant components of the expectations of the recreationists.

Recreation participation in all types of settings are experiencing growth. Often, growth is occurring among a number of different activities that occur at the same sites and in the same settings, resulting in conflicts and needs for carefully considered management strategies that offer everyone opportunities. The increases in participation that are occurring are not just in the numbers of people participating on occasion, they also represent growth in the number of days and trips in total that people take for their preferred recreation. Total days and numbers of trips for outdoor recreation by the U. S. population portray a huge market for the goods, services, and access to places for participation.

Both long-term and short-term past trends point to continued growth in outdoor recreation across all segments of the population, some more than others. Growth seems particularly strong in viewing and learning activities and in new activities. If these trends continue, pressures for places to recreate and for recreation infrastructure to support recreation seekers will continue to build. There is evidence particularly of growing pressures on the public lands and the recreation opportunities those lands represent. Growing pressure is likely to take many forms and will require a variety of management responses. Level to decreasing public funding for outdoor recreation access, service, and facility development and maintenance will represent major challenges in the near as well as long-term future. These growing pressures and the challenges they represent will likely include:

- The more popular beaches, forest sites, parks, and special attractions will experience greater congestion at peak times in the year, and these congestion levels and the situations resulting from them will eclipse the experience background of most outdoor recreation managers.
- There will likely be more conflicts among recreationists who will be competing at the same times for use of some of the same areas and sites for different forms of outdoor recreation. Some of these activities are not incompatible with one another, but others are.

- Because of persisting rises in the popularity of outdoor recreation, policies, and management practices, including those on public land such as timber and range management that are not directly aimed at recreation opportunities, will increasingly affect larger numbers of people with increasingly diverse interests and social and economic characteristics, making resource management more challenging and calling for increasingly innovative, collaborative approaches.
- Public- and private-sector providers will need to continue to provide viewing and learning, social gathering, and swimming opportunities to meet the rising demand by the majority of the American public. Many of these types of opportunities can be provided near the urban places where many of those seeking such opportunities live. Development and resource extraction activities may increasingly be viewed as conflicting with recreation and nature conservation interests.
- Access to developed sites and dispersed areas will almost certainly be an increasingly important and difficult issue to resolve, especially when different types of activities conflict and where universal accessibility must be a significant concern. As management tools such as charging fees continue to evolve, the access implications of such tools will increasingly be issues viewed differently by different social groups and by different types of recreation participants.
- Especially heavy pressures are likely to occur at water sites that have always been a major attraction for a wide variety of outdoor recreational activities. These pressures will take on added significance with advances of technology making them accessible to jet-propelled water craft.
- Scenic quality will increasingly be an issue that managers of recreation areas and of natural lands in general must address as growth and interest in sightseeing, viewing and learning activities, and other activities drive the demand for aesthetically pleasing settings.
- Markets for outdoor activities are changing as new forms of participation are discovered, as the backgrounds, perspectives, and tastes of recreationists change, and as constraints and opportunities shift. In that these changes are in part determined by the opportunities that are available, public land management policies will be under increased scrutiny to determine how well they meet the needs of Americans across all social strata, while at the same time providing private sector business opportunities.
- Rapid increases in the diversity of the population in race, culture, age, income, and other factors will change the demand for outdoor recreation, but not diminish the size of the overall market. Increasing population diversity will result in different preferences, expectations, and ways of seeking and participating in outdoor recreation. Management policies and solutions of the past will only partially fit the emerging shifts in demand and new forms of recreation people will pursue.
- Because most forms of outdoor recreation participation depend so heavily on natural settings, which differ among regions of the country, and because most of these forms continue to grow in popularity, domestic tourism and associated recreation travel can be expected to continue growth as long as transportation remains as affordable and as convenient as today and access to land and water areas is available.
- Continued increases in visits to most federal and state forests and parks will put added pressures on public managers to adopt new management policies and practices. Fees and reservation systems will spread. Information will be more available. Greater attention will be paid to the unequal effects of these policies on lower income, less well educated, and place-confined segments of our population.
- Increasingly, international travel to the United States for outdoor recreation will add to pressures on the U.S. supply of outdoor opportunities, particularly at the most popular national parks and other tourist destinations. International effects will be great near border and coastal states.
- Increasing domestic and international travel and tourism in the U.S. will create opportunities for large-scale private businesses to provide services, accommodations, and information. As the interest in defining and managing for sustainability in communities and in natural systems grows, ecotourism is likely to become a popular and viable approach for achieving both.
- Outdoor recreation contributes substantially to the economies of rural counties, and this contribution is likely to grow both in terms of countywide income and jobs, but also in terms of share of income and jobs among economic sectors.
- Organized groups representing specific outdoor recreation interests will grow in number and constituency represented. As public agencies continue to open up the planning and decision processes to public involvement, these organized groups will have increasing voice in public land management and the recreation interests they represent are likely to grow in numbers. Increasingly, organized groups will be integrated as partners in helping manage and protect public lands, access rights, and unique resources.
- New technologies and better modes of accessing backcountry will continue to shift the nature of the demand for outdoor recreation. Most impacted by these shifts will be the more traditional passive forms

of outdoor recreation where quiet, natural settings for learning, reflection, and nature appreciation are sought. Also impacted will be traditional forms of active participation where new technology enables more and different users onto the resource, for example, whitewater canoeists experiences impacted by jet ski use.

- Concerns about availability of outdoor recreation to inner city disadvantaged groups will grow with the realization that these groups participate substantially less in all forms of recreation because they do not have opportunities that are affordable and close enough to where they live.
- Research will become increasingly important in helping to understand changes that will occur across many different fronts. Ongoing national participation surveys, on-site studies of various user groups and interests, linking recreation behaviors and preferences with social changes, enabling recreation providers to understand market shifts as or before they happen, and monitoring access equity are among the vital research roles that will be needed.

Improved data, monitoring systems, and well understood management objectives that are in touch with the recreation demand shifts constantly occurring in the United States and internationally will be necessary to manage outdoor recreation in the future successfully. The decline in data and information on recreation visitation, customer satisfaction, and economic impact information has proven to be a detriment to effective, timely management, and policy specification. Greater attention to reliable information on trends, emerging issues, and effectiveness in delivering service and opportunities must emerge as high priority activities.

CONTRIBUTED PAPERS

The Recreation Vehicle Market

(By David J. Humphreys, Recreation Vehicle Industry Association, Reston, VA)

With nine million recreation vehicles (RVs) on the road according to a recent study by the University of Michigan Survey Research Center (Curtin, 1994), and 25 million RV users based on estimates by Recreation Vehicle Industry Association (RVIA), the RV industry is a dynamic component of the overall outdoor recreation market.

The typical RV owner is a 48-year-old homeowner with a household income just under $40,000 who buys an RV to travel and camp. RVIA research indicates RVers annually travel an average of 5,900 miles per year and spend over 23 days on the road.

There are two major groups of RV owners: empty-nesters and families with children. Forty-four percent of America's RVers are age 55 and up, while 39 percent are between the ages of 35 and 54.

In addition to the growing numbers of RV owners, the RV industry consists of 170 vehicle manufacturers, 295 supplier companies, 3,000 RV dealers, and more than 16,000 public or private campgrounds across the nation with RV facilities.

RVIA is the national association of RV manufacturers and component parts suppliers that together produce 95 percent of all recreation vehicles manufactured in the United States. An RV is defined as a vehicle designed as temporary living quarters for travel, recreation, and camping. RVs are either motorized vehicles, such as motorhomes and conversion vehicles, or towable units, such as travel trailers, folding camping trailers, and truck campers.

The Current RV Market

The RV market has enjoyed strong sales in the 1990s with shipments to retailers from 1994 to 1996 at their highest levels since the late 1970s. Most recently, 1996 saw RV manufacturers ship in excess of 466,000 new units. Retail sales of fifth-wheel travel trailers set a record in 1996 of nearly 45,000 units. Sales of upscale motorhomes were at an eight-year high of 36,500 units (RVIA, 1996).

The retail value of all RVs manufactured in 1996 exceeded $12.3 billion, the highest dollar volume in the industry's history. Including new and used unit sales, aftermarket components, and RV rentals, RVs are a $16 billion annual business.

Helping fuel this growth has been the aging of the baby boom generation with many consumers now beginning to reach prime RV-buying age; favorable economic trends such as strong consumer confidence, low inflation rates, and reasonable interest rates; and advances in RV technology and design.

The RV Market Future

RVIA and other segments of the RV industry are working to ensure the vitality of the market into the next century. Key among these efforts is the creation of the Go RVing Coalition, an inclusive industry group comprised of manufacturers, suppliers, dealers, and campground operators.

The Coalition is focusing on programs to introduce a greater number of people to RVing and improve the RV experience for current and future RV owners.

Marketing Strategies

The group recently launched a national advertising campaign, centered on the theme "Recreation Vehicles. Wherever You Go, You're Always at Home," to promote RV travel to baby boomer families.

The campaign was developed based on RV market research conducted by the University of Michigan Survey Research Center and Louis Harris and Associates that indicated baby boomer couples, who comprise 40 percent of the RV market, value the family time, stress reduction and convenience offered by RV vacations (Curtin, 1994). This campaign marks the first time the various segments of the RV industry united for an institutional advertising campaign.

The RVIA Seal

To assure an acceptable level of compliance with applicable safety standards is met within the RV industry, RVIA conducts an inspection program. As a condition of membership, all manufacturer members are subject to periodic, unannounced plant inspections by RVIA representatives.

Those in compliance with more than 500 safety specifications for electrical, plumbing, heating and fire and life safety established by the American National Standards Institute (ANSI) A119.2 Recreation Vehicle Standard display RVIA's seal on their vehicles. Members who fail to maintain an acceptable level of compliance can be expelled from the association.

Certified RV Technician Program

Through the Certified RV Technician Program conducted by RVIA and Recreation Vehicle Dealer Association (RVDA), the RV industry is working to create a nationwide network of well-trained, qualified service people to better serve the growing numbers of RV owners.

Since the program's inception in 1993, more than 500 technicians have been certified. To achieve certification, technicians must successfully complete a series of comprehensive tests. RVIA also conducts an industry education program to provide training to current and potential RV service technicians.

Public Land Usage

With the nation's public lands being magnets for RV owners, the proper funding of national parks, forests, and other public sites is critical to keeping these areas maintained and open to RVers. To ensure this funding, RVIA is a proponent of permanent fee legislation that re-invests revenues in the sites where they are generated.

RVIA also supports campgrounds, whether federally managed or operated by concessionaires, to exist on public lands. To assists RVers interested in camping on public lands, it might be wise to implement a national reservation system for campgrounds on federal lands

Future Trends Affecting the RV Industry

Over the next decade, the enormous baby boom generation will begin entering the highest ownership age group for RVs. This consumer group will continue to dominate the RV market for the next 20 years.

The University of Michigan Survey Research Center study shows that RV ownership rates rise significantly with age, peaking among 55 to 64-year-olds. This increase has significant long-term implications, considering the substantial growth potential within the prime RV ownership age groups. In the next 10 years, 12,000 Americans per day will turn 50 years old, bringing nearly 10 million more U.S. households into the ranks of prime RV prospects.

Interest in RV ownership is not confined to the 50-plus market, however. Research by Louis Harris and Associates found that more than half of those most likely to buy an RV in the future are 30 to 49 years old.

The University of Michigan study confirms this finding, also showing purchase intentions are strongest among younger age groups. Thirty percent of consumers age 18-34 expressed interest in buying an RV with 16 percent of those age 35-54 doing so.

Changes in the frequency and duration of vacations also favor the RV industry. Americans are traveling more often, but over shorter distances and with less planning. For RV owners, this is a natural travel pattern.

The growing American interest in outdoor recreation should positively impact the RV industry. A survey by the Recreation Roundtable in 1991 found that 77 percent of Americans view outdoor recreation as a priority in their lives, and 67 percent plan to increase their participation in camping. RVs are a natural focal point for many of these activities, especially camping.

With the growing interest in outdoor recreation, the impact of the baby boom generation and the industry's efforts to communicate the advantages of RV travel, RV sales and usage are expected to be robust through the remainder into the next century.

Four Wheel Drive Trends

(By Alan Lane, United Four Wheel Drive Association, Shelbyville, IN)

Important Issues to Four Wheel Drive Recreation

In 1991, the United Four Wheel Drive Association (UFWDA) commissioned a study of issues impacting the sport of "fourwheeling." Some of the major issues refined from a larger list of challenges submitted by fourwheelers from throughout the United States are off-highway recreation advocacy, public land recreational access and use protection, the right to operate older motor vehicles, and public funding for recreational trails on public lands.

The USDA Forest Service sponsored the National Access and Travel Conference in August of 1991 as a starting point for the "Report of the National Access and Travel Management Strategy Team, January, 1992." Various disciplines and interests were represented, including recreation, fisheries and wildlife, conservation, related businesses, associations, state and local governments, and federal agencies. From this cconference, a strategy team developed 14 situation statements. These statements covered situations such as the common perception, both internally and externally, that inadequate travel management results in unacceptable resource impacts, and that loss of public access has a major impact on programs and use on National Forest System lands.

A survey of conference participants indicated that these statements represented the majority opinion of conference participants about travel management. These statements were used to develop six goals regarding appropriate access to national forest lands and accommodation of a variety of user needs and expectations within resource limitations.

Current Interests, Programs, and Directions

As evidenced by responses to surveys and references made in reports, there is a continuing need to educate the public and four wheel drive enthusiasts regarding safe and proper use of their vehicles. This also entails working with land managers and decision makers to ensure an understanding of the needs of four-wheel-drive enthusiasts. Some programs have been in place to further the awareness of proper use and techniques in operating vehicles on varying terrain and areas where use is restricted. Two of the major programs being applied now are Tread Lightly! and Four Wheel Drive Safety Awareness Clinics.

Tread Lightly! is an educational program dedicated to increasing awareness of how to enjoy public and private lands while also minimizing impacts. Tread Lightly! emphasizes responsible use of off-highway vehicles, other forms of backcountry travel, and low impact principles in outdoor recreation. The Tread Lightly! program began in 1986 from the U.S. Forest Service and was later adopted by the Bureau of Land Management. A nonprofit corporation, Tread Lightly! Inc. was formed in 1990.

The Four Wheel Drive Awareness Program is another example that was adopted from the California Association of Four Wheel Drive Clubs, Inc. This safety and education program consists of two segments. The first is a classroom segment using workbooks and instructional videos, and the second is an outdoor, hands-on, instructional segment covering various driving techniques on a set course. These clinics are directed at the novice and at land managers and current enthusiasts wanting refresher training.

While these instructional courses are important tools, there are other approaches to working for access and use of public lands. Becoming involved in planning processes is one effective approach used to maintain a voice in decision making. Active participation in planning as well as collaboration in maintaining the resource and trails while recreating can be very helpful to understaffed land managers with tight budget constraints. In addition to working with local, state, or regional agencies, it has been effective and often necessary to share information and work with other user groups. Examples include agreements of mutual cooperation between users and agencies covering cooperation through volunteer work projects and promotion of educational and environmental programs.

Another example is formation of state recreational trail advisory boards as part of the requirement for funding from the National Recreational Trust Fund. These boards bring user groups together to generate new ideas—a sharing of purpose. Often the different groups represented identify similar goals that lead to shared corridors and multiple-use areas to meet a variety of user needs.

Another example that has been well-received by users and Forest Service personnel in the West is the Multiple Use/Shared Trail (MUST) Workshop. This Workshop brings public land users together to discuss ways they can share trails and other access opportunities. These diverse forest users include four wheelers, ATVers, equestrians, mountain bikers, motorcyclists, hikers, cross-country skiers, hunters, and snowmobilers. Classroom subjects include Adopt-A-Trail programs, agency expectations of user groups, public involvement in land management and project planning, wildlife habitat management, and official rules and regulations relating to off-highway recreation.

Field subjects would include concepts and examples from Tread Lightly!, rare/threatened/endangered (RTE) species identification, proper equipping of vehicles, shared trail ideas/demonstrations, and off-highway recreation user group demonstrations to include four wheel drive, ATVs, motorcycles, mountain bikes, hikers, cross-country skiers, snowmobilers, horses, and sportsmen.

Future Trends and Directions

According to the U.S. Forest Service, off-road vehicle driving is an activity that 13.9 percent of the population, or 27.9 million people 16 years or older, have participated in at least once in the past 12 months (Cordell, et al., 1997). Participation in this activity is expected to grow to over 32 million by the year 2050 (see tables in Chapter 6).

Further educational programs relating to recreational use of our natural resources will continue to be important in the protection and conservation of our public lands.

With funding a growing concern, combined efforts will be used in seeking funds. The National Recreational Trails Funding Program will likely be of great importance in providing funding to states. Four-wheel-drive enthusiasts will continue working with the Coalition for Recreational Trails, state trail administrators, and trail advisory boards to assure the success of programs.

With the growing demand for more recreational activities, innovative and unique alternatives will be explored as ways to provide access. In some cases, there will be an increasing need for fees to offset maintenance costs as public funding remains level.

People are spending a lot on their outdoor endeavors. According to a U.S. Fish & Wildlife report in 1991, more than 76 million Americans watched, photographed, and fed birds and other wildlife in 1991, spending $18.1 billion. Equipment and other expenditures accounted for $10.6 billion of the $18.1 billion in direct expenditures. Of this amount, nearly a third was for off-road vehicles, tent trailers, motor homes, and pickup trucks. These types of expenditures will continue into the future, emphasizing the importance of four-wheel-drive recreation in particular and outdoor recreation in general in our American society.

Paddle Sport Recreation in the United States

(By Jeffrey A. Yeager, American Canoe Association, Newington, VA)

Paddlesport includes canoeing, kayaking, and rafting. The National Survey on Recreation and the Environment (NSRE) released by the USDA Forest Service in 1996 indicated that 24.8 million Americans participate in these activities each year. The paddlesport industry consists of approximately 50 national paddle craft manufacturers that together sell an estimated 150,000 craft each year. There are an estimated one million privately owned paddle craft in the U.S.

Representing the interests of individual paddlesport enthusiasts are a number of national nonprofit organizations and approximately 500 local clubs around the country. The American Canoe Association (ACA), founded in 1880, is the largest and oldest of the nonprofit organizations serving the paddlesport community.

Current Trends

Currently, the overall paddlesport market appears to be growing at a modest 5-percent rate. While some segments of the market, including open canoe sales, are static or decreasing, the sale of kayaks, particularly sea kayaks, is offsetting this decline with strong growth.

Factors currently effecting private paddling opportunities include increased competition with other user groups for limited water resources, regulation of access to natural waters, continued pollution and water quality problems, evolution of equipment, and expansion of the market that requires corresponding expansion of safety education programs and delivery systems.

In addition to the above factors, paddlesport has benefited from significantly increased media visibility in recent years. One indication of this benefit is the ability of the paddlesport organizations to secure outside corporate sponsors where none existed a decade ago.

Current Activities

Organized paddlesport groups are emphasizing the following three activities in support of their membership. First, paddlers are pursuing enforcement actions under the Clean Water Act against polluters of the nation's rivers, lakes, and coastal waterways. Paddlers are also pursuing a coordinated legislative agenda on the federal, state and local level, which advocates for the interests of paddlers and protects the quality and enjoyment of the nation's recreational waterways.

Second, ACA and others are expanding emphasis on safety education to keep pace with market expansion and equipment design changes. This emphasis includes a curriculum of training for paddling instructors.

Third, paddlesport organizations are creating strategic alliances, particularly with the corporate sector, to generate new sources of financing and support.

Future Outlook

With the aging of the American public and a growing environmental ethic, paddlesport seems well positioned for continued growth into the next century. Paddlesport can provide an accessible, economical and healthful form of "green recreation" for middle-aged families and older adults. On the other hand, paddlesport expects to face continuing and even increasing competition for access to water resources in the future. This may be particularly true of protection of pristine wilderness areas such as Minnesota's Boundary Waters Canoe Wilderness Area, which is already under heavy pressure from commercial groups to allow increased usage as well as motorized water craft.

Unfortunately, the environmental forecast is relatively pessimistic for the years ahead. One of the primary concerns is the likelihood that water quality in the nation's rivers, lakes and coastal waterways may decline from weakened governmental efforts to enforce the Clean Water Act. To address this concern, the ACA has initiated plans to undertake independent enforcement actions under the act on behalf of its members.

The Horse Industry: Heading to the Next Century

(By Molly Chaffinch, American Horse Council, Washington, DC)

A decade after facing many changes prompted by economics, competition and a less agrarian society, the horse industry is showing signs of resurgence. Recreational use of horses in the United States is estimated at 2.97 million horses and 4.35 million participants, representing over $28.3 billion in annual economic impact. These figures reflect only the horseback riding segment of the industry, and do not incorporate the "professional" segments, which include horse racing, showing, polo, farm work, rodeos, and police work. Those activities are responsible for $83.8 billion in annual economic impact on the U.S. economy, generated by almost four million horses and 2.75 million participants, not including the millions of spectators at various horse events and their off-site spending when attending those events.

The Horse Industry

Almost two million Americans own horses, and more than five million others work in the industry. This industry is more diverse than most sporting and recreational opportunities. This diversity includes polo, rodeo, training, showing, recreational riding, and viewing the thousands of public horse events. Horse racing, which is conducted daily in 41 states across the nation, has tens of millions of spectators and millions more visit horse shows, rodeos and other horse competitions.

Every state has a horse "economy," and, in many instances, horses are a key part of a state's recreational base and a magnet for tourism. Consider, for example, states like Kentucky, Maryland, New York, California, Ohio, and Arizona, which host world-famous races, shows, and expositions.

Figure V.16: Number of Participants and Horses Involved in Four Areas of Activity

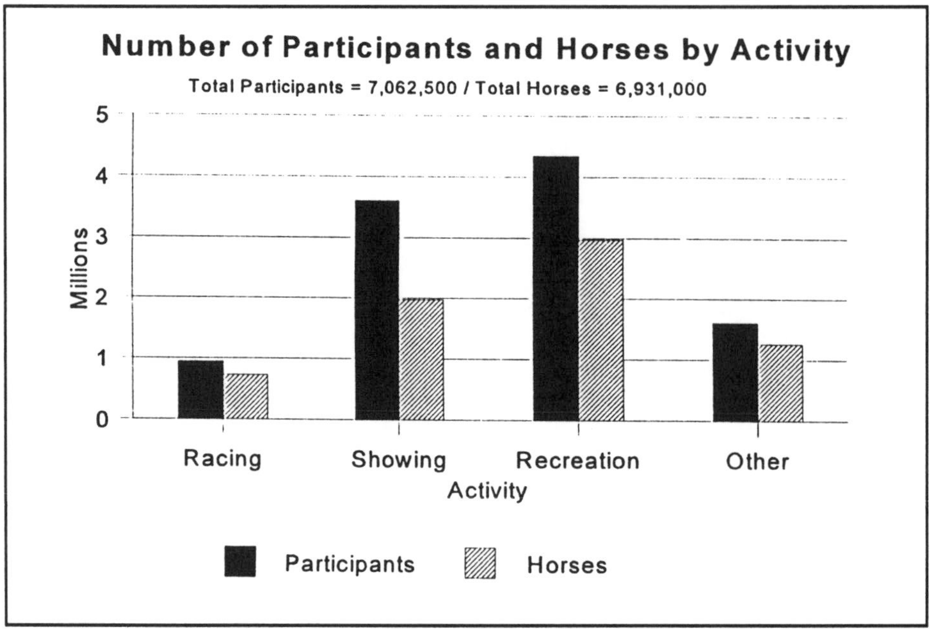

Horse Owners

Horse ownership has been commonly considered a pursuit of the wealthy, but current industry demographics dispute that notion, and indicate a trend that has led to a flourishing market for leisure expenditures on horses. A 1996 economic analysis of the industry sponsored by the American Horse Council Foundation, a Washington, DC-based organization, indicates that the median income for horse-owning households is $60,000 annually and that 64 percent of horse owners have yearly incomes of less than $75,000. Horse ownership has clearly become a middle-class leisure activity, and one that is growing steadily among families.

Participation in horse activities, which historically was based on farm use, has now swung heavily toward recreational use. This is a meaningful trend for the industry due to the rising availability of leisure dollars and the growing interest in seeking interesting and unique outdoor activities.

The challenge before the industry, and one being recognized more and more by industry institutions and professionals, is to develop public awareness of horses and the recreational potential they represent. In a society that is less agrarian than at any time in its history, Americans are not as routinely acquainted with horses as they were in previous generations. Once brought into contact with the horse world, many Americans, especially young people, become genuine enthusiasts and get involved in a variety of equine activities. The goal of the various segments of the horse industry is to find ways of increasing public awareness of horses through marketing, special events, and public relations programs.

Involvement with Government

The pleasure horse industry, while not regulated in the same way as racing, has found that it, too, must be more attentive to government. Areas such as tax policy, trails, use land management, environmental matters, use of government-owned parks and conservatories, agricultural regulations, and animal welfare concerns are among matters often of interest to horse enthusiasts in both the racing and pleasure areas. Industry groups have learned that it is often necessary to be pro-active in the legislative and regulatory arenas, rather than defensive, as has been the typical industry posture.

Recreational participants have long been quiet politically, but that is now changing. Issues such as trails, land management, and equine liability laws are driving pleasure horsemen to stand up and take action with legislative policies.

Learning to Act Collectively

With greater political sensitivity comes an understanding of the need to act collectively. The horse industry, as large as it is, consists of thousands of small businesses scattered across the country. There are no large, concentrated production operations such as one would find in many industries of comparable scope. This lack of brand identification, lack of broad scale product marketing, has been a matter of growing concern to industry participants in recent years.

The pleasure horse world, being less event-driven and comprised of more disparate elements, has nonetheless developed a strong sense of an industry-wide need for product identity and exposure. Lacking the economic engine that exists in parimutuel wagering, pleasure horse organizations have had to work harder at developing corporate sponsors for events. This has led to greater participation in industry marketing initiatives by those who sell products and services to the industry.

By getting people to attend or watch equine events, there will be exposure for the various breeds and disciplines involved and for the idea of participation in equine activities. Both live attendance and television programming of horse events provide a forum for industry segments to emphasize the variety of ways people can enjoy horses, either as spectators or in recreational activities.

Moving Toward Marketing

The evolution of information technology has seen rapid expansion of both print publishing and electronic information transmission. There are more than 200 equine publications in North America, not counting thousands of organizational newsletters, and the larger ones are now promoting web sites.

The horse industry is not unlike many other entertainment-driven entities in seeking to broaden its appeal. What is different is that industry participants are now acutely aware that the survival of their equine world may well depend upon their ability, and willingness, to market themselves and their horses to a bigger segment of the consuming public than ever before. There is much to like about horses—their beauty, athleticism, relationship to the outdoors and the nation's agricultural heritage—but in a society less in touch with its agrarian past than ever before, they have to be viewed as an entertainment and recreational commodity, and marketed as such.

Cycling Issues and Futures in Outdoor Recreation

(By Gary MacFadden, Adventure Cycling Association, Missoula, MT)

Overview

Bicycling is many faceted and includes racing, touring, mountain biking, commuting, motocross (BMX), day riding, local rides (like children visiting friends), and other lesser categories. Interest in these different styles of biking has fluctuated over the years. Recently, interest has been growing in mountain biking and racing and declining in long-distance touring. Day rides and BMX have remained strong for the past decade and show no signs of disappearing.

Local recreational riding and commuting have been on the upswing, partially due to an increased awareness of cycling in the transportation community and funding for bicycle routes through the Intermodal Surface Transportation Efficiency Act (ISTEA). According to a report by the Environmental Working Group in Washington, DC, more than 100 million Americans were expected to go bike riding in 1997. That study also notes that 10 million more Americans ride bikes today than in 1990, a 10 percent increase. Approximately four million adults ride their bikes to work, and 12 million more report they would ride to work if adequate cycling routes were available.

Changes in the Adventure Cycling Association (ACA) mirror general trends in cycling. The ACA began in 1974 as Bikecentennial to design the first cross-country bicycle route—the TransAmerica Bicycle Trail. Since then, ACA has identified and mapped nearly 23,000 miles of bicycle touring routes. Yet, as the interest changed in the late 1980s and early 1990s from road touring to mountain biking, the ACA began work on opportunities for off-pavement biking. There now are ACA trail systems in the Jackson Hole, Wyoming area, the Monongahela National Forest in West Virginia, and the Missoula, Montana region surrounding the organization's headquarters. Our newest long-distance route effort is the Great Divide Mountain Bike Route, taking cyclists from Canada to Mexico, paralleling the Continental Divide. This 2,500-mile route uses a mixture of jeep roads, abandoned rail beds, and single-track trails.

Recent Trends, Issues, and Forces Driving Change

The average age of cycling enthusiasts is rising. A study commissioned by ACA in 1995 found that the average member is 47 years of age; 41 percent of the membership is 50 years of age or older. Meanwhile, only three percent of the membership between the ages of 18 and 29. According to this study, seven of 10 members expect to bicycle tour within any given year. Approximately 64 percent said that tour would be two to seven days in length, and 23 percent said the typical cycling vacation was 7 to 14 days. In the past, when the membership was younger, the average tour length was much longer. Cyclists today cite family and employment pressures as the primary reasons for shorter cycling vacations.

Another factor affecting touring is harder-to-find cycling venues. Rural America is not as easy to find as it was 20 or 30 years ago. In many areas,k intense development is occurring, and most of the new pavement is not designed for cycling. In many states it is illegal to bicycle on a freeway shoulder. Without access to enjoyable and safe places to bicycle, people may not be able to participate as much as they would prefer.

Current Policies and Programs

The growing overlap of road touring and mountain biking has led directly to creation of the Great Divide Mountain Bike Route. Similar trends are at work in bicycle commuting. There is a fine line between the supposed drudgery of using a bicycle to commute to work and the enjoyment of following a well-designed bicycle path that carries one home without the stresses of automobile traffic. The bicycle industry in the early 1990s mounted a campaign to publicize the need for more safe places to ride. In response, federal officials included major funding for bicycle routes in ISTEA.

The Future

In late 1997, the ISTEA transportation bill will be re-authorized, either with or without the bicycling components intact. Members of cycling and pedestrian groups have joined together to encourage continued funding for design and construction of trails and support ofinfrastructure.

A new way that cycling activists communicate is the Internet. This has proved effective in networking at an extremely low cost. Cyclists looking for information can choose from dozens of specialty sites on the Internet. General interest cycling sites include BikeNet (an America On-Line site operated by ACA), advocacy information at the League of American Bicyclist's site (http://www.bikeleague.org), and touring information at Adventure Cycling's Internet site (http://www.adv-cycling.org.).

Family Campers and RVers

(By Barbara J. Turner)

Family Campers and RVers is a large, non-profit family camping association representing people interested in this form of outdoor recreation. FCRV is a member of American Recreation Coalition (ARC) and other associations that promote outdoor recreation and its expansion.

Recreation seems to be growing in importance in people's lives. In addition, recreation is big business, as evidenced by the billions of dollars of sales of outdoor clothing and equipment. There is a wide variety of camping and RV equipment now available. FCRV represents people using any type of camping equipment. Many other family camping groups tend to represent specific types of equipment or even particular brands. The RV industry is setting its sights on the target market of people in their 30s to 50s. These people are identified as potential first-time buyers, the target of the industry's new Go-RVing campaign. There will continue to be, however, large numbers of older campers and their numbers are even likely to increase.

Various recreation user groups hold festivals and events to promote their interests and to provide a setting for showing new equipment and social interaction. Each year FCRV holds a national rally called a Campvention. Traditionally, Campventions have been hosted by states or provinces, either individually or in combination with others. Beginning with 1998, Campvention will be rotated among regions to make it more accessible.

When looking at overall trends, issues, and the direction of family camping, one must first look at the trends of society. Leisure time and recreation seem to be increasing in importance in people's lives. Balancing work and vacation time and looking beyond work toward retirement are vital issues to people. Camping and RV recreation help provide recreational options at any stage in the lifecycle. As FCRV moves into the 21st century, the organization is striving to promote camping and RV recreation as a part of the RV industry in the United States.

Trends in American Fishing

(By Celeste McCaleb and BASS Inc. Staff, Bass Anglers Sportsman Society, Montgomery, AL)

A primary goal of fishing organizations, such as the Bass Anglers Sportsman Society (BASS), is to ensure the environmental safety of fish habitats. In 1970, BASS resurrected the 1899 Refuse Act and filed lawsuits naming over 200 polluters ranging from laundromats to large industries in Texas, Tennessee, and

Alabama. In that same year, the society created Anglers for Clean Water, where concerned fishermen could make tax-deductible contributions toward conservation causes of interest. One of the most recent projects involves efforts to prevent the draining of Rodman Pool, a bass fishery located in Florida. An effective method to work for water resource conservation is close communication with federal, state, and conservation agencies.

Because most pollution problems are not national in scope, state-wide networks have sprung up to handle regional challenges. For example, in the late 1970s, this organization helped organize affiliated clubs into 25 state federations. Currently, there are over 2,700 clubs and 50,000 chapter members.

Perhaps the most significant fisheries legislation in the recent past was the 1984 Wallop-Breaux Amendment to the Dingell-Johnson Sportfish Restoration Act. Since 1986, over $1 billion from additional taxes on motorboat fuel and fishing tackle have flowed back to state fish and wildlife agencies for management programs. Fishing organizations lobbied to pass and protect key provisions in that act.

Fishing Trends

Over the past few years, sportfishing has become more of a family activity than in the past. This may be the result of changing family structures and a desire to spend more time with the family. Two ways BASS has addressed this change is coordinating fishing programs and educational resources for children, and planning a theme park for fishermen and their families.

Another trend noted by sportfishing authorities is that anglers are participating more frequently than in the past (see chart). From 1989 to 1994, the annual number of anglers who fished only one to four days per year was declining, while the number of anglers who fished over 40 days increased. This increase and the fact that families are becoming more involved support strongly that bass fishing will continue to grow in the future.

Outdoor Recreation Trends for Motorized Vehicles

(By Adena Cook, BlueRibbon Coalition, Pocatello, ID)

The BlueRibbon Coalition works to ensure recreational access for motorized users on public lands. Motorized use on public lands has been affected by numerous acts and regulations over the last 40 years. For example, the Wilderness Act of 1964 prohibited motorized vehicles from congressionally designated wilderness. Subsequent designations to the system after 1964 has further prohibited motorized uses. Unfortunately, the debate over which lands should be designated Wilderness has polarized backcountry non-motorized and motorized interests.

In 1972, Executive Order 11644 authorized the secretaries of interior and agriculture to designate administratively "the specific areas and trails on public lands on which the use of off-road vehicles may be permitted, and areas in which the use of off-road vehicles may not be permitted." It further required that such designations "be based upon the protection of the resources of public lands, promotion of the safety of all users of those lands, and minimizing of conflicts among the various uses of those lands."

In 1977, Executive Order 11989 added a paragraph to EO-11644 stating in part "the respective agency head shall, whenever he determines that the use of off-road vehicles will cause or is causing considerable adverse effects on the soil, vegetation, wildlife, wildlife habitat, or cultural or historic resources, immediately close such areas or trails to the type of off-road vehicle causing such effects until such adverse effects have been eliminated and that measures have been implemented to prevent future recurrence."

Motorized recreationists formed local clubs to address access concerns and to enjoy motorized sports as a family activity. Local clubs work to promote actively ethical behavior and responsible use, as well as to perform volunteer maintenance of trails and facilities.

Local organization and volunteerism were effective, but continuing concern for access led to formation of the BlueRibbon Coalition in 1987. The BlueRibbon Coalition provides the *BlueRibbon Magazine* with news and information about public land policy. The magazine addresses issues of rural communities, natural resource users, and public access. BlueRibbon's land use program works with land managers to maintain and expand state and federal recreation opportunities. The BlueRibbon Coalition promotes cooperation among users and prevention of closures or restrictive access policies.

In addition to work on local and regional issues, the coalition works to affect the national land management policy. Attending national conferences, maintaining contact with public land agencies, working with members of Congress, and a variety of other methods are used to affect public land policy.

In the National Recreational Trail Fund Act (NRTFA) of 1991, Congress recognized the need to fund and provide recreational facilities for motorized recreationists. Patterned after off-highway vehicle funds successful in several states, NRTFA sets aside a portion of the federal gas tax for trails and facilities for all recreationist interests.

Much information is available on how to provide motorized recreation opportunities that are rewarding, yet not in conflict with other recreationists and resource management. Federal agencies are working to develop strategies for accommodating motorized recreationists needs. For example, the Forest Service has formulated principles and an action plan in the "National Off-Highway Vehicle Activity Review" (USDA Forest Service, Washington Office, File Code: 1410/2350). This review has led to development of a trail system by land managing agencies as outlined in the National OHV Activity Review which requires modified design to provide vehicle access as well as access for other uses. Based on Recreation Visitor Day (RVD) data and appropriate mileage for each type of trail experience, it is estimated that OHV trails should make up a minimum of 64 percent of a forest trail system. Exclusive use trails for equestrian, hiking, and bicycling should make up a maximum of 17 percent, 15 percent and four percent of the trail system, respectively. Groups such as the BlueRibbon Coalition will continue to face challenges and to work collaboratively to meet these challengers of access to motorized sports.

Technical Rock Climbing Trends in the United States

(By Sally Moser and Sam Davidson, The Access Fund, Boulder, CO)

Overview

Technical climbing is gaining popularity as a mainstream recreational activity. It is generally defined as the use of specialized equipment, including shoes, ropes, harnesses, and safety anchors, to provide a margin of safety and facilitate the physical efforts required for ascending and descending vertical rock faces.

It occurs on both public and private lands throughout the United States in a variety of settings, including high altitude mountains, ice flows, snow fields, boulders, constructed rock walls, and overhangs. There are several distinct forms of technical climbing, including bouldering (climbing close to the ground, generally without ropes and safety anchors), free climbing (holding on and moving up using one's equipment only to catch the climber in case of a fall), aid climbing (using one's ropes and safety anchors to support one's weight and assist in the ascent of terrain too steep or featureless to be free climbed), and sport climbing (a gymnastic blend of free and aid climbing on steep rock, generally over terrain so difficult that multiple attempts are often needed to climb a route without weighting one's safety anchors).

Technical climbers seek to explore the limits of their physical and mental skills in settings sometimes shared by other users of the public lands. However, they must be distinguished from the general public, who occasionally scramble without equipment or knowledge onto rock faces and boulders and may be the victims of climbing accidents. Technical climbers usually are less likely to be injured, killed, or require a rescue than hikers, swimmers, or skiers.

In the last ten years, the number of technical climbers has grown, as have climbers' impacts on natural and administrative resources. In some climbing areas, these impacts have resulted in use restrictions, including short- and long-term prohibitions.

The future of technical climbing in America depends on preserving the vertical "wilderness" and the diverse experiences climbers find in these environments. Technical climbing, more than many other types of outdoor recreation, is defined by personal freedom, self-reliance, and a minimum-impact ethic. To preserve the freedoms and responsibilities at the heart of the climbing experience, climbing enthusiasts are attempting to help in the resolution of public land management issues.

To keep climbing areas open and to conserve the climbing environment, the Access Fund was incorporated in 1990 to preserve the diversity of climbing resources and opportunities in the United States. Critical issues facing technical climbers include finding a solution to the question of whether "fixed" (semi-permanent) safety anchors will be prohibited or properly managed in designated Wilderness areas; developing a coalition of commercial and non-profit interests to promote human-powered recreation; forming alliances with other environmentally concerned users; and providing funding for grassroots advocacy efforts, climber education, impact-mitigation projects, and outreach programs.

Current Trends

Growth of Climbing

The number of climbers in the United States has risen dramatically in the past ten years, due partly to the growing interest in outdoor recreation generally and partly to the advent and rapid spread of indoor climbing facilities. In 1986, there were no known indoor climbing gyms; currently there are over 200. The popularization of climbing in the mainstream media has also contributed to the sport's growth. The voluminous sales of books about mountain climbing are evidence of the rising public fascination with technical climbing. Current estimates by nationally distributed climbing magazines suggest 300,000 to 400,000 climbers are active today, compared to fewer than 100,000 ten years ago. The Access Fund now has more than 7,200 members, with 16-percent growth in membership between 1995 and 1996.

Increased Regulation

As the number of active climbers continues to rise, public land management agencies have begun to pay more attention to climbing activities and impacts. On the federal level, the U.S. Forest Service, the National Park Service, the Bureau of Land Management, and the U.S. Fish & Wildlife Service all have developed or are considering new regulations as guidance for local authorities in managing technical climbing. Many state park systems now have climbing-specific policies as well. An emerging trend is for all public land units that have significant climbing resources to develop climbing management plans, which typically protect some traditional climbing freedoms but restrict others. Climbing management plans address the unique requirements and impacts of climbers, such as the use of fixed safety anchors, exploration of new routes, size of the climbing party, and commercial guide services. Other issues often addressed in climbing management plans are the protection of sensitive or rare plant and animal species and archeological or cultural sites.

Rock climbers prepare to face the challenges of rock climbing and rappelling. Photo courtesy of USDA Forest Service. Photo by Alan Ewert.

Liability Concerns

As the popularity of technical climbing grows, so do the liability concerns of public lands managers, private landowners, and climbing equipment manufacturers, even though landowner or government liability is no greater for climbing than for other recreational uses. Without exception, the courts have supported this protection from liability in the few instances in which the government has been sued by climbers or their estates. There is no record of any private property owner in the United States being sued by a climber for liability. Organizations such as the Access Fund, along with outdoor recreation industry trade groups, are working to reduce liability concerns by publicizing the protections offered by state recreational user statutes and by standardizing climbing equipment labels and warnings by the equipment manufacturers.

Mitigation of Environmental Impacts

Climbers are frequently in the vanguard of environmental activism, a trend that seems to grow in the outdoor recreation community. This activism derives from awareness that in order to preserve recreation opportunities, the natural resources that are the source and inspiration for these activities must also be safeguarded. This trend is evident in the increase numbers of volunteers who help with trail maintenance and clean-up projects. For example, in 1996, climbers logged over 500 volunteer days on Access Fund sponsored projects.

Policies, Programs, and Directions

Working in cooperation with local climbers, other recreational users, public land managers, and private property owners, the Access Fund promotes responsible use and management of climbing resources throughout the United States. Some steps taken toward these ends by rock climbing organizations include:

- *Monitoring proposed federal policies* and responding to these initiatives through administrative procedural channels and direct communications with government officials. Reduced public lands management budgets could lead to restrictions on public access and legitimate uses of the public domain. Providing direct comments on all management plans and regulations that pertain to technical climbing.
- Given the declining budgets for managing public lands, public agencies are seeking *partnerships* with private organizations such as the Access Fund to help provide essential facilities and services. Climbing preservation grants from climbing organizations provide funding for projects such as trails, toilets, signage, scientific studies, and educational materials. Since 1990, the Access Fund has provided over $1 million for such programs.
- Developing and distributing *climber education programs* and materials, such as climbing newsletters and booklets, which provide practical information for minimizing resource impacts and promoting long-term stewardship of the climbing environment.
- *Grassroots activism* promotes individual responsibility and local initiative in the expression and protection of climber interests through actions like a regional volunteer activist network that communicates between national groups and local climbers.
- *Preserving and restoring access to climbing areas* often focuses on climbing areas, particularly on private lands, that have been closed or restricted due to concerns about resource impacts. Property donations and purchases sometimes take place to keep an area open to climbing.
- Major rock climbing groups have begun nurturing *partnerships with mainstream environmental organizations* such as the Sierra Club, the Wilderness Society, and the National Parks & Conservation Association. The Access Fund has developed in-depth ties with the International Mountain Bicycling Association and the American Whitewater Association International as the three groups organize the Recreational Access Summit of 1997. By joining forces with groups that share the same concerns, the climbing community is broadening its perspective and gaining partners to preserve the quality and diversity of our natural heritage.

Trends for the Years 2000 and 2005

Trends that can have an affect on the climbing experience and management of climbing resources in the next five to eight years include:

It is expected that *the number of climbers will continue to grow,* but at a reduced rate, as many of those who learned to climb indoors move to the outdoors.

As the government seeks alternative ways of paying for the costs of managing outdoor recreation programs and resources, high-profile activities such as climbing will continue to be put under the microscope. Public lands management agencies will step up their cost-recovery efforts, especially with respect to rescues of stranded or injured climbers. *Special-use fees* to access parking areas, trails, and climbing resources will become standard or rise. Congressional appropriations for public lands administration will probably continue to decline if pilot user-fee programs prove successful, leaving individual national forests, parks, and land units to raise even more revenue at the local level.

As outdoor recreation in general becomes increasingly popular, there will be greater competition for access to limited resources. For example, there will be more interest in visiting popular designated wilderness areas, and land managers may respond by *imposing additional quotas* on day-use and overnight visitation. Climbers face the prospect of being required to reserve months in advance a day-use pass for national parks, and competing with other climbers for permits to explore new routes or even to climb established routes that are very popular.

As the climbing community expands and matures, it will become more cohesive and *increase its activism* in the continuing debate over how best to balance resource protection with recreational access. By the year 2005, for example, this organization expects membership to exceed 20,000 individuals and organizations.

Riding into the Future: Motorcycling Recreation on the Road Ahead

(By Eric J. Lundquist, American Motorcyclist Association, Columbus, OH)

Introduction

Except for competitive events in stadiums and arenas, recreational motorcycling depends on access to roads and open spaces. Broadly, there are three types of motorcycling categories: road riding (or touring), off-highway trail biking or all-terrain-vehicle recreation, and amateur or professional competition. Each of these groups is interested in a variety of outdoor recreation issues. For example, road-riding motorcyclists, many of whom enjoy camping and touring, have been highly supportive of the Federal Scenic Byways Program.

Off-highway enthusiasts are involved in land management planning activities and the American Motorcyclist Association (AMA) has successfully encouraged many to seek appointments to federal land advisory boards. These enthusiasts enjoy the same stimuli as other participants in strenuous trail-based recreation, such as the trail for the trail's sake, getting to the destination, viewing wildlife, scenic vistas, hunting, fishing, camping, and companionship.

Competition riders are interested in a variety of opportunities, from events at the Daytona International Raceway to small local tracks, to enduros, or to off-road endurance races traditionally held on public lands.

Forces Driving Significant Change

A variety of forces are driving change in motorcycling and influencing the demographics of participants, their activities, the opportunities available to them, and the types of machines they use.

As the nation's population ages, so do participants in motorcycling and AMA members. Most are well educated and financially secure (Lundquist, 1995). There has been heightened interest in cycling by female riders.

Motorcycling experienced a flat market from the late 1980s to the early 1990s. Sales since then have shown a modest rise. Participation in motorcycling associations, however, has risen over the past decade. AMA membership went from 147,000 in 1988 to 213,000 in 1997. There has been a concurrent rise in the numbers taking part in other rider organizations such as state off-highway vehicle coalitions. Also a number of newer rider groups have come into existence in recent years, such as the Motorcycle Riders Foundation, the National Off-Highway Vehicle Conservation Council, and the BlueRibbon Coalition.

The AMA sanctions about 3,500 motorcycling events of all types each year. Other sanctioning organizations present many thousands of other events. Trends in such events are varied. In road-riding, there is more interest in destination events related to races held in Daytona Beach and Sturgis, South Dakota. Professional and amateur racing is continually evolving new types of competition. Vintage racing and events based around antique motorcycles are growing also. Non-competitive events such as dual-sport scenic touring and field meets are becoming more popular. A dual-sport tour uses motorcycles that are street-legal but off-highway capable. Athletic events such as motocross remain popular with several hundred thousand entrants every year.

The motorcycle industry itself is undergoing dramatic changes. Besides the traditional U.S., Japanese, and European manufacturers, new manufacturers from Europe, the former Eastern Bloc, China, and Southeast Asia are emerging. These groups are joined in this country by a variety of new producers of off-highway motorcycles and more than a dozen smaller manufacturers building machines similar to the most popular U.S. brand with after-market parts available. Growing requirements for vehicle emission controls in Asia and Europe are forcing innovation in motor types.

One traditional source of concern, motorcycle noise, is being addressed by the manufacture of machines that are much quieter (Lundquist & Chapin, 1996). Interest in ATV recreation remains high, and while the industry has not released recent ATV sales information, past trends indicate sales equivalent to street motorcycles.

Key Current Interests, Campaigns, Programs, and Directions

Women and Motorcycling

While still a male-dominated activity, the past decade has seen a heightened interest by women. In the summer of 1997, the AMA hosted a conference on women and motorcycling. Recent years have also seen several new magazines devoted to women riders and a growing number of women's motorcycling clubs.

Cooperation with Land Management Agencies

Motorcycle organizations have encouraged their members to work locally with federal land management agencies. For example, the association developed a volunteer Trail Rider program with the Forest Service in 1988. A video advertising the program was funded with the Forest Service's first cost-share agreement. The program was upgraded in 1996 and has been modified to recognize participation with other state and federal agencies.

Safety and Education

Most states now have street rider education courses developed at the insistence of enthusiasts. They are generally self-funded through registration and license fees. Reduction of fatalities have been dramatic, down from 4,564 in 1985 to 2,221 in 1995, and accidents were down 60 percent over this same period (Motor Industry Council, 1986-1996). Similar reductions in ATV deaths and injury since 1988 may also be partly attributed to the more widespread availability of safety training for those vehicles.

Government

Motorcycling groups maintain a high interest in several areas, such as obtaining provisions against health insurance discrimination by employers in the Health Care Insurance Portability Act of 1996. Another of these interests is expressed through proposals in the 1997 reauthorization of the Intermodal Surface Transportation Efficiency Act relating to motorcycle safety, access to HOV lanes, cessation of federal mandates for states to require apparel, and funding for the National Recreational Trails Fund Act (the Symms Act).

One current focus is the push for "smart highways," which includes automated toll booths. Current state initiatives include promoting legislation authorizing off-highway vehicle management programs and the preservation of existing safety and education schemes.

The Future

The next ten years may bring additional change to recreational motorcycling. Due to the ready availability of automobiles, motorcycling has not generally been seen as part of the personal transportation mix. Rather, it has been viewed as another competitor for disposable consumer dollars. There are other competitors for these dollars, such as home computers and entertainment systems.

One project that could serve as a model for future outdoor user partnerships is the Hatfield-McCoy project in West Virginia, which could provide up to several thousand miles of multiple use trail through agreements with private property owners. There is also interest in this project from adjoining counties in Kentucky and Virginia (American Motorcyclist Association, 1996). These agreements may become trendsetters in other areas of the country with interspersed public and private land. Tourism agencies are interested in findings that off-highway vehicle recreation generates $0.5 billion in Colorado and $3 billion annually in California (Lundquist, 1995).

Motor sports of all types are enjoying surging popularity. Attendance at such events as Supercross and road racing is at its highest level in recent history. The AMA is working to develop new venues for participation at the amateur level. Motorcyclists are by nature interested in technology. A substantial Internet presence already exists, which will likely grow and become more useful in planning races or recreation trips.

REFERENCES

Absher, J., & Winter, P. L. (1997). *Evaluation of the 1995 Eco-Team Program*. Unpublished technical report supplied by the authors.

American Motorcyclist Association. (1996, Summer). West Virginia trail study completed.*The OHV Planner*, 1.

Baas, J. M., Ewert, A., & Chavez, D. J. (1993). Influence of ethnicity on recreation and natural environment use patterns: Managing recreation sites for ethnic and racial diversity. *Environmental Management, 17*(4), 523-529.

Bartels, S. (1994). *ABA survey of members.* Colorado Springs, CO: American Birding Association.

Bicycle Institute of America. (1993). *The Bicycle Institute of America reference book*. Washington, DC: Author.

Boyd, S., & Butler, R. W. (1996). Managing ecotourism: An opportunity approach. *Tourism Management, 8*, 557-566.

Brown, K. (1988). Wheels of fortune: Bicycle marketers shift into high gear to meet demand. *Adweek's Marketing Week, 29*(2), 2.

Bullard, R. (1995). *People of color environmental groups: 1994-1995 directory*. Flint, MI: Charles Stewart Mott Foundation.

Butler, M. (1990). *Rural-urban continuum codes for metro and nonmetro counties*. Washington, DC: United States Department of Agriculture, Economic Research Service, Agriculture and Rural Economy Division.

Caro, V., & Ewert, A. (1995). The influence of acculturation on environmental concerns: An exploratory study. *The Journal of Environmental Education, 26*(3), 13-21.

Carr, D. S., & Chavez, D. J. (1993). *Culture, conflict, and communication in the wildland-urban interface*. Boulder, CO: Westview Press.

Chase, J. (1987, January). Mountain bikes, the gnarly question of knobby tires. *Backpacker*, 36-37.

Chavez, D. J. (1992). Hispanic recreationists in the wildland-urban interface. *Trends, 29*(4), 23-25.

Chavez, D. J. (1993a). *Pilot studies of changing urban wilderness recreation use on the Cleveland National Forest: Past wilderness users and on-site wilderness users*. Unpublished report supplied by author.

Chavez, D. J. (1993b). *Visitor perceptions of crowding and discrimination at two national forests in southern California*. PSW-RP-216, Research Paper. Albany, CA: USDA Forest Service, Pacific Southwest Station.

Chavez, D. J. (1995). *Demographic shifts: Potential impacts for outdoor recreation management*. Proceedings of the International Outdoor Recreation and Tourism Trends Symposium and the 1995 National Recreation Resource Planning Conference, May 14-17, pp. 252-255. St. Paul, MN: University of Minnesota Press.

Chavez, D. J. (1996a). Mountain biking: Issues and Actions for USDA Forest Service managers. PSW-RP-226, Albany, CA: USDA Forest Service, Pacific Southwest Research Station.

Chavez, D. J. (1996b). *Leisure experiences of Hispanic families*. Abstracts from the 1996 Symposium on Leisure Research, held in conjunction with the 1996 Congress for Recreation and Parks, October 23-27, p. 67, Kansas City, MO.

Chavez, D. J., Baas, J., & Winter, P. (1993). *Mecca Hills: Visitor research case study*. Technical report BLM/CA/ST-93-005-9560, 31 pp. Sacramento, CA: California State University Press.

Chavez, D. J., & Mainieri, T. (1994). *Recreation day use series-report 1: San Bernardino National Forest, Summer 1992*. Unpublished report supplied by the authors.

Chavez, D. J., & Winter, P. L. (1993). *Report for the Applewhite picnic area, Cajon ranger district, San Bernardino National Forest*. Unpublished report supplied by the authors.

Chavez, D. J., & Winter, P. L. (1994). *The trappings of recreation: Is ethnicity the key variable?* Presented at the 36th annual conference of the Western Social Science Association, April 20-24, Albuquerque, New Mexico.

Chavez, D. J., Winter, P. L., & Baas, J. M. (1993a). Recreational mountain biking: A management perspective. *Journal of Park and Recreation Administration, 11*(3), 29-36.

Chavez, D. J., Winter, P. L., & Baas, J. (1993b). *Imperial Sand Dunes visitor research case study*. Technical report BLM/CA/ST-93-014-9560. Sacramento, CA: California State University Press.

Chavez, D. J., Winter, P. L, & Larson, J. (1995). *Managing recreation resources for changing urban populations*. Paper presented at the National Recreation and Park Administration Congress for Recreation and Parks, San Antonio, TX.

Chavez, D. J., Winter, P .L., & Mainieri, T. (1994). *Recreation day use series-report 2: Angeles National Forest, summer 1993*. Unpublished report supplied by the authors.

Chavez, D. J., Winter, P. L., & Mainieri, T. (1995). *Recreation day use series-report 3: Los Padres National Forest, summer 1994*. Unpublished report supplied by the authors.

Clawson, M., & Van Doren, C. (1984). *Statistics on outdoor recreation*. Washington, DC: Resources for the Future, Inc.

Cordell, H. K., Bergstrom, J. C., Hartmann, L. A., & English, D. B. K. (1990). *An analysis of the outdoor recreation and wilderness situation in the United States: 1989-2040*. GTR RM-189. Fort Collins, CO: USDA Forest Service, Rocky Mountain Forest and Range Experiment Station.

Cordell, H. K., McDonald, B. L., Briggs, J. A., Teasley, R. J., Biesterfeldt, R., Bergstrom, J., & Mou, S. (1997). *Emerging markets for outdoor recreation in the United States*. North Palm Beach, FL: Sporting Goods Manufacturers Association, Outdoor Products Council.

Cordell, H. K., McDonald, B. L., Lewis, B., Miles, M., Martin, J. & Bason, J. (1996). United States of America. In G. Cushman, A. J. Veal, & J. Zuzanek (Eds.), *World leisure participation: Free time in the global village*. Oxford, England: CAB International.

Coupland, D. (1991). *Generation X*. New York: St. Martin's Press.

Curtin, R. T. (1994). *The RV consumer*. Ann Arbor, MI: The University of Michigan, Survey Research Center.

Dwyer, J. (1994). *Customer diversity and the future demand for outdoor recreation*. GTR: RM-252. Fort Collins, CO: USDA Forest Service, Rocky Mountain Forest and Range Experiment Station.

English, D. B. K., & Bergstrom, J. C. (1994). The conceptual links between recreation site development and regional economic impacts. *Journal of Regional Science, 34* (4), 599-611.

English, D., & Cordell, H. K. (1985). A cohort-centric analysis of outdoor recreation participation changes. In A. E. Watson (Ed.), *Southeastern recreation research proceedings*. February 28-March 1, 1985, Myrtle Beach, SC. Statesboro, GA: Georgia Southern College, Department of Marketing.

Environmental Protection Agency. (1996). *Nature-based tourism*. OSEC Issue Brief 1. Washington, DC: Author.

Eubanks, T., Kerlinger, P., & Payne, R. H. (1993). High Isle, Texas: A case study in avitourism. *Birding, 25*(6), 415-420

Fennell, D. A., & Smale, B. J. A. (1992). Ecotourism and natural resource protection. *Tourism Recreation Research, 17*(1), 21-32.

Gerlach, L. P., & Bengston, D. N. (1994). If ecosystem management is the solution, what's the problem? *Journal of Forestry, 92*(8), 18-21.

Go, F. M., Milne, D., & Whittles, L. J. R. (1992, Spring). Communities as destinations: A marketing taxonomy for the effective implementation of the tourism action plan. *Journal of Travel Research*, 31-37.

Gordon, J. C. (1994). From a vision to policy, a role for foresters. *Journal of Forestry, 32*(7), 16-19.

Greene, W. H. (1993). *Econometric Analysis* (2nd ed.). Englewood Cliffs, NJ: Prentice Hall.

Heywood, J. (1993). *Studying social order on urban proximate forest lands*. Unpublished cooperative agreement report supplied by the author.

Hof, J. G., & Kaiser, H. F. (1983). Long-term outdoor recreation participation projections for public land management agencies. *Journal of Leisure Research, 15(1),* 1-14.

Hollenhorst, S. J., Schuett, M. A., Olson, D., & Chavez, D. J. (1995). An examination of the characteristics, preferences, and attitudes of mountain bike users of the national forests. *Journal of Park and Recreation Administration, 13*(3), 41-51.

Hollenhorst, S. J., Schuett, M. A., Olson, D., Chavez, D. J., & Mainieri, T. (1995). *A national study of mountain biking opinion leaders: Characteristics, preferences, attitudes and conflicts*. Unpublished draft supplied by authors.

Hsieh, S., O'Leary, J. T., & Morrison, A. (1994, 1991). A comparison of package and non-package travelers from the United Kingdom. *Journal of International Consumer Marketing*, 6(3), 79-102 and *TTRA CENSTATES News, 8*(3), 9-10 ().

Hutchison, R. (1993). Among leisure and recreation activity. In P. Gobster (Ed.), *Managing Urban and High-Use Recreation Settings* (pp. 87-92). Chicago, IL: USDA Forest Service, North Central Forest Experiment Station.

Jacoby, J. (1990). Mountain bikes: A new dilemma for wildland recreation managers? *Western Wildlands, 16*(1), 25-28.

Keller, K. D. (1990). *Mountain bikes on public land: A manager's guide to the state of the practice*. Washington, DC: Bicycle Federation of America.

Kellert, S. R. (1985). Birdwatching in American Society. *Leisure Sciences 7*, 343-360.

Kerlinger, P. (1993). Birding economics & birder demographics studies as conservation tools. In D. Finch & P. Stangel (Eds.), *Proceedings: Status & management of neotropical birds*. General Technical Report. Fort Collins, Colorado: Rocky Mountain Forest & Range Experimental Station.

Kerlinger, P., & Brett, J. (1994). Hawk mountain sanctuary: A case study of birder visitation & birding economics. In R. Knight & K. Gutzmiller (Eds.), *Wildlife & recreationists: Coexistence through management & research*. Washington, D.C.: Island Press.

Kerlinger, P., & Eubanks, T. (1995). Birds & Bucks. *Birding, 27*(1), 21-23.

Kerlinger, P., & Wiedner, D. S. (1991). The economics of birding at Cape May, New Jersey. In J. A. Kusler, (Ed.), *Ecotourism & resource conservation*, (vol. 1). Second International Symposium, Ecotourism & Resource Conservation, Miami, FL.

Lang, C. T. (1996). *A typology of international travelers to nature-based tourism destinations*. Unpublished doctoral dissertation. Purdue University, Lafayette, IN.

Lang, C. T., & O'Leary, J. T. (1990, May). *International travel and tourism: Analysis of overseas travelers to national parks/historic sites*. A series of reports to the U.S. National Park Service and Tourism Canada.

Leatherman, J. C., & Marcouiller, D. W. (1996). Persistent poverty and natural resource dependence: Rural development policy analysis that incorporates income distribution. *The Journal of Regional Analysis & Policy, 26*(2), 73-94.

Lieberson, S., & Wilkinson, C. (1976). A comparison between Northern and Southern blacks residing in the North. *Demography, 13*(2),199-224.

Lindsey, J., & Ogle, R. (1972). Socioeconomic patterns of outdoor recreation use near urban areas. *Journal of Leisure Research, 4*(1),19-24.

Lingle, G. R. (1991). History and economic impact of crane watching in central Nebraska. *Proceedings of North American Crane Workshop, 6*, 25-29.

Lundquist, E. J. (1995). Demographics and contributions of the off-highway motorcycling community. In J. L. Thompson, D. W. Lime, B. Gartner, & W. M. Sames (Comps.), *Proceedings of the Fourth International Outdoor Recreation and Tourism Trends Symposium and the 1995 National Recreation Resource Planning Conference, May 14-17*, pp. 300-303. St. Paul, MN: University of Minnesota, College of Natural Resources and Minnesota Extension Service.

Lundquist, E. J. (1995). *Off-highway motorcycle and ATV enthusiast demographics*. Pamphlet. Westerville, OH: American Motorcyclist Association.

Lundquist, E. J., & Chapin, B. (1996). *Testing closed-course competition motorcycles for compliance with Michigan trail bike regulations*. Paper presented at the meeting of the American Motorcyclist Association Congress, Westerville, Ohio.

Magill, A. W. (1995). Multicultural wildland users: A growing communication challenge. *The Environmental Professional, 17*, 51-54.

McDonald, B. L., & Van Horne, M. (1995). The moralists and the millennial generation: The crafting of outdoor recreation in the 21st century. In J. L. Thompson, D. W. Lime, B. Gartner, & W. M. Sames (Comps.), *Proceedings of the Fourth International Outdoor Recreation and Tourism Trends Symposium and the 1995 National Recreation Resource Planning Conference*, May 14-17, 1995, St. Paul, MN. St. Paul, MN: University of Minnesota College of Natural Resources and the Minnesota Extension Service.

McDonald, D., & McAvoy, L. H. (1996). In countless ways for thousands of years: Native American relationships to wildlands and other protected places. *Trends, 33*(4), 35-40.

McDonald, D., & McAvoy, L. (1997). *Outdoor recreation, racism, and Native Americans*. Unpublished cooperative agreement report supplied by the authors.

Motorcycle Industry Council (1986-1996). *Motorcycle industry council statistical annuals, 1986 through 1996*. Costa Mesa, CA: Author.

Murdock, S. H., Backman, K. E., Colberg, E., Hoque, M. N., &. Hamm, R. R. (1990). Modeling demographic change and characteristics in the analysis of future demand for leisure services. *Leisure Sciences, 12*, 79-102.

National Advisory Committee on Civil Disorders. (1968). Kerner commission report: Grievances. In J. A. Nesbitt, P. D. Brown, & J. F. Murphy (Eds.), *Recreation and Leisure Services for the Disadvantaged*, (pp. 41-48). Philadelphia: Lea & Febriger.

National Marine Manufacturers Association. (1997). *Inter/port*. Chicago, IL: National Marine Manufacturers Association.

Office of Policy Development and Research. (1994, September). *Urban policy brief* (1). Washington, DC: U.S. Department of Housing and Urban Development.

Orams, M. B. (1995). Towards a more desirable form of ecotourism. *Tourism Management, 16*(1), 3-8.

Outdoor Recreation Resources Review Commission (ORRRC). (1962). *National recreation survey*. ORRRC Study Report 19. Washington, DC: U.S. Government Printing Office.

Parker, J., & Winter, P. L. (1996). *Angeles National Forest wilderness visitors' characteristics and values*. Unpublished draft manuscript supplied by the authors.

Payne, R. H. (1991). Potential economic and political impacts of ecotourism: A research note. *Texas Journal of Political Studies, 13*, 65-77.

Propst, D. B., Gavrilis, D. G., Cordell, H. K., & Hansen, W. J. (1985). Assessing the secondary economic impacts of recreation and tourism: Work team recommendations. In D. B. Propst (Comp.), *Assessing the economic impacts of recreation and tourism*. Asheville, NC: U.S. Department of Agriculture, Forest Service, Southeastern Research Station.

Proshansky, H. M., Fabian, A. K., & Kaminoff, R. (1983). Place identity: Physical world socialization of the self. *Journal of Environmental Psychology, 3*, 57-83.

Rogers, E. M., Burdge, R. J., Korshing, P. F., & Donnermeyer, J. (1988). *Social change in rural societies: An introduction to rural sociology*. Englewood Cliffs, New Jersey: Prentice Hall.

Romero, A., & Stangel, P. (1997). *1997 directory of birding festivals*. Washington, D.C.: National Fish & Wildlife Foundation.

Scott, D., Stewart, W., & Cole, J. (1997). *An examination of activity preferences & orientations among serious birders*. College Station, TX: Texas A&M University, Department of Recreation, Park & Tourism Sciences, Texas Agricultural Extension Service.

Scott, D., Thigpen, J., Kim, S. S., & Kim, C. (1996). *The 1995 Rockport Hummerbird celebration: A survey of visitors including information about the Great Texas Coastal Birding Trail.* College Station, TX: Texas A&M University, Department of Recreation, Park & Tourism Sciences, Texas Agricultural Extension Service.

Shafer, E. L., Carline, R., Guldin, R. W., & Cordell, H. K. (1993). Economic amenity values of wildlife: Six case studies in Pennsylvania. *Environmental Management, 17*(5), 669-682.

Simcox, D. E. (1993). Cultural foundations for leisure preference, behavior, and environmental orientation. In A. W. Ewert, D. J. Chavez, A. W. Magill (Eds.), *Culture, Conflict and Communication in the Wildland-Urban Interface*. Westview Press.

Simcox, D. E., & Pfister, R. E. (1990). *Hispanic values and behaviors related to outdoor recreation and the forest environment*. Unpublished cooperative agreement report supplied by the authors.

Spiegler, M. (1996, December). Pop vulture: Gen X—not. *American Demographics*.

Sporting Goods Manufacturing Association. (1991). *Mountain biking—on the way up*. North Palm Beach, FL: Sporting Goods Manufacturing Association.

Strauss, W., & Howe, N. (1991). *Generations: The history of America's future, 1584-2069*. New York: William Morrow and Company.

Taylor, D. E., & Winter, P. L. (1994). *Factors influencing perceptions, expectations, and responses to depreciative behaviors in three national forests of the Pacific Southwest*. Unpublished draft manuscript supplied by the authors.

Tilmant, J. T. (1991). *Mountain bike use within national parks: A report on a 1990 survey*. Unpublished draft supplied by author.

Trembley, K. R., Jr., & Dunlap, R. E. (1978). Rural-urban residence and concern with environmental quality: A replication and extension. *Rural Sociology, 43*(3), 474-491.

U.S. Bureau of the Census. (1994). *Current Population Reports, P25-1095 and P25-1104*. Washington, D.C.: Author.

U.S. Department of Agriculture, Forest Service. (1994). *RPA assessment of the forest and rangeland situation in the United States—1993 update*. Report No. 27 . Washington, D.C.: Government Printing Office.

U.S. Department of Agriculture, Forest Service. (1995). *The forest service program for forest and rangeland resources: A long-term strategic plan*. Draft 1995 RPA Program. Washington, DC: Author.

U.S. Department of Agriculture, Forest Service. (1996). *Common social unit data base*. Golden, CO: Rocky Mountain Regional Office.

U.S. Department of the Interior. (1974-1992). *Federal recreation fee report*. Washington, DC: Author, National Park Service.

U.S. Department of the Interior. (1993). *The 1991 national survey of fishing, hunting, & wildlife-associated recreation*. Washington, DC: U.S. Fish & Wildlife Service.

Uysal, M., Oh, H. C., & O'Leary, J. T. (1995). Seasonal variation in propensity to travel in the U.S. *Journal of Tourism Systems and Quality Management*, 1(1), 1-13.

Van Horne, M. J., Szwak, L. B., & Randall, S. A. (1986). *1982-1983 nationwide recreation survey*. Washington, DC: U.S. Government Printing Office.

Viehman, J. (1990, August). Let's build trails, not walls. *Backpacker,* p. 3.

Walsh, R. G., Jon, K. H., McKean, J. R. & Hof, J. (1992). Effect of price on forecasts of participation in fish and wildlife recreation: An aggregate demand model. *Journal of Leisure Research, 21*, 140-156.

Washburne, R. F. (1978). Black underparticipation in wildland recreation: Alternative explanations. *Leisure Sciences, 1*(2), 175-189.

Watson, A. E., Williams, D. R., & Daigle, J. J. (1991). Sources of conflict between hikers and mountain bike riders in the Rattlesnake NRA. *Journal of Park and Recreation Administration, 9*(3), 59-71.

Wenger, K. F. (1997). What is ecosystem management? *Journal of Forestry, 95*(4), p. 44.

Western, D. (1993). Defining ecotourism. In K. Lindberg & D. Hawkins (Eds.), *Ecotourism: A guide for planners and managers* (pp. 7-11)., North Bennington, VT: The Ecotourism Society.

Wiedner, D., & Kerlinger, P. (1990). Economics of birdwatching: A national survey of active birders. *American Birds*, 44, 209-213.

Wilson, W. J. (1980). *The declining significance of race*. Chicago and London: The University of Chicago Press.

Wilson, W. J. (1987). *The truly disadvantaged*. Chicago: The University of Chicago Press.

Winter, P. L. (1995). *Visitor research case study: The Redding Resource Area final report*. Unpublished report supplied by the author.

Winter, P. L. (1996). *Environmental concern and environmental action: How do recreationists fare?* The Sixth International Symposium on Society and Resource Management: Social Behavior, Natural Resources, and the Environment, Pennsylvania State University, University Park Pennsylvania.

Winter, P. L. (1996). *San Gorgonio Wilderness visitor survey, summer and fall, 1994*. Unpublished report supplied by the author.

Woo, C. J. 1996. Asian immigrants: Attitude and behavior toward natural resources. In *The Sixth International Symposium on Society and Resource Management: Social Behavior, Natural Resources, and the Environment* (May 18-23, 1996). University Park: The Pennsylvania State University.

Woods & Poole Economics, Inc. (1997). 1997 Complete Economic and Demographic Data Source (CEDDS) on CD-Rom Technical Documentation. Washington, DC: Woods & Poole Economics, Inc.

CHAPTER VI

PROJECTIONS OF OUTDOOR RECREATION PARTICIPATION TO 2050

. . . .

J. M. Bowker[1]
Donald B. K. English
H. Ken Cordell

Acknowledgments:
The authors acknowledge the valuable suggestions of Dr. David Newman and Dr. Christopher McIntosh. The authors also thank Dr. Gajanan Bhat and Jo Anne Norris for technical assistance.

INTRODUCTION

Outdoor recreation in various forms has been and continues to be an important component of Americans' lives. Chapter V focused on the present situation, based primarily on descriptive findings from the National Survey on Recreation and the Environment (NSRE) (Cordell, McDonald, Lewis, Miles, Martin, & Bason, 1996). In addition, where possible, long-term trends in recreation participation were assessed by comparing NSRE findings with those of national recreation surveys dating back to 1960.

The intent of this chapter is to project future outdoor recreation participation and consumption, in days and trips, well into the next century as mandated by the Renewable Resources Planning Act (RPA). The chapter begins with a brief description of the data and methods used. Next, we report indexed projections of future recreation participation (by millions of participants aged 16 and over) and consumption (by millions of days annually and by millions of primary purpose trips taken) across the four assessment regions (see Figure II.1 in Chapter II) at 10-year intervals beginning in 2000 and ending in 2050. For convenience, we place projections for specific activities in the following groups: winter, water, wildlife, dispersed land, and developed land. Finally, we discuss some important findings, implications, and limitations of the analysis.

METHODS AND DATA

For projections, we developed two types of regional cross-sectional models. The first is a logistic regression model similar to those frequently used in recreation, economics, political science, and various other fields where individuals provide yes or no responses to behavioral questions (Greene, 1995). In this application, we used the model to estimate the probability that an individual will participate in a given recreation activity based on the individual's characteristics and the recreation opportunities near the individual's primary resi-

---

[1] J. M. Bowker and D. B. K. English are both research social scientists and H. Ken Cordell is a regional forester and project leader, USDA Forest Service, Athens, GA.

dence. We obtained a separate model for each activity across each of the four assessment regions. Model results were then combined with population information to obtain estimates of the total number of participants in an activity per region. These results were then indexed on the 1995 base year. A number of previous RPA studies have used logistic regression models to estimate activity participation including those by Hof & Kaiser (1983) and Walsh, Jon, McKean, and Hof (1992). In both of these studies, national rather than regional models were constructed.

The second type of model used in this analysis is a negative binomial form of a count data model. We used this model to measure consumption levels through reported days and reported primary purpose trips. This type of model is very popular in recreation and labor market research (Greene, 1995). It is designed to take into account the quantitative aspect of trip–taking behavior—i.e., the fact that people spend a countable number of days or trips per year participating in recreation activities. Here we used the model to estimate annual days an individual will spend in a given outdoor recreation activity and the number of annual trips an individual will take for the primary reason of participating in a selected activity. As with the logistic regression participation models, we combined the results of our models with population estimates to project the number of primary purpose trips for a given activity originating in each assessment region and the number of days participants from a given region would be involved in any given activity. We report these estimates in indexed form relative to the base year. A more detailed explanation of both logistic and negative binomial regression models is provided by Greene (1993).

To develop projections of future recreation activity, we created a structure based on today's behavior. We created models to explain today's behavior in terms of measurable factors. If the structure of today's behavior is a good indicator of future behavior, the models can be used to estimate future recreation participation, days, and trips by activity and region. While this assumption is not always accurate, it is a reasonable alternative when adequate cross-sectional time-series data are unavailable.

Recreation research shows that demographic factors such as age, age squared, race or ethnicity, sex, wealth or income, education, and previous experience influence recreation behavior (Hof & Kaiser, 1983; Walsh, Jon, McKean, & Hof, 1992; Cordell, Bergstrom, Hartman, & English, 1990). In Table VI.1, we provide indexed projections of demographic variables used in this analysis. These projections are based on U.S. Census estimates of population (Day, 1996) and macroeconomic estimates from the USDA Economic Research Service (Torgerson, 1996).

Table VI.1: Indexed Explanatory Variable Projections for Regional Model RPA Forecasts[1]

VARIABLE	YEAR						
	1995	2000	2010	2020	2030	2040	2050
Age	1	1.02	1.056	1.089	1.114	1.126	1.126
Age-squared	1	1.033	1.07	1.103	1.128	1.141	1.141
Real Income	1	1.067	1.209	1.357	1.515	1.691	1.888
Percent White	1	0.989	0.97	0.952	0.935	0.917	0.901
Percent Male	1	1.002	1.002	1.002	1.004	1.004	1.006
Population North	1	1.013	1.064	1.138	1.197	1.241	1.304
Population South	1	1.062	1.168	1.271	1.371	1.461	1.534
Population Rocky Mtn	1	1.064	1.17	1.272	1.369	1.457	1.53
Population Pacific	1	1.077	1.207	1.318	1.425	1.527	1.604
Population Nation	1	1.042	1.126	1.217	1.299	1.4	1.439

[1] Ref: Census publication p25-1130 (1996) and USDA-ERS mimeo (Torgerson, 1996).

The biggest changes expected to take place in factors influencing recreation behavior over the next half-century relate to increases in population and real income. Using the mid-level growth scenario from the U.S. Census, population increases in the continental United States through 2050 will range from a low of 30 percent in the North to a high of 60 percent along the Pacific Coast. Average income, after accounting for inflation, is expected to grow 88 percent over the same time period. This projection makes no attempt to identify changes in the distribution of income, which may have a profound influence on recreation behavior. Population, age, and sex ratio are expected to change relatively little, while percentage of whites in the population should decline somewhat as other racial groups grow at faster rates.

It has also been established that supply factors such as proximity and availability of recreation resources are important in determining whether and to what degree individuals recreate (Walsh, Jon, McKean, & Hof, 1992). Previous research has shown that the amount of outdoor recreation settings or opportunities available to an individual will affect the individual's choice and intensity of participation in given activities (Walsh, Jon, McKean, & Hof, 1992). For example, whether an individual skis and how often that individual skis can in part be explained by the proximity of skiing opportunities. Likewise, most dispersed outdoor recreation activities, such as viewing wildlife, require access to wildlife habitat on private and public forests, ranges, and wetlands. However, the supply of this habitat is finite. Thus, as population and participation in activities requiring its availability increase, relative scarcity of the habitat increases. Because there are no readily available and reliable measures of future land and water availability, we followed convention and assumed a fixed amount of habitat for the various outdoor recreation activities modeled herein.

Past efforts at predicting recreation participation have used fairly general resource availability measures (Cordell, Bergstrom, Hartmann, & English, 1990; Walsh, Jon, McKean, & Hof, 1992). The resource variables that are included in our availability measure are described briefly in Table VI.2. This set of resource variables covers the primary resource base for all of the recreation activities for which projections are made. For any given location, the availability measure for each of these variables equaled the sum of all acres within a 200-mile straight-line radius, divided by the total population within that area. The 200-mile limit has been observed to approximate the maximum market area for many types of recreation (Cordell, Bergstrom, Hartman, & English, 1990). By adjusting for population, we accounted for relative increases in the scarcity of recreation opportunities that occur with population increases from any combination of congestion, reduction in quality, loss of access, and physical conversion due to development.

Table VI.2: Resource Recreation Variables Used in Projection Models[2]

RUNWATER = acres of running water area including river, stream, or any running water.
FLATWATER = acres of standing water which includes lakes, ponds, and reservoirs.
BAYEST = acres of bay area and estuary area.
WILDALL = acres of federally designated wilderness area.
NONWILDAC = acres of federally-owned nonwilderness area including rangeland.
NRIFOR = acres of nonfederal land with forest cover.
NRIWETL = acres of nonfederal wetland area.
PVTAGAC = acres of nonfederal agricultural land including rangeland.
SPACRES = acres of State Park area.
DSKIACRE = acres of downhill ski slopes.
SNOWFOR = acres of forests covered with snow during winter season.
SNOWMTN = acres of mountains covered with snow during winter season.
SNOWAG = acres of agricultural land covered with snow during winter season.
BLYMTN = acres of mountains classified under Bailey's ecological classification.
CGSITES = number of developed camp-sites.
PUBFOR = WILDALL+ NONWILDAC + SPACRES.
SUMWATER = RUNWATER+FLATWATER.
SUMSNOW = DSKIACRE+SNOWAG+SNOWFOR.
FLATBAY = FLATWATER+BAYEST.
ALWATER = SUMWATER+FLATBAY
ALFRAGWT= PUBFOR + PVTAGAC+NRIFOR+NRIWETL
[2] All units are represented as the physical quantity within a 200-mile radius of the individual's origin divided by the population within the area defined by the same radius. Ref: Norsis Data Base (1997) USDA Forest Service, Athens, GA

RESULTS

Indexed values for recreation activity participation, annual days, and annual trips are presented in this section. The indexes represent changes from the 1995 baseline totals for millions of participants, millions of days, and millions of trips at 10-year intervals to the year 2050. Activity groupings include: winter, water, wildlife, dispersed land, and developed land. Indexed projections are reported by activity and assessment region as well as for the nation.

Model parameter estimates for all activities and regions and their asymptotic standard errors are available from the author.[3] Common to all models are the explanatory variables age (age in years of respondent), age squared, income (household annual pretax income), race (white or nonwhite), sex (male or female), and population density of the respondent's county. The latter variable serves as a continuous proxy for rural/nonrural variables commonly encountered in recreation demand models. In addition, each model contains up to two supply-type variables as listed in Table VI.2. Means by region for these explanatory variables are available from the author.

Projections for explanatory variables follow the indexes reported in Table VI.1. For example, mean income in any given region increases by 88 percent over the 55-year simulation time horizon, while the percent of whites decreases by about 10 percent over the same time frame. Population density increases in proportion to population growth, while relevant supply is discounted by population growth for any region. Projected changes in the explanatory variables are then combined at 10-year intervals with the static parameter estimates (available from the author) to arrive at the projections reported in this section.

Winter Activities

Three winter-based activities, cross-country skiing, downhill skiing, and snowmobiling were modeled by the methods described above. Model parameter estimates are available from the author.

Cross-Country Skiing

Nationally, participation in cross-country skiing is expected to increase by 95 percent by the year 2050 (Table VI.3). The Rocky Mountain region will have the biggest increase at approximately 144 percent. A considerable decrease in the number of participants in this activity is projected for the South, however this will have little effect on the national projection because of the small number of Southerners currently participating in this sport.

Table VI.3. Baseline Estimates in Millions and Projected Indexes of Change in Days, Trips, and Participants for Cross-Country Skiing, by Region and Decade 1995-2050

					Projection Index			
Unit	**Region**	1995	2000	2010	2020	2030	2040	2050
Cross Country Skiing								
Days	North	35.70	0.92	0.90	0.91	0.93	0.98	1.10
	South	1.40	0.89	0.66	0.49	0.39	0.34	0.32
	Rocky Mountain	4.20	1.08	1.44	1.89	2.42	2.92	3.42
	Pacific	7.80	0.99	0.96	0.93	0.89	0.85	0.81
	National	49.00	0.94	0.94	0.96	1.00	1.06	1.18
Trips	North	23.90	1.02	1.06	1.13	1.22	1.33	1.49
	South	0.70	1.08	0.66	0.55	0.46	0.48	0.29
	Rocky Mountain	3.30	1.09	1.45	1.93	2.48	2.64	3.57
	Pacific	5.90	1.03	1.00	0.97	0.96	1.02	0.97
	National	33.50	1.02	1.05	1.12	1.21	1.30	1.44

[3]Appendix tables and technical information are available upon request from the USDA Forest Service, Outdoor Recreation, 320 Green St., Athens, GA 30602-2044. Technical appendices herein shall be abbreviated to TAs.

Table VI.3 Cont.

Unit	Region	1995	Projection Index 2000	2010	2020	2030	2040	2050
Cross Country Skiing								
Participation	North	4.40	1.03	1.15	1.23	1.49	1.67	1.91
	South	0.40	0.91	0.77	0.66	0.59	0.54	0.52
	Rocky Mountain	0.70	1.07	1.31	1.41	1.88	2.16	2.44
	Pacific	1.10	1.06	1.23	1.33	1.57	1.74	1.90
	National	6.50	1.04	1.18	1.26	1.54	1.73	1.95

Activity days of cross-country skiing are estimated to increase by 18 percent over the next half century. Unlike participation, the estimated increase in days is less than the rate of growth of the population in general. However, the projected increase in the Rocky Mountain region is 242 percent, which is far greater than the 53 percent population growth projected for that region. Primary-purpose trips follow a pattern between participation and activity days. The national increase closely follows national population growth. Very large growth is projected in the Rocky Mountain region and growth greater than that of the population is projected in the North. The South and Pacific Coast regions will have sharp and moderate decreases, respectively, in primary-purpose trips for cross-country skiing. However, there are few significant parameter estimates for cross-country skiing models for these two regions. This result is not surprising given the small percentage of people in these regions partaking of this sport. Hence, the index projections for the South and Pacific Coast regions should be viewed cautiously.

Downhill Skiing

As reported in Chapter V, downhill skiing annually accounts for the most days (126.5 million) and primary-purpose trips (78.9 million) of all the major winter sports. Projections of days, trips, and participants are reported in Table VI.4. Following trends of recent years, participation in downhill skiing is expected to increase by 93 percent nationally over the next half century. Regional percentage increases in participants range from 82 percent in the North to 111 percent in the Pacific Coast region. Because the North currently accounts for as many skiers as all other regions combined, the North will continue to account for far and away the most participants in this sport.

Table VI.4: Baseline Estimates and Projected Indexes of Change in Days, Trips, and Participants for Downhill Skiing, by Region and Decade, 1995-2050

Unit	Region	1995	Projection Index 2000	2010	2020	2030	2040	2050
Downhill Skiing								
Days	North	67.20	1.00	1.09	1.21	1.36	1.55	1.86
	South	13.00	1.07	1.36	1.47	1.78	2.22	2.90
	Rocky Mountain	14.90	1.01	1.16	1.14	1.25	1.42	1.67
	Pacific	31.50	1.06	1.36	1.46	1.70	2.00	2.35
	National	126.50	1.03	1.22	1.31	1.51	1.75	2.10
Trips	North	40.90	1.03	1.12	1.28	1.48	1.53	2.15
	South	6.10	1.04	1.11	1.21	1.36	1.58	1.94
	Rocky Mountain	10.70	1.03	1.07	1.15	1.27	1.44	1.70
	Pacific	21.40	1.09	1.29	1.53	1.81	2.13	2.48
	National	78.90	1.06	1.18	1.36	1.58	1.85	2.22
Participation	North	8.40	1.00	1.09	1.16	1.36	1.54	1.82
	South	3.10	1.03	1.14	1.26	1.43	1.67	2.01
	Rocky Mountain	1.70	1.04	1.14	1.15	1.29	1.58	1.84
	Pacific	3.60	1.06	1.21	1.31	1.55	1.80	2.11
	National	16.80	1.03	1.13	1.22	1.43	1.63	1.93

Downhill skiing days for the nation, as well as for residents of each of the four assessment regions, are expected to increase much more than the general increase in population. The national increase in annual skiing days is expected to be about 110 percent, or an increase from 126.5 million in 1995 to over 265 million days annually by 2050. While the biggest proportional increase will come from the Rocky Mountain region, residents of the North will account for the most annual skiing days at about 125 million by the year 2050.

Trips by Americans for the primary-purpose of downhill skiing will also continue to increase faster than population growth. Nationally, an increase of 122 percent is expected by 2050. As with participation and days, each assessment region shows an increase, with the greatest increase expected in the Pacific Coast, 148 percent, followed by the North at 115 percent. A major factor accounting for the increase in downhill skiing appears to be the strong positive relationship to personal income and the rather large expected increase in real personal income over the next 55 years (see Table VI.1).

Snowmobiling

Snowmobiling is the last of the winter sports examined in this chapter. Snowmobiling is the second most popular major winter sport, accounting for approximately 65.8 million days and 38.6 million primary-purpose trips in 1995. Like the other winter sports, the North and Rocky Mountain regions are responsible for over 85 percent of the participants in this activity.

Indexed projections for snowmobiling are presented in Table VI.5. Nationally, forecasted increases in this activity equal or exceed the rate of population growth, but the increases in participants for the principal snowmobiling regions, the North and Rocky Mountain, are below projected population growth.

Table VI.5: Baseline Estimates and Projected Indexes of Change in Days, Trips, and Participants for Snowmobiling by Region and Decade, 1995-2050

			Projection Index					
Unit	**Region**	1995	2000	2010	2020	2030	2040	2050
Snowmobiling								
Days	North	51.10	1.00	1.18	1.42	1.68	1.92	2.21
	South	2.30	1.04	1.13	1.22	1.37	1.61	1.98
	Rocky Mountain	6.70	0.49	1.06	1.02	1.08	1.15	1.28
	Pacific	5.40	1.02	1.36	1.77	2.20	2.54	2.82
	National	65.80	1.00	1.14	1.32	1.53	1.74	1.99
Trips	North	28.10	1.00	1.15	1.34	1.54	1.75	2.06
	South	1.20	1.07	1.17	1.31	1.52	1.84	2.36
	Rocky Mountain	4.30	1.04	1.11	1.23	1.37	1.54	1.76
	Pacific	4.90	1.16	1.58	2.31	3.21	3.47	4.86
	National	38.60	1.02	1.16	1.35	1.56	1.77	2.10
Participation	North	4.90	0.98	1.00	1.05	1.08	1.13	1.22
	South	0.80	1.03	1.13	1.25	1.40	1.58	1.82
	Rocky Mountain	0.80	1.02	1.06	1.10	1.16	1.25	1.36
	Pacific	0.70	1.09	1.42	1.54	2.33	2.91	3.60
	National	7.10	1.00	1.04	1.09	1.18	1.27	1.40

Like downhill skiing, days and primary-purpose trips for snowmobiling are expected to increase in all regions by substantial amounts. As with the other major winter sports, however, results for the South and Pacific Coast regions should be viewed with some caution, because the statistical performance of the projection models for these regions is poor. Nevertheless, there appears to be strong evidence to support the notion that as long as real increases in household income continue, participation and intensity of participation will continue to make snowmobiling an increasingly popular winter recreation activity.

Overall, the three major outdoor winter recreation pursuits discussed in this section—cross-country skiing, downhill skiing, and snowmobiling—are projected to see increased participants and increased participation intensity over the next 52 years. In most cases, the rates of increase in participation, days, and primary-purpose trips will exceed those for population. Growth in income appears to be the factor most responsible for the projected increases. It is expected to offset both reductions in per-capita supply of opportunities due to increased population, and increasing proportions of nonwhites in the general population who are currently less likely to participate in winter sports.

Water-based Activities

The water-based activities for which indexed projections of participants, days, and trips are reported include canoeing, motorboating, nonpool swimming, and rafting. With the exception of pool swimming, these are the most popular of the water-based outdoor recreation activities, accounting for about 2,093 million activity days and 1,429 million primary-purpose trips annually. In addition, we include the more generic activity of visiting a beach or waterside, which is paramount to participating in any of the more specific activities listed. This activity is currently undertaken by over 124 million people each year in 1,667 million primary-purpose trips and 3,188 million activity days. Indexed projections for the water-based activities are reported below.

Canoeing

Nationally, participation in canoeing is projected to increase slightly more than population growth over the next 55 years, with the largest percentage increase in the Pacific Coast region. However, the North and the South will continue to account for the majority of canoeing given the current large numbers of participants in those regions (Table VI.6).

Table VI.6: Baseline Estimates and Projected Indexes of Change in Days, Trips, and Participants for Canoeing by Region and Decade 1995-2050

			Projection Index					
Unit Canoeing	Region	1995	2000	2010	2020	2030	2040	2050
Days	North	44.70	1.00	1.14	1.33	1.51	1.64	1.78
	South	17.60	1.04	1.09	1.13	1.21	1.35	1.57
	Rocky Mountain	2.90	1.04	1.14	1.25	1.36	1.47	1.59
	Pacific	9.70	1.08	1.18	1.29	1.42	1.59	1.80
	National	74.60	1.02	1.14	1.28	1.43	1.57	1.73
Trips	North	25.50	0.98	0.93	0.90	0.89	0.89	0.90
	South	14.20	1.02	1.07	1.12	1.18	1.25	1.36
	Rocky Mountain	2.10	1.07	1.12	1.20	1.29	1.37	1.52
	Pacific	7.60	1.11	1.15	1.24	1.33	1.41	1.41
	National	49.30	1.02	1.07	1.14	1.22	1.29	1.29
Participation	North	8.00	1.00	1.06	1.13	1.24	1.33	1.48
	South	4.20	1.03	1.07	1.11	1.16	1.23	1.34
	Rocky Mountain	0.70	1.03	1.11	1.20	1.25	1.32	1.39
	Pacific	1.20	1.06	1.21	1.30	1.51	1.69	1.89
	National	14.10	1.02	1.08	1.15	1.24	1.33	1.46

The number of days spent canoeing is expected to increase about 30 percent more than the population growth through the year 2050. The biggest increases, on the order of 80 percent, will be in the North and Pacific Coast regions. Currently, over half of the canoeing days nationally originate in the North, and this proportion should continue if not increase over the next half century.

Nationally, the number of primary-purpose canoeing trips is projected to increase by 29 percent over the same time period. Oddly, the number of trips by Northern residents is expected to decline by about 10 percent, while the number of days increases. These changes could mean that trips will be of longer duration or that canoeing will be done as a complementary or secondary activity within a multipurpose trip.

Motorboating

Motorboating currently is the most popular recreational boating activity with 47 million participants nationally, more than tripling its nearest competition. Projected changes in motorboating participation, days, and primary-purpose trips are reported in Table VI.7.

Table VI.7: Baseline Estimates and Projected Indexes of Change in Days, Trips, and Participants for Motorboating, by Region and Decade, 1995-2050

Unit Motorboating	Region	1995	Projection Index 2000	2010	2020	2030	2040	2050
Days	North	292.30	1.00	1.03	1.07	1.11	1.15	1.20
	South	294.00	0.99	1.00	1.02	1.05	1.10	1.16
	Rocky Mountain	31.10	1.06	1.19	1.34	1.50	1.68	1.90
	Pacific	82.20	1.11	1.38	1.69	2.06	2.52	3.09
	National	699.90	1.01	1.07	1.14	1.23	1.32	1.45
Trips	North	208.50	1.02	0.99	1.01	1.04	1.06	1.06
	South	190.10	1.04	1.07	1.15	1.23	1.31	1.42
	Rocky Mountain	24.20	1.08	1.21	1.37	1.55	1.64	2.02
	Pacific	58.90	1.14	1.35	1.63	1.98	2.40	2.94
	National	480.40	1.05	1.08	1.16	1.26	1.36	1.48
Participation	North	22.00	1.01	1.06	1.13	1.21	1.29	1.40
	South	15.50	1.04	1.13	1.24	1.33	1.45	1.59
	Rocky Mountain	3.20	1.06	1.17	1.26	1.40	1.54	1.70
	Pacific	6.30	1.07	1.22	1.32	1.52	1.69	1.88
	National	47.00	1.03	1.11	1.21	1.31	1.42	1.55

Nationally, participation, days, and trips are projected to increase slightly more than population growth up to 2050. The rate of increase in trips is expected to be greatest in the Pacific and Rocky Mountain regions at more than 194 percent and 102 percent, respectively. Likewise, these regions will account for the biggest rates of increase in activity days devoted to motorboating. However, because of the current popularity of the sport in the North and South, even a moderate increase like that reported in Table VI.7 will mean that the preponderance of motorboating activity will continue to be generated by people of the North and South.

Nonpool Swimming

Nonpool swimming is and will continue to be the single most popular water-based recreation activity taking place in natural settings, but the rate of growth in this activity will be more modest than motorboating. As reported in Table VI.8, participation and annual days of nonpool swimming should mostly keep pace with population growth, while primary-purpose trips for nonpool swimming should lag somewhat behind population growth, increasing only 25 percent out to 2050.

Examination of the model parameter estimates indicates that perhaps the biggest single factor slowing the growth of nonpool swimming is the importance of race in the model and the declining proportion of whites in the population expected over the next half century.

Table VI.8: Baseline Estimates and Projected Indexes of Change in Days, Trips, and Participants for Nonpool Swimming, by Region and Decade, 1995-2050

Unit	Region	1995	Projection Index 2000	2010	2020	2030	2040	2050
Nonpool Swimming								
Days	North	578.60	1.00	1.05	1.12	1.19	1.26	1.37
	South	410.90	0.96	1.02	1.08	1.15	1.24	1.35
	Rocky Mountain	56.10	1.04	1.12	1.20	1.29	1.41	1.57
	Pacific	196.60	1.06	1.15	1.23	1.31	1.43	1.56
	National	1241.40	1.00	1.05	1.12	1.20	1.28	1.40
Trips	North	385.40	1.00	1.01	1.06	1.11	1.15	1.22
	South	268.50	1.00	1.01	1.04	1.08	1.11	1.14
	Rocky Mountain	37.80	1.03	1.11	1.20	1.30	1.41	1.54
	Pacific	147.20	1.07	1.15	1.22	1.30	1.40	1.50
	National	837.90	1.01	1.04	1.09	1.14	1.19	1.25
Participation	North	38.40	1.01	1.08	1.16	1.28	1.37	1.51
	South	23.30	1.05	1.15	1.27	1.37	1.50	1.64
	Rocky Mountain	4.80	1.04	1.14	1.24	1.35	1.47	1.60
	Pacific	11.60	1.06	1.19	1.29	1.43	1.57	1.72
	National	78.10	1.03	1.12	1.21	1.33	1.45	1.58

Table VI.9: Baseline Estimates and Projected Indexes of Change in Days, Trips, and Participants for Rafting/Floating, by Region and Decade, 1995-2050

Unit	Region	1995	Projection Index 2000	2010	2020	2030	2040	2050
Rafting/Floating								
Days	North	35.00	0.99	1.02	1.08	1.16	1.26	1.43
	South	24.20	1.00	1.01	1.03	1.06	1.12	1.21
	Rocky Mountain	6.70	1.06	1.11	1.17	1.26	1.41	1.64
	Pacific	11.40	1.06	1.27	1.51	1.75	1.97	2.16
	National	77.30	1.01	1.08	1.17	1.27	1.39	1.55
Trips	North	27.50	0.97	0.90	0.88	0.86	0.86	0.80
	South	19.90	1.00	1.05	1.11	1.19	1.27	1.38
	Rocky Mountain	5.30	1.06	1.17	1.32	1.52	1.79	2.17
	Pacific	8.70	1.07	1.27	1.49	1.71	1.82	2.04
	National	61.50	1.01	1.03	1.10	1.17	1.23	1.30
Participation	North	6.90	0.97	0.94	1.01	0.93	0.94	1.00
	South	4.90	1.01	1.01	1.02	1.04	1.09	1.18
	Rocky Mountain	1.10	1.04	1.10	1.19	1.24	1.36	1.52
	Pacific	2.30	1.05	1.20	1.30	1.52	1.73	1.97

For decades recreationists have combed the beaches of Fire Island National Seashore, located along the New York City coastline. Of the coastline surrounding the city, only Fire Island remains relatively wild, roadless, and isolated. Photo courtesy of USDI National Park Service. Photo by Richard Frear.

Rafting

Rafting and floating projections are reported in Table VI.9. Nationally, the number of annual days spent rafting should increase about 10 percent faster than the population. The number of participants and primary-purpose trips, while increasing, will fall short of increases in population, indicating that fewer primary-purpose trips will be taken per capita and that the proportion of people rafting and floating will diminish somewhat.

These results are somewhat contrary to an apparent dramatic increase in this sport in recent years and may suggest a leveling after recent rapid growth. Nevertheless, fairly sizable increases are expected in the Rocky Mountain and Pacific Coast regions.

Visiting Beaches and Watersides

The final activity in the water-based section is visiting a beach or waterside. This activity is extremely popular and an essential ingredient for partaking of other activities in this section. Currently, an estimated 124.4 million people above the age of 16 report at least one visit annually to a beach or waterside. Moreover, this participation led to approximately 3,187.9 million days and 1,667.1 million primary-purpose trips in 1995. Not surprisingly, highest per-capita day and trip numbers are from the Pacific Coast region, but the North and South regions are fairly close behind and, because of greater populations, account for the majority of days and trips to a beach or waterside.

Indexed projections for beach and waterside participation, days, and trips are reported in Table VI.10. Nationally, participation is expected to outstrip population increases to 2050, and all regions will experience increases in participation at rates faster than population growth. Interestingly, by 2050 over 75 percent of the population 16 and over will make at least one visit per year to recreate at a beach or waterside.

Table VI.10: Baseline Estimates and Projected Indexes of Change in Days, Trips, and Participants for Visiting a Beach or Waterside, by Region and Decade, 1995-2050

			Projection Index					
Unit	**Region**	1995	2000	2010	2020	2030	2040	2050
Visiting a Beach or Waterside								
Days	North	1319.70	1.01	1.07	1.15	1.22	1.28	1.36
	South	1037.50	1.05	1.16	1.28	1.41	1.55	1.69
	Rocky Mountain	128.00	1.06	1.17	1.29	1.42	1.54	1.67
	Pacific	706.20	1.08	1.24	1.39	1.55	1.73	1.92
	National	3187.90	1.03	1.10	1.17	1.25	1.47	1.59
Trips	North	673.50	1.00	1.01	1.05	1.08	1.11	1.17
	South	536.80	1.05	1.11	1.18	1.27	1.33	1.44
	Rocky Mountain	80.00	1.06	1.23	1.40	1.58	1.68	1.96
	Pacific	382.10	1.08	1.22	1.35	1.49	1.59	1.80
	National	1667.10	1.03	1.10	1.17	1.25	1.31	1.42
Participation	North	57.70	1.01	1.09	1.17	1.28	1.35	1.45
	South	37.70	1.07	1.20	1.30	1.48	1.62	1.76
	Rocky Mountain	8.30	1.07	1.20	1.30	1.48	1.62	1.75
	Pacific	20.70	1.08	1.21	1.33	1.46	1.60	1.72
	National	124.40	1.05	1.15	1.24	1.38	1.49	1.61

Days and primary-purpose trips to beaches or watersides will also increase faster than population growth, with the exception of trips originating in the North. The biggest relative increase in days, 92 percent, will be in the Pacific Coast. The largest relative increase in primary-purpose trips will be 96 percent in the Rocky Mountain region.

Overall, the four major water recreation pursuits discussed in this section—canoeing, motorboating, nonpool swimming, and rafting—will experience an increase in the number of participants and an increase in participation intensity over the next 55 years. In most cases, the increase in participation, days, and primary-purpose trips will proceed at about the rate of population growth. Rafting will experience overall national growth but a slight decline in per capita participation in the populous North and South. Motorboating and nonpool swimming will remain the most popular water sports. The biggest relative increase in days of participation will occur in canoeing. Primary-purpose trips will, in general, lag population growth. Combined with increases in participation and days, this may indicate a trend to more multipurpose trips or a tendency toward longer trips.

Growth in income appears to be the factor most responsible for the projected increases in water recreation. Sex is also an important factor, but has little effect on projections because of the long-term stability of the sex ratio in the population. Growth is buffered by decreasing relative availability of water recreation venues and the increase of nonwhite members of the population who, in terms of current behavior, appear to prefer alternative outlets for recreation.

Wildlife-related Activities

In this section, we combine a number of smaller categories of wildlife-related recreation into three main groups—fishing, hunting, and nonconsumptive wildlife activity. Fishing and hunting are traditional consumptive forms of wildlife recreation, although an increasing number of people are participating in catch and release fishing. Nonconsumptive wildlife activity includes various forms of wildlife viewing such as birdwatching and wildlife photography.

Fishing

Fishing as a general category includes warm and cold freshwater species, saltwater and anadromous species, and catch-release fishing. Ice fishing, with about a two-percent participation rate nationally, was not included as day and trip data were unavailable in the NSRE. Nationally, participation in fishing is expected to increase 36 percent over the next 52 years, marginally less than projected population growth of 44 percent

(Table VI.11). The Rocky Mountain region will see the biggest relative increase in fishing, 57 percent, while the North will see the slowest growth in participation at 27 percent. The North and South will remain responsible for generating most of the fishing activity because of their large populations and high proportions of individuals participating in fishing (30 percent). Per-capita participation in fishing is projected to remain constant in all regions except the Pacific Coast, where a decline of 3.5 percent is forecast. Overall participation for those 16 and older is expected to grow from about 57.9 million today to about 79 million in 2050.

Table VI.11: Baseline Estimates and Projected Indexes of Change in Days, Trips, and Participants for Fishing, by Region and Decade, 1995-2050

Unit Fishing	Region	1995	Projection Index 2000	2010	2020	2030	2040	2050
Days	North	451.00	1.00	1.05	1.11	1.15	1.16	1.15
	South	491.50	1.02	1.11	1.19	1.26	1.29	1.29
	Rocky Mountain	76.00	1.05	1.16	1.28	1.40	1.50	1.59
	Pacific	119.10	1.05	1.16	1.25	1.33	1.40	1.44
	National	1135.40	1.02	1.09	1.17	1.23	1.26	1.27
Trips	North	367.50	0.99	0.99	1.01	1.01	0.97	0.95
	South	395.00	1.01	1.03	1.06	1.08	1.07	1.04
	Rocky Mountain	61.40	1.08	1.14	1.23	1.32	1.39	1.46
	Pacific	98.50	1.09	1.10	1.15	1.89	1.27	1.22
	National	919.50	1.03	1.05	1.10	1.12	1.14	1.13
Participation	North	25.60	1.00	1.05	1.12	1.17	1.21	1.27
	South	20.20	1.04	1.11	1.19	1.24	1.31	1.38
	Rocky Mountain	4.60	1.05	1.16	1.26	1.38	1.48	1.57
	Pacific	7.50	1.05	1.12	1.20	1.23	1.30	1.38
	National	57.90	1.03	1.09	1.17	1.23	1.29	1.36

Days of fishing should increase by about 27 percent nationally from an estimated current level of 1,135.4 million to about 1,442 million by the year 2050. The largest relative increase will be in the Rocky Mountain region at 59 percent, but the North and South will continue to account for upwards of 70 percent of all fishing days.

As with a number of other outdoor recreation pursuits, trips for the primary-purpose of fishing will not grow as fast as either participants or days. Nationally, the growth in fishing trips is estimated at about 13 percent over the next 52 years. In fact, in the North a decline of five percent over the same time period is forecast. Again, coupled with the increase in days, this could mean that fishing complements other activities on multipurpose trips or that trip lengths will be increasing.

Fishing model parameter estimates for participants, days, and trips indicate a strong negative relationship between fishing and population density, suggesting a decline in the activity as urbanization continues. Also, unlike winter and other water-based recreation, race does not affect participation very much, indicating the multiracial nature of this sport. Perhaps most important is the negative effect of income on many of the fishing models. The projected 88-percent increase in real income over the next 52 years has a strong negative influence on fishing activity.

Hunting

In this section, big game, small game, and migratory bird hunting are combined into a general hunting category. Hunting appears to be in a decline in popularity for those 16 and older. Nationally, it is projected that the next 52 years will see a reduction in the number of hunting participants by 11 percent, from today's level of nearly 19 million to about 16.5 million (Table VI.12). As a proportion of the general population, the decline is more apparent. The Rocky Mountain region will experience an increase in hunters of about 20 percent while the number of hunters in the North will remain constant. Participation will decline by about 35 percent in the Pacific Coast and South regions.

Table VI.12: Baseline Estimates and Projected Indexes of Change in Days, Trips, and Participants for Hunting, by Region and Decade, 1995-2050

Unit Hunting	Region	1995	Projection Index 2000	2010	2020	2030	2040	2050
Days	North	193.70	0.98	1.01	1.05	1.09	1.10	1.12
	South	150.90	0.92	0.89	0.86	0.82	0.76	0.70
	Rocky Mountain	34.50	1.00	1.05	1.10	1.15	1.18	1.22
	Pacific	36.00	0.94	0.95	0.96	0.95	0.88	0.81
	National	416.30	0.96	0.97	0.99	1.00	0.99	0.98
Trips	North	140.40	1.01	1.04	1.10	1.16	1.18	1.22
	South	112.40	1.02	0.92	0.91	0.88	0.83	0.78
	Rocky Mountain	26.60	1.09	1.06	1.12	1.19	1.26	1.35
	Pacific	26.00	1.05	0.86	0.82	0.77	0.69	0.62
	National	305.50	1.02	0.99	1.03	1.05	1.05	1.06
Participation	North	8.40	0.98	0.97	0.98	0.98	0.98	0.99
	South	6.50	0.93	0.82	0.74	0.68	0.65	0.64
	Rocky Mountain	2.00	1.01	1.05	1.12	1.22	1.16	1.20
	Pacific	1.70	0.94	0.85	0.79	0.73	0.67	0.64
	National	18.60	0.97	0.93	0.91	0.89	0.88	0.89

Hunting days should remain stable over the next half century in spite of the decline in participants. North and Rocky Mountain regions are projected to generate increases of 12 and 22 percent, while the South and Pacific Coast region will produce 30 and 19 percent fewer hunting days, respectively.

Primary-purpose trips for hunting are expected to increase slightly, 6 percent nationally, through 2050. As with days, the North and the Rocky Mountain region will generate increases in hunting trips of 22 and 35 percent, respectively. The increase in trips relative to days could signal that trip duration may shorten somewhat. The South will see a decline of 22 percent, while the Pacific Coast could see a reduction of 38 percent.

Hunting model parameter estimates suggest that the factors most closely related to hunting behavior are sex, race, and population density. While the percent of males in the population will remain stable, the increase in nonwhites will cause a decline in the sport. More importantly, the increase in population density will decrease the number of people living rural lifestyles and reduce available hunting venues. As a result, numbers of participants will decline in all regions except the Rocky Mountain region. Hunting days and hunting trips should increase for the North and Rocky Mountain regions, while decreasing in the South and Pacific Coast regions.

Nonconsumptive Wildlife Activities

This class of activities includes birdwatching, photography, and other forms of wildlife viewing. It claims upward of 116.7 million participants aged 16 and older across the country (Table VI.13). Participation in nonconsumptive wildlife activities is expected to increase 61 percent nationally over the next 52 years. In all regions, the number of participants should increase more rapidly than the population, with the largest relative increase coming in the South.

Table VI.13: Baseline Estimates and Projected Indexes of Change in Days, Trips, and Participants for Nonconsumptive Wildlife Activities, by Region and Decade, 1995-2050

			Projection Index					
Unit	**Region**	1995	2000	2010	2020	2030	2040	2050
Nonconsumptive Wildlife Activities								
Days	North	3319.30	1.04	1.22	1.44	1.63	1.72	1.76
	South	2322.10	1.09	1.32	1.59	1.85	2.06	2.20
	Rocky Mountain	578.90	1.09	1.28	1.49	1.68	1.84	1.94
	Pacific	838.50	1.10	1.33	1.58	1.82	2.01	2.14
	National	7057.10	1.07	1.27	1.51	1.73	1.88	1.97
Trips	North	1154.40	0.96	1.02	1.09	1.09	1.02	0.90
	South	746.30	1.04	1.08	1.14	1.18	1.17	1.11
	Rocky Mountain	180.60	1.08	1.11	1.16	1.21	1.26	1.30
	Pacific	212.80	1.03	1.23	1.39	1.53	1.61	1.62
	National	2277.10	1.00	1.07	1.15	1.18	1.15	1.08
Participation	North	56.00	1.01	1.10	1.21	1.30	1.35	1.40
	South	34.20	1.07	1.22	1.38	1.54	1.71	1.86
	Rocky Mountain	9.60	1.07	1.20	1.30	1.47	1.89	1.70
	Pacific	16.70	1.08	1.23	1.37	1.52	1.65	1.77
	National	116.70	1.04	1.16	1.29	1.41	1.51	1.61

Days of nonconsumptive wildlife activity are expected to increase by 97 percent nationally. The increases are similar across all regions but the biggest relative increases, 114 and 120 percent, are projected for the Pacific Coast and South, respectively.

Primary-purpose nonconsumptive wildlife trips are also projected to increase nationally, but at a rate well below population growth. In fact, in the North the number of trips is expected to decline by 10 percent over the next 52 years. The discrepancy between the tremendous increase in days and the relatively small increase in primary-purpose trips could be explained by the complementary or incidental nature of nonconsumptive wildlife activity in multipurpose recreation trips (U.S. Fish & Wildlife Service, 1997).

Race is not a strong predictor of nonconsumptive wildlife activity. Sex is a strong predictor, since women are more likely to be participants than men. The largest factor contributing to the increase in nonconsumptive wildlife recreation, however, appears to be the increasing age of the population.

Wildlife-related outdoor recreation will continue to be enjoyed by large numbers of Americans. Of the three general forms discussed above, nonconsumptive wildlife activity should experience the greatest relative growth in participation over the next 52 years. Fishing should provide about the same percentage increase in primary-purpose trips as nonconsumptive wildlife activity. Currently, fishing provides about twice as many primary-purpose trips as nonconsumptive wildlife activities and about three times as many trips as the various forms of hunting combined. The biggest relative increase in days for any of the wildlife-related activities will be in nonconsumptive wildlife activity. This growth is probably due to the complementary nature of this activity with other forms of outdoor recreation and to the year-round opportunities to observe wildlife.

Dispersed Land Activities

In this section, we report projections to 2050 for a number of dispersed land activities including backpacking, hiking, horseback riding, off-road driving, primitive camping, and rock climbing. In general, with the exception of horseback riding, these activities take place primarily in undeveloped or less developed outdoor environments. Except for primitive camping, these activities fall into the "Outdoor Adventure" category in Chapter V.

Backpacking

Backpacking is closely identified with undeveloped areas. Currently, an estimated 15 million outdoor enthusiasts across the country backpack. About 12 percent of the population over 16, living in the Rocky Mountain and Pacific Coast regions, enjoy this activity. Over the next half century, participation in backpacking is projected to increase by 26 percent (Table VI.14). The sport will grow at about the same rate as the population in the South, Rocky Mountain, and Pacific Coast regions, while decreasing about six percent in the North.

Table VI.14: Baseline Estimates and Projected Indexes of Change in Days, Trips, and Participants for Backpacking, by Region and Decade, 1995-2050

			Projection Index					
Unit Backpacking	**Region**	1995	2000	2010	2020	2030	2040	2050
Days	North	53.90	0.98	0.95	0.96	0.98	1.00	1.08
	South	25.20	1.01	1.23	1.48	1.76	2.03	2.31
	Rocky Mountain	14.50	1.00	1.03	1.07	1.11	1.17	1.24
	Pacific	36.40	1.03	1.11	1.17	1.22	1.25	1.26
	National	129.70	1.00	1.08	1.15	1.23	1.32	1.36
Trips	North	35.20	0.98	0.95	0.96	0.98	1.00	1.08
	South	15.60	1.06	1.30	1.66	2.08	2.21	2.87
	Rocky Mountain	8.70	1.03	1.07	1.13	1.21	1.25	1.38
	Pacific	19.70	1.09	1.08	1.11	1.14	1.22	1.22
	National	79.20	1.02	1.03	1.08	1.14	1.20	1.30
Participants	North	6.00	0.96	0.93	0.99	0.91	0.91	0.94
	South	3.60	1.01	1.08	1.15	1.23	1.31	1.42
	Rocky Mountain	1.80	1.03	1.11	1.18	1.28	1.38	1.51
	Pacific	3.80	1.05	1.12	1.23	1.24	1.34	1.46
	National	15.20	1.00	1.04	1.11	1.12	1.18	1.26

Backpackers hike along the Appalachian Trail through the Great Smoky Mountains in Tennessee. Photo courtesy of USDI National Park Service. Photo by Richard Frear.

Backpacking days are expected to increase faster than the rate of population growth in all regions. Primary-purpose backpacking trips, like days, are expected to increase nationally at a rate faster than population growth. With the exception of what appears to be a large increase in the South, growth in backpacking trips should be less than population growth in all other regions.

Race and income appear to be prime factors driving the backpacking forecasts. In general, an increase in nonwhites in the population will retard the growth of backpacking. Income, while insignificant in many models, appears to be the major factor leading to the large projected increases in days and trips in the South. Since income is not as statistically significant in the South models, the large projected increases in that region should be viewed with some suspicion.

Hiking

Like backpacking, hiking has long been a symbol of dispersed outdoor recreation. Of the "Outdoor Adventure" activities reported in Chapter V, it is the most popular, accounting for close to 50 million participants, 804.7 million days, and about 557.7 million primary-purpose trips in 1995 (Table VI.15). Nationally, hiking activity can be expected to increase marginally faster than population growth. Participation in hiking will increase from about 31 percent in the North to approximately 80 percent in the South and Pacific Coast regions.

Table VI.15: Baseline Estimates and Projected Indexes of Change in Days, Trips, and Participants for Hiking, by Region and Decade, 1995-2050

			Projection Index					
Unit Hiking	Region	1995	2000	2010	2020	2030	2040	2050
Days	North	330.30	0.99	1.04	1.11	1.17	1.19	1.23
	South	194.70	1.07	1.27	1.48	1.70	1.90	2.08
	Rocky Mountain	87.80	1.04	1.12	1.20	1.28	1.36	1.44
	Pacific	192.80	1.07	1.20	1.31	1.41	1.52	1.62
	National	804.70	1.03	1.14	1.24	1.34	1.43	1.51
Trips	North	240.60	0.98	0.97	1.01	1.02	1.01	1.00
	South	117.60	1.14	1.30	1.53	1.78	1.92	2.32
	Rocky Mountain	62.90	1.04	1.12	1.21	1.30	1.37	1.50
	Pacific	135.90	1.07	1.25	1.42	1.58	1.70	1.87
	National	557.70	1.04	1.12	1.23	1.33	1.39	1.52
Participation	North	20.60	0.99	1.04	1.11	1.19	1.24	1.31
	South	11.30	1.05	1.17	1.32	1.45	1.61	1.78
	Rocky Mountain	5.00	1.05	1.15	1.24	1.35	1.47	1.59
	Pacific	10.90	1.08	1.23	1.34	1.53	1.69	1.85
	National	47.80	1.03	1.13	1.23	1.34	1.45	1.57

Both days of hiking and primary-purpose trips will increase fastest in the South and Pacific Coast regions. The South will generate a 132-percent increase in trips by 2050, while the trips originating in the North will remain about constant over the next half century. In the South, hiking days will more than double. The large increases expected in the South should put the region on par with the North in terms of total days and total trips.

Interestingly, the supply variable for this activity is not significant for either the South or Pacific Coast regions, possibly suggesting that ample opportunities near population centers exist in both regions. The large increases projected for the South could change this relationship. Moreover, population density in many of the regional models is insignificant or significant and positive indicating that this sport is less associated with a rural lifestyle than activities like hunting, fishing, or motorboating.

Horseback Riding

Horseback riding may be considered a dispersed or developed land activity because it takes place in such diverse locations as suburban riding academies and stables, rural farms and ranches, and back country forest areas. While this activity currently has about the same number of enthusiasts as backpacking (about 15 million), it more than doubles backpacking in terms of primary-purpose trips and activity days. It is behind only hiking and off-road driving among dispersed land activities.

Based on the estimated models, participation in horseback riding is expected to increase faster than population growth in all regions, with the biggest relative increase coming in the South at 82 percent by the year 2050. Likewise, primary-purpose trips and activity days of horseback riding are expected to increase faster than the population in all regions (Table VI.16).

Table VI.16: Baseline Estimates and Projected Indexes of Change in Days, Trips, and Participants for Horseback Riding, by Region and Decade, 1995-2050

			Projection Index					
Unit	**Region**	1995	2000	2010	2020	2030	2040	2050
Horseback Riding								
Days	North	108.50	1.03	1.14	1.30	1.48	1.70	2.03
	South	104.10	0.97	1.06	1.15	1.23	1.26	1.27
	Rocky Mountain	48.20	1.00	1.06	1.14	1.22	1.34	1.51
	Pacific	76.70	1.00	1.10	1.21	1.34	1.49	1.70
	National	336.30	1.00	1.10	1.22	1.35	1.49	1.69
Trips	North	68.70	1.02	1.10	1.22	1.33	1.39	1.47
	South	55.00	1.02	1.20	1.43	1.67	1.78	1.97
	Rocky Mountain	23.00	1.01	1.05	1.11	1.21	1.38	1.66
	Pacific	38.00	1.00	1.18	1.37	1.59	1.82	2.09
	National	185.10	1.01	1.14	1.29	1.46	1.60	1.77
Participation	North	5.60	1.00	1.07	1.18	1.28	1.39	1.54
	South	4.70	1.04	1.15	1.28	1.42	1.60	1.82
	Rocky Mountain	1.70	1.04	1.13	1.23	1.34	1.46	1.60
	Pacific	2.40	1.05	1.18	1.29	1.46	1.61	1.77
	National	14.30	1.02	1.12	1.23	1.35	1.49	1.66

Forecast increases in this activity run somewhat contrary to trends reported in Chapter V. There is a strong positive relationship between income and riding. The forecast 88-percent increase over the 52-year period (Torgerson, 1996), suggests a large increase in horseback riding. A factor that may have led to the forecast of somewhat higher horseback riding than past trends would suggest is the lack of a buffering effect in the models from reduced availability of places to ride. In fact, for the populous North and South, no appropriate supply variable could be identified. Yet, horse riding groups make the point that trails for riding are increasingly scarce. Race influences the likelihood of horseback riding, but unlike many other outdoor recreation activities, sex is negative or insignificant in the majority of models. Horseback riding is not a male-dominated sport.

Off-Road Driving

Off-road driving is currently practiced by about 28 million Americans accounting for 522.6 million primary-purpose trips and 685.5 million activity days annually. Over 20 percent of Rocky Mountain region residents and close to 15 percent of Southern and Pacific Coast residents are involved in this activity.

Participation in this activity is expected to grow in all regions over the next half century. However, the national rate, at 16 percent, should be slower than that of population growth. The biggest increase, at 37 percent, will be in the Rocky Mountain region (Table VI.17).

Table VI.17: Baseline Estimates and Projected Indexes of Change in Days, Trips, and Participants for Off-Road Driving by Region and Decade 1995-2050

Unit Off-Road Driving	Region	1995	Projection Index 2000	2010	2020	2030	2040	2050
Days	North	308.30	0.94	0.87	0.82	0.76	0.70	0.66
	South	219.00	1.03	1.08	1.13	1.19	1.27	1.38
	Rocky Mountain	57.30	1.04	1.12	1.20	1.29	1.40	1.54
	Pacific	98.90	1.05	1.09	1.13	1.18	1.28	1.42
	National	685.50	0.99	0.99	0.99	1.00	1.03	1.07
Trips	North	211.40	0.92	0.79	0.69	0.60	0.52	0.45
	South	201.60	1.01	0.93	0.88	0.84	0.88	0.79
	Rocky Mountain	47.90	1.04	1.08	1.14	1.20	1.26	1.40
	Pacific	61.60	1.06	1.15	1.27	1.38	1.48	1.60
	National	522.60	0.98	0.91	0.86	0.82	0.82	0.78
Participation	North	11.20	0.99	0.99	1.06	1.03	1.04	1.09
	South	9.00	1.00	0.99	1.03	1.01	1.04	1.10
	Rocky Mountain	3.00	1.04	1.09	1.17	1.19	1.27	1.37
	Pacific	4.70	1.04	1.10	1.20	1.20	1.26	1.33
	National	27.90	1.00	1.02	1.05	1.06	1.10	1.16

Days of off-road driving should increase in all regions except the North, where a 34-percent decline is expected. The Rocky Mountain region will see the biggest increase in days at about 54 percent, followed by the Pacific Coast and South regions, at about 40 percent each. Nationally, the increase should be around seven percent.

Trips specifically for off-road driving are expected to increase in the Rocky Mountain and Pacific Coast regions, while decreasing by more than 50 percent in the North and by about 22 percent in the South. Overall, a 16-percent decrease is forecast nationally.

The two most apparent factors causing declining numbers of trips in the North and South appear to be age and income (TA VI.A). In the North, this sport appears to be more popular among lower income people. Hence, in a forecasting model, increasing income causes a drop in the number of trips. The activity also appears more popular with people who are younger than average. Thus as average age increases, the predicted number of trips decreases. The same is true for the South, but to a lesser extent.

Primitive Camping

Camping in primitive areas, while more popular than backpacking, lags behind many of the other dispersed land activities. It accounts for around 258.6 million days and 146.6 million primary-purpose trips annually. The number of participants in primitive camping should increase about 10 percent nationally through 2050. Increases will occur in the Rocky Mountain and Pacific Coast regions, while the North will experience a 16-percent decline from current levels (Table VI.18).

Table VI.18: Baseline Estimates and Projected Indexes of Change in Days, Trips, and Participants for Primitive Camping, by Region and Decade, 1995-2050

Unit	Region	1995	Projection Index 2000	2010	2020	2030	2040	2050
Primitive Camping								
Days	North	86.30	0.95	0.93	0.91	0.87	0.81	0.75
	South	80.70	0.97	0.97	0.99	1.00	0.99	0.97
	Rocky Mountain	34.60	1.01	1.09	1.15	1.22	1.26	1.29
	Pacific	57.50	1.07	1.26	1.46	1.67	1.88	2.08
	National	258.60	1.00	1.05	1.11	1.17	1.21	1.24
Trips	North	47.50	0.96	0.92	0.91	0.87	0.81	0.75
	South	50.90	1.02	1.00	1.02	1.02	1.07	0.94
	Rocky Mountain	21.30	1.04	1.06	1.11	1.15	1.21	1.20
	Pacific	27.60	1.06	1.11	1.18	1.24	1.28	1.29
	National	146.60	1.01	1.01	1.03	1.04	1.05	1.00
Participation	North	10.90	0.96	0.92	0.98	0.87	0.84	0.84
	South	8.00	0.98	0.98	1.01	0.98	0.99	1.02
	Rocky Mountain	3.60	1.03	1.12	1.20	1.29	1.37	1.44
	Pacific	5.60	1.05	1.13	1.23	1.27	1.35	1.44
	National	28.00	1.00	1.01	1.04	1.05	1.07	1.10

Nationally, days of primitive camping are projected to increase 24 percent over the forecast period. A doubling is projected for the Pacific Coast region, while a 25-percent decrease is expected in the North. The number of days of primitive camping for residents of the South should remain relatively stable.

Primary-purpose trips for primitive camping should also remain about constant nationally. As is the case for days, the North and South can be expected to see a decline from current levels, while the Rocky Mountain and Pacific Coast regions should see increases of 20 and 29 percent, respectively.

Factors affecting projections of primitive camping are similar to those for hunting and fishing. With the exception of the Pacific Coast, this activity decreases as income increases. Moreover, sex and race affect participation in that the activity is more often done by white males. It is also apparent that primitive campers are more likely to be from more rural, less–populated areas. Hence, with expected increases in income, urbanization, and non–whites in the population, primitive camping activities could decline somewhat from current levels.

Rock Climbing

Rock climbing is the least popular and most physically challenging of the dispersed land activities examined in this chapter. This activity has about the same number of participants as cross-country skiing. While the residents of the North take more rock climbing trips than those of any other region, the proportion of rock climbers in the population is highest in the Pacific Coast and Rocky Mountain regions.

Participation in rock climbing is expected to grow a little faster than the population over the next 52 years—about 50 percent nationally. This activity will grow the most rapidly (by 83 percent) in the South. The North could experience a decline of 13 percent (Table VI.19). The Rocky Mountain and the Pacific Coast regions should both see growth close to 30 percent.

Table VI.19: Baseline Estimates and Projected Indexes of Change in Days, Trips, and Participants for Rock Climbing, by Region and Decade, 1995-2050

Unit Rock Climbing	Region	1995	Projection Index 2000	2010	2020	2030	2040	2050
Days	North	13.50	0.98	1.00	1.06	1.12	1.20	1.34
	South	6.10	1.07	1.24	1.45	1.72	2.10	2.64
	Rocky Mountain	8.30	1.01	1.04	1.06	1.09	1.14	1.19
	Pacific	9.90	1.03	1.07	1.09	1.14	1.25	1.42
	National	37.70	1.01	1.07	1.15	1.24	1.39	1.60
Trips	North	10.90	0.96	0.87	0.83	0.79	0.77	0.78
	South	5.90	1.12	1.27	1.51	1.86	2.43	3.40
	Rocky Mountain	8.70	1.05	1.05	1.07	1.11	1.16	1.24
	Pacific	8.30	1.06	1.09	1.14	1.23	1.40	1.65
	National	34.00	1.02	1.00	1.03	1.09	1.19	1.38
Participation	North	3.00	0.96	0.91	0.97	0.86	0.85	0.87
	South	1.80	1.06	1.19	1.32	1.47	1.64	1.83
	Rocky Mountain	1.00	1.03	1.06	1.15	1.13	1.19	1.28
	Pacific	1.70	1.03	1.06	1.16	1.12	1.21	1.34
	National	7.50	1.03	1.10	1.21	1.26	1.36	1.50

Nationally, days and primary-purpose rock climbing trips should both increase about 60 percent and 38 percent, respectively, over the coming half century. Major increases for both trips and days are forecast for the South, while the North may see a decrease in the number of trips by around 20 percent. The Pacific Coast region will also see an increase in trips that exceeds population growth.

The statistical models project growth in the Pacific Coast and South because of positive relationship between income and involvement in this activity. These relationships do not appear to hold in the North or the Rocky Mountain region. As with a number of other outdoor–dispersed land activities, race is a strong explanatory variable.

Developed Land Activities

Participation projections are reported for seven land-based activities that occur in developed settings. These activities include developed camping, biking, family gathering, visiting historical places, picnicking, sightseeing, and walking. Four of these (family gathering, picnicking, sightseeing, and walking) are among the five most popular activities in the nation. Together, these seven developed land activities account for over 20 billion activity days.

Biking

Nationally, the number of biking participants is expected to grow by 70 percent by the middle of the next century. In the South, the percentage growth in participants is expected to be greatest, with the number of participants nearly doubling in the next 52 years (Table VI.20). Although percentage growth in the North will be the lowest among the regions (58 percent increase), the greatest increase in absolute number of participants will occur in that region.

Table VI.20: Baseline Estimates and Projected Indexes of Change in Days, Trips, and Participants for Biking, by Region and Decade, 1995-2050

Unit Biking	Region	1995	Projection Index 2000	2010	2020	2030	2040	2050
Days	North	1055.20	1.01	1.09	1.19	1.29	1.40	1.55
	South	599.60	1.08	1.21	1.36	1.53	1.74	1.98
	Rocky Mountain	180.30	1.04	1.13	1.21	1.29	1.36	1.42
	Pacific	400.90	1.06	1.16	1.24	1.33	1.43	1.55
	National	2237.00	1.04	1.14	1.25	1.36	1.49	1.66
Trips	North	656.20	1.03	1.17	1.35	1.52	1.67	1.85
	South	362.00	1.12	1.33	1.59	1.88	2.20	2.54
	Rocky Mountain	115.30	1.05	1.10	1.17	1.26	1.36	1.48
	Pacific	250.40	1.14	1.34	1.60	1.89	2.23	2.60
	National	1386.80	1.08	1.24	1.45	1.67	1.90	2.16
Participation	North	27.90	1.01	1.10	1.17	1.33	1.43	1.58
	South	15.20	1.07	1.22	1.38	1.55	1.74	1.95
	Rocky Mountain	4.50	1.05	1.17	1.26	1.40	1.53	1.65
	Pacific	9.80	1.06	1.19	1.29	1.41	1.53	1.65
	National	57.40	1.04	1.15	1.28	1.41	1.54	1.70

The national number of days of biking participation is expected to increase by nearly 70 percent between 1998 and 2050. Regionally, the percentage growth in days of participation will be slightly less than growth in participants for all regions except the South. In the South, since participation is possible year-round for the most part, participation days will increase slightly faster than participant growth. Nevertheless, residents of the North will continue to account for more days of participation than will residents of any other region.

Trips for biking are expected to more than double in the next 52 years for the nation as a whole. In both the South and Pacific Coast regions, the number of trips taken for biking in 2050 is expected to be more than 2.5 times the current level. By comparison, an increase in the number of trips of fewer than 50 percent is expected for Rocky Mountain region residents. Residents of the North and South will continue to account for over two-thirds of all biking trips.

Developed Camping

In 1995, about 41.5 million people participated in developed camping (see Chapter V). Over the next 52 years, this number is expected to increase by about 50 percent (Table VI.21). Participant growth will be very uneven across regions. The number of participants will nearly double in the South, while increasing less than 10 percent in the North. These regional differences in rates are directly tied to differences in the estimated relation between income and participation. For example, in the South and Pacific Coast, income has a strong and positive relationship on the likelihood of participation. As income rises, therefore, so does participation. In the North, however, income growth exerts a slightly downward influence on participation projections. Currently, there are more participants in the North than in any other region. By 2050, it is expected that more participants will live in the South than in any other region.

Table VI.21: Baseline Estimates and Projected Indexes of Change in Days, Trips, and Participants for Developed Camping, by Region and Decade, 1995-2050

Developed Camping Unit	Region	1995	Projection Index 2000	2010	2020	2030	2040	2050
Days	North	195.00	1.00	1.09	1.19	1.27	1.31	1.32
	South	115.50	1.10	1.37	1.68	2.03	2.41	2.82
	Rocky Mountain	39.30	1.04	1.14	1.25	1.35	1.43	1.50
	Pacific	92.90	1.07	1.23	1.39	1.56	1.73	1.88
	National	442.40	1.04	1.19	1.36	1.53	1.68	1.83
Trips	North	88.50	0.99	1.06	1.16	1.24	1.28	1.34
	South	56.70	1.09	1.38	1.74	2.16	2.66	3.28
	Rocky Mountain	19.10	1.04	1.14	1.25	1.35	1.44	1.51
	Pacific	45.30	1.03	1.11	1.19	1.26	1.33	1.41
	National	209.60	1.03	1.15	1.30	1.46	1.62	1.80
Participation	North	18.00	0.98	1.11	1.04	1.06	1.07	1.09
	South	10.70	1.06	1.22	1.34	1.58	1.77	1.97
	Rocky Mountain	4.00	1.03	1.16	1.17	1.23	1.29	1.34
	Pacific	8.80	1.06	1.19	1.32	1.45	1.59	1.73
	National	41.50	1.02	1.12	1.19	1.30	1.39	1.49

Days of participation in developed camping are expected to increase by over 80 percent from 1995 to 2050. This rise is led by an increase of over 2.8 times current levels in the South. In all regions, activity days will increase more rapidly than numbers of participants. This growth is especially true in the eastern regions. In the North, percentage growth in activity days is more than three times the rate of participant growth. In the South, activity days are expected to grow twice as fast as participants. This comparison indicates that people who camp in developed campgrounds will do so more often in the future than they do now.

The number of trips for developed camping is expected to increase 80 percent from 1995 to 2050. In the South, the number of trips is expected to triple in the next 52 years. In all other regions, trips will grow between 34 and 51 percent during the same time period. Since the number of trips grows at the same rate as the number of days, we expect the average length of a camping trip will remain stable in the future.

Family Gathering

Family gathering in the outdoors ranks among the four most popular outdoor recreation activities in the country. Between now and 2050, about a 60-percent increase is expected in the number of people who participate in this activity (Table VI.22). In each region, the percentage increase in participation outpaces population growth, indicating that the proportion of the population that participates in this activity will increase in the future. There is expected to be a 41-percent increase in the number of participants who live in the North, a 65-percent increase in both western regions, and a 76-percent increase in participants from the South. Even though percentage growth will be slowest in the North, in 2050 that region will still be the home for over 40 percent of all participants in this activity.

Table VI.22: Baseline Estimates and Projected Indexes of Change in Days, Trips, and Participants for Family Gathering, by Region and Decade, 1995-2050

Family Gathering		Projection Index						
Unit	**Region**	1995	2000	2010	2020	2030	2040	2050
Days	North	500.80	1.01	1.07	1.15	1.21	1.27	1.34
	South	311.20	1.06	1.18	1.30	1.43	1.58	1.75
	Rocky Mountain	92.30	1.06	1.18	1.30	1.42	1.54	1.65
	Pacific	180.40	1.07	1.19	1.29	1.40	1.54	1.71
	National	1084.50	1.04	1.13	1.23	1.32	1.42	1.54
Trips	North	400.70	0.92	0.76	0.65	0.55	0.46	0.40
	South	240.40	1.01	0.92	0.85	0.81	0.86	0.77
	Rocky Mountain	70.40	1.04	1.08	1.14	1.20	1.26	1.40
	Pacific	144.20	1.07	1.17	1.30	1.43	1.53	1.66
	National	855.60	0.98	0.89	0.83	0.79	0.79	0.75
Participation	North	58.10	1.02	1.09	1.16	1.26	1.33	1.41
	South	37.00	1.07	1.20	1.34	1.48	1.62	1.76
	Rocky Mountain	9.40	1.07	1.19	1.29	1.43	1.54	1.65
	Pacific	19.30	1.07	1.20	1.30	1.42	1.54	1.65
	National	123.80	1.04	1.14	1.24	1.36	1.46	1.57

Activity days for family gathering are projected to increase at about the same rate, both nationally and regionally, as participant growth. Nationally, activity days are expected to grow by 54 percent over the next 52 years. Growth in activity days is expected to be about 75 percent in the South, 71 percent in the Pacific Coast, 65 percent in the Rocky Mountain region, and 34 percent in the North.

Despite projected growth in participation and activity days, the models indicate a steady decline in the national number of trips for this activity. Curiously, there are dramatic differences between projections for western and eastern regions. In the Pacific Coast and Rocky Mountain regions, trips for the primary purpose of a family gathering are projected to increase by 66 and 40 percent, respectively. In the North and South, trips for the primary purpose of a family gathering are expected to decline by 60 and 23 percent, respectively. This difference may indicate that in the eastern regions, family gathering activities will increasingly be incidental parts of longer or multipurpose recreation trips.

Picnicking

Picnicking is enjoyed by more than half of the population over the age of 16 in the United States. Over the next 52 years, that percentage will continue to increase. The projected 54-percent increase in number of participants exceeds population growth in that age category (Table VI.23). As is the case with most developed land activities, percentage growth in participants will be the greatest in the South (80 percent), and the least in the North (35 percent).

Table VI.23: Baseline Estimates and Projected Indexes of Change in Days, Trips, and Participants for Picnicking, by Region and Decade, 1995-2050

Unit Picnicking	Region	1995	Projection Index 2000	2010	2020	2030	2040	2050
Days	North	500.80	1.00	1.07	1.16	1.22	1.24	1.23
	South	311.20	1.07	1.19	1.32	1.47	1.64	1.83
	Rocky Mountain	92.30	1.05	1.17	1.29	1.40	1.48	1.54
	Pacific	180.40	1.06	1.21	1.35	1.48	1.57	1.62
	National	1084.50	1.03	1.14	1.26	1.35	1.42	1.49
Trips	North	400.70	0.91	0.72	0.58	0.48	0.40	0.30
	South	240.40	0.94	0.76	0.65	0.57	0.52	0.49
	Rocky Mountain	70.40	1.01	0.99	1.00	1.03	1.08	1.16
	Pacific	144.20	1.06	1.15	1.26	1.38	1.47	1.57
	National	855.60	0.94	0.79	0.70	0.63	0.59	0.55
Participation	North	47.00	1.01	1.08	1.15	1.25	1.29	1.35
	South	27.40	1.06	1.21	1.38	1.52	1.67	1.80
	Rocky Mountain	8.10	1.06	1.18	1.28	1.42	1.53	1.62
	Pacific	15.80	1.07	1.20	1.31	1.44	1.54	1.63
	National	98.30	1.04	1.14	1.25	1.37	1.45	1.54

Growth in activity days for picnicking is projected to be about the same as participant growth. Nationally, a 49-percent growth in activity days is projected by 2050. In the South, the growth rate is expected to be about 83 percent during that time period. By comparison, growth in activity days for western residents is expected to be about 60 percent, and only about 23 percent for the North.

Like family gatherings, a sharp decline in the number of primary-purpose trips for picnicking is predicted for both of the eastern regions. For both of these regions, the number of primary purpose trips for picnics in 2050 will be less than half of the current levels, despite increases in both participants and activity days. In contrast, both western regions are projected to have increases in the number of trips taken by residents for the primary purpose of picnicking, including a 16-percent increase by residents of the Rocky Mountain region, and nearly a 60-percent increase by residents of the Pacific Coast region.

Picnicking remains one of the most popular outdoor activities. Photo courtesy of the USDA Forest Service.

Sightseeing

For the nation and for each region, the growth in number of sightseers is expected to be between 50 and 96 percent (Table VI.24). Overall, a 71-percent increase in the number of participants is expected between now and 2050. Percentage growth is expected to be nearly twice as high in the South as in the North.

Table VI.24: Baseline Estimates and Projected Indexes of Change in Days, Trips, and Participants for Sightseeing, by Region and Decade, 1995-2050

			Projection Index					
Unit Sightseeing	**Region**	1995	2000	2010	2020	2030	2040	2050
Days	North	904.80	1.04	1.27	1.38	1.55	1.68	1.80
	South	605.40	1.07	1.23	1.40	1.58	1.78	1.99
	Rocky Mountain	163.30	1.08	1.24	1.41	1.58	1.73	1.85
	Pacific	363.50	1.12	1.38	1.67	1.98	2.29	2.59
	National	2036.30	1.06	1.27	1.43	1.63	1.81	1.98
Trips	North	511.20	1.03	1.14	1.29	1.43	1.48	1.62
	South.	379.50	1.08	1.19	1.53	1.79	1.90	2.31
	Rocky Mountain	95.00	1.07	1.23	1.40	1.57	1.66	1.90
	Pacific	225.20	1.11	1.36	1.62	1.89	2.03	2.38
	National	1209.50	1.06	1.20	1.43	1.63	1.72	1.98
Participation	North	52.30	1.02	1.11	1.23	1.33	1.41	1.50
	South	33.90	1.08	1.25	1.43	1.61	1.79	1.96
	Rocky Mountain	8.70	1.07	1.21	1.32	1.49	1.63	1.74
	Pacific	18.50	1.09	1.26	1.42	1.58	1.74	1.87
	National	113.40	1.05	1.18	1.32	1.47	1.59	1.71

The number of activity days for sightseeing is expected to double in the U.S. by 2050. Activity days by residents of the Pacific Coast region will increase 260 percent. However, the relatively small number of participants in that region means that the national average will be closer to the growth rate in the North and South. Even in the slower-growing North, however, activity days are expected to increase by about 80 percent.

Sightseeing trips are also expected to double nationally over the next 52 years. Trips taken by residents of the North and Rocky Mountain regions will not quite double in that period. However, in the South and Pacific Coast regions, the number of trips taken by residents for sightseeing will increase by more than 130 percent of current levels.

Visiting Historic Places

The number of people who visit historical places is expected to increase steadily by 13 to 17 percent of the 1995 total during each 10-year period from the turn of the century to 2050 (Table VI.25). By 2050, the total number of participants will be more than 75 percent above 1995 levels. Both the South and Rocky Mountain regions will show growth above the national average. Even in the North and Pacific Coast regions, which will have the lowest levels of growth, rates of increase in numbers of participants will be greater than population growth.

Table VI.25: Baseline Estimates and Projected Indexes of Change in Days, Trips, and Participants for Visiting Historic Places, by Region and Decade, 1995-2050

Visiting Historic Places Unit	Region	1995	Projection Index 2000	2010	2020	2030	2040	2050
Days	North	203.20	1.03	1.20	1.42	1.60	1.71	1.79
	South	172.90	1.11	1.35	1.63	1.97	2.36	2.83
	Rocky Mountain	38.70	1.07	1.23	1.40	1.57	1.72	1.84
	Pacific	68.40	1.09	1.23	1.37	1.52	1.70	1.89
	National	482.40	1.07	1.26	1.48	1.71	1.93	2.16
Participation	North	40.80	1.02	1.13	1.20	1.38	1.47	1.59
	South	26.90	1.08	1.28	1.48	1.70	1.90	2.09
	Rocky Mountain	6.90	1.08	1.23	1.34	1.54	1.69	1.83
	Pacific	13.80	1.08	1.22	1.33	1.46	1.58	1.68
	National	88.40	1.06	1.19	1.32	1.49	1.63	1.76

Across the country, activity days spent visiting historic places will increase at a steady rate. In the South, growth in days of activity for visiting historic places will be much greater than for the other three regions, doubling in a little more than 35 years. Growth in the other three regions will be roughly equal—about 80 percent over the next 52 years.

Walking

Walking is also among the four most popular activities in the United States, with over 140 million participants. Over the next 52 years, growth in the number of participants will be at roughly the same level as population growth (Table VI.26). However, participant growth rates will not be even across regions. Participant growth will be about 64 percent in the Rocky Mountain region and about 73 percent in the Pacific Coast. These levels are about 10 percent higher than projected population growth. In the North, the increase in the number of participants will be about equal to the increase in the total population. In contrast, in the South the number of participants is expected to grow by about 34 percent in 52 years, while the population grows 53 percent.

Table VI.26: Baseline Estimates and Projected Indexes of Change in Days, Trips, and Participants for Walking, by Region and Decade, 1995-2050

Unit Walking	Region	1995	Projection Index 2000	2010	2020	2030	2040	2050
Days	North	6568.70	1.04	1.14	1.27	1.37	1.44	1.52
	South	4395.40	1.07	1.20	1.33	1.47	1.60	1.72
	Rocky	1077.70	1.06	1.15	1.24	1.32	1.37	1.40
	Pacific	2340.60	1.09	1.22	1.34	1.46	1.58	1.68
	National	14381.40	1.06	1.17	1.29	1.40	1.50	1.58
Participation								
	North	62.60	1.01	1.07	1.15	1.22	1.27	1.33
	South	40.00	1.03	1.07	1.11	1.16	1.23	1.34
	Rocky Mountain	10.00	1.06	1.18	1.28	1.41	1.53	1.64
	Pacific	21.10	1.08	1.23	1.34	1.49	1.62	1.73
	National	133.70	1.03	1.12	1.21	1.30	1.39	1.46

Activity days of walking are expected to grow by about 30 percent over the next 25 years, and by an equal amount in the subsequent 30 years. Percentage growth in activity days is expected to be above the rate of participant growth for both the North (52 percent) and South (72 percent). In the western regions, the percentage growth in activity days will be less than the growth in participants.

In general, the number of participants in developed land activities will increase at least as fast as population growth rates for the next half century. Thus, we can expect an increasing proportion of the U.S. population to engage in this type of recreation activity. In the South the proportion will grow the fastest for most of these activities. Fewer primary-purpose trips for several activities combined with increases in activity days indicate that these activities increasingly will be parts of multipurpose recreation trips. Projections for developed camping indicate a continuation of the trend of the last 30 years: a departure from multiple-week vacation trips and toward weekend and long-weekend trips for many Americans.

KEY FINDINGS

National

The five fastest growing outdoor recreation activities through the year 2050 measured in activity days are expected to be: visiting historic places (116 percent growth), downhill skiing (110 percent growth), snowmobiling (99 percent growth), sightseeing (98 percent growth), and nonconsumptive wildlife activity (97 percent growth). The five slowest growing outdoor recreation activities through the year 2050 as measured in activity days are expected to be: fishing (27 percent growth), primitive camping (24 percent growth), cross-country skiing (18 percent growth), off-road vehicle driving (seven percent growth), and hunting (minus-two percent growth).

In terms of annual primary-purpose trips, the five fastest growing outdoor recreation activities through the year 2050 are expected to be: downhill skiing (122 percent growth), biking (116 percent growth), snowmobiling (110 percent growth), sightseeing (98 percent growth), and developed camping (80 percent growth). The five slowest growing outdoor recreation activities as measured by primary-purpose trips are expected to be: hunting (six percent growth), primitive camping (zero percent growth), off-road vehicle driving (minus 22 percent growth), family gatherings (minus 25 percent growth), and picnicking (minus 45 percent growth).

The five fastest growing outdoor recreation activities through the year 2050 as measured by number of participants are projected to be: cross-country skiing (95 percent growth), downhill skiing (93 percent growth), visiting historic places (76 percent growth), sightseeing (71 percent growth), and biking (70 percent growth). The five slowest growing outdoor recreation activities as measured by the number of participants are projected to be: rafting (26 percent growth), backpacking (26 percent growth), off-road vehicle driving (16 percent growth), primitive camping (10 percent growth), and hunting (minus 11 percent growth).

Regional

Growth in activity days should be fairly consistent across regions—faster than population growth in every region for about 60 percent of the activities. The Pacific Coast will see the greatest number of activities for which primary-purpose trips grow faster than the population, about 13 out of 22. The North will see the fewest, about seven out of 22. Participants should increase in all regions faster than the population growth for at least 60 percent of the activities. The Pacific Coast will have the most activities (75 percent), growing at a rate faster than the population.

Activities

Days spent and numbers of participants in winter, water-based, and developed land activities will, in general, grow faster than the population. Hunting and fishing, along with other dispersed land activities, are not expected to increase in activity days or participation numbers as fast as the population is growing. Nonconsumptive wildlife activity is an exception to this trend; however, it is not limited to dispersed settings. With the exception of winter sports, there appears to be a general shift toward fewer primary-purpose trips per capita while at the same time more days and participants per capita.

Factors

Race and sex are important predictors of behavior for a number of outdoor activities. White males are, in general, more likely to engage in winter, water-based, hunting, and dispersed land activities, females are more likely to engage in horseback riding, picnicking, and nonconsumptive wildlife activity. Race is not an important factor in describing fishing, walking, picnicking, and nonconsumptive wildlife activity.

Population density has a strong negative effect on more rural activities like fishing, horseback riding, hunting, motorboating, off-road vehicle driving, and primitive camping. Income has a strong positive effect on activities generally considered expensive to participate in, such as downhill skiing, snowmobiling, horseback riding, motorboating, and sightseeing. Projected reductions in indexes of available supply have noticeable negative effects on the growth of land-intensive activities like hunting, hiking, off-road vehicle driving, and primitive camping.

REFERENCES

Cordell, H. K., Bergstrom, J. C., Hartmann, L. A., & English, D. B. K. (1990). *An analysis of the outdoor recreation and wilderness situation in the United States: 1989-2040*. General Technical Report RM-189. Fort Collins, CO: USDA Forest Service, Rocky Mountain Forest and Range Experiment Station.

Cordell, H. K., McDonald, B. L., Lewis, B., Miles, M., Martin, J., & Bason, J. (1996). United States of America. In G. Cushman, A. J. Veal, & J. Zuzanek (Eds.), *World leisure participation: Free time in the global village*. Oxford, England: CAB International.

Day, J. C. (1996). *Population projections of the United States by age, sex, race, and Hispanic origin: 1995 to 2050*. U.S. Bureau of the Census, Current Population Reports, P25-1130. Washington, D.C.: U.S. Government Printing Office.

Greene, W. H. (1993). *Econometric analysis* (2nd ed.). Englewood Cliffs, NJ: Prentice Hall.

Greene, W. H. (1995). *LIMDEP version 7.0 user's manual.* Bellport, NY: Econometric Software, Inc.

Hof, J. G., & Kaiser, H. F. (1983). Long-term outdoor recreation participation projections for public land management agencies. *Journal of Leisure Research, 15*(1), 1-14.

Torgerson, D. (1996, May). [Macroeconomic projections]. Unpublished memo. USDA Economic Research Service, Macroeconomics Team, Commercial Agriculture Division 1996.

U.S. Fish & Wildlife Service. (1997). *1996 national survey of fishing, hunting, and wildlife-associated recreation: National overview.* Washington, D.C.: U.S. Government Printing Office.

Walsh, R. G., Johnson, D. M., & McKean, J. R. (1992). Benefit transfer of outdoor recreation demand studies, 1968-1988. *Water Resources Research, 28*(3), 707-713.

Walsh, R. G., Jon, K. H., McKean, J. R., & Hof, J. (1992). Effect of price on forecasts of participation in fish and wildlife recreation: An aggregate demand model. *Journal of Leisure Research, 21,* 140-156.

CHAPTER VII

DEMAND FOR AND SUPPLY OF WILDERNESS

. . . .

John Loomis[1]
Kenneth Bonetti
Chris Echohawk

Acknowledgments:

Valuable guidance and much assistance was provided by Kenneth Cordell and Michael Bowker of the Southeast Forest Experiment Station, U.S. Forest Service (USFS) in Athens, GA. Carter Betz and Linda Langner of the USFS provided future demographic data used as inputs for the visitor use projections. David Cole of the Intermountain Station, USFS, was most gracious in sharing his long-time series of data on wilderness use. Without these data no statistical model would have been possible. Wes Henry of the National Park Service (NPS) provided information on potential wilderness acreage in the National Park System. Don Applegate of the Bureau of Land Management (BLM) in Arizona single-handedly provided Wilderness visitation data for all BLM lands. Geographic Information Specialists Jack Johnson of the BLM in Arizona, Dave Mensing of New Mexico BLM, Kim Foiles of USFS Region 1, and Dave Prevendel of USFS Region 4 were quite helpful in providing access to their areas' wilderness maps. In addition, Dr. Dean Tucker, NPS, provided much data and assistance, including a 1994 data set organized by the National Geographic Society (supplied by Russ Little of the Society). Peter Fix, Colorado State University, was instrumental in estimating recreation use at Wilderness areas on National Wildlife Refuges. Armando Gonzalez-Caban, USFS, and Thomas Stevens, University of Massachusetts, provided many valuable suggestions for improving the clarity and flow of an earlier version of this chapter. The first two authors owe an intellectual debt of gratitude to Richard Walsh, Professor Emeritus, Colorado State University, who taught us a great deal about wilderness economics. Any errors are, of course, the responsibility of the authors.

INTRODUCTION

In 1974, Congress passed the Renewable Resources Planning Act (RPA) to provide long-term direction for the management of the National Forest System and other U.S. Forest Service (USFS) programs. As part of that act, Congress required a nationwide assessment of the supplies of and demand for natural resources every 10 years. This assessment compares the current supply of renewable natural resources—range, recreation, timber, water, wildlife, and wilderness—with current and likely future demands on these resources. Since all land ownerships together provide these renewable natural resources, the assessment looks at private lands as well as public lands, from state to federal agencies. The assessment provides the overall context for the Forest Service to develop its own five-year RPA program for managing National Forests and related programs. Given that many of the values of natural resources on public lands are non-market, the price mechanism is unavailable to balance the quantity demanded with the quantity supplied.

[1] John Loomis is a professor and Kenneth Bonetti is a doctoral student, Department of Agricultural and Resource Economics, Colorado State University, Fort Collins, CO; and Chris Echohawk is a graduate student, Department of Earth Resources, Colorado State University, Fort Collins, CO.

The comprehensiveness of the RPA assessment is typically broader than individual state and federal agencies, which look at just their own resource base and management mandate. However, the findings of the comprehensive RPA assessment should be of use to all state and federal natural resource agencies in performing ecosystem management. The intention of ecosystem management is that agencies will coordinate their resource management activities with each other so that they complement rather than conflict with each other's action. The comprehensiveness of the assessment is of particular importance for the country's wilderness resource. Federal agencies are required to manage their congressionally designated Wilderness as a part of the National Wilderness Preservation System (NWPS). As such, agency decisions are influenced, in part, by how their recommendations of roadless areas contribute to the overall diversity of the system.

This chapter provides an overview of the NWPS in the United States. This information should prove useful to state and federal land management agencies responsible for wilderness recommendations and management. The chapter describes the current status of the NWPS and how it contributes to recreation and ecosystem protection in the United States.

HISTORICAL TRENDS AND CURRENT STATUS

Wilderness Supply Trends 1965 to 1994

More than 30 years have passed since the 1964 National Wilderness Preservation Act designated 54 areas totaling just over nine million acres to comprise the NWPS. Today, the system covers almost 104 million acres in 630 areas and is managed by four federal agencies (Cole 1996). The USFS manages nearly 29 million acres in the lower 48 states (36 million when Alaska is included). The National Park Service (NPS) manages another 10 million acres (39 million when Alaska is included). These two agencies manage over 80 percent of the acreage in the NWPS in the lower 48 states and nearly all of the documented Wilderness recreation occurs in their jurisdictions.

National Forest Wilderness

USFS designations began in 1964 with the passage of the Wilderness Act. As Table VII.1 shows, Wilderness designation of national forest land occurred sporadically as Congress acted upon recommendations of the USFS and environmental groups. Growth was relatively moderate after the initial enactments. Twenty-five percent was added over 10 years to make a total of 15 million acres in 1975. Between 1975 and 1985 designations grew significantly, increasing the total on national forests to 27 million acres in 1985. From 1975 to 1985, the average annual growth rate was 13.2 percent. Between 1985 and 1995, the annual rate of USFS designations slowed to about 1.1 percent. During that period, significant additions occurred in the Rocky Mountain, Pacific Coast and the Southern regions (see Table VII.1). The vast majority of USFS growth occurred in the Rocky Mountain and Pacific Coast regions, which held 93.3 percent of USFS Wilderness by 1995. In 1995, the USFS managed 28.9 million acres in 40 of the lower 48 states and 5.8 million acres in Alaska.

Table VII.1: Total Acres of National Forest Land in the National Wilderness Preservation System for the U.S. and by Region and Year

Year	Continental U.S. Total	Regions			
		North	South	Rocky Mountains	Pacific Coast
1965	12,158,586	804,828	29,425	7,123,389	4,200,944
1970	13,301,846	804,828	29,425	7,130,468	5,337,125
1975	15,214,040	888,247	197,898	8,448,654	5,679,241
1980	22,144,504	941,540	220,636	14,392,495	6,589,833
1985	27,147,329	1,167,003	573,861	16,869,257	8,537,208
1990	28,076,738	1,300,010	683,777	17,551,951	8,541,000
1995	28,941,072	1,307,200	692,200	17,890,100	9,051,572

Figure VII.1: The 1998 RPA Wilderness Assessment Study Areas

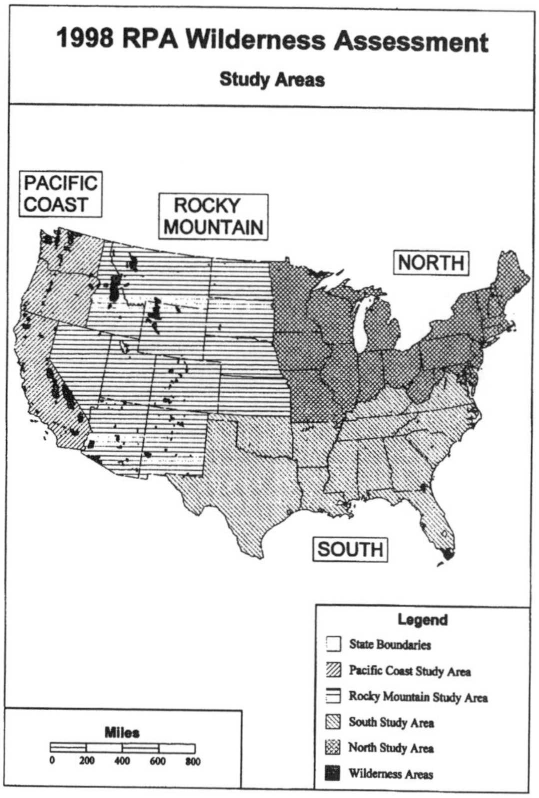

National Park Service

NPS acreage has increased sporadically, with large additions in the late 1970s (Table VII.2). The NPS Wilderness growth pattern is similar to the USFS, with most (five million acres) occurring between 1978 and 1988. There were no additions to NPS Wilderness from 1988 until 1994, when the long-delayed California Wilderness Act added 3.8 million acres. In 1994, NPS holdings totaled 10 million acres or about 9.8 percent of the NWPS. In 1994, the majority of NPS Wilderness acreage was in the Pacific Coast region (77 percent), but the South had a significant share (14 percent), more than double that in the Rocky Mountain region. The North region contained only a little more than one percent of NPS Wilderness in 1994.

Other Federal Agencies

The U.S. Fish and Wildlife Service (USFWS) manages slightly more than 20 million acres of Wilderness on its refuges, with 18.6 million of its Wilderness acreage in Alaska. The Bureau of Land Management (BLM) became eligible to recommend land for Wilderness designation in 1976 with the passage of the Federal Land Policy and Management Act. To date, 5.2 million acres have been designated and many acres identified as having wilderness potential await consideration. Of BLM managed Wilderness, 3.5 million are in California and 1.4 million are in Arizona.

The Madison River offers some of Montana's most challenging white water as it cuts through Bear Trap Canyon. Part of the Lee Metcalf Wilderness, Bear Trap is the first area administered by the Bureau of Land Management to receive Wilderness designation. Photo courtesy of the USDI Bureau of Land Management.

FEDERAL WILDERNESS

Across all four agencies, about 104 million acres of federal land are designated Wilderness. About half of this total is in Alaska; about 40 percent is in the contiguous western states; and 10 percent is in the East.

Table VII.2: Total Acres of National Park Land in the National Wilderness Preservation System for the U.S. and by Region and Year

Year	Continental U.S. Total	Regions North	South	Rocky Mountains	Pacific Coast
1965	0	0	0	0	0
1971	93,503	0	0	93,503	0
1975	203,862	0	0	96,420	107,442
1980	3,111,257	133,243	1,435,258	693,152	849,604
1985	4,534,677	133,243	1,444,098	693,152	2,264,184
1990	6,227,825	133,243	1,459,108	693,152	3,942,322
1993	6,227,825	133,243	1,459,108	693,152	3,942,322
1994	10,081,063	133,243	1,459,108	693,152	7,795,560
1995	0	0	0	0	0

Qualified Roadless Areas by Agency

Information was obtained from a variety of agency sources on acreages of proposed Wilderness. For the USFS and BLM, we were able to obtain both recommended acreages as well as Wilderness Study Area (WSAs) acreages not recommended. Since WSAs met the criteria of being suitable for Wilderness, we were able to estimate an upper limit on acreage and recreation visitor use if all potential wilderness acreage was designated by Congress. For the NPS, data are available only for recommended acres.

In the lower 48 states, the NPS has over seven million acres recommended for but not yet designated as Wilderness. If all of its recommended acres are designated, NPS Wilderness acreage in the lower 48 states would double. For the Rocky Mountain region, the increase would be quite dramatic with an increase in official Wilderness by nearly a factor of 10 (from 700,000 acres to 6,594,500 acres because of large additions in Yellowstone, Glacier, and Rocky Mountain National Parks). In the South, designation of recommended acres would result in a 30 percent increase in Wilderness. Much of this increase is in the Great Smoky Mountains National Park. Increases for the West Coast are much smaller, representing just two percent increases.

Increases in National Forest Wilderness would be modest, representing a 10 percent (three million acres) overall increase if all recommended acres were designated by Congress. The Rocky Mountain region would gain the most acreage (2.6 million acres), representing a gain of 14 percent in that area.

The BLM has 26 million acres of WSAs and recommended about one third of them, or 9.5 million acres as Wilderness. About six million of these acres are in the Rocky Mountain region and 3.5 million are in the Pacific Coast region. As discussed briefly below, addition of these BLM lands would improve the ecological representation in the NWPS. Much of BLM's WSAs are high desert, an ecosystem that is currently under-represented in the system.

Ecosystem Representation by the Federal System

In recent years, policymakers have become more aware of the importance of preserving natural diversity in plants and animals and physical environments. Biological diversity includes both species diversity and genetic diversity within species. Natural diversity incorporates the physical environment and climate within which species interact with biological diversity. Natural diversity therefore depends on the preservation of a full range of functioning ecosystems.

Two methods are used to preserve natural diversity: manipulative management and preservation management. Davis' (1989) previous analysis of Wilderness addresses preservation management, specifically the inclusion of representative samples of naturally occurring ecosystems in the NWPS. Preservation management ensures diversity through the preservation of unrestrained ecological processes. Wilderness protection, however, is only one mechanism for protecting selected portions of the natural landscape. National parks, nature preserves, and similar legal reservations also play important conservation roles.

In its second Roadless Area Review and Evaluation (RARE II) in 1977, the USFS decided to give preference to additions of areas that would increase the diversity of the NWPS. RARE II adopted the Bailey-Kuchler ecosystem classification system, which considers physical (climate and soil) and biological (vegetation) factors. The number of ecosystems identified under the Bailey-Kuchler system total 261. The USFS defines adequate representation of an ecosystem to include two or more distinct examples of at least 1000 acres (400 hectares). In addition, the areas selected must epitomize that particular ecosystem.

As a result of RARE II and subsequent designations by Congress, 157 of the country's ecosystems were represented in the NWPS by 1989. The Bureau of Land Management (BLM) has also adopted the Bailey-Kuchler system for its wilderness studies. Additions of BLM land have the potential to increase the diversity within the NWPS. Davis anticipated that up to 200 ecosystems would be represented by the year 2000. While forest and desert ecosystems are well represented in the NWPS, few of the fertile native grassland ecosystems have been included because most of these lands are privately owned and lack the scenic splendor that encourages citizens to support wilderness designations.

Davis performed the last analysis of ecosystem representation in 1989. Discussions with Davis indicated he had not updated the analysis since then. Discussions with others, such as the GAP GIS project at the University of Idaho, indicated that such an analysis was not complete for the U.S. Therefore, we undertook an updated analysis using Bailey's ecoregions at the province level and federal agency Wilderness GIS data.

Data Sources

The data were collected from several sources with the help of many people in the federal land management agencies. GIS coordinators in the USFS, BLM, and NPS provided map layers. Geographic Information System (GIS) analysis was conducted using Arc/Info, Arc View, and Atlas GIS software. Data sets were provided from sources in one of three formats: Arc/Info coverages, Arc export files, or Atlas GIS .agf files. After these sources were converted to common projections, analysis and display of the data was accomplished using Atlas GIS. Statistics were calculated using Microsoft Excel from the Atlas files. The results were compared with figures obtained independently of the GIS analysis and were found to be satisfactory (5 to 10 percent difference). This analysis was acceptable since the level of detail and accuracy in the GIS data available was highly variable from agency to agency and source to source.

The results of the GIS work are summarized in the maps provided and in the accompanying table. These show the result of overlaying the final wilderness coverage with the Bailey's Ecoregions coverage. The maps show the spatial distribution of the data, including a low wilderness representation in the Great Basin relative to the other western regions. This study is striking considering the large proportion of federal ownership. The greatest representation is in the western mountains and southwestern deserts, and the lowest amounts in the high prairie and southern forests.

Table VII.3: Comparison of Wilderness Acreage by Ecoregion

Ecocode	Province	% of Total U.S. Lower 48 Wilderness	% of U.S. in Ecoregion	Wilderness to Ecoregion Area ratio	Ratio over 1?	% Ecoregion as Wilderness	Wilderness (ac)	Total Ecoregion Area (ac)
322	American Semi-Desert and Desert Province	21.0%	2.9%	7.17	Yes	16.4%	9,197,580	56,238,396
M331	Southern Rocky Mountain Steppe-Open Woodland-Coniferous Forest-Alpine Meadow Province	17.4%	3.4%	5.10	Yes	11.6%	7,635,330	65,613,296
M332	Middle Rocky Mountain Steppe-Coniferous Forest-Alpine Meadow Province	13.7%	2.7%	5.04	Yes	11.5%	6,021,600	52,324,240
M261	Sierran Steppe-Mixed Forest-Coniferous Forest-Alpine Meadow Province	11.8%	2.3%	5.17	Yes	11.8%	5,164,810	43,748,392
M242	Cascade Mixed Forest-Coniferous Forest-Alpine Meadow Province	11.4%	1.8%	6.40	Yes	14.6%	5,001,910	34,242,360
411	Everglades Province	3.0%	0.3%	11.35	Yes	25.9%	1,299,350	5,014,900
M313	Arizona-New Mexico Mountains Semi-Desert-Open Woodland-Coniferous Forest-Alpine Meadow Province	2.9%	1.7%	1.75	Yes	4.0%	1,287,300	32,182,260
212	Laurentian Mixed Forest Province	2.8%	4.9%	0.57	No	1.3%	1,226,870	94,418,672
313	Colorado Plateau Semi-Desert Province	2.5%	2.5%	1.01	Yes	2.3%	1,115,840	48,280,396
M262	California Coastal Range Open Woodland-Shrub-Coniferous Forest-Meadow Province	2.5%	0.8%	3.00	Yes	6.9%	1,094,610	15,966,126
M333	Northern Rocky Mountain Forest-Steppe-Coniferous Forest-Alpine Meadow Province	2.3%	1.3%	1.84	Yes	4.2%	1,022,580	24,375,970
341	Intermountain Semi-Desert and Desert Province	1.4%	3.6%	0.39	No	0.9%	616,502	68,719,944
331	Great Plains-Palouse Dry Steppe Province	1.2%	9.7%	0.12	No	0.3%	529,926	186,315,184
232	Outer Coastal Plain Mixed Forest Province	1.2%	5.8%	0.21	No	0.5%	527,653	111,395,924
M341	Nevada-Utah Mountains-Semi-Desert-Coniferous Forest-Alpine Meadow Province	1.1%	1.5%	0.77	No	1.8%	492,072	27,947,022
321	Chihuahuan Semi-Desert Province	0.8%	2.8%	0.28	No	0.6%	354,299	54,607,684
342	Intermountain Semi-Desert Province	0.7%	5.3%	0.13	No	0.3%	304,501	101,961,848
M221	Central Appalachian Broadleaf Forest-Coniferous Forest-Meadow Province	0.6%	2.3%	0.26	No	0.6%	259,940	43,615,616
261	California Coastal Chapparral Forest and Shrub Province	0.5%	0.3%	1.35	Yes	3.1%	202,972	6,608,040
M212	Adirondack-New England Mixed Forest-Coniferous Forest-Alpine Meadow Province	0.3%	1.5%	0.23	No	0.5%	147,172	27,986,370
222	Eastern Broadleaf Forest (Continental) Province	0.2%	9.0%	0.02	No	0.1%	97,687	172,911,328
242	Pacific Lowland Mixed Forest Province	0.1%	0.5%	0.26	No	0.6%	57,497	9,534,571
315	Southwest Plateau and Plains Dry Steppe and Shrub Province	0.1%	5.4%	0.02	No	0.0%	39,815	103,129,536
221	Eastern Broadleaf Forest (Oceanic) Province	0.1%	3.5%	0.03	No	0.1%	38,808	66,889,328
263	California Coastal Steppe-Mixed Forest-Redwood Forest Province	0.1%	0.2%	0.52	No	1.2%	34,481	2,918,990
M222	Ozark Broadleaf Forest - Meadow Province	0.1%	0.2%	0.28	No	0.6%	26,369	4,100,165
231	Southeastern Mixed Forest Province	0.1%	6.4%	0.01	No	0.0%	26,353	123,644,224
M231	Ouachita Mixed Forest - Meadow Province	0.0%	0.3%	0.09	No	0.2%	11,908	5,644,113
332	Great Plains Steppe Province	0.0%	4.5%	0.01	No	0.0%	10,148	85,891,360
311	Great Plains Steppe and Shrub Province	0.0%	0.6%	0.03	No	0.1%	8,504	11,252,168
234	Lower Mississippi Riverine Forest Province	0.0%	1.5%	0.01	No	0.0%	4,122	28,361,032
251	Prairie Parkland (Temperate) Province	0.0%	7.3%	0.00	No	0.0%	0	139,783,520
255	Prairie Parkland (Subtropical) Province	0.0%	2.7%	0.00	No	0.0%	0	51,247,280
262	California Dry Steppe Province	0.0%	0.6%	0.00	No	0.0%	0	12,323,812
M334	Black Hills Coniferous Forest Province	0.0%	0.1%	0.00	No	0.0%	0	2,353,896
				Median				
	Totals	100.0%	100.0%	0.26		2.3%	43,858,509	1,921,547,962

Table VII.3 presents a tabulation of total acres in the continental U.S. by province and the corresponding amount of this in Wilderness areas. This table provides several key types of information: (1) percentage of the ecoregion protected as Wilderness, (2) percentage of lower 48 Wilderness in each province, (3) percent of total lower 48 Wilderness by ecoregion. These data provide several interesting perspectives.

The first is the proportion of an ecoregion protected in Wilderness. Overall, about two percent of the land areas in the continental United States are protected as Wilderness. At the upper end, about 26 percent of the Everglades province and 16.4 percent of the American Desert province are Wilderness (with the latter high percentage occurring just recently with the recent California National Parks Wilderness legislation). High percentages of alpine provinces in the Cascades, Rocky Mountains, and Sierras also are protected. The top five provinces (just 15 percent) contain 75 percent of Wilderness, leaving the other 85 percent of provinces with 25 percent of U.S. Wilderness. This disparity is even more apparent when one looks at Figure 2 (map), which shows that large provinces have essentially no Wilderness protection (20 of the 60 provinces have zero or fewer than 1 percent protected as Wilderness). Plains and Southeastern mixed forest represent substantial portions of U.S. land areas with almost no Wilderness. However, much of these provinces are in areas with limited acreage of federal lands, so the opportunities for Wilderness designation may be limited.

Figure 2 also indicates a large "gray doughnut" in the public states of Utah and Nevada. Under-representation of the Intermountain Desert province could be reduced if BLM WSA's are designated. Figures 3-4, 5-6, 7 and 8 provide a mapping of the Wilderness areas by province for the North, South, Rocky Mountains and Pacific Coast, respectively.

To provide some policy perspective on underrepresentation, we calculate the ratio of Wilderness to ecoregion area. A ratio of one means that the province has equal percentages of the NWPS and continental United States land area. For example in the case of Province M331, a ratio of 5.1 means that this province has five times as much representation in the NWPS as it has in the land area in the Continental United States. Thus this province is well represented in the NWPS. Conversely, Province 341, Intermountain Desert, represents 3.6 percent of the U.S. land area but only 1.4 percent of the NWPS. Thus, this province has a ratio of 0.39, indicating it is underrepresented in the NWPS and underprotected. Addition of another acre would be more important in Province 341 than in M331 in terms of the contribution to protecting diversity of landscapes.

Figure VII.2: The Relative Protection of Ecoregions by Wilderness

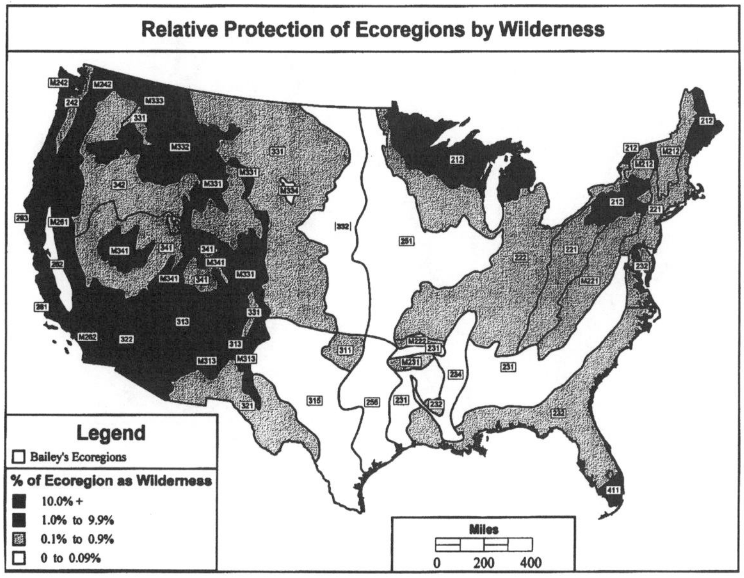

Figure VII.3: Wilderness Ecoregions Within the Eastern Portion of the North Study Area

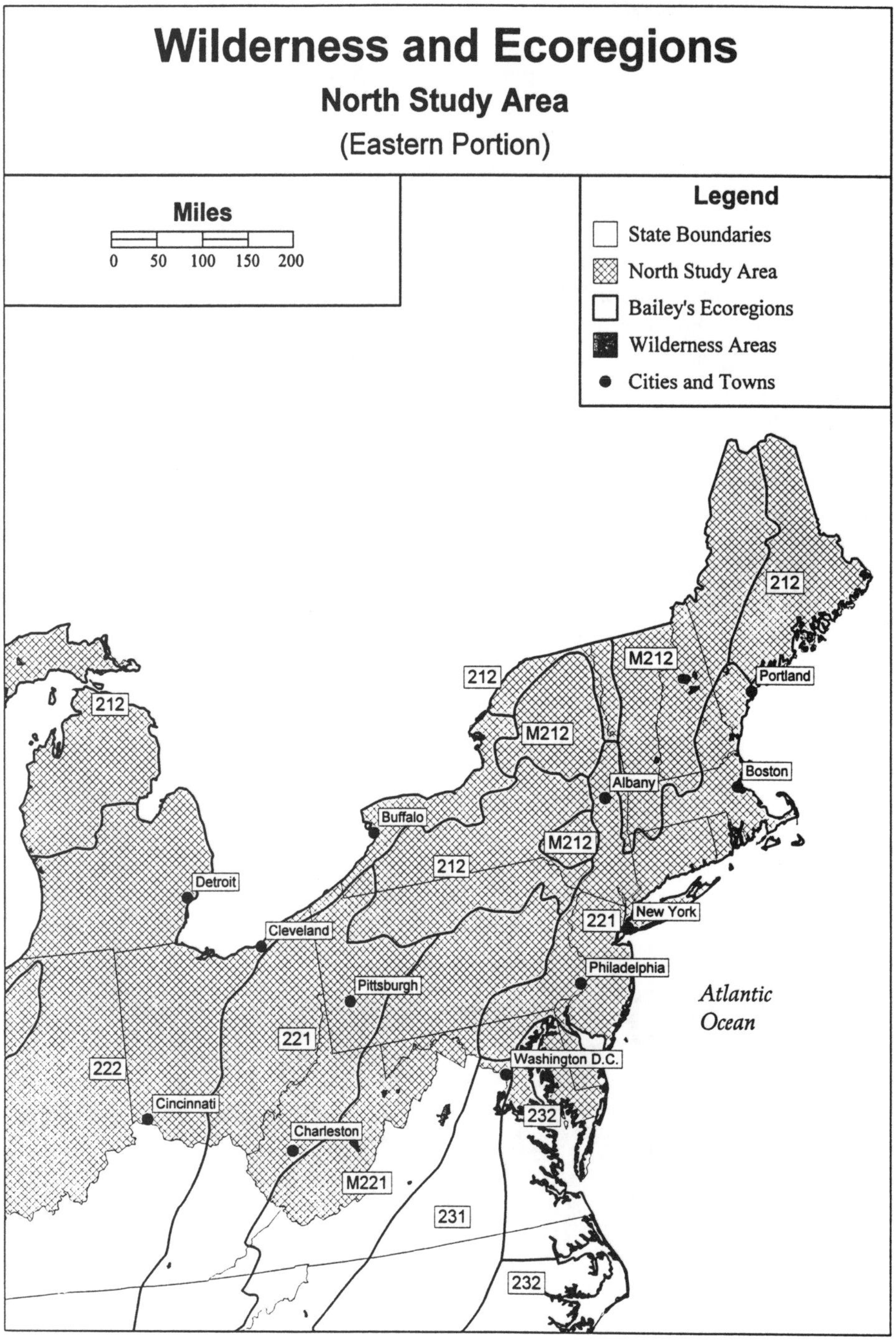

Figure VII.4: Wilderness Ecoregions Within the Western Portion of the North Study Area

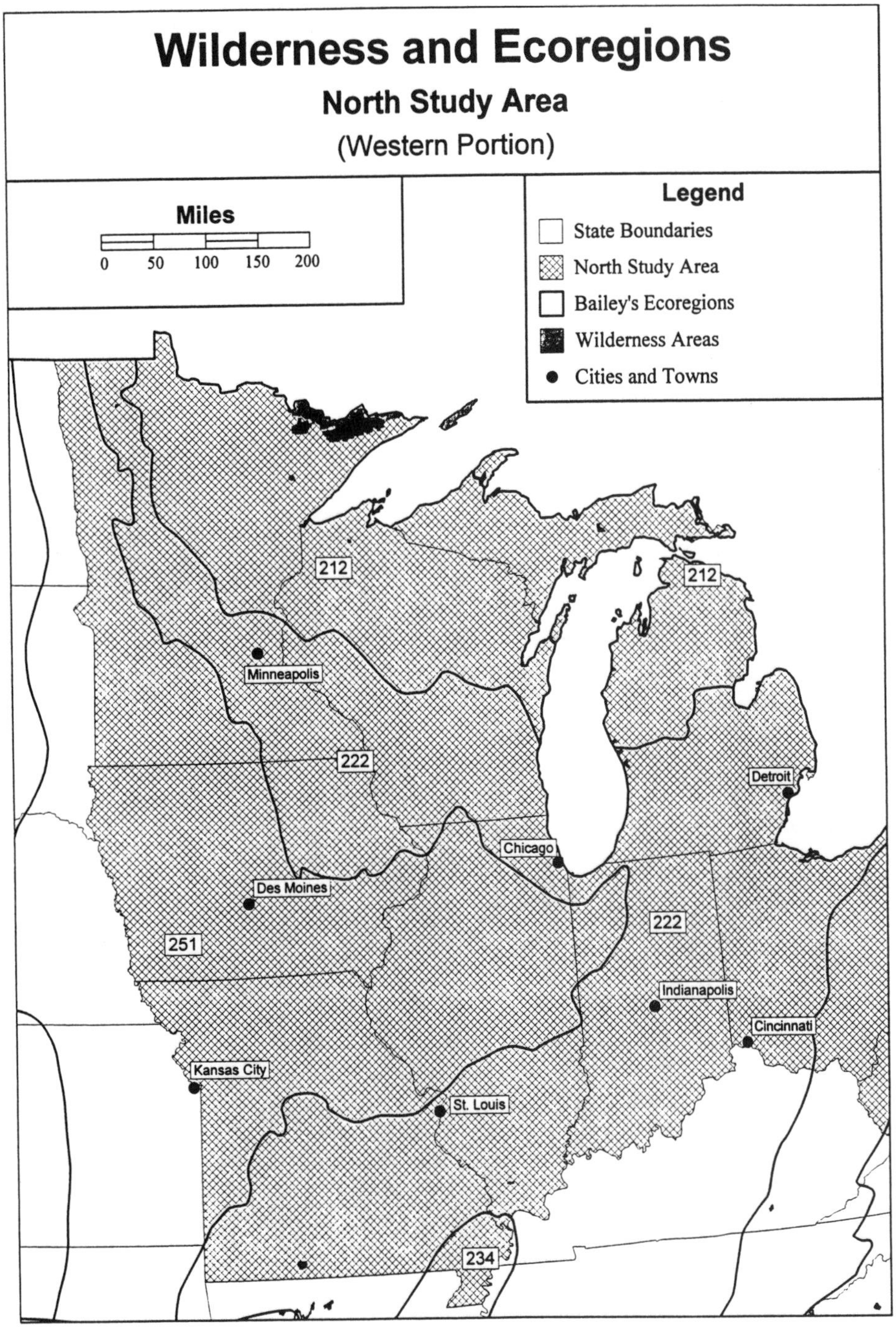

Figure VII.5: Wilderness Ecoregions Within the Eastern Portion of the South Study Area

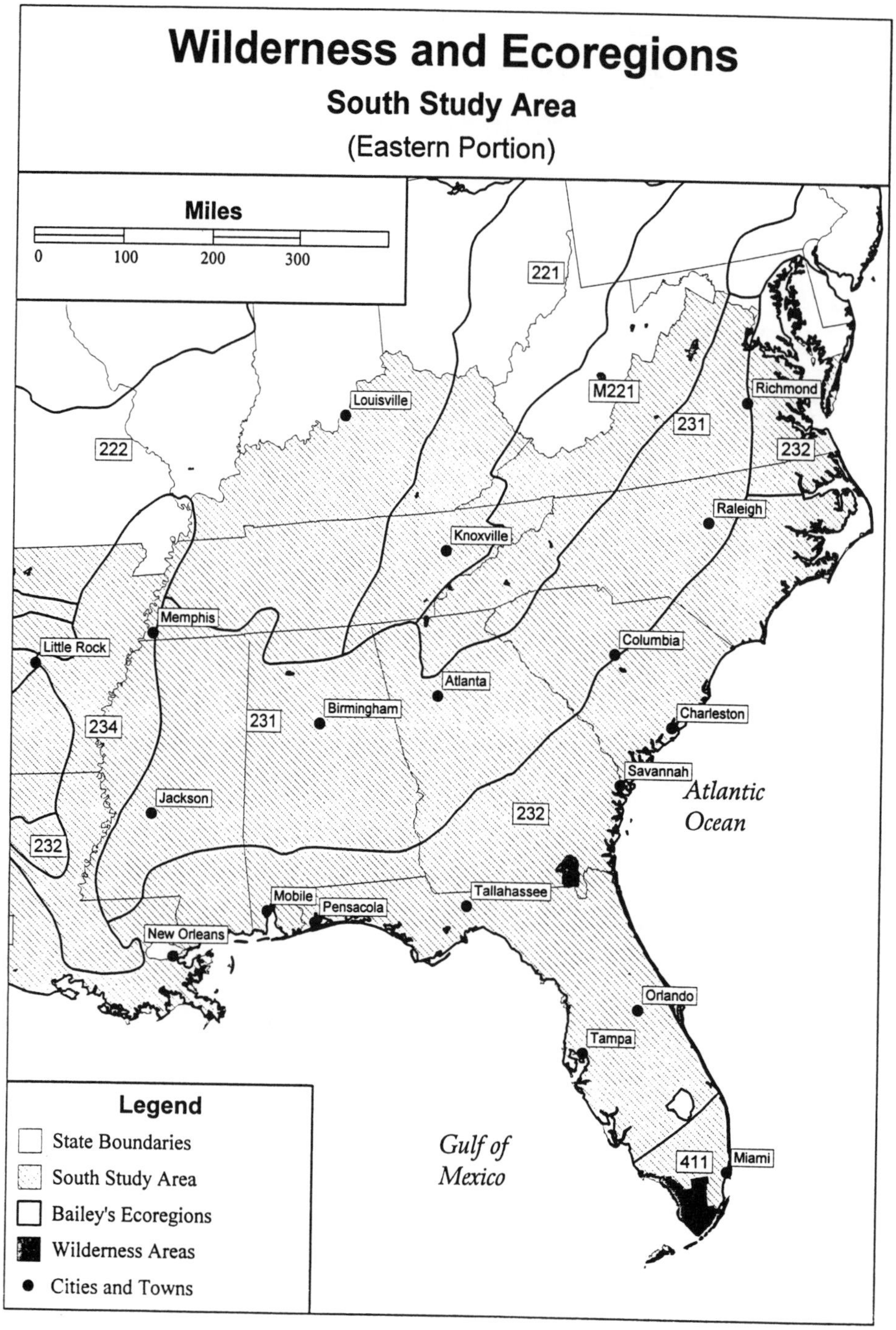

Figure VII.6: Wilderness Ecoregions Within the Western Portion of the South Study Area

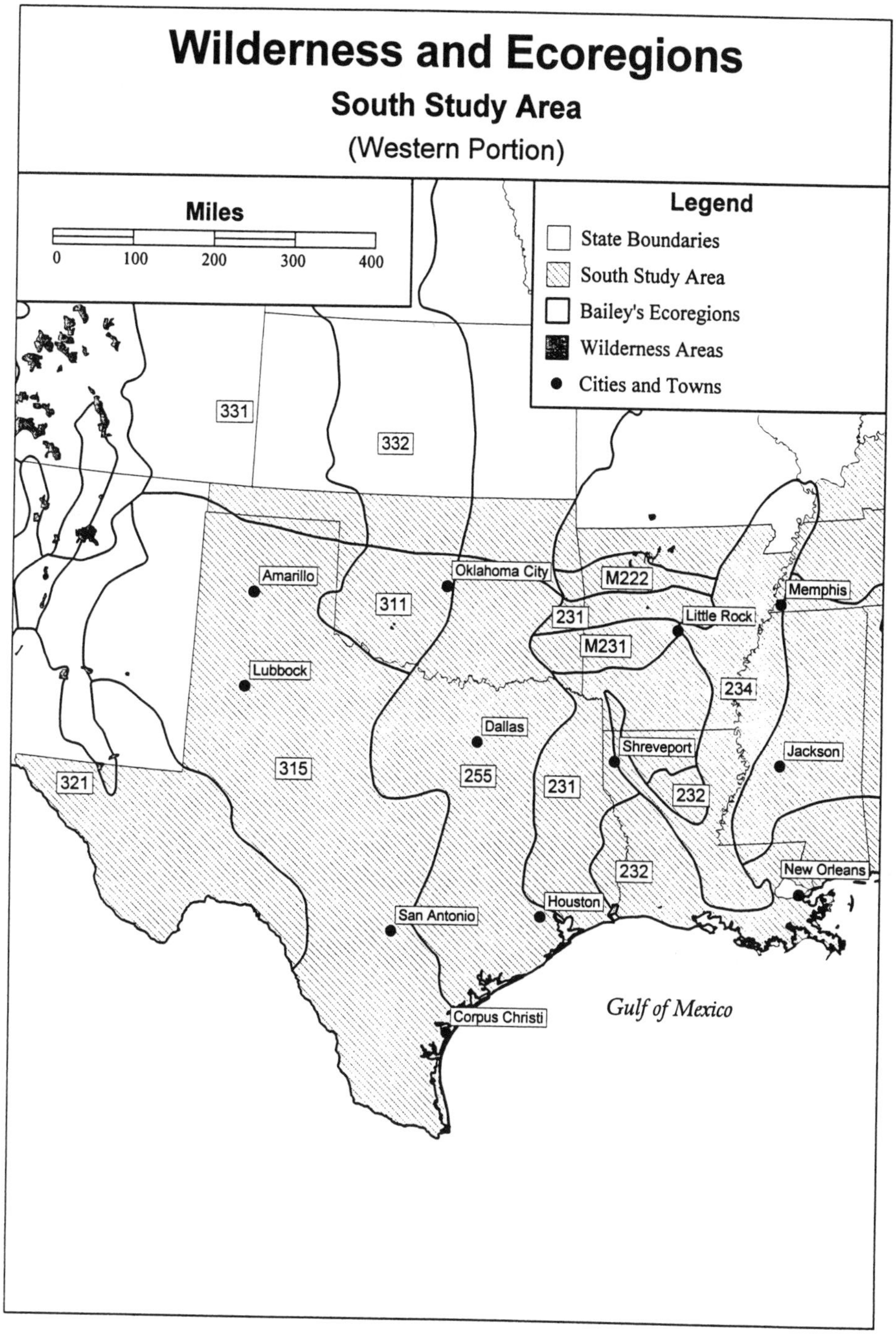

Figure VII.7: Wilderness Ecoregions of the Rocky Mountains Study Area

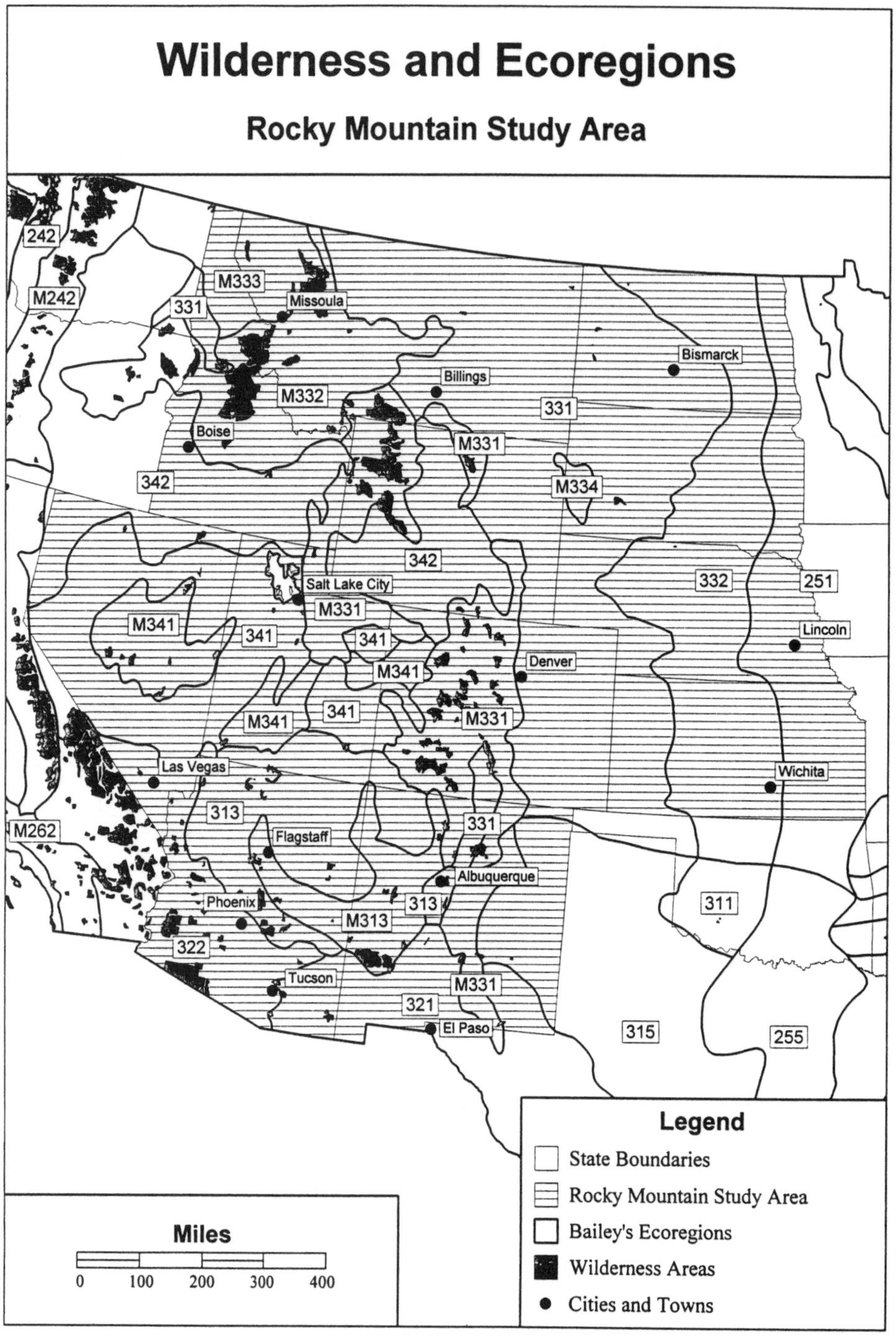

Figure VII.8: Wilderness Ecoregions of the Pacific Coast Study Area

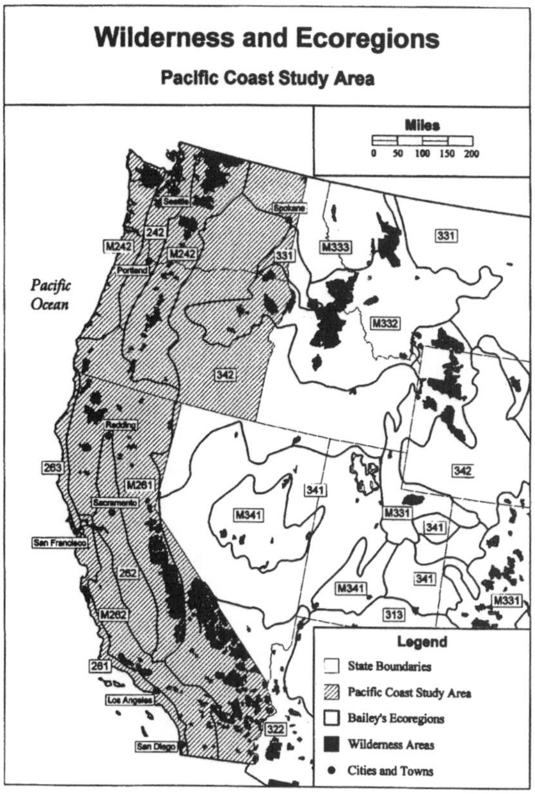

STATE AGENCY WILDERNESS

Resource Base and Ecosystem Representation

Since 1970, eight states have designated 3,289,077 acres of wilderness in 59 areas (Table VII.4) (Peterson, 1996). State wilderness includes areas that are part of recognized state programs that: (a) preserve natural qualities and primitive recreation opportunities, (b) prohibit resource development activities, (c) specify minimum area size criteria, and (d) recognize other values (e.g. historic, educational, scientific) compatible with wilderness management. Five wilderness areas in Florida, where that state's wilderness act was repealed in 1989, were not included in the survey.

Table VII.4: Number of Areas and Total Acreage Protected as Wilderness by State Agencies, 1996

State	Areas	Acres
Alaska	5	1,397,000
California	7	443,770
Maryland	11	144,400
Michigan	3	52,056
Minnesota	1	100,000
Missouri	11	22,671
New York	20	1,122,822
Wisconsin	1	6,358
Total	59	3,289,077

Source: Peterson, 1996.

About 40 percent of 261 major terrestrial ecosystems recognized by a combination of Bailey's ecoregions and Kuchler's potential natural vegetation are not protected in the National Wilderness Preservation System. State wilderness can serve an important recreation role where federal land holdings are scarce or nonexistent, particularly in the Eastern U.S., which holds one half of the country's population but less than five percent of the federal Wilderness.

Current Recreation Use

Data on state Wilderness visitation is sparse: only Alaska and New York systematically collect information on visitation levels. According to Wilderness managers, 34 percent of areas are in the "high" use category, 39 percent are in "medium" use, and 27 percent are rated as "low" use areas (Peterson, 1996). Despite relatively high levels of use experienced in several states, only California, Michigan, and New York limit the number of people entering a Wilderness Area (Peterson, 1996). Most states have not adopted a comprehensive visitor management strategy such as Limits of Acceptable Change, Visitor Impact Management, or the Recreation Opportunity Spectrum (ROS).

Visitor impacts are monitored by most states except California and Maryland. Of 14 biophysical and sociocultural wilderness resources identified in the survey, seven were identified to be unacceptably impacted by visitor use in one or more states. Impacts include campsite spreading, erosion, vegetation impacts, increasing trail depth and width, overcrowding, and declining user satisfaction. Sixteen issues not related to direct use were reported to impact wilderness resource values at least to a "medium" magnitude. These impacts included: subdivision of land on wilderness boundaries, limitations to public access through private lands, disruption of wildlife corridors due to adjacent land uses, noise and visual impacts from nearby activities, exotic plant species, unnatural plant succession, use of toxic chemicals by adjacent land owners, nontraditional, motorized or illegal uses; inadequate staffing of field stations; and political pressures from local governments regarding wilderness management policies. Managers report that funding for state Wilderness areas is not formalized in state budgets, and appropriations for management are not adequate.

A backpacker in Ernie Creek Valley glances toward Gates of the Arctic Wilderness Preserve in Alaska, which is managed by the National Park Service. Photo courtesy of USDI National Park Service. Photo by John M. Kauffmann.

TRENDS IN RECREATION USE OF FEDERAL WILDERNESS AREAS

USFS and NPS Wilderness Use Trends 1965 to 1994

Time series data were obtained from Cole (1996). These data are the best available, consistently compiled data for the USFS and NPS. However, Wilderness use trends are difficult to measure accurately for several reasons. For example, methods for collecting visitor-use data at non-permit Wilderness areas have sometimes changed from year to year. The quality of data–collection efforts varies with funding and staffing devoted to the task. Further, the USFS and NPS use different units of measurement—the Recreation Visitor Day (RVD) and the Overnight Stay (OS), respectively. The Overnight Stay is considered to be a better indicator of intensity, although a factor of 2.5 is often employed to obtain equivalent RVDs (Cole, 1996).

Generally speaking, the trend in recreation visits to National Forest Wilderness has paralleled designations. Use grew at more than 9.4 percent annually between 1965 and 1974. In the Pacific Coast region, use grew at a faster pace (nearly 17 percent annually) than designations. Between 1975 and 1985 the rate of growth in use increased to roughly 10 percent per year. USFS Wilderness visits increased by about 4.5 million RVDs, led by a 298.4 percent gain (3.3 million visits) in the Rocky Mountain region, and a 700,000 RVD increase in the Pacific Coast region. Large increases in the South during that period closely follow substantial acreage additions. After 1985, as growth in supply leveled off, USFS Wilderness use grew more slowly, rising 8.4 percent by 1993. Recreation visitor days at USFS Wilderness between 1965 and 1993 are shown in Table VII.5.

Table VII.5: National Forest Wilderness Visitor Use in 12-Hour Recreation Visitor Days for the U.S. and Regions for Selected Years

Year	Continental U.S. Total	Regions			
		North	South	Rocky Mountains	Pacific Coast
1965	2,951,500	717,200	13,700	996,500	1,224,100
1970	4,646,000	1,171,500	15,300	1,054,500	2,404,700
1975	6,465,000	1,205,200	169,900	1,635,900	3,454,000
1980	9,079,360	1,421,300	422,600	3,751,460	3,484,000
1985	10,954,170	1,352,920	527,850	4,917,400	4,156,000
1990	11,569,821	1,821,800	519,783	5,136,700	4,091,538
1993	12,028,873	1,837,800	507,716	5,959,575	3,723,782

Use of NPS Wilderness (Table VII.6) closely follows large acreage designations, but a large number of additions in 1978 did not seem to affect total use. After 1983, use of NPS Wilderness jumped with each new designation, fell slightly, then leveled off or grew slowly in subsequent years until the next designation. The largest increase in NPS Wilderness use occurred in 1984 with the addition of Yosemite and Sequoia-Kings Canyon in California to the NWPS.

Table VII.6: National Park Service Wilderness Overnight Stays and Recreation Visitor Days Statistics, U.S. Total, and Regions for Selected Years

Year	Overnight Stays				
	U.S.	Regions			
		North	South	Rocky Mountains	Pacific Coast
1965	0	0	0	0	0
1971	73			73	
1975	15,244			282	14,911
1980	179,763	28,043	89,101	15,801	46,684
1985	417,774	32,313	73,570	13,065	298,826
1990	559,093	37,489	81,459	11,631	428,504
1993	688,208	40,690	106,921	14,966	525,625
1994	738,434	43,673	109,174	17,976	567,611

Table VII.6 Cont.

Year	U.S.	Recreation Visitor Days North	South	Regions Rocky Mountains	Pacific Coast
1965	0	0	0	0	0
1971	183			183	
1975	38,110			705	37,278
1980	449,408	70,108	222,753	39,503	116,710
1985	1,044,435	80,783	183,925	32,663	747,065
1990	1,397,733	93,723	203,648	29,078	1,071,260
1993	1,720,520	101,725	267,303	37,415	1,314,063
1994	1,846,085	109,183	272,935	44,940	1,419,028

The intensity of use, usually expressed as RVD/Acre, is another indicator of Wilderness use. By accounting for increased acreage, this measure modifies changes in observed use resulting from new additions to the NWPS. The intensity of overall USFS Wilderness use has been fairly constant when observed between 1971 and 1993. The national average fluctuates between 0.39 and 0.44 RVD/Acre over the 22-year period. However, there is substantial variability between regions (Figure 9). The North and the South have high RVD/Acre, while the Rocky Mountains have the least. After 1984, when few additions occurred, use intensity was virtually constant at about 0.4 RVD/Acre.

Observed use intensity for NPS Wilderness areas also has fluctuated. Large additions of well-used NPS areas in the Rocky Mountain and North regions resulted in a near doubling of national average use intensity from 0.19 to 0.36 RVD/Acre (see Figure 10). Addition of several less intensely used areas, including the 1.3 million acre Everglades Park, brought the national average back down to 0.14 RVD/Acre in 1978 where it remained fairly constant at about 0.15 RVD/Acre until 1984 with the addition of the big, heavily used California parks. Between 1984 and 1993 intensity remained between 0.21 and 0.27 RVD/acre. The addition of the lightly used 3.2 million acre Death Valley reduced overall intensity to 0.18 RVD/acre in 1994.

Intensity of use varies significantly among regions. Not surprisingly, the North has substantially higher RVD/Acre than the other regions. Designation of much of Yosemite National Park as Wilderness in 1983 boosted the RVDs per acre in the Pacific Region. As in USFS Wilderness, the Rocky Mountains have the least use per acre. Part of the reason for the region's low value, however, is the most intensively used areas, such as Rocky Mountain National Park, have not been designated.

Figure VII.9: Number of Recreation Visitor Days (RDVs) per Acre on USDA Forest Service Land

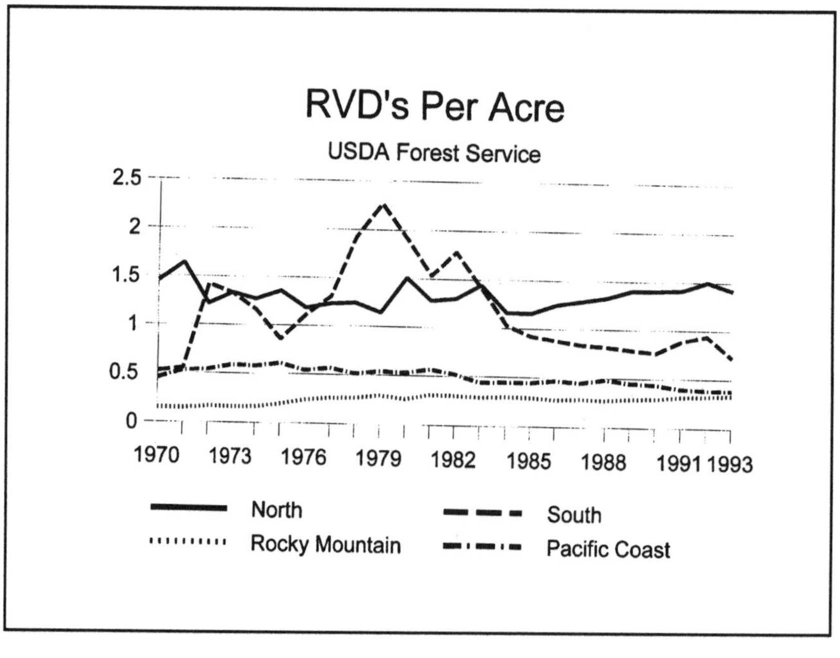

Figure VII.10: Number of Recreation Visitor Days (RDVs) per Acre on National Park Service Land

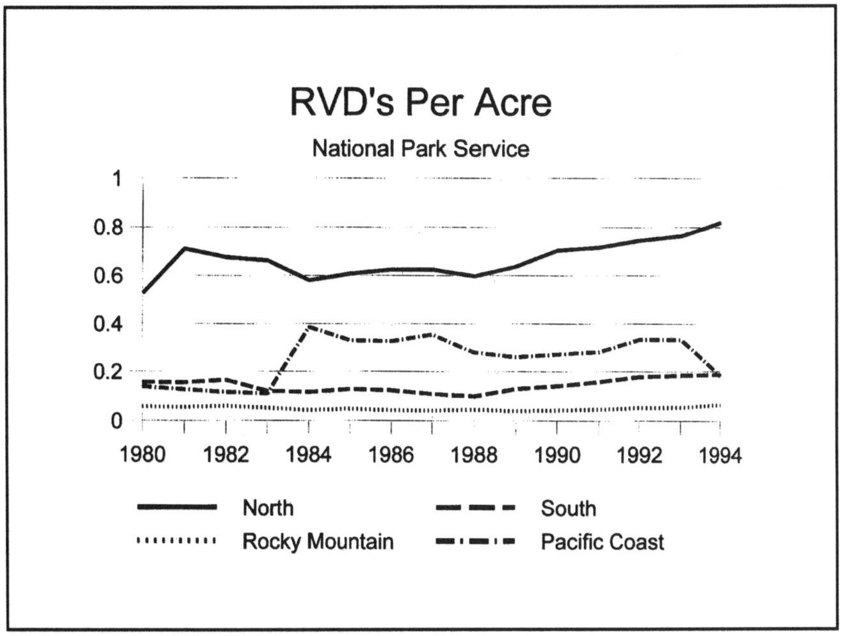

U.S. Fish and Wildlife Service Visitor Use

The USFWS does not maintain or report data on visits to Wilderness areas within its National Wildlife Refuges. It reports only total visits to an entire refuge. To determine the visitor days occurring in Wilderness areas in National Wildlife Refuges, we obtained information on the Wilderness acres within each refuge and then individual refuges were contacted to determine the number of total visits that are attributable to the Wilderness acres. While 63 refuges have designated Wilderness acreages, only the 14 that have substantial percentages of wilderness acres were contacted for two reasons. First, only on refuges where Wilderness acreage represents a large percent of the refuge or a large absolute amount of acreage would managers likely be able to provide accurate estimates of the proportion of refuge visits attributable to Wilderness. Second, refuges with only a few hundred acres of Wilderness would likely contribute such a small amount to total visits that it was not deemed worthwhile to contact the refuge managers for such information. Thus, managers for each of the 14 refuges were contacted and asked about the percentage of activities that take place in the Wilderness areas.

We surveyed most of the Wilderness acreage in National Wildlife Refuges in the Rocky Mountain and Southeast regions (Table VII.7). The areas in these refuges account for nearly all of the Wildlife Refuge acreage in the lower 48 states. Combining each refuge manager's estimates yields a total of about 350,000 visits to Wilderness Areas on refuges. About 80 percent of the visits occur in the South. More accurate assessment of Wilderness use on National Wildlife Refuges will not be possible unless the USFWS makes Wilderness data collection a priority.

Table VII.7: Total Acreage and Estimates of Visitor Use in National Wildlife Refuge Wilderness Areas, 1996

Region	Total Wilderness Acres	Acres Surveyed	Estimated Use
Alaska	18,676,320	None surveyed	—
Pacific	1,475	None surveyed	—
Rocky Mountain	1,473,384	1,405,251	66,785
Northeast	63,528	25,150	2,170
Southeast	461,630	403,693	283,328
Total	20,676,340	1,834,094	352,283

Bureau of Land Management Visitor Use

The BLM recently developed a database system for recording recreation use at its Wilderness Areas. However, the system is not accessible to either BLM staff nor the public on any centralized computer system. Not surprisingly, the visitor use data is incomplete and the lack of access provides little incentive for agency personnel to use or update the system.

The most detailed data available are for Arizona Wilderness Areas. Combining the data for Arizona, Colorado (only three areas reported), Montana, and Utah (only one area each is reported) yields 63,000 visits in 1996 on 1.15 million acres. The Pacific Coast region reports 53,700 visits in 1996 on 735,200 acres, with the majority of the visits being in California.

The visitor use statistics in the BLM database are very likely substantial underestimates of use as zero visitation is reported for thousands of acres of Wilderness Areas located in several BLM districts in California. Wilderness visitation data is reported in the database for less than half the designated acreage. Given that much BLM Wilderness is high desert with spring and fall seasons of use that complement rather than substituting for Forest Service and Park Service alpine Wilderness Areas (e.g., primarily summer use), one would expect total visits to be in the millions, not 116,000 visits as reported for 1996. Knowing visitor use is part of the foundation of an agency's Wilderness management program. Without knowing current use, it is difficult to assess trends for monitoring impacts and to evaluate the merits of designations of additional areas objectively.

Other Sources of Visitor Use Data

Given the variable reliability of Wilderness visitor use information, especially from BLM and USFWS, it is useful to have other independent estimates of visitation. One available estimate is provided by Cordell and Teasley (1997) using data from the 1994-95 National Survey on Recreation and the Environment. Their approach employed a telephone survey of U.S. households, so it is based on these individuals' self-reported number of visits to areas they perceived to be Wilderness areas. Based on these responses, Cordell and Teasley conservatively estimated 40.4 million visits to Wilderness areas in 1995. Since the sum of USFS and NPS RVDs is about 14 million, and with about 100,000 visits from BLM and 352,000 from the USFWS, the combined agencies' reported total is about 14.5 million visits. Thus, the agency-derived estimates appear to be conservative. Given the heated debates over Wilderness acreage recommendations, it would seem that agencies would want to have data on visitor use. This is particularly true for BLM. This agency has more acres being debated for Wilderness than any other agency, yet it knows the least about visitor use of its Wilderness areas. This discrepancy contributes to the debates being based on emotion rather than data.

OFF-SITE PUBLIC GOOD BENEFITS OF WILDERNESS

Undeveloped and pristine environments cannot be created. As a result, Weisbrod (1964) suggested that preservation of natural environments might have an option value—preserving them maintains the opportunity to visit them in the future.

The Wilderness Act of 1964 emphasizes many societal benefits to Wilderness preservation that go well beyond recreation. Wilderness preservation also provides benefits to the nonvisiting general public who take comfort in knowing that particular natural environments exist and are protected. This motivation leads to existence benefits. As the empirical examples below indicate, it is likely to be one of the more dominant motivations for maintaining Wilderness in the future. Another off-site benefit is the benefit the current generation obtains from knowing that protection today will provide Wilderness to future generations. Existence and bequest motivations are sometimes referred to as nonuse or passive use benefits. Passive use benefits of Wilderness have all of the required characteristics of a pure public good. For example, such benefits can be simultaneously enjoyed by millions of people without reducing the passive use benefits of others. In addition, no one can be prevented from enjoying the knowledge that a particular Wilderness is protected.

The economic theory underlying these existence motivations allows us several generalizations. First, a Wilderness area need not be absolutely unique to generate existence benefits (Freeman, 1993). However, the more unique the area is, the fewer the possible substitutes, and the higher the passive use benefits. The more unique the Wilderness is, the rarer or scarcer it is, so we would expect this would result in higher benefits. Second, the potential loss of the resource need not be irreversible to generate existence benefits (Freeman, 1993), but existence benefits are likely to be largest when the resource is both unique and irreplaceable (i.e., without effective substitutes). Preservation of a Wilderness jointly produces recreation and passive use benefits. Lastly, active users can also receive existence benefits (Loomis, 1988).

Empirical Examples of the Relative Importance of Passive Use Values

Walsh, Loomis, and Gillman (1984) made the first attempt to measure the option, existence, and bequest benefits as well as the recreation benefits of Wilderness. They conducted a mail survey of Colorado residents in 1980. In the survey booklet, they asked sampled individuals about their household's willingness to pay (WTP) annually into a fund for continued preservation of the current (at the time of the study) 1.2 million acres of Wilderness in Colorado. They were also asked about their WTP for 2.6 million acres, five million acres and finally designating all roadless areas in Colorado (10 million acres) as Wilderness. Following these questions, individuals were asked what percent of their WTP was for recreation use this year, maintaining the option to visit in the future, knowing that Wilderness areas exist as a natural habitat for plants, fish and wildlife, and finally, knowing that future generations would have Wilderness areas. Results are summarized in Table VII. 8.

The second study of the benefits of Wilderness preservation was performed by Pope and Jones (1990) in Utah. They conducted telephone interviews of Utah households regarding designation of alternative quantities of BLM land as Wilderness. While these authors did not split out the different motivations for payment to preserve Wilderness, they did find households willing to pay substantial amounts.

The most recent U.S. Wilderness preservation study was conducted by Gilbert, Glass, and More (1992) to value Wilderness Areas in the eastern U.S. A mail questionnaire was sent to a sample of Vermont residents; after two mailings the overall response rate was 30 percent. The questionnaire asked respondents to value protection of all Wilderness areas east of the Mississippi River. Respondents indicated that 84 percent of their value was related to such passive uses as existence and bequest.

Table VII. 8 shows the decomposition of total value individual motivations. It is evident that a majority of the value of Wilderness is related to option, existence, bequest, and Gilbert et al.'s new category, related to altruism (defined as protecting it for use by others).

Table VII.8: Distribution of Motivations for Paying For Wilderness Designation

	Own Recreation	Option Benefit	Existence Benefit	Bequest Benefit	Altruistic Benefit
			Percentages		
Walsh, et al. Colorado Wilderness	43	16	20	21	not asked
Gilbert, et al. All Eastern Wilderness	16	17	21	29	17

ESTIMATING FUTURE RECREATION USE OF WILDERNESS

A multiple regression model was constructed to estimate future use of Wilderness areas with and without designation of eligible roadless areas. In the regression model, visitor use is the dependent variable and demographic variables, along with Wilderness acreage, are the explanatory variables. Combining the estimated coefficients with projections of future values of the demographic variables, we forecast future recreation use with the current Wilderness acreage and proposed Wilderness acreage.

Dependent Variable

Visits per capita are an appropriate measure of wilderness demand. To calculate visits per capita, data are needed on visits and population. Data on RVDs from 1965 to 1993 were obtained from the Intermountain Research Station of the USFS. These data are of varying quality, only 13 percent come from systematic counts such as permits or counters (McClaan and Cole, 1993). This was one reason to take as the unit of observation, RVDs of all Wilderness areas in a given U.S. Census region. We believe this aggregation of individual areas would net out much of the variability in use arising from inconsistencies in administrative estimating procedures across areas. Cole (1996) also suggests that aggregating areas will improve the reliability of the recreation use data. Trend relationships are more evident in aggregate data. Data on National Park Service Wilderness visits also were obtained from the Intermountain Research Station. This agency's data were originally collected as overnight visits and then converted to visitor-days by Cole using average length of stay. Then day use was added to this figure (see Cole, 1996 for more details).

Population is perhaps one of the most important determinants of total demand for nearly any product. We collected state population statistics from the U.S. Census and the *Statistical Abstract of the U.S.*

Since it is unlikely that population would simply have a linear additive effect on visits irrespective of other factors, we choose to divide visits by Census region population to yield visits per capita. This is a common formulation for many recreation demand models, such as the zonal travel cost model (Hellerstein, 1995; Loomis & Walsh, 1997). In addition, by moving population from the right-hand side into the left-hand side eliminates the multicolinearity between acres and population on the right hand side.

Finally, the natural log of visits per capita was used to estimate a nonlinear relationship between visits per capita and the independent variables.

Independent Variables

Per Capita Income

Per capita income is a commonly investigated determinant of recreation behavior. It measures the ability of households to incur the travel cost to visit Wilderness areas as well as purchase the appropriate equipment.

To allow for comparability across years, income was deflated and put into 1992 dollars. The natural log of income was used to allow for a nonlinear effect of changes in income on quantity of visitation. Since the dependent variable is logged the coefficient on income can be interpreted as an elasticity. Per capita personal disposable income data are found in *State Personal Income 1929-1993,* U.S. Bureau of Economic Analysis (1995).

Unemployment Rate

This variable was included to reflect the possibility that the performance of the overall economy, and specifically labor market conditions, might influence Wilderness use. Since Wilderness trips are relatively inexpensive but quite time intensive, it may be that the opportunity costs of such trips are lower when the unemployment rate is high. That is, with high unemployment rate, many people are without jobs and wages tend to be lower. This factor would make the travel and on-site time cost of Wilderness visits less. In addition, with a high unemployment rate people may substitute Wilderness visits for more expensive forms of outdoor recreation such as staying at resorts. The unemployment rate by state was taken from the *Statistical Abstract of the U.S.*

Acreage

The acres of Wilderness can serve as a proxy for quality or for supply of Wilderness recreation opportunities. The more acres there are, holding everything else constant, the less crowding and hence more opportunities for solitude there are. Crowding has been shown to result in a statistically significant reduction in the value of a Wilderness recreation experience (Walsh & Gilliam, 1983). If acreage is statistically significant, it will allow forecast of future visitor days with different Wilderness designation scenarios. Scenarios range from no additional acreage to designation of the all-qualified roadless areas. Since economic theory suggests diminishing marginal value for additional acres of Wilderness, the natural log of acres was used as the independent variable. Thus the coefficient can be interpreted as an elasticity. We expect this elasticity to be less than one.

Year

Many other demographic factors and preferences may have influenced recreation use of Wilderness areas over the past 30 years and may continue to influence future recreation use as well. Unfortunately it is difficult to get annual data on such variables as ethnicity of the population and education. These variables are collected at the state level only each decade during the U.S. Census. Wilderness users tend to have above-average levels of education (Hendee, et al., 1990), and they tend to be non-minorities (National Park Service, 1986:21). The trend in the U.S. and particularly in populous states like California is toward increasing percentages of the population being minority. As Cole (1996) notes, use slowed at Forest Service Wilderness areas and actually declined at National Park Wilderness areas during the 1980s. However, use accelerated at National Park Wilderness areas in the early 1990s. Given the lack of consistent data on demographic variables such as ethnicity, a trend variable is used to capture all of these influences.

Regional Influences

The fixed effects regression model estimates a separate constant for each of the Census/RPA regions for the NPS model and eastern versus western regions for the USFS model. If these regional constants are significantly different from zero (using a standard t-test) and contribute significantly to model fit (using a likelihood ratio test and F-test), then each region has specific factors that are different from each other but vary in a systematic way. These variables then reflect the unquantified influences that vary across Census or RPA regions. For consistency, we estimated and compared fixed effects models for the NPS and USFS using both Census/RPA region and eastern-western U.S. as regional constants. The logic of the eastern-western division was developed by recognizing that a separate Eastern states Wilderness Act was passed by Congress about 10 years after the Wilderness Act of 1964. The Eastern States Wilderness Act was necessary because much of the potential Wilderness land in the East could not meet the same standards of being pristine and untouched that western roadless areas did. Thus, including a geographic constant or variable would allow for testing differences between regions. Region is indexed as in the regression models that follow.

Age

Hendee et al. (1990) suggested that the aging of the population may influence wilderness use trends. However, research by English and Cordell (1985) suggests that recreation participation rates among all age cohorts have risen steadily since 1960. We assembled data on percentage of the population in the 18-44 age categories to test if the percentage of this prime-age Wilderness use group had any influence.

Use Estimating Model

To take full advantage of the available data and to allow for estimation of the effect that acres have on wilderness visits, time series data over the four U.S. Census/RPA regions was pooled. The time series nature of the data and the pooling of time series and cross section raise several econometric issues that are dealt with at length in a technical appendix available from the USDA Forest Service.[1]

The basic multiple regression model estimated is:

(1) $\ln(RVD/POP)_{it} = \alpha D_i + \beta X_{it} + (\rho\varepsilon_{it-1} + \eta_{it})$

where D_i are the regional constants reflecting the fixed effects and i= 1, 2, 3, 4 reflecting Northeastern, Southeastern, Rocky Mountain and Pacific Coast regions in the NPS model and i =1, 2 represents eastern U.S. and western U.S. in the USFS model. $_{it-1}$ + $_{it}$ is the error term. The difference in region-specific constants between USFS and NPS resulted from comparative analysis of the same fixed effects structure for the two agencies.[1]

Statistical Results

The multiple regression results of RVDs of Wilderness areas administered by the USFS are quite satisfactory.[1] Log of acres is significant at the 0.01 level, while log of disposable per capita income is significant at the 0.02 level. Because of the double log specification, the coefficient on acres can be interpreted as an elasticity. Thus, a 10-percent increase in Wilderness acres results in a nine-percent increase in recreation visitor days. This variable allows us to predict changes in visits with additions to the NWPS. Technical Appendix VII table A-3 presents the results of the multiple regression analysis for visitor use of Wilderness areas administered by the National Park Service. Here, log of acres, log of disposable per capita income and year are statistically significant at the 0.01 level.[1]

Forecasting

Source of input values

The accuracy of future forecasts of visits is as dependent on the future estimates of the independent variables as it is on the coefficient estimates themselves. As part of the RPA Assessment process, the USFS commissioned the USDA Economic Research Service's Macroeconomics Team to estimate several future demographic variables, including disposable personal income and unemployment rates (Torgeson, 1996). State-

---

[1]This technical appendix is available in table form from the USDA Forest Service, Outdoor Recreation and Wilderness Assessment Group, 320 Green Street, Athens, GA 30602-2044. Herein all references to Technical Appendices shall be abbreviated as TAs.

level population forecasts were developed from U.S. Census projections and Bureau of Economic Analysis data by Dr. Linda Langner of the USFS RPA staff. Generally, the forecasted future values of the input variables are in line with recent trends. For example, disposable income is projected to grow at two percent a year, which is well below the historic time period but consistent with the experience of the last six years.

One of the biggest unknowns is future Wilderness acreage. Our initial forecast starts with the current quantity of Wilderness as a baseline. Future visits are then estimated with acreage at its current level in each of the four regions for each agency. The resulting estimate is the number of visits in absence of any additional Wilderness designation. The change in visits, therefore, is due to changes in population and income.

Figures VII.11 and VII.12 illustrate the forecasted future use of Forest Service Wilderness at three different Wilderness acreages: (a) holding acreage fixed at the current level, (b) adding the Wilderness acreage recommended for designation, and (c) adding all WSA acreages.

Figure VII.11: Forecasted Wilderness RVDs with Alternative Acreage Supply for National Forests in the Northeast and Southeast Region

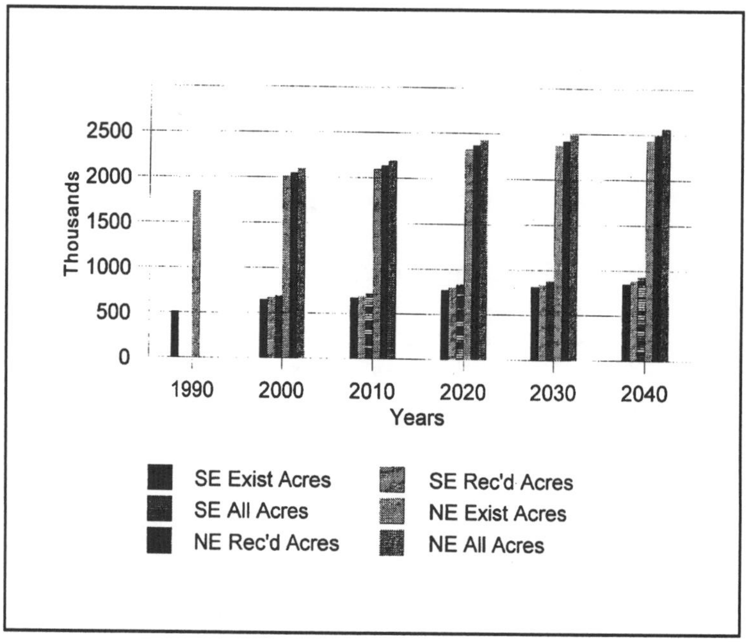

Figure VII.12: Forecasted Wilderness RVDs with Alternative Acreage Supply for National Forests in the Pacific Coast and Rocky Mountain Regions

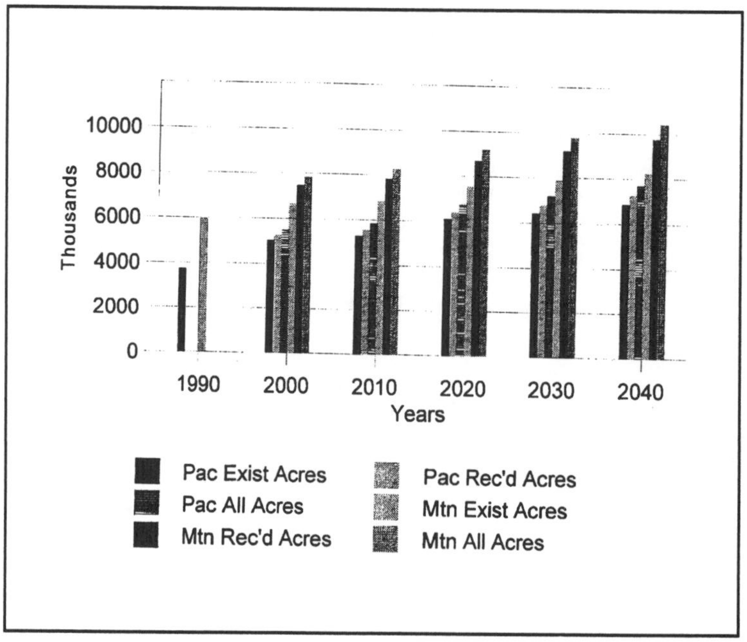

When acreage is held constant at current levels, recreation use is forecast to increase by about 0.5 percent per year during the next 50 years (cumulative increase of 24 percent and 27 percent, respectively, over the 50 years) in the Northeast and Rocky Mountain regions. In the Southeast and Pacific Coast, recreation use is forecast to increase by just slightly less than one percent per year for a cumulative increase of 40 percent and 45 percent, respectively.

Designating additional acres generally shifts the pattern of use upwards. In the North and Southeast, total use would rise from 24 percent to 26 percent and 40 percent to 42 percent, respectively, if recommended acres were designated. In the Pacific Coast, the additional acres are estimated to increase visits from 45 percent to 49 percent over the 50-year period, a net gain of four percent from the added acres. In the Rocky Mountain region, the large recommended increase in Wilderness (2.6 million acres) would result in a 12-percent increase in visitor use, from 27 percent to 39 percent over the 50-year period.

National Park Service Wilderness use is estimated to increase substantially over the next four decades (Figures VII.13 and 14). Holding acres constant, use would grow by about four percent per year. Whether the NPS will accommodate this increased demand will depend upon its management strategy. The increase in NPS Wilderness use results from the sizeable positive trend variable in the national park regression. As illustrated in these figures, designation of recommended acreages as Wilderness reinforces this trend. A large part of the forecasted increase in visits in the Rocky Mountain region with recommended acres is due to additions of backcountry areas in heavily visited Parks, such as Yellowstone (two million acres).

Figure VII.13: Forecasted Wilderness RVDs with Alternative Acreage Supply for National Forests in the Northeast and Rocky Mountain Regions

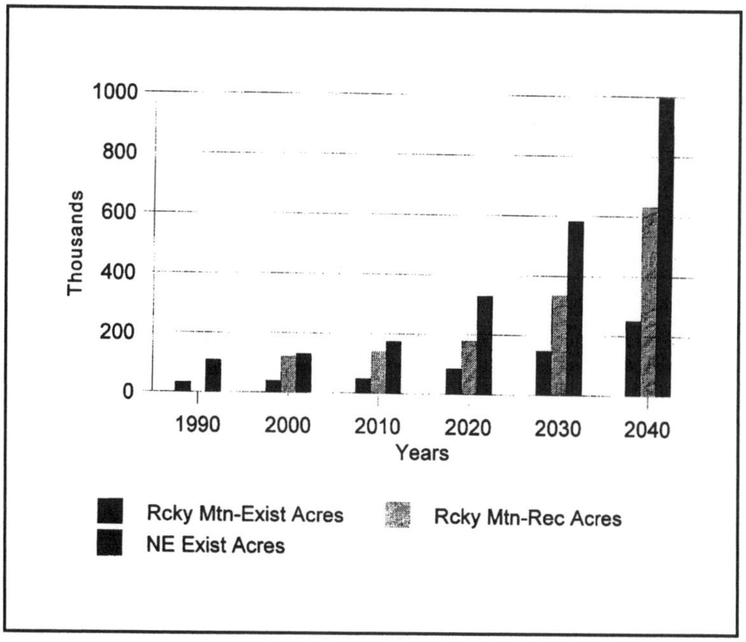

Figure VII.14: Forecasted Wilderness RVDs with Alternative Acreage Supply for National Forests in the Southeast and Pacific Coast Regions

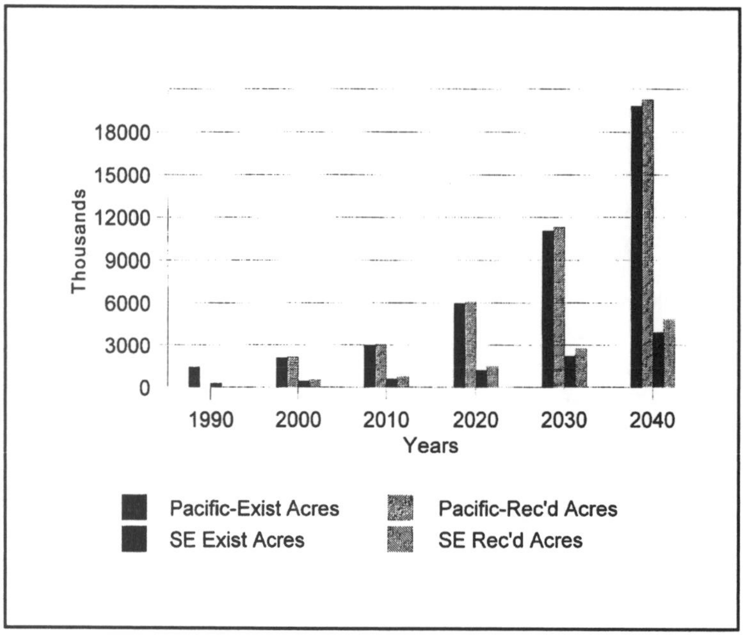

CONCLUSION AND MANAGEMENT IMPLICATIONS

There are four main management implications of this analysis:

1. The benefits of Wilderness to society go far beyond recreation. The current imbalance of ecoregion representation in the National Wilderness Preservation System can be rectified with strategic designations of low elevation and high desert Wilderness Study Areas. In this way, Wilderness can contribute to protecting the diversity of ecoregions located throughout the U.S. In addition, these areas offer differing seasons for recreation (e.g., spring and fall) to the current high elevation Wilderness areas of the USFS and NPS (e.g., primarily summer).

2. A review of the literature on passive use values, such as existence and bequest values, provided by Wilderness protection suggests that the nonrecreation benefits of Wilderness are larger in percentage terms and in the aggregate than the recreation use benefits of wilderness. Accurate assessment of the benefits of Wilderness management and designation requires inclusion of these benefits. Otherwise, benefits of Wilderness are underestimated by at least 50 percent.

3. The multiple regression model for predicting future recreation use showed a statistically significant positive influence of additional Wilderness acreage on recreation use. Thus, additions to the National Wilderness Preservation System will be used by recreationists.

4. Recreation use of both USFS and NPS Wilderness areas is expected to increase in the future. Visitor use of Wilderness areas on national forests are forecast to grow between 0.5 percent and one percent each year for the next 50 years. If current trends continue, NPS Wilderness areas will see substantially increased visitor demand. Whether the National Park Service can accommodate this additional demand within the carrying capacity of these areas is a question that may require further research by that agency.

In the course of assembling visitation data and GIS maps it became clear that Wilderness management has fallen from being a serious priority of the federal land management agencies. The data available to the agencies themselves for making wilderness management decisions are often incomplete, and little effort appears to be made to make it more complete. Much of the existing data are often not consistently maintained or accessible to agency personnel or the public. Data on and trends in visitor use, along with knowledge of the ecological representation of the current Wilderness areas are critical to informed decision making about Wilderness management and allocation issues. The consequences of this lack of basic data on the current status of Wilderness will make it difficult to put wilderness management and allocation decisions on an objective rather than emotional level.

REFERENCES

Cole, D. (1996). *Wilderness recreation use trends 1965 through 1994.* USDA Forest Service Research Paper INT-RP-488. Ogden, UT: USDA Forest Service, Intermountain Research Station.

Cordell, K., & Teasley, J. (1997). *Estimating recreational trips to wilderness in the U.S.: Results from the National Survey on Recreation and the Environment.* Athens, GA: USDA Forest Service, Southern Research Station.

Davis, G. D. (1989). Preservation of Natural Diversity: The Role of Ecosystem Representation Within Wilderness. In *Wilderness Benchmark 1988: Proceedings of the National Wilderness Colloquium; 1988 January 13-14, Tampa, FL, GTR SE-51* (pp.76-82). Asheville, NC: USDA Forest Service, Southeastern Forest Experiment Station.

English, D. & Cordell, K. (1985). A cohort-centric analysis of outdoor recreation participation changes. In A. Watson (Ed.), *Proceedings: Southeastern Recreation Research Conference* (pp. 93-110). Statesboro, GA: Dept. of Recreation and Leisure Services, Georgia Southern College.

Freeman, M. (1993). Nonuse Values in Natural Resource Damage Assessment. In R. Kopp & V. K. Smith (Eds.), *Valuing natural assets: The economics of natural resource damage assessment.* Washington, DC: Resources for the Future.

Gilbert, A., Glass, R. & More, T. (1992). Valuation of Eastern Wilderness: Extramarket Measures of Public Support. In C. Payne, J. Bowker, & P. Reed, *Economic Value of Wilderness*, GTR-SE78, (pp. 57-70). Asheville, NC: USDA Forest Service, Southeastern Forest Experiment Station.

Greene, W. (1990). *Econometric analysis.* New York: Macmillan.

Greene, W. (1995). *Limdep, Version 7.0.* New York: Econometric Software Inc.

Hellerstein, D. (1995). Welfare estimation using aggregate and individual observation models. *American Journal of Agricultural Economics,* 77, 620-630.

Hendee, J., Stankey, G., & Lucas, R. (1990). *Wilderness management* (2nd ed.). Golden, CO: North American Press.

Kmenta, J. (1986). *Elements of econometrics* (2nd ed.). New York: Macmillan.

Loomis, J. (1988). Broadening the concept and measurement of existence value. *Northeastern Journal of Agricultural Resource Economics,* 17,23-29.

Loomis, J. (1993). *Integrated public lands management: Principles and application to national forests, parks, wildlife refuges and BLM lands.* New York: Columbia University Press.

Loomis, J., & Walsh, R. (1997). *Recreation economic decisions* (2nd ed.). State College, PA: Venture Press.

National Park Service. (1986). *1982-1983 Nationwide Recreation Survey.* Washington, DC: U.S. Department of the Interior.

Peterson, M. R. (1988). The Evolution of State-Designated Wilderness Programs in *Outdoor Recreation Benchmark 1988: Proceedings of the National Outdoor Recreation Forum,* Tampa FL. Asheville, NC: USDA Forest Service SE-51, Southeastern Forest Experiment Station.

Peterson, M. R. (1996). Wilderness by state mandate: A survey of state-designated wilderness areas. *Natural Areas Journal*, 16,192-197.

Pope, C., Jones, A., & Jones, J. (1990). Value of wilderness designation in Utah. *Journal of Environmental Management,* 30,157-174.

Stynes, D., Peterson, G., & Rosenthal, R. (1986). Log transformation bias in estimating travel cost models. *Land Economics,* 62, 94-103.

Torgerson, D. (1996). U.S. macroeconomic projections to 2045. Washington, DC: USDA Economic Research Service, Commercial Agriculture Division.

U. S. Bureau of the Census. (1995). *Statistical abstract of the United States, 1966 to 1995.* Washington, D.C.: U.S. Government Printing Office.

U.S. Bureau of Economic Analysis. (1995). *State personal income, 1929-1993.* Washington DC: U.S. Department of Commerce.

Walsh, R., Loomis, J., & Gillman, R. (1984). Valuing option, existence, and bequest demand for wilderness. *Land Economics,* 60, 14-29.

Walsh, R., & Gilliam, L. (1983). Benefits of wilderness expansion with excess demand for Indian peaks. *Western Journal of Agricultural Economics,* 7, 1-12.

Weisbrod, B. (1964). Collective consumption services of individual consumption goods. *Quarterly Journal of Economics,* 78, 471-477.

CHAPTER VIII

WILDERNESS USES, USERS, VALUES, AND MANAGEMENT

. . . .

Invited Papers:

Alan Watson and David N. Cole, USDA Forest Service
Gregory T. Friese, Camp Manito-wish YMCA, and Michael L. Kinziger and John C. Hendee, University of Idaho Wilderness Research Center
Alan Watson and Peter Landres, USDA Forest Service
Thomas F. Geary and Gerald L. Stokes, USDA Forest Service
Jeff Jarvis, Bureau of Land Management
Wes Henry, National Park Service

This chapter is a compendium of six papers written to add further depth to our national assessment of Wilderness, begun with the previous chapter. The first three papers summarize research and experience about the identity of Wilderness users and how Wilderness is used, use of Wilderness for personal growth, and changes of Wilderness values. The second three papers summarize the management situations and policies of three of the federal Wilderness management agencies–the U.S. Forest Service, the Bureau of Land Management, and the National Park Service. With these papers much can be learned about the significance of and issues surrounding Wilderness in the United States.

WILDERNESS USERS AND USE: RECENT ADDITIONS TO UNDERSTANDING

(By Alan Watson and David N. Cole, USDA Forest Service, Missoula, MT)

Scientists at the Leopold Institute, a research unit maintained in Missoula, MT, by the departments of the Interior and Agriculture, have recently conducted or sponsored studies intended to measure aspects of Wilderness visits and visitors at areas where there are comparable data from earlier studies dating back to the 1960s and 1970s. Such areas with comparable historic data include the Boundary Waters Canoe Area Wilderness in Minnesota, the Desolation Wilderness in California, the Shining Rock Wilderness in North Carolina, the Bob Marshall Wilderness Complex in Montana, and the Eagle Cap Wilderness in Oregon. The text that follows summarizes the trends found through comparisons of past and more current studies.

Things That Have Changed

Many demographic and user pattern variables were studied, but only a few strong, consistent changes were found. These changes were in age, gender, and education and in the proportion of visitors with previous experience at other Wildernesses.

Age

The average age of Wilderness visitors increased across most areas. Average ages of Wilderness hikers in the early years of the National Wilderness Preservation System were most typically in the mid-20s. In the 1990s, the average age of wilderness hikers is in the mid-30s.

Gender

Women are found in increasing numbers in Wilderness today. In most Wilderness studies of the 1960s and 1970s, the proportion of women usually was not over 25 percent. In the 1990s, the proportion was close to one third, and sometimes exceeded that number.

Education

Education levels of the general U.S. population have risen since the NWPS was created, and Wilderness users have always been more highly educated than the general population. Over the 30 years of the NWPS's existence, however, education levels of visitors have changed at an even higher rate. For example, at the Boundary Waters Canoe Area Wilderness, the proportion of the sample indicating some graduate-level education (study beyond the BS/BA degree) rose from 15 percent in 1969 to 41 percent in 1991. Most Boundary Waters visitors come from Minnesota, where Census data show that the proportion of the state's population with some graduate education increased from four to six percent between 1970 and 1990. For Boundary Waters visitors, the median level of education increased from 13.1 years in 1969 to 16.4 years in 1991.

Previous Wilderness Experience

The proportion of today's Wilderness visitors who have visited other Wildernesses has grown significantly. At the Desolation Wilderness, where only 61 percent of visitors in 1972 reported previous visits to other Wilderness locations, 94 percent of 1992 visitors reported such experiences.

Things That Have Not Changed

A few factors did not change in most areas. These included the size of population centers people live in, the number of days spent in wilderness during a year, the proportion of visitors who hike, photograph, or swim, the typical distance traveled off-trail, the number of groups encountered around campsites, the ability to find campsite solitude, evaluations of impacts, and support for outhouses, cement fireplaces, interpretive signs, natural fisheries, and restriction of number of visitors.

Although wilderness visitation is thought of primarily as a male activity, an increasing number of wilderness enthusiasts are women. Female camper in Isle Royale National Park Wilderness area in Michigan. Photo courtesy of USDI National Park Service. Photo by Richard Frear.

Current Residence

While there are regional differences in the sizes of communities people are coming from to visit Wildernesses, at specific Wilderness Areas the types of places people come from have been consistent across time. In North Carolina, where the Shining Rock Wilderness is located, the median type of origin in both 1978 and 1990 was a city with a population of about 30,000. For North Carolina this is a big place. In that state the median population level of communities was 7,500 in 1980. Nationally, it was 70,000. In California, Wilderness visitors came predominantly from the large population centers of that region, much larger places than origins for Shining Rock visitors.

Number of Days Spent in Wilderness in the Past Year

The total amount of time visitors spend in any Wilderness in a year has remained constant. Of course, differences exist across regions and even across users at a particular area. For instance, at the Desolation Wilderness, day users averaged a little fewer than five days in the past year and campers averaged around 11.

Proportion of Visitors Who Hike, Photograph, or Swim

From the many activities that Wilderness visitors participate in, the frequency of hiking, photographing, and swimming have not changed at most areas. These activities have remained extremely popular.

Distance Traveled Off-Trail

Studies across time suggest that visitors have not varied the distances they travel off-trail during a Wilderness visit. While overnight visitors sometimes travel farther within Wilderness now than they once did, the amount of off-trail travel has not increased. Reports of off-trail travel varied greatly between parties, but the average remains about two to 2.5 miles for overnight visitors to the Desolation Wilderness.

Number of Groups Encountered Around Campsites

Overall, reports of number of campsite encounters with other visitors have not changed across time for most areas. Use densities, and therefore encounters, vary considerably across areas and across different zones of individual Wildernesses.

Campsite Solitude

The proportion of those who were able to find the level of solitude they desired at campsites has remained constant over time at most areas. Despite reported increases in use levels, this aspect of solitude achievement was consistent. At the Boundary Waters Canoe Area Wilderness, about one-third of the visitors still see more people than they desire to see nearby.

Evaluations of Impacts

Visitor perceptions of the seriousness of resource impacts from recreation use did not change appreciably at most places. On a scale from "very poor" to "very good," Desolation Wilderness visitors in 1972 and 1990 evaluated wear-and-tear conditions to be "very good." More experienced users, however, typically have significantly poorer evaluations of resource conditions than less experienced users.

Support for Outdoor Facilities, Interpretive Signs, Natural Fisheries and Visitor Restrictions

Some of these management actions can be quite controversial. While overall support has remained constant, types of users differ in their views of visitor support. Day users often demonstrate a fairly neutral attitude toward outhouses, while campers feel slightly negative about them; day users are slightly supportive of interpretive signs in wilderness, and campers are slightly negative.

Visitor Attitudes and Beliefs

Several studies have been conducted at specific places to understand how visitors feel about Wilderness, but only one study was conducted to investigate how attitudes and beliefs have changed over time.

Attitudes Toward Appropriate Behaviors

At the Eagle Cap Wilderness in Oregon, it was found that between 1965 and 1993 visitors demonstrated consistent increases in evidence of a deep commitment to "an enduring resource of Wilderness" and a more purist attitude toward appropriate behaviors. When appropriate behaviors were explored, visitors were asked if they should be able to camp wherever they please in Wilderness. Nearly two-thirds of the 1965 visitors agreed with that statement, but less than one-fourth of the 1993 sample agreed. A similar level of change was exhibited in response to a question about appropriateness of cutting wood for a campfire or tree boughs for a bed. Attitudes toward the necessity of a campfire, burying noncombustible trash, bringing radios into the wilderness, and taking shortcuts all showed similar shifts in perceptions of appropriateness. Current visitors have become much more concerned about their impacts on wilderness.

Values of Wilderness Visitors

Support for allowing lightning-caused fires to run their course increased from about three percent in 1965 to 44 percent in 1993 at the Eagle Cap Wilderness. Similarly, over one-third (44 percent) of the 1993 sample supported allowing heavy infestations of native insects to run their course in wilderness, compared to only five percent support in 1965. The apparent value placed on risk and being self-sufficient is reflected in the decrease in support for placing highest priority on the rescue of injured or lost visitors. Some items with less dramatic changes, but still demonstrating significant shifts in a more purist direction, include reduced support for allowing pack animals, livestock grazing, hunting, and building corrals for livestock in Wilderness. Support for charging fees to visit Wilderness decreased.

Conclusions

While some demographics of both the U.S. population and Wilderness users have changed substantially, there are no corresponding shifts in kinds of trips or preferences for Wilderness conditions encountered. This finding suggests the possibility that most visitors keep returning to the same Wildernesses while getting older, more experienced, and more educated. Alternatively, different people may be visiting Wilderness, taking similar types of Wilderness trips and showing comparable attitudes about what they encountered there. In either case, managers may need to worry relatively little about the sociodemographic shifts predicted in the future. Further changes in age distribution, educational achievement, gender distribution, and past wilderness experience would not be expected to lead to changes in how visitors enjoy Wilderness. However, there could be a relationship between other changing sociodemographic variables and changes in Wilderness visitors, values, and views about appropriate Wilderness behaviors. For instance, there is very little historic information on ethnicity trends of Wilderness visitors. If this character of society changes in most parts of the country as it is predicted, unanticipated shifts in use characteristics and values could occur.

HISTORY AND STATUS OF USE OF WILDERNESS FOR PERSONAL GROWTH

(By Gregory T. Friese, Camp Manito-wish YMCA, and Michael L. Kinziger and John C. Hendee, University of Idaho Wilderness Research Center, Moscow, ID)

The use of Wilderness for personal growth, education, therapy, and leadership development has grown significantly since the 1962 arrival of Outward Bound® in the United States. A nationwide survey of the Wilderness Experience Program (WEP) industry identified 700 organizations offering Wilderness programs for personal growth (Friese, 1996). Another nationwide survey of Wilderness managers revealed in their estimate that WEP use was increasing an average of 15 percent per year (Gager, 1996). WEPs use Wilderness as both teacher and classroom with various impacts. The growth of WEPs will create Wilderness management challenges as well as opportunities for increasing Wilderness benefits for people.

Introduction

For several years, some researchers have suspected that use of Wilderness for personal growth, education, therapy, and leadership development was growing. This perception was fed by publicity about accidents, frequent encounters with advertisements, and literature about diverse Wilderness experience programs (WEPs), such as Outward Bound® and the National Outdoor Leadership School (NOLS). In an investigation by the authors, a number of questions were addressed: How fast is personal growth use increasing? How many WEPs operate in designated Wilderness? What kind of methods do they use? How many WEPs practice Leave No Trace methods? How many people participate? And collectively, what are the characteristics and dynamics of the WEP industry these programs represent?

Wilderness Experience Programs

A Wilderness Experience Program (WEP) takes customers into Wilderness or comparable areas to develop their human potential through personal growth, education, therapy, and leadership or organizational development activities (Hendee & Brown, 1987; Roberts, 1989). Potential aims of WEPs include therapy and rehabilitation, changing delinquent behavior, breaking chemical dependency, acceptance and adjustment to disabilities, spiritual renewal, physical challenge, and character building. All are based on the healing and inspirational elements and challenge opportunities of Wilderness experiences. Technical skills development may be an integral part of a WEP, but such benefits are secondary to the central goals of personal growth, education, therapy, leadership development, or organizational development. WEPs use either designated Wilderness or other public or private areas that have the characteristics of naturalness and solitude.

In a national survey of WEPs, snowball sampling was used to identify potential WEPs from a variety of data sources, including previous research, advertising and listings in popular literature, association directories, and WEP referrals (Friese, Hendee & Kinziger, 1997; Friese, 1996). By this method, 700 potential programs were found. The total was much higher than anticipated, especially since the sample did not include Boy Scout or Girl Scout troops, community or church recreation programs, outfitters and guides, adventure travel businesses, or Wilderness skills instruction or work programs. In the spring of 1995, potential WEPs were contacted and asked to respond to a short postcard survey and return examples of their promotional material. Nearly 70 percent (484) of the programs contacted responded. Of the respondents, 366 were classified as WEPs. Thus, if the classification were proportionally correct, there are more than 500 WEPs for personal growth operating in the United States.

Historical Background of WEPs

Changing views of wilderness, from being an obstacle to conquer to a healing and rejuvenating environment, have contributed to the growth of the WEP industry. Youth camping organizations and the Boy Scouts extensively use the outdoors to stimulate personal growth. The development of trail and campsite networks, the leisure boom after World War II, and creation of the NWPS contributed to the rapid expansion of WEPs following the arrival of Outward Bound® in 1962. In the last three decades, such schools have continued to expand, and hundreds of other organizations have adapted their methods and philosophies.

The rapid expansion of the WEP industry has been fed by acceptance of the idea of Wilderness as a restorative environment. For example, the Wilderness Education Association (1995) "promotes national Wilderness education and preservation programs by providing expedition-based Wilderness leadership courses through affiliated colleges, universities, and private organizations nationwide" (p. 3). At Catherine Freer's Wilderness Therapy Expedition (1995), students "learn to recognize and deal with their behavioral and emotional problems throughout the trek." Wilderness Transitions, Inc. (1994) describes the Vision Quest as a "time and natural, quiet place to look within to see again who you are, what you think and feel, where you are going." In Earlham College's Southwest Field Studies program, students "study natural history, resource management, and outdoor education while backpacking through American deserts" (Earlham College, 1995). Longacre Expeditions (1995) employs challenge adventure activities, such as "ropes and initiatives, backpacking, mountaineering, rock climbing, and white water rafting," to meet personal growth goals.

WEP Industry Dynamics

The industry is characterized by a few large, well-established organizations and many new smaller ones. In this study, nearly one-fourth (25 percent) of the WEP respondents run five or fewer trips per year, and nearly 40 percent (39 percent) offer fewer than 10 trips per year. This number is balanced by the one-third (33 percent) of respondents, the larger, more prominent WEPs, who offered more than 31 trips or programs annually.

Additionally, 17.1 percent of all WEPs had fewer than 25 clients participate in their trips or programs in 1994, and 41 percent served fewer than 100. One-third (30 percent), however, served more than 500 clients that year. The large mean number of clients (1,435) and modest median number (169) reflect the influence of the largest of the WEP organizations on the industry totals. For example, some large operators, such as the Glacier Institute and Teton Science School, serve thousands. They couple Wilderness trips with education programs, visitor and interpretive centers, conference facilities, or other non-WEP attractions.

WEPs serve a broad spectrum of people in society, including youth, executives, women, people in therapy, people with disabilities, and many more. The leading clientele categories for all types of WEPs are either youth, youth-at-risk, or college students. Thus, although they serve a full spectrum of people, WEPs focus primarily on youth.

Hikers along a trail in Isle Royale National Park Wilderness area in Michigan trek through virgin forests. Photo courtesy of USDI National Park Service. Photo by Richard Frear.

Several large, well-known organizations, such as Outward Bound® and the National Outdoor Leadership School, lead the industry in several ways: number of clients they serve, prevalence in research and popular literature, and setting operating standards. For example, since 1962, more than 300,000 people have participated in U.S. Outward Bound® programs (New York City Outward Bound® Center, 1995). There has been widespread adoption of the Outward Bound® model, philosophies, and methods by WEPs focused on self-improvement and behavior modification, which may contribute to the inaccurate notion among the public and land managers that WEPs are few in number and have similar aims and methods. The exact number of direct adaptations and modified adoptions by public and private schools, colleges, universities, correctional institutions, and private organizations of Outward Bound® has been estimated to range from 200 to thousands (Conger, 1992; Krakauer, 1995; Messier, 1984; Powch, 1994; Wilson, 1981; Zook, 1987).

The WEP industry is characterized by frequent turnover of smaller programs entering and exiting the industry. These changes make it difficult to maintain a current directory of programs. Miner (1995, p. 175) found that "only 20 percent of provider organizations appearing in a 1989 listing of outdoor–based training providers remained in the 1993 edition." O'Keefe (1989) found that in three years, 20 of the 58 possible academic orientation programs using Wilderness were no longer operating, mostly due to financial and staffing problems. The recent *Directory of Wilderness Experience Programs* assembled in this study will also soon be obsolete as WEPs continually enter and exit the industry (Friese, 1996).

It is difficult to achieve financial success with revenue from only a few trips and participants. There are numerous barriers to increasing the number of trips and participants due to limited operating seasons on the areas they use and the time constraints of their participants. A good example are WEPs that primarily serve youth and are limited to the summer or nonschool season. The time required for WEPs may limit trips and revenue. For example, Wilderness Transitions' Vision Quests require a two-month trip cycle, including four pretrip meetings, an eight-day wilderness trip including a four-day solo fast, and a post-trip reunion two weeks after returning (Riley, 1997). Limited permit allocations and the seasonality of activities, such as whitewater rafting and some Wilderness areas, can also limit trips.

WEP Land Use and Management Issues

Over half (57 percent) of all WEP survey respondents indicated they used designated Wilderness. More than half (61 percent) of all WEPs said they use private land, which may indicate only that respondents have offices, ropes course facilities, or staging areas on private land, not just that they run trips on private land. Despite the large number of WEPs using designated Wilderness, only 65 percent of WEP respondents said they provide minimum impact training. Also, a recent study of Wilderness managers of areas reporting WEP use found that virtually all managers who believe that WEP Wilderness use is increasing also believe that WEPs frequently dodge the permit system (Gager, 1996). Better understanding of the WEP industry will help managers improve communication with WEPs, help reduce WEP impacts on the land and other users, and help address other WEP issues.

How WEPs Use Wilderness: Teacher Vs. Classroom

WEPs use of and impact on Wilderness vary. From our survey, a conceptual model (continuum) was created based on how WEPs use Wilderness, a continuum of methods with "Wilderness as Teacher" at one extreme and "Wilderness as Classroom" at the other. A method is in essence the way a WEP pursues its goals. WEPs employ a variety of methods that help determine activities, required setting, leadership, outcomes, learning transfer, and goals. It is difficult to pinpoint any single WEP on the continuum because many programs utilize a range of methods, i.e., Wilderness as both teacher and classroom.

The continuum of WEP methods for using Wilderness, as teacher vs. classroom, and associated attributes are proposed in Figure VIII.1. For example, trip leadership refers to the role of the trip leader in facilitating or guiding participant outcomes. Activity emphasis, whether soft skills or hard skills, is closely related to the role of the trip leader.

In the "Wilderness as Teacher" approach, the trip leader is relatively passive, allowing the wilderness to teach. Presumably, therefore, the program's success depends heavily on Wilderness characteristics. For example, Kent Mountain Adventure Center (1995) states, "We provide the gear and the supervision, but the Wilderness is the big teacher." Wilderness Discovery, a program designed for youth-at-risk in the Federal Job Corps, is touted as a low-risk, soft skills Wilderness experience (Russell & Hendee, 1997). Thus, the "Wilderness as Teacher" approach lends itself to passive leadership, soft skills, and reflective activities.

In a "Wilderness as Classroom" approach, trip leadership is more proactive, setting up activities and situations. Wilderness becomes a classroom for learning, combining some of the characteristics of Wilderness, the components of the activity, and the aptitude of the instructor. The S.O.A.R. program (1996) brochure states, "the out-of-doors provides an ideal classroom where relevant learning can occur and life skills can be taught." Active trip leadership and using "Wilderness as Classroom" lends itself to challenge adventure and hard skills activities.

Figure VIII.1: Proposed Continuum of WEP methods from "Wilderness Is Teacher" to "Wilderness Is Classroom," Based on 246 Programs Classified (n=246)

Wilderness is Teacher — **Kind of Program** — **Wilderness is Classroom**

Method n=246	Mountains speak for Themselves (1)	Reflection (17)	Rite of Passage and Initiation (24)	Expedition Learning (11)	Environmental Education (37)	Field Classroom (33)	Counseling (14)	Challenge Adventure Activities (106)	Conscious Use of Metaphor (3)
Self	determine and reflect own issues and outcomes	realize and affirm goals, talents, and values	reflecting, preparing, and celebrating	individual has group responsibilities	understand connection to nature	set individual learning objectives	focused on correcting behavior	success and accomplishment lead to growth	experience is metaphoric
Group	logistical and safety purpose	may help individuals	supports the individual	depends on group cooperation	part of connection	team learning and research	feedback to group members	encourage success	metaphoric to other groups
Nature	gives logical consequences	reflects goals and talents	mirrors back to them	gives performance feedback	used to demonstrate connection	classroom	environment for diagnosis and correction	setting for activity	setting for metaphoric activities
Leader	passive	creating success and reflection situations	passively guides transition	transfers leadership to participants	actively teaches connections	guides educational experience	gives feedback and actively engages	actively creates success experiences	actively facilitates and debriefs

Role of Trip Leadership

Passive trip leadership ⟵⟶ Active trip leadership

Relative Dependence on Wilderness Characteristics

Greater dependence ⟵⟶ Lower dependence

Do WEPs Need Wilderness?

Wilderness dependence refers to the relative degree to which a WEP requires the defining characteristics of Wilderness, such as naturalness and solitude, to meet goals. The typology implies that "Wilderness as Classroom" methods may have relatively low Wilderness dependence, since they have more proactive leadership. But it is clear from promotional materials gathered in the study that such programs also see Wilderness as vital for designing metaphors, creating a positive environment for growth, and providing opportunities for challenge adventure activities. Furthermore, the physical features on which challenge adventure activities rely, such as whitewater rivers or mountain peaks, are often only available in Wilderness.

Summary and Conclusion

The WEP industry has grown significantly since the 1962 arrival of Outward Bound®. Today more than 500 organizations offer Wilderness experiences aimed at personal growth, education, therapy, and leadership development. Continued growth seems likely in a fast-paced, complex, and stressful society, for which WEPs can provide an antidote. The fact that WEPs are numerous and diverse reveals adaptation in the industry to meet different needs and goals.

While WEPs serve a diverse spectrum of society, youth have been the dominant clientele. Despite the diversity of the industry, a few large operators account for most use, have been the focus of most of the research, and are the most familiar to land managers. Dominance by large operators may contribute to a lack of full understanding of the WEP industry by Wilderness managers, despite their responsibility for allocating and regulating use through permits and fees.

Growth in the WEP industry suggests that training trip leaders and clientele in minimum impact methods and a positive and cooperative relationship with agency Wilderness managers will be increasingly important. Fewer than two-thirds of WEP respondents in our study provide such training, and over half of Wilderness managers in another survey think WEPs dodge the permit system (Friese, et al., 1997; Gager, 1996).

As Wilderness areas grow more crowded, WEPs that require the Wilderness characteristics of naturalness, solitude, and primitive challenges to meet their goals will have the most difficulty finding substitutes for designated Wilderness as suitable locations to operate. Efforts to protect naturalness and solitude are of greatest value to these WEPs, which feature the healing qualities of "Wilderness as Teacher." Likewise, WEPs that feature "Wilderness as Teacher," emphasizing reflective activities, would seem to impact Wilderness the least. Finally, WEP use of Wilderness to teach social values and healing has large benefits for society as a whole. Wilderness managers will be able to consider these benefits when evaluating Wilderness regulations, restrictions, and use allocations.

CHANGING WILDERNESS VALUES

(By Alan Watson and Peter Landres, USDA Forest Service, Missoula, MT)

In addition to work on Wilderness use and users as reported earlier in this chapter, scientists at the Leopold Institute have conducted or sponsored other studies aimed at understanding the values of Wilderness protection in the United States. Biologists, ecologists, and social scientists have merged their knowledge in terminology and perspective to seek ways to improve Wilderness management in the future. Current knowledge suggests that values are constantly changing. The source of this change is a combination of general societal trends and specific influences on Wilderness values.

Creation of a National Wilderness Preservation System, with instant classification of over nine million acres of Forest Service lands as Wilderness, reflected the values of U.S. society at that time. Emphasis was on preserving and protecting for the American people of present and future generations an enduring resource of Wilderness. Wilderness was to be administered for future use and enjoyment by the American people. The act stressed both preservation and use of these places, particularly for recreation.

Wilderness areas are receiving increasing numbers of visits by backpackers, day hikers, anglers, horseback riders, canoeists, berry pickers, photographers, and hunters. Recreation use increased steadily through the 1960s and 1970s, into the early 1980s, when it appeared to level off. By the late 1980s, a resurgence of growth in Wilderness visits occurred and it continues today. Along the way, nearly 100 million additional acres were legally classified as Wilderness, adding land managed by the NPS, BLM, and USFWS, as well as more FS land, and that system of protected lands continues to be considered for additional growth today. With many changes in society and how people view protected areas, what are the values we associate with Wilderness today? How has society changed, what forces have worked to influence our beliefs about Wilderness?

Wilderness in 1964: Preserved and Managed for Human Values

When supporters of the NWPS in the early 1960s spoke of future generations, they were talking partially about today's society. Hubert H. Humphrey introduced the original legislation in the House of Representatives. Senator Humphrey passed away in 1978. Howard Zahniser, the person who authored much of the original legislation and who campaigned for passage of the Wilderness Act all through the 1950s and early 1960s died just shortly before passage. The influential philosophers and scientists who were commonly quoted during Wilderness debates (Muir, Leopold, Marshall, Marsh, Thoreau) were mostly of an even earlier era. The baby boom generation was hardly a part of the movement. We are, however, the beneficiaries and stewards of their work, just as future generations will be beneficiaries and stewards of our work.

When the first textbook on Wilderness management appeared in 1978, it relied strongly upon the foundation of these Wilderness philosophers and champions. In the textbook by John Hendee, George Stankey, and Robert Lucas, three major values of Wilderness in our society were acknowledged.

Experiential Value

Muir referred to forests as temples with the trees singing psalms and with these words gave the Wilderness a spiritual quality, with abilities to inspire and provide insight into the connection of all things. Leopold advocated preservation of the American packtrain experience, and Olson found feelings of timelessness important to understanding the ways of the past.

Mental and Moral Restoration Values

Carhart believed that these values contributed to building individual and national character. Leopold, Muir, and Thoreau advocated understanding the challenges of self-sufficiency in order to increase one's self-confidence. The therapeutic values of Wilderness to members of a society challenged by the stresses of modern life were frequently acknowledged.

Scientific Value

At the turn of the century, Marsh thought that there was a scientific value to protecting intact forests. The scientific uses most often mentioned were as baselines for comparison with altered areas. There, complex biological processes could be studied in environments that have escaped the impacts of human progress. Wilderness offered opportunities to study the complex relationships between all organisms and the impacts human activities were causing in areas that were not protected.

General Societal Changes Since Wilderness Protection Began

Many things have changed in our society since 1964. We cannot expect our children to value experiences or places in the same ways we do. And our grandchildren will have different values than our children. With changes in the culture we live in, advances in technology, dramatic changes in the environment, and diversification of the economy, our attitudes toward Wilderness protection are bound to change.

Changing Culture

A spreading U.S. population converts about one million acres of farmland to urban housing, businesses, and roads each year. In our lifetimes we have all experienced basic changes in orientation to the landscape as a result of increasing conversions. Articles commonly appear in National Geographic and local newspapers about the rapid increases in home construction in formerly rural areas. Las Vegas, NV, is adding 6,000 new residents each month. Home construction is proceeding rapidly. From all this development a new culture is evolving. Expectations for recreation, public services, and taxes place new challenges before local administrators. In the United States, education levels are rising. People are improving their understanding of natural processes and how we all fit into the global situation. The racial and ethnic mix of our society is changing rapidly. These cultural changes, among many others, are having profound effects on how our society values protection of wildlands.

Technological Advances

We have advanced technology beyond our expectations of 20 years ago. The World Wide Web provides overwhelming amounts of information for trip planning. The dominant value of our society has been described as efficiency, which is evident in communications (cellular phones, Internet, satellite television, FAX, etc.), transportation (gas mileage, mountain bikes, llamas in trekking groups, etc.) and in medicine (from prevention to treatment). We are a culture that seeks every technological advantage. Some of this efficiency may reduce our impact on natural places and increase our enjoyment of time we have there. Others, possibly in unexpected ways, threaten our ability to protect unique places and experiences there.

Environmental Changes

Although the environmental awareness movement arose when the Wilderness Act was moving toward passage, we are much more aware of environmental issues today than people were in the 1960s. Commodity extraction impacts are commonly discussed in public arenas. We have changed everything from our deodorants to our vehicle air conditioners to protect the ozone layer. Our attitudes toward beef and the fast-food restaurants that prepare it in quantity have changed due to relationships between tropical deforestation and agriculture.

Diversification of the Economy

Our economy has become much less dependent upon commodity extraction. Just a few years ago, we had many more communities than we do now that were entirely dependent upon the resource base as a source of income. Today, our economy is highly diversified, and we have improved our understanding of how natural amenities influence the local tax base and the local economy.

Specific Influences on Wilderness Values

Some specific things have happened since 1964 that influence how we value Wilderness, and these things seem to continue to affect the beliefs we hold about wildland protection. These changes include our awareness of impacts caused by recreation, media coverage on the beneficial role of natural ecological processes, scientific understanding about the functions of ecological systems, and the loss of natural areas to development.

Awareness of Impacts Caused By Recreation

The images we have of early Wilderness visits often include campsites adjacent to streams or lakes, bedrolls spread on freshly cut boughs of fir trees, heavy cooking utensils, several head of pack or riding stock, and a huge campfire. Times have changed. There is now a higher percentage of solo visitors to Wilderness. The trend is for shorter stays with predominance of day use, and a lower proportion of use depends on pack animals.

While many preferences for naturalness of conditions and lack of crowding persist, Wilderness values have changed. In one in-depth study of values and codes of behavior, Wilderness users in Oregon had changed tremendously in 28 years. In 1965, just one year after passage of the Wilderness Act, 64 percent of visitors believed that they should be able to camp wherever they please in Wilderness. By 1993, that proportion had dropped to only 22 percent. Likewise, 53 percent thought it was appropriate to cut brush or limbs for a bed and wood for a campfire in 1965. In 1993, however, that acceptance rate was down to 17 percent. The symbolic presence of an evening campfire was accepted by 76 percent in 1965, but only 37 percent in 1993. The largest change was in beliefs about appropriateness of burying noncombustible trash. Almost everyone believed it was appropriate in 1965 (87 percent) and almost no one thought it was appropriate in 1993 (9 percent).

In part, these changes in attitudes have resulted from agency-sponsored education programs. Educational signs have been mounted at trailheads and campgrounds to promote Woodsy Owl and a national Leave No Trace program, and we have seen commitment to improved ethics by organizations such as the National Outdoor Leadership School.

Media Coverage on the Beneficial Role of Natural Ecological Processes

At the Eagle Cap Wilderness, only three percent of a 1965 sample of visitors felt lightning-caused fires should be allowed to run their course in Wilderness. By 1993, 44 percent of the visitors expressed that belief. A similar change in attitudes was evident toward native insect infestations. In 1965, five percent of visitors supported allowance of heavy infestations of native insects to run their course in Wilderness, while in 1993, 43 percent of visitors supported that action. It is believed that regional coverage of insect issues and national and regional coverage of fire issues are largely responsible for these swings in attitudes. In fact, there is evidence that accuracy of knowledge about fire effects is closely linked to positive support of prescribed natural fire policies, and that knowledge and support is highest in the regions where wildland fires occur most often and receive press coverage regularly.

Scientific Understanding

Biodiversity, a common goal of ecosystem management today, normally is not highest in currently designated Wilderness Areas. Greater diversity exists in lower elevation areas, which often are privately owned. Ecosystem management reflects concern about the often severe impacts of human activities on natural systems. Today, many people can engage in intelligent conversations about the costs of habitat fragmentation and the impacts of fire exclusion for so many years on the integrity of biological systems.

Development and Loss of Natural Areas that Lack Formal Protection

From the local to the national level, there has been a reduction in natural areas. We see it locally in clearing of lands for housing tracts, we hear it regionally when the timber industry and preservation interests debate on the future of remaining, unprotected, roadless lands in the Northern Rockies, and we hear it in stories about wetland development, offshore mineral exploration, and tourism development. Scarcity increases the value of natural landscapes in an urban society that is rapidly developing its unprotected places.

The Importance of Understanding Changes in Attitudes Toward Wilderness

Figure VIII.2 shows how values are modified and eventually contribute to understanding personal and societal benefits of Wilderness protection. In this flow chart the word *values* appears twice. In one place it is equated with *attitudes*. In this case, the general societal trends and specific influences described above combine to influence the beliefs people have about the advantages of protecting Wilderness lands and experiences. These beliefs, attitudes, and values influence formation of legislation, interpretation of legislation into policy, and on-the-ground management activities. In the last few years we have seen increasing mountain bike traffic in nonroaded areas, proposals to open up Wilderness Areas for more motorized access, salvage logging bills that promote commodity values in roadless areas, and increased debate over extending protected status to additional public lands. The challenge of the Resources Planning Act Assessment is to describe societal values accurately in order for the program to prescribe policy for the future. The attitudes of today's society are very different than those found in 1964 due to the many societal and specific influences that have come into existence since that time, and they continue to evolve. That is the difficult aspect of development of policy for the future.

Figure VIII.2: Flow Chart to Understand the Role of Values in Wilderness Management

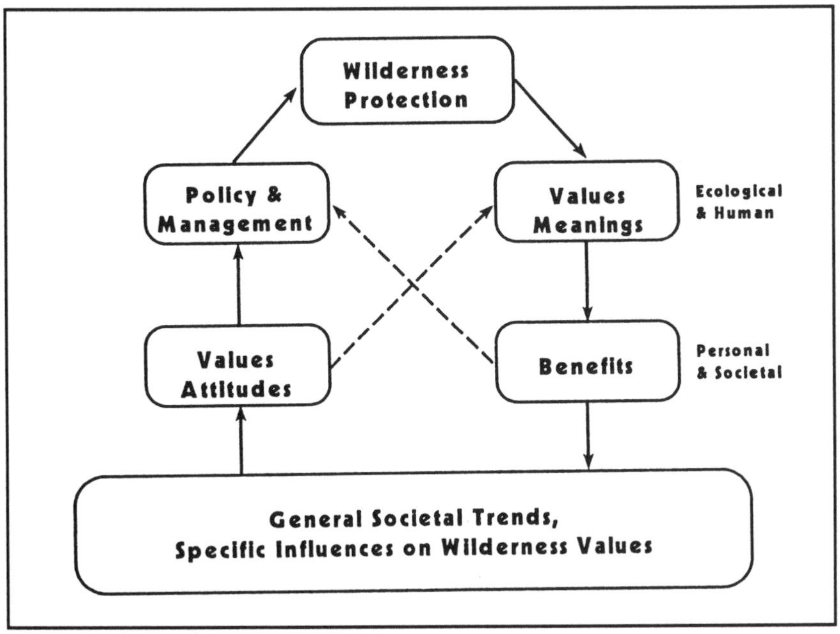

The second use of "values" can be applied to describe the positive ecological and human services of Wilderness protection. Biodiversity has been judged by humans as a desirable value of Wilderness protection and management. Humans sometimes visit Wilderness for functional reasons, such as hunting, berry picking, or escaping crowds. On the other hand, some people go to places we call Wilderness because they have personal relationships with that place, or because they desire to acknowledge the significance of entering a place our society has deemed appropriate to protect. These values give rise to either personal or societal benefits, those long-term, higher-order positive purposes of Wilderness protection. Society can benefit ultimately through maintenance of cultural traditions, through physical subsistence, through scientific advancement of knowledge, and through extension of ethical considerations to the natural world. These benefits are ultimately to humans and are constantly changing due to changes in society and specific things we do to influence the beliefs of people about the advantages of providing these benefits. Understanding these changing attitudes toward Wilderness and the human and ecological meanings Wilderness has in our rapidly changing society will continue to be a challenge for public land managers.

FOREST SERVICE WILDERNESS MANAGEMENT

(By Thomas F. Geary and Gerald L. Stokes, USDA Forest Service, Washington, DC)

Since passage of the Wilderness Act in 1964, the National Wilderness Preservation System (NWPS) has grown from its initial 9.1 million to 103.5 million acres. The system now includes nearly 4.5 percent of the total areas of the United States. Four hundred of the total 630 units in the NWPS are managed by the Forest Service, a total of 35 million acres. The Wilderness managed by the Forest Service represents 63 percent of the NWPS in the contiguous 48 states and more than one-third of the entire NWPS when Alaska is included. This amount is 18 percent of the 191 million acres of national forests in the National Forest System (NFS). Forest Service Wilderness areas are found in 38 states and range in size from the 2.3-million-acre Frank Church River of No Return Wilderness in Idaho to the 994-acre Leaf Wilderness in Mississippi.

Forest Service Policy and Management

Forest Service wilderness managers follow agency policy and regulations, derived from the Wilderness Act, to ensure mandated preservation of the Wilderness resource. Increasingly, however, Wilderness decisions are challenged by administrative oversight, judicial and legislative review, and public involvement. These challenges result from provisions in the Wilderness Act that seem at odds with each other in contemporary interpretations. Today's challenges to Wilderness management are best displayed by reviewing parts of the Wilderness Act itself.

Section Two of the Wilderness Act defines a somewhat poetic management ideal. In Sec.2(a),

> Wilderness areas . . . shall be administered for the use and enjoyment of the American people in such a manner as will leave them unimpaired for the future use and enjoyment as Wilderness, and so as to provide for the protection of these areas, the preservation of their Wilderness character.

In the definition of Wilderness articulated in Sec.2(c), the following key phrases provide the philosophical framework to guide managers in implementing the Act

> an area where the earth and its community of life are untrammeled by man, where man himself is a visitor who does not remain; land retaining its primeval character and influence, without permanent improvements or human habitation, which is protected and managed so as to preserve its natural conditions; and which generally appears to be primarily affected by the forces of nature, with the imprint of man's work substantially unnoticeable.

The act provides the fundamental basis and intent for Wilderness management in Section 4(c). In this section is the clause entitled, "Prohibition of Certain Uses." This clause generally limits commercial enterprises, permanent roads, motorized equipment, and mechanical transport. However, the act is complicated by the political compromises that were necessary for its passage. These compromises are embodied in Sec.4(d), "Special Provisions," which provides for exceptions to the prohibitions found elsewhere in the act. Special provisions allow, under certain conditions subject to regulation by the secretary of agriculture, the continued use (where established prior to Wilderness designation) of aircraft and motorboats, livestock grazing, mineral exploration, and mining. Commercial outfitter and guide operations may also be allowed "for activities that are proper for realizing the recreational or other Wilderness purposes." These allowances require Wilderness managers to revisit Congressional intent and interpretation of the act continuously, and of other legislation adding units to the NWPS, using management policy set forth in Forest Service Manual direction.

Several current situations illustrate the inherent dilemma these definitions and provisions pose to managers and the trend toward more administrative, legal, and political challenges to Wilderness management decisions. These situations include proposed legislation to abrogate Forest Service regulations limiting motorized use in the Boundary Waters Canoe Area Wilderness in Minnesota and the Sylvania Wilderness in Michigan; a court decision limiting the facilities and structures the Forest Service could allow to support outfitter and guide operations in the Frank Church River of No Return Wilderness in Idaho; and administrative and judicial decisions that uphold Forest Service management of livestock grazing in the Gila and Aldo Leopold Wildernesses in New Mexico. The conflict between Wilderness and human development is sure to increase.

The Benefits from Protecting Wilderness

Wilderness provides habitat for some of the country's rare and endangered species to sustain their gene pools. In Wilderness, natural processes dominate, within practical limits. Wilderness protects geological resources, is a unique repository of historical sites, and is a laboratory for research on mostly unaltered natural systems. The water supply of many cities and rural communities comes from the headwaters of streams and rivers flowing from Wilderness. Activities that conflict with Wilderness character, such as mining and grazing, are permitted if they existed before a Wilderness was designated by Congress. Local and regional economic development benefits from hunting, fishing, livestock grazing, mining, irrigation, and tourism in Wilderness. Wilderness provides solitude, recreation, and a resource for teaching conservation and ecosystem management.

Growth of the NWPS and increased understanding of the physical, biological, and social interactions between Wilderness and surrounding landscapes has brought increased recognition of the complexity of managing these wildlands. The uniqueness of Wilderness requires an approach different from that used over the rest of the NFS in managing grazing, mining, and oil exploration; resolving fish and wildlife management issues; administering access across NFS lands to private inholdings; management of structures and other modern, unnatural intrusions; conducting research; dealing with adjacent development and its associated effects; regulation of fire, in particular, facilitating the role of fire as a natural process; and preserving environments of primeval character that offer unique, primitive and unconfining human experiences.

The Forest Service objectives in Wilderness management are:

- to preserve and protect the physical, biological and social values of designated Wilderness on NFS lands;
- to provide Wilderness experience opportunities to the public that increase their awareness and understanding of themselves and Wilderness;
- to train agency personnel for their Wilderness stewardship role;
- to maintain strong professional leadership in Wilderness stewardship;
- to improve efficiency in administration;
- and to enhance public and interagency partnerships.

Management actions are taken when necessary to maintain acceptable conditions as specified in land and resource management plans. Many national forests utilize the limits of acceptable change approach.

Recreational Use

Trends in recreation use of Wilderness are not clear at this time. The last major RPA assessment of Wilderness was completed in 1989 and focused on the recreation value of Wilderness (Cordell, et. al, 1990). The assessment found the rate of increase in Wilderness recreation visits had slowed to where use had leveled or even declined in some areas. However, non-recreational use of wilderness for education, scientific study, habitat preservation, and ecosystem preservation was increasing. Since 1989, however, recreation use of Wilderness has increased, especially in backpacking. Patterns of recreation use have also changed. Shorter, more frequent trips are common. Use is more intense on weekends, holidays, and during favorable weather than in past years, especially in Wilderness areas near cities. These changes in how Wilderness is used are expected to continue, but the meaning of these trends for management of overall recreational use remains unknown.

Conflicts abound in the management of recreation in Wilderness. Many hikers dislike encountering horses or even the evidence of horse use in Wilderness. Non-hunters do not want hunting. Subsistence users in Alaska resent recreational use. Some climbers resist efforts to preserve solitude on popular peaks. A "light-handed" educational approach is typically used with some success in reducing offensive behaviors, changing attitudes based on misconceptions, and increasing tolerance for others. However, strong polarization of values suggests the need for greater efforts at conflict resolution. Increased management actions to minimize unnecessarily severe impacts now caused by recreation are also needed.

Fire in Wilderness

The role of fire in Wilderness is of increasing importance to both managers and the public. Air quality and fire management were major concerns expressed by the public through comments on the 1995 draft RPA program. Public concern about fire and air quality is supported by information obtained through the Forest Service's annual Wilderness reporting process. Only the management of impacts from recreation is a more important issue to the public.

Fire exclusion policies of recent decades threaten Wilderness preservation by interfering with the free play of natural processes specified in the 1964 Wilderness Act. When fire is excluded, fuels accumulate and Wilderness ecosystems become unnaturally dense and dominated by species different from those present under historical fire regimes. These synthetic plant communities are easily damaged by droughts, insects, diseases, and fires.

The conflict between the values of clean air and good visibility and the ecological value of fire is a management challenge. Smoke from fires is a significant but intermittent source of fine particulates that can threaten human health and decrease visibility. The Environmental Protection Agency (EPA) and the states, through implementation of the Clean Air Act, are developing programs to reduce emissions of fine particulates and protect Wilderness from unacceptable effects of air pollution, particularly from industrial sources. The Forest Service is also working with other regulatory agencies to develop practices that better balance the ecological benefits of fire while protecting human health and scenic values.

Forest Service goals for management of fire in Wilderness are to permit lightning-caused fires to play their natural role, yet reduce to an acceptable level the risks and consequences of wildfire. Under these goals, all fires in Wilderness must be prescribed. A prescribed fire is a fire burning under planned, specified conditions to accomplish specific, planned resource management objectives. It may be ignited by nature, for example, by lightning (Prescribed Natural Fire—PNF) or management (Management Ignited Prescribed Fire—MIPF). All other fires are wildfires. PNFs are the preferred means of assuring the role of fire as a natural ecosystem process. Where PNF occurrences are not adequate to accomplish these goals, a MIPF may be needed to supplement the PNF within Wilderness and on adjacent lands. The total land area burned by PNFs has been highly variable in recent years, but remains a tiny portion of that needed to maintain understood natural and historical fire regimes.

Training and Research

The Forest Service seeks to develop excellence in Wilderness stewardship through implementation of the national Interagency Wilderness Strategic Plan (1995). This plan was written by a devoted group of Wilderness experts, and endorsed by leaders of the Bureau of Land Management, National Park Service, U.S. Fish & Wildlife Service, U.S. Forest Service, and the previous National Biological Service. The Arthur Carhart National Wilderness Training Center fosters interagency excellence in Wilderness stewardship by improving managers' and the public's understanding of Wilderness. The Aldo Leopold Interagency Wilderness Research Institute provides improved scientific understanding needed to improve Wilderness management.

In recognition of the importance of Wilderness management and to raise the profile of the Wilderness resource in the agency, in 1996 the Forest Service established the position of assistant director for Wilderness in the Forest Service's Recreation, Heritage, and Wilderness Resources staff.

Future Trends

The greatest challenge facing managers of Forest Service Wilderness in the 21st century will be the continuing increases of human population and associated development surrounding areas of the National Wilderness Preservation System. Population growth, fueled by immigration, and shifting cultural values may bring unforeseen views on how Wilderness should be used and managed. Threats to Wilderness and impacts from human use may particularly impact opportunities for solitude, the role of natural fire, and levels of ambient air pollution.

Additional designation of lands in the National Forest System as Wilderness is a political process usually involving confrontations between commodity and environmental interests. The amount of land area to be added to the NWPS is decided by Congress; the Forest Service only recommends additions. The NFS has an additional 54 million acres of undeveloped, roadless area that might qualify for inclusion in the NWPS. Of this area, Congress has identified more than four million acres covering 40 areas for study and possible inclusion. The Forest Service has already recommended to Congress that 19 of these 40 study areas, an area of 2.5 million acres, be designated as Wilderness. In its forest plans, the Forest Service has identified another 2.1 million acres for consideration. More areas could be recommended as forest plans are revised (usually on a 10-year cycle) and roadless areas are reconsidered.

Given the political complexities of adding to the NWPS, it is impossible to predict how much of the remaining national forest roadless area will be designated. But a conservative estimate would be an increase from today's 35 to 39 million acres in 2045, a rate of increase much less than that predicted for recreation use. The result will be more visitors per unit acre of Wilderness, with possible losses of quality in Wilderness experiences, particularly in the more accessible areas.

Air quality and fire issues, as noted previously, are closely linked. The Forest Service's goal is for natural visibility conditions in Wilderness, including visibility conditions resulting from prescribed natural fire. Managing fire to minimize its effects on visibility and visual quality within and around Wilderness will be a challenge. But without prescribed fire, fuel loads will accumulate and increase the intensity of fire occurrences, perhaps to levels unacceptable for protecting visibility and human health in Wilderness.

Besides addressing fire issues, a huge task will remain for protecting Wilderness from air pollution from industries and cities. It will become necessary to identify specific air quality-related values of Wilderness and the species and resources sensitive to pollutants that should be protected.

Baseline and trend information is needed for all critical values of Wilderness, social, biological, and physical, so they can be monitored for unacceptable changes and effectiveness of management strategies. Currently, no widely accepted set of Wilderness condition indicators have conceptualized, nor is a monitoring system in place.

Under current levels of appropriated funding, the Forest Service may be severely challenged to complete desired actions in the Interagency Wilderness Strategic Plan. If there is stable funding, there may be a steady reversal of extant unacceptable conditions in Wilderness. However, slow, steady progress toward restoration of recreational and solitude values, reintroduction of fire, and mitigation of air pollution effects may be unacceptable to the public. Although conflicts over use, fire, and air pollution may often be resolved in the courts, the Forest Service could resolve an increasing proportion of conflicts if there were better monitoring and research to improve understanding of conditions and trends.

The following individuals provided assistance in the development of the RPA issue paper from which this paper was adapted: Dave Barone, Harry Croft, Jim Saveland, Susan Sater, Liz Close, and the staff of the Aldo Leopold Wilderness Research Institute.

WILDERNESS IN THE BUREAU OF LAND MANAGEMENT

(By Jeff Jarvis, Bureau of Land Management, Washington, DC)

The Bureau of Land Management (BLM) was not included in the original Wilderness Act of 1964 because long-term retention or disposal of land under its jurisdiction had not yet been resolved. By 1976, however, the retention issue had been resolved with passage of the BLM's organic act, the Federal Land Policy and Management Act (FLPMA). In FLPMA, Section 102 directed that extant public land would be retained in federal ownership. Section 603 required the review of BLM land for Wilderness characteristics and required the BLM recommend which lands were suitable for inclusion in the National Wilderness Preservation System. With enactment of FLPMA, BLM joined the other three agencies as a full partner in management of Wilderness. Currently, BLM manages 5.2 million acres as Wilderness.

As directed by FLPMA, an inventory of BLM land was completed and 27.5 million acres (865 areas) in the lower 48 states were identified as Wilderness Study Areas. Study of these potential areas was completed in 1991 and recommendations were made to the president and Congress for designation as Wilderness (Dombeck, 1995). As a result of these recommendations, Congress passed Wilderness legislation for Arizona (1984 and 1990) and southern California (1994), as well as numerous smaller bills designating Wilderness in other states.

As of the writing of this book, the BLM manages 135 areas in the National Wilderness Preservation System in 10 western states. Approximately 22 percent of areas and five percent of the acreage in the National

Wilderness Preservation System are managed by BLM. Wyoming is the only western state without BLM-managed Wilderness. In addition to designated Wilderness, BLM manages 17 million acres made up of 622 Wilderness Study Areas that await Congressional action.

Characteristics of BLM-Managed Wilderness

Although it is impossible to describe the typical BLM Wilderness, they generally differ from other agency Wilderness areas in size; topography, water, and vegetation; accessibility; and historical uses and developments.

Size

The average BLM Wilderness area is 38,500 acres in size, similar to those of the Fish and Wildlife Service in the lower 48 states. Average sizes of Forest Service (76,000 acres) and Park Service (270,000 acres) areas in the lower 48 tend to be larger. BLM Wilderness areas range in size from the 209,000-acre Palen McCoy Wilderness in California to small areas designated as additions to other agency Wilderness areas. These areas include an 800-acre addition to the Frank Church River of No Return Wilderness and a 240-acre addition to the Ishi Wilderness. Twenty percent of the BLM's "stand alone" Wilderness areas are fewer than 15,000 acres. This smaller size increases the miles of boundary relative to the total acres under Wilderness management and increases the potential impacts of outside uses on Wilderness values.

Topography, Water, and Vegetation

In contrast to the rugged headwater landscapes that typify other agencies' Wilderness areas, most BLM Wilderness areas are in lower elevation desert lands. Many are dry. Seldom do the headwaters of a river or minor creek reside within a BLM Wilderness. Springs are often the only source of surface water. Trees may be limited, with the dominant vegetation being brush, cactus, or grasslands. Consequently, many BLM Wilderness areas have values that differ from the prototypical mountainous or alpine wilderness. Numerous ecosystems that otherwise would not be represented in the National Wilderness Preservation System have now been protected as BLM Wilderness.

Accessibility

Locations at lower elevations mean that many BLM Wilderness areas are closer in proximity to local communities. Boundaries are often defined by a highway, road, or vehicle trail, increasing the areas' accessibility to local residents. In many cases, the areas may be more accessible to some local communities than to the widely dispersed BLM offices responsible for management. A large number of the BLM's Wilderness areas are in locations where climate, weather, and elevation ensure virtually year-round access and use. Many BLM areas, due to their size, accessibility, proximity to population centers, and lack of water are essentially used for day use or weekend use instead of longer, two-week, pack trips.

Historical Uses and Developments

Most BLM Wilderness areas have a use history that includes grazing, mining, oil and gas exploration, off-road vehicle use, or other vehicle-based recreation activities. Few BLM Wilderness areas contain developed horse or hiking trails or other facilities designed to support nonmotorized recreation.

Current Management Issues

The BLM is concentrating on three areas: designated Wilderness area management, interim management of Wilderness study areas, and participation in the legislative process. Of these, the first priority is management of the Bureau's 135 Wilderness areas. Immediately after designation, management emphasis is on completing surveys, boundary maps, and legal descriptions; locating and signing boundaries; notifying individuals and groups directly affected by designation; training employees to understand Wilderness management responsibilities; and ongoing patrols and monitoring. Over time, management emphasis shifts to long-term upgrading of staffing, field patrols, monitoring resource conditions, and compliance with use authorizations. Special projects include monitoring mineral operations, restoring past disturbances, public education, completing land exchanges with state and private inholders, and responding to the various requested uses of Wilderness areas. A long-term goal of Wilderness management is to protect or restore the biodiversity of each individual area. This aim includes managing Wilderness in the context of the larger landscape, restoring fire to a natural role, and managing exotic plants and animals.

The second priority for the Wilderness program is management of study areas awaiting congressional action. Section 603 of FLPMA directed the BLM to manage Wilderness study areas, "so as not to impair the suitability of such areas for preservation as wilderness." This "Interim Management" is designed to ensure that wilderness values remain intact until Congress can determine whether a study area warrants Wilderness designation or release.

The legislative phase of the BLM's Wilderness designation process will continue to be dominated by controversy among special interests. With rare exceptions, Congress will likely continue to deal with BLM Wilderness nominations state-by-state, perhaps taking decades to resolve. Legislative issues will include topics such as specific language for releasing areas from study status, aircraft overflights, water rights, acreage to be designated as Wilderness, use of motorized equipment, vehicular access, grazing of domestic livestock, acquisition of or access to privately-owned inholdings, and mining. The BLM will participate in the legislative process to ensure that Congress and the public are informed about the resource values involved and to assist whenever possible in specifying the final law.

Prospects for Wilderness Expansion

Congress is increasingly interested in BLM Wilderness issues and will likely continue to designate new Wilderness areas. Depending on the future actions of Congress, the BLM could ultimately manage 15-25 million acres of Wilderness in the lower 48 states, 20 percent of the total system acreage. More important than total acreage, are the contributions BLM Wilderness makes to the diversity and quality of the National Wilderness Preservation System. These contributions include:

- Expanding the diversity of representation of ecosystems
- Creating linkages with other agencies' Wilderness, which in some cases may complete a mountain Wilderness area and protect surrounding lower elevation lands
- Ensuring the long-term protection of numerous, easily accessible areas in the West
- Expanding Wilderness-based recreation opportunities
- Creating nontypical Wilderness areas in some of the more arid, lower-elevations in western states.

The Future of BLM–Managed Wilderness

Combined, the above factors create a fundamentally different wilderness management challenge for BLM than those faced by the other Wilderness managing agencies. These issues are expected to affect BLM Wilderness in the following ways:

Wilderness Management Emphasis

The unique physical characteristics and management complexities of BLM Wilderness areas represent a departure from more traditional Wilderness management. For many areas, the emphasis will be on restoration of natural values, protection of natural processes, and enhancement of biological values, as opposed to mostly focusing on managing visitor use.

Recreation Opportunities in Natural Settings

Since most of BLM's Wilderness areas have not been managed previously for recreation, the agency has the option of starting with a clean slate. For many areas, priority will be given to protection of the basic Wilderness ecosystem and management of biological values, rather than providing a recreation opportunity. In the long term, this change will mean that these areas will not have traditional recreation facilities such as developed trails, trail heads, or directional signs. Few will contain developments such as bridges or require entry permits. Users will be free to chose travel routes and campsites, and after entering the area can freely travel through and experience completely wild landscapes. Less visited areas are likely to continue to offer freedom to experience outstanding opportunities for solitude. Management to emphasize natural conditions will reduce ongoing construction, maintenance, and management costs.

Creative Management

The BLM is expanding use of field manager positions for Wilderness. Eleven new Wilderness field positions have recently been created to manage areas in the California desert. However, the BLM will not likely have the funding or personnel needed for intensive management in coming years. Indirect management methods such as offsite education, use of volunteers to assist in management, and partnerships will be emphasized. Management will be undertaken cooperatively with adjacent landowners and communities.

Planning

The era of isolated Wilderness planning is ending. Planning focused exclusively on the area within Wilderness boundaries and exclusion of external issues from Wilderness plans has seemed to hamper effective management. Because Wilderness does not exist in a vacuum, the BLM will continue an ecosystem approach to Wilderness planning. Sound management decisions must consider the larger landscape, and include participation by adjacent land owners, other agencies, state and local governments, tribes, and interested citizens. For example, the BLM in Arizona has developed creative approaches to planning that have immediately improved on-the-ground management.

Science

BLM, along with all other land managing agencies, will be challenged to improve the use of scientific research in wilderness management. With the majority of BLM study areas still awaiting congressional action, BLM has an opportunity to consider recent research results relating to such issues as biological diversity, biological corridors, and plant and animal habitats in decisions on Wilderness designation. Incorporating existing scientific research and developing a Wilderness management process that will quickly adapt to new science as it becomes available will be emphasized.

Special Legislative Language

BLM Wilderness bills often contain special management provisions that deviate from the Wilderness Act of 1964. For example, the California Desert Protection Act and the Arizona Desert Wilderness Act allow motor vehicles for wildlife management and to conduct law enforcement, border patrol, and surveillance operations. The 104th Congress considered a Utah Wilderness bill that would have allowed unprecedented motorized access for a wide variety of uses. Expanded motorized uses were considered to have had valid existing rights, and the bill would have allowed the maintenance and repair of vehicle routes without consideration of Wilderness values or resources.

If the trend toward more legislative direction that differs from the intention of the Wilderness Act of 1964 continues, the long-term effect is expected to be that BLM-managed Wilderness will have a higher incidence of inconsistent uses, greater vehicle use, and more miles of vehicle trails than other agencies. This trend would ultimately lead to creation of two types of Wilderness, with areas designated after 1990 allowing generous use of motorized vehicles and other exceptions to the original Wilderness Act. This practice would, of course, deviate from the earlier stated goal of providing more solitude in undisturbed setting, as well as reducing other Wilderness values.

With addition of Wilderness areas, BLM's responsibilities for management will grow. BLM is committed to improvement of Wilderness management and supports the Aldo Leopold Wilderness Research Institute and the Arthur Carhart National Wilderness Training Center in Montana. The BLM also helps sponsor the *International Journal of Wilderness* and is active in implementation of the Interagency Wilderness Strategic Plan of 1995. The BLM will continue to be a full and equal partner with the Forest Service, National Park Service, Fish and Wildlife Service, and the Biological Division of the U.S. Geological Service to foster stewardship of the Wilderness resource.

NATIONAL PARK SERVICE WILDERNESS MANAGEMENT

(By Wes Henry, National Park Service, Washington, DC)

The Wilderness Act of 1964 significantly strengthened protection and management of National Park Service (NPS) areas designated or recommended as Wilderness. While the NPS administers the largest portion of the U.S. National Wilderness Preservation System, many environmental constituencies believe that NPS Wilderness management has not been effective. Despite the devotion of many field staff, strong leadership in regional or national offices has been lacking to provide needed policy consistency across the agency. A Wilderness task force in 1986 acknowledged a lack of collective understanding of the relationship between the mandates of the 1916 NPS Organic Act and the 1964 Wilderness Act. Wilderness management has not been differentiated from basic park management. Many NPS Wilderness studies and recommendations have languished for longer than 20 years. Recently, however, this passivity has begun to change.

Director Kennedy convened an NPS Task Force in November, 1993, to develop recommendations for improving wilderness management through leadership, partnerships, communication, training, planning, resource management, and designation. The director endorsed the Task Force recommendations on September 3, 1994, the Thirtieth Anniversary of the Wilderness Act. He highlighted them at the Sixth National Wilderness Conference in New Mexico, in November, 1994. Progress toward implementation of these recommendations is continuing.

Leadership

The key task force recommendation for improving NPS Wilderness management concerned better leadership. One specific recommendation was to form a National Wilderness Steering Committee (NWSC). Formed in 1995, this committee is made up of four senior superintendents (Rocky Mountain, Mount Rainier, Great Smoky Mountains, and Saguaro National Parks), the associate director for operations and education, and staff specialists from across the service. The NWSC is providing much needed leadership in four critical areas:

- Revising Wilderness management policies for the National Park Service.
- Developing guidelines for Wilderness management that address Wilderness planning, minimum requirements, cultural resource management, rockclimbing, and scientific uses.
- Ensuring Wilderness management is a critical performance element for superintendents, identified as a major duty for positions with Wilderness management assignments, and incorporated into park plans in response to the Government Performance and Results Act.
- Initiating a Wilderness awards program to honor employees and private sector organizations for excellence in leadership.

In addition to the NWSC, leadership is provided through the national program leader and the intermountain region wilderness coordinator, who also serve on the steering committee.

Wilderness Training

A second major series of recommendations of the Wilderness task force recognized that investing in training is one of the best long-term ways to improve Wilderness management. The NPS now has a full-time trainer stationed at the interagency *Arthur Carhart National Wilderness Training Center* to provide Wilderness-related training to the National Park Service.

The mission of the Arthur Carhart National Wilderness Training Center is to foster interagency excellence in Wilderness stewardship by cultivating knowledgeable, skilled, and capable Wilderness managers and by improving public understanding of Wilderness. Program areas offered include advanced management for line officers and staff, planning, wilderness fire planning, cultural resources management, rehabilitation and restoration, K-12 wilderness box curriculum, management correspondence courses, and Leave No Trace.

The National Park Service has been an active participant in most courses, especially recent National and Regional Wilderness Training courses. This emphasis on training will likely continue as the method because an assessment conducted by the Carhart Center of NPS Wilderness managers and staff show the choice to build skills in planning, public education/awareness, Leave No Trace ethics, resource management, and use management.

Planning

Improved Wilderness planning was another priority identified by the NPS Wilderness Task Force and the Carhart Center. Progress is being made by identifying needed changes to policy, implementing the director's orders on Wilderness, and providing Wilderness guidelines. This three-tiered guidance addresses identification of the Wilderness resource, establishment of accountability, identification of minimum-requirement alternatives, establishment of planning policy, and identification of critical issues in interagency relationships.

In a March 1997 memorandum to superintendents with Wilderness units, the NPS director requested that management and protection of Wilderness be integrated into the individual park strategic plans being developed in response to the Government Performance and Results Act. He asked that completion of an approved Wilderness management plan by 2002 be one of the objectives.

The National Wilderness Steering Committee has authorized the national office to help parks in developing Wilderness management plans where circumstances warrant. One example is the assistance being provided to Cumberland Island National Seashore to address the extreme complexity of that planning effort.

Partnerships and Improving Communications

The task force also urged the NPS to forge Wilderness management partnerships with industry, educators, environmental groups, and other organizations. Many important and creative partnerships have been formed for improving the NPS Wilderness management program. Partnership will likely become even more important in the future as urbanization and population diversification continue.

The 30th anniversary of the Wilderness Act was the springboard for a campaign to bring more attention to Wilderness. The NPS and other agencies developed a cost-share agreement with the National Geographic Society to develop Wilderness education programs for teachers through the Geographic Education Program's *Wilderness Workshop.* Educators were selected from state *geographic alliances* to participate in annual summer institutes. The theme for the 1994 institute was to give participants knowledge and skills about Wilderness and related environmental issues so they can more effectively provide professional development opportunities to their colleagues.

Following the summer institute, workshop participants, working with interagency personnel and the National Geographic Society, spearheaded a campaign to promote enthusiasm and awareness about the importance of Wilderness protection and management during National Geography Awareness Week. The cost-share agreement also produced educational materials, including lesson plans, posters, a banner, and a map. These materials were used by the agencies and by the educators for the 30th Anniversary of the Wilderness Act and National Parks Week. These efforts reached an estimated 72 million citizens, 85,000 teachers, and perhaps 20 million students.

The Leave No Trace program is another important NPS partnership. Leave No Trace (LNT) is a nationwide partnership between four federal agencies, the National Outdoor Leadership School (NOLS), and numerous representatives from industry, education, and recreation groups. The mission of the LNT program is to develop a national backcountry system to educate wildland users, land managers, and the public. NOLS assists with the LNT program by working with the Arthur Carhart National Wilderness Training Center to provide LNT master courses, distribute LNT materials, and conduct research on use impacts. NOLS also runs courses in 21 national parks and preserves.

The NPS Leave No Trace program has made progress through grants from the *Parks as Classrooms* program. LNT employs the "train the trainers" strategy to train LNT masters who in turn train others. NPS LNT masters have been introducing LNT to the public, park employees, industries, and other organizations. In addition to LNT masters training, NPS is exploring how to incorporate LNT into other training programs.

The Leave No Trace program is also being used as a vehicle for partnerships with industry. Newly formed Leave No Trace, Inc., is a non-profit organization to work with manufacturers, outdoor retailers, user groups, educators, and individuals who share a commitment to maintaining and protecting public lands. Important progress has resulted from NPS and other agency participation at outdoor marketing shows where LNT trainers explain opportunities for participating in the program.

The Internet is another likely area where Wilderness management agencies can partner. It is critical that Wilderness managing agencies and institutions capitalize on the Internet's unique opportunity to further understanding of Wilderness both within managing organizations and with the external public. The NPS is working as part of an interagency project with the University of Montana School of Forestry, the Arthur Carhart National Wilderness Training Center, and the Aldo Leopold Wilderness Research Institute to make Internet connections. These connections would help move users among different levels of information and communication to serve managers, educators, students, researchers, wilderness users, and advocates. The network could also link to agency home pages and to external sources. An issue is making the partnership work while addressing the ethical dilemma of potential intrusion of the *information superhighway* on basic Wilderness values.

Improving Resource Management

The NPS Wilderness Task Force also recommended improving understanding and management of Wilderness. This goal requires that the NPS recognize Wilderness as a component of both visitor and resource management. It also involves use of resource management plans to identify needs in the budget process and encouragement of use of the Aldo Leopold Wilderness Research Institute (ALWRI) for research, technology transfer, technical assistance, education, and cooperative studies.

The mission of the institute is improving ability to sustain Wilderness resources, both ecologically and socially. A strategic plan has been developed and core issues identified to focus ALWRI research. Topics include recreational and non-recreational uses of Wilderness; physical, ecological, and social impacts on the Wilderness resources; National Wilderness Preservation System monitoring; and development of information useful for Wilderness management and education.

Wilderness Designation

Passage of the California Desert Protection Act (P.L. 103-433) in 1994 was significant for NPS Wilderness. The percentage of NPS acreage designated as Wilderness rose to nearly 52 percent. The NPS now has the largest wilderness unit in the lower 48 states, the 3,158,038-acre area in the Death Valley National Park. The measure also changed the Joshua Tree National Monument to a National Park, increased the park by 234,000 acres, and designated 132,000 Wilderness. The act also established the 1,419,800-acre Mohave National Preserve and designated 695,000 acres of the new preserve as Wilderness. The NPS now has 44 designated Wilderness Areas, 10,170,455 acres in the lower 48 states and Hawaii and 32,979,370 acres in Alaska. The current listing of Wilderness areas in the National Park System is shown as Table VIII.1.

Table VIII.1: Wilderness in the National Park Service

Field Area	Park/Wilderness	Acres of Wilderness	Year of Designation
Alaska	Denali	2,124,783	1980
	Gates of the Arctic	7,167,192	1980
	Glacier Bay	2,664,840	1980
	Katmai	3,384,358	1980
	Kobuk Valley	174,545	1980
	Lake Clark	2,619,550	1980
	Noatak	5,765,427	1980
	Wrangell-St. Elias	9,078,675	1980
	(All Alaska Areas)	(32,979,370)	
Intermountain	Bandalier	23,267	1976
	Black Canyon of the Gunnison	11,180	1976
	Carlsbad Caverns	33,125	1978
	Chiricahua	9,440	1976
	Great Sand Dunes	33,450	1976
	Guadalupe Mountains	46,850	1979
	Mesa Verde	8,100	1976
	Organ Pine Cactus	312,600	1978
	Petrified Forest	50,260	1970
	Rocky Mountain	2,917	1980
	Saguaro	71,400	1976
	(All Intermountain Areas)	(602,589)	
Midwest	Badlands	64,250	1976
	Buffalo River	34,993	1978/1993
	Isle Royale	132,018	1976
	Theodore Roosevelt	29,920	1978
	(All Midwest Areas)	(261,181)	
Northeast	Fire Island	1,363	1980
	Shenandoah	79,579	1976
	(All Northeast Areas)	(80,942)	

Table VIII.1 Cont.

Field Area	Park/Wilderness	Acres of Wilderness	Year of Designation
Pacific West	Craters of the Moon	43,243	1970
	Death Valley	3,158,038	1994
	Haleakala	19,270	1976
	Hawaii Volcanoes	123,100	1978
	Joshua Tree	561,470	1976/1994
	Lassen Volcanic	78,982	1972
	Lava Beds	28,460	1972
	Mohave	695,200	1994
	Mount Rainier	228,498	1988
	North Cascades	634,614	1988
	Olympic	876,669	1988
	Pinnacles	12,952	1976
	Point Reyes	25,370	1976
	Sequioa-Kings Canyon	736,980	1984
	Yosemite	677,600	1984
	(All Pacific West Areas)	(7,900,436)	
Southeast	Everglades	1,296,500	1978
	Congaree Swamp	15,010	1988
	Cumberland Island	8,840	1982
	Gulf Islands	4,957	1978/1994
	(All Southeast Areas)	(1,325,307)	

In 1996 President Clinton addressed the long-standing backlog of Wilderness designation proposals for the National Park Service in his *Parks for Tomorrow* initiative. He urged Congress to act on previous Wilderness recommendations and directed the secretary of the interior to work with Congress to make necessary changes to these proposals during the legislative process. President Clinton stated that the National Park Service and Presidents Nixon, Ford, and Carter recommended Wilderness designations in 17 national parks, covering some five million acres, which Congress has never really seriously considered. These areas include such well-known parks as the Yellowstone, Glacier, Grand Teton, Great Smoky Mountains, Zion, Bryce Canyon, and Canyonlands National Parks.

Emerging Issues

Democratic government is, by nature, an evolving experiment, and Wilderness is one of the pieces that will continue to evolve. Major challenges include the following:

1. Wilderness issues are shifting from primary allocation (how many acres and where) to stewardship (seeing the Wilderness condition perpetuate itself). The NPS will continue to press for park Wilderness designations, but we must impress our considerable land stewardship experience into the service of Wilderness management. Land stewardship is not independent from social and political realities, but entwined with our history, culture, economy, politics, and faith. Knowing this, the NPS will reach out for new partners to help inform Americans of both their legacy and continuing need to steward the land.
2. Dramatic demographic changes in the West are influencing and will influence Wilderness. The proportion of total U.S. population living in the West has tripled since 1950. Were the 20 counties in and adjacent to the Greater Yellowstone Ecosystem a state, it would be the nation's fastest growing one. The NPS will need to approach the stewardship of parklands, Wilderness and other resources in ever more collegial fashion. The NPS should seek to lend rather than to insist upon use of NPS expertise. Many new residents are now drawn to the West because of its wildland character.
3. The U.S. population is aging, growing more ethnically diverse, and growing in numbers. The NPS needs to broadcast the benefits from Wilderness that accrue, whether one visits a Wilderness area or not. The

NPS will need to seek out, learn, and carefully enfranchise the wildland connections and heritage of ethnic groups as partners and stakeholders. The NPS must continuously examine its own cultural assumptions. The NPS will aggressively impress upon Wilderness users the Leave No Trace and other zero impact awareness ethics. The NPS will need to become apostles for sensitive, sustainable, environmental stewardship among all who share park boundaries or live upwind and upstream.

4. How the public and our other federal agencies view public lands is shifting. Federal land policy in general has shifted toward retention and management and away from disposal. But multiple claims continue to be asserted for public land resources from timber and mining to tourism, outdoor recreation, vision questing, scientific research, and Wilderness. The NPS will need to seek cooperation, not competition, with other land management agencies. Long-term social agreement on Wilderness values may well prove unlikely or at least unstable over time. The Park Service will reach out in both public debate and education to clarify public land values. The NPS must do a better job of engaging in this debate and provide education where people actually live, work, and learn. The NPS can no longer merely wait for people to come to parks before pressing the case.
5. American politics has shifted toward adversarial struggles for privilege and away from shared commitments to civic responsibility and the common good. Recent politics challenge our public school textbook assumption that Americans in fact constitute a people and, moreover, a people somehow committed to a common good. The Park Service will no longer simply assume it stands for the common good. The NPS must seek out partners among those who also affirm a common good, particularly among nonprofit and nongovernmental organizations who share heritage concerns and commitments.
6. Public involvement in public land management has increased greatly. When powerful opponents of Wilderness at the eleventh hour injected the review process into the Wilderness Act, they hoped thereby to stymie the Wilderness System. Quite the opposite happened. They motivated citizens to learn how to influence federal decision making and soon put an end to the old closed-committee mode of the Congress. The Park Service appreciates the voice of citizens as individuals and members of nonprofit organizations as wholesome expressions of the common good. Again, the NPS must both share expertise with and work to encourage public involvement for Wilderness allocation and management. As proponents of biodiversity, the NPS can have no argument with the rich mix of interests at the grassroots of politics.
7. The role of science is changing in America. Since World War II, scientists in the United States began a half-century expansion of their role in policy making. Conservation biology and the new forestry express this expansionism today. The concept of limits-of-acceptable-change (LAC) is a good example of the injection of social science concepts into resource policy. But increasing numbers of Americans now reject science and have lost faith in technology. The Congress is also often impatient with science. The Park Service must continue to make use of good science to inform Wilderness management decisions. Responsible science in Park Wilderness should be encouraged. (Source: Gary Machlis, U. of Idaho.)

These seven challenges will influence both NPS stewardship of Wilderness and its overall heritage-protection mission. Indeed, the meaning and value of Wilderness stewardship will continue to be challenged in the future, just as national parks themselves have faced recent challenges. To the extent that Wilderness remains the exclusive concern of a small cadre of professionals, aficionados, and Wilderness users, such challenges are better assured. The same democracy that raised the Wilderness system can also raze it. It is incumbent on the National Park Service, steward of 51 percent of the Wilderness system, to involve ever more citizens. Stewardship intended to last in perpetuity, as the Wilderness Act clearly mandates, must keep asking, "Who benefits? Who loses? Who has the power?" and perhaps most of all, "Who cares?" The National Park Service will continue to improve its caring stewardship of the 43 million acres of Wilderness assigned to it by the Congress.

REFERENCES

Catherine Freer Wilderness Therapy Expedition. (1995). *Catherine Freer therapy expeditions: A wilderness therapy experience for troubled youth* [Brochure]. Albany, OR: Author.

Cole, D. (1996). *Wilderness recreation use trends 1965 through 1994*, USDA Forest Service Research Paper INT-RP-488. Ogden, UT: USDA Forest Service.

Conger, J. A. (1993). Personal growth training: Snake oil or pathway to leadership? *Organizational Dynamics.*

Cordell, H. K., Bergstrom, J. C., Hartmann, L. A., & English, D. B. K. (1990). *An analysis of the outdoor recreation and wilderness situation in the United States: 1989-2040*. General Technical Report RM-189. Fort Collins, CO: U.S. Department of Agriculture, Forest Service, Rocky Mountain Forest and Range Experiment Station.

Cordell, H. K., & Teasley, J. (1997). Estimating recreational trips to wilderness in the U.S.: Results from the National Survey on Recreation and the Environment. Athens, GA: USDA Forest Service, Southern Research Station.

Davis, G. D. (1989). Preservation of natural diversity: The role of ecosystem representation within wilderness. In *Wilderness Benchmark 1988: Proceedings of the National Wilderness Colloquium; 1988 January 13-14,* Tampa, FL (pp. 76-82). GTR SE-51. Asheville, NC: U.S. Department of Agriculture, Forest Service, Southeastern Forest Experiment Station.

Earlham College. (1995). *Earlham College* [Brochure]. Richmond, IN: Author.

English, D., & Cordell, H. K. (1985). A cohort-centric analysis of outdoor recreation participation changes. In A. Watson, (Ed.), *Proceedings: Southeastern Recreation Research Conference* (pp. 93-110). Statesboro, GA: Georgia Southern College, Dept. of Recreation and Leisure Services.

Freeman, M. (1993). Nonuse values in natural resource damage assessment, In R. Kopp & V. K. Smith, (Eds.), *Valuing natural assets: The economics of natural resource damage assessment*. Washington, DC: Resources for the Future.

Friese, G. T., Hendee, J. C., & Kinziger, M. L. (In press). The wilderness experience program industry in the United States. *Journal of Experiential Education.*

Friese, G. T. (1996). *An inventory and classification of wilderness experience programs*. Unpublished masters thesis, University of Idaho, Moscow.

Friese, G. T. (1996). *Directory of wilderness experience programs*. Moscow, ID: University of Idaho, Wilderness Research Center.

Gager, D. (1996). *Agency policies and wilderness managers attitudes towards wilderness experience programs*. Unpublished masters thesis, University of Idaho, Moscow.

Gilbert, A., Glass, R., & More, T. (1992). Valuation of eastern wilderness: Extramarket measures of public support. In C. Payne, J. Bowker, & P. Reed, *Economic value of wilderness*, (GTR-SE78) (pp. 57-70)Athens, GA: USDA Forest Service, SE Forest Experiment Station.

Greene, W. (1990). *Econometric analysis*. New York: Macmillan Publishing.

Greene, W. (1995). *Limdep, version 7.0*. New York: Econometric Software Inc.

Hellerstein, D. (1995). Welfare estimation using aggregate and individual observation models. *American Journal of Agricultural Economics,* 77, 620-630.

Hendee, J. C., & Brown, M. (1987). How wilderness experience programs work for personal growth, therapy, and education: an explanatory model. In J. C. Hendee (Ed.), *The highest use of wilderness: Using wilderness experience programs to develop human potential.* Proceedings of the special plenary session at the 4th world wilderness congress Estes Park, CO September 16, 1987 (pp. 5-21). On file University of Idaho, Wilderness Research Center, Moscow, ID 83844.

Hendee, J., Stankey, G., & Lucas, R. (1990). *Wilderness Management* (2nd ed.). Golden, CO: North American Press.

Kent Mountain Adventure Center. (1995). *Kent Mountain Adventure Center* [Brochure]. Estes Park, CO: Author.

Kmenta, J. (1986). *Elements of Econometrics* (2nd ed.). New York: Macmillan.

Krakauer, J. (1995, October). Loving them to death. *Outside, 72-82*, 142-143.

Longacre Expeditions. (1995). *Longacre Expeditions 1995* [Brochure]. Newport, PA: Author.

Loomis, J. (1988). Broadening the concept and measurement of existence value. *Northeastern Journal of Agricultural Resource Economics, 17*, 23-29.

Loomis, J. (1993). *Integrated public lands management: Principles and application to national forests, parks, wildlife refuges, and BLM lands*. New York: Columbia University Press.

Loomis, J., & Walsh, R. (1997). *Recreation economic decisions* (2nd ed.). State College, PA: Venture Press.

Messier, S. (1984). The wilderness code of ethics and troubled youth. In D. P. Teschner, & J. J. Wolter (Eds.), *Wilderness challenge: Outdoor education alternatives for youth in need* (pp. 87-91). Hadlyme, CT: The Institute of Experimental Studies.

Miner, T. (1995). The providers of outdoor-based training. In C. C. Roland, R. J. Wagner, & R. J. Weigand (Eds.), *Do it...and understand! The bottom line on corporate experiential learning* (pp. 173-176). Dubuque, IA: Kendall/Hunt Publishing Company.

National Park Service. (1986). *1982-1983 Nationwide Recreation Survey*. Washington DC: U.S. Department of Interior.

O'Keefe, M. A. (1989). *An assessment of freshman wilderness orientation programs in higher education: A descriptive Delphi study*. (ERIC Document Reproduction Service No. ERIC ED 252 368). Boston: Boston University, School of Education.

Peterson, M. R. (1988). The evolution of state-designated wilderness programs. In *Outdoor recreation benchmark 1988: Proceedings of the national outdoor recreation forum,* Tampa FL. Asheville, NC: USDA Forest Service Southern Research Station.

Peterson, M. R. (1996). Wilderness by state mandate: A survey of state-designated wilderness areas. *Natural Areas Journal, 16*,192-197.

Pope, C. A., & Jones, J. (1990). Value of wilderness designation in Utah. *Journal of Environmental Management, 30, 157-174.*

Powch, I. G. (1994). Wilderness therapy: What makes it empowering for women? In E. Cole, E. Erdman, & E. Rothblum (Eds.), *Wilderness therapy for women: The power of adventure* (pp. 11-27). New York: Harrington Park Press.

Riley, M. R. (1997). Wilderness vision quests tap the spiritual values of wilderness. *Women in Natural Resources, 18*(1): 11-13.

Roberts, A. R. (1989). *Juvenile justice: Policies, programs, and services*. Chicago: The Dorsey Press.

Russel, K., & Hendee, J. C. (1997). *Testing wilderness discovery: A wilderness experience program for youth-at-risk in the Federal Job Corps*. Technical report 24. Moscow, ID: University of Idaho.

S.O.A.R. (1996). *S.O.A.R. 1996 adventure opportunities* [Brochure]. Balsam, NC: Author.

Stynes, D., Peterson, G., & Rosenthal, R. (1986). Log transformation bias in estimating travel cost models. *Land Economics, 62*, 94-103.

Torgerson, D. (1996). U.S. Macroeconomic Projections to 2045. Washington, DC: USDA Economic Research Service, Commercial Agriculture Division.

U. S. Bureau of the Census (1966 to 1995). *Statistical Abstract of the United States.* Washington, DC: U.S. Government Printing Office.

U.S. Bureau of Economic Analysis. (1995). *State personal income 1929-1993.* Washington D.C: U.S. Department of Commerce.

Walsh, R., & Gilliam, L. (1983). Benefits of wilderness expansion with excess demand for Indian peaks. *Western Journal of Agricultural Economics, 7*,1-12.

Walsh, R., Loomis, J., & Gillman, R. (1984). Valuing option, existence, and bequest demand for wilderness. *Land Economics, 60*, 14-29.

Weisbrod, B. (1964). Collective consumption services of individual consumption goods. *Quarterly Journal of Economics, 78*, 471-477.

Wilderness Education Association. (1995). *Wilderness Education Association* [Brochure]. Fort Collins, CO: Author.

Wilderness Transitions, Inc. (1994). *Wilderness transitions: The vision quest* [Brochure]. Ross, CA: Author.

Wilson, R. (1981). *Inside outward bound*. Charlotte, NC: The East Woods Press.

Zook, L. R. (1987). Outdoor adventure programs build character five ways. In J. F. Meier, T. W. Morash, & G. E. Welton (Eds.), *High adventure outdoor pursuits* (pp.8-15). Columbus, OH: Publishing Horizons.

CHAPTER IX

MOTIVATIONS, ATTITUDES, PREFERENCES, AND SATISFACTIONS AMONG OUTDOOR RECREATIONISTS

. . . .

Michael A. Tarrant[1]
Alan D. Bright
Erin Smith
H. Ken Cordell

INTRODUCTION

This chapter is presented in two sections. The first by Bright and Tarrant describes visitor preferences and examines users' perceptions of encountering other visitors in outdoor recreation settings. The second by Tarrant and others reviews visitor preferences for, and satisfactions with, outdoor recreation experiences.

Outdoor recreation experiences are investigated by means of an in-depth review of the published literature since 1986, focusing upon (1) measurement and application of the Recreation Experience Preference (REP) scales developed to measure user motives for outdoor recreation involvement, and (2) user attitudes toward social encounter levels. Encounter levels were examined because of the vast amount of literature in the past 10 years devoted to determining recreation use carrying capacities. The second part of the chapter is an analysis and summary of data from the Customer Use and Survey Techniques for Operations, Management, Evaluation, and Research (CUSTOMER) study, which resulted in interviews of over 11,000 visitors to 31 outdoor recreation sites across the country between 1990 to 1994. Using the framework of importance and performance, this section explores visitor preferences for, and satisfactions with, site attributes for six types of outdoor recreation settings (general, developed, dispersed, water, roaded, and winter).

RECREATION VISITOR EXPERIENCE PREFERENCES AND ATTITUDES

(By Alan D. Bright, Washington State University, Pullman, WA, and Michael A. Tarrant, University of Georgia, Athens, GA)

Outdoor recreation has become a defining aspect of U.S. society. To a large extent, the connection many Americans feel to the "Great Outdoors" is an underlying theme of our culture. Such a kinship exists for the individual who actively enjoys the outdoors by venturing into a wilderness area every weekend, as well as one who enjoys and values nature without directly experiencing any aspect of it. The increase in outdoor recreation participation continues as it was during the post-World War II years. For the most part, increases in many activities mirror the slowing rate of population increase (Cordell, Bergstrom, Hartmann, & English, 1990). In addition to the increase in demand for outdoor recreation experiences, there is potential for other highly

---

[1]Michael A. Tarrant is an associate professor and Erin Smith is a former graduate research assistant, University of Georgia, Athens, GA; Alan D. Bright is an assistant professor, Washington State University, Pullman, WA; and H. Ken Cordell is a research forester and project leader, USDA Forest Service, Athens, GA.

significant changes in outdoor recreation. Cordell et al. (1990) suggested that factors such as an aging population, a decline in leisure time, geographically uneven population growth, increasing immigration, changes in family structures, and increasing levels of education, among other factors, have significantly changed the way Americans recreate in the outdoors. Examples include (a) a change in the nature of vacations with a trend toward shorter, more frequent excursions, (b) an increasing diversity of participation patterns across groups, (c) a resurgence in wilderness recreation visits, (d) a growth in non-recreational values of wilderness such as scenic, scientific, educational, conservation, and historical, and (e) an increase in more passive activities appropriate for an aging population. Such significant change in the way Americans recreate in the outdoors holds significant implications for not only the public, but also for recreation professionals. According to McLellan and Siehl (1988), "recreation managers, researchers, and policymakers will find need to cope with rapid change; recreation resource concerns increasingly will be people issues and not resource issues alone."

The growing complexity of society coupled with the change in outdoor recreation participation have resulted in a greater emergence of social-psychological research aimed at understanding outdoor recreation behavior and exploring factors that underlie such behavior. These factors include reasons why people participate in outdoor recreation as well as how individuals evaluate various aspects of an outdoor recreation experience.

The first section of this chapter discusses what is currently known about experiences the public is looking for in outdoor recreation and public perceptions related to recreation in outdoor settings. Since these are very broad areas of research, we focus on two specific objectives. First, we examine the reasons why people participate in outdoor recreation, that is, their motivations for participation. Second, we examine attitudes toward, or evaluations of encounters with, other people while recreating in the outdoors.

Motivations for Participating in Outdoor Recreation

Recreation researchers have long been interested in understanding why people participate in outdoor recreation. While it once appeared evident that an angler fishes to catch fish and a hunter hunts to "bag" game, it is clear that outdoor recreation motivations are, in reality, much more complex.

The Meaning of Motivation

While research on the motives behind outdoor recreation participation has been going on for several years, definitions of motivation have varied. Stankey and Schreyer (1987) considered motives to be a predisposition to fulfill specific types of needs. Reasons for participating in outdoor recreation have also been called recreation experience preferences (REP) (Driver 1976), emphasizing the voluntary nature of behavior based on those preferences. That is, we engage in specific recreation behavior because we desire outcomes that we perceive will occur as a result of that behavior. Focusing on these outcomes, motivations have been referred to as desired psychological outcomes (Driver & Brown, 1978) and desired consequences (Driver & Knopf, 1976). The meaning of motivations has also focused on the user's expectation that he or she will encounter desirable conditions, or experience expectations (Schreyer & Roggenbuck, 1978). The importance of studying motivations for outdoor recreation lies in their potential to influence satisfaction through meeting individual's needs, preferences, expectations, and/or desired outcomes.

Early Research on Motivations for Outdoor Recreation

The search for motivations for outdoor recreation was abundant during the 1960s, but it was generally limited to a description of participation in specific activities, such as hunting, fishing, camping, or canoeing. A conceptual foundation for explaining why people recreate in the outdoors was lacking. While a number of researchers began to explore the theoretical nature of motivations during the 1960s and 1970s (e.g., Burch, 1969 & Hendee, 1974), the most comprehensive study of motivations for outdoor recreation was by Driver and his associates. In their approach, recreation was perceived not as an activity, but as an experience derived from recreational engagements (Driver & Tocher, 1970). Such an "experiential approach" suggests that people participate in outdoor recreation in order to realize any number of psychological outcomes. Research in this area was primarily interested in understanding how basic motivations, or psychological outcomes, influence the choices people make about what activities they participate in and what settings they prefer. Results would aid managers in identifying the "product" recreationists desire, and enable them to take steps to provide that product.

This research developed psychometric scales that could be used to measure the dimensions of people's recreation experience. These measurements have become known as the recreation experience preference

(REP) scales (Driver, 1977). The assumption in using these scales is that several scale items correlate to provide information about a broader experience preference domain. For example, obtaining information about the extent to which an individual values an *escape from physical pressure* in outdoor recreation activities requires determining the importance of several correlated items designed to measure needs for (a) tranquility, (b) privacy, (c) escaping crowds, and (d) escaping physical stress.

Early empirical work on motivations focused on (a) describing recreation experience preferences in various activities, (b) identifying different types of experiences enjoyed by different recreationists engaging in the same activity, (c) establishing a relationship among setting and activity preferences, (d) identifying a relationship between non-leisure conditions and recreation experience preferences, (e) exploring the relationship between experience preferences and subject characteristics, and (f) methodological development of the REP scales (Manfredo, Driver, & Tarrant, 1996).

Recent Research on Motivations for Outdoor Recreation

More recent work examining experience preferences has focused on (a) testing the REP scales, and (b) examining experience preferences by activity, setting, and group type.

Testing the REP scales

Some researchers have questioned the validity of the experience preference scales. For example, Williams, Schreyer, and Knopf (1990) found that the extent to which specific experience items correlated with each other (therefore defining a particular experience preference domain) differed depending on the past experience of the user. To address questions regarding such validity, Manfredo et al. (1996) conducted a meta-analysis of the structure of the REP scales. These researchers examined the results of 36 different studies that had applied the REP scales during the middle to late 1970s. Analyses supported the *a priori* domain and scale structures of the recreation experiences (Table IX.1).

The kind of outdoor recreation experience people seek often depends upon the type of setting in which the activity takes place. Photo courtesy of the Appalacian Trail Conference. Photo by Theodore C. Viars.

Table IX.1: List of Recreation Experience Preference Domains and Scales

Domains	Scales	Domains	Scales
Achievement/ Stimulation	1. reinforcing self-image 2. social recognition 3. skill development 4. competence testing 5. excitement 6. endurance 7. telling others	Enjoy Nature	1. scenery 2. general nature experience
		Introspection	1. spiritual 2. introspection
		Creativity[1]	1. creativity
Autonomy/ Leadership	1. independence 2. autonomy 3. control-power	Nostalgia[1]	1. nostalgia
		Physical Fitness[1]	1. physical fitness
Risk Taking[1]	1. risk taking	Physical Rest[1]	1. physical rest
Equipment[1]	1. equipment	Escape Personal-Social Pressures	1. tension release 2. slow down mentally 3. escape role overloads
Family Togetherness[1]	1. family togetherness		
Similar People	1. being with friends 2. being with similar people	Escape Physical Pressure	1. tranquility 2. privacy 3. escape crowds 4. escape physical stressors
New People	1. meeting new people 2. observing other people		
		Social Security[1]	1. social security
Learning	1. general learning 2. exploration 3. geography study 4. learn more about nature	Teaching-Leading Others	1. teaching-sharing skills 2. leading others
		Risk reduction	1. risk moderation 2. risk avoidance

Items on the left represent experience preference domains while numbered items represent experience preference scales. Individual items for each scale may be found in Manfredo, Driver, and Tarrant (1996).
[1] One-scale domains.

Manfredo et al. (1996) identified three desirable uses of the validated scales: (a) to determine why people took a particular trip, (b) to determine why people engage in a particular activity, and (c) to measure the satisfaction obtained from a particular trip or activity. Differences in researcher objectives may be illustrated by differences in response scales used. Furthermore, Manfredo et al. (1996) suggested that identifying a link between attained recreation experiences and broader beneficial human consequences, such as positive mental and physical health, would be an important use of the scales in future research.

Given the potential importance of identifying experience preferences that outdoor recreationists desire, research in the past decade has attempted to identify just what those preferences are in various situations. This work led to attempts to identify experience preferences across different outdoor settings and activities.

Experience preferences across settings

Attempts have been made to identify consistency in experience preferences across settings. Much of this research has examined whether desired experiences were consistent with the chosen setting, focusing primarily on settings defined by the Recreation Opportunity Spectrum. The most notable trend in findings is that such consistency does exist to some extent, but that the relationship between experience preferences and setting can be complex. For example, Floyd and Gramann (1997) found that four hunter types (categorized based on experiences desired) systematically differed on setting characteristics such as desired accessibility, amount of regimentation, preferred use density, desired presence of nonrecreational uses, and preferred site management. However, Virden and Knopf (1989) found that four-wheelers, hikers, anglers, and campers all held experience preferences that depended somewhat on the setting they were participating in, but these preferences were (a) very different for each activity, and (b) did not include all the important preferences held by participants. That is, only some of the preferences required a particular setting. Similar evidence for such a nonlinear relationship between setting and experience preferences was found by Yuan and McEwen (1989) and Heywood, Christensen, and Stankey (1991).

Experience preferences within activities

Further complicating attempts to describe outdoor recreationists' motivations for participation is the recognition that many different experience preferences exist for different people participating in the same activity. Factors that influence desired experience preferences fall into four distinct categories: (1) *general differences in experiences desired*, (2) *type of trip taken*, (3) *characteristics of the participants*, and (4) *outcome of the trip*.

First, for outdoor recreation activities, several distinct groups of users can be identified based on *general differences in experiences desired*. Floyd and Gramann (1997) identified four types of hunters, based on experience preferences: outdoor enthusiasts, high-challenge harvesters, low-challenge harvesters, and non-harvesters. Similarly, Manfredo, Bright, and Stephenson (1991) identified four types of wildlife viewers (positivists, creativity-focused, generalists, and occasionalists) based on various levels of preferred experiences, related activities engaged in, activities combined with wildlife viewing, preferred wildlife, and constraints to taking trips to view wildlife. Similar categorizations have been constructed for hunters (Hazel, Langenau, & Levine, 1990) and anglers (Zwick, Glass, & More, 1993).

Second, experience preferences may differ by the *type of trip taken*. For example, Ewert (1993, mountaineering) found that people who went on guided or commercial trips valued adventure and excitement most highly, while those on private trips were more likely to prefer a quiet or escape experience.

Third, *characteristics of the participants* appear to influence preferences for experiences from a given activity. For example, the *age* of the participants has been found to influence experience preferences. For example, Decker and Connelly (1989) found that deer hunters under 30 years of age were the most likely group to prefer "achievement," or success experiences, those between 30 and 44 years of age preferred "appreciative," or nature enjoyment experiences, while those over 45 years old preferred "affiliative," or social experiences. In addition, experience preferences may differ across levels of *experience* of the participants. For example, Ewert (1993) found that advanced, intermediate, and beginning climbers preferred different experiences from climbing Mount McKinley in Denali National Park, Alaska. Decker and Connelly (1989, deer hunters) and Williams, Schreyer, and Knopf (1990, river floaters) also found differences in experience preferences across experience levels. Related to experience levels, the level of *specialization* has also been found to influence experience preferences desired by outdoor recreationists (Ewert & Hollenhorst, 1994, whitewater rafters and rock climbers; Fisher, 1997, anglers; McFarlane, 1994, birdwatching). Other participant characteristics that influence experience preferences are *ethnicity and acculturation*. For example, Carr and Williams (1993) found that Anglos and Hispanics with longer generational tenure and high acculturation scores in the U.S. were more likely to visit national forests to (a) be with friends, (b) escape from the city, and (c) respect the forest than less acculturated Hispanics.

Fourth, the *outcome of the trip* has been found to influence reported experience preferences. Both Ewert (1993, mountaineers) and Stewart (1992, hikers) found that success in achieving certain experience preferences influenced the subsequent report of the importance of those experiences.

Identifying consistent user preferences for an activity probably is not possible, but the benefit to managers is understanding what factors influence experience preferences and how these factors differ across recreation user types and groups. Identification of users across several experience dimensions allows for a deeper understanding of the socio-cultural meanings behind activities and, on a practical level, provides market segmentation advantages for managers who desire to attract or communicate with certain types of recreation users. The attention to motivations in research over the past several decades is related to a significant amount of research in related areas that directly or indirectly address the extent to which motivations or desired experiences are satisfied. These areas include user preferences and expectations while on-site and evaluations of the extent to which these preferences and expectations are met.

Attitudes Toward Recreation Encounters

The importance of research focusing on experience preferences, or motivations, lies in the extent to which outdoor recreationists are satisfied with their experience, that is, the extent to which experience preferences are fulfilled. Originally, attempts at measuring such satisfaction resulted in a general measure of "user satisfaction." Often, the recreationists were simply asked if they were satisfied with their trip. However, the general inability of such a global measure to differentiate between levels of experience fulfillment has resulted in attempts to gain a more specific understanding of the attitudes and perceptions of outdoor recreationists. Studies have examined perceptions of a variety of social and ecological impacts. Here we will focus on attitudes or evaluations of encounters with other individuals or groups while recreating, which is perceived crowding.

Perceived Crowding in Outdoor Recreation

Much of the research on perceived crowding arose from early attempts to determine social carrying capacities for outdoor recreation settings. Social carrying capacity has been defined as "the level of use beyond which social impacts exceed acceptable levels specified by evaluative standards" (Shelby & Heberlein, 1986), where one of those evaluative standards might address the number of people encountered. Early research on carrying capacity attempted to identify factors that might influence perceived crowding, including density and use levels (Hammitt, McDonald, & Noe, 1984), encounter preferences (Ditton, Fedler, & Graefe, 1983), tolerance norms (Stankey, 1973), and experience expectations (Gramann, 1982). More recently, research on social carrying capacity has focused on establishing specific evaluative standards for satisfactory levels of use.

Recent Trends in Perceived Crowding

There is evidence that the tolerance of meeting other groups or individuals while participating in outdoor recreation is changing in this country. However, the direction of that tolerance is unclear given the mixed results across different areas. For example, in a longitudinal study of visitor use at three Wilderness Areas, Cole, Watson, and Roggenbuck (1995) examined changes in evaluations of encounters with several types of groups in each Wilderness area. While the level of interparty contacts in the Boundary Waters Canoe Area Wilderness had changed little between 1969 and 1991, twice as many 1991 respondents felt crowded as in 1969. Tolerance for paddle canoe, motor canoe, and motorboat groups also decreased from 1969 to 1991. Contrasting results were found for the Shining Rock Wilderness (1978 vs. 1990) and Desolation Wilderness (1972 vs. 1990), where tolerance for a specific encounter level was higher for more recent visitors. The ambiguity of these results illustrates the need to examine factors that may influence perceived crowding. Research of the last decade has identified such factors that can be classified as situational and personal.

Situational Factors Affecting Perceived Crowding

Several situational factors influence the extent to which individuals feel crowded in an outdoor recreation setting. While these factors may interact, they will be identified separately here. These factors include the *number of encounters*, the *location of the encounter*, the *type of group encountered*, and the *type of activity engaged.*

The Number of Encounters

A fundamental assumption of the social interference model is that use levels are a key factor in determining the number of encounters, which in turn influence perceived crowding (Tarrant, Cordell, & Kibler, 1997). Although self-reports of the levels of encounters generally provide lower estimates than more objective measures of encounters, perceived crowding appears to be best explained by an individual's perception of a situation in terms of encounter levels. In a review of crowding research, Graefe, Vaske, and Kuss (1984) found that more than three-fourths of the studies examining the relationship between use levels and perceived crowding reported a positive, yet only moderate, correlation between these factors. The number of perceived encounters, on the other hand, showed a significantly higher correlation with perceived crowding than use level. Other researchers have continued to identify situations that support the ability of encounters to predict crowding over use levels (Shelby, Vaske, & Heberlein, 1989; Stewart, Chen, & Cole, 1996; Tarrant, et al., 1997).

The Location of the Encounter

In addition to the actual number of encounters, the extent to which individuals experience crowding also depends on where the encounter took place. In studies of backcountry use, Stankey (1973) found that encounters had a greater negative effect on user's experiences in the interior of a Wilderness than in the periphery. Since then, several studies have continued to support these findings in a number of different settings, including put-in and take-outs versus campsites for boating experiences (Ditton, Fedler, & Graefe, 1983; Hammitt, Shafer, & Bixler, 1992; Freeman, Tarrant, & Cordell, 1996; Tarrant, et al., 1997), trailheads versus trails (Patterson & Hammitt, 1990), and en-route to versus actual visit to a historical park (Anderek & Becker, 1993).

The Type of Group Encountered

The type of group encountered also influences perceived crowding. For example, encountering one large party in an outdoor area has been found to result in greater perceived crowding than meeting several smaller parties separately (Manning, 1985a; Tarrant, et al., 1997), for experienced users encountering inexperienced users (Ditton, et al., 1983), and for specialists encountering generalists (Hammitt, et al., 1984). An explanation for this influence is that when a group is perceived to have different values and goals than one's own party, perceived crowding increases and factors such as method of travel and group size are the most visible signs of assessing the similarity of that group to one's own (Graefe, et al., 1984).

The Type of Activity

Finally, the type of activity one is engaged in influences the level of crowding an outdoor recreationist feels. For example, canoeists were found to experience crowding more when encountering motorboaters than other canoers (Schreyer & Roggenbuck, 1978). However, the type of activity most likely interacts with one of the previously discussed factors that influence perceived crowding. For instance, perceived crowding of boaters and backcountry users has differed between campsite and trail (Ditton, et al., 1983; Patterson & Hammitt, 1990), and differences between kayakers and canoers were found across put-ins versus rapids (Tarrant, et al., 1997). In addition, there have been differences in perceived crowding identified across groups such as innertubers, anglers, and hunters (Shelby & Heberlein, 1986). More global descriptions of activities may provide generalizable information about the effects of activity on perceptions of crowding. For example, outdoor recreationists participating in activities considered as specialized (activities that require more development in skills and equipment) are likely to perceive crowding differently in given situations than those in nonspecialized activities (Hammitt, et al., 1984).

Personal Factors Affecting Perceived Crowding

An important and often-studied personal factor that influences an individual's perceived crowding is the perception or evaluation of the number of contacts with other individuals or groups while recreating in the outdoors. Often referred to as a normative approach to perceived crowding, several writers have suggested that norms are strongly related to experience parameters such as perceived crowding and satisfaction (Graefe, Vaske, & Kuss, 1984; Manning, 1985a; Vaske, Shelby, Graefe, & Heberlein, 1986). Research attempting to connect an individual's reported norms for encounter levels to satisfaction has been somewhat mixed. For example, Patterson and Hammitt (1990) and Tarrant et al., (1997) found low correlations between the extent to which an individual's actual encounters exceeded reported tolerances and decreased satisfaction with the trip. Similarly, Williams, Roggenbuck, and Bange (1991) found significant correlations only in extreme discrepancies between tolerance for and actual encounters. On the other hand, a substantial amount of research has found high correlations between norms for tolerable contacts and evaluations of an outdoor recreation experience (Hammitt & Rutlin, 1995; Lewis, Lime, & Anderson, 1996; Manning, Johnson, & Van de Kamp, 1996; Manning, Lime, Friemund, & Pitt, 1996; Vaske, Donnelly, & Petruzzi, 1996). Research on norms for encounter levels has most generally addressed two key questions: (1) Who can identify norms for encounter levels? (2) For what activities and settings are norms for encounter levels highest or lowest?

Who Can Identify Encounter Norms?

Although many indicate that the level of contacts is important to their satisfaction, not all outdoor recreationists are capable of identifying specific levels of tolerable contacts with other individuals or groups. For example, Hall and Shelby (1996) indicated that fewer than one-half were able to give a specific number of tolerable contacts, and Tarrant et al. (1997) found that no more than one-fourth could give a number. In what circumstances are individuals capable of accurately identifying the number of contacts with other individuals or groups before the quality of their experience diminishes?

One factor that has been examined is the *type of activity*. Overall, studies that explore the existence of norms across activities support the notion that recreationists who participate in different activities show different levels of tolerance for encounters. This result has been found for a variety of activities including hunting and boating (Heberlein & Vaske, 1977; Roggenbuck, Williams, Bange, & Dean, 1991). Closer inspection of these findings, however, suggests that the relationship between activity and ability to report tolerable levels of encounters is more complex.

The most common factor that influences the ability of outdoor recreationists to identify tolerable encounter levels is the *type of setting* in which the activity is to take place. That is, individuals who are recreating in a low density setting are more able to identify a certain level of contacts with others than those participating in a high density, or high use, area. This result has been found for a variety of activities, including hikers (Hall & Shelby, 1996; Patterson & Hammitt, 1990), whitewater boaters (Roggenbuck, Williams, Bange, & Dean, 1991; Tarrant, et al., 1997), canoeists (Heberlein & Vaske, 1977; Lewis, Lime, & Anderson, 1996; Shelby & Stein, 1984), and anglers (Martinson & Shelby, 1992; Shelby, 1981; Shelby & Stein, 1984). Other factors that influence the ability to provide a level of tolerable contacts are the *experience and/or knowledge levels of the recreationists* (positive correlation, Basman, Manfredo, Barro, Vaske, & Watson, 1996; Hall & Shelby, 1996), the *size of the group* (negative correlation, Hall & Shelby, 1996), and the *level of specialization* (negative correlation, Tarrant, et al., 1997).

For What Activities and Settings Are Norms for Encounter Levels Highest or Lowest?

Research has explored the ability of recreationists to identify encounter norms for various types of boaters (Manning, et al., 1996; Shelby & Heberlein, 1986; Tarrant, et al., 1997; Vaske, Donnelly, Freimund, & Miller, 1995), hunters and anglers (Heberlein & Vaske, 1977; Shelby, 1981). Typically, tolerance for encounters depends on the nature of the recreationist encountered. In general, the more "obtrusive" a recreation activity is (e.g., motorboats versus kayaks), the lower the tolerance for encountering people or groups engaging in that activity. However, this effect depends to some extent on the nature of the recreationist encountering the "obtrusive" activity. As would be expected, as the desired setting moves from low density to high density, the levels of encounters that an individual can tolerate increases for boaters (Lewis, Lime, & Anderson, 1996; Martinson & Shelby, 1992; Shelby, 1981), hikers (Hammitt & Rutlin, 1995; Patterson & Hammit, 1990), and others (Vaske, Donnelly, & Petruzzi, 1996).

Summary

Motivations and Experience Preferences

At least four general conclusions may be drawn from work identifying the experiences that the public prefers when recreating on public land:

(1) While it is evident that different resources, or settings, can provide varying experiences, recent research suggests that the relationship between desired experiences and specific settings may be more complex than outdoor recreation management models often assume. Common sense might suggest that a primitive, backcountry setting provides better opportunities for solitude and getting back to nature than an area with developed trails and facilities. In reality, public recreation users often differ in (a) the types of setting that will give them a particular experience and (b) their definition of what, precisely, a specific experience is. Solitude for one individual might mean seeing no one else for an entire day, while another individual may perceive an experience of solitude as seeing other parties but only at the campground, or trailhead. Others may define this experience as spending time with specific types of people (such as family or friends) rather than focusing on a number of people.

(2) The complex nonlinear nature of experience preferences not only applies to various settings but also to activities. Desired experiences form complex interactions with a number of characteristics, such as the size and composition of the group, type of trip, and experience level. In addition, the desire for multiple types of experiences, or satisfactions, within a single activity has resulted in the identification of user types based on many criteria. Notwithstanding the ability of statistical techniques to identify a limited number of experience factors, the number of groups that can be identified on the basis of experience preferences is limited primarily by the number of experience preferences that are thrown into the analysis. This result underscores the complex nature of motivations for specific experiences.

(3) Identifying experience preferences across settings and activities ignores the fluid nature of desired experiences in a given setting and activity. As an individual enjoys a specific setting by engaging in an equally specific activity, experience preferences may shift as a result of other changes in the immediate environment, such as success in achieving desired experiences or interactions with other users.

(4) The appropriate use of existing experience preference scales continues to attract research. While domains of existing scales appear to be relatively stable, research on specific activities has found that the factor structures may, in fact, depend on the activity, setting, or user group being studied. Furthermore, the ever-evolving nature of outdoor recreation in America suggests that research addressing the complex nature of desired experiences will continue to be relevant for quite some time.

Overall, the focus on motivations is an attempt to understand why people value opportunities to participate in outdoor recreation. According to Schreyer (1986), outdoor recreation behavior is directed toward the attainment of an outcome ultimately to satisfy various needs. It is simply a subset of all human behavior. Needs filled in outdoor recreation are tied to "the broader sphere of needs which people seek to fulfill in everyday life". Several implications exist for policymakers and administrators. As input to policy discussions, identifying the needs of people in outdoor settings allows us to understand what the most important unmet needs are in society as a whole. These needs vary with values, culture, and physical abilities. Identifying unmet needs may also clarify government's role in the provision of public social services as well as the role of the private sector. Also, given that much of the public land in this country is managed for multiple resource uses, a better understanding of outdoor recreation needs improves public land planning and decision making. Finally, identifying salient motives for recreating in the outdoors contributes to improved understanding of the ultimate value of outdoor recreation to society. This contribution is one reason why research into long-term benefits of outdoor recreation is growing.

Understanding the nature of motivations for outdoor recreation participation is important in the planning, inventory, and provision of opportunities for recreation. Americans expect diverse experiences in outdoor recreation settings because motivations vary among people, settings, and times. Such motivations relate strongly to the attitudes, preferences, and expectations that ultimately drive the satisfaction people get from recreation.

Attitudes Toward Recreation Encounters

Several conclusions may be drawn about attitudes toward encountering other recreationists. First, while it appears that recreationists are generally able to identify norms for encounters, this ability is influenced by factors such as the type of activity, the amount of experience the individual brings to a recreation activity, the type of group encountered, the nature of the recreation trip, and the setting in which the activity takes place. Furthermore, the ability to identify a norm is positively related to concern about other types of impacts. Given that many recreationists can identify norms for appropriate encounters, different levels of tolerance exist depending on the activity engaged in and the activity with which one comes into contact.

Research on normative standards has identified several managerial benefits from using attitudinal information in decision making. First, in identifying what experiences and preferences are most desirable for a particular site, such as opportunities for a wilderness experience, normative information can focus management actions on satisfying preferences. Second, understanding user preferences helps identify the most important characteristics of settings. Third, identifying acceptable impacts helps to define standards and target management. Targets can be quantifiable measures, such as "three or fewer contacts with other parties in a four-hour period." Fourth, attitudinal information can identify minimal and optimal conditions for experiences at different times, providing flexibility for seasonal and climatic changes. Fifth, the

Visitor perceptions of overcrowding at recreation areas are subjective estimates relating to visitor expectations of the recreation place. Boone Dam Reservation. Photo courtesy of the Tennessee Valley Authority.

intensity of people's attitudes toward on-site conditions can help managers identify the most important impacts to address. Finally, attitudinal information can provide managers with a sense of how much agreement there is among the public about on-site conditions. Attitudinal findings have been applied in management frameworks such as Limits of Acceptable Change (LAC), Recreation Opportunity Spectrum (ROS), Visitor Impact Management (VIM), Carrying Capacity Assessment Process (C-CAP), Quality Upgrading and Learning (QUAL), and Visitor Experience and Resource Protection (VERP).

Implications

An understanding of recreationists' motivations for and attitudes about recreation experiences is essential to improving management of public outdoor recreation. A primary goal of recreation management is to provide a diversity of recreation experiences. To do so, managers need information about what those experiences are and what user perceptions influence the quality of their experiences. Managers also need information about the nature of future recreation use in order to determine needs for funding, staffing, and facilities. Future recreation demand can be projected by gathering information about experiences people desire. Finally, studies of motivations and experiences identify things managers do not know about existing and new user groups. For example, the traditional user of outdoor recreation areas has been white and middle class. Minorities have generally been underrepresented in resource-based, nonurban outdoor activities. In addition, some activities and experiences are culturally more popular with one racial group than another (Cordell, et al., 1990). As the U.S. population becomes increasingly diverse due to immigration and high birth rates among minority populations, there will be significant effects on the way outdoor recreation managers approach their responsibilities.

RECREATION VISITOR PREFERENCES FOR AND PERCEPTIONS OF OUTDOOR RECREATION SETTING ATTRIBUTES

(By Michael A. Tarrant and Erin Smith, University of Georgia, and H. Ken Cordell, USDA Forest Service, Athens, GA)

Between 1990 and 1994, a comprehensive national survey was conducted by the USDA Forest Service (FS), Southern Research Station, to measure visitor preferences for, and perceptions of, setting attributes at a variety of outdoor recreation sites. Over 11,000 visitors at 31 outdoor recreation sites across the country were interviewed in this study. The study was entitled CUSTOMER, which is an acronym for Customer Use and Survey Techniques for Operations, Management, Evaluations, and Research. Sites included those managed by the FS, the Bureau of Land Management (BLM), and the Tennessee Valley Authority (TVA). This section presents results of analysis of CUSTOMER data on visitor preferences for, and satisfaction with, site attributes corresponding to five specific recreation settings (developed, dispersed, water, roaded, and winter) and one general outdoor setting.

Developed areas were the most evenly distributed (across the U.S.) of the five specific settings sampled and includes sites and services such as campgrounds, RV hook-ups, picnic sites, and roads. Dispersed settings are primarily roadless areas and are more widely available in the Western than in the Eastern U.S. Water settings include lakes, rivers, and streams that are either near or adjacent to roads as well as intensively developed water sites. Roaded recreation areas are within 0.5 mile of roads, and most uses are trail dependent (for example, walking, biking, and horse riding). Winter settings provide snow and ice-based recreation opportunities and are more widely distributed in the West.

Each interviewed visitor responded to a list of 15-24 specific attributes of the setting in which he or she was recreating (e.g., visitors to a winter setting completed the list of winter setting attributes). In addition, all visitors completed a list of 14 general attributes common to all outdoor recreation settings, such as clear signs to the area, reasonable fees, and safety and security on site. Respondents reported (1) their preferences (on a scale of 1, "not important," to 5, "extremely important") and (2) their perceptions (on a scale of 1, "terrible," to 5, "delighted") for each of the settings. Visitors were contacted on-site and asked to complete a mail-back survey, which measured their preferences and satisfactions with the setting attributes.

Figure IX.1: Importance-Performance Framework (Martilla & James, 1977)

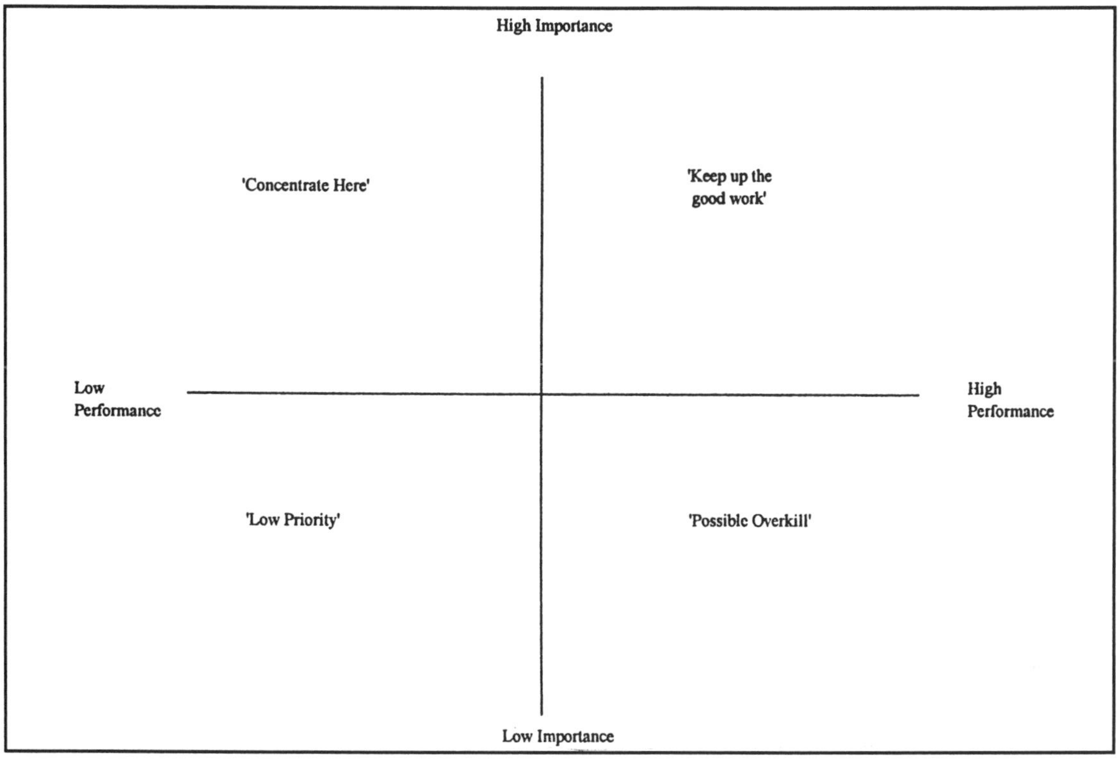

The CUSTOMER data were analyzed using the importance-performance method, in which the satisfaction scale was considered analogous to a performance criterion. The importance-performance framework is derived from the marketing literature, especially works in market segmentation (Martilla & James, 1977), and provides an effective procedure for evaluating customer satisfaction with products or services comprised of multiple attributes. Display of analysis results uses a 4-quadrant grid (Figure IX.1). Attributes in the "keep up the good work" quadrant are ones that the visitor considers to be important and satisfactory. "Possible overkill" items are those that perform well, but are not rated as important by visitors. Resources may be wasted on increased management of the attributes in this quadrant. The "low priority" items are those that receive low performance and importance ratings. The "concentrate here" quadrant represents attributes with low perceived performance, but high importance. The "concentrate here" quadrant contains the attributes that may be of greatest concern to outdoor recreation managers because their poor performance is most likely to reduce visitor satisfaction.

Purpose and Objectives

This section provides an overview to visitor satisfactions with, and preferences for, attributes of specific and general outdoor recreation settings using an importance-performance framework. Three objectives were addressed:

1. Determine specific setting attributes that outdoor recreation managers should target, i.e., the "concentrate here" quadrant of the importance-performance framework.
2. Determine the effect of visitor demographic characteristics on their importance and performance ratings.
3. Determine the effect of trip characteristics on visitor importance and performance.

Demographic Characteristics

Socio-demographic variables have traditionally explained some of the variance in outdoor recreation participation (Manning, 1985a). White, able-bodied, well-educated, and middle-income individuals comprise the "typical" participant (Cordell, Bergstrom, Hartmann, & English, 1990). Communities with proportionately higher black and low-income residents have fewer opportunities for dispersed and winter recreation. Communities with a higher percentage of whites have lower participation in developed land and water recreation. Males and higher-income individuals are associated with the most recreation opportunities of all groups. Disabled populations participate less per capita than any other social group (Cordell, et al., 1990). Clearly, as the U.S. population becomes more ethnically, socially, and economically diverse, recreation managers will have to modify the attributes of many outdoor settings to accommodate new demands.

The following demographic variables were used in objective two and categorized into dichotomous groups: gender (male versus female), education (<16 years versus 16+ years), disability (disabled versus non-disabled), race (white versus non-white), and employment (full-time or part-time employment versus unemployed).

Trip Characteristics

As society becomes more urbanized, travel patterns (including length of stay, repeated visitation, and distance traveled) will be increasingly dependent upon the quality of the recreation opportunities and settings provided. Urban residents typically have fewer recreation opportunities than rural dwellers, culminating in increased pressures on, and demand for, recreation opportunities closer to metropolitan areas. The following trip characteristics (used to address objective three) were categorized into dichotomous groups: number of previous visits to site (first-time versus return visits), distance traveled from primary residence (<30 miles versus 30 or more miles),[2] length of stay (day versus overnight visitors), and day of visit (weekday versus weekend). A final trip characteristic, origin of visitor, was grouped into the four assessment regions (See Figure II.1, Chapter II.).

General Setting

Objective One: Attributes Requiring Management Attention

Figure IX.2 shows that three of the 14 general setting attributes fell into the "concentrate here" quadrant for the general setting: cleanliness of restrooms, facilities and grounds (7), clear directional signs (3), and maps, informational signs and bulletin boards (13).[3] These factors represent attributes where managers should direct most of their attention because they are likely to reduce visitor satisfaction. Only one attribute fell in the "possible overkill" quadrant: location of area, it is near to my home (2). Items that fell in the "keep up the good work" quadrant were quality of the scenery (11), reasonable fees (12), helpfulness of employees (9), good roads and parking (4)), and safety and security (10). Attributes within the "low priority" quadrant were access to supplies and shopping (14), information and programs about the area history (8), barrier-free access for disabled visitors (5), presence of a ranger (6), and information for planning a trip to the area (1).

---

[2]In states east of the Mississippi River, *local* was defined as 30 miles or less traveled from primary residence. In states west of the Mississippi, *local* was defined as <50 miles.

[3]Item numbers in Figure IX.2 match the order in which the attributes are listed in the corresponding tables (TATs IX.1-IX.8). For example, item two in Figure IX.2 (which falls into the "possible overkill" quadrant) is the second attribute (location of area, it is near to my home) listed in TATs IX.1-IX.8.

Figure IX.2: Importance-Performance of General Settings

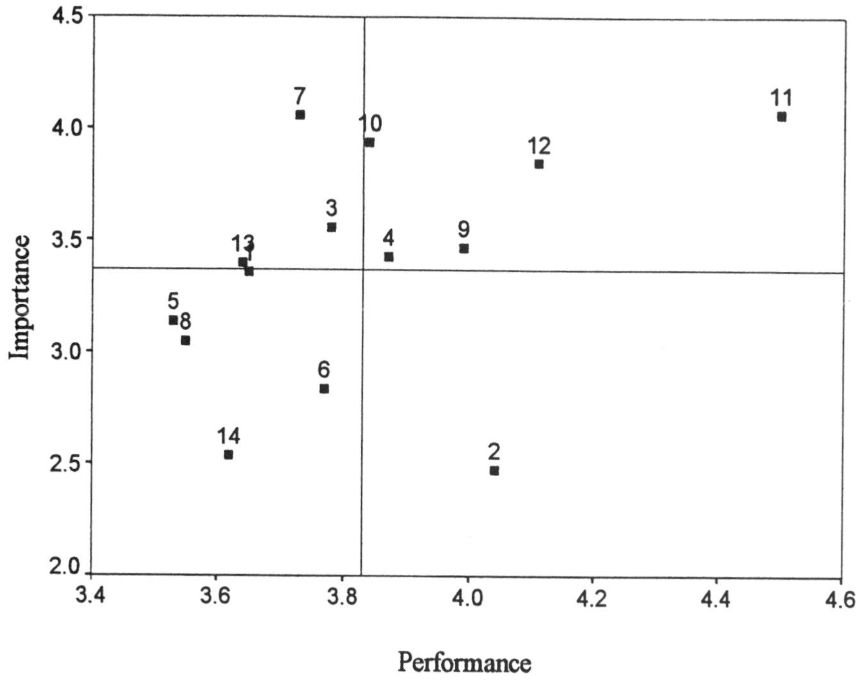

Objective Two: Effect of Demographic Characteristics on Attribute Ratings

With the exception of disabled visitors, importance-performance charts for all demographic groups were very similar. The same three attributes found in objective one (cleanliness of facilities, clear directional signs, maps, and information) appeared in the "concentrate here" quadrant for gender (males and females), education (<16 versus 16+ years), race (white and non-white), employment (employed versus unemployed), and nondisabled visitors. For disabled visitors, managers should address barrier-free access and cleanliness of facilities.

In the remainder of this chapter, referenced tables (herein abbreviated to TAT—Technical Appendix Table)[4] may be seen by requesting a copy from the USDA Forest Service. The Tables IX.1-8 show differences in performance and importance scores for the different demographic groups. Generally, females rated setting attributes as more important than males (TAT IX.1), especially clear directional signs, cleanliness of facilities, safety and security, and barrier-free access. Females also rated performance on seven of the 14 attributes higher than males (TAT IX.2), especially location of the area, safety and security, and presence of a ranger. Interestingly, the differences between the two groups on performance ratings (TAT IX.2) were not as highly significant as for importance ratings (TAT IX.1).

Eight of the 14 attributes were rated more important by less (than highly) educated visitors (especially access to supplies, barrier-free access, and good roads and parking), two are rated more important by highly (versus less) educated visitors (quality of the scenery and planning information) and four have no significant difference (TAT IX.1). Fewer differences occurred for performance ratings: six attributes were rated higher for highly (versus less) educated visitors (especially quality of the scenery and reasonable fees) (TAT IX.2). Less (versus highly) educated visitors rated safety and security lower.

[4]These technical appendices are available upon request to USDA Forest Service, Outdoor Recreation and Wilderness Assessment Group, 320 Green Street, Athens, GA 30603-2044.

Attributes falling in the "concentrate here" quadrant differed by disability. For disabled visitors, managers should address barrier-free access and cleanliness of facilities. For nondisabled visitors, the same three attributes identified in objective one occurred (i.e., cleanliness of facilities, clear directional signs, maps, and information). Disabled visitors rated seven of the 14 attributes as more important than nondisabled visitors, especially barrier-free access, ranger presence, and access to supplies (TAT IX.1) and rated one attribute as performing lower (barrier-free access) (TAT IX.2). No other significant differences were found. Access to supplies and barrier-free access were rated as more important by non-whites than whites (TAT IX.3). Only one attribute (information for planning a trip) was rated as performing significantly differently for whites than non-whites (TAT IX.4).

Nine of the 14 attributes were rated as significantly more important by employed versus unemployed visitors (TAT IX.3), the most highly significant were good roads and parking, ranger presence, and barrier-free access. Employed visitors rated one attribute (scenic quality) as more important than unemployed visitors. Seven attributes were rated in better condition by unemployed visitors, especially maps and signs, information about the area's history, and helpfulness of employees (TAT IX.4). Employed visitors rated one attribute (scenic quality) higher.

Objective Three: Effect of Trip Characteristics on Attribute Ratings

The same three attributes identified in objective one also occurred in the "concentrate here" quadrant for length of stay (overnight and day), day of visit (weekday versus weekend), origin (Pacific Coast, Rocky Mountain, South, and North), and non-locals. Four attributes fell in the "concentrate here" quadrant for first-time visitors (information for planning a trip, clear directional signs, cleanliness of facilities, and maps and information signs) and two attributes for return visitors (cleanliness of facilities and safety and security). For locals, there were only two attributes (cleanliness of facilities and safety and security).

As expected, return visitors rated location of the area as more important than first-time visitors. First-time visitors, however, rated six of the 14 attributes as more important than return visitors (especially, information for planning a trip, maps and information signs, information about an area's history, and clear directional signs) (TAT IX.3). TAT IX.4 shows that, overall, first-time visitors rated the setting in better condition than return visitors, especially helpfulness of employees, reasonable fees, safety and security, and cleanliness of facilities.

Local visitors rated location of the area, good roads and parking, and barrier-free access as most important, while non-locals rated information for planning a trip and information about the area's history as more important (TAT IX.5). For 12 of the 14 attributes, non-local visitors rated the condition of the setting higher than local visitors (TAT IX.6), especially cleanliness of facilities, safety and security, helpfulness of employees, and information (maps and history). As expected, location of the area was highest for locals.

Day users rated seven of the 14 attributes as more important than overnight users (TAT IX.6), especially location of the area, good roads and parking, information (maps and history), barrier-free access, and clear directional signs. Day visitors also rated the condition of the setting better than did overnight visitors on three attributes, especially location of the area. They rate conditions significantly worse than overnight visitors on four attributes (TAT IX.6).

Only two attributes have significant differences for importance ratings (TAT IX.5). Weekend visitors rated location of the area and scenic quality as more important than weekday visitors. Generally, weekday visitors (TAT IX.6) gave higher performance ratings. Overall, visitors from the Pacific Coast and Rocky Mountain regions rated the attributes least important, while visitors from the South and North gave the highest importance ratings (TAT IX.7). This trend was particularly evident for the following attributes: ranger presence, access to supplies, safety and security, location of the area, information (maps and history), clear directional signs, information for planning a trip, good roads and access, and cleanliness of facilities. A similar trend as for importance ratings was found for condition ratings. Southern visitors rated general recreation settings in better condition than (in the following general order) Northern, Pacific Coast, and Rocky Mountain visitors (TAT IX.8). The most pronounced differences occurred for the following attributes: information (maps and history), cleanliness of facilities, helpfulness of employees, good roads and parking, and location of area.

Figure IX.3: Importance-Performance of Developed Settings

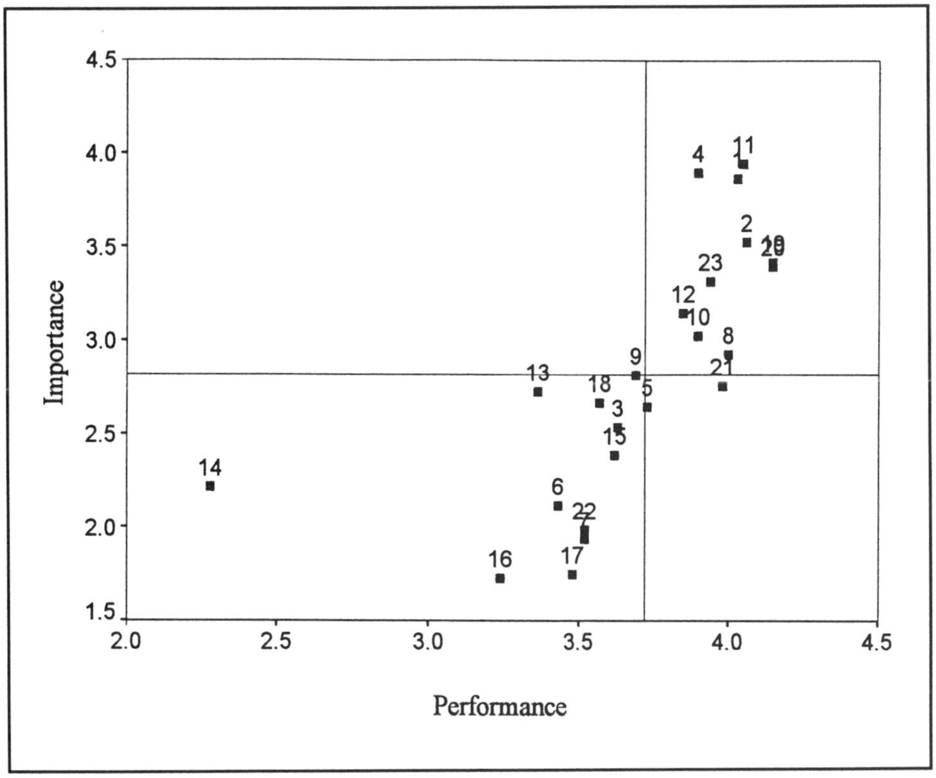

Developed Setting

Objective One: Attributes Requiring Management Attention

The importance-performance chart for the developed setting (Figure IX.3) shows that none of the 23 attributes fell in the "concentrate here" quadrant and only two items [cabin and campsite reservations (5), and cooking grills available (21)] occurred in the "possible overkill" zone. These results suggest that visitors are generally satisfied with setting conditions.[5] Attributes falling in the "keep up the good work" quadrant are associated with the most basic services and facilities provided at a developed recreation setting [e.g., drinking water available (11), an uncrowded and quiet setting (1), fire rings available (20), picnic tables available (19), adequate parking spaces (2), clean, well-maintained facilities (4), well maintained trails (23), flush toilets (10), lighting (12), and campsite access (8)]. Items in the "low priority" zone included more supplemental services and facilities such as electrical hook-ups (14), RV dump stations (15), laundry facilities (16), recreation equipment rentals (17), hot showers (13), group shelters (7), food stores (3), educational programs (6), playground (22), telephones (18), and firewood (9).

Objective Two: Effect of Demographic Characteristics on Attribute Ratings

No attributes were in the "concentrate here" quadrant for gender (males and females), employment status (employed and unemployed), and for visitors who were nondisabled, <16 years education, and white. However, the following attributes did occur in the "concentrate here" quadrant for disabled visitors (availability of hot showers), 16+ years education (availability of firewood), and non-whites (availability of telephones).

Females rated most developed setting attributes as significantly more important than did males (TAT IX.9), especially parking, clean facilities, and availability of group shelters and picnic tables. However, there were negligible differences between males and females on performance ratings (TAT IX.10). Visitors with <16 years of education rated most developed setting attributes as significantly more important than visitors with 16+ years education (TAT IX.9), especially RV sewage dumps, electrical hook-ups, nearby store for food and supplies, and availability of hot showers. Only one attribute was rated more important by highly (versus less)

---

[5]Item numbers in Figure IX.3 match the order in which the attributes are listed in the corresponding tables (TATs IX.9-IX.16).

educated visitors: an uncrowded and quiet setting. There were negligible differences between high versus low education groups on performance ratings (TAT IX.10).

Few differences existed in mean importance or performance scores for disabled versus nondisabled visitors (TAT IX.9 and IX.10). One reason may be the relatively low sample size for disabled users (ranging from n = 50 to 68). Bathroom facilities (flush toilets and lighting) were more important to disabled than nondisabled visitors (TAT IX.9), but it was the condition of campsite facilities (availability of picnic tables, fire rings, firewood, and campsite access) that disabled visitors rated significantly lower than visitors without a disability (TAT IX.10).

Generally, non-whites prefer more supplemental services (e.g., recreation equipment rentals, telephones, cooking grills, and playground/sports fields) than whites (TAT IX.11). There were no differences in performance scores for whites versus non-whites (TAT IX.12). Again, one reason for the lack of statistical significance may be the relatively low sample size for non-whites.

Attributes related to RV camping (e.g., gravel/paved camping access, electrical hook-ups, RV sewage dump stations, and laundry facilities) were rated as more important for employed versus unemployed visitors (TAT IX.11). This difference may reflect the higher proportion of retired visitors who drive RVs. There were no significant differences between the two groups on performance ratings (TAT IX.12).

Developed recreation areas provide picnic areas and other facilities such as running water and electric hookups.

Objective Three: Effect of Trip Characteristics on Attribute Ratings

No attributes were in the "concentrate here" quadrant for day of the week (weekend versus weekday users) or for nonlocals, day users, and first-time visitors. However, the following attributes did occur in the "concentrate here" quadrant for locals, overnight, Southern and Northern visitors (availability of hot showers), return, overnight, and Rocky Mountain visitors (availability of firewood), local users (area and restroom lighting), and Pacific Coast visitors (well-maintained trails).

Few differences existed in mean importance (TAT IX.11) or performance scores (TAT IX.12) for first-time versus return visitors. First-time visitors rated educational and laundry facilities as more important, while return visitors rated campsite features (availability of fire rings, picnic tables, and cooking grills) as more important (TAT IX.11).

As expected, overnight visitors rated attributes associated with longer stays (e.g., availability of fire rings, firewood, hot showers, drinking water, and sewage dump stations) as more important, while day users rated trails and educational programs as more important (TAT IX.13). Overnight (versus day) users (TAT IX.14) also rated performance for long-stay attributes lower (e.g., availability of picnic tables, fire grills, drinking water, and flush toilets).

No significant differences in importance scores (TAT IX.13) and few significant differences in performance ratings (TAT IX.14) were found for weekday versus weekend users. Setting attributes related to use levels (e.g., an uncrowded and quiet setting, adequate parking spaces, and cabin/campsite reservations) were rated higher in performance for weekday versus weekend visitors (TAT IX.14).

Local visitors were more concerned with short-stay attributes (e.g., availability of picnic tables and grills, and group shelters), while nonlocals exhibited a greater preference for long-stay attributes (e.g., availability of educational programs, hot showers, and laundry facilities) (TAT IX.13). Nonlocals tended to rate the performance of many (nine of 23) attributes more highly than locals, especially availability of drinking water, area and bathroom lighting, RV sewage stations, and an uncrowded and quiet setting (TAT IX.14).

Generally, visitors from the West (Pacific Coast and Rocky Mountain Regions) rated developed setting attributes as least important and eastern (North and South) visitors rated the attributes as most important (TAT IX.15). Attributes of most importance to eastern visitors focused on visitor comfort and convenience and included availability of hot showers, bathroom lighting, flush toilets, playground/sports facilities, recreation equipment rentals, and nearby stores.

While there are fewer significant differences between the groups on perceived condition of the settings, performance ratings were generally highest from eastern than western visitors (TAT IX.16). Differences were particularly apparent for the following attributes: availability of flush toilets, lighting, firewood, and telephones, RV sewage dump stations, uncrowded/quiet setting, adequate parking, and proximity of stores.

Figure IX.4: Importance-Performance of Water Settings

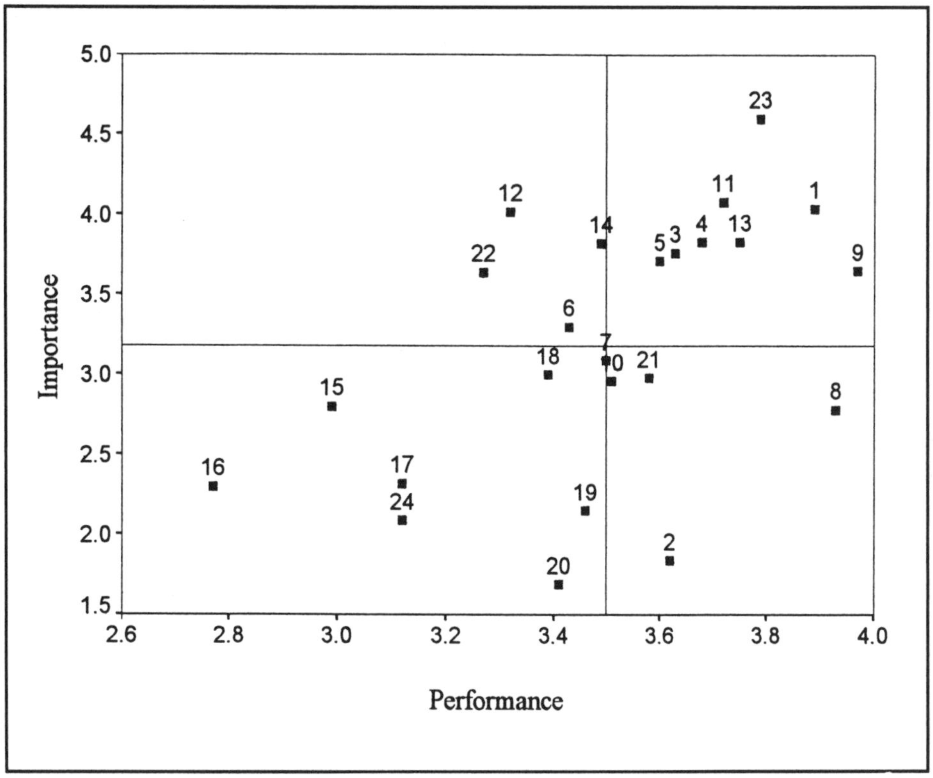

Water Setting

Objective One: Attributes Requiring Management Attention

The importance-performance chart for the water setting (Figure IX.4) shows that four of the 24 attributes fell in the "concentrate here" quadrant: take-out/beaching spots (6), information on hazards and conditions (12), restrooms (14), and stable water levels (22).[6] Attributes falling in the "possible overkill" zone were activity-based (challenging rapids (2), waterskiing in the area (8), designated swimming area and beach (21), and boat-in camping opportunities (10). "Keep up the good work" attributes were associated with natural-

[6]Item numbers in Figure IX.4 match the order in which the attributes are listed in the corresponding tables (TATs IX.17-IX.24).

ness of conditions: clean, unpolluted water (23), safe drinking water (11), hazard-free water (1), fishing opportunities (9), uncrowded conditions (3), adequate road access (13), adequate and secure parking (4), and boat ramps/launching facilities (5). "Low priority" attributes were related to services and amenities on-site (fuel services (7), fish cleaning stations (16), showers (15), mechanic services (17), docking facilities (18), equipment rentals (19), commercial outfitters (20), and fishing piers (24).

Objective Two: Effect of Demographic Characteristics on Attribute Ratings

All demographic groups in the "concentrate here" zone identified many of the same attributes. Males, those with fewer than 16 years education, nondisabled, nonwhite, and employed visitors identified the same attributes listed in objective one (take-out/beaching spots, information on conditions and hazards, restrooms, stable water levels). Visitors who were female, 16+ years education, and unemployed listed two attributes (information on hazards and stable water levels), white visitors listed take-outs and restrooms, and disabled visitors did not identify any attributes falling in the "concentrate here" zone. Females rated most attributes more important than males (TAT IX.17), especially those concerned with safety (e.g., designated swimming area, hazard-free water, safe drinking water, and information on hazards). Males rated only one attribute more importantly (fishing opportunities). In contrast, males and females rated performance of the setting similarly, with only a few exceptions (TAT IX.18).

Water recreation includes boating, swimming, and fishing activities.

In general, visitors with <16 years education rated most water setting attributes more importantly than those with 16+ years education (TAT IX.17), especially attributes related to fishing (e.g., fishing opportunities, fish-cleaning stations, fishing piers). Visitors with 16+ years education rated only one attribute more important (uncrowded conditions). Again, performance ratings were more closely aligned between the two groups (TAT IX.18). Few significant differences were found for importance (TAT IX.17) and performance (TAT IX.18) ratings between visitors with and without a disability. No significant differences between white and non-white visitors were found for importance (TAT IX.19) and performance (TAT IX.20) ratings. Few significant differences between employed and unemployed visitors were found for importance (TAT IX.19) ratings. Unemployed visitors generally rated the setting in poorer condition than employed visitors did (TAT IX.20).

Objective Three: Effect of Trip Characteristics on Attribute Ratings

Again, there was much overlap in the type of attributes in the "concentrate here" zone by trip characteristics. First-time, previous, local, and nonlocal visitors as well as weekend users identified the same attributes listed in objective one (take-out/beaching spots, information on conditions and hazards, restrooms, and stable water levels). Attributes listed in the "concentrate here" quadrant were information on hazards, restrooms, and stable water levels for day users and visitors from the Rocky Mountain Region; take-out/beaching spots, information on hazards and stable water levels for overnight, weekday, and Pacific Coast visitors; information on hazards and restrooms for Southern visitors; and boat ramps and information on hazards for Northern visitors.

First-time visitors rated support services (equipment rental and commercial outfitters) more importantly than return visitors did, while return visitors rated stable water levels and boat ramps as more important (TAT IX.19). First-time visitors consistently rated performance of the water setting attributes higher than return visitors did (especially uncrowded conditions, adequate and secure parking, and stable water levels).

Importance ratings for local and non-local visitors were somewhat similar (TAT IX.21). Locals rated swimming areas and fishing piers more important, while nonlocals rated uncrowded conditions and challenging rapids as more important. In contrast, performance ratings for the two groups differed considerably: nonlocals consistently rated the setting attributes higher than locals did (TAT IX.22).

Overnight visitors attached greater importance to water setting attributes (especially supplies, shower facilities, and mechanic services) than did day users (TAT IX.21). They also rated actual conditions higher than day users, especially safe drinking water, equipment rentals, restrooms, and uncrowded conditions (TAT IX.22). No significant differences occurred between weekday and weekend visitors on importance ratings (TAT IX.21). A few significant differences were seen for performance ratings, with weekday visitors giving higher scores for parking, road conditions, and equipment and supplies than weekend visitors (TAT IX.22).

In comparison with other outdoor recreation settings, there were fewer differences in importance ratings for water attributes by origin of visitors. Once again, however, visitors from the East gave consistently higher importance scores than visitors from the West (TAT IX.23). While the highest performance ratings were typically given by Northern visitors and the lowest by Rocky Mountain visitors (similar to other recreation settings), Pacific Coast visitors generally rated water conditions better than Southern visitors (in contrast to other recreation settings) (TAT IX.24).

Figure IX.5: Importance-Performance of Dispersed Settings

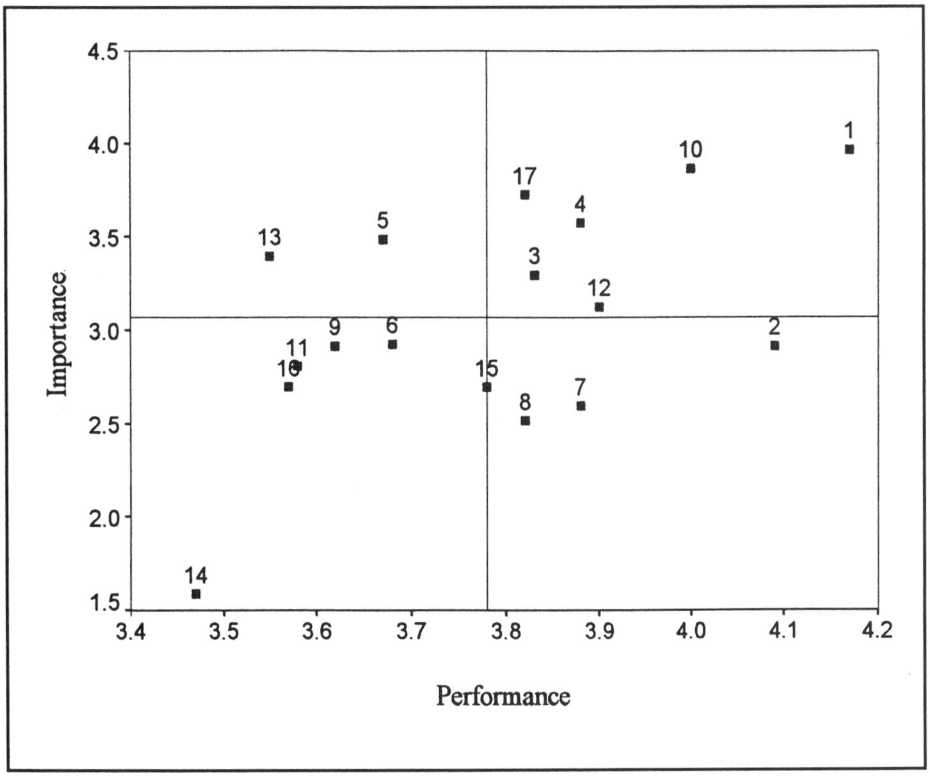

Dispersed Setting

Objective One: Attributes Requiring Management Attention

The importance-performance chart for the dispersed setting (Figure IX.5) shows that only two of the 17 attributes fell within the "concentrate here" quadrant (safe drinking water (5) and information on conditions and hazards (13)). Three items (physically challenging environment (2), designated campsites (7), and motorized access (8)) were in the "possible overkill" zone, suggesting visitors were satisfied with some, but not all, setting conditions.[7] Attributes falling in the "keep up the good work" quadrant were associated with naturalness (an undisturbed and natural setting (1) and presence and evidence of wildlife (10)) and travel facilities (absence of motorized vehicles (4), well-maintained trails (12), separation of motorized and nonmotorized

[7]Item numbers in Figure IX.5 match the order in which the attributes are listed in the corresponding tables (TATs IX.25-IX.32).

uses (17), and adequate and secure parking (3)). "Low priority" attributes included supplementary services (commercial outfitters and guide services (14), primitive toilet facilities (16), connecting or loop trails (15), information and access to historic sites (11), directional signs (9), and see/hear others (6)).

Most dispersed recreation areas exist in a natural, unfettered state.

Objective Two: Effect of Demographic Characteristics on Attribute Ratings

Two attributes (safe drinking water and information on conditions and hazards) were located in the "concentrate here" quadrant for education (<16 years and 16+ years) and employment (employed versus unemployed) groups as well as for male, non-disabled and white visitors. However, additional attributes occurred in the "concentrate here" quadrant for females (adequate and secure parking). For disabled and non-white visitors, the following attributes only fell in the "concentrate here" quadrant: safe drinking water, information on conditions and hazards, and separation of motorized and non-motorized uses.

Females consistently rated dispersed setting attributes as more important than did males, especially the need for well-maintained trails, information on conditions and hazards, and safe drinking water (TAT IX.25). Males gave a higher importance rating than females for only one attribute (the presence of a physically challenging environment). While there were fewer differences by gender for performance ratings (TAT IX.26), women generally gave higher ratings for the attributes to which they gave high importance scores (i.e., safe drinking water and well-maintained trails) as well as natural conditions (e.g., an undisturbed natural setting and presence of wildlife). Visitors with <16 years education exhibited greater importance for items related to a more developed camping experience, such as motorized access, safe drinking water, primitive toilet facilities, and designated campsites (TAT IX.25). In contrast, visitors with 16+ years education rated items associated with solitude and naturalness as more important (e.g., undisturbed natural setting, absence of motorized vehicles, see/hear others, presence of wildlife). Higher-educated visitors generally rated the actual setting in better condition than less educated visitors (TAT IX.26).

No significant differences in importance ratings were found between visitors with and without a disability (TAT IX.25), but, disabled visitors typically rated the performance of the dispersed setting much lower than visitors without a disability (TAT IX.26). No significant differences between whites and non-whites were observed for either the importance or performance ratings (Technical Appendix Tables IX.27 and IX.28).

Attributes associated with naturalness (undisturbed natural setting, physically challenging environment, see/hear others, and presence of wildlife) were rated as more important by employed than by unemployed visitors (TAT IX.27). Unemployed visitors were more concerned with safety issues (adequate and secure parking and safe drinking water). Employed and unemployed visitors did not significantly differ on performance ratings of the dispersed setting (TAT IX.28).

Objective Three: Effect of Trip Characteristics on Attribute Ratings

Two attributes (safe drinking water and information on conditions and hazards) were in the "concentrate here" quadrant for both first–time and return visitors, for both locals and nonlocals, for weekend and weekday users, and for day-use, Rocky Mountain, and Southern visitors. An additional attribute occurred in the "concentrate here" quadrant for overnight and Pacific Coast visitors (separation of motorized and nonmotorized uses). For Northern visitors, attributes in the "concentrate here" quadrant were adequate for secure parking, information on conditions and hazards, and separation of motorized and nonmotorized uses.

First-time visitors rated attributes about information (on conditions and hazards, historic sites, and directional signs) and safety (safe drinking water and well-maintained trails) as more important, while return visitors rated opportunities for a physically challenging environment and motorized access as more important (TAT IX.27). Generally, return visitors rated the setting's performance higher than did first–time visitors (TAT IX.28).

Local visitors also rated attributes about information (on conditions and hazards, historic sites, and directional signs) as more important than did nonlocals (TAT IX.29), but they generally rated the setting in worse condition than nonlocals did (TAT IX.30). Day visitors placed greater importance on information (about hazards and conditions, historic sites, and directional signs) and management services (well-maintained trails, commercial outfitters, and toilet facilities) (TAT IX.29). Overnight visitors exhibited stronger preference for naturalness (physically challenging environment, see/hear others, and presence of wildlife). There were relatively few differences between day and overnight visitors on performance ratings (TAT IX.30). No significant differences were found between weekday and weekend visitors on either importance (TAT IX.29) or performance ratings (TAT IX.30).

The highest mean importance scores were given (in the following descending order) by Southern, Northern, Pacific Coast, and Rocky Mountain visitors (TAT IX.31). Generally, there were similarities in importance ratings for visitors from the East and West. Visitors from the Pacific Coast and Rocky Mountain regions reported similar scores, and Southern and Northern visitors exhibited similar scores. A similar trend was observed for performance ratings: Northern and Southern visitors typically reported higher perceived condition scores than Western visitors.

Figure IX.6: Importance-Performance of Roaded Settings

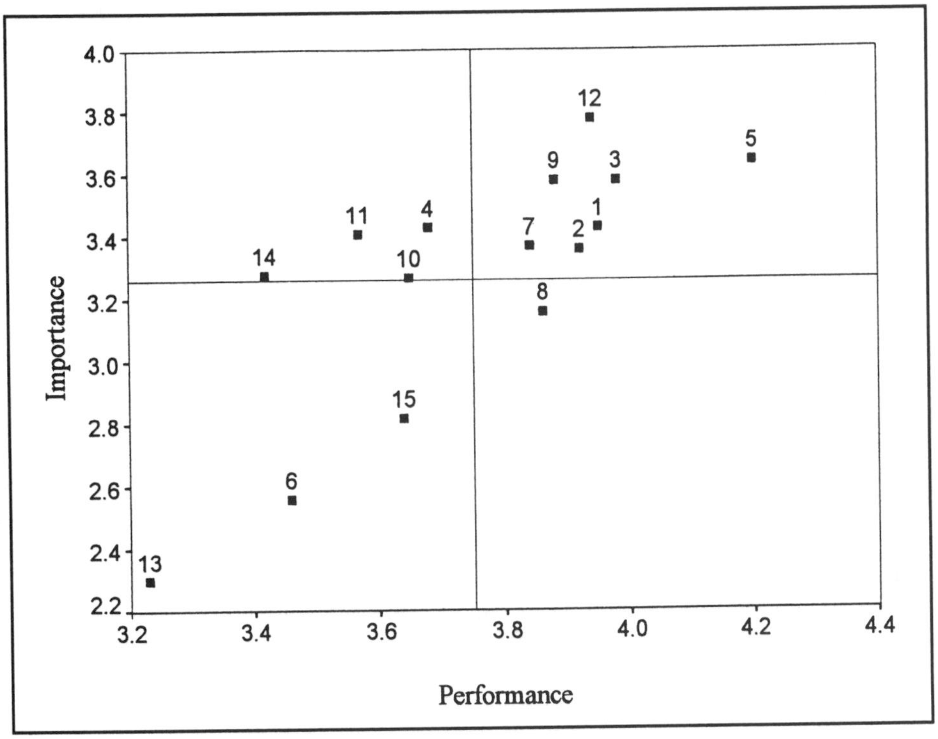

Roaded Setting

Objective One: Attributes Requiring Management Attention

In the importance-performance chart for the roaded setting (Figure IX.6), four of the 15 attributes fell in the "concentrate here" quadrant (convenient restrooms (4), interpretive signs (10), information about historic sites (11), availability of drinking water (14)), while only one item (roaded access (8)) was in the "possible overkill" zone.[8] Attributes in the "keep up the good work" quadrant were associated with scenic quality and access (distant views (5), scenic overlooks (3), wildlife viewing (12), absence of human modification to landscape (1), uncongested traffic (9), good all-weather roads (2), and walking trails (7)). "Low priority" items were picnic facilities (15), passing lanes (6), and bicycle lanes (13).

Well-built and maintained roads wind through the national forests and national parks.

Objective Two: Effect of Demographic Characteristics on Attribute Ratings

The same four attributes as in objective one (convenient restrooms, interpretive signs, information about historic sites, and availability of drinking water) fell in the "concentrate here" quadrant for gender (males and females), education (<16 years and 16+ years), race (whites and non-whites), and employment (employed versus unemployed) groups. These same attributes occurred for visitors without a disability (with the exception of drinking water availability) and for disabled users (except that opportunities for viewing wildlife replaced interpretive signs).

Females consistently rated roaded attributes as more important than did males, especially convenient restrooms, interpretive signs, drinking water, and good all-weather roads (TAT IX.33). There were no significant differences between the two groups on performance ratings (TAT IX.34). Visitors with <16 years education rated attributes related to roadside conveniences as more important (good all-weather roads, passing lanes, picnic facilities, convenient restrooms, and drinking water) (TAT IX.33). There were no significant differences between the two education groups on performance ratings (TAT IX.34).

Disabled visitors consistently assigned greater importance for attributes related to roadside conveniences (good all-weather roads, scenic overlooks, passing lanes, and picnic facilities) than visitors without a disability (TAT IX.33). Again, there were no significant differences between the two groups on performance ratings (TAT IX.34). There were no significant differences between whites and non-whites on importance (TAT IX.35) and

[8]Item numbers in Figure IX.6 match the order in which the attributes are listed in the corresponding tables (TATs IX.33-IX.40).

performance ratings (TAT IX.36). Few significant differences between employed and unemployed visitors were found on importance (TAT IX.35) and performance ratings (TAT IX.36). However, unemployed visitors did rate roadside conveniences (good all-weather roads, passing lanes, and convenient restrooms) as more important than did employed visitors (TAT IX.35).

Objective Three: Effect of Trip Characteristics on Attribute Ratings

The same four attributes as in objective one (convenient restrooms, interpretive signs, information about historic sites, and availability of drinking water) fell in the "concentrate here" quadrant for both first-time and return, day and overnight, and weekday and weekend visitors, as well as for nonlocals and visitors from the Rocky Mountain, North, and South regions. Local visitors identified convenient restrooms and drinking water, while Pacific Coast visitors only placed information about historic sites in the "concentrate here" zone.

Generally, first-time visitors rated roaded setting attributes as being of greater importance than did return visitors, especially interpretive signs, scenic overlooks, and good all-weather roads (TAT IX.35). There were few significant differences between the two groups in performance ratings (TAT IX.36). There were very few significant differences between locals and nonlocals in importance (TAT IX.37) and performance ratings (TAT IX.38). Day users rated roadside conveniences (convenient restrooms, good all-weather roads, picnic facilities, passing lanes, and scenic overlooks) more important than did overnight users (TAT IX.37). Day visitors also tended to rate the performance of roaded attributes higher than overnight users (TAT IX.38). There were no significant differences between weekday and weekend visitors in importance (TAT IX.37) and performance ratings (TAT IX.38).

Mean importance ratings for roaded attributes by origin of visitor were given in the following descending order: South, North, Rocky Mountain, and Pacific Coast. The greatest differences were for good all-weather roads, convenient restrooms, availability of drinking water, and picnic sites (TAT IX.39). Relatively few significant differences were found for performance ratings, but the ratings were typically lowest from the Rocky Mountain region and highest from Northern visitors (TAT IX.40).

Figure IX.7: Importance-Performance of Winter Settings

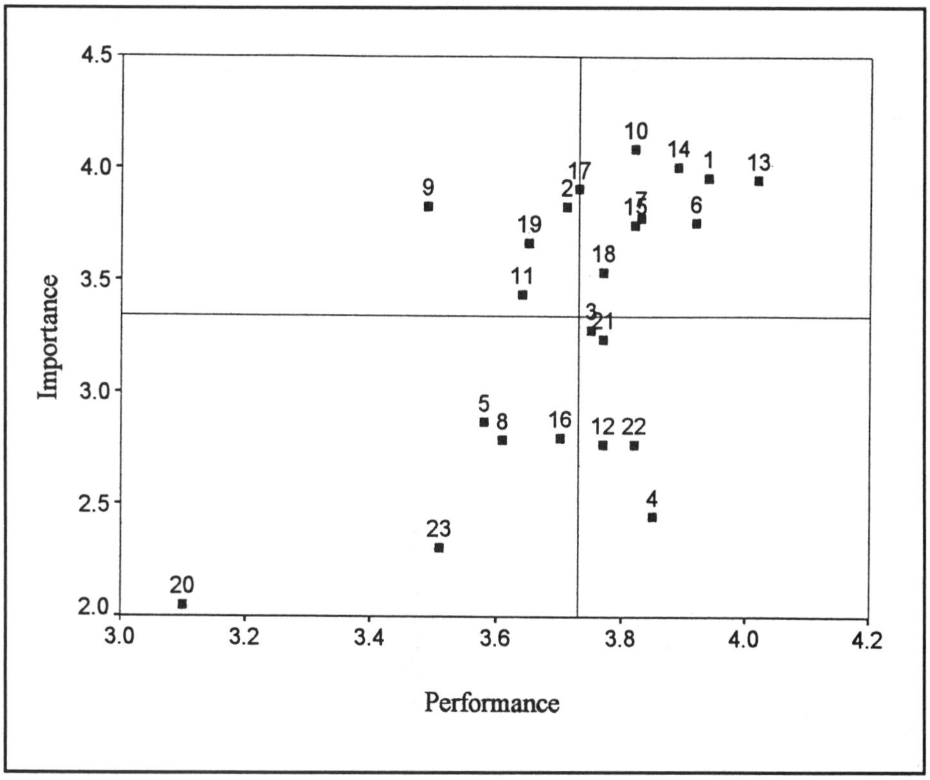

Winter Setting

Objective One: Attributes Requiring Management Attention

In the importance-performance chart for the winter setting (Figure IX.7), four of the 23 attributes fell in the "concentrate here" quadrant (information on conditions and hazards (9), restrooms (19), presence of wildlife (11), and adequate parking (2)). Five items (equipment rental (4), lighted trails (22), instruction staff (12), presence of rangers (21), and warming facilities (3)) were in the "possible overkill" zone, suggesting that managers should attend to almost 40% of the winter setting attributes.[9] Attributes falling in the "keep up the good work" quadrant were associated with management of use levels (variety of challenging trails (13), uncrowded areas (1), short wait for lifts (14), avalanche control (6), plowed/maintained roads (10), trail grooming (7), emergency rescue (15), absence of development (18), and separation of motorized/nonmotorized uses (17)). "Low priority" items were restaurants/groceries (5) and lodging nearby (8), evening activities (23), campgrounds with electricity (20), and snowmaking capabilities (16).

Winter recreation opportunities are more plentiful in the North and Rocky Mountain regions than in other parts of the country.

Objective Two: Effect of Demographic Characteristics on Attribute Ratings

Relative to other settings, there was tremendous variation in the attributes falling in the "concentrate here" zone by demographic characteristics. Variables of concern to all groups of visitors were information on conditions/hazards and public restrooms. Additional attributes in the "concentrate here" quadrant included separation of motorized and non-motorized use (for employed and unemployed, females, and users with and without disabilities), presence of wildlife (males and females, <16 and 16+ years education, unemployed, white, and users without disabilities), and adequate parking (females, users without disabilities, unemployed, <16 years education, and white).

As with other settings, females placed greater importance on safety (avalanche control) and convenience (restrooms) than males (TAT IX.41). No other significant differences occurred between the two groups. Performance ratings were also very similar for males and females (TAT IX.42). There were no significant differences between visitors with <16 years and 16+ years education for importance (TAT IX.41) and performance (TAT IX.42) ratings. There were no significant differences between visitors with and without a disability on importance (TAT IX.41) and performance (TAT IX.42) ratings. There was only one significant difference between white and non-white visitors on importance scores (instruction staff) (TAT IX.43) and there were no significant differences on performance ratings (TAT IX.44). There were no significant differences between employed and unemployed visitors for importance (TAT IX.43) and performance (TAT IX.44) ratings.

---

[9] Item numbers in Figure IX.7 match the order in which the attributes are listed in the corresponding tables (TATs IX.41-IX.46).

Objective Three: Effect of Trip Characteristics on Attribute Ratings

Again, there was large variation in the type and number of attributes in the "concentrate here" zone by trip characteristics. Variables of concern for most groups included presence of wildlife, information on hazards/conditions, and public restrooms. For locals, day, weekend and weekday, and Pacific Coast visitors, adequate parking and separation of mechanized and non-mechanized uses were additional concerns. (Because of the relatively small sample sizes for visitors from the Rocky Mountain (n = 8 to 30), Southern (n = 2 to 9), and Northern (n = 4 to 10) regions, only Pacific Coast visitors (n = 180 to 324) will be reviewed here.) Attributes in the "concentrate here" zone for first-time visitors were uncrowded areas, instruction staff, and lighted trails. For return visitors they were warming facilities, equipment rental, instruction staff, snow-making facilities, presence of rangers, and lighted trails. There was only one significant difference between first-time and return visitors on importance scores (absence of development) (TAT IX.43) and on performance ratings (variety of challenge) (TAT IX.44). Local visitors placed greater importance on support services and facilities (lighted slopes, warming facilities, snowmaking equipment, emergency rescue, avalanche control, and instruction staff) (TAT IX.45), and rated parking conditions worse (TAT IX.46) than nonlocals.

There was only one significant difference between day and overnight visitors on importance scores (overnight visitors rated the need for overnight lodging higher) (TAT IX.45). There were two significant differences in performance ratings (overnight visitors rated overnight lodging and plowed roads/parking in better condition) (TAT IX.44). Weekday visitors typically rated winter setting attributes as more important than did weekend visitors, especially emergency rescue, warming facilities, lighted trails, restrooms, and avalanche control (TAT IX.45). Fewer differences between the two groups were observed for performance ratings; weekday visitors (TAT IX.46) rated only avalanche control and public restrooms more highly.

Conclusions and Implications

There are at least seven major findings with implications for outdoor recreation management:

(1) Relatively few (fewer than one-quarter) of all setting attributes occurred in the "concentrate here" quadrant. This finding indicates that, for the most part, visitors are generally satisfied with the way outdoor recreation settings are managed.

(2) There are, however, some exceptions to the general finding above. Restroom facilities (clean bathrooms, availability of restrooms), safety (safe drinking water, stable water levels), and information (directional signs, information on conditions and hazards, and on-site interpretation) appeared in the "concentrate here" quadrant for all settings except developed, suggesting that these attributes warrant additional attention by outdoor recreation managers. Visitor needs for information and clean facilities (particularly restrooms) are consistent with previous studies, which have revealed that users are more concerned with basic managerial than physical conditions such as type and extent of vegetative erosion (Cordell, et al., 1990; Hendee, Stankey, & Lucas, 1990; Manning, 1985b). However, our findings extend this conclusion to include a visitor concern for more improved on-site communication and information, especially with regard to hazards and conditions at the setting. At a time when funding for on-site interpretation has decreased, it is interesting that visitor demand for this type of information remains high. If visitors are willing to pay for on-site interpretation as suggested by Cordell et al. (1990), our findings suggest the greatest information needs may be related to safety and setting conditions. In 1988, the Domestic Policy Council recognized the need for information on local area recreation that was not addressed by the tourism industry. Our results also support this conclusion.

(3) Greater differences between groups (on demographic and trip characteristics) were found for attribute importance than performance (i.e., perceived ratings of setting conditions). This finding suggests that while visitor preferences may differ, setting conditions are perceived similarly by most groups of visitors.

(4) Across most settings, females and visitors originating from eastern states rate attributes more important than do males and western visitors. Yet, their perceptions of setting conditions are quite similar. This finding implies that if managers wish to increase the number of setting attributes in the "keep up the good work" quadrant, they must recognize that certain groups of visitors (especially females and eastern visitors) place greater importance on many setting attributes than do other types of visitors. Previ-

ous research has shown contradictory findings with regard to the importance and performance of setting attributes for Wilderness areas. Roggenbuck, Williams and Watson (1993), for example, demonstrated that eastern and Western visitors place similar importance on various site indicators for Wilderness, while Tarrant and Shafer (in review) found considerable differences in visitor perceptions of, and preferences for, Wilderness setting attributes. Although our chapter examined a broad array of recreation (and not Wilderness) settings, the question of regional differences in visitor preferences and perceptions remains.

(5) Visitors appear more satisfied with settings on the opposite ends of the Recreation Opportunity Spectrum (ROS) (i.e., developed and dispersed) than with settings nearer the middle of the spectrum (water, roaded, and winter).

(6) For the most part, visitors from the South and North regions of the U.S. gave similar importance and performance ratings, as did visitors from the Pacific Coast and Rocky Mountain regions. Southern visitors consistently reported the highest importance and performance scores for setting attributes, while Pacific Coast visitors typically gave the lowest ratings.

(7) One of the most striking findings was the similarity in demographic and travel groups. With the exception of two settings (winter and dispersed), there were very few differences between groups on the attributes rated in the "concentrate here" quadrant. For winter and dispersed settings, females were less satisfied with parking conditions than males. Disabled, overnight, and Pacific Coast visitors were all less satisfied with the separation of motorized and nonmotorized uses than nondisabled visitors, day-visitors, and visitors from other regions.

Potential differences in outdoor recreation users across the settings investigated here suggest the possibility that outdoor recreation settings might be managed to different standards in the East and West and for males and females. The issue of uniformity in standards has been raised for management of areas in the National Wilderness Preservation System (see for example, Higgins, 1990; Mitchell, 1990; Tarrant & Shafer, 1997). There also are implications for managing outdoor recreation areas using the ROS. ROS recognizes that a diverse array of recreation opportunities should be provided for the American public (Driver, Brown, Stankey, & Gregoire, 1987). ROS provides the basis for establishing minimum standards for setting conditions using a LAC (Limits of Acceptable Change) framework (Stankey, Cole, Lucas, Petersen, & Frissell, 1985). Our study provides an initial step toward determining minimum acceptable standards by (a) identifying indicators of setting conditions that managers should be concerned about (i.e., attributes that fall in the "concentrate here" quadrant) and (b) recognizing that standards may vary by visitor demographic and trip characteristics.

At least two notes of caution should be raised when interpreting the results of CUSTOMER: (1) Failure to find significant differences between racial and disabled groups may be a function of unequal and low sample sizes. Additional research using larger sample sizes for non-whites and for visitors with a disability is clearly necessary. (2) Statistical significance does not necessarily equate with managerial significance. The large sample sizes for many groups in our analysis suggest some of the differences between groups may be an artifact of the type of statistics we used and do not represent a substantial or "real-world" difference that managers should be concerned about. While there is some validity to this argument, it should be recognized that: (a) part of our analysis did not involve statistical inference (i.e., the use of an importance-performance framework), and (b) the magnitude of difference (as indicated by the size of the t-value) provides a good indicator of critical differences (e.g., a t-value of 4.0 has more questionable statistical significance than a t-value greater than 6.0 or 7.0).

Overall, managers of outdoor recreation settings should be somewhat concerned about the results of CUSTOMER presented here. Although most setting attributes fell outside the "concentrate here" quadrant, two of the most important attributes (visitor safety and information), along with cleanliness of facilities (especially restrooms), were consistently rated as highly important but in relatively poor condition. In the future, managers should give additional attention to water, roaded, and winter recreation settings, where the number of attributes in the "concentrate here" quadrant was considerably higher than in dispersed or developed outdoor recreation settings.

REFERENCES

Anderek, K. L., & Becker, R. H. (1993). Perceptions of carry-over crowding in recreation environments. *Leisure Sciences, 15*(1), 25-35.

Basman, C. M., Manfredo, M. J., Barro, S. C., Vaske, J. J., & Watson, A. (1996). Norm accessibility: An exploratory study of backcountry and frontcountry recreational norms. *Leisure Sciences, 18*(2), 177-192.

Burch, W. R., Jr. (1969). The social circles of leisure: Competing explanations. *Journal of Leisure Research, 1*(2), 125-147.

Carr, D. S., & Williams, D. R. (1993). Understanding the role of ethnicity in outdoor recreation experiences. *Journal of Leisure Research, 25*(1), 22-38.

Cole, D. N., Watson, A. E., & Roggenbuck, J. W. (1995). *Trends in wilderness visitors and visits: Boundary Waters Cane Area, Shining Rock, and Desolation Wildernesses*. (Res. Pap. INT-RP-483). Ogden, UT: US Department of Agriculture, Forest Service, Intermountain Research Station.

Cordell, H. K., Bergstrom, J. C., Hartmann, L. A., & English, D. B. K. (1990). *An analysis of the outdoor recreation and wilderness situation in the United States: 1989-2040.* (Gen. Tech. Rep. RM-189). Fort Collins, CO: US Department of Agriculture, Forest Service, Rocky Mountain Forest and Range Experiment Station.

Decker, D. J., & Connelly, N. A. (1989). Motivations for deer hunting: Implications for antlerless deer harvest as a management tool. *Wildlife Society Bulletin, 17*, 455-563.

Ditton, R. B., Fedler, A. J., & Graefe, A. R. (1983). Factors contributing to perceptions of recreational crowding. *Leisure Sciences, 5*, 273-288.

Driver, B. L. (1976). A better understanding of the social benefits of outdoor recreation participation. *Proceedings of the Southern States Recreation Research Applications workshop*, September 15 - 18, 1975, Asheville, NC. (Gen. Tech. Rep. SE-9, 163-189). Asheville, NC: US Department of Agriculture, Forest Service, Southeastern Forest Experiment Station.

Driver, B. L. (1977). *Item pool for scales designed to quantify the psychological outcomes desired and expected from recreation participation*. Ft. Collins, CO: USDA Forest Service Rocky Mountain Forest and Range Experiment Station.

Driver, B. L. & Brown, P. J. (1978). The opportunity spectrum concept and behavioral information in outdoor recreation resource supply inventories: A rationale. In *Integrated inventories of renewable natural resources*. (Gen. Tech. Rep. RM-55, 24-31). Fort Collins, CO: US Department of Agriculture, Forest Service, Rocky Mountain Forest and Range Experiment Station.

Driver, B. L., Brown, P. J., Stanley, G. H., & Gregoire, T. G. (1987). The ROS planning system: Evolution, basic concepts, and research needed. *Leisure Sciences, 9*, 201-212.

Driver, B. L., & Knopf, R. C. (1976). Temporary escape: One product of sport fisheries management. *Fisheries, 1*(2), 21-29.

Driver, B. L. & Tocher, R. C. (1970). Toward a behavioral interpretation of recreational engagements, with implications for planning. In B. L. Driver (Ed.), *Elements of outdoor recreation planning* (pp. 9-31). Ann Arbor, MI: University Microfilms.

Ewert, A. (1993). Differences in the level of motive importance based on trip outcome, experience level and group type. *Journal of Leisure Research, 25*(4), 335-349.

Ewert, A., & Hollenhorst, S. (1994). Individual and setting attributes of the adventure recreation experience. *Leisure Sciences, 16*(3), 177-188.

Fisher, M. R. (1997). Segmentation of the angler population by catch preference, participation, and experience: A management oriented application of recreation specialization. *North American Journal of Fisheries Management, 17*(1), 1-10.

Floyd, M. F., & Gramann, J. H. (1997). Experience-based setting management: Implications for market segmentation of hunters. *Leisure Sciences, 19*(2), 113-128.

Freeman, P. A., Tarrant, M. A., & Cordell, H. K. (1996). The reliability of the perceived crowding scale. *Abstracts from the Proceedings of the 1996 NRPA Symposium on Leisure Research, October 23-27, 1996.* Kansas City, MO: National Recreation and Park Association.

Graefe, A. R., Vaske, J. J., & Kuss, F. R. (1984). Social carrying capacity: An integration and synthesis of twenty years of research. *Leisure Sciences, 6*(4), 395-432.

Gramann, J. H. (1982). Toward a behavioral theory of crowding in outdoor recreation: An evaluation and synthesis of research. *Leisure Sciences, 5*(2), 109-126.

Hall, T. & Shelby, B. (1996). Who cares about encounters? Differences between those with and without norms. *Leisure Sciences, 18*(1), 7-22.

Hammitt, W. E., & Rutlin, W. M. (1995). Use encounter standards and curves for achieved privacy in wilderness. *Leisure Sciences, 17*(4), 245-262.

Hammitt, W. E., McDonald, C. D., & Noe, F. P. (1984). Use level and encounters: Important variables of perceived crowding among nonspecialized recreationists. *Journal of Leisure Research, 16*, 1-8.

Hammitt, W. E., Shafer, C. S., & Bixler, R. (1992). Perceived crowding of whitewater rafters during three phases of the recreation experience. *Abstracts of Proceedings from the 1992 NRPA Symposium on Leisure Research, October 15 - 18, 1992*. Cincinnati, OH: National Recreation and Park Association.

Hazel, K. L., Langenau, E. E., Jr., & Levine, R. L. (1990). Dimensions of hunting satisfaction: Multiple satisfactions of wild turkey hunting. *Leisure Sciences, 12*, 383-393.

Heberlein, T. A. & Vaske, J. J. (1977). *Crowding and visitor conflict on the Bois Brule River*. (Report WISC WRC 77-04). Madison, WI: University of Wisconsin Water Res. Center.

Hendee, J. C. (1974). A multiple-satisfaction approach to game management. *Wildlife Society Bulletin, 2*(3), 104-113.

Hendee, J. C., Stankey, G. H. & Lucas, R. C. (1990). *Wilderness management*. Golden, CO: North American Press.

Heywood, J. L., Christensen, J. E., & Stankey, G. H. (1991). The relationship between biophysical and social setting factors in the Recreation Opportunity Spectrum. *Leisure Sciences, 13*, 239-246.

Higgins, J. F. (1990). A case for national standards for wilderness management. In B. Shelby, G. Stankey, & B. Schindler (Eds.), *Defining wilderness quality: The role of standards in wilderness management* (pp. 76-78). (USDA Forest Service Technical Report PNW-GTR-305). Portland, OR: USDA Forest Service, Pacific Northwest Station.

Lewis, M. S., Lime, D. W., & Anderson, D. H. (1996). Paddle canoeists' encounter norms in Minnesota's Boundary Waters Canoe Area Wilderness. *Leisure Sciences, 18*(2), 143-160.

Manfredo, M. J., Bright, A. D., & Stephenson, M. (1991). Public preferences for non-consumptive wildlife recreation in the Denver area. Fort Collins, CO: Colorado State University, Human Dimensions in Natural Resources Research Unit.

Manfredo, M. J., Driver, B. L., & Tarrant, M. A. (1996). Measuring leisure motivation: A meta-analysis of the recreation experience preference scales. *Journal of Leisure Research, 28*(3), 188-213.

Manning, R. E. (1985a). Diversity in a democracy: Expanding the recreation opportunity spectrum. *Leisure Sciences, 7*(4), 376-398.

Manning, R. E. (1985b). Studies in outdoor recreation: A review and synthesis of the social science literature in outdoor recreation. Corvallis, OR: Oregon State University Press.

Manning, R. E., Johnson, D., & Van de Kamp, M. (1996). Norm congruence amount tour boat passengers to Glacier Bay National Park. *Leisure Sciences, 18*(2), 125-142.

Manning, R. E., Lime, D. W., Freimund, W. A., & Pitt, D. G. (1996). Crowding norms at frontcountry sites: A visual approach to setting standards of quality. *Leisure Sciences, 18*(1), 39-59.

Martilla, J. A. & James, J. C. (1977). Importance-performance analysis. *Journal of Marketing, 41*(1), 77-79.

Martinson, K. S., & Shelby, B. (1992). Encounter and proximity norms for salmon anglers in California and New Zealand. *North American Journal of Fisheries Management, 12*, 559-567.

McFarlane, B. L. (1994). Specialization and motivations of birdwatchers. *Wildlife Society Bulletin, 22*(3), 361-369.

McLellan, G., & Siehl, G. (1988). Trends in leisure and recreation: How we got where we are. *Trends, 25*(4), 4-7.

Mitchell, J. M. (1990). Do we really want wilderness management standards to be uniform? In B. Shelby, G. Stankey, & B. Schindler (Eds.), *Defining wilderness quality: The role of standards in wilderness management* (pp. 76-78). (USDA Forest Service Technical Report PNW-GTR-305). Portland, OR: USDA Forest Service, Pacific Northwest Station.

Patterson, M. E. and Hammitt, W. E. (1990). Backcountry encounter norms, actual reported encounters, and their relationship to wilderness solitude. *Journal of Leisure Research, 22*, 259-275.

Roggenbuck, J. W., Williams, D. R., Bange, S. P., and Dean, D. J. (1991). River float trip encounter norms: Questioning the use of the social norms concept. *Journal of Leisure Research, 23*(2), 133-153.

Roggenbuck, J. W., Williams, D. R., & Watson, A. E. (1993). Defining acceptable conditions in wilderness. *Environmental Management, 17*(2), 187-197.

Schreyer, R. (1986). Motivation for participation in outdoor recreation and barriers to that participation: A commentary on salient issues. In *The President's Commission on Americans outdoors: A literature review* (pp. Motivations 1-8). Washington, D.C.: US Government Printing Office.

Schreyer, R., & Roggenbuck J. W. (1978). The influence of experience expectations on crowding perceptions and social psychological carrying capacities. *Leisure Sciences, 1*(4), 373-394.

Shelby, B. (1981). Encounter norms in backcountry settings: Studies of three rivers. *Journal of Leisure Research, 13*, 129-138.

Shelby, B., & Heberlein, T. A. (1986). *Carrying capacity in recreation settings*. Corvallis, OR: Oregon State University Press.

Shelby, B., & Stein, K. (1984). Recreational use and carrying capacity of the Klamath River. Report WRRI-92. Water Res. Res. Institute, Oregon State University, Corvallis, Oregon.

Shelby, B., Vaske, J. J., & Heberlein, T.A. (1989). Comparative analysis of crowding in multiple locations: Results from 15 years of research. *Leisure Sciences, 11*, 269-291.

Stankey, G. H. (1973). *Visitor perception of wilderness recreation carrying capacity* (USDA Forest Service Research Paper INT-142). Ogden, UT: International Forest and Range Experiment Station.

Stankey, G. H., Cole, D. N., Lucas, R. C., Petersen, M. E., & Frissell, S. S. (1985). The limits of acceptable change (LAC) system for wilderness planning. (USDA Forest Service General Technical Report INT-176). Ogden, UT: Intermountain Research Station.

Stankey, G. H., & Schreyer, R. (1987). Attitudes toward wilderness and factors affecting visitor behavior: A state-of-knowledge review. In *Proceedings of the National Wilderness Research Conference: Issues, State-of-Knowledge, Future Directions*, 1985 July 23-26, Fort Collins, CO. (Gen. Tech. Rep. INT-220). Fort Collins, CO: US Department of Agriculture, Forest Service, Intermountain Research Station.

Stewart, W. P. (1992). Influence of the onsite experience on recreation experience preference judgments. *Journal of Leisure Research, 24*(2), 185-198.

Stewart, W. P., Chen, P. T., & Cole, D. (1996). Crowding revisited: Evidence from Grand Canyon. Abstracts from the *Proceedings of the 1996 NRPA Symposium on Leisure Research*. October 23-27, 1996. Kansas City, MO: National Recreation and Park Association.

Tarrant, M. A., Cordell, H. K., & Kibler, T. L. (1997). Measuring perceived crowding for high density river recreation: The effects of situational conditions and personal factors. *Leisure Sciences, 19*(2), 97-112

Tarrant, M. A. & Shafer, C. S (In press). Condition indicators for distinct wilderness: Is there uniformity? *Journal of Wilderness, 3*(4), 29-33.

Vaske, J. J., Donnelly, M. P, Freimund, W. A., & Miller, T. (1995). *The 1995 Gwaii Haanas visitor survey*. (HDNRU Rep. No. 24). Fort Collins, CO: Colorado State University.

Vaske, J. J., Donnelly, M. P., & Petruzzi, J. P. (1996). Country of origin, encounter norms, and crowding in a frontcountry setting. *Leisure Sciences, 18*, 161-176.

Vaske, J. J., Shelby, B., Graefe, A. R., & Heberlein, T. A. (1986). Backcountry encounter norms: Theory, method, and empirical evidence. *Journal of Leisure Research, 18*, 137-153.

Virden, R. J., & Knopf, R. C. (1989). Activities, experiences, and environmental settings: A case study of Recreation Opportunity Spectrum Relationships. *Leisure Sciences, 11*, 159-176.

Williams, D. R., Roggenbuck J. W., & Bange, S. P. (1991). The effect of norm-encounter compatibility on crowding perceptions, experience and behavior in river recreation settings. *Journal of Leisure Research, 23*(2), 154-172.

Williams, D. R., Schreyer, R. C., & Knopf, R. C. (1990). The effect of experience use history on the multidimensional structure of motivations to participate in leisure activities. *Journal of Leisure Research, 22*(1), 36-48.

Yuan, M. S., & McEwen, D. (1989). Test for campers' experience preference differences among three ROS setting classes. *Leisure Sciences, 11*, 177-185.

Zwick, R. R., Glass, R. J., & More, T. A. (1993). Motivation/importance typology of natural resource harvesters. In G.A. Vander Stoep (Ed.), *Proceedings of the 1993 Northeastern Recreation Research Symposium, 1993 April 18-20, Saratoga Springs, NY* (pp. 145-150). (Gen. Tech. Rep. NE). Radnor, PA: US Department of Agriculture, Forest Service, Northeastern Forest Experiment Station.

CHAPTER X

IMPLICATIONS OF THIS ASSESSMENT

Donald B. K. English[1]
H. Ken Cordell
J. M. Bowker

Outdoor recreation is complex and difficult to summarize fully. It includes a wide variety of activities and interests, ranging from canoeing to watching wildlife. In addition, many outdoor activities often occur in a variety of settings. These settings may have different characteristics and thus provide different kinds of recreation experiences. Similarly, one setting often supports an array of activities, often at the same time. Having the opportunity to participate in a mix of activities and settings is important to people as they seek satisfying and varied recreation experiences. On any given day or recreation trip, a single individual or group may participate in a number of activities across more than one setting.

A further complexity of outdoor recreation is that the meanings of and benefits from participating can be very different for different people who are doing the same activity in the same place at the same time. Research has shown that people engage in recreation activities for a variety of reasons, such as amusement, spiritual growth, better health, or relaxation. Different people may choose greatly different combinations of activities and settings to reach the same goal.

Differences in the benefits recreationists seek can translate into significant differences in their preferences for setting attributes, their perceptions of crowding or other conditions at the recreation site, their expectations about resource quality and service delivery, and their attitudes regarding management goals and methods. Different types of recreation users do share some of the same concerns about facilities and general perceptions about the quality of managed sites. However, research presented in earlier chapters has indicated that segmenting user markets based on setting-specific preferences for recreation experiences, although difficult to do, may be a managerially useful way to understand recreation site users better. As a result of their differences in preferences, visitors to the same recreation site are likely to exhibit different reactions to management prescriptions or resource changes.

Over and above the direct benefits participants get from their recreation experience, there is mounting evidence of indirect benefits of wild areas, scenic amenities, and recreation itself. There is an expanding definition of outdoor recreation participation and the scope of people who benefit from someone else's participation. Beyond the direct benefits of actual participation, economists and other social scientists have identified benefits to persons other than the visitor when measuring the values of the natural resources that support recreation. It also recognized that visitors benefit not only at the time they are participating in recreation, but also before and sometimes long after their visit to a recreation area. In addition, maintaining the quality of Wilderness and other undeveloped or unique natural or historic resources can provide benefits into the future for those who may make use of them. A growing class of beneficiaries of recreation, wildlife, and Wilderness resources includes those who engage in sightseeing, wildlife viewing, nature study, or other activities in "virtual" settings.

[1]Authors are listed alphabetically by first name, indicating equally–shared first authorship. Donald B. K. English is a research social scientist, H. Ken Cordell is a research forester and project leader, and J. M. Bowker is a research social scientist, USDA Forest Service, Athens, GA.

SOME GENERAL FINDINGS

Wilderness Benefits Are Expanding

Wilderness continues to be important to the American public. On-site recreational use of Wilderness provides interesting, fun, and relaxing experiences to those who venture in for hikes, backpacking, or horseback trips. In addition, Wilderness users often indicate they experience spiritual growth and therapeutic healing. And beyond the benefits visitors to Wilderness receive, many people who do not actually visit Wilderness areas obtain passive benefits based on knowing the areas are preserved as a natural or environmental trust fund.

Recreation use of Wilderness is difficult to measure. Some estimates of Wilderness use are on the order of 40 million visits per year. Forecasts of future use indicate a trend of increased use per acre. This trend is driven by decreasing amounts of publicly-owned land parcels that are large enough and wild enough to be classified as Wilderness, relatively slow growth in additions of qualified roadless areas to the National Wilderness Preservation System (NWPS), and an ever-increasing number of people who want access to the unique opportunities afforded Wilderness settings. Moreover, access to substitute venues on private lands are diminishing more rapidly than public venues, so more of the total use pressure is shifting to publicly–owned Wilderness. As this trend continues, easily accessed Wilderness areas will likely be pushed to their limits in accommodating human use while still maintaining their wild character.

The contributions of Wilderness to national welfare through passive and off-site benefits will likely become more important in the future as these wild areas become increasingly scarce and unique. Preserving the ecological integrity of Wilderness areas is paramount to maintaining the benefits they provide as a form of environmental trust fund. To this end, the need to preserve ecological integrity may take precedence over and thus limit recreational use of Wilderness areas in the future. Further, for the NWPS to be a complete system, there is pressure to have all ecological types found in the United States represented by areas within the system. Currently, four ecoregions that together comprise over 20 percent of the land area of the continental United States are not represented in the NWPS.

The Outdoor Recreation Market Is Expected to Continue to Grow

Both recent trends and future projections point toward continued increases in the number of participants, trips, and activity days for outdoor recreation across almost all activities and among all regions. Among the top activities in trips, activity days, and percent of the population participating are visiting a beach or waterside and swimming in lakes, oceans, and streams. Both of these activities are expected to grow at or above the rate of the increase predicted for population, meaning that they will continue to be among the most important activities for most Americans. However, the water resource base that supports these activities is finite. In order to minimize crowding and likely reduction in enjoyment of water-based recreation, it will be necessary to maintain the availability of as many as possible of the areas now provided. Thus, water quality improvement and various means of access to water resources are issues that can be expected to remain and grow in importance in the future.

For over half the activities examined in the previous chapters, projections indicate that participant growth will be faster than population growth. This trend implies that a growing proportion of the population will participate in the future. But growth across types of activities is not expected to be equal among regions. The greatest percentage of increases in winter and water activities will likely come from residents of the two western regions. However, the majority of participants, trips, and activity days will continue to be accounted for by residents of the eastern regions, given their much larger population base. For almost all developed and dispersed land activities, the greatest percentage increases in participation will be in the South. The slowest growth rates will be in the North, due primarily to the slowing rates of population growth predicted for that region.

Across all types of activities and all regions, the outdoor recreation activities that occur in developed settings, including developed water and developed winter settings, are expected to show the greatest absolute increase in numbers of participants and recreation trips. Percentage increases in these activities are expected to exceed population growth rates. Along with projected population increases, projected increases in mean income of almost 90 percent by the year 2050 are likely to have strong positive effects on both participation rates and intensity for many activities. However, these projections assume that the distribution of income within the population will remain constant, which it has not in recent years. The proportion of people in the "middle class" has gotten smaller, and there has been a widening gap between the very rich and the very poor.

Should this trend continue, participation could be greatly altered. In addition, because the baseline levels of participants, trips, and activity days are relatively high, even small percentage increases in the proportion who participate can mean fairly large absolute changes.

As is the case with outdoor recreation in general, Wilderness visitation is also expected to increase quite rapidly, particularly for National Park System-managed areas. Other than visits to designated Wilderness areas, growth in activities that require extensive open spaces, such as hunting, backpacking, snowmobiling, and primitive camping, are expected to grow fairly slowly. Even so, there will be increases in participants and activity levels for most of these activities, albeit at rates somewhat less than population growth and the rate of growth of many other forms of outdoor recreation participation.

Access to the Private Land Base for Recreation Continues to Decline

A key resource supporting many different types of outdoor activities in the past has been private forest land. But ever fewer landowners allow public access to their lands. In three of the four assessment regions, the proportion of owners allowing public use declined by at least 35 percent from 1985 to 1995. Couple this decrease with the continued conversion of forest and agricultural land around cities into housing, shopping venues, and other developments, and that leaves large tracts of undeveloped public land to support a growing share of dispersed forms of recreation activity. Because the public lands, and especially the federal resource base, are generally not located near cities, visiting these types of settings is likely to involve a greater amount of travel and hence domestic tourism activity.

The extra pressure on large public holdings to support dispersed forms of recreation is likely to be especially heavy in the eastern portion of the country. The North and South contain the majority of recreation participants, but have a relatively small public land base. Thus, declines in access to undeveloped private forest lands in those regions will likely press a proportionately greater amount of dispersed recreation use pressure onto public lands.

Increased Demand for Nearby Recreation Resources

Across a fairly high proportion of the activities examined in the previous chapters, the projected increases for activity days (days during which some time is spent in an activity) are far greater than projected increases for trips. One interpretation of this projection is that fewer days of recreation participation will occur during a trip, while more days of participation will take place close enough to home that a trip is not necessary. For example, an evening walk or bike ride on one of the many greenways or rail trails that have been completed in suburban areas in the last 10 years would count as a participation day in those activities, but would not require a trip. As a result, neighborhood or other local outdoor spaces, possibly including forested land owned by family or friends, will be under greater pressure to serve a higher proportion of overall recreation demand. It is reasonable to expect that less affluent people in our population in particular will make greater use of nearby recreation opportunities. Transportation to recreation opportunities serving local areas is usually inexpensive and often has low or no user fees.

Another finding of this assessment is a continued trend toward multiple-activity but shorter-length trips. The increased frequency of two-income households has two important effects that support this trend. First, long (two or more weeks) vacations are more difficult to plan, because both workers must coordinate vacation time. Second, the added stress of parenting in a two-income household makes more frequent getaways desirable. The emphasis of the trip shifts to providing a variety of activities on any given trip. Indeed, nearly 10 percent of those surveyed in the NSRE about their last trip reported that the trip had no primary activity. This trend will likely mean that there will be increasing demand for easily accessed (drive to) recreation opportunities, and for recreation areas that can serve multiple needs and support a variety of activities near one another. An example might include areas that have both developed and dispersed setting opportunities in close proximity.

The recent Southern Appalachian Assessment found that many of the "hot spots," areas with consistently high levels of visitation, had both land and water features. Examples include campgrounds, trails, or other land resources adjacent to lakes or rivers. It is expected that managing such areas will become increasingly complex as more users and more diversity in types of use lead to increased conflicts among visitors.

People have always engaged in the types of recreation activities that they are most familiar with, often those most readily available to them. This practice is clear from the regional differences in participation among activities (for example, less winter activity by Southerners and more camping and adventure participation in

Western regions) and higher participation rates among rural people in activities such as hunting, fishing, and primitive camping. Further evidence is the frequency that inadequate time or insufficient access are listed as primary constraints to participation. Without doubt, the search for variety and increases in participation across a broader array of activities will be a force in the future that shapes many recreation trips and drives an ever-increasing level of recreation participation.

Resource Changes Have not Been Equal Across Regions or Settings

There has been a relatively large increase in developed facilities over the last 10 years, particularly in the East, which has greater population. Obviously related is growth of participation in developed site activities at rates exceeding other types of participation over the same time period. Higher levels of services and facility development are continuing to occur at private recreation facilities, including campgrounds and marinas. In addition, more development is occurring in state park systems and in federal systems. These changes are likely to reinforce the projected increased demand for developed recreation settings across the country, regardless of whether the providers are in the public or private sectors.

Two forces helping to fuel increases in developed recreation opportunities are the expanding needs for new sources of funding for state and federal providers and the increased emphasis on outdoor recreation as a rural development tool. At the federa,l and even more so at the state level, inflation-adjusted funding for management and operation has leveled or declined in recent years. Increasingly, user fees are being instituted as a way to augment appropriated financial resources. However, assessing fees for use of undeveloped public lands is usually more difficult than charging for access to developed facilities. In addition, contracts for concessions or "privatizing" the operation of public parkland usually requires some sort of developed facility through which the private partner can generate revenue.

Using recreation for rural development means having nonlocal visitors travel to and spend money in the rural areas where the recreation attraction exists. Undeveloped lands provide only modest opportunities for visitors to spend money on goods and services associated with a recreation trip and may not draw many outside visitors. A variety of developed recreation attractions greatly increases the tourist draw of an area and increases the amount of money visitors could be expected to spend while visiting. Thus, developed recreation facilities are a necessary component in the more successful rural development strategies.

Losses of access to private land through land-use conversions, closure, or leasing, have reduced opportunities for dispersed recreation on extensive tracts of undeveloped lands for many Americans. Increased facility development on state parklands has further reduced this type of opportunity. Public Wilderness areas are less and less able to accommodate increases in recreational uses. As a result, other publicly-owned undeveloped lands are receiving a growing share of the pressure for natural settings for engaging in activities that require extensive acreages of land or water.

Regional per capita availability of opportunities for recreation participation has been declining most noticeably in the Pacific Coast region. That decline has been largely due to population increases. In contrast, despite significant population growth in the last 10 years in the South, per capita resource availability has been relatively stable in that region. A fairly high degree of demand growth is expected by residents of the South in the future. The expected participation growth in the North may offset the relatively large recent gains in state parklands and trail resources in that heavily populated region.

SOME MORE SPECIFIC OBSERVATIONS

In addition to the more general observations offered in the preceding section, there are a number of more specific points worthy of mention.

Access

Rising levels of outdoor recreation activity, coupled with increased diversity in equipment, user groups, and modes of participation, are resulting in increased competition for the recreational resources of this country. A common theme of the user groups writing for Chapter V is the increasing challenge of having and keeping access to the most desirable places and spaces. Competition is especially evident between motorized and nonmotorized users (water, snow, and land), on-foot and riding participants, fast-moving versus slow-moving styles, highly specialized versus novice participants, risk/adventure versus sensing/learning-motivated users, and commercial versus private users. Fair approaches to allocating the increasingly limited per capita opportunities will be central issues in both public and private recreation management in the future.

Resource Impacts

Public land managers, environmental interests, and recreation users all cite in one way or another concern over how natural resources are recreationally used in this country. Greater numbers of users, more use of mechanized equipment, and easier access to backcountry are combining to impact the resource base, especially in fragile ecosystems. Resource impacts are likely to intensify in some of the more popular places and widen to others as use pressures increase.

Management Evolution

Approaches to providing and managing recreation resources will have to evolve and adapt if recreation opportunities are to keep pace with demand growth. New approaches will need to account for reduced or stagnant funding, shrinking access to private lands, greater frequency and intensity of crowding, and unprecedented patron levels, diversity, and styles. The fiscal, policy, and customer need environment in which managers operate is itself new and constantly evolving. Charging fees and doing so in different ways, improved education techniques about recreation and historic resources, improved use of electronic media for information dissemination, and comanagement between users and providers are among many options for adapting to these changing conditions.

Benefits-based Management

Increasingly, there is interest in doing a better job in the public sector of providing high quality recreation experiences. The private sector receives market signals to guide its investment and operational decisions. The public sector must employ other means to understand what the customer of recreation opportunities is looking for and what attributes and services are most important to satisfying experiences. All recreation visitors to public lands and water seek to obtain benefits from their participation. Managing the benefits received from recreation resources transcends the more traditional approach of managing to provide capacity for recreational use. Benefits-based management is spreading to all levels of government, in part because of the efforts of committed scientists and other professionals to help the recreation management community better understand the merits of this innovative approach.

Improved Data

In the 1960s and 1970s there was growing and widespread interest in creating workable and comprehensive data bases covering recreation facility amounts, access, condition, use levels, and demand. Federal and state agencies worked hard at creating national and statewide systems for keeping track of outdoor recreation. At the time, the recreation industry relied very heavily on government statistics for information to guide investments. Interest in extensive data systems at government levels waned in the 1980s and has only very recently waxed anew. Private industry, however, has continued to improve its capabilities. Neither the private nor public sectors, however, have fully addressed the need to develop a system for tracking the markets, use patterns and levels, emerging trends, inventory of opportunities, complementarity of opportunities, and other macro aspects of outdoor recreation. All agree, however, that good data on these issues are needed for planning, investing, and adaptive management. The current rise in interest in improved data and analytical capability is very likely to continue and will include innovations such as GIS and GPS capabilities, real-time tracking, integration of industry, and public sector data bases and reporting.

Better Understanding the Enthusiasts

Outdoor recreation is a part of life for almost 95 percent of the people living in the United States. But for most of those who participate, involvement is not frequent. The enthusiasts described in Chapter V (the one-third of participants who participate the most) account for between 60 and 90 percent of all days and trips for outdoor recreation. Yet, enthusiasts are typically only 10 to 15 percent of the participant population for many activities. Particularly for some activities where enthusiasts account for at least 80 percent of the participation days and trips, a much better understanding of their motivations, expectations, and outlook on management is needed. First of all, for these devoted participants, assuring they receive high quality service depends on knowing what they are looking for in their recreational experiences. Second, comanagement (or user participant management) is most likely to come from the enthusiasts most interested in the resources they use, for example, protecting white water segments of rivers.

Collaboration

Increasingly, interest groups will collaborate with public agencies to set the course of management of natural resources. Collaboration in this sense does not mean just one agency working with one user group on a single project or site. Rather, it means all parties interested in better outdoor opportunities will work together to meet common goals. This broader notion of collaboration must include stakeholders across the spectrum of resources and management challenges. Broad-based and broad-scoped collaboration with open sharing of ideas, concerns, and proposed solutions to issues is the approach most likely to succeed in the long run as competition for open space and facilities continues to be a major trend. With collaboration at the planning and policy levels, comanagement becomes a more viable option.

The Underserved

Participation in some forms of outdoor recreation is possible for only a small portion of the United States' population. Some activities, such as horseback riding or sailing, require huge monetary investments. Other forms, including rock climbing, white water kayaking, and fly fishing, require a high degree of physical ability and/or skill for participation. Some others require ownership, acquisition of a lease, or other special access rights to large rural tracts in order to have a place for participation. In general, however, participation in most activities is possible for the majority of Americans. Despite that, there are growing numbers of people in the United States who face significant barriers to participating in recreation. These people include the very poor, inner-city residents with little access to or information about outdoor opportunities, and people with disabilities of one form or another. While local governments provide a considerable amount of opportunities for these segments of society, we need to know more about the needs and lifestyles of underserved populations. Then all providers can be aware of how well their services and opportunities are being delivered.

COMPARING TRENDS IN PARTICIPATION AND RESOURCE AVAILABILITY

Across the country, there are two types of resource settings for which it seems likely that an imbalance between recreation demand and the available amount of recreation opportunities will occur. These imbalances can be identified as those for which there is declining per capita availability of opportunities for the outdoor activities that occur in those settings, while at the same time there is expected increases in demand for those activities at rates that exceed expected rates of population growth. The two settings for which imbalances are most likely are flatwater resources, such as lakes and reservoirs, and extensive, undeveloped land settings.

Across all regions, participation in water-based recreation is expected to increase at rates at least as fast as population. Although there have been significant increases in availability of river resources for recreation in the last 10 years, in three of four regions the great majority of people have experienced declining per capita availability for flatwater and coastal resources. Opportunities for activities that require an extensive land base have also been declining for most people in the country. Participation in some activities, such as hunting, that make use of this resource setting are expected to decline. However, there are a number of other activities that occur in this setting, such as backpacking, hiking, off-road driving, and snowmobiling, that are expected to increase significantly.

Each region has some supply-demand imbalances that are of particular regional interest. Regional differences in trends in resource availability result in expectations of different settings being more or less abundant among the regions in the future. Variation across regions in predicted population changes and income growth are the factors primarily driving expected differences among regions in the predicted growth rates in participation.

North

The most important imbalance between recreation supply and demand in this region is in flatwater resources. More than half of the region's populations live in areas where the availability of such resources is less than the national average. Fewer than two percent of the population have experienced increases in resource availability over the last 10 years. However, the number of participants and days of participation for most water activities, including motor boating, canoeing, swimming, and rafting, are expected to increase faster than population growth in the future. Declining per capita availability coupled with increased demand likely signals a situation that will need focused attention by resource planners in the future. Competition for these types of resources may be exacerbated by the greater demand for domestic uses of water that will result from population increases.

Fishing opportunities per capita are also declining in the North. However, the number of days of participation for fishing and the number of fishing participants is predicted to grow in the future. This disparity will further heighten the focus on water-based recreation in the North. From a social equity standpoint, addressing any imbalance between fishing demand and available opportunities may be salient because all races participate in fishing at about the same rates. Because some racial groups have less access to other types of opportunities, imbalances regarding this activity are more likely to affect minorities negatively.

There have been reductions in the availability of privately–owned rural land through its conversion to other uses. There have also been reductions in the per capita availability of large tracts of federal land because population has increased but the resource base has not. Dispersed activities such as backpacking, snowmobiling, and hiking are predicted to grow faster than population. To the extent that dispersed activities occur in these resource settings, a potential imbalance could result.

South

Similar to the North, coastal and flatwater resources are recreation settings that are finite, and opportunities to recreate in them have not increased as fast as population in the South. However, access issues are not as prominent for the resources of this region as they are in the North. Participation in water-based activities, including motorboating, swimming, canoeing, and visiting beaches, are all predicted to grow faster than population for Southern residents. Fishing participation is also predicted to grow. Thus, for the same reasons as listed for the North, water-based recreation settings may represent potential gaps between demand pressures and supply availability in the South.

Corps of Engineers, Tennessee Valley Authority, and private utility companies are prominent providers of water-based recreation opportunities in the South. Their reservoirs and other projects are typically close to population centers, and they represent vast areas of water surface. Their properties provide opportunities for developed camping and many other activities. It is possible that the more rapid growth in demand for water-based recreation will put additional pressure on these agencies not only to expand access to water resources, but also to meet additional demands for camping, fishing, hiking, and other activities that people often combine during their visits to lakes and reservoirs.

A second resource area that may be of concern for residents of the South is availability of winter opportunities. Participation in both downhill skiing and snowmobiling are predicted to increase much faster than population growth over the next 50 years. Per capita resource availability to support these activities, for obvious reasons, is going to be relatively stable for most of the population in the region. For most residents of the South, there are no winter sport areas close by that consistently support winter recreation. It is not likely that much can be done about improving opportunities within the region. The portions of the region where such resources are found, such as in western North Carolina, and those in easily accessible portions of other regions, such as southern West Virginia, could well experience excessive levels of demand.

Rocky Mountains/Great Plains

In this region, there are four types of recreation resources that have shown declining per capita availability over that last 10 years. For two of these four resource types, flatwater resources and urban, developed resources, most residents of the region have below-average levels of availability now. However, for the other two, agricultural and range lands and developed camping, the majority of the region's residents still have greater than average levels of availability compared to the nation as a whole. As a result, it is not clear that the availability reductions for the first two resource settings will lead to significant constraints on recreation activity. About the only activity that could be constrained by this resource situation and that is predicted to grow at a relatively high rate in the region is developed camping.

Several water-based activities are expected to grow at rates that outpace expected population growth in the region. These activities include motorboating, non–pool swimming, canoeing, and visiting a beach or waterside. Unfortunately, this is a region that is not widely endowed with resources to support such activities.

Fewer than five percent of the region's residents live in areas that have had stable per capita availability for flatwater resources over the last 10 years. Further, more than three-fourths of the region's residents have below-average accessibility to this resource setting.

Developed, urban resources have increased less rapidly than population growth in this region. As a result, per capita availability has declined. These types of resources are important for many people and are used frequently because of their proximity. Activities including biking, picnicking, family gathering, sightseeing, and walking are predicted to grow relatively rapidly in this region. In addition, many of these same activities are done now by a large portion of the population and are done very frequently by those people who participate in them.

Pacific Coast

Per capita availability has declined for a number of resource settings in this region over the last 10 years, including developed urban resources, coastal resources, developed camping opportunities, and agricultural and range lands. However, for all of these settings, almost all residents in this region still have a greater level of availability than do residents of the other three regions. So while there have been reductions, those reductions have come in resource settings for which residents had a relative abundance of opportunities. As a result, it is not clear whether reduced availability of outdoor recreation opportunities will lead to any imbalance between supply and demand. Quite a large number of activities dependent upon the above settings are predicted to have increases in participation at rates faster than population growth. It is therefore possible that imbalances for some or all of them may occur. But it is not clear how likely imbalances are to occur in these activities that include downhill skiing, visiting a beach or waterside, developed camping, picnicking, family gathering, sightseeing, off-road driving, hiking, and backpacking.

PERPETUAL MOTION, UNICORNS, AND MARKETING IN OUTDOOR RECREATION

Francis Pandolfi observed in the beginning of this book that "perpetual motion, unicorns, and marketing outdoor recreation all have one thing in common—many people believe them to be fiction." We have seen in the data, analysis, and discussions as this book has unfolded that outdoor recreation is still a strong growth area in our American economy and in American life. We observe that far from the "maturing market" image some have portrayed, it is a growing market. For both the private and public sectors, this growth offers both challenge and opportunity.

For the private sector, growing and widening interest in outdoor recreation is expected to offer opportunity for growth in many existing markets and the emergence of new markets for services, equipment, and facilities. The United States economy is currently strong and is expected to remain so for the foreseeable future. The challenge facing the private sector is to influence both the political and market systems such that access to outdoor settings remain available and can expand to meet predicted demand growth.

For the public sector, the challenge will be to find ways that work for continuing to provide opportunities for recreation participation for a growing and diversifying American public. Marketing outdoor opportunities in proven ways that result in better user as well as provider stewardship of the natural resource base, on which much of outdoor recreation depends, is likely to become an increasingly workable and acceptable approach. The opportunity is to change approaches that no longer work and create new approaches to meet conditions unlike those of the past.

As both sectors march into the 21st century, we can see the lines between private and public sectors blurring as both increasingly work together to provide appropriate and adequate outdoor recreation opportunities. Neither will relinquish its basic motivation for operation—profit for one, public service for the other. But as demand for outdoor recreation continues to grow, it seems it will take a collaborative effort to provide the opportunities Americans seek in their lives.

Ken Cordell earned his Ph.D. degree in economics and forestry at North Carolina State University. As a Forest Service scientist, he has worked on the application of social science theory and methods in outdoor recreation, wilderness, and generally, natural resources management. Recently, Dr. Cordell directed an ongoing series of national studies, including the U.S. National Recreation Study. He is a national authority on recreation demand and supply trends and serves as adjunct faculty at several major universities.

INDEX

A

B

C

D

E

F

G

H

I

K

L

M

N

O

P

R

S

T

U

V

W

Y